D1233777

Paul

and His Letters

Paul

and His Letters

John B. Polhill

ACADEMIC

NASHVILLE, TENNESSEE

ISBN: 978–0-8054–1097–6

Published by B&H Publishing Group, Nashville, Tennessee
Editorial Team: Leonard G. Goss, John Landers, Sandra Bryer
Page Design and Typesetting: TF Designs, Mount Juliet, Tennessee

Dewey Decimal Classification: 225
Subject Heading: NEW TESTAMENT

Unless otherwise noted, Scripture quotations are from the Holy Bible, New International Version, copyright © 1973, 1978, 1984 by International Bible Society.

Scripture quotations marked NKJV are from the New King James Version, copyright © 1979, 1980, 1982, Thomas Nelson, Inc.

Library of Congress Cataloging-in-Publication Data

Polhill, John B., 1939–
  Paul and his letters / by John B. Polhill.
    p. cm.
  Includes bibliographical references and indexes.
  ISBN 0-8054-1097–X
  1. Bible. N.T. Epistles of Paul—Theology. 2. Paul the Apostle, Saint.
  I. Title.
BS2651.P55 1999
225.9'2—dc21

99–26826
CIP

22 23 24 25 26 27   14 13 12 11

Contents

༺❦༻

INTRODUCTION

NOT A "LIFE OF PAUL"

$\mathcal{T}$his book is in no sense a "life of Paul." A biography of the apostle is impossible. Our sources are too limited to compose one. We know virtually nothing of his birth and childhood. Reliable sources for Paul begin only with his persecution of the Christians and his conversion, probably some time around his thirtieth year. These sources are the canonical Acts of the Apostles and the thirteen Pauline epistles. Even these are selective. Acts does not cover all of Paul's ministry. It has major gaps, such as the long "silent period" of ten years or so after his conversion, when he ministered in his native Cilicia. The Pauline epistles provide an even slimmer picture of his ministry. We have letters to only a few of his congregations; much of his correspondence has probably been lost. The last years of Paul's life are particularly difficult to reconstruct. The narrative of Acts stops short, not treating the last five years or so of the apostle's life. The Pastoral Epistles give us some glimpse into the final period of his ministry, particularly 2 Timothy. For his death we have only noncanonical writings like *The Acts of Paul* and testimonies from the early church fathers, all of which are heavily encrusted with legend.

PURPOSE

The purpose of this book is to provide a survey of all the information we have on the life and thought of the apostle Paul—from Acts, from his epistles, and from seemingly reliable traditions that have been preserved in the noncanonical sources. The book is designed for a college survey course on Paul or a seminary course in New Testament introduction. It has been arranged to serve as a general reference work on Paul and his letters and, as such, will prove useful not only to students but also to pastors and church Bible teachers as well.

APPROACH

Comprehensive treatments of the apostle Paul generally follow one of two approaches. The first approach has been to divide the book into two parts, the first dealing with what might be termed the "history" of Paul—his life and ministry. The second part deals with the "thought" of Paul as reflected in his epistles. This part usually follows one of two formats: either an introduction to each of the epistles,[1] or a summary of the main theological themes of Paul drawn from all the epistles viewed together as a whole.[2] The second approach is to weave the Pauline epistles into the Acts narrative to produce a continuous story line for the life and ministry of Paul. A number of scholars have taken this approach, such as the influential volume by Conybeare and Howson at the turn of the twentieth century,[3] and the more recent contribution of F. F. Bruce.[4] This is the approach that is followed in the present volume. It must be readily admitted that it has its pitfalls. The dating of Paul's epistles is often uncertain. In cases such as Galatians for instance, one cannot even be sure to what location Paul was writing. Thus, it is not always clear where the letters should be worked into the Acts narrative of Paul's ministry. I have endeavored to list the various options when they occur. The student should realize that in many instances the placement of the letters is at best tentative and always subject to revision. In some instances, I have deliberately treated an epistle at a point where it almost certainly does *not* fit into the chronology of Paul's ministry. For example, this is true of Philippians and Galatians. I have treated them in the chapters that deal with the establishment of the congregations at Philippi and Galatia. This provides a good background for understanding the letters. Obviously both were written at a later period, subsequent to the church's establishment.

PROCEDURE

The first two chapters of the book cover what we know of Paul's early years in Tarsus and Jerusalem. Our knowledge of these years is scant and is based mainly on a few random comments in Paul's speeches in Acts 22 to 26 and in his letters. The bulk of these two chapters broadly considers the Roman, Greek, and Jewish influences which would have helped shape Paul. Chapter 3 deals with Paul's conversion, based both on the three accounts in Acts and in Paul's references in his epistles. Chapters 4 through 6 deal with Paul's early ministry and are largely based on Acts, supplemented by material from Paul's epistles that seems to allude to these events. Chapter 7 is an excursus, an introduction to the literary features of Paul's letters. There are a number of excurses throughout the book on various topics related to Pauline studies. They can be located by consulting the table of contents as well as the index.

In the remainder of the volume, the Acts narrative serves as the organizing principle for presenting the Pauline material. The Pauline epistles are introduced, either in the context of when the church was established (Galatians, Philippians, 1 and 2 Thessalonians) or at the point where we have placed Paul's writing of them (the rest of the epistles).

I do not share the prevalent scholarly skepticism about the historical reliability of Acts. I assume that it was written by Luke, the physician, Paul's traveling companion. He was with Paul at those places where a first-person narrative occurs in Acts (the "we" passages)—at places like Troas and Philippi on Paul's second mission, and as Paul's constant companion from the journey to Jerusalem in Acts 20 to the very end of Acts.[5]

I also do not share the skepticism about whether Paul wrote some of the epistles which bear his name. I would argue that Paul wrote all thirteen of the letters that carry his name in their address. In particular, I consider him the author of those epistles which many consider deutero-Pauline (written by a later disciple of Paul). These are Colossians, Ephesians, 2 Thessalonians, and the three Pastoral Epistles. The size of a person's Pauline corpus (body of letters) will greatly affect his or her view of Paul's theology. I would argue for a large corpus and a great theological breadth on the apostle's part. I would *not*, however, include Hebrews among the epistles of Paul. It does not identify itself as being by Paul. In style, form, and content, it is wholly unlike any Pauline epistle.[6] It is thus not included in our treatment of the letters of Paul.

In this volume, each epistle is provided with an introduction, designed to set it in context and to introduce the student to the main scholarly issues surrounding it. A study outline is provided for each epistle. This is followed by "highlights," which summarize the main ideas in the epistles. This section is very tight. It assumes that the student will study it *with Bible open to the text being discussed.* It will be difficult to follow apart from the biblical text.

This book is more historically and exegetically oriented than theologically oriented. Major Pauline theological themes are treated in the various "highlight" sections, however. Chapters which introduce Paul's letters conclude with a listing of Pauline commentaries currently available. These cover the gamut of scholarship, running from the short and popular to the very heavy and scholarly. In a number of instances better older commentaries have been listed, ones which have stood the test of time. In chapters that do not cover an epistle, a listing of suggested supplementary reading has been provided.

FEATURES TO NOTE

Notes are given at the end of each chapter. They are primarily of three types: informational, documentary, and bibliographical. Informational notes supply additional, less essential detail to matters mentioned in the text. They have been held to a minimum. Documentary notes are provided to indicate noteworthy, pioneering, or unique scholarly contributions on a given topic. Where a particular viewpoint is not available in English, the French or German source is provided. These also have been kept to a minimum. The bulk of the notes are of the bibliographical type. They are designed to provide the student with further reading on a given subject. Since the notes are primarily supplementary, they are provided in endnote rather than footnote form, so as not to detract from the main text.

All biblical citations follow the New International Version, unless specified otherwise. Citations from nonbiblical ancient sources, such as Josephus and Eusebius, follow the system of book, chapter, and sectional enumeration found in the Loeb Classical Library. Occasionally a Greek word has been given in the text, transliterated into the English alphabet. The transliterated words are provided for students who have an acquaintance with Greek. English translations are always provided next to the Greek words. No knowledge of Greek is necessary or assumed for making full use of this book.

PUTTING THE PIECES TOGETHER

Because of the limited and varied nature of our sources, assembling them into a picture of Paul and his ministry is neither an easy nor a certain task. It is much like assembling the shards from an ancient piece of pottery. Pieces are often missing altogether, making it difficult to determine how the existing pieces fit together. We will probably never have certainty about the location of many of the pieces for the life and ministry of Paul. Where was Galatia? Where was Paul located when he wrote

3

the Prison Epistles? Was he released from his first imprisonment in Rome? Did he ever fulfill his desire to witness in Spain? Was Galatians or 1 Thessalonians the first of the thirteen Pauline epistles to be written? Was Philippians written from Ephesus in A.D. 53 or from Rome a decade later, or was it written halfway between (A.D.58) from Caesarea? For many of the epistles, we know neither when they were written nor the order of their relationship to the others. I have attempted to piece them together into a plausible reconstruction. In places, it may seem a bit idiosyncratic. I trust, however, that I have been fair in listing the alternatives. Each student is challenged to reconstruct her or his own picture of the life and letters of the apostle to the Gentiles.

The overall framework of Paul's ministry is clear from the narrative of Acts. Fitting the epistles into the framework is what gets tricky. Some scholars would cut Paul's epistles free from the framework of Acts altogether. The end result of this procedure is total subjectivity and chaos. Fortunately, the theological task is less fraught with uncertainties than the historical task. The *message* of Paul's epistles does not depend on the contingencies of our historical reconstructions. Ultimately, it is the message of the apostle which continues to challenge us. Hopefully this book will make some small contribution for the student seeking to understand the mind and message of this great Christian missionary and theologian.

NOTES

1. This is the approach of M. L. Soards, *The Apostle Paul: An Introduction to His Writings and Teachings* (New York: Paulist, 1987).
2. G. Bornkamm, *Paul*, trans. D. M. G. Stalker (New York: Harper and Row, 1971).
3. W. J. Conybeare and J. S. Howson, *The Life and Epistles of Saint Paul* (Hartford, Conn.: S. Scranton, 1902).
4. F. F. Bruce, *Paul: Apostle of the Heart Set Free* (Grand Rapids: Eerdmans, 1977).
5. For a fuller discussion, see J. B. Polhill, *Acts*, New American Commentary (Nashville: Broadman, 1992), 23–27.
6. See D. A. Carson, D. J. Moo, and L. Morris, *An Introduction to the New Testament* (Grand Rapids: Zondervan, 1992), 394–397.

1

⁓⁓⁓

A Citizen of Two Cities

*T*hree very different influences contributed to the early formation of Paul. All three are emphasized in a single thirty-verse section of the Book of Acts. The setting is the grounds of the temple in Jerusalem. An angry mob had attacked Paul, accusing him of desecrating the temple. The Roman troops responsible for maintaining order in the city had just rescued Paul from the crowd and taken him into custody. The soldiers were garrisoned in a tower located at a corner of the temple. As they carried Paul up the stairs that led from the temple grounds into their barracks, Paul requested permission to address the crowd below. The Roman commander was surprised to hear Paul speaking in fluent Greek. Paul quickly informed him that he was a native Greek speaker. In fact, he was a citizen of the city of Tarsus in the province of Cilicia. He described it as "no ordinary city," or, as we might say "not just any old city" (Acts 21:39).

The Roman commander granted Paul permission to address the Jewish crowd. Paul began by introducing himself to the crowd. He also pointed out that he came from Tarsus. But he emphasized that he was also a Jew, in fact, that he had come to Jerusalem at a young age to study under Gamaliel, a leading teacher of the Jewish law (Acts 22:3). A citizen of Tarsus, a Jew educated in Jerusalem—there was more. The commander soon learned about it. Paul's address did not appease the Jewish crowd, who screamed for his death (Acts 22:22). Determined to learn the reason for this major disturbance of the peace, the commander ordered a centurion to examine Paul by beating him. It was illegal to scourge a Roman citizen without a hearing and formal charges. Paul quickly informed the centurion that he was a Roman citizen (Acts 22:25). Immediately the centurion stopped the scourging procedure and went to the commander to inform him of Paul's citizen status. Coming to Paul, the commander learned that Paul was indeed a "high status" citizen: he had been *born* with a citizen's rights (Acts 22:28).

Paul's self-identification on all three accounts was directly suited to the occasion. Initially, before the Roman commander his *Tarsian* citizenship explained why he spoke fluent Greek. Before the Jewish crowd, Paul emphasized his *Jewish* heritage. He wanted them to know that he had always been true to his Jewish faith and still was faithful to God's leading. In face of an imminent scourging, Paul appealed to his *Roman* citizen's rights. Paul did indeed share all three identities. Each contributed to the success of his mission to the Gentiles. To his Tarsian heritage he owed his fluency in the Greek language and probably much of his cultural orientation. His ministry would mainly be in hellenistic cities like Tarsus; his early years in that city prepared him. To Paul's Roman heritage he owed the legal protection that assisted him throughout his ministry. Even more, the Roman world order facilitated his extensive travels. To his Jewish heritage, Paul owed his faith and his perspective on life. More than anything else, Paul was, and always remained, a faithful Jew.

This chapter will examine the influence of Tarsus and Rome upon Paul. Chapter 2 is devoted to Paul's Jewish heritage.

TARSUS

Scholars are divided over the extent to which Tarsus influenced Paul. Some argue that Paul was formed almost totally by his background in the Jewish Diaspora and that Diaspora Judaism was more lax and Hellenized in its attitude toward the Jewish law than was Palestinian Judaism.[1] Others argue that Paul left Tarsus as a young boy and received all his training from elementary school on in Jerusalem.[2] The truth likely lies somewhere in between these extremes. Paul was reared in Tarsus by a pious Jewish family who sent him to study the Jewish Torah in Jerusalem, probably while he was in his early teens. In his earlier years, Paul would not have been wholly sheltered from the hellenistic culture of Tarsus; it would have influenced him in various and subtle ways.

A BRIEF HISTORY OF TARSUS

Our knowledge of ancient Tarsus is limited. The city thrives today and is still called by its ancient name. The modern city lies over the ruins of the old, preventing excavation. Literary references to the ancient city are almost as sparse as the archaeological evidence.

Tarsus lies on the fertile Cilician plain in the southeastern corner of modern Turkey. The ancient city was located about ten miles north of the Mediterranean Sea. The river Cydnus flowed from the Taurus mountains located to the north of the city. Its course went through the center of the city. Several miles south of the city, the river widened into a natural inland lake. At an early stage of the city's history, the Tarsians dug a channel connecting the lake to the sea, thus providing a spacious, protected harbor. In Roman times the whole area around the lake was extensively populated, and there were settlements northward all the way to the city. Some twelve miles farther north of the city began the foothills of the Taurus mountains. In Paul's day there was an extensive settlement in these foothills as well. One scholar estimates that in Paul's day the population of the whole area around Tarsus was "not less than half a million."[3]

Another twenty-five miles north the road from Tarsus led up into the Taurus mountains through the famous pass known as the Cilician Gates. A natural river channel, the pass had been widened by the Tarsians to provide a wagon trail, which they chiseled out of sheer stone. This pass was on the main route from Syria to Asia Minor, the primary trade route connecting the east with the west. With its fine harbor and famous pass, Tarsus was a major center of commerce. As a boy Paul must have observed the traders on their journeys through the Cilician Gates. His own propensities for travel may well have been first engendered in Tarsus.

The earliest mention of the area around Tarsus is in ancient Hittite records from around 1200 B.C. where the Cilician Plain is referred to as Kizzuwatna. Not long after, Greeks seem to have settled around Tarsus, having come from Ionia. The people of Tarshish mentioned in Genesis 10:4–5 were probably the inhabitants of the Cilician plain. In the ninth century B.C., the area was subjugated by the Assyrians and subsequently by the Medes and the Persians. Tarsus is mentioned in the Persian records. Persian domination lasted until the time of Alexander the Great. In 333 B.C. Alexander defeated the Persian forces decisively at the battle of the Issus River, not far to the east of Tarsus. After the death of Alexander a decade later, Tarsus came under the domination of Seleucus, one of Alexander's generals, whose empire centered in Syria. The later Seleucid kings granted Tarsus the status of a Greek *polis*, which gave it a measure of independence and self-government. More important, it was during this period that "Hellenism" came to Cilicia, Syria, and Palestine. Alexander dreamed of a world united around Greek culture, and his successors did much to make that dream come true. The Greek language became the common tongue for communication throughout the civilized world. Greek institutions were established everywhere—baths, gymnasiums, theaters, marketplaces (*stoa*), and architecture. This spread of Greek culture is known as "Hellenism." Entire cities were built in Greek style with the full repertoire of Greek institutions. The Decapolis in Palestine, which Jesus visited, consisted of ten such hellenistic cities (Mark 5:20). Tarsus was another. Every city where Paul ministered was influenced by the hellenistic culture and spirit, even Jerusalem. Paul first came into contact with Hellenism in his native Tarsus.

Rome was the next great power to exert its influence over Tarsus. The Romans first created a province of Cilicia in 102 B.C. This consisted primarily of the western part of Cilicia, where the Taurus mountains extended all the way to the Mediterranean. The eastern plain, where Tarsus was located, was not yet incorporated into the early Roman province but retained its Greek "free city" status under the Seleucid kings. Roman political control by this time was being exerted everywhere in the Mediterranean world. The Seleucids were basically "tribute kings," wholly subservient to Rome. For a time in the early part of the first century B.C., the kings of Pontus and Armenia succeeded in resisting Roman rule. During this period, the king of Armenia subjugated the city of Tarsus. His rule was short-lived, as he was decisively defeated by the Roman general Pompey in 67 B.C. On this occasion Pompey reorganized the old province of Cilicia, expanding it by the addition of the eastern portions of the Cilician plain. He also incorporated the areas of Syria and Phoenicia into the province under a single governor, the imperial legate of Syria. From this time until A.D. 72, and thus throughout all of Paul's life, Syria, Cilicia, and Phoenicia comprised a single Roman Province.

Julius Caesar visited Tarsus in 47 B.C. and was enthusiastically received by the city. The Tarsians even renamed their city Juliopolis for a while after their famous visitor. When civil war broke out in Rome in 44 B.C., the Tarsians naturally allied with Antony and Octavian, the defenders of the murdered Caesar against his assassins Cassius and Brutus. This brought some grief to Tarsus when Cassius and his troops arrived in the city in 43 B.C. At that time Cassius exacted a very heavy tribute payment from the city, so heavy that a number of citizens had to be sold into slavery to pay for the levy. Their slave status was short-lived, however. Antony and Octavian defeated Brutus and Cassius at the battle of the Plains of Philippi in 42 B.C.

Soon thereafter Antony arrived in Tarsus, freed those who had been enslaved, and declared Tarsus a "free Roman city."

This status of a "free city" brought many privileges with it, including local law, self-government, and exemption from the heavy provincial taxes. Tarsus still retained its "free city" status when Paul grew up there. Antony returned to Tarsus in 38 B.C. when he had a rendezvous there with the Egyptian queen Cleopatra. It must have been a colorful occasion when she sailed up into the harbor of the Cydnus beneath a purple canopy in her royal barge with its gilded stern and golden oars.

One of the most extensive literary references to Tarsus is the description of the city's government by the Greek geographer Strabo (54 B.C.–A.D. 24).[4] Strabo wrote that Tarsus "surpassed" Athens and Alexandria in its love for philosophy. This is sometimes mistakenly interpreted to mean that Tarsus was superior to all the Greek cities in its philosophical training. Strabo, however, was not referring to the quality of the education so much as the zeal for education. The Tarsians outstripped everybody else in their love for the study of philosophy. He went on to say that only natives studied in Tarsus. Outsiders did not come to study there. Even the natives usually went elsewhere to study after they had exhausted the courses available in their home city. Seldom, says Strabo, did they return.

One who did return was Athenodorus, a Stoic philosopher who taught the emperor Augustus and was attached to the imperial court in Rome for many years. Athenodorus (ca. 74 B.C.–A.D. 7) retired from the court of Augustus some time around 15 B.C. and returned to his native Tarsus. In the meantime, Tarsus was experiencing particularly bad government from an oligarchy that had come to power in the time of Antony. Augustus entrusted Athenodorus with the power to expel the old government and initiate his own reforms. Strabo praises Athenodorus for his reforms and his own enlightened rule. After his death, he was succeeded by another philosopher-ruler, Nestor, also a Stoic. Tarsus seems to have been unique among hellenistic cities in having such a rule by philosophers for a time. And, that time was the period of Paul's youth.

PAUL'S FAMILY

Neither Acts nor Paul says much about his family except to mention the strict Judaism under which he was reared. That will be discussed in chapter 2. But do we know anything else about them?

Writing in the third century A.D., the Christian scholar Jerome mentioned a tradition that Paul migrated to Tarsus with his family from Gischala in Judea.[5] Jerome added that they fled because the area was being laid waste by the Romans. This tradition presents two problems. The first is the easiest to treat. Gischala was in Galilee, not Judea. However, there is ample evidence that the term *Judea* was used to refer to all of Palestine in the first century. The second problem is more difficult. Paul told the Jewish crowd that he was *born* in Tarsus (Acts 22:3), not carried there from "*Judea*." Jerome's tradition must be corrected at this point. The most likely time for a Jewish family to flee Roman repression in Palestine was that of Pompey (around 67 B.C.). If Jerome's tradition has any historical basis, we must assume that the family went to Tarsus before Paul's birth, perhaps as much as two generations earlier.

Paul's family were Diaspora Jews; that is, they were Jews who lived outside Palestine. Also referred to as the Jewish Dispersion, Jews had from the time of the Babylonian captivity been living in communities outside the Holy Land. Many did not return from Babylon when Cyrus permitted the return from exile. There were other periods of major Jewish migrations from Palestine; for instance, to Alexandria in the third century B.C. and to Syrian Antioch in the second. Antiochus IV seems to have settled a number of Jews in Cilicia and also in Rome.[6] By the first century, Jews lived in every major city of Asia and Syria-Cilicia.[7]

Unfortunately, we do not know a great deal about Diaspora Jews. There are few sources of information—some writings which seem to have originated in the Diaspora, such as the Wisdom of Solomon, the apocalyptic book of IV Ezra, the little fictional writing called Joseph and Asenath, and the writings of the Alexandrian apologist Philo. Their religion does not seem to have differed much from that of Palestine, either in belief or in practice. Philo, for instance, used elaborate allegorical methods derived from the Greeks. He employed them to expound the Jewish faith to the hellenistic world. His own faith, however, was squarely centered in what could be called "orthodox" observance of the Jewish law. Diaspora Jews usually lived in Jewish quarters with other Jews. The synagogue was the center of their community life.

Did Paul come from a family of means? There really is little evidence to go by. Some scholars have argued that his family was wealthy. This conclusion is based on one or both of two considerations. The first is the fact of their Tarsian citizenship. According to the Stoic philosopher Dio Chrysostom, who visited Tarsus in the late first century, one of the measures initiated by Athenodorus a century earlier was to restrict the right of voting to those who were able to pay a 500 drachma poll tax.[8] This was a considerable amount, equivalent to 18-months' wages for a working-class person. A second consideration is Paul's tent-making trade (Acts 18:3). It is possible that Paul worked with the material known as cilicium, which was made of woven goat's hair. Named for Cilicia, where it originated, it was used for tents and saddles. It was durable and expensive.[9] Tarsus was famous for its textile business. The Jewish rabbinic writings record that there was extensive commerce in textiles between Judea and Cilicia.[10] Paul's family may have had connections with this trade. It is also possible that Paul's family was not involved in tent making at all. Paul studied in Jerusalem to be a rabbi, a teacher of the law. The Jewish ideal for teachers was that they be self-supporting and not earn their livelihood by teaching. In this way they remained unencumbered and free to teach as they saw fit. Paul may have learned his tent making in Jerusalem in order to fulfill this ideal.

The life of a pious Diaspora Jewish family like Paul's would have centered around the synagogue. Religious instruction took place there on a regular basis through the readings of Scripture and the prayers in the worship every Sabbath. There may also have been synagogue instruction in Scripture for young Jewish boys. They were expected to learn large portions of the Pentateuch. We know that by the second century elementary schools existed for teaching boys aged six through twelve the written books of Law. These were known as the "houses of the book" (beth ha'sepher). We have little evidence for educational practices in first-century Diaspora Judaism. Religious education was a family responsibility, and Paul may have received his primary instruction in the family circle. One thing is certain: he learned his Greek Bible well. Paul cited Scripture consistently from the Septuagint, the Greek translation of the Scripture. Of course, Paul ministered among Jews and Gentiles outside Palestine for whom Greek would have been their primary language. His use of the Greek Scripture was thus natural. He had probably first become acquainted with it in Tarsus.

9

Another influence on Paul in Tarsus would have been the presence of Gentile proselytes and God-fearers in the synagogue. Proselytes were converts to Judaism who had been circumcised and who agreed to live by the Torah. God-fearers were synagogue adherents, Gentiles who believed in the one God and who participated in synagogue worship but who had not been circumcised and become full converts to Judaism. A good example of a God-fearer is the centurion Cornelius: he worshiped God, prayed constantly, and gave generously to the needy (Acts 10:2). God-fearers were usually present in the synagogues where Paul later witnessed as a Christian missionary. They were probably present in the synagogue of Paul's youth in Tarsus. It may well have been there where he first developed a burden for the salvation of the Gentiles, a burden which would become the passion of his life.

PAUL'S GREEK EDUCATION

Did Paul have any formal education in Greek schools? Hellenistic cities like Tarsus had a long tradition of primary education. Boys between the ages of six and fourteen, were sent to elementary schools, where they were trained in the basic skills of reading, writing, simple arithmetic, and music. Moral formation was also a major component of their studies. The writings of the Greek poets were emphasized. Does Paul show any evidence of such training? His literary skills are beyond question, as demonstrated in his letters. They are written in a fluent, educated Greek, neither the careless style of the popular papyri nor the artificial, verbose style of first-century schools.

Only rarely does Paul show any awareness of the Greek writers. In fact, there are only three instances where he quoted them. In his speech to the philosophers of Athens he quoted the third-century B.C. Stoic poet Aratus: "We are his offspring" (Acts 17:28). Aratus was a "local," a Cilician poet from the town of Soli, not far from Tarsus. In his first epistle to the Corinthians, Paul quoted from one of the comedies of Menander, a playwright of Athens (ca. 341–290 B.C.): "Bad company corrupts good character" (1 Cor. 15:33). Finally, in his letter to Titus, Paul quoted Epimenides, a Cretan religious teacher from around 500 B.C. Epimenides described the bad character of his fellow Cretans: "Cretans are always liars, evil brutes, lazy gluttons" (Titus 1:12).

These are the only three instances where Paul reflected any clear awareness of Greek writers. Even these need not have come to Paul through formal schooling. They had become proverbial tradition, well known by the general public. Paul's literary background was elsewhere. Throughout his letters he drew from the Greek Old Testament, the Septuagint. He quoted from it, he alluded to it, his choice of words reflected that he was thoroughly steeped in it. His primer was not the Greek writers but the Greek Bible. Did Paul attend grammar school in Tarsus? Perhaps some judgment such as that of Martin Hengel is on target: he received his elementary education in Tarsus, but it was in a Jewish school, not a Greek school.[11]

Greek secondary education was attended only by the rich. It was designed to prepare a young man for public service. Advanced mathematics and literature were a part of the curriculum. A major component was the study of rhetoric. Rhetoric was the art of persuasive speech for use in the legislature, the law courts, and for public occasions such as funerals. By Paul's time formal handbooks had been developed for teaching rhetorical method. Especially valued were those of Aristotle, Cicero, and, later, Quintilian. In recent years a number of scholars have noted how Paul seems to have employed a number of devices from formal hellenistic rhetoric. His speeches in Acts can be analyzed according to the major divisions of classical rhetoric.[12] Rhetorical method was also applied to written as well as oral communication, always with an emphasis on persuasion. The use of such devices as irony, various figures of speech, and appeals to emotion and common knowledge were all designed to carry an argument.[13] Some scholars have attempted analyses of entire Pauline epistles according to the major categories of classical rhetoric.[14]

Greek rhetoric was taught on the "high school" level, from ages fourteen to eighteen. But Paul probably never studied rhetoric in the schools of Tarsus. He was most likely already in Jerusalem studying under Gamaliel at this point in his life. Any formal training would have been in that city. Hellenism had penetrated the entire civilized world by the first century. The Romans were its most ardent supporters. Jerusalem would have been familiar with Greek culture. Paul's teacher Gamaliel had a reputation of being open to the study of Greek learning. Paul, however, may not have studied formal rhetoric. Rhetoric was above all an oral medium. In Tarsus especially Paul would have been exposed to the popular Cynic and Stoic street philosophers and their artful methods of persuasion.

Part of Paul's education as a boy in Tarsus would have been his exposure to the various institutions of Hellenism like the theater and the gymnasium. Paul doesn't show much interest in the former. Once he described his suffering as an apostle as being a "spectacle" (Gk., *theatron*) to the world. That is about it for his acquaintance with drama, but it is quite different with the gymnasium (1 Cor. 4:9). Every hellenistic city had its gymnasium, its center of athletic training. There men and youths engaged in athletic competition in the nude. This was where the institution derived its name, *gymnos* being the Greek word for "naked." For Jews, nakedness was religiously offensive. When the Seleucid king Antiochus Epiphanes sought to introduce a gymnasium into Jerusalem, it contributed to the revolt that eventually led to the Maccabean wars. Diaspora Jews seem to have been more open to Greek athletic events. The Alexandrian Jew Philo attended the games. Paul may have done so as well.

A number of times in his epistles, Paul employed athletic images. Some of these may have been mere metaphors, such as his frequent references to running. Other passages, however, reveal his clear awareness of Greek athletics. Particularly is this true of 1 Corinthians 9:24–27, where Paul combined images of the foot race, boxing, and training for competition. Philippians 3:12–14 presents a developed picture of the runner with eyes fixed on his goal, straining to reach it. The Pastoral Epistles frequently employ athletic images, such as physical training (1 Tim. 4:8), competing by the rules (2 Tim. 2:5), fighting the good fight (1 Tim. 6:12), and winning the race (2 Tim. 4:7). Paul's athletic references are too pervasive in his letters for him to have shared the antipathy that some Jews felt toward the games. His love for sports may have been a part of his Tarsian legacy.[15]

PAUL AND THE MYSTERY RELIGIONS

In the late nineteenth century, the history of religions school of biblical interpretation flourished. This school investigated early Christianity against the background of the pagan religions of that day. At the height of this method of study, much of Paul's theology and practice were explained as heavily influenced by or even produced by these non-Jewish and non-Christian religions. In particular, it was argued that Paul's teachings were derived from the contemporary mystery religions. These were cults which were widespread throughout the Roman Empire in the first centuries after Christ. They were developments from ancient native religions, and they came from nearly every part of the empire. From Greece came the oldest of the cults, the Eleusinian mysteries. From Asia Minor came the cult of Dionysus. It had its roots in the worship of the ancient Mother Goddess. From Persia came the worship of the "invincible sun," Mithraism. The cult of Isis originated in the worship of Isis and Osiris in Egypt. Behind all these was usually some form of ancient nature religion which celebrated the dying and coming to life of the seasonal agricultural cycle. In their first-century form, they had been uprooted from their original setting and universalized. They were called "mysteries" because secret rites lay at their heart. They flourished in an age when the old local gods were no longer considered protectors because of the dominance of Rome. They promised protection and deliverance on an individual level. Through undergoing the secret rites, adherents were "perfected" and guaranteed immortality.

Those people initiated into a mystery formed local brotherhoods called *thiasoi*. From the second century B.C., most of the mysteries had brotherhoods in all the major cities of the Roman Empire. Not much is known about the rites of the individual mysteries because of their esoteric nature. Initiates were sworn to secrecy. One of the few testimonies is that of Lucius Apuleius, who was initiated into the Isis mysteries at Cenchrea, a port of Corinth.[16] Most of the mysteries probably followed a pattern similar to Lucius's experience, which involved purification, extensive esoteric instruction, a sacred meal, and a vision of the goddess. The rites of Dionysus were particularly notorious for their frenzied dancing and drunken revelry.

History-of-religions scholars argued that Paul virtually turned Christianity into a mystery religion. The Lord's Supper was seen as a cultic meal in which initiates consumed the god. Baptism was traced to the *Taurobolium*, a mystery rite involving the slaughter of a bull and the bathing of the initiate in its blood. Paul's view of the believer's union with Christ was seen to come from oriental mysticism with its goal of the believer being totally absorbed into the being of the deity. Even the early Christian confession of Christ as "Savior" and "Lord" was seen to come from the local and imperial Greco-Roman cults.[17] Today the excesses of the history-of-religions school are largely ignored. There are a few scholars who would argue that Paul was exposed to the mystery cults in Tarsus. But there is no evidence that there were any brotherhoods of any of the mysteries in Tarsus in Paul's day. In fact, one cannot be sure of any fully developed mystery rites in the first century anywhere. All our sources for them date from the second century and later.[18]

There were undoubtedly remnants of the old Cilician gods in Tarsus in Paul's day. In the coinage of ancient Tarsus a native god often appears. He is usually depicted seated, holding out grapes or ears of grain. He was a typical near-eastern agricultural god. The Great Mother cult, an ancient fertility religion, originated in Phrygia, not far west of Tarsus. The sacred object of the goddess, a meteorite, was taken to Rome in 191 B.C. Veneration of the Great Mother lay behind the worship of Artemis in Ephesus with which Paul clashed (Acts 19:23–41). Paul almost certainly encountered the indigenous Greek religions from an early age. They seem to have contributed nothing to his religious thought beyond a possible word or two in his vocabulary. The content of his faith came from the Old Testament and from his conviction that Christ was the risen Messiah.

PAUL AND THE PHILOSOPHERS

Paul related easily to the Greek philosophers. Acts 17:16–21 depicts him holding his own with Epicurean and Stoic philosophers in the Athenian marketplace. His address from the Areopagus held the philosophers' attention until he came to the inevitable "offense" of the gospel—the death and resurrection of Christ and the final judgment (Acts 17:22–31). Paul even quoted a Stoic philosopher (v. 28). Is this an accurate picture? Was Paul that well acquainted with the philosophical currents of the time? The answer seems to be "yes."

There is much in Paul's letters which bears favorable comparison with the contemporary philosophers, particularly with the Stoics and Cynics. These were the most familiar to the general population. It is often hard to distinguish between the two, and so they are often put together—Stoic/Cynic. In Paul's day, both were peripatetic street philosophers. They used similar methods of argument, and both emphasized moral teaching. The Cynics were the original street preachers. They abandoned all luxuries, living lives of poverty, dressed in ragged cloaks, depending on begging for sustenance. They were particularly known for their sharp social critique. Stoics were perhaps the most popular philosophers of the day. They sought detachment from the world and total self-sufficiency as the greatest virtue. They believed that the world was permeated by a rational spirit which held everything in balance. Every human was believed to possess this spirit and thus to participate in divinity. Because the divine was seen to pervade everything, they emphasized living in harmony with nature and with one's fellow human beings. This emphasis on brotherhood made Stoicism especially popular with the military.

As we have seen, Tarsus was a major center of Stoic education and was even ruled for a time by the Stoics during the period of Paul's boyhood. One would not be surprised to see him being familiar with Stoic thought and manners. Some common Stoic themes do occasionally appear in his letters. For example, Stoics would have agreed with Paul's argument in Romans 1:19–20 that God is "clearly seen" in his creation. They, too, believed in a divine design that pervades all nature. They likewise would have agreed with Paul's reference to those who "do by nature things required by the law" and to those whose "consciences" bear them witness (Rom. 2:14–15). The idea of natural law was at the heart of the Stoic system. A Stoic, however, would have found Paul's use of these concepts incomprehensible. Paul used the ideas of God's visibility in creation and of human conscience to argue human responsibility for sin. For the Stoic, they were a sign of humanity's divinity; for Paul, they pointed to human lostness. The same can be said for Paul's statement in Philippians 4:11 that he had "learned to be content whatever the circumstances." Paul even used the Stoic terminology, *autarches* (self-sufficient). The goal of the Stoic was to become totally self-reliant, detached from the world, dispassionate, able to take whatever life might dish out. For a Stoic, this could be accomplished by tapping on one's inner resources, on the divine spark within each one of us. Paul shared no such view of human divinity. His sufficiency indeed came from divinity—not his own, but God's (Phil. 4:13).

Paul did not share the basic viewpoint of the Stoic philosophers. His debt to them was more in form than in substance. For instance, he often used their style of argumentation. Known as the *diatribe* style, this was a method of arguing by extensive use of rhetorical questions. A development of the Socratic method of teaching by asking questions, it was perfected by the Cynics in their street preaching and adopted by the Stoics. The Stoic diatribe often set up an imaginary dialogue partner, a sort of "straw person" who would ask questions, often in rapid succession. The Stoic would advance his argument by responding to these "straw" questions. Paul frequently used the method, particularly in Romans. A good example is Romans 6:1. Paul had been maintaining that we are saved by God's grace, not by our own good works. Now he wished to address the issue of whether this means that morality has no role in the Christian life. He used the diatribe method to raise the issue. The imaginary dialogue partner asked, "Shall we go on sinning so that grace may increase?" Paul answered his own question with a strong "by no means!" and proceeded to argue that a Christian no longer sins, because the sinful life has been buried with Christ. Paul's "by no means" (Gk., *mē genoito*) often accompanies the diatribe style. Paul used it three times in the space of nine verses in the diatribe argument of Romans 3:1–9.[19]

In Paul's day the major component of Stoic teaching was moral instruction. This often followed certain standard forms. Paul was familiar with the forms and often used them. For example, there were the virtue and vice lists, lists which enumerated various good qualities to be nurtured and bad traits to be avoided. The "acts of the sinful nature," which he listed in Galatians 5:19–21, take the form of a traditional vice list. The "fruit of the Spirit," which follow in verses 22 and 23, are a "virtue" list. A related form of hellenistic moral instruction were the lists of qualifications for leaders. These often took a rather stereotypical form, listing the various characteristics which made for a good leader in specific professions. Paul followed this form in his lists of qualifications for overseers and deacons in the Pastoral Epistles (1 Tim. 3:2–13). A final form of moral teaching was that of the "household order," where instruction was given to various members of the household as to their responsibilities toward one another. Paul likewise used this form of teaching (Col. 3:18–4:1).

In all these instances, Paul followed the *form* of hellenistic moral teaching. His *content* was generally quite different. For example, in the household order the philosophers usually furnished advice to only one party in the relationship, generally the subordinate member in the social order of the day (wives, children, slaves). In the household orders of Colossians and Ephesians, Paul addressed the responsibilities of *both* parties (husbands as well as wives, parents as well as children, slaves as well as masters). For the Stoic, the advice was always based on what was believed to be in accordance with nature. For Paul, the instruction derived from one's relationship to Christ (what was seen to be fitting in light of one's Christian status).

Paul may have been influenced by the philosophers in other ways as well. For instance, it has been argued that Paul combated his opponents in 2 Corinthians 10–13 with an ironical type of argument which emphasized that the true philosopher often appears in weakness rather than arrogance, a type of ideal that ultimately went back to Socrates.[20] Others have noted how Paul's methods of dealing with his churches exemplify a sort of "pastoral care" that had much in common with the communities of the philosophers.[21] Again, it must be emphasized that lines of dependence are difficult to establish. The influence of the philosophers may have been communicated to Paul indirectly, mediated through the Diaspora synagogue or even in his schooling in Jerusalem. It should also be noted that sometimes the connection was negative. For example, in the first century some of the traveling philosophers had become virtual charlatans, preying on the innocent for their personal gain. Paul may have had to dissociate himself from them on occasion. At Corinth, it might have been the bad taste of itinerant philosophers that led him to forego the material support of the church (1 Cor. 9:3–18).

14

We will never know for certain how much and in what ways Paul was influenced and formed by his years in Tarsus. In the cross-fertilization characteristic of the age, Paul could have been exposed to hellenistic influences in Jerusalem as well as in Tarsus. One legacy he almost certainly owed to Tarsus, however: There he was exposed to Gentiles to an extent he never could have been in Jerusalem. It was probably not by accident that a Diaspora Jew like Paul became the apostle to the Gentiles (Rom. 1:5).

ROME

Politically, Paul's world was a Roman world. Rome's conquest of the Mediterranean basin was complete by the first century A.D. The only areas not under Roman control were the Parthians to the east of Syria and the barbarian tribes of northern and eastern Europe. The Romans established strong borders to keep the latter out. Within those borders there was relative peace throughout the Mediterranean world. Rome's administration of its empire took various forms, but the one constant was the Roman presence.

ROMAN CITIZENSHIP

Paul grew up in a world ruled by Rome. His native Tarsus was a free city under Rome, which meant that it had a measure of independence and self-government. Still, it was within the Roman administrative province of Syria-Cilicia; the supreme local authority was the imperial legate of Syria. When Paul moved to Jerusalem, he lived in a city which was even more directly controlled by the Romans. Judaea was under a Roman procurator, who resided in Caesarea and periodically came to Jerusalem to hold court and attend to affairs. Roman troops were permanently garrisoned in the city. Though the Jewish Sanhedrin had probably been delegated a degree of jurisdiction in local matters, the supreme authority lay with the Romans, particularly in more serious matters like capital crimes. Jesus, for instance, was formally condemned by the Roman procurator Pilate and executed on a Roman cross.

Paul had even closer ties with Rome; he possessed the coveted Roman citizenship. He never mentioned his citizenship in his epistles; he had no occasion to do so. In Acts Luke related several incidents involving Paul's status as a citizen—his informing the Philippian magistrates that they had violated his citizenship by scourging him (16:37–39), his divulging his citizenship to avoid another beating in Jerusalem (22:25–29), and the Roman tribune's advising the governor Felix of the prisoner Paul's Roman citizenship (23:27). Paul's citizenship was not mentioned but was obviously implied when he appealed to Caesar (25:10–12). A number of questions naturally arise over Paul's citizenship.[22] What privileges did it carry? How did Paul's family acquire it? How could he prove he had it?

Roman citizenship was not common when Paul was born into it. It was granted on an increasing basis through the course of the first century and thereafter. Finally, in A.D. 212 it was extended to all inhabitants of the Roman empire (the *Constitutio Antoniana*). But in Paul's day it was uncommon in the provinces of the empire, where even high-ranking officials often did not possess the coveted status. Citizenship carried a number of advantages. Perhaps the primary one was that citizens were subject to Roman law, not to the local laws of the provincial cities. A citizen could agree to trial by local law but always retained the right to be heard before a Roman tribunal. Only a Roman citizen had the legal right to marry another Roman citizen.

A citizen could not be scourged or imprisoned without a hearing and the establishment of sufficient cause. In capital offenses, a citizen had the right to appeal the decision of a lower court to the emperor.[23] In general, citizens were exempt from cruel punishments like crucifixion.[24]

There were various ways by which citizenship could be granted. Freeborn natives of Rome were automatically citizens. When they took up residence in the provinces, they carried their citizenship with them. One could become a citizen through military service. Veterans of ten or more years were granted citizenship. Sometimes individuals or whole territories were granted citizenship by vote of the Roman senate or by imperial decree. Usually this was in gratitude for some special service rendered to the state. Some have suggested that Paul's family may have obtained the status in this manner—through services rendered to the military in their tent-making trade. Direct purchase of citizenship does not seem to have been possible. When the tribune Lysias told Paul that he had obtained his citizen's rights by paying a large sum of money (Acts 22:28), he was probably referring to the bribes he had to pay the "right people" to obtain the coveted status.

One of the most common means by which people became Roman citizens was by being freed from slavery. When a Roman citizen freed a slave, the slave legally obtained his patron's citizenship along with freedom. The patron's name now became his own legal name. It is very possible that Paul's father or grandfather obtained Roman citizenship in this fashion. Philo, for example, told how a number of Jews had been carried captive to Rome by Pompey in 63 B.C. and how they were later set free and continued to live in the city.[25] Paul's family may have obtained citizenship in some such fashion. In the case of such "freedmen," their citizen's rights were limited in some respects. They could not hold public office, for example. Children born to them, however, had no such restrictions, being full citizens in every respect. Paul's situation was the latter; he was *born* a Roman citizen.

How did a person prove Roman citizenship? During the time of Augustus, a policy was adopted whereby newborn citizens in the provinces were registered in the office of the provincial governor. Registry had to be completed within thirty days of birth and in the presence of seven witnesses. A permanent record was kept in the official archives. Presumably a copy was furnished to the family. It may have been like the small diptych which military veterans carried with them to confirm their citizenship. It consisted of a pair of folded wooden tablets inside which was inscribed the official record of their citizenship.[26] Citizens probably did not have to produce proof of citizenship on demand. Penalties were severe for imposters, serving as a deterrent to deception.

One badge of citizenship was a person's name. Roman citizens had three names, as in the following examples: Gaius Julius Caesar, Marcus Tullius Cicero. The first name, called the *praenomen* (Gaius, Marcus), was little more than a formality. In the first century only a handful of praenomina were used. The second name (Julius, Tullius) was called the *nomen*. It denoted the Roman tribe to which one belonged. Every citizen belonged to a tribe (or gens). This tribal name linked individuals to their ancestry or to the patron from whom they obtained their citizenship. The third name (Caesar, Cicero) was known as the *cognomen*. This was the name which carried the most weight for actually identifying the individual. Often it was a name which was commonly used in a given family.

The tripartite name was distinctly Roman. Jews and Greeks normally used only a single name. A full three-part Roman name never appears in the New Testament. Latin names are common in the New Testament but never the full formal name. Three praenomina occur: Gaius, Lucius, and Titus. Only two nomina occur: Cornelius and Julius. Twice a double name (nomen and cognomen) appears: Sergius Paulus and Claudius Lysias. Paul (Paulus) is a cognomen. It is a Latin, not a Jewish name. It is significant that Paul always called himself by this Roman name in his epistles. He never used Saul, which is found only in Acts.[27]

Many have speculated about Paul's possible full name. Pompey, Julius Caesar, and Marc Antony were all patrons who bestowed benefits on Tarsus. If Paul's ancestors were granted citizenship by one of these, they would have taken on the first two names of the patron. The resulting name for Paul would then be Gaius Julius Paulus, or Marcus Antonius Paulus. Others have noted that Paulus is a common cognomen found among the Aemilius tribe. They suggest that Paul's name may then have been L. Aemilius Paulus. The church fathers speculated about Paul's name as well. Jerome suggested that Paul took it from Sergius Paulus, Paul's first convert on the first missionary journey. It is indeed at the place where Luke mentioned Sergius Paulus that he first introduced the name Paul into the narrative of Acts (13:9). But Paul was himself a Roman citizen and would have had his Latin name from birth. Augustine preferred to play on the etymology of Paul's name, noting that the Latin word *paulus* means "small," and suggesting that Paul preferred to be known as the "least" of the apostles (1 Cor. 15:9) rather than by the name of the arrogant king Saul.[28] All speculation aside, Paul's Roman name would have served him well as he ministered in the provinces of the Roman Empire as the apostle to the Gentiles.

ROMAN GOVERNMENT

For the first few hundred years of its existence, Rome had a republican form of government with a senate as its governing body. With the burgeoning empire and with the growing power of the military, in the first century B.C. the republic eventually gave way to rule by a single individual—first Julius Caesar and then his nephew Octavian. Octavian, better known as Augustus ("revered"), ruled from 31 B.C. to A.D. 14. He was emperor when Jesus was born (Luke 2:1) and probably at Paul's birth as well. Paul lived under three other Roman emperors. Tiberius Caesar (A.D. 14–37) was emperor when Jesus began his ministry (Luke 3:1). Jesus was crucified during his reign, and Paul was probably converted while Tiberius was emperor. The emperor throughout most of Paul's missionary activity was Claudius (A.D. 41–54). He is mentioned twice in Acts—in connection with a worldwide famine (11:28) and with his expulsion of the Jews from Rome (18:2). The emperor to whom Paul appealed was Nero (A.D. 54–68), and, if early tradition is correct, he was the emperor responsible for Paul's death.

The emperor was *princeps*, "first" in command. But under him was an extensive imperial retinue. At the top were the governors of the various provinces. For administrative purposes, Rome's subject territories had been divided into a number of provinces. These were of two types: senatorial and imperial. Senatorial provinces tended to be the older, more settled districts. They were ruled over by a governor of senatorial rank who was appointed by the Roman senate. The governor was called a proconsul and generally served a term of one year. Gallio was the proconsul of the province of Achaia (southern Greece) around A.D. 52. The Jews of Corinth made a formal accusation against Paul before Gallio, who quickly dismissed the case (Acts 18:12–17). Since the government of the senatorial provinces was well established and stable, Roman troops were usually not stationed in them. Most of Paul's missionary activity was conducted in senatorial provinces. In his day, the senatorial provinces were Sicily, Sardinia, Spain, Pamphylia, Africa, Macedonia, Asia, Bithynia, Achaia, Crete, and Cyprus.

Imperial provinces were those that had only recently come under Roman administration. Their governors were called procurators and were appointed by the emperor. Often these provinces lay along the borders of the empire or in areas where there was instability or resistance to Roman rule. Correspondingly, troops were regularly stationed in these territories. Syria-Cilicia, Gaul, Galatia, and Britain were among the imperial provinces in Paul's time.

In addition to provinces, there were small "client" kingdoms where the Romans allowed local kings to retain their rule. These kings were little more than puppets who swore their allegiance to Rome. Herod the Great (40–4 B.C.) is a good example of a client king. He owed his rule over Judaea to the Romans. He served as a "benefactor" of Rome throughout his reign, paying for lavish building enterprises in cities all over the Roman Empire. During most of Paul's ministry, Judaea was not ruled by a local king but was directly administered by Roman procurators/governors, except for the brief three-year reign of Herod's grandson Agrippa I (A.D. 41–44). Agrippa is the "king Herod" of Acts 12. Paul had close dealings with two of the Judaean governors: Felix (Acts 23:26–24:26) and Festus (Acts 24:27–26:32).

In his epistles Paul consistently used official Roman provincial designations. He referred to Philippi and Thessalonica as "Macedonia" (2 Cor. 8:1), to Corinth as "Achaia" (2 Cor. 9:2), and to Ephesus as "Asia" (Rom. 16:5). Likewise, he addressed the Galatian epistle to the province and not the particular cities where the Galatian churches were located. If he had done the latter, we would not have the problem of determining whether the Galatians were located in the northern or in the southern portion of the province.[29]

Paul ministered in many hellenistic cities. The majority of these were of two types: *free cities* and *colonies*. *Free cities* were based on the Greek model of the independent city-state. The Roman policy was to allow as much local autonomy as possible, to encourage cities to govern themselves as long as they maintained allegiance to Rome. Well-established hellenistic cities which had a history of self-government and had demonstrated their loyalty to Rome were often given the status of free cities. Among the cities where Paul ministered, Syrian Antioch, Thessalonica, and Athens were all free cities. Being a free city carried a number of advantages. In theory, free cities were allowed to pass and to enforce their own laws. Roman troops were not to be quartered within the city limits. The city was exempt from provincial taxation and allowed to levy its own taxes. Since free cities were allowed to determine their own government, they varied widely in their laws and administration. For instance, Luke referred to the officials of Thessalonica as "politarchs" (Acts 17:6), a term which has been found in inscriptions at Thessalonica and that seems to have been unique to that city.

Colonies were the highest status of cities in the Roman Empire. As the name implies, colonies were little islands of Roman culture and government scattered throughout the empire. Like free cities, colonies enjoyed self-government and exemption from provincial taxes. But the government and law were uniform in the colonies. They all had Roman law and Roman government. Colonies were always comprised of a nucleus of Roman citizens, who alone had the vote and who were responsible for the administration of the city. Colonies were particularly numerous along the frontiers of the empire. Troops and veterans would be located there to ensure the integrity of the empire's borders. Among the colonies where Paul witnessed, Pisidian Antioch and Lystra were of this type of military border colony. Another type of colony was the veteran colony. These colonies consisted of settlements of retired Roman soldiers. One of the rewards of serving in the military was the receipt of a pension and a homestead upon retirement. These veteran communities were usually located on land which Rome had acquired through its conquests. They were "colonies" of the mother city; their law, their administration, and often their language were Roman.

Among the veteran colonies where Paul served were Corinth and Philippi. Corinth had been destroyed by the Romans in 146 B.C. in reprisal for its leadership in the Greek wars against Rome. It was rebuilt in 44 B.C. by Julius Caesar. A number of veterans were settled there. In addition, many of the indigenous Greek population were granted Roman citizenship by Caesar. The new city was organized as a Roman colony. Philippi was an ancient city located close to the plain where in 42 B.C. the decisive battle of the Roman civil war took place, Octavian and Antony prevailing over the republican forces of Brutus and Cassius. Philippi was at that time reorganized as a colony, and veterans of the victorious forces were settled there.

The scene of Paul's imprisonment in Philippi (Acts 16:19–40) illustrates a typical Roman colony. Paul and Silas were accused of a crime and taken before the magistrates of the colony. Every colony had this Roman governmental structure of two chief judicial officers (called *duoviri*). The two Christian missionaries were beaten with rods and then cast into prison. The rods were the typical Roman instruments for scourging. They were carried about by the police (called *lictors*) and were bound in bunches called *fasces*. (Mussolini's government was called "fascist" because it used this symbol of the fasces, the bundles of rods carried by the police of ancient Rome). Quite understandable was the great concern of the magisrates over having improperly scourged the two Roman citizens, Paul and Silas. Roman law prevailed in the Philippian colony, and scourging without a hearing was a serious breach of law. It is possible that Paul's letter to Philippi reflects the city's colonial status. A great deal of military language appears in Philippians. Paul spoke of the Roman palace guard (1:13) and described Epaphroditus as a "fellow soldier" (2:25). He used the language of citizenship (3:20) and may even have reflected Roman laws regulating partnerships in his references to the Philippians serving as his partners in the gospel (1:7; 4:10–20).[30]

In the Roman provinces, even cities which enjoyed neither colonial nor free city status were often given considerable local autonomy. This was the case for both Jerusalem and Ephesus in Paul's day. The account in Acts of Paul's encounter with the Ephesian silversmiths illustrates the interplay of local and imperial jurisdiction that prevailed in these cities (Acts 19:23–41). Luke referred to the crowd which gathered in the theater as the *dēmos* (v. 30) and the *ecclēsia* (v. 32). These are both technical terms for the assembly of voting citizens in a Greek city. The city clerk (v. 35) was the presiding officer of the assembly. Under Roman rule, the clerk was the liaison officer between the town assembly and the Roman administration. He was thus concerned that the Ephesians might fall under Roman suspicion through having an unlawful assembly (vv. 39–40). He reminded them of the regular courts to which they could appeal, presided over by the Roman proconsul (v. 38). The Romans preferred that locals administer their own internal affairs as much as possible, but they were always on guard against disturbances of the peace and possible revolts. Riots would inevitably result in tighter Roman control, and this was the main concern of the Ephesian town clerk.

OTHER ROMAN INSTITUTIONS[31]

The military. Paul frequently encountered the Roman military. Legions were regularly stationed in the imperial provinces where he ministered, like Syria-Cilicia and Galatia. He would have come in contact with the military especially in border colonies like Lystra and Pisidian Antioch and with the veterans of Philippi. There were likely many Christian converts from among the military in these places. Paul received good treatment from the various Roman officers who were responsible for him during his periods of imprisonment, officers like the tribune Lysias (Acts 22–24) and the centurion Julius (Acts 27).

It is striking how wide a variety of the various ranks Paul encountered, and it may prove helpful to give an overview of the Roman military organization. The basic unit of the Roman army was the legion, which consisted of from five thousand to six thousand personnel. During the time of Augustus, the number of active legions within the empire varied from eighteen to twenty-five. Within a legion were two types of officers: nobility and career military. Nobility held the high-ranking positions. They had to be of equestrian (knight) rank. The imperial legate was the commander of the legion. He was answerable to the governor of the province in which his legion was stationed. Under the legate were six tribunes. Claudius Lysias, the officer under whom Paul was arrested in Jerusalem, was a tribune and the top-ranking officer over the forces in Jerusalem. He may have begun as a career officer. His obtaining Roman citizenship was essential to his climbing the ranks, a possibility open only to the nobility. The career ladder for nobles usually started with the rank of tribune. From there it led to the position of a minor officer in the administration of a province, then to the rank of legate, from there to a major civil post such as a consulate, and finally to the top status of provincial governor (proconsul).

The backbone of the Roman legions were the career military. These were of two types. *Regular* legions in the republican and early imperial periods were comprised only of Roman citizens, nobility holding the top ranks, plebians the lower. *Auxiliary* legions were comprised largely of noncitizens, drawn from the natives of the province in which the legion was located and from mercenaries who came from elsewhere. From the time of the emperor Claudius, veterans of the auxiliary forces were granted citizenship upon their retirement.

The smallest unit of a legion was a squadron of eight soldiers, known as a *contubernium*. Ten squadrons comprised a *centuria*. A centurion was its ranking officer. Centurions appear often in the New Testament, such as the centurion Julius who accompanied the prisoner Paul to Rome (Acts 27:1). The largest division within the legion was the *cohort*. There were ten cohorts within a legion. The centurion Cornelius, to whom Peter witnessed, was a member of the "Italian Regiment" (Acts 10:1), a contingent of native Italians stationed in Caesarea. No legion was stationed in Italy, just as there were none in the senatorial provinces. The only forces in Italy were the emperor's own elite corps, known as the Praetorian Guard, which consisted of nine cohorts. In Philippians Paul mentioned witnessing to the Praetorian Guard (Phil. 1:13), and he may have been under their custody during his confinement in Rome (Acts 28:16).

Roman legions were often on the move, trained to move quickly from one region to another as the circumstances demanded. The very favorable picture the New Testament consistently gives of the Roman military is evidence that many like Cornelius became Christians. They carried their faith wherever they went. Many places, perhaps even Rome itself, doubtlessly first heard the gospel from military personnel.

Travel. A by-product of the Roman military was the extensive system of roads which crisscrossed the empire. Largely built by the military, the primary purpose of the roads was for the rapid deployment of troops. By the end of the first century, there were over fifty thousand miles of primary (paved) Roman roads. As the proverbial statement goes, all roads *did* eventually lead to Rome. Augustus erected a golden milestone for point zero in the middle of the forum in Rome. On Roman roads throughout the empire, mile markers were erected measuring the distance to the central marker in Rome. Many thousands of these markers still remain today as do long stretches of the ancient stone roads and bridges, a testimony to their durability and the skill of those who engineered them. The Roman roads interconnected, all eventually leading to Rome. Paul traveled them often.

For instance, he walked the Via Augusta between Pisidian Antioch and Lystra and the Via Appia on his trip from Puteoli to Rome (Acts 28:15). One of the roads he traveled most was the Via Egnatia, which ran from Byzantium west to the Adriatic coast at Dyrrhachium. At this point a person caught a ship, which sailed across the Adriatic directly to Brundisium on the eastern coast of Italy. From there he or she proceeded north to Rome. Paul traveled the Via Egnatia between Neapolis, Philippi, and Thessalonica. The ancient road ran through the center of Philippi, and extensive remnants of it can still be viewed from the modern road that links Philippi with Kavala (ancient Neapolis). Paul traveled thousands of miles by foot. His extensive journeys would not have been possible in an earlier day before the advent of the Roman road system.

Paul frequently traveled by sea as well. Ancient navigation was not without its dangers. Paul spoke of being shipwrecked three times and being adrift at sea for a day and a night (2 Cor. 11:25), and all this took place *before* the catastrophic wreck on his voyage to Rome (Acts 27). In an earlier day, however, Paul may not have escaped with his life. Piracy had made voyage on the Mediterranean extremely precarious. In the first century before Christ, Pompey rid the eastern Mediterranean of its pirates, and by the early first century A.D. Augustus had virtually eliminated piracy. What was true of the sea was also true of land travel. In an earlier day, Paul could not have traveled unmolested on such precarious routes as those of his first missionary journey. The passes through the rugged Taurus mountains and the sparsely inhabited territory made the area a haunt for brigands. The Romans, however, cleared the land routes as well as the seas of thieves. Paul may have been directly assisted by Romans in some of his travels. His journey to Rome may have been on ships involved in the imperial grain trade. Egypt was the breadbasket of the Roman Empire. To ensure that there was adequate distribution of grain throughout the empire, the emperor employed a large fleet of ships. Both ships on which Paul sailed to Italy came from Egypt and may well have been imperial grain ships (Acts 27:38; 28:11).

In many other ways the Roman rule made Paul's missionary travels possible. The Romans regulated the excessive duties and taxes which once plagued the traveler who crossed the borders of each tiny territory. They initiated uniform standards of weights and measures. They brought a standard coinage to the world that was recognized and accepted everywhere. Such undertakings as Paul's collection for Jerusalem would have been virtually impossible without such currrency standards. Rome regulated and unified the Mediterranean world. It brought relative peace and enabled a traveler like Paul to make his extensive journeys in a manner never before possible. Paul owed little to Rome for his message; he owed much to Rome for his mission.

NOTES

1. This view is often taken by Jewish scholars, who see Paul as an "apostate" Jew. An example is H. J. Schoeps, *Paul* (Philadelphia: Westminster, 1961).
2. W. C. Van Unnik, "Tarsus or Jerusalem: The City of Paul's Youth," trans. G. Ogg, *Sparsa Collecta*, Part 1 (Leiden: Brill, 1973), 259–320.
3. W. M. Ramsay, *The Cities of St. Paul* (London: Hodder and Stoughton, 1907), 97. For a full treatment of Tarsus, see pp. 3–240 of this volume.
4. Strabo, *Geography*, 14.5.13–15.
5. Jerome, *Commentary on the Epistle to Philemon*, on verse 23, and *De viris illustribus*, 5.
6. Ramsay, *Cities*, 182–86. Ramsay thinks Antiochus settled Jews in Cilicia to maintain order and that he granted them Tarsian citizenship at that time.
7. V. Tcherikover, *Hellenistic Civilization and the Jews* (Philadelphia: Jewish Publication Society of America, 1961), 287–289.
8. Dio Chrysostom, *Orations*, 34.1–23.
9. F. F. Bruce, *Paul, Apostle of the Heart Set Free* (Grand Rapids: Eerdmans, 1977), 35–36.
10. M. Hengel, *The Pre-Christian Paul*, trans. John Bowden (Philadelphia: Trinity Press, 1991), 99.
11. *Ibid.*, 38.
12. For Stephen's speech in Acts 7 as an example, see J. B. Polhill, *Acts*, NAC (Nashville: Broadman, 1992), 188, n. 38.
13. For a clear rhetorical analysis of a short Pauline passage, see James Hester, "The Use and Influence of Rhetoric in Galatians 2:1–14," *Theologische Zeitschrift* 42 (5, 1986): 386–408. For a useful introduction to rhetorical criticism of the New Testament, see George Kennedy, *New Testament Interpretation Through Rhetorical Criticism* (Chapel Hill: University of North Carolina Press, 1984).
14. For example, see the analysis of Galatians by Hans Dieter Betz, *Galatians*, Hermeneia (Philadelphia: Fortress, 1979).
15. For a thorough treatment of Paul's athletic imagery, see V. C. Pfitzner, *Paul and the Agon Motif: Traditional Athletic Imagery in the Pauline Literature* (Leiden: Brill, 1967).
16. Preserved by Ovid, *Metamorphoses*, 11.18–25.
17. This was the main thesis of W. Bousset, *Kyrios Christos*, trans. J. E. Steely from the 1913 German edition (Nashville: Abingdon, 1970).
18. For a thorough treatment of the mystery religions that sees little influence on Paul, see H. A. A. Kennedy, *St. Paul and the Mystery Religions* (London: Hodder and Stoughton, 1913). See also C. A. A. Scott, *Christianity According to St. Paul* (Cambridge: At the University Press, 1961), 22–33.
19. For Paul's diatribe style, see S. K. Stowers, *The Diatribe and Paul's Letter to the Romans*, SBL Dissertation Series, 57 (Chico, Calif.: Scholars Press, 1981).
20. H. D. Betz, *Der Apostel Paulus und die sokratische Tradition* (Tübingen: Mohr/Siebeck, 1972).
21. A. J. Malherbe, *Paul and the Thessalonians: The Philosophic Tradition of Pastoral Care* (Philadelphia: Fortress, 1987).
22. Very few scholars question the historical reliability of the tradition in Acts that Paul was a Roman citizen. One exception is W. Stegemann, "War der Apostel Paulus ein romis-

cher Burger?" *Zeitschrift für die neutestamentliche Wissenschaft* 78 (3–4, 1987): 200–229. Stegemann argues that it is unlikely there was a significant number of Jewish citizens in the early principate.

23. Paul's appeal will be examined in detail later. His case was somewhat unusual in that it involved a change of venue and not an appeal of a decision already rendered. See P. Garnsey, "The Lex Julia and Appeal under the Empire," *Journal of Roman Studies* 56 (1966): 167–189.

24. There were exceptions. For example, Jews of Roman citizenship (equestrian rank) were crucified by Florus in A.D. 66 at the outbreak of the Jewish war: Josephus, *War*, 2.308.

25. Philo, *Embassy to Gaius*, 155–157.

26. A. N. Sherwin-White, *The Roman Citizenship* (Oxford: Clarendon Press, 1973), 314–316.

27. Paul may have deliberately avoided using the name Saul (Gk., *saulos*) in his Greek letters. The Greek word *saulos* refers to personal affectation, especially in one's walking. It was sometimes used of the seductive sauntering of prostitutes. See T. J. Leary, "Paul's Improper Name," *New Testament Studies* 38 (3, 1992): 467–469.

28. Cited in W. J. Conybeare and J. S. Howson, *The Life and Epistles of Saint Paul* (Hartford, Conn.: S. S. Scranton, 1902), 137.

29. This is a major issue of scholarly discussion which will be covered in the chapter on Galatia.

30. J. P. Sampley, *Pauline Partnership in Christ: Christian Community and Commitment in Light of Roman Law* (Philadelphia: Fortress, 1980), 51–77.

31. The following material and much of the preceding is a summary of my article, "Political Background of the New Testament," in *Foundations for Biblical Interpretation*, ed. Dockery, Matthews, and Sloan (Nashville: Broadman & Holman, 1994), 524–544.

SUGGESTED FURTHER READING

Hengel, Martin. *The Pre-Christian Paul*. Trans. John Bowden. Philadelphia: Trinity Press International, 1991.

Kennedy, George. *New Testament Interpretation through Rhetorical Criticism*. Chapel Hill: University of North Carolina Press, 1984.

Kennedy, H. A. A. *St. Paul and the Mystery Religions*. London: Hodder and Stoughton, 1913.

Malherbe, Abraham J. *Paul and the Popular Philosophers*. Minneapolis: Fortress, 1989.

Polhill, John. "Political Background of the New Testament." *Foundations for Biblical Interpretation*. Ed. Dockery, Matthews, and Sloan. Nashville: Broadman and Holman, 1994, pp. 524–544.

Ramsay, William M. *The Cities of St. Paul*. London: Hodder and Stoughton, 1907. Reprinted by Baker, 1979, pp. 3–240.

Sherwin-White, A. N. *Roman Society and Roman Law in the New Testament*. Oxford: Clarendon, 1963.

Stowers, Stanley K. *The Diatribe and Paul's Letter to the Romans*. SBL Dissertation Series, #57. Chico, Calif.: Scholars Press, 1981.

2

~⁊e9⁊~

HEBREW OF THE HEBREWS

The previous chapter treated the Greek and Roman influences on Paul, the cultural and political matrix in which he conducted his ministry. Although this material was presented under the heading of Paul's heritage in Tarsus, one must not get the impression that these influences were exclusive to that context. On the contrary, hellenistic culture and the Roman political presence were as evident in Jerusalem as in Tarsus. We cannot be sure *where* Paul was most influenced in any particular respect. His religion, of course, was Jewish. But again we cannot be sure how much he learned in the context of his family in Tarsus. We do know, however, that he pursued advanced studies in the Jewish law and that those studies took place in Jerusalem. This chapter will focus on Paul's Jewish heritage. It also contains a brief discussion of the little we know about his physical appearance.

PAUL THE JEW

Several times in his epistles Paul referred to his Jewish heritage. Most of these references occur in contexts where his Jewish background was important to his argument. The main texts are Philippians 3:4–6, Galatians 1:13–17, 1 Corinthians 15:8–10, 2 Corinthians 11:22, and Romans 11:1. In addition to these, there are Paul's autobiographical comments in his speeches to the Jewish mob in the temple yard (Acts 22:3–5) and before King Agrippa (Acts 26:4–5). The material in these testimonies is of three types. First, there are those characteristics which were Paul's Jewish heritage by birth: his circumcision, membership in Israel (a "Jew"), Benjamite tribal affiliation, descent from Abraham, and "Hebrew" background. Second, there were those things which Paul owed to his Pharisaic connections. Third, Paul referred to his zeal in persecuting the Christians. In the following treatment, the "birth" heritage will be considered first, then Paul's Pharisaic training, and finally, his past as a persecutor of the Christians. Philippians 3:4–6 is the most comprehensive of Paul's autobiographical statements. It will serve as a convenient organizing text.

CIRCUMCISED ON THE EIGHTH DAY (PHIL. 3:5)

Paul mentioned his circumcision only in the letter to the Philippians. He was warning them against Judaizers, those who would insist on their being circumcised and living by the Jewish law in order to be full Christians. Paul's response was that he could himself claim circumcision and a full Jewish pedigree, but none of that was of any importance to him any longer in comparison with his relationship to Christ.

Circumcision was the external mark which set a person apart as a Jew. It was viewed as the badge of membership in the covenant people of God. A boy born into Judaism was normally circumcised on the eighth day after birth. There were exceptions, of course. Converts to Judaism (proselytes) were circumcised at the time of their conversion, usually as adults. Some Jewish males were not circumcised at all, like Timothy, who was technically a Jew because he had a Jewish mother (Acts 16:1–3). Paul could boast that his own circumcision was "by the book." Literally, he said that he was an "eighth-dayer" with respect to his circumcision. Some Jewish males who wanted to participate in the nude Greek athletic events tried to "undo" their circumcision by undergoing a painful operation. Paul was referring to such a practice when he urged the circumcised not to "become uncircumcised" (1 Cor. 7:18).

Greeks and Romans neither understood nor appreciated Jewish circumcision. They considered it a defacing of the human body. As a Jew, Paul never denied his own circumcision. He even insisted on Timothy being circumcised because he was a Jew (Acts 16:1–3). But he never asked that Gentiles be circumcised in order to become Christians. In fact, he insisted that they *not* do so. Paul had come to see that circumcision was no longer essential to God's people in the light of Christ. True circumcision for the Christian is not a mark of the flesh but a spiritual dedication of the heart to God (Rom. 2:28–29).

OF THE PEOPLE OF ISRAEL (PHIL. 3:5; 2 COR. 11:22; ROM. 11:1)

Paul's claim that he belonged to the people of Israel could be taken in several senses. First, it was a racial term. It referred to the physical descendants of Abraham. When Paul referred to himself as Abraham's descendant, it was in close parallel to the term *Israelite* (Rom. 11:1; 2 Cor. 11:22). The term *Jew* was used in the same way (Acts 22:3). The designations Israelite/Jew/descendant of Abraham could also be taken in a political sense. The Jews of Judaea constituted a nation within the Roman sphere. Even the Diaspora Jews had a political identity, usually living within enclaves in the cities of the empire and often with certain privileges and a degree of self-jurisdiction. Finally, and primarily, being a Jew was a matter of religion. Jews, descendants of Abraham, were those who shared Abraham's covenant with God. This, of course, is where Paul redefined what it was to be a "Jew" in the light of Christ. In the religious sense, he maintained, a "Jew" is not the Jew of physical descent but rather of spiritual descent (Rom. 2:28–29). The real descendant of Abraham is the person who shares the faith of Abraham, and this includes both Jews and Gentiles (Rom. 4:16).

OF THE TRIBE OF BENJAMIN (PHIL. 3:5; ROM. 11:1)

Paul's Jewish pedigree included his membership in the tribe of Benjamin. Only two Jewish tribes survived the exile, Judah and Benjamin, the two tribes of the southern kingdom. Lying to the north of Jerusalem, Benjamin was the only tribe to remain with Judah when the northern tribes separated from the southern kingdom after the death of Solomon. The first Jewish king, Saul, was a Benjamite, and Paul may have received his Jewish name in memory of him. Paul's teacher Gamaliel was also a Benjamite. Benjamites seem to have retained their identity after their return from the exile. Their families are mentioned along with those of Judah and Levi in the post-exilic censuses of Nehemiah 11:7–9, 31–36. It is interesting that Paul never referred to himself as Saul in his letters. Only Acts calls him Saul. On the other hand, Acts never mentions that Paul was a Benjamite. Only Paul does so. Not all first-century Jews would have been able to trace their tribal roots. Paul's family could; it was proud of its heritage. But Paul had come to see that all of this was only "refuse" in the light of his relationship to Christ (Phil. 3:7–8).

A HEBREW OF THE HEBREWS (PHIL. 3:5; 2 COR. 11:22)

When Paul described himself as a "Hebrew," he may have been referring to his facility in the Hebrew language. It is true that the word *Hebrew* need not mean any-thing more than "Jew" or "Israelite." In 2 Corinthians 11:22 Paul may have used the three terms *Hebrews/Israelites/descendants of Abraham* as virtually synonymous desig-nations for "Jews." In Philippians 3:5, however, he seemed to use each of his terms with a different nuance. How does "Hebrew" differ from the phrase "of the people of Israel" or "of the tribe of Benjamin"? The most likely answer is that it refers to the ability to speak the Hebrew language. It seems to have that meaning in Acts 6:1 where the early Jewish Christian community in Jerusalem is described as consisting of two language groups—those who spoke Greek and those who spoke the native Hebrew/Aramaic of Palestine. Contemporary Jewish writings also used the term *Hebrew* to refer to those who spoke the Hebrew language in contrast to those who spoke a different tongue.[1]

If Paul was referring to his ability to speak Hebrew, where did he attain it—as a boy in Tarsus, or in Jerusalem? The former would seem to be indicated by his expres-sion "Hebrew of Hebrews" in Philippians 3:5—that is, a Hebrew speaker from a fam-ily that spoke Hebrew. Hebrew may have been spoken in his family circle. He may have learned some in connection with his education in Scripture. All of this is guess-work. We simply don't know much about Diaspora Jewish education. It is highly likely that Paul would have spoken Hebrew in connection with his education in Jerusalem. The related Semitic language Aramaic was the common language of Pal-estine in the first century. Hebrew was certainly nurtured in religious circles. (Of the enormous library found at Qumran, the vast majority of the manuscripts are in Hebrew, with some in Aramaic and very little in Greek.) Whether Paul brought his Hebrew with him to Jerusalem or whether he learned it all there is of little conse-quence. He surely knew it. He could not have studied Torah without some facility in Hebrew.

Paul remained a Jew even as a Christian. He kept the Jewish festivals (1 Cor. 16:8). He maintained Jewish practices, like taking a Nazarite vow (Acts 18:18) and participating in the vows of others (Acts 21:26). He insisted on the circumcision of Timothy because of his Jewish mother (Acts 16:3). Although he saw himself as called by Christ to be the apostle to the Gentiles, he always viewed the Gentile par-ticipation in God's salvation in terms of God's election of Israel. For him, it was always "first for the Jew, then for the Gentile" (Rom. 1:16; 2:9–10). Indeed, the greatest agony of his Christian life was to see most of his fellow Jews fail to respond to the gospel (Rom. 9:1–5).

PAUL THE PHARISEE

The last three terms Paul used in the third chapter of Philippians to describe his Jewish pedigree are closely related. "In regard to the law," he was "a Pharisee" (v. 5). "As for zeal, persecuting the church; as for legalistic righteousness, faultless" (v. 6). Pharisees were a religious, political, and social movement within Judaism that emphasized the keeping of the Jewish law—not just in its written form but also in their extensive oral tradition of interpreting it. Paul studied the law, became "faultless" in keeping it and passionate in his endeavor to protect it from any would-be enemies. Paul did not explicitly call himself a Pharisee in Galatians 1:13–14 when he spoke of his pre-Christian life as persecutor of the church. He said there that he was "extremely zealous for the traditions of [his] fathers." Those "traditions" were the oral laws of the Pharisees. Paul "advanced in Judaism" beyond his fellow students in his knowledge and zeal for the law. In his own experience, the three fitted closely together—Pharisee, zeal for the law, and persecutor of the church.

THE PHARISEES

There is an extensive discussion in contemporary scholarship about who the Pharisees were, when they originated, what their influence was in Paul's day, and how they relate to subsequent rabbinic Judaism. It is not our purpose here to go into this debate.[2] We will attempt enough of a sketch, however, to provide some understanding of Paul's Pharisaic heritage.

History. The most significant element in the Pharisaic system was Torah, the Jewish law. It was an emphasis which lay at the heart of Jewish religion from the time of Moses. It became particularly important during the exilic period, when Israel no longer had a king or a temple at the center of its life. After the return from the exile, Torah continued to occupy a central place. For several hundred years Israel was dominated by foreign powers—at first the Persians, then the Greek successors of Alexander (the Syrian Seleucids and Egyptian Ptolemies), and finally the Romans. Torah became essential for maintaining Israel's distinctiveness, for keeping it from being totally assimilated by the foreign powers which dominated it. Some time during the Greek period a movement arose in Judaism known as the *Hasidim.* Feeling that there was too much laxity among the people in keeping the law, they emphasized strict Torah observance. Not surprisingly, this group joined the Jewish forces who revolted against the Syrian king Antiochus IV ("Epiphanes") when in 167 B.C. he initiated policies aimed at completely suppressing Judaism. The Jewish forces succeeded in gaining their independence from the Syrians. The *Hasidim* remained a significant political force during the reigns of the independent Jewish Maccabean and Hasmonean kings who ruled for the next century.

Around 152 B.C. the Maccabean king Jonathan took over the high priesthood in addition to his kingship. Jonathan did not come from a priestly family. The Essenes seem to have withdrawn from the Hasidim at this time in protest of this illegitimate priesthood. The Pharisees likewise seem to have come from the ranks of the Hasidim. They first appear as a political force during the reign of John Hyrcanus (134–104 B.C.). Josephus tells how Hyrcanus was originally sympathetic to the Pharisees but later transferred his support to the Sadducees because of the Pharisees criticizing his illegitimate priesthood (*Ant.* 13, 288–298). Pharisaic opposition to the Maccabean kings came to a head in a civil war under the Hasmonean king Alexander Jannaeus (103–76 B.C.) that ended in Alexander's crucifying some eight hundred Jews. Presumably, they were Pharisees (Josephus, *Ant.* 13.372–383). On his deathbed, Alexander advised his wife and successor Alexandra to come to terms with the powerful Pharisees. Alexandra (76–67 B.C.) did indeed make peace with the Pharisees, so much so that they virtually ran the nation during her reign. Josephus says that Alexandra may have ruled the nation, "but the Pharisees ruled her" (*War*, 1.110–114). It was the period of the Pharisees' greatest political clout. It was also a very bloody time, when the Pharisees took vengeance on their old enemies from the time of Alexander.

The Pharisees seem to have become increasingly less political in the Roman period (after 63 B.C.). In the early part of his reign, Herod the Great seems to have been well disposed to them. For instance, he exempted them from having to take an oath of loyalty (Josephus, *Ant.* 15.370). Herod probably found Pharisaic support advantageous in his struggle against the high priestly aristocracy. Josephus estimated the number of Pharisees during Herod's time at six thousand (*Ant.* 17.42). After Herod, the Pharisees do not seem to have been directly involved in politics. They were, however, very popular with the masses. Josephus says that even though the Sadducees held all the major offices, they never made any important decisions without first consulting with the Pharisees (*Ant.* 18.16–17).

The Pharisees seem to have split in the year A.D. 6 when a certain Judas the Galilean led a tax revolt against Rome. The movement known as the Zealots began at this time, founded by Judas and a Pharisee named Saddok. This movement seems to have been thoroughly Pharisaic in its theology, only differing in its political agenda. From the time of Hillel (late first century B.C.) Pharisees had pursued a policy of tolerance toward the government as long as it allowed them free pursuit of their religion. The Zealots disagreed with this policy, maintaining that the land needed to be totally freed of foreign domination. Many Pharisees seem to have gone over to the zealot persuasion. Eventually, it was Zealotism that led to the outbreak of the war with Rome in A.D. 66. The more quietistic Pharisees, the true successors of Hillel, did not join the revolt against Rome. It was to this group that the Romans turned for the reconstruction of Judaism after the Roman victory of A.D. 70. The Pharisees were allowed to establish the school at Jamnia, which consolidated all of Judaism around the Torah and produced what we know as rabbinic Judaism.

Emphases. Josephus listed three distinct movements within Judaism in the first century when he wrote. These were the Pharisees, the Essenes, and the Sadducees (*Ant.* 13.171–173). In one place he called the Zealots a fourth "school" but admitted that except for their political agenda they differed "in no respect" from the Pharisees (*Ant.* 18.23–25). Actually we now know that Josephus's picture is a simplification. There were many individual groups in first-century Judaism before the war of 66–70. There were political groups like the Herodians, priestly groups, baptizing groups, apocalyptic groups. Josephus's were probably the largest and were representative of the others.

The different groups had much in common. Probably no views were absolutely unique to any one group. But each had its own combination of characteristics. Josephus listed the following Pharisaic distinctives. He noted that they believed in living in harmonious relationships with one another (*War* 2.166). The latter is a reflection of their practice of forming *haberim,* "brotherhoods," close communities of common interest, especially for the study of Torah. Pharisaism was a lay movement. Even the most reputed teachers received no pay but were wholly self-supporting through their adopted trade or profession. Josephus also noted that they lived simply, eschewing all luxuries (*Ant.* 18.12–15). They believed in a life after death, angels, and spiritual powers (Acts 23:8). Their canon of Scripture included not only the books of the Law but the Prophets and the Writings as well. Several times Josephus noted the particular Pharisaic understanding of providence: a perfect blending of the divine with the human will (*War* 2.162–163). Josephus also referred to the Pharisaic doctine of rewards and punishments in the afterlife and to their emphasis on their own laws "not recorded in the law of Moses" (*Ant.* 13.297–298). The latter is, of course, the oral tradition of the Pharisees, which Jesus also mentioned on several occasions (Mark 7:8–9).

The Pharisees developed the oral law as a further explication of the written law. It was seen as a "fence around the Torah," a means of determining the exact application of the written law to all possible circumstances. The oral law was a living tradition in Paul's day, passed on by word of mouth from teacher to pupil. A school for learning the oral law was called a *beth ha'midrash* (a "house of interpretation"). Teachers preserved the opinions of former scholars and added their own interpretations. The oral law was not written down until the publication of the *Mishnah* in A.D. 200. One of the difficulties in tracing the viewpoints of the Pharisees is the late date of the rabbinic writings. One cannot be sure that individual sayings in the *Mishnah* or *Talmud* go back to a tradition in force in the first century unless the name of an early scholar is attached to it.

The name *Pharisee* seems to have derived from the word meaning "separate," *perush*. The Pharisees were the *perushim* (the "separate ones"). They scrupulously observed the Torah and kept apart from the ordinary people, the *am ha'aretz* (the "people of the land," the nonobservers). Particularly important to them were laws maintaining separateness and Jewish distinctiveness—purity laws, Sabbath laws, food laws, tithe laws. It is easy to see how Jesus would have come into conflict with those who held such an orientation. Like the Old Testament prophets, he considered that such scrupulousness over external matters missed the weightier matters of justice and mercy that were God's real concern. Jesus was himself a Jew, and his criticism of the Pharisees was very much an intramural concern, a prophetic critique. Jesus had much in common with the Pharisees—faith in an afterlife, in God's providence, in God's justice, in the coming Messiah. They of all people should have understood his message. That is why his critique was so harsh. It is not by accident that Jesus directed his energy to the Pharisees and not the Sadducees, with whom he had little in common.

The same can be said for the stereotypical view that is often taken regarding Paul's picture of the Pharisees. Pharisees are seen as willful, prideful, and self-righteous. They are depicted as attempting to pull themselves up by their own bootstraps to gain God's acceptance through their scrupulous observance of the law. Recent studies have emphasized that in most instances this is not an accurate picture of Pharisees. Most of them were well aware of their own sinfulness and dependence on God. Most tended to view the law as an expression of God's mercy, as a gift within his covenant relationship with his people.[3] This is probably true. Still, the depth of Paul's encounter with Christ led him to see *all religion* in a new light. Whether through law or worship or whatever, religion often becomes a human endeavor to reach God. For Paul, the only true encounter comes when God first reaches out to us. He could not but see his former Pharisaic faith as wrongheaded.

PAUL THE PHARISEE

Was Paul a Pharisee when he went to Jerusalem, or did his Pharisaism derive exclusively from his studies in Jerusalem? If one takes Acts 23:6 literally, it must mean that Paul's family were Pharisees: he was "son of a Pharisee." It is true that "son of" can mean "a disciple or a student," but since Paul had already told the Sanhedrin that he was a Pharisee, he seemed to be saying more. The difficulty here is that there is no evidence for Pharisaic *haberim* outside Palestine in the first century. It is thus argued that Paul's family could not have been of a Pharisaic orientation.[4] As we have seen, our evidence for Diaspora Judaism is scant, so this is an argument from silence at best. But who is to say that Paul's forebear who went (or was taken) to Tarsus had not been a Pharisee in the home country back in Hasmonean times? And why did they send Paul to Jerusalem to study under a famous Pharisee? There probably was no *beth ha'midrash* in Tarsus. If Paul wanted to study Torah, he had to go to Jerusalem. His family, however, may well have already shared a Pharisaic viewpoint.

Paul was probably in his early teens when he went to Jerusalem. Years later his nephew lived in Jerusalem (Acts 23:16), and Paul may already have had family there. The normal age for studying in the house of Torah interpretation was fifteen, according to a late Mishnaic tradition (*Aboth* 5.21). It may have been so in Paul's day, or perhaps he began his studies around the time of his *bar mizpah*, his coming of age as an Israelite. Josephus says that he himself entered into formal study in the three schools of Judaism around the age of sixteen (*Life* 9–12). So perhaps around the age of fourteen to sixteen Paul went to Jerusalem to study under Gamaliel (Acts 22:3).

Gamaliel was the outstanding teacher of the law in Paul's day. There were two main schools of interpretation, both dating from their historical founders, who lived in the time of Herod the Great. Hillel headed the more liberal school, which emphasized flexibility and tolerance. Hillelites were more open to hellenistic influence and advocated cooperation with the Roman authorities. Shammai headed the more conservative, stricter school of interpretation. Shammaites were not so open to outside influences or dominion. It is likely that most Shammaites participated in the war with Rome. At the end of the war, the Romans favored the Hillelites, probably because of Shammaite involvement in the war.

Gamaliel I was of the school of Hillel. He may have been a grandson of Hillel, although this is not certain. Gamaliel conducted his school from A.D. 22 to 55. He was the outstanding teacher of his generation and was greatly revered in the tradition. The Mishnah says of him: "When Rabban Gamaliel the Elder died, the glory of the law ceased and purity and abstinence died" (*Sotah* 9.15). Several of his rulings are recorded in the Mishnah. Some of them dealt with marriage, such as a regulation requiring the use of legal names and forbidding false names and nicknames on bills of divorce (*Gittin* 4.2) and laws which sought to ensure that widows received the proper payment of their dowries (*Gittin* 4.3). One wonders if Paul's concern for Christian marriage in 1 Corinthians 7 was not in some part influenced by his teacher's similar concerns. Another Mishnaic tradition from Gamaliel provided for the setting aside of portions of fields to provide produce for the poor (*Peah* 2.6). The most interesting ruling preserved from Rabban Gamaliel was his insistence that a woman had the right to remarry upon the testimony of a single witness that her husband had died (*Yebamoth* 16.7). Paul enunciated precisely the same principle in Romans 7:2. The Mishnah records another quotation from Gamaliel which concerned the quantity of leaven it takes to render dough forbidden for passover (*Orlah* 1.12). It is possible that Paul remembered his teacher's ruling when he used the analogy of yeast and dough (Gal. 5:9; 1 Cor. 5:6).

Gamaliel is best known to New Testament students for his advice to the Sanhedrin when the apostles were hauled before that body for having preached in the name of Christ (Acts 5:27–28). Gamaliel was a member of the Sanhedrin, which at that time was comprised of a majority which came from the Sadducees and the high priestly families. Gamaliel was among the Pharisaic minority. The Sanhedrin had already forbidden the apostles to speak or teach in Jesus' name (Acts 4:18). The apostles had not heeded this interdiction. The majority of the Sanhedrin were thus of a mind to condemn the apostles to death. Gamaliel advised against this, pointing out that God would not allow any movement to persist that ran counter to his will. He cited examples from Israel's recent past where false messianic movements had ended in disaster. This would happen to the Christians, he argued, if God were not behind them. On the other hand, if God *were* behind them, there would be little the Sanhedrin could do to stop them (Acts 5:34–39).

In giving this advice, Gamaliel was enunciating a principle attested in the later Mishnaic tradition: "Any assembling together that is for the sake of Heaven shall in the end be established, but any that is not for the sake of Heaven shall not in the end be established" (*Aboth* 4.11). Gamaliel was very much in the line of Hillel, who also would have counseled nonviolence and leaving the matter up to God. Gamaliel's pupil Paul may have sat at his feet, but in the matter of how to deal with the Christians, Paul had more in common with the intolerant Shammaites than with his teacher.

Paul's methods of interpretation. In his writings, Paul reflected his Pharisaic Torah training. Sometimes he used Jewish Midrashic methods of interpretation, methods which often appear in the later rabbinic writings. For example, in Romans 11:12, 24 Paul used a *qal wahomer* argument, one which argued from the lesser to the greater. This type of reasoning went thus: if this lesser thing is true, how much more will this greater thing be true? Jesus himself often used this form of teaching. An example is his argument that if sinful human parents give good gifts to their children, how much more can God be expected to give good things to *his* children (Luke 11:13).[5] In Romans 11 Paul reasoned that if the failure of the Jews to receive the gospel had brought riches (of the gospel) to Gentiles, how much greater riches of salvation could be expected when the Jews embraced the gospel.

An oft-cited example of Paul's use of Midrashic technique is 2 Corinthians 3:12–18 where he spoke of the veil with which Moses covered his face at Sinai. Moses' face so shone from his having witnessed the shekinah glory of God that the children of Israel could not look upon it. So Moses covered his face with a veil when he appeared before them. He removed it in the privacy of his tent when he spoke to "the Lord" (v. 16). Paul then applied the lesson. First, he noted that the veil still exists. It formerly covered Moses' face at the time he received the law. Now it covers the face of the Israelites when they read the law. At Sinai Moses would remove the veil when he approached "the Lord." Now, Paul said, Christians can remove the veil (reinterpreted as blindness) by turning to the Spirit. For, "the Lord" is really "the Spirit" (v. 17). When we approach God through the Spirit, the veil is removed, our eyes are uncovered, and we have direct access to the full glory of God.

Sometimes Jewish interpreters would build elaborate arguments around small points of grammar. Such is the case in Galatians 3:16 where Paul interpreted God's promise to Abraham in Genesis 12:7. In Paul's Greek Bible the word *seed* (offspring, descendants) appeared. The Greek word for "seed" (*sperma*) is singular in the Genesis passage. In Greek the singular form often is used in a collective sense. (The same is true in English. *Seed* can refer to a single grain or to a whole pack.) But Paul used the occurrence of the single rather than the plural form (*spermata*) to argue that the promise to Abraham was ultimately fulfilled by a single individual—Christ, the Messiah. Of course, Paul's basic point was true. God's promises to Abraham were ultimately fulfilled in Christ; that was Paul's Christian conviction. His intricate grammatical argument may seem strained to us, but it was well within the guidelines of first-century Jewish methods of interpretation.

Paul not only used Jewish methods of interpretation; sometimes he reflected teachings found in Jewish traditions from his time. For example, in 1 Corinthians 10:4 Paul spoke of a rock which followed Israel and furnished them water in the wilderness period. In Exodus 17:6 and Numbers 20:11–13 there are traditions of water gushing from a rock when Moses struck it. There is also the tradition of the pillars of cloud and fire which followed Israel (Exod. 13:21), but there is no reference in the Old Testament to a water-producing rock which followed Israel. There was such a tradition, however, in the later Jewish Midrashic literature, and Paul seems to have been aware of it.[6]

In a very influential book, W. D. Davies demonstrated that many of Paul's key concepts reflect his familiarity with Jewish theological traditions.[7] His book was written largely in response to the history-of-religions scholarship which argued that hellenistic ideas were the formative influence on Paul's thelogy and that these ideas were mediated through hellenistic philosophy, the mystery religions, and Gnostic currents. Davies showed that many of the main ideas that had been traced to hellenistic sources had far more in common with rabbinic Judaism—basic concepts like the first and the second Adam (Rom. 5:12ff.), Christ as the wisdom of God (1 Cor. 1:18–30), and Paul's frequent contrast of flesh and spirit. Though Davies has sometimes been critiqued for his use of later rabbinic traditions, his basic thesis has largely carried the day: the main background to Paul's thought was his Jewish world.

OTHER CURRENTS

Paul would have encountered other forces in Judaism which also contributed to his formation. As we have seen, Pharisaism did not enjoy the dominance over Judaism in Paul's day that it later came to have. There were many other groups as well.

Sadducees. Of Josephus's three parties, the Sadducees probably had the least influence on Paul. They seem to have been largely restricted to the upper classes, particularly the high priestly circles. With respect to the Roman occupation, their policy was one of cooperation to the largest extent possible. Since the Romans controlled the government, it is no surprise that the Sadducees generally held the top posts. Josephus noted, however, that they rarely accomplished anything. The Pharisees so controlled popular opinion that the Sadducees had to bend to their will on most matters (*Ant.* 18. 16–17). Josephus depicted them as rather boorish, rude, and self-satisfied. They did not believe in a life after death nor a place of divine reward and punishment (*War 20.* 164–166). Josephus's statement is confirmed by the dispute that arose in the Sanhedrin between the Pharisees and Sadducees when Paul mentioned the resurrection (Acts 23:6–10). Luke informs us in that context that the Sadducees believed neither in the resurrection, nor in angels, nor in spirits (v. 8). The Sadducees were in the majority on the Sanhedrin. Once again, as the apostles had experienced with Gamaliel, the Christians found themselves backed by the Pharisaic minority.

According to Josephus, the Sadducees did not believe in divine providence. They believed that everything occurred in accordance with human free will and "fate" (*Ant.* 13. 171–173). They accepted as Scripture only the Pentateuch, the books of the Law. They did not accept either the Prophets or the Writings. Nor did they accept the oral traditions of the Pharisees. It is obvious that Paul would have had little in common with Sadducees. There was one area, however, where he might have sought them out. From the start, they had been the main enemies of the Christians. They feared that the Christians might develop into a popular messianic uprising that would bring Roman reprisals (cp. Acts 4:1–2). It is not by accident that when Paul sought assistance in persecuting the Christians he went to the high priest, who almost certainly was a Sadducee (Acts 9:1–2).

The Essenes. Along with the Pharisees and Sadducees, the Essenes constituted the third of Josephus's "parties" in Judaism. As we have seen, this group seems to have originated with the *hasidim* of the Macabbean period and to have split off from them when Simon declared himself high priest. Of the three groups, Josephus dedicated by far the most space to his description of the Essenes (*War* 2.119–162). In his lengthy treatment he described them as a largely monastic movement, for the most part celibate, practicing common ownership, conducting a self-supporting communal existence, with a rigid heirarchical structure, a strong emphasis on purity and a devotion to the study of the sacred writings. Before 1947, we only knew of the Essenes through literary sources like Philo, Josephus, and the Roman writer Pliny the Elder. With the discovery in that year of the first of the Dead Sea Scrolls and the subsequent uncovering of the monastery at Qumran and its extensive library, we now know them more intimately than any other first-century Jewish group.

Most scholars are now agreed that the Qumran community were Essenes. They seem to have occupied the site from the early first century B.C. until the time of the Jewish war with Rome (A.D. 66–70). Their large library was found stored in eleven caves, located in the cliffs across from the monastery. Most of the writings are sacred Scripture: canonical, apocryphal, and pseudepigraphic. Also found were a number of the distinctive writings of the Essene community—its Manual of Discipline, an apocalyptic War Scroll, a commentary on Habakkuk, a book of psalms, a temple scroll, and others. The Qumran discovery has made accessible to us for the first time an extensive library of Jewish writings dating from the time of Christian origins.

From the time of its discovery, attempts have been made to link Jesus, John the Baptist, or Paul to the Essenes. Some have maintained that one or the other of them may have at least spent some time in the Qumran community. For instance, it has been suggested that Paul may have spent his period in Arabia after his conversion (Gal. 1:17) in the Dead Sea monastery. All of this is most unlikely. There is no evidence that Jesus, John, or Paul had any significant influence from Essenism. This is not to say that the Dead Sea Scrolls are not important. To the contrary, they constitute our most extensive source of knowledge for Jewish religion contemporary with Jesus and Paul.

There are many similarities between things found in the Dead Sea Scrolls and in the writings of Paul. In no instance does it seem to be a matter of dependence. There are no verbal "parallels." What *is* there are similar concepts, similar language, similar methods of interpretation. For instance, one finds in both Paul and the scrolls a strong dualism—the language of good and evil, light and darkness, God and Satan. Both emphasize the idea of "mystery," and in both the mystery is God's revelation. A strong emphasis in the scrolls is the idea of God's predestination of his people, an idea found in Paul as well. In speaking of the community of believers, both Paul and the scrolls describe it as a temple. Qumran insisted that its members seek legal redress only in their own courts, not in the courts of outsiders, much as Paul argued in 1 Corinthians 6:1–8.

A number of similarities have been noted between the scrolls and Paul's epistles to the Colossians and Ephesians. This may be due to the nature of the writings. Paul used the language of worship extensively in these two epistles, and the similarities with the scrolls may be due to their common background in Jewish liturgy. One passage which has been seen as particularly close to the scrolls is Paul's treatment of the purity of the Christian community in 2 Corinthians 6:14–7:1. It has been argued that the passage was taken directly from the Essenes.[8] No area of New Testament study is complete without some consideration of the scrolls. This is certainly the case for Pauline studies. The scrolls have proved useful in considering individual passages within Paul's epistles. Essenism itself does not seem to have had a major impact on Paul's thought, though some would argue that ideas very much like those of the Essenes may have influenced some of Paul's congregations, such as Colosse. These possibilities will be considered later in the context of the individual epistles.

Apocalyptic thought. "Apocalyptic" was a major force in first-century Judaism. It wasn't a particular party like Pharisees or Essenes. It was an outlook that influenced many groups. The Essenes, for instance, were an "apocalyptic" group. So were the Christians. The term *apocalyptic* is somewhat slippery and is defined differently by different people. One way of defining it is as an outlook on life. Seen this way, an apocalyptic group is one which has a pessimistic view of the world order. It views the present as being so evil that it is beyond the ability of humans to reform it. Only God, breaking in from beyond, can destroy the forces of evil and deliver his people. One can also view apocalyptic as a particular type of writing, a literary genre. In this sense, apocalyptic usually involves a seer who is given a divine revelation of the events of the end time. This type of literature usually employs a specialized symbolic language and stereotypical images. A number of passages in the New Testament are written in this apocalyptic style—Mark 13; 2 Thessalonians 2:3–12, and all of Revelation, except for chapters 2–3. Apocalyptic generally involved God's sending a messianic figure to deliver his people.

There were strong apocalyptic currents in first-century Judaism. The Roman presence seemed unbearable, and many Jews looked to God's intervention to rid the land of the hated occupiers. The Essenes are representative of an apocalyptic group. One of the Dead Sea Scrolls is entitled The War Between the Sons of Light and the Sons of Darkness. This "War Scroll" looks to God's intervention and calls the members of the community to battle alertness in preparation for the final great battle led by God against his enemies. The Messianic expectation that usually accompanied the apocalyptic viewpoint is perhaps best represented in Psalms 17 and 18 of the Psalms of Solomon, a Jewish writing which originated in Palestine in the first century B.C.

about the time the Romans first seized the land under Pompey. Psalms 17 and 18 describe how God will come and deliver the land by sending the Messiah, the Son of David. The Messiah will drive the enemy and all sinners from the land. He will then restore all the tribes of Israel to their former tribal borders. He will bring all the Jews home from the Diaspora. He will purify and restore the true and legitimate worship of the temple, and all the Gentile nations will come to Israel to worship.

Albert Schweitzer was considered radical by his contemporaries when he suggested that the message of both Christ and Paul was apocalyptic.[9] Though few would follow his understanding of Paul's "mysticism," most scholars today would agree with him about Paul's apocalyptic orientation.[10] The first Christians embraced an apocalyptic viewpoint. They believed that Jesus Christ had come as the promised Messiah. They believed that he had risen from the dead and that his resurrection was the firstfruits of the general resurrection of the end time. They believed that God had poured out his Spirit on all who belonged to Jesus Messiah, and this was also an unmistakable sign that they were living in the final times of history (Acts 2:16–21). When Paul met the risen Christ on the road to Damascus, he realized the truth of the Christian apocalyptic message. And he drew a very natural conclusion from it: if he was indeed living in the final messianic times, it was time to reach out to the Gentiles and lead them to the worship of God.

PAUL THE PERSECUTOR

The Book of Acts first mentions Paul in connection with the stoning of Stephen. Paul was the "young man" at whose feet Stephen's assailants laid their garments (Acts 7:58). At this point Luke referred to him by his Hebrew name *Saul*. He did not switch to Paul's Roman name until the outset of Paul's first missionary journey (Acts 13:9). Paul's connection with Stephen does not appear to be incidental. It was Stephen's fellow "Hellenists" whom Paul targeted as a persecutor, and he may already have clashed with them before Stephen's martyrdom.

STEPHEN AND THE HELLENISTS

The group of Christians known as "Hellenists" (NIV "Grecian Jews") are first encountered in Acts 6:1–7. They seem to have been Greek-speaking Jews who had become Christians. Their Greek language reflected their Diaspora background. It is not surprising to find them among the Christians. Among those who heard the gospel preached at Pentecost were many Diaspora Jews (Acts 2:5–11). Because Greek was their primary language, they likely met in their own house churches, much like ethnic language-group churches in today's cities. They are first mentioned in Acts in connection with a failure in the church's charity system. The hellenist widows were being neglected in the daily distribution of food, because it was administered by the Aramaic-speaking apostles. At this point in Acts, all the Christians were Jews or converts to Judaism. The church had not yet reached out to Gentiles. The Hellenists became the key figures in that mission.

To solve the breakdown in communication, the apostles directed the Hellenists to choose seven men from their own ranks to administer the food distribution to the Greek-speaking widows. The Hellenists did so, and the apostles endorsed them. Luke listed their names (Acts 6:5). All seven are Greek names. Only two of the seven have any further role in Acts. These two were Stephen and Philip. They became the main subjects of the narrative in Acts 6–8, where their role is evangelism, particularly in the wider outreach of the church beyond Jerusalem.

In the narrative of Acts, the church does not seem to have witnessed beyond the confines of Judaism until the Hellenists appear on the scene. Stephen had a vision of a wider mission; at least his defense before the Sanhedrin would indicate that he did. Philip definitely reached beyond the Jews of Jerusalem, conducting a successful mission among the Samaritans and leading a Gentile, an Ethiopian, to Christ (Acts 8:4–40). Fellow Hellenists took the gospel to the coastal cities, notably to Antioch, where they conducted a successful outreach to Gentiles (Acts 11:19–21). It is quite likely that the Damascus Christians whom Paul sought to persecute were also Hellenists. Paul probably owed much of his own dedication to a Gentile mission to the Hellenists. It was one of their churches, that of Antioch, which sponsored his first mission (Acts 13:1–3). Stephen conducted no witness outside Jerusalem, but he shared the vision.

THE MARTYRDOM OF STEPHEN

Stephen began his Christian testimony in the Diaspora-Jewish synagogues of Jerusalem. These would have been comprised of Greek-speaking Jews like himself. It is unclear exactly how many synagogues Luke intended in Acts 6:9. The construction of the Greek is very loose and could refer to one, two, or as many as five different synagogues. The NIV translation assumes only one synagogue, known as "the Synagogue of the Freedmen." It consisted of Jews from two main areas—North Africa (Cyrene and Alexandria) and the eastern provinces of Cilicia and Asia (both in modern Turkey). Paul himself came from Cilicia. His family may well have derived its Roman citizenship from an ancestor who had been made a freedman.[11] It is thus conceivable that Paul participated in the Synagogue of the Freedmen, where he would have been with fellow Cilicians. It would have been his natural "church family" when he came to Jerusalem to study. Paul may already have encountered Stephen in the latter's debates in the Diaspora synagogues of Jerusalem.

Whether Paul was or was not among the men of the synagogue who opposed Stephen, their resistance reached such a point that they trumped up charges against Stephen and dragged him before the Sanhedrin. Their charges were twofold: that he spoke against the law (Moses), and that he spoke against the temple (Acts 6:12–14). Stephen responded to their charges with a long summary of Israel's history from Abraham to Solomon's temple (Acts 7:2–53). At first glance it seems to have no relation to the charges against him. On closer scrutiny, however, one can see that Stephen turned the accusations back on his accusers. They, not he, were the real lawbreakers. He showed how their history depicted them as consistent idolaters and resisters of the leaders whom God had sent them. Now once more they were turning the worship of God into idolatry and were rejecting God's ultimate deliverer, Christ, the "Righteous One" (vv. 51–53).

Another theme ran consistently through Stephen's speech: in Israel's history, some of the most decisive moments of God's relationship with his people took place outside the Holy Land—in God's call of Abraham, in Egypt, at Sinai, in the tabernacle worship of the wilderness. This theme is summed up in Stephen's unusual statement that Abraham owned not so much as a foot of ground in the promised land (v. 5). Stephen's point was that God could not be tied down to a single place or people: "heaven is [his] throne and the earth is [his] footstool" (v. 49). God is God of all the world. This "universal" note was an essential assumption for the Christian outreach to the Gentiles. Stephen enunciated it. His fellow Hellenists carried through on it.

Stephen did not complete his defense speech. He was cut short by the fury of his listeners. Dragged out of the city, he was stoned to death. It does not seem to have been a formal Jewish execution by stoning. The scene has more the traits of lynch justice. The Sanhedrin did not have the right to execute in the first place; the Roman procurator alone could pass a capital sentence (John 18:31). One thing that did resemble a Jewish execution was the participation of the witnesses who had testified against Stephen. Paul held *their* garments (Acts 7:58). In his speech before Agrippa, Paul talked about his days as a persecutor. He mentioned that when Christians were condemned to death he "cast [his] vote" against them (Acts 26:10).

Many have seen this as evidence that Paul was a member of the Sanhedrin with a formal vote. Paul, however, could have been expressing himself metaphorically, meaning that he went along with the decision, that he was "consenting" to the death penalty, as was the case with Stephen (Acts 8:1). If Paul were a member of the Sanhedrin, Luke would have most likely said so. It could only have enhanced his picture of Paul the persecutor. And Paul never claimed Sanhedrin membership in his epistles. It would be hard to account for his silence had he been a member, especially in those autobiographical passages where he boasted of his Jewish pedigree. Paul's presence at Stephen's martyrdom was probably not due to his membership on the Sanhedrin but rather to his participation in the delegation from the Synagogue of the Freedmen that brought charges against Stephen.

PAUL AS PERSECUTOR

On the day of Stephen's martyrdom "a great persecution broke out against the church at Jerusalem, and all except the apostles were scattered throughout Judea and Samaria" (Acts 8:1). The persecution seems to have been focused against the Hellenists, the associates of Stephen. Some like Philip went to Samaria, others to the cities along the coast (Acts 11:19). Those who stayed experienced the full fury of the persecution, especially as it was embodied in Paul. Acts describes Paul as being intent on destroying the Christians, entering the homes where their house churches met, dragging them off to prison, both men and women (8:3). His very breath spewed threat and murder against the Christians (9:1). He "raised havoc" (Gk., *portheō*) (9:21). Paul referred to his days as a persecutor in his speeches before the Jewish mob (Acts 22:4) and before King Agrippa (Acts 26:10–11). In both he testified how he had thrown men and women into prison, even consenting to the death penalty. He told Agrippa that he attempted to get the Christians to blaspheme (26:11), that is, to deny Christ.

Paul spoke of his persecuting days in his epistles as well. In Galatians 1:13 and 1:23 he used the same word for his attempt to destroy the church (*portheō*) that Luke used in Acts 8:3. In Philippians 3:6, he referred to his persecuting as the supreme manifestation of his zeal as a Pharisee. In 1 Timothy 1:13–16 Paul spoke of his persecution of the church and his blasphemy of Christ, both done in ignorance, both evidence of God's mercy and forgiveness. It is that same divine grace which Paul highlighted when he told how Christ had appeared to him, the persecutor, the least and last, and called him to be an apostle (1 Cor. 15:9). When Paul thought of his pre-Christian past, he above all thought of his role in persecuting the church.

Why did Paul persecute the Christians with such intensity? Why did he not follow his teacher's advice and leave it to God to determine the outcome of the young messianic movement? Paul certainly showed more the attitude of the zealots than of Gamaliel. There was, of course, ample precedence in Judaism for the sort of zeal that Paul showed. Moses ordered the execution of the immoral Israelites at Baal-peor (Num. 25:1–5), and on the same occasion God commended Phinehas for his zeal in killing the immoral Israelite man and Midianite woman (Num. 25:11–13). In a number of places the Maccabean writings depict the *hasidim* as purifying the nation by their slaughter of apostate Jews (1 Macc. 2:2–28, 42–48; 2 Macc. 6:13).[12] There is ample precedent for such zeal. But what was it about the Christians that seemed such a threat to Paul? Unfortunately, Paul never told us. Although he often spoke of his persecuting, he never said why. Perhaps the closest he came was in Philippians 3:5–6, where he referred to his persecuting in close connection with his zeal for the law. One of the charges against Stephen was that he criticized the law. Had the Hellenists already come to a less than rigid application of the law? Had they already concluded, as Paul later came to do, that Christ was the "end" of the law?

Stephen's temple critique may also have bothered Paul. As a Jew from the Diaspora, Paul may have had something in common with modern "Zionists," a yearning for the independence of the nation and the restoration of the glory of the temple by the Messiah. Indeed, Paul may have possessed a strong messianic hope. The Messiah would be no indifferent matter for him. False messianic movements should be eliminated to make ready for the true. And Christ must have seemed a false Messiah to Paul. As he later stated in Galatians 3:13, anyone who dies "on a tree" as did the crucified Christ stands under a curse according to the Scriptures (Deut. 21:23). Who ever heard of a Messiah who stood under a curse? Paul was surely a messianic Jew. There is a strong likelihood that it was his messianic fervor that fueled his fury against what he saw as a dangerous false Messianism.

A number of scholars believe that Paul persecuted the Hellenists of the Diaspora, as in Damascus, but that he never persecuted the Jerusalem Christians. This is based on Galatians 1:22–23 where Paul referred to his first visit to Jerusalem three years after his conversion in Damascus. Paul stated that on that occasion he only met briefly with Peter and James and was "personally unknown to the churches of Judea." He added that they only "heard the report" that the former persecutor was now preaching the faith. This is taken to mean that Paul never persecuted in Judea, that the Christians there only "heard about" the former persecutor. This conclusion is a misunderstanding of the Galatian context. Paul was simply stating there that his first postconversion visit to Jerusalem was a brief one. He saw only Peter and James, none of the other Christians. They only heard that he had visited Jerusalem. They only received the report that their former persecutor was now proclaiming the gospel. He did not visit them on that occasion. Indeed, they probably knew him all too well from his former role as persecutor, by reputation if not by face.[13]

PAUL'S APPEARANCE

We have precious little information on Paul's physical traits. Occasionally in his letters he referred to some personal characteristic, but these remarks are often in a polemical context and are not necessarily to be taken at face value. For instance, in the second letter to the Corinthians Paul noted how some of them had talked about the unimpressiveness of his physical presence and his speech in comparison to the power of his letters (10:10; 11:6). Throughout the letter he spoke of his "weakness" (4:7–11; 11:30; 12:10). He gave long lists of his sufferings as an apostle to illustrate this "weakness"(e.g., 6:3–10; 11:23–28). These very lists, however, show that his physical condition was anything but weak. Only the strongest of constitutions could have survived such trials. His emphasis on weakness was part of his message to the Corinthians that they not place their confidence in human "strength" but in God's. In two instances, however, Paul did seem to speak of an actual physical ailment, and we will look at them. But first let us examine an actual description of Paul found in an early Christian writing.

THE ACTS OF PAUL

The description occurs in a writing from the last half of the second century known as The Acts of Paul. It is a primarily fictional writing, but may preserve some reliable traditions about Paul. One is inclined to be cautious in using it, particularly when informed that the church elder who produced it was removed from his office for giving a distorted picture of Paul and a lopsided emphasis on celibacy. Still, the description is so uncomplimentary that many feel it has to be valid. The church would not have fabricated such a portrait of its hero. The description runs thus: "a man small of stature, with a bald head and crooked legs, in a good state of body, with eyebrows meeting and nose somewhat hooked, full of friendliness; for now, he appeared like a man, and now he had the face of an angel."[14] A couple of later traditions give further descriptions—one from the sixth century describing him as having blue eyes, a thick gray beard, a fair and flushed complexion, and a winsome smile. A fourteenth-century description speaks of his beard being pointed and of his frame being slight and somewhat stooped.[15]

Probably none of these reliably reflects the historical Paul. Like the Byzantine icons of Paul, they are flat and stereotypical. But they communicate an understanding of the apostle. It is interesting to note that other ancient figures are portrayed with many of the same traits. A general from the seventh century B.C. is also described as short and bowlegged. A Celtic warrior of the second century A.D. is depicted with meeting eyebrows, a hooked nose, and bowed legs. Suetonius even portrayed Caesar Augustus as having these same three traits. What did Paul have in common with these three? Probably nothing as far as physique is concerned but perhaps a great deal of the same character traits. The descriptions are not uncomplimentary. They are stock pictures of desirable personality characteristics in ancient Mediterranean culture.[16]

Looked at from this perspective, what does the portrait of Paul in the Acts communicate about the apostle? His short stature tells us that he was active. In first-century thought tallness was sometimes seen as leading to slowness, but short people got things done. That is why generals and even the emperor could be described as short. Paul's "bald" or "shaven" head pointed to his piety. Holy men were often depicted as shaven, perhaps related to the monk's tonsure or even to Paul's shaving himself in his vows (Acts 18:18; 21:24). Crooked legs pointed to resoluteness. One's feet were planted firmly on the ground. Bowlegged persons were seen to be fearless, unyielding. Paul's "good state of body," his health, was a trait that denoted his higher social status. Healthy people were those who could afford the gymnasium, who could train their bodies and minds for leadership and civic responsibility.

Paul's meeting eyebrows were a mark of beauty and manliness for his culture. The hooked nose was also regarded as a sign of manliness. The ideal male had a hooked, aquiline nose. The ideal female's nose was a snub nose. Paul's hooked nose marked him off as virtuous and handsome. He was also described as "friendly." Friendliness in Paul's day as in ours is seen as a mark of leadership. Leaders are outgoing and winsome. Finally, it is said that sometimes Paul appeared to be an ordinary man, but sometimes he had the face of an angel. This would mark him off as one who represented a powerful patron. Like Stephen, Paul was full of grace and power and favor among the people (Acts 6:8). Also like Stephen, the divine power shown through so much that his face became "the face of an angel" (Acts 6:15). In the Acts of Paul we almost surely do not have an actual physical description of Paul. We have an assessment of Paul's character. Such stereotypical descriptions communicated more about a person to the ancients than our photographs do to us.

THE THORN IN THE FLESH

In two of his epistles Paul seems to have referred to a chronic physical ailment. The clearest reference is Galatians 4:13–15, where he discussed the first occasion of his preaching to the Galatians. He had not intended on stopping there, but an illness forced him. The illness was such that it could have offended them. Rather than repulsing them, they welcomed Paul, receiving him "as if [he] were an angel." Indeed, they would have "torn out [their] eyes" and given them to Paul. The second reference is more ambiguous. In 2 Corinthians 12:7–10 Paul spoke of a "thorn in my flesh, a messenger of Satan," which was sent to "torment" him (literally, to "beat on" him). He went on to relate how on three occasions he had begged the Lord to remove it. Instead of removing it, the Lord assured him of his grace, and so this evidence of weakness became a constant reminder of the sufficiency of God's grace at work in Paul's ministry. God's strength worked through his weakness. In the context, Paul had been "boasting" to the Corinthians of a visionary experience in which he was caught up into paradise and heard "inexpressible things" (vv. 2–4). He went on to say that the thorn in the flesh served to keep him from "becoming conceited because of these surpassingly great revelations" (v. 7).

The two passages are generally taken as referring to the same physical problem. They need not be doing so, especially if the Corinthian "thorn" is taken to mean something other than an ailment. In fact, the "thorn in the flesh" has been interpreted in three distinct ways. All three have had their supporters from the time of the church fathers on down to the present.

A first interpretation sees the thorn as a fleshly temptation, particularly the sexual impulses. This seems to have come from the Latin Vulgate translation, where "thorn in the flesh" is translated *stimulus carnis meae*. In Latin *stimulus* can be either a "goad or prod" (something that "sticks") or it can be an "impulse." The idea of temptation results from this "impulse" sense.[17] This view has had the fewest advocates, not least because of God's failure to respond to Paul's plea for help with his temptations. Is grace "sufficient" in such a case? This sounds more like the Roman libertines than Paul's own teachings on the matter (cp. Rom. 6:1).

A second more widely advocated view of Paul's "thorn" is that it was his enemies, in particular the opponents whom he was combating at Corinth. In support of this, it is noted that the description of the thorn as a "messenger" of Satan sounds more like a person than a sickness. Likewise, the word for *tormenting* (*punching*) is used only of human tormenters/beaters in the New Testament.

Finally, the metaphor of a "thorn" is used in the Old Testament as a description of Israel's enemies (Num. 33:55; Ezek. 28:24).[18] A major problem with this view is that the word *flesh* seems to point to something in Paul's body. Also, it is hard to see how his "weakness" would be related to his failure to overcome the opponents of the gospel. How could this be seen as evidence of God's grace? Paul uses the weakness motif in Corinthians not as evidence of his enemies but as a means of overcoming them and their false reliance on human power.

Most interpreters are inclined to see Paul's thorn in the flesh as a physical ailment. At that point the agreement ends. Every conceivable sickness has been suggested.[19] A number of scholars have suggested epilepsy. This is seen to account for the possible revulsion of the Galatians. It also is often applied to the conversion of Paul, which is viewed as an epileptic seizure. But there is no evidence that Paul suffered from a progressive, degenerative disease like epilepsy. It must be remembered that there were no treatments or medications available for it in Paul's day. Certainly Paul's visions do not resemble the typical epileptic blackout.[20] A suggestion first made by W. M. Ramsay was that Paul suffered from malaria, contracting it in the Pamphylian lowlands and suffering an attack shortly thereafter in Galatia.[21] He noted that the throbbing head pains connected with malarial fever attacks fit the tormenting pounding of Paul's thorn in the flesh. Another suggestion has been that Paul suffered from neurasthenia, a paralysis of the facial nerves that would account for his stumbling speech (2 Cor. 10:10; 11:6). A number of scholars have seen Paul as suffering from a distress of his eyes. This is based on his regular use of an amanuensis (secretary) and his reference to writing in "large letters" (Gal. 6:11). Particularly has this been related to the willingness of the Galatians to tear out their own eyes for him (Gal. 4:15), though it is recognized that this expression may be metaphorical and not literal. One thing this view has going for it is that it would not be a debilitating illness.

The vigor with which Paul pursued his ministry and the hardships which he conquered (2 Cor. 11:23–29) would indicate that his overall health was robust. One can only speculate about his thorn in the flesh. The significant matter is not *what* it was but *how* he came to see that even adversity could be a strength for his ministry, a constant reminder that whatever was accomplished was not through his own human frailty but through God's empowering grace.

A WIFE?

Some have suggested, usually with tongue in cheek, that Paul's thorn in the flesh was his wife. This is not seriously advocated: how did Paul propose that God "remove" her when he prayed so fervently on those three occasions? It does raise the issue of Paul's marital status. What was it? Almost every possibility has been suggested—that Paul was single, that he was married, that he was widowed, that he was divorced.

Those who maintain that Paul was single point to 1 Corinthians 7:8, the only passage in Acts or Paul's epistles where his marital status is explicitly addressed: "Now to the unmarried and the widows I say: It is good for them to stay unmarried, as I am." In verse 7 he described his unmarried status as his "gift" from God (*charisma*). At the time he wrote 1 Corinthians, Paul did not seem to have been married.

The view that Paul was married is an old one. In his *Church History* (3.30) Eusebius approvingly quoted Clement of Alexandria to the effect that Paul was married. He pointed as proof to Paul's addressing his "loyal yokefellow" in Philippians 4:3. Today, most scholars would see Paul's Philippian yokefellow as his coworker or perhaps even a person with the name *Yokefellow* (*Syzygus*). The view that it refers to Paul's wife has persisted, however. Some Victorian exegetes even maintained that since she lived in Philippi, she almost certainly was Lydia. The usual argument for Paul's being married is based on inference from Paul's Jewish background. Appeal is made to the Mishnaic tradition (*Aboth* 5.21) that the normal age of marriage was around eighteen and to sayings in the Talmud which emphasize that one must be married in order to fulfill God's command to be fruitful and multiply. Those who believe that Paul was a member of the Sanhedrin note the requirement that judges be at least thirty years of age and have children. It must be noted that all of these traditions are late (from scholars of the second century and later) and do not reflect marriage customs for first-century Judaism. The Essenes, for instance, were celibate. The later marriage expectations reflect post-Jamnian Judaism.

Most contemporary scholars who maintain that Paul was married admit that he was single when he wrote 1 Corinthians. They argue either that he was a widower or that he was divorced. The latter view is often connected with Paul's allowing for divorce at the insistence of an unbelieving partner (1 Cor. 7:15). It is maintained that Paul's wife left him when he became a Christian. She would be among the things of which he suffered loss when he became a Christian (Phil. 3:8).

Paul's marital status will always remain a speculative issue based on arguments of probability and from the silence of the sources. Clearly Paul was single when he wrote 1 Corinthians. Whether he had been previously married we will never know for sure. Neither Luke nor Paul was concerned with giving biographical details about Paul's life. They were concerned rather with his Christian witness and the spiritual health of his churches. Personal details were at best incidental.

NOTES

1. For example, the prologue of Ecclesiasticus/Ben Sirach, Philo in *de Abrahamo* 28, and 4 Maccabees 12:7 and 16:15.
2. For further reading, see the Jewish scholars J. Neusner, *From Politics to Piety: The Emergence of Pharisaic Judaism* (Englewod Cliffs, N.J.: Prentice-Hall, 1973) and E. Rivkin, *A Hidden Revolution: The Pharisees' Search for the Kingdom Within* (Nashville: Abingdon, 1978). For a standard treatment, see E. Schuerer, *The History of the Jewish People in the Age of Jesus Christ*, new English version revised by Vermes, Millar, and Black, vol. 2 (Edinburgh: T. and T. Clark, 1979), 381–403.
3. Particularly associated with this view is E. P. Sanders, *Paul and Palestinian Judaism* (Philadelphia: Fortress, 1977).
4. R. A. Martin, *Studies in the Life and Ministry of the Early Paul and Related Issues* (Lewiston, N.Y.: Mellen Biblical Press, 1993), 35–37.
5. *Qal Wahomer* was one of seven rules of interpretation proposed by Hillel and expanded into thirteen by the later rabbis. For a good discussion of first-century Jewish interpretation, see R. N. Longenecker, *Biblical Exegesis in the Apostolic Period* (Grand Rapids: Eerdmans, 1975), 19–50, 104–32.
6. All in all, Paul's use of the Old Testament is independent of most Jewish tradition. See E. E. Ellis, *Paul's Use of the Old Testament* (Grand Rapids: Eerdmans, 1957).
7. W. D. Davies, *Paul and Rabbinic Judaism* (London: S.P.C.K., 1958).

8. For a balanced introduction to the issue of Paul's relation to the scrolls, see J. Murphy-O'Connor and J. H. Charlesworth, eds., *Paul and the Dead Sea Scrolls* (New York: Crossroad, 1990).

9. A. Schweitzer, *The Mysticism of Paul the Apostle*, trans. William Montgomery (New York: Macmillan, 1931).

10. In his influential book, J. Christiaan Beker sees apocalyptic as the center which gives coherence to all of Paul's writings: *Paul the Apostle: The Triumph of God in Life and Thought* (Philadelphia: Fortress, 1980).

11. P. Van Minnen, "Paul the Roman Citizen," *Journal for the Study of the New Testament* 56 (1994): 43–52.

12. R. N. Longenecker, *Paul, Apostle of Liberty* (New York: Harper and Row, 1964), 101–103.

13. For a thorough refutation of this view, see M. Hengel and A. M. Schwemer, *Paul Between Damascus and Antioch* (Louisville: Westminster/John Knox, 1997), 36–37.

14. *Acts of Paul* 3.3 in E. Hennecke and W. Schneemelcher, *New Testament Apocrypha*, trans. and ed. R. M. Wilson, vol. 2 (Philadelphia: Westminster, 1964), 354.

15. Both cited in M. Grant, *Saint Paul* (London: Weidenfeld and Nicolson, 1976), 13.

16. This discussion is largely dependent on B. Malina and J. Neyrey, *Portraits of Paul: An Archaeology of Ancient Personality* (Louisville: Westminster John Knox, 1996), 127–152.

17. Among modern advocates of this "sexual temptation" view, see M. Grant, *St. Paul*, 32–35 and A. D. Nock, *St. Paul* (New York: Harper and Brothers, 1937), 71.

18. T. Mullins, "Paul's Thorn in the Flesh," *Journal of Biblical Literature* 76 (1957): 299–303.

19. For a comprehensive summary of the various suggestions, see W. M. Alexander, "St. Paul's Infirmity," *Expository Times* 15 (1903–1904): 469–473, 545–548.

20. For a refutation of the epileptic view, see W. M. Ramsay, *The Teaching of St. Paul in Terms of the Present Day* (London: Hodder and Stoughton, 1913), 306–328.

21. W. M. Ramsay, *St. Paul the Traveller and the Roman Citizen* (London: Hodder and Stoughton, 1897), 94–97.

SUGGESTED FURTHER READING

Bruce, F. F. *Paul: Apostle of the Heart Set Free.* Grand Rapids: Eerdmans, 1977, pp. 41–73.

Davies, W. D. *Paul and Rabbinic Judaism.* London: S.P.C.K., 1958.

Ellis, E. E. *Paul's Use of the Old Testament.* Grand Rapids: Eerdmans, 1957.

Longenecker, R. N. *Biblical Exegesis in the Apostolic Period.* Grand Rapids: Eerdmans, 1975.

Malina, B. and J. Neyrey. *Portraits of Paul: An Archaeology of Ancient Personality.* Louisville: Westminster/John Knox, 1996.

Murphy-O'Connor, J. and J. H. Charlesworth, eds. *Paul and the Dead Sea Scrolls.* New York: Crossroad, 1990.

Neusner, J. *From Politics to Piety: The Emergence of Pharisaic Judaism.* Englewood Cliffs, N.J.: Prentice-Hall, 1973.

3

SEIZED BY CHRIST

*I*n Philippians 3:12 Paul spoke of Christ having "taken hold" of him. He probably had his conversion in mind. On the Damascus road Paul was literally seized by Christ. The persecutor of Christians was transformed into proclaimer of Christ. It was a miraculous event, solely due to the power and grace of God. The three conversion accounts of Acts depict it as such, and Paul's allusions to his conversion in his epistles confirm that picture. Paul's conversion and call was a single experience and the key event for his ministry and probably for his theology as well. This chapter will examine it in some detail. It will then consider Paul's witness immediately after his conversion—in Damascus, Arabia, and Jerusalem. A final section will consider the extent to which Paul was influenced by the life and teachings of the earthly Jesus.

PAUL'S CONVERSION
Paul's conversion is narrated with some detail in three accounts in Acts. In his epistles Paul refers to it on several occasions. In addition, his conversion seems to lie behind many of Paul's references in his letters to his apostleship and ministry. There are differences in detail within the three accounts of Acts, and even more so between the Acts accounts and the references in Paul's letters. For the most part these do not offer serious conflicts but are mainly due to differing contexts. They complement one another, giving a multifaceted view of this pivotal event in Paul's life as a Christian.

THE THREE ACCOUNTS IN ACTS
Paul's conversion is related three times in Acts. The first is Luke's *narrative* of the event (9:1–19). It is located in the center of chapters 6 through 11, chapters which relate how the Christian witness began to expand beyond the borders of Judea and the bounds of Judaism, first with Stephen's programmatic speech (chap. 7), then with Philip's witness to the Samaritans and the Ethiopian (chap. 8), then with Peter's testimony to the Gentile Cornelius (10:1–11:18), and finally with the outreach to the Gentiles conducted by the Antioch church (11:19–30). Paul had a role in Antioch's Gentile mission (11:25–26). Luke appropriately placed the story of Paul's conversion in the middle of this section of Acts, because Paul more than any other single person was responsible for the church's mission to the Gentiles. Beginning with chapter 13, the story of Acts is wholly the story of Paul's mission.

The two other accounts of Paul's conversion are of a different genre. Both are *testimonies* of Paul, parts of speeches delivered by the apostle in defense of his ministry. The first is his speech before a Jewish mob in the temple square (22:3–16). The mob had just attempted to kill Paul, accusing him of having taught disloyalty to the law and of violating the sanctity of the temple. Rescued by the Roman garrison and placed under protective custody, Paul secured permission from the commander to address the mob. He wanted to witness to Christ and to convince the crowd that faith in Christ was in no way antithetical to Judaism. The third account in Acts is a part of Paul's address before the Jewish king Agrippa II (26:4–18). Under accusation of a capital crime by the Jewish authorities, Paul had appealed his case to Caesar. The Roman governor Festus requested the hearing before the Jewish king, hoping that the king could clarify the Jewish charges against Paul. Paul gave his personal testimony before the king and governor in order to clarify that the matter was wholly a religious issue within the Jewish community involving Jesus' messianic role as the fulfillment of the Jewish hope.

Though obviously parallel, the three accounts differ in detail, largely due to their different contexts. In the treatment that follows, we will examine all three together, noting the elements they have in common and where they differ.

Paul's persecuting (9:1–2; 22:3–5; 26:4–5, 9–12). In his two testimonies, Paul began by noting his Jewish heritage. He was brought up in a Jewish family in Tarsus, trained in the law under Gamaliel, zealous for God (22:3; 26:4). He had lived by the "strictest sect" of the Jewish religion—a Pharisee (26:5). Paul's Jewish background was essential to the argument of his speeches before the temple mob and Agrippa. It was not necessary in the conversion narrative of Acts 9. What *was* essential there was Paul's preconversion role of being the ravager of the church. So that is where Luke began. Paul was "breathing out murderous threats against the Lord's disciples" (9:1). Paul was so intense in his persecution of the Christians that he drew his very breath from the threats and slaughter which he harbored against them. Paul's testimonies go into greater detail: he persecuted the Christians "to death," dragging off both men *and* women to prison (22:4); when it was a question of the death penalty, he "cast [his] vote against them" (26:10). Paul's persecuting in Jerusalem is not elaborated in Acts.[1] The only death detailed by Luke is that of Stephen. Paul need not have been a member of the Sanhedrin, even though his testimony would indicate that the chief priests gave him authorization for his persecuting activities (26:10). Paul went into the greatest detail about his persecuting in his testimony before Agrippa. There he noted how he had consistently attempted to make the Christians "blaspheme"; that is, to renounce the name of Christ (26:11a). He added that he extended his persecution "even . . . to foreign cities" (25:11b).

The persecution in Jerusalem probably did not last long. It erupted after Stephen's martyrdom and may have been conducted by the Greek-speaking Jews of Jerusalem who had brought Stephen to trial (Acts 6:8–14). Paul may well have been a member of their synagogue. The main target of the persecution were the "Hellenists," the Greek-speaking Jewish Christians like Stephen and Philip. Because of the persecution, they quickly were "scattered" away from the center of the persecution in Jerusalem (Acts 8:1). One of them, Philip, went to Samaria (Acts 8:5). Others went to the coastal cities like Antioch (Acts 11:19). Still others probably went to Damascus. In any event, when they fled from Jerusalem, Paul determined to pursue them wherever they might go. All three accounts in Acts mention that Paul went to Damascus on the authority of the high priests. Specifically, he obtained from them "letters" addressed to the synagogues of Damascus, requesting their assistance in bringing back to Jerusalem for trial any Christians whom he might find in the city (9:2; 22:5). This sounds very much like an official right of extradition. There is evidence that the high priest was granted such rights in earlier times, but no indication that the Romans had granted him such power in Paul's time.[2] It is more likely that the high priest had granted Paul *letters of introduction* to the Damascus synagogues, requesting their assistance in his persecuting effort. In the Roman period, local synagogues were permitted to discipline their members.[3] Later Paul would experience himself the severe synagogue discipline of the thirty-nine lashes on five separate occasions (2 Cor. 11:24).

Paul's letters from the high priest may have requested that the Damascus synagogues defer their disciplinary prerogatives to the Jerusalem Sanhedrin, allowing Paul to take his Christian prisoners there for trial. At this point in the life of the early church, the Christian movement was still closely identified with Judaism and attached to both temple and synagogue. Luke indicates as much by referring to the Christians as "the Way" (9:2). This term was also used as a self-designation by the Essenes of Qumran. For Essenes and Christians alike, it indicated the conviction that theirs was the true "way of the Lord" within the larger Jewish community.[4]

Why would the Christian Hellenists have fled to *Damascus*? There was an extensive Jewish community in Damascus. Josephus mentions pogroms against the Jews during the time of the Jewish War with Rome. He stated that some 10,500 Damascene Jews were slaughtered by the Gentiles of Damascus at that time (*War*, 2.559–561). In the same passage he noted that "with few exceptions" the Gentile wives of Damascus had become Jewish proselytes. Josephus was prone to exaggerate and probably did so in this account. Allowing for this, he still seems to indicate that there was an extensive Jewish community in Damascus with a significant component of God-fearers and proselytes in their synagogues, all of which would have made the city a prime place for the witness of the hellenist Christians.

Damascus had a close relationship to Israel throughout its history. The oldest continually occupied city in the world, it is first mentioned in the Old Testament in connection with Abraham (Gen. 14:15; 15:2). It was within the borders of David's empire, and he garrisoned troops there (2 Sam. 8:6). In the period of the divided kingdom, it was the main enemy of the northern tribes and like them was eventually captured by the Assyrians. In fact, its political history largely parallels that of Israel thereafter, with subsequent occupation by the Babylonians, Persians, Ptolemies, and Seleucids. In 66 B.C., it came under Roman control and was listed among the cities of the Decapolis. During the Roman period, Damascus had close ties with Israel. Herod the Great built a gymnasium and a theater there. Damascus was on the major north-south trade route, and Israel allied with the city to protect their mutual commercial interests, particularly against the Nabatean tribes of Arabia. Jewish client kings like Agrippa I were given small holdings in the vicinity of Damascus by the Roman emperors, who probably felt that the Jewish presence would help contain the Nabateans. Its long history of relationship with Israel, its extensive Jewish community, and its commercial alliances with the Jews all made Damascus attractive for the missionary work of the hellenist Christians. In many ways, it was a natural extension of their Judaean witness.

There were two main routes between Jerusalem and Damascus in Paul's day. One led through Samaria and forded the Jordan at Bethsean (Scythopolis). There was a southern ford at Bethany near Jericho, which went directly north through Perea and Batanea. This was the shorter of the two, a six- to seven-day journey of around 140 miles. This is probably the route that Paul followed.[5]

The appearance of Jesus to Paul (9:3–9; 22:6–11; 26:12–16a). As Paul's caravan proceeded to Damascus, suddenly a bright light flashed from heaven (9:3; 22:6; 26:13). The time of day was noon (22:6; 26:13). The light was overwhelming, "brighter than the sun" (26:13). In the Old Testament, light often accompanies an epiphany (an appearance of God), as with the fire of the burning bush and the radiance that shone from Moses' face after his meeting with God on the mountain (Exod. 34:29–35). Paul fell to the ground (9:4a; 22:7). Evidently his companions did the same (26:14). Paul then heard a voice from heaven. Only in his account before Agrippa did Paul mention that the voice spoke in the Aramaic tongue (26:14). This is implicit, however, in Paul's being addressed in all three accounts by his Hebrew name, "Saul, Saul." Then came the startling words, "Why do you persecute *me?*" (9:4b; 22:7b; 26:14). Not "my church," not even "my brothers and sisters," but "why do you persecute *me?*" There is a strong identification here of Christ with his followers. When his disciples suffer, Christ suffers. When Christians are persecuted, their Lord is persecuted. Here is the germ of Paul's later teaching on the unity of the church with its Lord.

At this point in his testimony before Agrippa, Paul added the proverb, "It is hard for you to kick against the goads" (26:14). It is a proverb found in Greek writers like Aeschylus and Euripides but was probably well-known by the public at large. Perhaps it is of some significance that Paul reserved this detail for his testimony before the hellenistic king. The basic meaning of the saying is that one resists a stronger power only to one's own detriment. The reference is *not* to Paul's past, to pangs of conscience or second thoughts about his persecution of the Christians, not even to the searing memory of the dying Stephen begging the Lord's forgiveness of his murderers. These memories surely later brought tears to the eyes of the *Christian* Paul, but not now, not to the zealous persecutor of God's "enemies," the proud vindicator of God's right. No, the proverb means that it is futile and hopeless to kick against God's movement in one's life. Christ was taking hold of Paul, irresistibly. He could not stop it. It was futile and foolish to try.

Paul did not resist. He answered, "Who are you, Lord?" (9:5; 22:8a; 26:15a). This was not a confession. Paul did not recognize that the Lord was Jesus or even God. He only recognized a visitation of a heavenly being and addressed him appropriately as "Lord." He did not know him: "Who are you?" He immediately found out: "I am Jesus, whom you are persecuting" (9:5; 26:15). Before the Jewish mob Paul elaborated slightly on Jesus' self-disclosure. Jesus/Jeshua was a common Jewish name. This, however, was not just any Jeshua: it was "Jesus *of Nazareth*" (22:8b). Imagine how those words must have impacted the zealous persecutor. He had sought to stamp out the Christians for their proclamation of a *dead* Messiah. How it must have cut Paul to the quick. Jesus of Nazareth, the "King of the Jews" (John 19:19), who died on that Roman cross, was not dead at all. He was alive! He was indeed the King of the Jews, the long-awaited Messiah. In his pride and misguided zeal, Paul had persecuted the Messiah!

There was no more comment from Paul. He was completely broken. Jesus continued by directing him to rise and go into the city, where he would receive further instructions (9:6; 22:10). The account before King Agrippa stops with Jesus' command for Paul to arise (26:16a). In fact, at this point the testimony in chapter 26 moves to Paul's commission to witness in Jesus' name, an element that appears only later in the other two accounts in Acts. The other two relate the state of Paul's traveling companions, but in different detail. The narrative of chapter 9 says that they "stood there speechless; they heard the sound but did not see anyone" (v. 7). Chapter 22 states: "My companions saw the light, but they did not understand the voice of him who was speaking to me" (v. 9). The two are often seen to be in conflict, one referring to their hearing but not seeing, the other to their seeing but not hearing. The conflict is only *apparent*. The point is that the companions did not see the *vision* of Jesus; they only saw a light. They did not hear the *conversation* between Jesus and Paul; they only heard voices. The epiphany was something only Paul experienced. But it was not something in his imagination. His companions could verify that something objective took place—they saw a light; they heard a sound.

When Paul arose from the ground, he could see nothing. Blinded by the vision, he was hand-led into Damascus (9:8; 22:11). Only the narrative of chapter 9 supplies the detail that Paul remained sightless for three days. He did not eat or drink during that period (v. 9). This indicates the depth of his encounter with the Lord. His fasting marked his meditation and prayer as he awaited further revelation from his Lord.

Ananias (9:10–19a; 22:12–16). As we have seen, Paul did not elaborate further on his Damascus experience before King Agrippa (chap. 26). After relating the initial vision, he proceeded directly to the Lord's commissioning him to be a missionary. Chapters 9 and 22 tell how a pious Jewish Christian of Damascus named Ananias was sent to Paul to assist in restoring his sight and to baptize him. The two accounts differ because of their different forms. As a narrative, chapter 9 relates God's appearance to Ananias in a vision. Chapter 22 is Paul's personal testimony. The vision that came to Ananias was not a part of his personal experience, so Paul dealt only with Ananias's visit to him.

We begin with Ananias's vision as related in 9:10–16. Ananias is introduced only as a "disciple," that is, as a follower of Christ. Paul described him in more detail in his speech before the Jewish mob: "He was a devout observer of the law and highly respected by all the Jews living there" (22:12). Just as Paul had emphasized his own thoroughly Jewish background (22:3–5), he wished to impress before the Jewish crowd that the person who first introduced him to the Christians was also not a renegade but as faithful a Jew as himself. We know nothing more about Ananias. He seems to have been much like James, the brother of Jesus and leader of the Jerusalem church. He was respected by all the Jews for his faithful observance of the Jewish law. We don't know where or from whom Ananias received his Christian faith.

Jesus appeared to Ananias in a vision, evidently as suddenly and unexpectedly as in Paul's vision outside Damascus. Verse 10 speaks of "the Lord" calling out to him. In Acts "Lord" can refer either to God or to Jesus. Since "Lord" seems to refer to Jesus in verse 15, it is likely Jesus who appears to Ananias throughout the narrative of his vision. Like Paul, Jesus addressed him by name, "Ananias!" (v. 10). Ananias's response, however, was decidedly *not* like Paul's. He *recognized* Jesus. He did not ask "Who is it, Lord?" but responded "Yes, Lord." Ananias's response was that of a believer. It was the "here am I, Lord" of other great figures of faith like Abraham

(Gen. 22:1) and the boy Samuel (1 Sam. 3:4–14). Jesus responded with precise directions: he was to go to Straight Street to the house of a man named Judas and to ask for a man who was staying there and praying who was named Saul (v. 11). We know nothing more about Judas. He evidently was a Jew, for Paul had not yet been introduced to the Damascus Christians. The Street called Straight is believed to be still in existence. Known today as the Darb-el-Mostakim, it is somewhat to the north and several levels higher than the ancient street.

Jesus continued by informing Ananias that this Saul had had a vision of his own that a man named Ananias would come and lay hands on him that he might receive his sight (v. 12). This phenomenon of a vision within a vision is found also in Acts 10, where the dual visions of Cornelius and Peter intersect. Their significance is to legitimize the experience. Visions received independently by two persons confirm each other, demonstrating that the information that is revealed is correct and backed by divine authority.[6] The laying on of hands is sometimes associated with commissioning in Acts (6:6; 13:3). Here it is connected with the healing, as was the case with Jesus' healing of the blind (Mark 8:25).

Ananias responded to the Lord's directions by reminding him how Paul was the archenemy of the Christian community, how he had come to Damascus to persecute the Christians, just as he had in Jerusalem (vv. 13–14). His words parallel the description of Paul in verses 1 and 2. They remind us of the remarkable turnabout in Paul's life. He had indeed been the archenemy of the church. But all that had changed now because of the Lord's intervention in his life. This is the central emphasis in the conversion narrative of chapter 9: the persecutor of Christ had become the witness to Christ.

Verses 15–16 summarize the Lord's commission for Paul. He is Christ's "chosen instrument to carry [his] name before the Gentiles and their kings and before the people of Israel."[7] Verse 15 is programmatic for the rest of Acts. Chapters 13–28 depict Paul's mission in which he indeed witnessed before Gentiles, the Jewish king Agrippa, and regularly in the synagogues to the sons of Israel. Above all, Paul was called to be the apostle to the Gentiles, and they are mentioned first. Paul's call to the Gentile mission is central to the other two conversion accounts as well. In his speech before the Jewish crowd, Paul mentioned it obliquely ("witness to *all men*," v. 15) in connection with Ananias, then explicitly in his description of how the Gentile call was confirmed subsequently in a vision he had in the temple (22:21). In his speech before Agrippa, the call to a Gentile mission constitutes the center of the conversion account. Paul is sent forth as the servant and witness of Christ (26:16). He is promised protection from hostile Jews and Gentiles alike (26:17). He is sent to "turn them from darkness to light, and from the power of Satan to God" (26:18). This last statement reflects Paul's understanding that God had called him to fulfill the role of the Isaianic Servant in being a light to the Gentiles/nations (Isa. 49:6; cp. Acts 13:47).

Verse 16 of chapter 9 concludes the vision of Ananias. Paul, who had inflicted so much suffering on the young Christian community, had now become its chief sufferer. The theme runs throughout the account of Paul's conversion in chapter 9. Paul began by persecuting Christ (vv. 4–5). Then came the great reversal of his life, and he became one who would himself suffer for the name of Christ (v. 16). Indeed, he does—immediately. His first preaching in Damascus evoked a violent response. Paul the pursuer became Paul the pursued, and he had to flee the city (vv. 23–25). He then bore his witness in Jerusalem, but an attempt was made on his life there as well, and he again had to flee (vv. 29–30).[8] Indeed, Paul came to see that a faithful witness can expect to be persecuted. Suffering is the way of the cross, but it is a suffering which leads to resurrection and life (Rom. 8:17; 2 Cor. 4:7–12).

Verses 17–19 conclude the conversion narrative of Acts 9, describing Ananias's visit to Paul. Paul's testimony of his conversion picks up again at this point in chapter 22 (vv. 12–16). Ananias went to the house where Paul was staying. On entering it, he placed his hands on Paul so that he might receive his sight again (cp. 9:12). Paul was immediately healed. "Something like scales" fell from his eyes, and he saw again (9:18; 22:13). But Ananias brought more than the recovery of his physical sight. He saw to it that Paul was baptized (9:18; 22:16) and received the gift of the Spirit (9:17); he introduced him into the Christian community (9:19b). His acceptance into the circle of Christian disciples is perhaps no better indicated than by Ananias' addressing Paul as "brother Saul." Jews also addressed one another as "brother," but here Ananias was accepting his former enemy as a brother in Christ. That was surely the greatest miracle that occurred that day in Judas's house.

According to Acts 22:14–15, Ananias shared with Paul the vision Christ had revealed to him of his future ministry (cp. 9:15–16). Luke does not repeat it in chapter 22; it would have been superfluous. God had revealed Christ ("the Righteous One") to Paul; he had "chosen" Paul (22:14). Paul would be Christ's witness to all people of what he had seen and heard (22:15). In all three accounts of Acts, Paul's conversion and his call to the Gentiles go together. They are inseparable aspects of the single experience on the Damascus road.

The three accounts in Acts: An Overview. How are we to understand the relationship between the three accounts of Paul's conversion in Acts? In an era when source criticism of Acts was in vogue, the differences between the three were attributed to Luke's use of sources. A popular theory was that of Emanuel Hirsch.[9] He argued that chapter 26 was Paul's own account. He saw chapter 9 as less reliable and coming from the Christian community of Damascus. Chapter 22 was attributed to Luke and seen to be his combination of the other two. Source-critical theories tended to be rather subjective and to have a rationalistic bias.

Others pursued a history-of-religions approach to the Acts conversion narratives, seeking possible parallels in ancient literature which could have served as a pattern for Luke. One popular theory was that Luke based the conversion of Paul on the Heliodorus legend of 2 Maccabees 3. Heliodorus was an emissary of the Syrian king who was sent to Jerusalem to confiscate the temple treasure. He was prevented from doing so by a blinding vision which knocked him to his feet. He departed the scene hastily, convinced of the power of Israel's God. About the only element in common between Heliodorus and Paul is the motif of God protecting his people from a persecutor.[10] If one is seeking a background for the conversion narratives, the most natural place to look is the Old Testament. As we have already seen, the Acts accounts of Paul's conversion have much in common with Old Testament forms such as that of a divine epiphany.

One Old Testament form of particular note is the prophetic call. The accounts of Paul's conversion share patterns found in the calls of the Old Testament prophets. Note the following elements in common between Paul and the prophets' calls. First, there is the appearance of blazing light (Ezek. 1:26–28). Second, there is a vision of the Lord on his throne (Ezek. 1:26–28; Isa. 6:1). Third, the prophet falls to the ground or protests his unworthiness (Ezek. 1:28; Isa. 6:5; Jer. 1:6). Fourth, the Lord lifts the prophet up and affirms him (Ezek. 2:1–2; Isa. 6:6–7; Jer. 1:7–8). Finally, the Lord calls him to mission (Ezek. 2:3–7; Isa. 6:9–10; Jer. 1:9–10).[11] That the Acts conversion narratives resemble the calls of the Old Testament prophets comes as no surprise. In his epistles also, Paul describes his call in terms reminiscent of the prophets.

Perhaps the most fruitful recent research on the Acts conversion narratives have been investigations from the viewpoint of Luke's literary technique. The three accounts build on one another and assume a knowledge of the ones which come before them. Chapter 9 is the initial and basic account. It highlights the miraculous nature of Paul's conversion. The emphasis is on the complete turnabout of Paul from persecutor to witness. Paul's commission to preach to the Gentiles is present, but secondary, imbedded in the vision of Ananias (v. 15). In chapter 22, the miracle is present but less emphasized. More prominent is Paul's commission to witness to "all" (v. 15), a commission which is underlined immediately by Paul's vision in the temple that reinforces his call to the Gentiles (v. 21). In chapter 26, Paul's commission to the Gentiles holds central place (vv. 16–18). It becomes clear that this is ultimately the central theme for Paul's traveling companion Luke—the apostle's call as missionary to the nations. But the story begins with his miraculous conversion; so that is highlighted in chapter 9. As Paul's mission to the Gentiles is related in the subsequent chapters of Acts, the significance of his call unfolds and comes to take center stage in his final conversion account.[12]

PAUL'S REFERENCES TO HIS CONVERSION

Several times in his epistles Paul made explicit reference to his conversion. He never related the experience as an event in itself. His allusions to his conversion were always made in support of some other point that he wished to make.

Galatians 1:13–16. In the first chapter of Galatians Paul argued that his gospel was received as a direct revelation from Jesus Christ; he neither received it nor was he taught it through human mediation (vv. 11–12). In order to drive this point home, he spoke of his earliest days as a Christian—in Damascus and in Jerusalem. He emphasized that at this time he was not instructed by others, particularly by those who were apostles before him (vv. 13–24). Paul's early Christian period in Damascus and Jerusalem will be discussed at length in the second division of this chapter. At this point we will focus on verses 13–16, which relate to his conversion.

The differences between Paul's Galatian account and the Acts account have often been noted. Galatians does not present the sort of personal testimony found in Acts 22 and 26. There is no blinding light, no falling to the ground, no conversation with Christ. In Galatians Paul was not concerned with the details of his conversion experience—only its significance for his subsequent ministry. In particular, he wished to show the *independence* of his call. What is really striking is how much Paul's Galatian conversion account has *in common* with those in Acts.

All the major emphases of Galatians 1:13–16 are found in Acts. First, Paul pointed to his former life as persecutor of the Christians (Gal. 1:13; cp. Acts 9:1–2; 22:4–5; 26:9–11). Next, Paul told the Galatians how he had "advanced in Judaism" and outstripped many of his peers in his knowledge of and zeal for the Jewish traditions (v. 14). The same emphasis on his Jewish zeal and Pharisaic training in the law is found in both his testimonies in Acts—before the Jews at the temple (22:3) and before Agrippa (26:5). Galatians 1:15–16 elaborates Paul's call in terms reminiscent of the Old Testament prophets. Paul spoke of how he had been "set . . . apart from birth" (literally, "from my mother's womb") and how he had been called "to preach [Christ] *among the Gentiles.*" Both these emphases are found in the call experiences of the Old Testament prophets, particularly Jeremiah (1:4–5) and the Servant of God (Isa. 49:1–6). Though the concept of being called by God even before birth is not found in the Acts accounts, the form of the prophetic call narrative *is*, as we have seen. And the nature of his call as being a call to witness to the Gentiles is found in all three conversion accounts in Acts (9:15; 22:15, 21; 26:16–18).

Finally, the *content* of his vision is the same in Galatians and Acts. In Galatians Paul spoke of God's "revealing his Son in me" (v. 16). Paul had a vision of God's Son, of Christ. There are those who would argue that the Acts accounts do not depict Paul as having a vision of Christ, only of his seeing a blinding light and hearing the voice of Jesus.[13] This, however, is to ignore the references in Acts which describe Paul as having experienced an appearance of Jesus and of having seen the Lord (9:7; 9:17; 22:14; 26:16). Acts and Paul's letters are in agreement that the *center* of his conversion experience was a vision of the risen Jesus. Both agree that his vision was inseparable from his call to proclaim Christ to the Gentiles.

1 Corinthians 15:8–10. To the Corinthians Paul made a brief allusion to his conversion. All of 1 Corinthians 15 is devoted to Paul's rebuttal of those who were denying that there would be a resurrection of the dead. Paul began his argument by pointing to the resurrection of Jesus and then showing how his rising was the "firstfruits" of the resurrection of those who had died in Christ (v. 20). In order to establish the certainty of Christ's resurrection, he pointed to the early tradition that had been passed to him, listing those who had seen the risen Lord (vv. 5–7): He appeared first to Peter, then to all twelve of the disciples, then to more than five hundred brethren in a single appearance, then to James (the Lord's brother), then to "all the apostles" (a wider group than the Twelve, who had already been listed). Finally, Paul said, "He appeared to me also, as to one abnormally born" (v. 8). Paul saw his vision of Christ as being on the same level as the other appearances of the risen Lord. He was surely referring to his vision of Jesus at his conversion and call. But what did he mean by referring to it as being as though he had been "abnormally born"? In the context the most likely understanding would be that it referred to the *lateness* of Jesus' appearance to Paul. The appearances to the others occurred earlier, probably all during the forty-day period before Jesus' ascension (Acts 1:3). Christ appeared to Paul much later. He was "last on the list."

The problem with this view is that the Greek word translated by the NIV as "abnormally born" (*ektrōma*) never means a "late birth" but always refers to a birth too early—a premature birth, a stillbirth, or an abortion. Because of its use for an aborted birth, it sometimes was given the meaning of "monstrous." Some would interpret Paul's reference that way—as referring forward to the next verse where Paul described his activity as a persecutor (v. 9). His apostleship was something of a "monstrosity," because he persecuted the church. Since *ektrōma* seems always to refer to a preterm birth of some sort, it has been suggested that Paul may have had in mind the same concept of his being called "from the womb" that one finds in Galatians 1:15. Then the idea would be that Paul was called from before birth but that the call had "aborted," so to speak, when Paul persecuted the church rather than proclaiming Christ.[14] But Christ's appearance to Paul turned all that around, and the previously aborted Paul became the hardest working apostle of them all.

Even if we cannot determine with certainty the precise meaning of *ektrōma*, the general drift of 1 Corinthians 15:8–10 is clear. It has much in common with Paul's reference to his conversion in Galatians 1. In both it is described as a vision of Christ—as God's revelation of his Son (Galatians), as an appearance of the risen Christ to Paul (1 Corinthians). Both accounts refer to Paul's preconversion activity of persecuting the church. Both emphasize that Paul's experience was solely due to God's grace. Both depict it as Paul's call to apostleship.

Philippians 3:4–11. In Philippians 3 Paul warned his Gentile converts at Philippi against those who would insist on their circumcision and living by the Jewish law. He spoke of his own Jewish pedigree and how he once had prided himself on such things. But now he had given all that up in order to be found in Christ Jesus. The passage is not as obviously a "conversion" narrative as the preceding two, but it is usually grouped with them because of its sharp contrast between the pre-Christian and the Christian Paul. Verses 5–6 have the closest resemblance to other conversion narratives, particularly to Galatians 1 and the three Acts accounts. They depict Paul's former life as a Pharisee and as a zealous persecutor of the church. Verse 10 could perhaps link with Acts 9:16 in its references to Paul's suffering. But the central elements in Paul's conversion experience which we found in all the other accounts are lacking in Philippians—his seeing the vision of the risen Christ and his call to be an apostle to the Gentiles. What is distinctive about the Philippian passage are the emphases on Paul's "loss" and on his having his righteousness through faith in Christ (vv. 8–9).

By human standards, Paul did "suffer the loss" of much when he "gained Christ." Rising star among the Pharisees that he seems to have been, he surrendered any promise of leadership in contemporary Judaism when he embraced Christ. But such things came to mean nothing for Paul after he met Christ. Nothing in his former life could make him right with God. Only Christ could do so; Paul had found the divine acceptance ("righteousness") in Christ alone. Nothing else mattered, not even the law, which once he cherished. Did this understanding come at once to Paul in a blinding flash of light on the Damascus road? Or was it the product of long reflection as a Christian and of experience as a missionary of Christ? We will consider this question in the next section.

2 Corinthians 4:4–6. The allusion to Paul's conversion is even less direct in 2 Corinthians 4:4–6. The context is one in which Paul was contrasting the glory of the old covenant and the even greater glory of the new covenant of the Spirit in Christ (3:7–18). In 4:4–6 he rounded off the section by praising the glory of God which has shone in the face of Christ. Paul was talking about the experience of every believer who has come to know God through the revelation in Christ. The Spirit enlightens the believer, who receives "the light of the knowledge of the glory of God in the face of Christ" (v. 6). Paul could well have had his own conversion in mind. Light flooded his soul in his encounter with Christ on the Damascus road. He had seen the Lord. He had seen the very glory of God in the face of Jesus Christ.[15]

1 Timothy 1:12–16. A final direct allusion to Paul's conversion appears in the first epistle to Timothy. In words reminiscent of 1 Corinthians 15:8–10, Paul spoke of his apostolic call to serve Christ. He emphasized his sense of unworthiness. He had been "chief of sinners" because he had blasphemed Christ and persecuted the church. Again Paul emphasized that his transformation was not of his own doing but was solely due to God's grace. The unique note in this passage is Paul's insistence that his former role as blasphemer and persecutor was done in ignorance and in unbelief (v. 13).

Call to the Gentiles. In a number of places Paul's letters speak of his role as apostle to the Gentiles. These could by extension be considered as relating to his conversion. As we have seen, Paul's call to the Gentile mission was an integral part of his conversion in both Acts and his epistles. Particularly when Paul spoke of his ministry in terms of sharing a "mystery," he had in mind the inclusion of the Gentiles in God's people and his own call to share the gospel with them (Rom. 16:25–26; Col. 1:26–27; Eph. 3:1–13). The text in Ephesians is especially noteworthy. It should probably be considered a conversion text.[16] Paul emphasized that he had received his gospel directly, *by revelation* (Eph. 3:3; cp. Gal. 2:2). At the heart of his gospel was the now-revealed mystery that in Christ the Gentiles were partakers in the divine promises (v. 6, cp. Gal. 1:16). Also by extension one could include as being related to his conversion the many places where Paul referred to himself as an apostle (e.g. Rom. 1:1; 1 Cor. 1:1; 2 Cor. 1:1; Eph. 1:1; Col. 1:1; Gal. 1:1). In his vision of Christ, Paul was called to be an apostle (1 Cor. 9:1). In particular, he was called to be Christ's apostle to the Gentiles (Rom. 1:5; Rom. 11:13; Rom. 15:15–16; Gal. 2:7–8; 1 Tim. 2:7).

Summary. The following composite can be drawn from Paul's references to his conversion in his epistles. First, Paul depicted it as a *vision* of the risen Christ (Gal. 1; 1 Cor. 15; 2 Cor. 4). Second, it was a radical *reversal* for Paul, from persecutor of Christ to proclaimer (Gal. 1; 1 Cor. 15; Phil. 3; 1 Tim. 1). Third, Paul considered himself *unworthy* of the commission given him by Christ; he owed it all to *God's grace* (1 Cor. 15; Eph. 3; 1 Tim. 1). Finally, he linked his conversion with his *call to be an apostle to the Gentiles*; they were inseparable (Gal. 1; 1 Cor. 15).

THE NATURE AND SIGNIFICANCE OF PAUL'S CONVERSION

The conversion of Paul is a central topic in much of the contemporary scholarship on the apostle. The following are some of the main questions in the discussion.

What was the nature of Paul's conversion? A former generation of scholars speculated about the form of Paul's conversion. Some sought natural explanations. For instance, it was argued that Paul was blinded by flashes of lightning in a violent thunderstorm over the hills outside Damascus. Others argued that Paul suffered from epilepsy, and his blindness and vision of light constituted the final state before a seizure.[17] Few today would engage in such speculation. A number of recent scholars, however, have suggested that Paul may have been predisposed toward his visionary experience through his involvement in practices of Jewish mysticism. Jewish *merkabah* mysticism practiced meditation on the wheel visions of Ezekiel. Contemporaries of Paul like Johanan ben Zakkai practiced this form of meditation. According to this theory, Paul would have been engaged in meditation as he traveled on his journey to Damascus and been in a trancelike state when the vision of Christ appeared to him.[18]

Is it proper to call Paul's experience a conversion? Many today would prefer to label Paul's experience a "call" rather than a "conversion." This was suggested in an influential article by Krister Stendahl, who argued that Paul was not "converted" from one religious group to another but remained a faithful Jew after his vision of Christ.[19] Stendahl noted that Paul's experience was much like the call experience of the Old Testament prophets. One would freely grant him that Paul saw his call along prophetic lines. But Paul might himself have accepted the designation of conversion for his experience. He saw it as a radical change of mind-set, a turning from persecutor to proclaimer of Christ. One *can* be "converted" to a radically new viewpoint within a larger community of faith. Many recent interpreters have thus insisted that it *is* accurate to describe Paul's Damascus road encounter as a conversion.[20] From what, though, was Paul converted? Perhaps one could take a clue from the Renaissance painters, who characteristically depicted the converted Paul as a fallen horseman, lying completely vanquished at the feet of his horse.[21] The willful, prideful, self-directed Paul was seized by Christ on the Damascus road and completely turned around. Paul's conversion was the quintessential conversion experience—from a self-centered to a Christ-centered life.[22]

Did anything prepare Paul for his conversion? Was Paul "predisposed" to his conversion experience? It has often been suggested that influences in his pre-Christian life prepared Paul for his Damascus road encounter. The most time-honored of these depicts Paul before his conversion as a tortured Pharisee, despairing over his inability to fulfill the letter of the Torah.[23] The picture of the divided self in Romans 7:13–25 is taken to be Paul's autobiography of his pre-Christian life. Despairing of ever finding the demanding God's acceptance because of his incapacity to fulfill the law, Paul was prepared for his encounter with the gracious God on the road to Damascus. It is the classic paradigm of Lutheran theology: despair over the law drove Paul to grace. The above-mentioned article of Krister Stendahl was particularly intent on refuting this paradigm. Stendahl attributed it more to the guilt-ridden consciences of Luther and Augustine than to the historical Paul. Romans 7 is probably not autobiographical,[24] and Paul's own statements indicate that he was not at all tortured by his inability to fulfill the law. Before he met Christ, he was proud of his fidelity to the law, "first" in his Torah class (Gal. 1:14), "faultless" with respect to legal righteousness (Phil. 3:6).

Other "preparatory" factors have been suggested. It has been argued, for instance, that Paul suffered from a tortured conscience. The figure of the dying martyr Stephen haunted him. He could not get the picture of the persecuted Christians from his mind, especially the families he disrupted as he dragged fathers and mothers off to prison. The godly zeal of the "Grand Inquisitor" Paul would scarcely have been moved by such things. After all, he was doing this for the glory of God. Paul was on his high horse. He needed someone to knock him off. That is exactly what happened on the Damascus road. The Renaissance painters had it right. Christ needed nothing to prepare Paul for this encounter. He only needed to appear to Paul. He did, and Paul was changed forever.

There is a general consensus among most contemporary researchers that Paul had a "radical" conversion experience, something for which he was totally unprepared. There is less agreement, however, on what immediate meaning it had for Paul. Most would agree that Paul's conversion would have forced a radical revision in his viewpoint, but they differ as to what that revision might be. Some would see Paul as having to exchange the center of his religion from Torah to Christ.[25] Others would see Paul having to revise his eschatology. Whereas before he had looked to a future Messiah coming to deliver Israel from exile and oppression, now he had to revise his understanding in light of the Messiah/Christ who had already come.[26] Most would agree that Paul conceived his call as an apostle to the Gentiles in terms of his conversion, but viewpoints differ widely as to how the Gentile mission should be connected with the conversion.

What is the link between Paul's conversion and his mission to the Gentiles? It is possible that Paul was already prepared for his mission to the Gentiles *before* his Damascus road encounter. Diaspora Jews were accustomed to having Gentile God-fearers in their synagogues. Some even became proselytes, and it is likely, though not easy to document, that there was some attempt by Jews to make proselytes.[27] It has been suggested that Paul himself may have been involved in such a mission in his pre-Christian period. He is seen as having referred to this earlier proselytizing activity in Galatians 5:11, where he denied that he was "still" practicing circumcision.[28]

Other avenues to Paul's Gentile mission have been suggested. In his popular book on Paul, Martin Dibelius suggested that the pre-Christian Paul's main contention with the Christians was their inclusiveness. He could neither condone nor fathom their easy acceptance of the common people, of the tax collectors and sinners who were so lax in keeping the law. His vision of Christ forced him to realize that the inclusiveness actually reflected God's own openness to all. It was an easy step for the Diaspora Jew to extend the inclusiveness to the Gentiles.[29] Some have suggested that the Christian community into which Paul was converted was already accepting Gentiles.[30] That may be, but Acts would indicate that the Gentile outreach was a slower process and did not reach full flower until much later with the Antioch church and with Paul. Paul's eschatology was certainly a factor in his call to the Gentiles. A major part of the Jewish expectation for the end time was that the Gentiles would turn to Israel's God. An outreach to the Gentiles/nations was part of the call of Jeremiah (1:5–6) and the Servant of God (Isa. 49:1–6). As we have seen, Paul identified closely with these prophets who were "called from their mother's womb" (Gal. 1:15). It was a small step from his new awareness that Christ was Lord and Messiah to his mission to the Gentiles.[31]

What influence did Paul's conversion have on his subsequent theology? There is no doubt that Paul's conversion profoundly influenced his theology. But how immediate was it, and how exclusive was it of other factors, such as his missionary experience? Scholars differ greatly on these questions. At one extreme are those who argue that the germ of *all* Paul's major teachings fell into place in his vision of Christ at his conversion, such as his Christology, his soteriology, his view of the Spirit, his eschatology, his concepts of righteousness and reconciliation.[32] At the other extreme are those who see Paul's theology as being almost totally influenced by his subsequent life in the Christian community, his conversion having little if any effect on his later thinking.[33] The truth probably lies somewhere between these extremes. Paul's epistles reflect that he himself traced his call, his ministry, and his gospel to the revelation of Jesus Christ at his conversion (Gal. 1:12–13). His letters, however, were written fifteen years after that experience at the earliest. It is likely that his missionary experience over these years and his reflection over his life both past and present contributed to his subsequent understanding of his encounter on the Damascus road.

PAUL'S EARLY WITNESS

Paul remained in Damascus for some time after his conversion. Galatians speaks of a period when he was in Arabia as well. Both Acts and Paul (2 Cor. 11:32–33) describe how a threat to his life forced him to leave Damascus. He went on to Jerusalem, where he met with at least two apostles. The accounts differ considerably at this point, but they are in agreement that Paul's life was threatened in Jerusalem as well. Leaving there, he went for a long sojourn in his home territory of Cilicia.

IN DAMASCUS AND ARABIA (ACTS 9:19B–22; GAL. 1:16B–17)

In Acts, Luke describes how Paul witnessed in the synagogues of *Damascus* immediately after his conversion. In Galatians, Paul speaks of going to *Arabia* after his conversion and call.

The witness in Damascus (Acts 9:19b–22). As the result of Ananias's visit, Paul received back his sight, was baptized, and ended his three-day fast by taking food (Acts 9:18–19a). He then "spent several days with the disciples in Damascus" (v. 19b). The "disciples" mentioned here were the Christian community in Damascus, the group that Paul had come to the city to persecute. One would assume that during this time the Damascene disciples shared their Christian knowledge with Paul. Paul would already have known a great deal about the Christians. As their persecutor, he must have questioned Christians closely in his attempt to stamp out what he then saw as a false teaching. But now he would have heard the traditions about Christ from a different perspective—not as an enemy but as a fellow believer.

Paul began his Christian witness "at once" (Acts 9:20). He began in the synagogues of Damascus. They were Diaspora Jewish synagogues like the Greek-speaking synagogues of Tarsus and Jerusalem that Paul was accustomed to attending. It was a pattern which Paul would continue throughout his ministry. He always began his witness in the synagogues. Not only would he find fellow Jews there with whom to share his message about Jesus the Messiah; there would also be Gentile God-fearers and proselytes for whom Paul had his special calling. Already believing in Israel's God, they would have been especially open to Paul's proclamation of the "mystery" that in Christ God had made the Gentiles "fellow heirs" of his promises (Eph. 3:4–6).[34] In the Damascene synagogues, Paul preached that Jesus was the "Son of God" (Acts 9:20). His message was truly astonishing to the Jews of Damascus. They had heard of his reputation. Had he not carried on an extensive persecution of Christians in Jerusalem on the grounds that they were proclaiming a *false* Messiah? Was he now arguing that this same Jesus was the Son of God? Had he not come to Damascus to ask them to assist him in the arrest of the Christians (v. 21)? Now he was trying to convince them to become Christians themselves. The words of the Jews are closely parallel to those of Ananias (9:13–14). At the risk of narrative redundancy, Luke impresses upon us the radical nature of Paul's conversion experience. The persecutor had been completely turned around: from pursuer to proclaimer.

Paul continued in the synagogues, "proving that Jesus is the Christ" (v. 22). (The Greek word *Christ* [*Christos*] is a translation of the Hebrew word for Messiah—the *anointed* of God.) Paul would have used Old Testament texts which show that Jesus fulfilled the promises and prophecies regarding the Messiah. Paul became more and more "powerful" in his arguments. The old student of Gamaliel was now filled with the Spirit, just like Stephen in his witness in the Jerusalem synagogues (Acts 6:8–10). As had been the case with Stephen, the Jews in the Damascus synagogues were unable to refute Paul's arguments (v. 22).

The witness in Arabia (Gal. 1:16b–17). In the Galatian account of his conversion Paul did not mention preaching in the synagogues of Damascus. Instead, he said that he "did not consult any man" (v. 16b). This would seem to contradict the statement in Acts that he spent a brief time with the Christian disciples in Damascus. The contradition may be only apparent, however. Paul's whole purpose in his autobiographical statements of Galatians 1 was to establish that he had not received his apostleship through human mediation but through a direct revelation of Christ. Paul was not denying all contact with other Christians. He was denying consultation with other apostles and insisting he was neither indoctrinated by them nor received his apostolic commission from them. That is why he emphasized that immediately after his conversion he did *not* go to Jerusalem or consult with the apostles there (v. 17a).

It is probably likewise an error to take Paul's denial that he consulted anybody as an indication he went into a period of isolation and meditation in Arabia in which he hammered out his gospel.[35] Paul's Arabian sojourn is only mentioned in Galatians. How long he spent there is uncertain. Paul's time references are vague. He said that he "immediately" (after his conversion) went to Arabia and "later returned to Damascus" (v. 17). The only time reference occurs in verse 18, which states that he went to Jerusalem "after three years." The whole period in Damascus and Arabia lasted three years. There is no way of determining how much of the three years was spent in Arabia and how much in Damascus. Some feel that Paul may have been in Arabia as long as two years; others argue for a much briefer period.

A more important question is what Paul was *doing* in Arabia. Arabia at this time consisted of the Nabatean Kingdom, ruled by the powerful Bedouin king Aretas IV. It stretched out on the desert side of the three easternmost cities of the Decapolis (Damascus, Raphana, and Philadelphia) and went south all the way to the Arabian Gulf. Its capital was Petra. King Aretas wielded considerable power. His daughter married Herod Antipas of Galilee, who divorced her to marry Herodias, the wife of his half-brother Philip. Herod imprisoned and eventually beheaded John the Baptist for his criticism of the affair (Mark 6:14–29). Aretas declared war on Antipas over the insult to his daughter and would have decimated his kingdom had not the Romans intervened. Aretas's kingdom was wealthy and extensively populated. The Jews considered the Arabs as the descendants of Abraham's son Ishmael and thus as distant relatives. Paul probably considered them a mission field. His Arabian period was most likely a time of witness, the beginning of his ministry to the Gentiles.[36]

The flight from Damascus (Acts 9:23–25; 2 Cor. 11:32–33). According to Galatians 1:17, Paul returned to Damascus after his time in Arabia. It may well have been this time that he preached in the synagogues of Damascus (Acts 9:20–22). In any event, Paul's testimony to Christ evoked the resistance of both the Jews and the Arabians. Acts 9:23–25 relates how the Jews conspired to kill Paul. Like Stephen (Acts 6:10–11), unable to refute him, they plotted to silence him by other means. Learning of their plot, Paul attempted to flee the city. The Jews, however, guarded the gates "day and night." His followers ("disciples") assisted him in an alternate escape plan, lowering him in a basket through an opening in the city wall. Paul must have had a ministry of some length in Damascus to have gathered a band of disciples around him.

The incident is also related in Paul's epistle to the Corinthians. There Paul also spoke of having to flee from the city of Damascus (2 Cor. 11:32–33). He also mentioned the same unusual manner of escape—being lowered in a basket through a window in the wall. In Corinthians Paul related the incident as an example of personal embarrassment. He used himself as an example to the Corinthians of how true Christian ministry is often performed in weakness. So his own life had often been a spectacle by the standards of the world. Paul did not mention the Jews in his account of the incident in 2 Corinthians. Instead, he noted that the governor (literally *ethnarch*) of King Aretas watched the gates to seize him. It is uncertain what authority Aretas's "ethnarch" had in Damascus. In Paul's day Damascus was a "free city" of the Decapolis under the Romans. The Nabateans had ruled it briefly more than a century earlier, but not in the Roman period. There may have been a Nabatean quarter in Damascus over which the ethnarch had jurisdiction.[37] Who watched the city gates—the Jews (Acts) or the Nabateans (2 Corinthians)? Quite possibly both, either independently or in some kind of mutual pact against their common enemy.

IN JERUSALEM (ACTS 9:26–30; GAL. 1:18–24)

Paul fled "from the frying pan into the fire," so to speak. Things proved no better for him in Jerusalem than in Damascus. He quickly evoked opposition and had to flee that city as well. Luke and Paul both give accounts of this first visit of Paul to Jerusalem after his conversion. There are significant differences between the two accounts, but they are obviously dealing with the same period.

Acts 9:26–30. Luke's time references in Acts are often vague. For instance, he refers here to Paul spending "many days" in Damascus (9:23). Paul informs us that the period in Damascus and Arabia lasted a total of three years (Gal. 1:18). According to Acts 9:26, Paul fled from Damascus to Jerusalem, where he attempted to join the Christian community ("the disciples"). Like Ananias, they were hesitant to receive him, uncertain that the raging persecutor could really now be a Christian like themselves. But Barnabas intervened for Paul and introduced him to the circle of apostles. Note what Barnabas told them about Paul. It is a summary of Paul's experience, highlighting the most significant elements of Paul's conversion: (1) he had "seen the Lord" and spoken with him, and (2) he had "preached fearlessly in the name of Jesus" in Damascus. Paul had encountered the risen Lord and been completely transformed, from persecutor to bold witness.

Barnabas plays a role here consistent with his role throughout Acts. First introduced in Acts 4:36–37, his nickname is given as "Son of Encouragement." He is exactly that throughout Acts—the encourager, the advocate of others. Here he serves as Paul's advocate before the apostles. In chapter 11, he is the encourager of the Antioch church in its efforts to reach the Gentiles with the gospel (Acts 11:22–23). He later serves as Paul's companion on the latter's first missionary journey, consistently playing a supporting role there. Finally, he supports and encourages the youthful Mark, even when Paul would have abandoned him (Acts 15:36–40).

Barnabas evidently succeeded. Paul was accepted by the apostles and able to come and go freely among the Christian community in Jerusalem (Acts 9:28). Ananias "legitimized" Paul's conversion experience and introduced him into the Damascus Christian community. Here through Barnabas the apostles are shown to endorse Paul's ministry as well, allowing him to move freely among them. Paul continued to bear his bold witness to Christ in Jerusalem. Luke used the word *parrēsiazō* in verse 28, which throughout Acts means to speak boldly through the power of the Holy Spirit. Paul's witness took him back to the Greek-speaking synagogues of Jerusalem, the synagogues which had turned on Stephen, the synagogues to which he had himself formerly been attached (v. 29). As had happened in the synagogues of Damascus, they turned against Paul and plotted to kill him. Again, the plot became known to the Christian community, and Paul was hastened from the city. He was taken to Caesarea, where he departed for his native Tarsus, presumably by ship (v. 30).

Acts 9:1–31 is something of an "interlude" in the narrative of Acts. It depicts the conversion of the church's greatest enemy, who in subsequent chapters will become its greatest advocate. Verse 31 aptly summarizes the result of Paul's conversion from the perspective of the Christian community. Its persecutor was now a brother; and the church throughout all Judea, Galilee, and Samaria was at peace and prospered.

Galatians 1:18–24. Paul's account of his first visit to Jerusalem after his conversion is significantly different from that of Acts. Luke and Paul recounted the event for reasons almost diametrically opposed. Luke wanted to show Paul's *acceptance* by the apostles. Paul emphasized his *independence* of them. Thus, he stated that he went to Jerusalem to visit (NIV "get acquainted with") Peter (Cephas). He noted that his visit was quite short—only fifteen days (Gal. 1:18). He added that he saw no other apostles, "only James, the Lord's brother" (v. 19). He underlined his statement with a mild oath: "before God," he was not lying! (v. 20). Paul wanted the Galatians to understand that his message to them was his own message for the Gentiles. It was not taught him by the apostles but revealed to him by Christ. His calling was directly from Christ, not mediated by others. His orders did not come from Jerusalem. In truth, he only spent fifteen days there three years after his conversion and didn't return for another fourteen years (Gal. 2:1).

Paul concluded his account in Galatians by noting that from Jerusalem he went to "Syria and Cilicia" (v. 21). His statement is in accord with the note in Acts that he was sent home to his native Tarsus (Acts 9:30). Tarsus was in Cilicia, and Cilicia was a part of the Roman province of Syria at this time. In Galatians Paul did not mention his preaching in the Greek-speaking synagogues; it would have served no purpose in his argument for his apostolic independence. He did, however, attest to the hesitancy of the Christians in Judea to accept the fact that their former persecutor was now a preacher of the faith (vv. 22–23; cp. Acts 9:26).

A couple of side issues arising from the Galatian account are worthy of consideration. One is whether Paul called James an "apostle" in verse 19. The most likely rendering of the Greek would indicate that he did: "I saw none of the other apostles, *except for* James, the Lord's brother." Some would render it: "I saw none of the other apostles (than Peter)—but I did see also James, the Lord's brother." The hesitancy to follow the most natural reading is the feeling that only the Twelve and Paul can legitimately be called apostles. Such is simply not true to Paul's own usage. In Acts, the title of "apostle" is restricted to the twelve disciples, to those who witnessed Jesus' earthly ministry (Acts 1:21–22). Not even Paul is called an apostle except for two places in Acts 14 (vv. 4, 14) where he and Barnabas are called apostles, probably in the sense of "those sent" by the Antioch church.

The word *apostle* comes from the Greek word meaning "one who is sent." Paul used it to refer to a wider group than the Twelve. For example, "all the apostles" of 1 Corinthians 15:7 are a different group from the Twelve, who are already listed in verse 5. In Romans 16:7, Paul listed Andronicus and Junia as "outstanding among the apostles." For Paul, an apostle seems to have been one who saw the risen Lord and was commissioned by him (1 Cor. 9:1). Paul seems to have viewed apostles as those to whom Christ had given their own unique sphere of work (Gal. 2:8) and who did not labor in the fields of others (Rom. 15:20).[38] The difference between Luke and Paul is basically semantic. Luke used the word in a more restricted sense, reserved only for the Twelve; Paul employed the term in a broader sense. In Paul's more embracing usage, he called the Lord's brother James an apostle. James had seen the risen Lord (1 Cor. 15:7) and been called to leadership in the church of Jerusalem.

A second question arising from Paul's account of his postconversion Jerusalem visit is more difficult to answer: What did Paul and Peter discuss during those fifteen days? It is hard to believe Paul didn't learn much about Jesus from Peter over those two weeks. The next section will examine the question of Paul's knowledge of Jesus in more detail. Of course, the reverse may be true as well. The apostle to the Gentiles might have had a thing or two to teach Peter. Could Paul have prepared Peter for Cornelius? Certainly the Peter who spoke at the Jerusalem Conference sounded like someone who had been talking with Paul (Acts 15:10–11).

PAUL AND JESUS

A long-standing debate has raged over the extent to which Paul knew and was influenced by the teachings of Jesus. Paul doesn't seem to quote much from the Gospel traditions, and many feel that his basic theology is poles apart from the message of the earthly Jesus. How well did Paul know the teachings of Jesus? How closely did he follow them? The issue of "Paul and Jesus" has two aspects. The first is the easier of the two.

Did Paul know Jesus? Did Paul meet Jesus during his earthly life? Was he sitting in on the Sanhedrin at the trial of Jesus (Luke 22:66)? Was he among the crowd mocking at the foot of the cross? It is of course a question "from silence," and such questions are ultimately unanswerable. Some have argued that Paul's references to "seeing" Jesus would indicate that he had known him and thus could recognize him (1 Cor. 9:1; 15:8).[39] The accounts in Acts would indicate that Paul did *not* recognize Jesus but had to inquire as to his identity. Others have maintained that when Paul said in 2 Corinthians 5:16 that he now no longer knew Jesus "according to the flesh" (NKJV), it would indicate that once he *had* known the fleshly, historical Jesus. The NIV is surely correct in translating the passage, "From now on we regard no one from a wordly point of view." Paul was not talking about acquaintance with the earthly Jesus but about a manner of knowing Jesus. There is a human, sinful, "fleshly" way of viewing him. Paul had once regarded Jesus through those kind of eyes and *persecuted* him. Now he saw Jesus through new eyes, the eyes of the new creation which saw all things differently through the transforming power of Christ. All things considered, there is little evidence that Paul had seen the earthly Jesus.

Did Paul know the tradition about Jesus and his teachings? This second aspect of the Jesus/Paul question is more difficult to answer. Do Paul's letters reflect a knowledge of the life of Jesus and his teachings? One might first consider the *facts about Jesus' life* which Paul mentions. He knew that Jesus was born under the law (Gal. 4:4) and that he came from a Davidic lineage (Rom. 1:3). Paul knew that Jesus had brothers (1 Cor. 9:5), and he knew James personally (Gal. 1:19; 1 Cor. 15:7). He knew in detail the tradition of Jesus' words at the Last Supper (1 Cor. 11:23–25). He knew the tradition about Jesus' death—his crucifixion, burial, resurrection, and many appearances (1 Cor. 15:3–7). In particular, the crucifixion and resurrection were central to his Christian understanding, and he referred to them frequently throughout his letters. Sometimes Paul appealed to the *example of Jesus*—to his obedience and humility (Phil. 2:5–9), to his love (Gal. 2:20), to his becoming poor in order that others might be rich (2 Cor. 8:9), to his willingly bearing reproach for the sake of others (Rom. 15:3).

Only three times does Paul *explicitly appeal to the teachings of Jesus*. In 1 Corinthians 7:10 he cites Jesus' teaching on divorce and distinguishes between the Lord's teaching and his own opinion (v. 12). First Corinthians 9:14 draws from Jesus' teaching that the workman is worthy of his hire (Matt. 10:10). Finally, 1 Corinthians 11:23–25 repeats the tradition of the Lord's words at the Last Supper. As with the other two, Paul identifies these words as coming "from the Lord." In one other place Paul specifically refers to a tradition as coming from the Lord—1 Thessalonians 4:15. The tradition deals with the state of dead Christians at the time of the Lord's return. None of the Gospels preserves a saying of Jesus that deals with this issue. Some scholars believe Paul is referring to a teaching revealed by the *risen* Christ. It is just as possible that Paul has preserved a saying in Thessalonians that is not included in the Gospels, like the saying about giving and receiving which he cited in his Miletus address (Acts 20:35). All of this is to say that the four Gospels do not contain *all* of Jesus' deeds and teachings (John 21:25). There may well be echoes of other teachings of Jesus in Paul's epistles not found in the four Gospels.[40]

Besides Paul's explicit references, many passages seem *to echo Jesus' teachings*. For instance, Paul's direction that the Corinthians "eat what is set before you" may draw from Jesus' teaching preserved in Luke 10:8. The ethical sections of Paul's letters are the places which most seem to draw from Jesus' teachings. In Romans 12–14 there are at least eight possible allusions to the teachings of Jesus: (1) Romans 12:14, "bless those who persecute you" (cp. Matt. 5:44); (2) Romans 12:17, "do not repay anyone evil for evil" (cp. Matt. 5:39); (3) Romans 12:21, "overcome evil with good" (Matt. 5:39–42); (4) Romans 13:7, "Give everyone what you owe him: If you owe taxes, pay taxes" (Mark 12:13–17); (5) Romans 13:8–10, all the commandments can be summed up in "love your neighbor as yourself" (Matt. 22:39–40); (6) Romans 14:10, "Why do you judge your brother?" (Matt. 7:1); (7) Romans 14:13, "[do not] put any stumbling block or obstacle in your brother's way" (Matt. 18:6); (8) Romans 14:14, "no food is unclean in itself" (Matt. 15:11).[41] Some scholars have detected an abundance of allusions to Jesus' teachings in Paul's letters. The extreme example is Alfred Resch, who found nearly twelve hundred allusions in the thirteen Pauline epistles. As an example, he traced twenty-four supposedly parallel phrases between Ephesians 2:1–19 and the parable of the prodigal (Luke. 15:11–32).[42]

At the opposite extreme are those who see almost no contact between Jesus and Paul. An example is Wilhelm Wrede. In a short book on Paul published in 1908, Wrede claimed that the apostle's theology was far removed from the teachings of Jesus, that Jesus had more in common with his non-Christian Jewish contemporaries than with Paul, and that Paul was really the second founder of Christianity.[43] Rudolf Bultmann's estimate was not far removed from Wrede. Though granting some echoes of Jesus' teachings in the epistles, he felt that the Palestinian traditions about Jesus and his preaching were largely lacking in Paul. Even more significantly, he maintained that the central themes of Jesus' message like the kingdom of God are not to be found in Paul. On the other hand, Paul's central teaching of justification by faith is not to be found in Jesus.[44] Bultmann was certainly right in his insistence that one should not expect an exact correlation between the historical Jesus and the later teachings of Paul and the early church. The latter stood on *this* side of the cross and saw everything in the light of the central salvific event of Jesus' death and resurrection. Still, one feels that Bultmann understated the continuity between the proclaimer (the historical Jesus) and the proclaimed (the risen Christ).

Recent research has drawn attention to the continuity between Jesus' style of ministry and Paul's. For instance, Jesus' inclusive outreach to the fringes of society like prostitutes and tax collectors is seen to be extended in Paul's Gentile mission, and the servant model of Paul's ministry (1 Cor. 9:19) is seen to be foreshadowed in Jesus' teaching on servanthood (Mark 9:35).[45] But even beyond that, it has been shown that central themes in Paul are closely related to the teachings of Jesus—Paul's Christology, his understanding of God's kingdom, of the death of Jesus, of the mission of the church, Paul's ethical teachings, his eschatology—all have close affinities with the Jesus of the Gospels.[46] Bultmann was wrong about Paul's doctrine of justification. It is very much present in the parables of Jesus which depict God's mercy to sinners—the prodigal son, the workers in the vineyard, the Pharisee and the Publican. Each in its own way depicts those who owe everything to a gracious, forgiving God who does for them what they neither deserve nor could accomplish for themselves. Surely Jesus' work of dying and rising for sinners stood at the center of Paul's theological reflection, but that atoning work was one with the message of the merciful God proclaimed by the historical Jesus.

NOTES

1. Some scholars have questioned the Acts account by arguing that Paul indicated in Galatians 1:23 that the Jerusalem Christians did not know him. But the reference to Paul's persecuting "us" in Galatians 1:23 would indicate the Jerusalem Christians knew Paul well as their persecutor. See H. E. Dana, "Where Did Paul Persecute the Church?" *Anglican Theological Review* 20 (1938): 16–26.
2. Extradition from Egypt was granted for Simon the high priest by Ptolemy VII in 142 B.C. (1 Macc. 15:15–21). Julius Caesar formally acknowledged the sovereignty of the high priest in all matters of Jewish religion in a decree of 47 B.C. (Josephus, *Ant.* 14. 192–195).
3. M. Hengel and A. M. Schwemer, *Paul Between Damascus and Antioch: The Unknown Years* (Louisville: Westminster John Knox, 1997), 50.
4. S. V. McCasland, "The Way," *Journal of Biblical Literature* 77 (1958): 222–230.
5. D. Smith, *The Life and Letters of St. Paul* (New York: Doran, n.d.), 47.
6. S. Lundgren, "Ananias and the Calling of Paul in Acts," *Studia Theologica* 25 (1971): 117–122.
7. The word *their* before *kings* in the NIV does not occur in the Greek text and does not belong. The only king before whom Paul testified in Acts was not a Gentile but the Jewish king Agrippa II.
8. D. Gill, "The Structure of Acts 9," *Biblica* 55 (4, 1974): 546–548.
9. E. Hirsch, "Die drei Berichte der Apostelgeschichte über die Bekehrung des Paulus," *Zeitschrift für die neutestamentliche Wissenschaft* 28 (1929): 305–312.
10. For a critical examination of the possible parallels to the accounts of Paul's conversion in Acts, see H. Windisch, "Die Christusepiphanie vor Damaskus (Act. 9, 22 und 26) und ihre religionsgeschichtlichen Parallelen," *Zeitschrift für die neutestamentliche Wissenschaft* 31 (1932): 1–23.
11. This pattern is outlined by J. Munck, "La Vocation de l'Apotre Paul," *Studia Theologica* 1 (1947): 131–145.
12. C. W. Hedrick, "Paul's Conversion/Call: A Comparative Analysis of the Three Reports in Acts," *Journal of Biblical Literature* 100 (1981): 415–432.
13. For example, J. Knox, *Chapters in a Life of Paul* (Nashville: Abingdon, 1950), 111–127.
14. G. W. Nickelsburg, "An 'ΕΚΤΡΩΜΑ,' Though Appointed from the Womb: Paul's Apostolic Self-Description in 1 Corinthians 15 and Galatians 1," *Harvard Theological Review* 79 (1986): 198–205. See also M. Schaefer, "Paulus, 'Fehlgeburt' oder 'unvernunftiges Kind'?" *Zeitschrift für die neutestamentliche Wissenschaft* 85 (3–4, 1994): 207–217.

15. For many contemporary interpreters, Paul's vision of the divine glory at his conversion is seen to be the key to his theology. See S. Kim, *The Origin of Paul's Gospel* (Tübingen: Mohr-Siebeck, 1981).

16. P. T. O'Brien, *Gospel and Mission in the Writings of Paul* (Grand Rapids: Baker, 1993), 19–22.

17. J. Klausner, *From Jesus to Paul* (Boston: Beacon Press, 1964; reprint of 1943 edition), 325–330.

18. J. W. Bowker, "'Merkabah' Visions and the Visions of Paul," *Journal of Semitic Studies* 16 (1971): 157–173.

19. K. Stendahl, "The Apostle Paul and the Introspective Conscience of the West," *Harvard Theological Review* 56 (1963): 199–215.

20. A. F. Segal, *Paul the Convert: The Apostolate and Apostasy of Saul the Pharisee* (New Haven: Yale, 1990).

21. B. Corley, "Interpreting Paul's Conversion—Then and Now," in *The Road from Damascus*, ed. R. N. Longenecker (Grand Rapids: Eerdmans, 1997), 8.

22. T. W. Manson, *On Paul and John: Some Selected Theological Themes*, Studies in Biblical Theology, 38 (London: SCM Press, 1963), 11–14.

23. For example, see P. Gardner, *The Religious Experience of St. Paul* (London: Williams and Norgate, 1911), 20–39.

24. W. G. Kümmel, *Römer 7 und das Bild des Menschen im Neuen Testament* (München: Kaiser Verlag, 1974; revision of 1929 edition).

25. J. Dupont, "The Conversion of Paul and its Influence on his Understanding of Salvation by Faith," in *Apostolic History and the Gospel*, ed. W. W. Gasque and R. P. Martin (Grand Rapids: Eerdmans 1970), 176–195.

26. N.T. Wright, *What Paul Really Said* (Grand Rapids: Eerdmans, 1997), 35–37.

27. Often cited as evidence is the incident recounted by Josephus (*Ant.* 20, 34–48) where the Jew Eliezer persuaded the Gentile king Izates to undergo circumcision and become a full proselyte.

28. M. L. Soards, *The Apostle Paul: An Introduction to His Writings and Teachings* (New York: Paulist, 1987), 21–25.

29. M. Dibelius, *Paul* (Philadelphia: Westminster, 1953), 50–51.

30. H. Räisänen, "Paul's Conversion and the Development of His View of the Law," *New Testament Studies* 33 (1987): 404–419.

31. For a thorough discussion of the various views over the connection between Paul's conversion and Gentile mission, see T. L. Donaldson, "Israelite, Convert, Apostle to the Gentiles: The Origin of Paul's Gentile Mission," in *The Road from Damascus*, 62–84.

32. S. Kim, *The Origin of Paul's Gospel*. See also his article, "God Reconciled His Enemy to Himself: The Origin of Paul's Concept of Reconciliation" in *The Road from Damascus*, 102–124.

33. P. Fredriksen, "Paul and Augustine: Conversion Narratives, Orthodox Traditions, and the Retrospective Self," *Journal of Theological Studies* 37 (1, 1986): 3–34.

34. For God-fearers, see Hengel and Schwemer, *Paul Between Damascus and Antioch*, 61–76.

35. R. A. Martin, *Studies in the Life and Ministry of the Early Paul and Related Issues* (Lewiston, N.Y.: Mellen Biblical Press, 1993); 127–135.

36. Hengel and Schwemer postulate an intriguing theory that Paul designed his early ministry according to the Jewish traditions of the lands God granted Abraham, which included Arabia, Syria, and Cilicia (*Paul Between Damascus and Antioch*, 106–120).

37. For a full discussion of the problem, see J. Taylor, "The Ethnarch of King Aretas at Damascus: A Note on 2 Cor. 11:32–33," *Revue Biblique* 99 (1992): 719–728.

38. R. Schnackenburg, "Apostles Before and During Paul's Time," in *Apostolic History and the Gospel*, 287–304.

39. W. Ramsay, *The Teaching of St. Paul in Terms of the Present Day* (London: Hodder and Stoughton, 1913), 20–30.

40. S. J. Patterson, "Paul and the Jesus Tradition," *Harvard Theological Review* 84 (1991): 23–41.

41. R. N. Longenecker, *Paul, Apostle of Liberty* (New York: Harper and Row, 1964), 188–190.

42. A. Resch, *Der Paulinismus und die Logia Jesu in Ihrem Gegenseitigen Verhältnis Untersucht* (Leipzig: Hinrichs'sche, 1904), 274.

43. W. Wrede, *Paul* (Lexington, Ky.: American Theological Library Association, 1962; reprint of 1908 edition), 179–180.

44. R. Bultmann, *Theology of the New Testament*, vol. 1 (New York: Scribners, 1951), 188–189.

45. See the articles by Wedderburn and Wolff in *Paul and Jesus*, ed. A. J. M. Wedderburn (Sheffield, U.K.: JSOT Press, 1989), 117–160.

46. D. Wenham, *Paul: Follower of Jesus or Founder of Christianity?* (Grand Rapids: Eerdmans, 1995).

SUGGESTED FURTHER READING

Hengel, Martin and Anna Maria Schwemer. *Paul Between Damascus and Antioch: the Unknown Years*. Louisville: Westminster John Knox, 1997, pp. 1–150.

Kim, Seyoon. *The Origin of Paul's Gospel*. Tübingen: Mohr-Siebeck, 1981.

Longenecker, Richard N., ed. *The Road from Damascus: The Impact of Paul's Conversion on His Life, Thought and Ministry*. Grand Rapids: Eerdmans, 1997.

Munck, Johannes. *Paul and the Salvation of Mankind*. Richmond: John Knox, 1959, pp. 11–86.

O'Brien, Peter T. *Gospel and Mission in the Writings of Paul. An Exegetical and Theological Analysis*. Grand Rapids: Baker, 1993.

Stendahl, Krister. *Paul Among Jews and Gentiles*. Philadelphia: Fortress, 1976.

Wedderburn, A. J. M., ed. *Paul and Jesus: Collected Essays*. Sheffield, U.K.: JSOT Press, 1989.

Wenham, David. *Paul: Follower of Jesus or Founder of Christianity?* Grand Rapids: Eerdmans, 1995.

Wright, N. T. *What Paul Really Said*. Grand Rapids: Eerdmans, 1997.

4

~e9~

"Speaking to Greeks Also"

$\mathscr{A}$cts 11:19–21 tells how a group of Christians began to evangelize the area of the Mediterranean coast. They had been "scattered by the persecution in connection with Stephen" (v. 19). This is a flashback to Acts 8:1. The main group against whom the persecution was directed was the Greek-speaking Jewish Christians, the Hellenists. In Acts 11 we are told that some of them began to witness in the coastal region—in Phoenicia, on the island of Cyprus, as far north as Antioch, the capital of the province of Syria-Cilicia. This most likely refers to separate witness in each area: some settled in Phoenicia, others set up work on Cyprus, still others established a church at Antioch. Most of them confined their evangelism to the Jewish synagogues, following the pattern of the witness in Jerusalem. At Antioch, however, there was a new breakthrough in the Christian outreach: they began to preach to Greeks as well.[1]

Christians had already begun to reach out beyond the limits of Judaism. Philip had witnessed to the "half-Jewish" Samaritans (Acts 8:4–25). He had baptized a full-fledged Gentile, a eunuch of Ethiopia (Acts 8:26–39). Peter's testimony led to the conversion of a Gentile military officer and a number of his family and acquaintances (Acts 10:1–11:18). Cornelius was already a God-fearer attached to the synagogue (Acts 10:2), and the eunuch was himself either a God-fearer or a proselyte, having gone to Jerusalem to worship. These were individual cases of witness to Gentiles, carefully orchestrated by the Holy Spirit, and exceptional at best. They involved those already acquainted with Judaism and Israel's God. What was exceptional at Antioch is that they did not confine their testimony to the synagogues, where their exposure to Gentiles would have been limited to proselytes and God-fearers. They reached beyond the Jewish community in a direct witness to the Gentile population. They were very successful: "The Lord's hand was with them, and a great number of people believed and turned to the Lord" (v. 21).

Where was Paul, the "apostle to the Gentiles," while all this was going on at Antioch? According to Acts 9:30, after leaving Jerusalem he went to his hometown of Tarsus. Paul says in Galatians 1:21 that at that time he went to the region of "Syria and Cilicia." This was a single political entity in Paul's day. Syria was the official Roman province. It included within its bounds the region of Cilicia where Tarsus was located. The time involved between Paul's departure from Jerusalem and the beginning of his first missionary journey (Acts 13–14) may have been a decade or more. Acts tells us very little about this "Cilician" period of Paul's ministry. We learn about his involvement in the church of Antioch toward the end of this period (Acts 11:25–30; 13:1–3) but nothing about his activity in Tarsus and Cilicia. Consequently, this period is often dubbed the "silent years" of Paul's Christian life. It is possible, however, that Paul's epistles make an occasional allusion to events of these years.

This chapter deals with the scant references and allusions we have in Acts and in the epistles to this obscure period of Paul's ministry. It begins with his arrival in Tarsus after leaving Jerusalem upon his first visit there after his conversion (Acts 9:30). It concludes with his and Barnabas's departure on their first missionary journey (Acts 13:4). A concluding section of the chapter considers matters of Pauline chronology and provides a suggested timetable to serve as a framework for the remainder of the book.

PAUL IN SYRIA AND CILICIA

Galatians 1:21 speaks of Paul's going to the regions of Syria and Cilicia after his brief fifteen-day visit in Jerusalem with Peter and James. Paul did not continue his autobiography at this point. He only resumed his story with a reference to his *next* visit to Jerusalem some fourteen years later (Gal. 2:1). Acts does not provide much more on this phase of Paul's ministry—only a brief treatment of his association with the Antioch church toward the end of the period. It is altogether silent about the early years in Tarsus and Cilicia.

THE SILENT YEARS (ACTS 9:30; GAL. 1:21)

There are several possible hints in Paul's epistles which might pertain to the "silent years" of his ministry in Syria and Cilicia. The first is found in the address of the Jerusalem church's letter outlining for Gentile Christians the minimum rules to observe in their fellowship with Jewish Christians. This so-called "apostolic decree" is addressed to the churches of "Antioch, Syria and Cilicia" (Acts 15:23). In the previous chapters of Acts, however, only *one* church in Syria has been mentioned—the Antioch church. No Cilician churches are spoken of. The other Syrian churches addressed in the letter were quite possibly missions of the Antioch church. Paul may have helped start some of them. And what about the churches of Cilicia that the letter addresses? Did they go back to Paul's ministry during his "silent years," when he worked out of Tarsus?

Another possible allusion to events of Paul's silent years is his long list of his "trials" as an apostle which he gives in 2 Corinthians 11:22–33. Many of the events mentioned by Paul are not related in Acts. For instance, in Corinthians Paul speaks of "frequent imprisonments." Up to the point in his ministry when he wrote 2 Corinthians, Acts has mentioned only *one* imprisonment—Philippi (16:25–30). Paul likewise spoke of being beaten with rods on three occasions. This was a Roman punishment. Luke does mention Paul's being punished in this fashion at Philippi (16:23) but makes no reference to any other floggings of this sort. Acts does mention the occasion when he was stoned—by the Jewish mob at Lystra (14:19). However, it only mentioned his experiencing one shipwreck (Acts 27), and that took place several years *after* Paul wrote 2 Corinthians. In the latter Paul spoke of three shipwrecks and being a day and a night adrift at sea. Could some of these events have taken place during Paul's silent years?

Particularly relevant is Paul's statement that on five different occasions he received "from the Jews the forty lashes minus one" (2 Cor. 11:24). This was the standard discipline of the local synagogues—thirty-nine lashes on the bare flesh with a leather whip. (Forty were prescribed, but the law directed that the count should be one short to ensure that the one being punished not receive more than the number required.) Nowhere in Acts is there mention of Paul's receiving a lashing from a synagogue. There is no doubt that Luke was selective in narrating the events of Paul's life. It is striking, however, that he mentioned none of the five lashings. It may be that some of them were received during the period of his Cilician ministry. This would be particularly likely if he worked exclusively out of the synagogues during this period, which seems to have been the case. His leaving the synagogues and turning primarily to Gentiles was a development of his first missionary journey, according to the picture furnished by Acts (13:46–48).

A final possible allusion to an event of his "silent years" is Paul's mention of a vision in 2 Corinthians 12:1–10. He dated the vision as occurring fourteen years earlier. It was a powerful experience; he says that he was "caught up" into heaven. Verses 2 and 3–4a are best taken as being parallel. Paul referred to himself obliquely in the third person—"I know a man." He was snatched up into the "third heaven," into "paradise." In contemporary Jewish thought paradise represented the final resting place of the blessed. Paul was elaborating his vision in opposition to certain false apostles at Corinth who put great stock on visions and experiences in the Spirit. They may have claimed that to rise above the confines of the body represented the ultimate state of spiritual perfection. That is quite possibly why Paul said two times that he didn't know whether he was in or out of his body when he had the vision. Such things didn't matter to him. He did, however, have an amazing auditory experience. He heard "inexpressible things," holy things he was not permitted to share with others.

Paul felt that visions and other experiences in the Spirit were personal matters. Acts depicts him as having a number of visions of the Lord directing him in his mission (9:12; 18:9–11; 22:17–21; 23:11; see also 16:9–10; 27:23). Evidently Paul felt the same about his visions that he did about tongue-speaking; such experiences were matters of private devotion (cp. 1 Cor. 14:19). Though he evidently had many such experiences (2 Cor. 12:7), he only related them this one time in his letters. Even here, he was speaking ironically, as a "fool" (2 Cor. 11:21), only boasting because his Corinthian opponents had forced him to do so. He was putting himself on their level. Though his experience was real and powerful for him personally, he spoke of it almost in parody.[2] It was an "empty" vision, hardly something he could boast about, for it was "inexpressible," something he was not allowed to share. Unlike his Corinthian opponents, he would not use it to exert his power over others. Ultimately, the only power that counted for Paul was the power of God's grace at work in him in spite of his human frailty. His thorn in the flesh reminded him of that (2 Cor. 12:7–10).

This "third heaven" experience stood out above all other such events for Paul. He could even date it; it was fourteen years before he wrote 2 Corinthians. When was that? Some have wanted to see this as a reference to Paul's conversion,[3] but his conversion was not a revelation of "inexpressible things." It was quite the opposite—a call to preach. It also took place too early to have been this event. The same holds true for his vision in the temple related in Acts 22:17–21.[4] That vision was associated with his visit to Jerusalem after his conversion. It also occurred too early to have been the vision of 2 Corinthians. Paul's third-heaven experience occurred fourteen years before he wrote 2 Corinthians. That would place it around A.D. 42—during his "silent years" in Cilicia.

It has been argued that Paul's vision was an example of Jewish mysticism, either of the *Merkabah* variety, which contemplated the throne of God in the wheel vision of

Ezekiel 1, or in the *Hekhalot* tradition, which involved the mystic's ascent to heaven in a journey through several concentric heavens. In particular, Paul's vision has been compared to a Talmudic tradition about four rabbis who shared in an ascent to Paradise (*Pardes*). Only one of them, Rabbi Akiba, was truly prepared for the beatific vision and able to return to earth "in peace." Of the other three, one went mad, one became apostate, and the third died.[5] It is questionable whether these Jewish mystical traditions can be found as early as Paul's time. The more likely background to Paul's experience is apocalyptic Judaism, which had its own tradition of the prophet's ascent to receive a revelation of the mysteries of God.[6] One wonders if Paul's thorn in the flesh had some sort of connection with his experience in the third heaven. Paul certainly joined them closely together in 2 Corinthians. Did he perhaps see his "thorn" as a legacy of the experience, like Jacob's limp after having wrestled with God (Gen. 32:25)?

How long did Paul's silent period last? Most see Paul as having worked in Cilicia for a decade or so before Barnabas took him to Antioch. It is possible that it was a much shorter period, perhaps no more then three or four years.[7] Paul's ministry in Antioch would then have been much longer than the usual view—six or seven years before his departure on the first missionary journey. One can only speculate; they *were* "silent" years. Why did Luke not relate Paul's experiences during those years? Perhaps he knew little about them. More likely, it was not germane to his purpose. He wanted to show how Paul's Gentile mission unfolded—above all, how it progressed through the western world to the capital city of Rome itself. Cilicia was not a major breakthrough in this regard. It was part of the province of Syria, at the doorstep of Israel. More significantly, Paul probably did not begin his concentration on the Gentiles in his Cilician ministry. He still worked mainly out of the synagogues. The Gentile mission only began in earnest on the first missionary journey, and that is where Luke began his story of the Pauline mission.

THE CHURCH AT ANTIOCH (ACTS 11:19–30)

Antioch. Antioch on the Orontes was a natural place for the Christian outreach to the Gentiles to begin. It was a hellenistic city, established by the Seleucid successors of Alexander the Great. It had a large Jewish community. It was the third most populous city of the Roman empire, exceeded only by Rome and Alexandria. It was thoroughly cosmopolitan, a mix of many cultures, a suitable place of witness for the successors of Stephen, who shared his vision of a God who cannot be tied down to any particular people or place.

Legend attributed the founding of the city to ancient Argive Greeks who came there in search of their lost priestess-princess Io, who, pregnant with the child of Zeus, had fled the wrath of Hera.[8] Though this is obviously pure myth, archaeology has confirmed its witness to a Greek presence in the area from as early as 1000 B.C. The Antioch of Paul's day was established around 300 B.C. by the first Seleucid king, Seleucus I Nicator (305–291 B.C.). Seleucus established a number of cities in various parts of his empire, naming them after himself and various members of his family. He is said to have established nine Seleucias, one of them being the port city of Syrian Antioch, some fifteen miles downstream at the point where the Orontes River flowed into the Mediterranean. Antioch was named after Seleucus's father Antiochus; so were fifteen other cities, including Pisidian Antioch, which Paul visited on his first missionary journey. Seleucus established six Laodiceas, which were named for his mother. Near Syrian Antioch he founded the city of Apamea, named for his wife.

Ancient Antioch was located on a large fertile plain with the Orontes River forming its western border and a mountain range to the east. The Orontes was navigable from the Mediterranean all the way up to Antioch. Some five miles south of the city was the community of Daphne, which had natural springs that provided ample water supply through aqueducts to the city. The city was an important commercial center, located on the main trade route between Asia and Egypt. Its population in Paul's day has been estimated at between three hundred thousand and five hundred thousand persons.

Antioch was a model hellenistic city. From the start it seems to have been designed with its streets in the grid pattern devised by the Greek architect Hippodamus of Miletus. Streets ran at right angles, forming rectangular blocks with uniform dimensions of 367 by 190 feet. Seleucus's original city was divided into two main quarters, one on each side of the main street, which ran from north to south. By Strabo's time there were four quarters. He called the city a *tetrapolis* ("four cities"), explaining that each quarter had its own city walls with a larger wall enclosing the entire city. The most imposing quarter in Paul's day was the one to the south of the city known as the *Epiphania*. It was begun by and named for the Seleucid king Antiochus IV "Epiphanes," the same king who provoked the Jewish Maccabean revolt. The Epiphania was provided with beautiful homes, an elaborate new agora, and extensive government buildings. Under Antiochus, the city reached its greatest glory of the entire Seleucid period. After Antiochus, it seems to have dimmed in splendor, as the power and wealth of the Seleucid kings diminished under an increasing Roman presence.

The city was richly patronized by the Romans. Coming under direct Roman control after 64 B.C. under Pompey, it was favored successively by Julius Caesar, Antony, Augustus, and the succeeding Roman emperors. Pompey granted it the status of a free city. Caesar and the subsequent emperors affirmed Antioch's free status and erected lavish buildings on the site. Caesar, for instance, built a theater in the center of the town at the foot of Mt. Silpius. To the south he constructed an amphitheater. He also erected a temple for the veneration of the Roman imperial cult, in which he placed a statue of himself. Perhaps the most impressive architectural wonder of the city was its wide main street, which split the city in half. It was paved in splendid marble provided by Herod the Great. Tiberius later erected beautiful colonnades which ran the length of the street on both sides.

Antioch had a mix of many religions. In the region of Daphne was a sacred grove where Seleucus erected a temple to Daphne (Artemis) and her consort Apollo. Originally this may have been the site of ancient Syrian fertility worship of Astarte, in which sacred prostitution played a part. Antioch had something of a reputation for immorality. The Roman satirist Juvenal, for instance, spoke of the "filth of the Orontes" when referring to Antioch (*Satire* 3.62). By the time of the empire, all the Olympian gods were venerated in Antioch and it was a center of the imperial cult. The patron goddess of the city was Tyche, the goddess of fortune—"lady luck." Her image depicted her with a wreathed head and a swimming youth at her feet, who represented the Orontes River. The mountains to the east made Antioch vulnerable to attack. The Orontes often flooded. The area was subject to frequent earthquakes. One occurred around A.D. 37, the time of Paul and the emperor Caligula, who rebuilt the city. Another occurred during the reign of Claudius (A.D. 41–54). Perhaps it was appropriate that Antioch had lady fortune as its patron. It needed her.

According to Josephus, the Jewish community in Antioch was the most populous Jewish settlement in the whole area. He also noted that Antiochus Epiphanes had granted the Jews of Antioch rights of citizenship equal to those of the Greeks in the city. He spoke of the Jews' wealth as evidenced by the lavish gifts which they sent to the temple in Jerusalem. He said the Antiochene Jews were highly respected by the Gentiles of the city, many of whom were attracted to their synagogues (*War*, 7.43–45). In another place Josephus stated that the Jews had been given citizen rights by Seleucus I when he established the city (*Ag. Apion*, 2.39). Josephus's references to the Jewish citizenship probably do not refer to their belonging to the *dēmos* (voting citizenry) of the Hellenistic city but to their being recognized as an autonomous political entity within the city with control of their own internal affairs. They probably had their own quarters along the analogy of the four main divisions of the city. Their number has been variously estimated at between forty-five thousand and sixty thousand.

In Paul's day relations between the Jews and Gentiles of Antioch were probably as good as in any major city of the ancient Near East. This is not to say that there weren't periods of difficulty. One time of tension occurred in A.D. 39–40 during the reign of Caligula. In an effort to enforce emperor worship, Caligula ordered Petronius, the imperial legate of Syria, to place an image of the emperor in the temple in Jerusalem. This provoked violent protests from the Jewish populations throughout the empire and equally severe Gentile responses to the Jews. Extensive pogroms against the Jews occurred in Alexandria in A.D. 39. The unrest spread up the coast to Jamnia, where the Jews smashed the emperor's image. At Dor, the Gentile population attempted to set up the emperor's image in the Jewish synagogue. The sixth–century Byzantine historian John Malalas wrote that a pogrom was launched against the Jews of Antioch at this time. Much of Malalas's history is fantastic, and one must examine his testimony with a critical eye, but a Jewish pogrom at this time is not out of the question. Petronius's headquarters were in Antioch. He set out from there on his way to Jerusalem to enforce Caligula's order. One can imagine Jewish riots in Antioch at this time and possible Gentile reprisals. Petronius was a wise commander, however. He played a delaying game, and lady Tyche favored him. Caligula died, and his successor Claudius rescinded the order.[9]

Barnabas in Antioch (Acts 11:22–24). Josephus spoke of many Gentiles attending the synagogues of Antioch. It might be their success in witnessing to these proselytes and God-fearers within the synagogues which led the Hellenist Christians to turn directly to the Greek-speaking Gentile community. In any event, the Jerusalem church soon learned of Antioch's new outreach. The church had never before undertaken a mission solely to Gentiles. This was something new. Previously the Jerusalem church sent Peter and John to Samaria when Philip undertook a new mission there (Acts 8:14). The Jerusalem church was the "mother church." It maintained relationship with the other churches, kept track of their affairs, and encouraged their witness. New missions always interested Jerusalem. This time they sent Barnabas as their representative to Antioch. Barnabas was an apt choice. He had connections with both churches. He had long been associated with the Jerusalem apostles (Acts 4:36–37; 9:27). He had family in Jerusalem; John Mark was his cousin, and Mark's family was from Jerusalem (Col. 4:10; Acts 12:12). Barnabas also had links with Antioch. He was a Diaspora Jew himself, from Cyprus (Acts 4:36). Some of the leaders in the Antioch outreach to the Greeks were Cypriots, whom Barnabas would likely have known (Acts 11:20).

When Barnabas arrived in Antioch and witnessed the success of their mission, he immediately joined in their effort. Acts 11:23 says that he "encouraged" them, using the same word that served as his nickname, "Son of Encouragement" (Acts 4:36). This is the light in which Barnabas appears throughout Acts—always the encourager, supporting others and bringing the best from them. Luke further describes him as a "good" man (v. 24); no other person in Acts is called "good." Barnabas did not return to Jerusalem. He stayed in Antioch to assist in their mission. But Barnabas surely always maintained his ties with the mother church. Paul did so also. He took Barnabas with him on his first mission. In a sense, Barnabas continued to represent the Jerusalem church. In the same way, on his second journey Paul took Silas as his companion. Silas likewise had once served as an official representative of the Jerusalem church (Acts 15:27).

The year in Antioch (Acts 11:25–26). With the increasing success of the Antioch witness, Barnabas looked for additional help. He immediately thought of Paul, the Greek-speaking Diaspora Jew like himself. He remembered how persuasively Paul had preached in Damascus and in the Greek-speaking synagogues of Jerusalem (Acts 9:27, 29). Who would be a more natural worker among the Gentiles of Antioch? Barnabas's last contact with Paul was probably a decade earlier, but he recalled that Paul had gone to his native Tarsus (Acts 9:30). Barnabas went off to Tarsus to get Paul. He may have had some difficulty in finding him. Luke used a word which means to "seek someone out" (v. 25). Paul may have been involved in work throughout Cilicia, using Tarsus as home base. Luke finally located him and persuaded him to come to Antioch.[10] Paul and Barnabas are described as "teaching" in Antioch for a whole year (v. 26). Everything we know about Paul would indicate that he was heavily involved in the evangelism of the Antioch church. The reference to his teaching should remind us that the tasks of leading people to faith and of instructing them in the faith are inseparable.

First called Christians in Antioch (11:26b). Luke adds almost as a footnote that the disciples were first called "Christians" in Antioch. The term in Greek is *Christianos*. It is a hybrid form, built on the Greek word for Messiah (*Christos*, "anointed one") and the Latin suffix *-ianus*, which means "belonging to." A number of *-ianus* formations are found in the contemporary Latin literature, generally referring to followers or partisans of someone. For instance, the term *Herodianoi* is found in Mark 3:6. It refers to the partisans of King Herod. The term *Augustiani* came from the imperial title *Augustus* ("revered"). It was borne by a group of avid young devotees of Nero in the early years of his reign. The *-ianus* suffix was sometimes used of freedmen to denote the patrons to whom they owed their liberty.

Christian appears only twice in Acts—here and in Acts 26:28 on the lips of King Agrippa II. It is found one other time in the entire New Testament—1 Peter 4:16, where Peter urged his readers to be willing to suffer for bearing the name "Christian." Elsewhere in the New Testament other names are regularly used for Christians—disciples, believers, brothers and sisters, the "Way," Nazarenes, saints, and the like. On the other hand, the term is found with some frequency in contemporary Roman writers, like Tacitus, Suetonius, Pliny, and Lucian. Sometimes it occurs with the spelling *Chrestiani*, which betrays the Roman unfamiliarity with *Christos*, the Greek word for the Jewish concept Messiah. Instead, *Chrestiani* is built on the Greek word *Chrestos*, which was a common slave name, meaning "useful." Christians do not seem to have used the word *Christian* widely until the latter part of the first century. Interestingly, the first to use it with any frequency was Ignatius, bishop of *Antioch* at the turn of the second century.

Some have argued that the *Christians* of Antioch originated the name, using it as a self-designation. This is based on the observation that the word usually translated "were called" is generally active in Greek and should be translated "called themselves Christians." The basis for this self-designation is seen as being the Christian conviction that believers "belong to," are "slaves" of Christ.[11] It has sometimes been argued that the term originated with the Roman *officials* of Antioch and reflects that they saw the Christians as a political entity that presented some possible threat to Roman law and order.[12] Most commentators attribute the term to the Gentiles of Antioch. Their use of the term would reflect two things about the growing Christian community. First, it distances them from Judaism. The movement which began as a Jewish sect was now taking on an identity of its own. Second, it reflects Antioch's outreach to Gentiles. The mission of the church was gaining a reputation in the Gentile community, and the Gentiles applied their own label to it: they were those who belonged to Christ.

The "famine collection" for Jerusalem (11:27–30). Acts 11:27 speaks of prophets coming down from Jerusalem to Antioch. One of them was Agabus (v. 28), who appears again in Acts 21:10–11. Acts also mentions that four of Philip the Evangelist's daughters had the gift of prophecy (Acts 21:9). Prophecy was an important spiritual gift in the life of the early church. In 1 Corinthians 12:28 Paul listed it as second only to the gift of the apostolic calling. In 1 Corinthians 14:1–5 Paul ranked prophecy above all the other spiritual gifts. Prophecy was sometimes predictive, as in this instance. It always consisted of bringing God's word to the community of faith through the inspiration of the Spirit.

Agabus was the spokesperson for this particular group of prophets. He predicted that a worldwide famine was on the horizon. Luke added as a footnote that such a famine did indeed occur under the reign of Claudius (A.D. 41–54). There is ample evidence of famines in various parts of the empire throughout the reign of Claudius.[13] Some argue, however, that there is no evidence for a "worldwide" famine, as Luke seems to indicate. This is to misunderstand the nature of food shortage in the Roman imperial period. The empire depended on certain "breadbasket" areas like Egypt to provide grain throughout its territory. Crop failure in a critical supply area would drive prices up throughout the empire, making food hard to obtain and unaffordable for the masses. The result was widespread famine, not just in the areas where crops failed.

Agabus came from Jerusalem, so he must have predicted that the famine would be particularly acute in that area. The Antioch Christians concluded as much and began taking up an offering for the Jerusalem Christians (v. 29). Barnabas may have been especially aware of the problems of poverty among the Jerusalem Christians; he had already given sacrificially to the community (Acts 4:36–37). Luke says that they were encouraged to give according to their own ability. One wonders if Paul was not influenced by this principle in his directions to Corinth when he gathered another collection for Jerusalem a decade later (1 Cor. 16:2; 2 Cor. 9:7). Antioch sent the gift off "to the elders" of Jerusalem by Barnabas and Saul. In earlier days the apostles had handled the church's funds. They seem to have surrendered that responsibility at the time the seven were chosen (Acts 6:2). Now the elders were responsible for the administration of the Jerusalem congregation, particularly under the leadership of Jesus' brother James (cp. Acts 12:17).

The problem of the Jerusalem visits. The "famine visit" of Barnabas and Paul to Jerusalem presents a major problem for New Testament scholarship. How does one reconcile the visits of Paul to Jerusalem in Acts with those which Paul lists in the first chapters of Galatians? In Galatians, Paul mentioned two visits to Jerusalem—one taking place three years after his conversion (Gal. 1:18), the other occurring fourteen years later (Gal. 2:1). These were the only two times he went to Jerusalem, he insisted; there were no others, he wasn't lying (1:20). The problem is that Acts 15 speaks of a visit of Paul and Barnabas to Jerusalem that sounds very much like the *second* visit of Galatians (2:1–10)—same people involved, same issue (circumcision), same resolution. Only, this is the *third* visit mentioned in Acts: (1) three years after conversion (Acts 9:26), (2) the famine visit (Acts 11:30), and (3) the "circumcision" conference (Acts 15). If Luke had not mentioned the famine visit, there would be no problem. Everyone would assume that Galatians 1:18 and Acts 9:26 were about the same visit and that Galatians 2:1 and Acts 15 were referring to the same conference in Jerusalem. How does one deal with the "extra" visit of Acts 11:30?

There are about as many "solutions" to the problem as there are scholars who have tackled it. Here are a few of their suggestions. A first and very popular view is that the famine visit of Acts 11:30 and the circumcision visit of Galatians 2:1 are one and the same; Galatians omits the offering and Acts omits the discussion over circumcision. Acts 15 is a second meeting about circumcision that took place later; there is no conflict.[14] A second more radical solution is to argue that the visits of Acts 11 and Acts 15 are doublets of the same visit and that the visit took place at the chronological point of Acts 11:30—*before* Paul's first missionary journey. Acts 15 is seen as being out of place; it deals with a conference that took place earlier in connection with the famine visit.[15] A third line of solution also sees a doublet but argues that the correct positioning of this dual famine visit (chap. 11) and circumcision conference (chap. 15) is *after* the first missionary journey—that is, at the chronological point of Acts 15 in the Acts narrative.[16] A fourth line of solution sees the famine visit as a Lukan construction of a visit which never took place.[17] The fifth solution is almost as hard on Luke. It suggests that the famine visit is really Luke's account of Paul's Jerusalem collection from his Gentile churches. It thus belongs in the later context of Paul's last visit to Jerusalem (Acts 21).[18]

A sixth line of solution shifts the burden of proof from Luke to Paul. It argues that Paul did not mention the famine visit because he did not consider it a visit. Paul was arguing his independence of the apostles in Galatians. He saw no apostles, only elders (Acts 11:30) at the time of the famine. The visit was not germane to Paul's argument, and so he overlooked it in the account in Galatians.[19] Or Paul may not actually have visited Jerusalem at this time. He may have only journeyed part of the way to Jerusalem, or he and Barnabas may have turned the funds over to the elders outside the city. It may still have been too dangerous for Paul within the city walls.[20] Something like this sixth line of solution is followed in this book. Reconciliation of the Jerusalem visits is in the final accounting a small matter. On the other hand, the circumcision conference of Acts 15 and Galatians 2 was a watershed in Paul's ministry. The two accounts will be treated together in this book as twin reports of a single event.

Antioch's extended mission (Acts 13:1–3). The twelfth chapter of Acts concludes Luke's traditions about the church in Jerusalem. It relates the martyrdom of James the son of Zebedee under King Herod Agrippa I, who ruled over all of Judea, Samaria, and Galilee between A.D. 41 and 44. It tells the story of Peter's escape from Herod's clutches and of Herod's own grisly death. Herod died in A.D. 44. The Judean famine seems to have occurred a couple of years later. Luke inserted the Jerusalem stories at this point in his narrative with the rather imprecise designation that the events occurred "about this time" (the time of the famine visit). He resumes the narrative about Paul and Barnabas's famine visit at 12:25. When they had completed their mission to Jerusalem, the pair returned to Antioch. From that point on, the narrative of Acts centers on Paul.

The first three verses of chapter 13 relate how the Antioch church was led to set Paul and Barnabas aside for an extensive "foreign" mission. The church had already evangelized Syria and had even begun a mission on Cyprus (11:19). Paul and Barnabas would expand the witness on Cyprus and travel by sea to the mainland province of Roman Galatia. It was a bold new mission. The Spirit led, but Antioch sought the Spirit's leading. From the evidence of Acts, it was the great missionary congregation of the early church. It had already reached out to Gentiles in its own environs. Through Paul and Barnabas it set its sights on the "ends of the earth."

Acts 13:1 seems to show that Antioch had a different sort of leadership than Jerusalem. Jerusalem was originally led by the apostles. As they began to leave the city on their own missions, the leadership gradually passed over to a group of "elders," probably following the pattern of Jewish synagogues. (Acts 11:30 and 12:17 seem to reflect this transition.) On the other hand, Luke describes Antioch as being led by "prophets and teachers." This reflects the more "charismatic" organization of Paul's mission churches like Corinth (1 Cor. 12:27–30), where leadership was more by spiritual endowment than by fixed offices. One might note that Paul himself embodied the first three of his "gifts" as listed in 1 Corinthians 12:29—apostle, prophet, teacher. This is the most natural reading of Acts 13:1: all five of the people listed were *both* prophets and teachers.

Of the five names listed in Acts 13:1, we know Paul and Barnabas. We know very little about the other three, although there has been much speculation about them. First, there is "Simeon called Niger." *Niger* is the Latin word for the color black. Simeon is a form of Simon. There is the temptation to equate him with another famous Simon who was a black, Simon of Cyrene, who carried Jesus' cross (Matt. 27:32). Simon's sons Alexander and Rufus are mentioned by Mark (15:21), since they were evidently Christians known to the Roman church where Mark wrote his Gospel. One of them may well be the same Rufus to whom Paul sent greetings in his Roman epistle (16:13). That is more likely than that his father was the Simeon of Antioch. (Luke would surely have drawn our attention to it had he been the cross-bearing Simon.)

The second figure has evoked even more speculation. From ancient times there have been those who would connect "Lucius of Cyrene" with the Luke who authored Luke and Acts. It has often been argued on this basis that Luke came from Antioch.[21] The "we," which is seen to indicate Luke's presence, however, does not occur until Troas on Paul's second missionary journey (Acts 16:10).[22] Also, *Lucius* is a very common Latin praenomen. It is not equivalent to the Greek *Luke*. If anything, the Lucius of Antioch may be the same as the Lucius of Romans 16:21, but even that is unlikely.

We know nothing else of Manaean. He is identified as a *suntrophos* of King Herod the Tetrarch, that is, Herod Antipas, the ruler of Galilee during the time of Jesus. Literally *suntrophoi* means "those who are suckled by the same nurse as babies." The word has derivative meanings of being someone's childhood playmate or one's close associate, such as a courtier in a king's retinue. Whatever the sense intended in Acts, it is evidence that already in this early period there were converts to Christianity from influential circles.

Verse 2 may describe the regular spiritual activity of the Antiochene prophets and teachers, but the "fasting" would indicate a period of intense devotion and expectation. They were not disappointed. The Holy Spirit directed them to set Paul and Barnabas apart for a special ministry. In both verses 2 and 3 Luke used plural participles, and it is not altogether clear who were involved—whether just the five, or the whole congregation. One manuscript (codex Beza) clarifies the matter by adding the word *all* at the beginning of verse 3. Following this reading, the five prophets would be engaged in the worship and prayer which anticipated the Spirit's directive (v. 2). The whole congregation ("all") would then have joined them in fasting and prayer as they prepared to send Paul and Barnabas on their mission. This is probably the correct understanding. The laying on of hands was not an ordination in any sense. Paul and Barnabas were already prophets, teachers, and evangelists. The whole congregation laid hands on the pair, expressing their solidarity in and their prayer for their mission. In a real sense, this was the first "commissioning" service for missionaries.

PAULINE CHRONOLOGY

Few areas of New Testament research are more difficult or the results more tenuous than matters of chronology. The New Testament writers were not interested in providing dates or in linking salvation history with world history. Luke shows more of such concerns than anyone else, but even his efforts were limited. Consequently, the various chronologies offered by scholars often differ radically from one another. None is set in stone. They are always subject to revision when a new piece of evidence is uncovered. This certainly applies to Pauline chronology. The following chronology is provided only as a framework for consideration of the ministry and writings of Paul in subsequent chapters. All suggested dates are tentative and debatable. The *sequence* of events is more significant than the dates assigned to them.

SOURCES

There are three main sources for Pauline chronology. First, several of Paul's epistles refer to events and time sequences in his life. These are limited, but of primary significance—the apostle's own testimony. Next comes the account of Paul's ministry provided by *Acts*. It furnishes a continuous narrative from Paul's conversion (chap. 9) to his arrival in Rome (chap. 28). It, too, has some claim to personal testimony as it was written by Luke, Paul's traveling companion for much of his ministry. Finally, there are parallels with *secular history*, either in the epistles or in Acts. Though limited in number, they are of vital importance, since they are often datable.

Paul's epistles. Paul's epistles provide us with very few explicit time references. Galatians 1:15–2:10 is the most important text. It outlines Paul's conversion (1:15–16), a visit to Jerusalem three years later that lasted only fifteen days (1:18), followed by a period of ministry in Syria and Cilicia (1:21). The account concludes with a reference to Paul's returning to Jerusalem again some "fourteen years later" (2:1). The "fourteen years" is ambiguous. It could mean fourteen years after the conversion or fourteen years after the previous visit to Jerusalem (which would make it seventeen years after the conversion). This second visit involved a major meeting of Paul with the Jerusalem leadership in which they acknowledged his mission to the Gentiles. Paul's testimony in Galatians is central for any reconstruction of a Pauline chronology. A conference in Jerusalem involving Paul's apostolate to the Gentiles took place either fourteen or seventeen years after his conversion.

Other important data for Pauline chronology are the apostle's frequent references to a collection for the "saints" in Jerusalem. The collection is mentioned explicitly in four of Paul's epistles: Galatians 2:10; 1 Corinthians 16:1–4; 2 Corinthians 8–9; and Romans 15:23–33. Romans indicates that Paul anticipated possible danger from unbelievers in Judea when he delivered the collection. This fits the occasion of Paul's last visit to Jerusalem in Acts, where he was attacked by a Jewish mob and arrested by the Romans (Acts 21:27–32).

In his epistles Paul often referred to relationships between himself and his congregations—his plans to come to see them, his reasons for not doing so, and the like. In particular, he went into detail in 2 Corinthians in discussing his strained relationship with the congregation, which evidently involved a brief, unhappy visit with them. (The visit is not related in Acts.) Such references do not provide any kind of *external* points upon which one could hang a chronological framework. Once given a framework, however, such references are invaluable for filling in the details of the events transpiring between the apostle and his congregations. We will not consider them at this point. They will be treated in detail later in considering Paul's ministry to the individual churches.

Acts. The sequence of Paul's ministry is given in detail in the Book of Acts. It is not our purpose to discuss this in full at this point. It might prove helpful, however, to take a sweeping glance at the outline of Paul's ministry from his conversion to his Roman imprisonment as presented in Acts. This will eventually serve as our basis for a chronological framework.

We have already treated the early part of Paul's ministry according to Acts—his conversion (9:1–19a), his witness in Damascus and escape from that city (9:19b–25), the visit to Jerusalem and flight to Tarsus (9:26–30). He next appeared in connection with the Antioch church (11:25–26), where he joined Barnabas in taking an offering from Antioch to Jerusalem (11:27–30; 12:25). Paul and Barnabas were then sent by the Antioch church on a mission, the so-called "first missionary journey," which took them to the island of Cyprus and the mainland cities of Pisidian Antioch, Lystra, Iconium, and Derbe (13:1–14:25). They returned to Antioch (14:26–28) from which they went to Jerusalem for a conference involving the status of Gentile believers (15:1–29).

Returning to Antioch, Paul set out on a second missionary journey, this time with Silas (15:29–41). He revisited the churches of his first mission (16:1–5) and was led by the Spirit to a ministry in Macedonia that included the cities of Philippi, Thessalonica, and Berea (16:6–17:15). After a brief visit in Athens (17:16–34), he went to Corinth, where he ministered for at least eighteen months (18:1–18a). Paul's second missionary period ended with his sailing to Caesarea and then "going up and greeting the church" (18:22). ("The church" was Jerusalem.)

Again starting from Antioch, Paul departed on his third mission, during which he spent two and one-half to three years in Ephesus (chap. 19) and three months in Corinth (20:1–6). Luke related his journey to Jerusalem at the end of this period in great detail (20:7–21:16). In Jerusalem Paul was arrested and eventually transferred to Caesarea (21:17–23:25). Paul was in prison in Caesarea at least two years (24:27), during which time his case was heard by the Roman procurators Felix and Festus and the Jewish King Agrippa II (chaps. 24–26). Appealing to Caesar, Paul was transferred to Rome, incurring a major shipwreck en route (chaps. 27–28). At the end of Acts, Paul is under house arrest for two years in Rome.

External data. A few of the events mentioned in Acts are datable from external sources. As we have seen, the famine under Claudius seems to have hit Judea a year or so after Agrippa's death, that is, around A.D. 45 to 46.[23] Agrippa's death (Acts 12:23) is another datable event; it occurred in A.D. 44. More significant for Pauline chronology are two pieces of evidence connected with Paul's ministry in Corinth. The first is Luke's note concerning Aquila and Priscilla's having gone to Corinth from Italy after Claudius had expelled the Jews from Rome (Acts 18:2). The Roman historian Suetonius referred to this event in his *Life of Claudius*, 25. The date seems to have been A.D. 49.[24] A.D. 49 would thus be the earliest possible date for Paul's arrival in Corinth.

Even more significant is Luke's reference to Paul appearing before the proconsul Gallio at Corinth (18:12). An inscription discovered at Delphi helps to date the period of Gallio's administration as proconsul of Achaia. The inscription is found in several fragments which originally seem to have been located on the south side of the temple of Apollo. It preserves a letter sent by the emperor Claudius to Gallio and is dated during the "26th acclamation of Claudius as Emperor." Inscriptions found elsewhere fix the period of Claudius's 26th acclamation between January 51 and August 52. Proconsuls of senatorial provinces like Achaia seem to have held one-year terms and to have entered upon office in the late spring or early summer. The most likely date for Gallio's service is thus spring/summer 51 to spring/summer 52.[25] Taking the Claudius and Gallio dates together, Paul's period in Corinth would have fallen between A.D. 49 and 52.

One final external dating point has to do with the accession of Festus as governor of Judea (Acts 24:27). Paul made his appeal before Festus, evidently soon after the latter replaced Felix (Acts 25:5–12) and after having spent two years in prison in Caesarea. But when was this? Festus's predecessor Felix was appointed by Nero in A.D. 52, and Festus's successor Albinus came to office in A.D. 62. Festus is known to have died in office. But the date is uncertain. A date around A.D. 59 is often suggested for Felix's removal and Festus's accession.[26] In sum, these few dates seem to provide the most significant external evidence for establishing a chronology of Paul.[27]

A SUGGESTED CHRONOLOGY

The chronology provided here is fairly traditional, basically following the outline of Acts and incorporating the data from Paul's epistles where applicable. Others have maintained that the proper procedure is to begin with Paul's epistles and then consider the evidence of Acts or to eliminate Acts altogether and follow only the "primary source"—Paul. The problem with the latter approach is that Paul's epistles are *not* autobiographies; in no sense does Paul attempt to give a sketch of his ministry in his letters. To illustrate the problem with this approach: it has been maintained that Paul's epistles only speak of three visits of Paul to Jerusalem, whereas Acts speaks of five. A chronology is then constructued assuming that there were *only* three visits, in accordance with the "primary source" Paul.[28] But Paul never says that he made only three visits to Jerusalem after his conversion. It just happens that three visits are mentioned in the extant epistles of Paul, which is not to say that there weren't others. The "three visit" chronology is an argument from silence at best, and it does violence to the account in Acts. Acts purports to be what Paul's epistles are not—a sequential treatment of Paul's missionary activity. Granted, Luke was selective. There are holes in his story of Paul. (For instance, Paul's relationship with the church at Colosse is never hinted at in Acts.) Acts *should be* filled in from the epistles. The principle that the epistles should be the *primary source* for Paul is sound. Given the nature of the two types of literature, however, it makes sense to follow Acts in reconstructing a picture of Paul's ministry and to adjust it in the light of Paul's epistles where needed.[29]

If one were writing a biography, one would start with Paul's birth. But neither Acts nor the epistles are biographies, and we have no idea when Paul was born. Some older interpreters cite a dubious sixth-century source which says that Paul served Christ for 35 years and died at the age of 68. If he died during the persecution of Nero around A.D. 67, as tradition has it, then he would have been born around A.D. 1.[30] Others date his birth as early as 6 B.C.,[31] but this is all guesswork. Unfortunately, much the same applies to the time of his conversion. Obviously it took place after the crucifixion of Jesus. But when did the crucifixion take place? Good cases have been made out for A.D. 27, A.D. 30 and A.D. 33.[32] Assuming A.D. 30, which is the date most commonly followed, it is still not at all clear how long after Jesus' resurrection Paul's conversion came—one year, two years, three or more years? The early chapters of Acts give no real indications of time lapses. Feeling that at least two years are needed for the events of Acts 1–8 to take place, most who assume a 30 crucifixion/resurrection date place Paul's conversion at 32 or 33. (Those who assume a 27 resurrection date place the conversion in 30 or 31).

The first Jerusalem visit of Paul is easier to calculate. It took place three years after Paul's conversion, according to Galatians 1:18–19. One need only add three years to whatever was set as the conversion date. Then, calculations get difficult again. We enter the period of the "silent years" in Syria and Cilicia (Gal. 1:21). When did Barnabas go to Tarsus to bring Paul back to Antioch? Acts only speaks of a one-year ministry of Paul and Barnabas in the city (Acts 11:26). The pair could have worked elsewhere in Syria for much longer. Barnabas could have brought Paul to Antioch as early as 40 or as late as 44. When did the "famine visit" occur? The period around 45 or 46 seems to fit. The first missionary journey (Acts 13–14) probably lasted a couple of years. Again, Luke gives no precise time references, but surely several months each should be allowed for the establishment of the work in Cyprus and the cities on the mainland. Acts would indicate the mission began shortly after the famine collection, thus from about 45/46 to 47/48. Paul and Barnabas returned to Antioch and soon went to Jerusalem for the Apostolic Conference (Acts 15). We have dated the conference at A.D. 48, allowing for some sixteen years since Paul's conversion. This assumes that the three years and the fourteen years mentioned in Galatians are consecutive and that Acts 15 and Galatians 2 refer to the same conference. (Sixteen rather than seventeen is based on the Jewish method of counting a partial year as a full year.) The dispute in Antioch over Jewish-Christian table fellowship with Gentile Christians (Gal. 2:11–14) probably took place after the Jerusalem Conference, though Luedemann may be correct in seeing it as the event which precipitated the conference.[33]

The key element in considering the chronology of Paul's second missionary journey is his stay in Corinth. The edict of Claudius and the Gallio inscription set limits between A.D. 49 and 52. Paul spent at least eighteen months there on his founding visit (Acts 18:11), perhaps significantly longer (Acts 18:18). The second mission *must* have lasted for a period of at least four years. The distance Paul traveled between Jerusalem and Corinth was some 2,700 kilometers by land and another 775 by sea.[34] He revisited the congregations established on the first missionary journey, and he established a number of others. The Jerusalem Conference must have occurred in early 48, allowing time for a limited stay in Antioch (Acts 15:25) before his departure with Silas on the second mission in the same year. Paul perhaps arrived in Corinth in early 51 and departed by sea in late summer 52, while travel was still safe. This would allow the better part of two and one-half years for his ministry between Antioch and his arrival in Corinth.

Paul's third mission again started from his sponsoring congregation of Antioch (18:23). As on the second journey, he went by foot, perhaps in the fall of 52 or spring of 53. The journey took him to Ephesus, where he spent the greater part of the period, some two and one-half to three years all told (Acts 19:8; 10; 20:31). After leaving Ephesus, he seems to have spent a year or so visiting the churches of Macedonia and Achaia, gathering his collection for Jerusalem. He spent the winter in Corinth (Acts 20:2–3) and then departed for Jerusalem via Philippi, Troas, and Miletus (Acts 20:7–38). It was spring; Paul was hastening to make Jerusalem by Pentecost (Acts 20:16). The year was 57. Arrested in Jerusalem, Paul was quickly sent to Caesarea, where he spent two years in prison. When Festus succeeded Felix as governor in 59, Paul appealed to Caesar. In late summer of 59 he began his voyage to Rome, which was curtailed by a shipwreck. Wintering on Malta, in early spring his party secured passage to Italy. He arrived in Rome the spring of 60. Here the New Testament account of Paul's ministry stops. We will end our chronology at this point. In the final chapters of the book, we will examine the traditions of Paul's release and subsequent martyrdom and the evidence of his further ministry furnished by the Pastoral Epistles.

A Suggested Time Chart

32	Conversion
35	First Jerusalem Visit after Conversion
35–43	Silent Years
43–44	Ministry with Barnabas in Antioch
44	Death of Herod Agrippa I
45/46	Famine Visit
45/46–47/48	First Missionary Journey
48	Return to Antioch
48	Jerusalem Conference
48–52	Second Mission
48–49	Antioch to Troas
49–51	Macedonia and Athens
51–52	Corinth
52	Return to Antioch via Caesarea and Jerusalem
52/53–57	Third Mission Period
53–56	Ministry in Ephesus
56–57	Administering the Collection
57	Arrival in Jerusalem and Arrest
57–59	Caesarean Imprisonment
59–60	Voyage to Rome
60	Arrival in Rome
60–62	House Arrest in Rome

NOTES

1. A number of the better ancient manuscripts have the reading "Hellenists" (*Hellenistas*) rather than "Greeks" (*Hellenas*). But, the church had for a long time witnessed to Hellenists (Greek-speaking Jews). This verse indicates that something *new* happened at Antioch, namely, the outreach to Gentiles. Those manuscripts which read "Greeks" are thus to be preferred on the grounds of intrinsic probability.

2. H. D. Betz argued that it *was* a parody. Paul was using a Socratic method throughout 2 Corinthians 11–12, based on the idea that weakness and humility are the signs of a true philosopher: *Der Apostel Paulus und die sokratische Tradition* (Tübingen: Mohr/Siebeck, 1972).

3. See C. H. Buck and G. Taylor, *Saint Paul: A Study in the Development of His Thought* (New York: Scribner's, 1969), 220–226.

4. C. R. A. Morray-Jones sees Paul's vision as occurring within the tradition of Jewish Merkabah mysticism and connects it with this temple vision: "Paradise Revisited (2 Cor. 12:1–12): The Jewish Mystical Background of Paul's Apostolate; Part II: Paul's Heavenly Ascent and Its Significance," *Harvard Theological Review* 86 (3, 1993): 265–292. For arguments against a background in Jewish mysticism, see P. Schafer, "New Testament and Hekhalot Literature: The Journey into Heaven in Paul and in Merkavah Mysticism," *Journal of Jewish Studies* 35 (1, 1984): 19–35.

5. For a full treatment of this tradition, see Part I of the article cited above by Morray-Jones, "The Jewish Sources," *Harvard Theological Review* 86 (2, 1993): 177–217.

6. W. Baird, "Visions, Revelation and Ministry: Reflections on 2 Corinthians 12:1–5 and Galatians 1:11–17," *Journal of Biblical Literature* 104 (4, 1985): 651–662.

7. M. Hengel and A. M. Schwemer, *Paul Between Damascus and Antioch: The Unknown Years* (Louisville: Westminster John Knox, 1997), 174.

8. See Strabo, whose discussion of Antioch is found in his *Geography*, 16.2.4–7. For a thorough treatment of ancient Antioch, see G. Downey, *A History of Antioch in Syria* (Princeton University Press, 1961) and his abridged version, *Ancient Antioch* (Princeton University Press, 1963). A useful short introduction is provided in J. E. Stambaugh and D. L. Balch, *The New Testament in its Social Environment*, Library of Early Christianity (Philadelphia: Westminster, 1986), 145–149.

9. Hengel and Schwemer, 180–191. On the Jews of Antioch, see C. H. Kraeling, "The Jewish Community at Antioch," *Journal of Biblical Literature* 51 (1932): 130–160.

10. Traditionally Paul's arrival in Antioch is dated around A.D. 45–46. Hengel and Schwemer (pp. 221–224) date it much earlier—around A.D. 40, allowing for a short "silent period" of three to four years and a much longer mission of Paul and Barnabas in the towns of Syria.

11. E. J. Bickerman, "The Name of Christians," *Harvard Theological Review* 42 (1949): 109–124.

12. J. Taylor, "Why Were the Disciples First Called 'Christians' at Antioch? (Acts 11, 26)" *Revue Biblique* 101 (1, 1994): 75–94. One writer argued that the first to use it was Agrippa I, who coined it in parody of Nero's *Augustiani*: Harold B. Mattingly, "The Origin of the Name Christiani," *Journal of Theological Studies* 9 (1958): 26–37.

13. Suetonius stated that famines occurred throughout Claudius's principate (*Claudius* 18.2). Harvest records from Tebtunis in Egypt reflect crop failure in A.D. 45–46, and Orosius records a Syrian crop failure at the same time. Josephus (*Ant.*, 20.51–53) spoke of a Palestinian famine during the procuratorships of Fadus and Alexander (that is, around A.D. 46). For the evidence, see Kenneth S. Gapp, "The Universal Famine Under Claudius," *Harvard Theological Review* 28 (1935): 258–265.

14. W. M. Ramsay, *St. Paul the Traveller and the Roman Citizen* (London: Hodder and Stoughton, 1897), 61–64.

15. P. Benoit, "La deuxième visite de saint Paul à Jérusalem," *Biblica* 40 (1959): 778–792.

16. J. Jeremias, "Sabbathjahr und neutestamentliche Chronologie," *Zeitschrift für die neutestamentliche Wissenschaft* 27 (1928): 98–103.

17. G. Strecker, "Die sogennante zweite Jerusalemreise des Paulus (Act 11:27–30)," *Zeitschrift für die neutestamentliche Wissenschaft* 53 (1962): 67–77.

18. R. W. Funk, "The Enigma of the Famine Visit," *Journal of Biblical Literature* 75 (1956): 130–136.

19. A. T. Robertson, *Epochs in the Life of Paul* (New York: Scribner's, 1909), 101.

20. Hengel and Schwemer, *Paul Between Damascus and Antioch*, 244–275. See Also B. W. Robinson, *The Life of Paul* (Chicago: Chicago University Press, 1918), 71.

21. This is often combined with the observation that the western text of Acts includes a "we" at Acts 11:28—"as we were gathered together, one of them, Agabus. . . ." From this poorly attested reading it is then argued that Luke was a member of the Antiochene congregation.

22. D. Smith (*The Life and Letters of St. Paul*, 667–670) argues that the ancient tradition of Luke's Antiochene origin may ultimately go back to Luke's having come from *Pisidian* Antioch, which Paul *did* visit shortly before the "we" narratives begin (Acts 16:4–5).

23. A. Suhl would date it in 43/44, *before* Agrippa's death, "Der Beginn der selbständigen Mission des Paulus: ein Beitrag zur Geschichte der Urchristentums," *New Testament Studies* 38 (3, 1992): 430–437.

24. G. Luedemann challenges this dating, arguing that Dio Cassius dates Claudius's enactments against the Jews at A.D. 41 rather than 49: *Paul, Apostle to the Gentiles: Studies in Chronology* (Philadelphia: Fortress, 1980), 164–177. For a rebuttal, see D. Slingerland, "Acts 18:1–17 and Luedemann's Pauline Chronology," *Journal of Biblical Literature* 109 (4, 1990): 686–690.

25. See A. Deissmann, *Paul: A Study in Social and Religious History* (New York: George H. Doran, 1926), 261–286.

26. R. Jewett, *A Chronology of Paul's Life* (Philadelphia: Fortress, 1979). Most assume a short tenure of two to three years by Festus. D. Moody is an exception, arguing Festus was procurator from 57–62 ("A New Chronology for the Life and Letters of Paul," *Perspectives in Religious Studies* 3 [3, 1976], 252).

27. I cannot concur with Jewett and Murphy-O'Connor that Aretas's rule over Damascus had to be in A.D. 37, thus fixing Paul's escape from the city at that time. See the discussion of the "basket" incident above. It is doubtful that Aretas *ever* had any jurisdiction over Damascus. See J. Murphy-O'Connor, *Paul, A Critical Life* (Oxford: Clarendon, 1996), 4–8. Even less likely is the dating of 2 Thessalonians at A.D. 44, based on Caligula's attempt to set up his image in the temple (Buck and Taylor, *St. Paul: A Study in the Development of His Thought*, 146–152).

28. See J. C. Hurd, "Chronology, Pauline," *Interpreter's Dictionary of the Bible, Supplementary Volume*, ed. Keith Crim (Nashville: Abingdon, 1976), 166–167.

29. A very popular current reconstruction takes Acts 18:22 as the time of the Jerusalem Conference mentioned in Galatians 2:1–10, *not* Acts 15, which is seen as unhistorical or out of place. Moving the conference to the time of Acts 18:22 (A.D. 51 of 52) allows for the full seventeen years since Paul's conversion. More important, it allows for *all* the missionary activity of the first and second missionary journeys to take place before the Jerusalem Conference and thus avoids the "inactive" years of the silent period. Suggested by J. Knox (*Chapters in a Life of Paul* [Nashville: Abingdon, 1950]), this chronological sequence has been adopted in the works cited above by Hurd, Jewett, Luedemann, and O'Connor. A modified version is also adopted by N. Hyldahl, *Die paulinische Chronologie* (Leiden: Brill, 1986). Hyldahl also holds that *all* the Pauline epistles except 1 and 2 Thessalonians were written in a one-year period between January 54 and January 55.

30. D. Smith, *Life and Letters of Paul*, 645.

31. Murphy-O'Connor, *Paul, A Critical Life*, 1–4, dates it at 6 B.C., reasoning that Paul called himself a *presbutēs* ("old man"—i.e. around 60) when he wrote Philemon and that Philemon was written in 53 (which is questionable itself).
32. J. Gunther, *Paul: Messenger and Exile. A Study in the Chronology of His Life and Letters* (Valley Forge, Penn.: Judson Press, 1972), 19–24.
33. Luedemann, *Apostle to the Gentiles*, 44–80.
34. Figures are Jewett's, *Chronology of Paul's Life*, 59–62.

SUGGESTED FURTHER READING

THE CITY OF ANTIOCH

Downey, Glanville. *Ancient Antioch*. Princeton: Princeton University Press, 1963.
Stambaugh, J. E. and D. L. Balch, *The New Testament in its Social Environment*. Library of Early Christianity. Philadelphia: Westminster, 1986, pp. 145–149.

PAUL'S MINISTRY IN SYRIA AND CILICIA

Hengel, Martin and Anna Maria Schwemer. *Paul Between Damascus and Antioch: The Unknown Years*. Louisville: Westminster John Knox, 1997, pp. 151–301.
Polhill, John B. *Acts*. New American Commentary. Nashville: Broadman, 1992, pp. 268–276, 288–290.

PAULINE CHRONOLOGY

Gunther, John J. *Paul, Messenger and Exile. A Study in the Chronology of His Life and Letters*. Valley Forge, Penn.: Judson Press, 1972.
Jewett, Robert. *A Chronology of Paul's Life*. Philadelphia: Fortress, 1979.
Riesner, Rainer. *Paul's Early Period: Chronology, Mission Strategy, Theology*. Trans. Doug Stott. Grand Rapids: Eerdmans, 1998.

5

THE FIRST MISSION

*T*he mission of Paul and Barnabas related in Acts 13 and 14 is usually referred to as Paul's "first missionary journey." It was certainly not his *first* mission, however. Luke had already mentioned others—the work in Damascus, the silent years in the area of Tarsus, the work with Barnabas in Antioch. What was different about this new undertaking was its pushing into new frontiers, moving ever westward. And Paul continued to make new breakthroughs, particularly in his outreach to Gentiles. At least, this is the picture furnished in Acts.

On this mission, patterns were set which continued throughout Paul's missionary efforts as presented by Acts. Beginning on the island of Cyprus, Paul's main encounter there was with a Roman proconsul and a magician in the official's entourage. Throughout his mission work, Paul found himself opposing practitioners of magic. He also continued to encounter the chief regional governing officials, usually in a positive manner. Moving to the mainland of what is today southern Turkey, Paul was next opposed by the synagogue in Pisidian Antioch. Leaving the synagogue, he turned his witness exclusively to the Gentiles. Yet in the very next town, Iconium, he is shown as beginning his witness again in the synagogue. This pattern continues throughout Acts: beginning in the synagogues, rejected there, turning to the Gentiles, starting all over again in the synagogues of the next town.

Another recurring pattern is Paul's revisiting his congregations. At the end of this mission period, Paul did not proceed back to Antioch by the easiest and most direct route. Instead, he retraced his steps, revisiting and strengthening the newly established congregations. Paul's continuing nurture of his congregations is well attested throughout Acts and in the epistles as well. A section of this chapter is devoted to Paul's missionary strategy; its main emphases appear already in this first mission with Barnabas.

Acts is our primary source for this phase of Paul's missionary activity. In 2 Timothy 3:11 Paul alluded to his suffering at the hands of the Jews in Antioch, Iconium, and Lystra, which almost certainly is a reference to the events of this journey. Many scholars believe that these churches of southern Asia are the congregations to whom Paul addressed Galatians, since they were all located in the Roman province of Galatia. But Luke never referred to this area as Galatia. Throughout Acts 13 and 14 he used other territorial designations, such as Pisidia, Phrygia, and Lycaonia. The term

Galatia does not appear in Acts until Paul's second missionary journey. It is assumed in this book that the Galatian churches were established at *that* time, *not* on the first journey. A concluding section of this chapter will consider this "north or south" Galatian question.

THE FIRST MISSIONARY JOURNEY
(ACTS 13:4–14:28)

Commissioned by the church of Antioch in Syria and sent off by the Holy Spirit, Paul and Barnabas began their witness on the island of Cyprus. From there they sailed to the coast of Pamphylia (southern Turkey today). They progressed northward to Antioch in Pisidia, and from there eastward to Iconium, Lystra, and Derbe. Retracing their steps, they revisited Lystra, Iconium, and Pisidian Antioch and set sail from Attalia on the return voyage to Syrian Antioch.

CYPRUS (13:4–12)

The island. Cyprus is a large island, with a coastline of 390 miles and a length of 160 miles at its broadest point. It was occupied as early as the eighteenth century B.C. and was colonized successively by Egyptians, Phoenicians, Greeks, Assyrians, Persians, and the Egyptian Ptolemies. Its fertile central plain provided agricultural products for export. It also exported salt and copper from mines on the island. Cyprus came under Roman influence as early as 100 B.C., when it allied with Roman Cilicia in the war against the Mediterranean pirates. It was annexed by Rome in 59 B.C. and made a senatorial province by Augustus in 22 B.C.[1]

Initial work on Cyprus (13:4–5). Paul and Barnabas set out from Seleucia, the port city of Syrian Antioch. They sailed directly the seventy miles to the city of Salamis, the closest Cypriot port. Cyprus was a natural place to begin their mission. Barnabas was a native of the island (Acts 4:36), and some of the hellenist Christians had already begun work there (Acts 11:19). Paul and Barnabas started their work in the synagogues of Salamis. Acts does not elaborate on the ministry. The Hellenists had probably already established a significant witness there, and it was Paul's principle *not* to work on a field started by others but to break new ground (Rom. 15:20; cp. 2 Cor. 10:15). John Mark, Barnabas's cousin (Col. 4:10) was with them as "helper." His role is uncertain. He was young and perhaps something of a missionary apprentice. He does not seem to have been a part of Antioch's commissioning service (13:2–3).

Sergius Paulus and Elymas at Paphos (13:6–8). The three evidently did not tarry in Salamis but went on to Paphos. They probably took the southern Roman road from Salamis to Paphos, which was the most direct route at a distance of around 115 miles.[2] The city was known as "New Paphos," the Roman capital and seat of the proconsul. An older Paphos was located some six miles to the southeast of New Paphos. It was famous for its ancient temple dedicated to Aphrodite. At Roman Paphos, the missionaries encountered two people, the Roman proconsul, named Sergius Paulus, and a magician in his entourage by the name of Bar-Jesus, or Elymas. Not a great deal is said about the proconsul. He is described as being "intelligent," which is perhaps indicated by his sending for the two missionaries to hear more about the word of God. This evidently posed a threat to Bar-Jesus. He is characterized in much greater detail. Six things are said about him.[3]

First, he is described as being a "magician," or "sorcerer" (Gk., *magos*). Sorcerers could be respectable astrologers, like the Magi who attended Jesus' birth (Matt. 2:1). Or they could be hucksters, charlatans. The word was used in both senses. Bar-Jesus seems to fit the latter category. Second, we are told that he was a "false prophet." In the Old Testament, false prophets usually speak their *own* word, not God's, and generally for their own self-interest (cp. Jer. 23:9–40). Third, he is described as being "Jewish." Josephus mentions a number of Jewish sorcerers. Jews evidently had a reputation among the Romans for having unusual powers of prophecy and magic.[4] Fourth, he is shown to be "an attendant of the proconsul." Roman emperors often had astrologers in their retinue, and Bar-Jesus probably held a similar role with Paulus. Fifth, he is given the name Bar-Jesus ("son of Jeshua/Jesus"). The name Jesus/Jeshua was common, but the pun is obvious when Paul refers to him as a "child of the devil" (v. 10). Finally, his by-name is given as Elymas, which Luke interprets as "sorcerer." The etymology is uncertain. The most popular explanations are that it comes either from an Arabic word (*alim*) meaning "sage," or from an Aramaic word (*haloma*) meaning "interpreter of dreams." Why this elaborate description of the old charlatan? Probably as a warning to Luke's readers. Superstition in the kinds of practices done by Bar-Jesus plagued the first-century world. Luke wanted to impress his readers that Christianity has nothing to do with such things, that it opposes and overcomes charlatans and deceivers like Elymas.

Paul's confrontation with Elymas (13:9–12). Paul's scathing denunciation of Elymas reminds one of Peter's similar rebuke of Simon the magician, who also practiced his trickery for personal gain (Acts 8:20–23). Elymas's blindness is reminiscent of Paul's own experience at his conversion when he too had to be led by the hand (Acts 9:8). Did Paul perhaps hold out some hope for the charlatan? If the light of Christ could enlighten the heart of the old persecutor of the church, could it not also change the direction of a two-bit trickster like Elymas? In any event, Elymas's blindness was only temporary ("for a time," v. 11). It was an "object lesson," for him and for the proconsul. It had its effect on the proconsul. He "believed" (v. 12), but not so much because of the "sign" as from hearing Paul's teaching about the Lord. Some would see verse 12 as only meaning that the miracle amazed Sergius Paulus, making "a believer" out of him. It is more likely it was a genuine conversion—the first example of an individual conversion connected with Paul in Acts. And he was an influential *Gentile*.

In connection with this encounter Luke mentions that Saul was "also called Paul." From this point on, he is always referred to as Paul in Acts.[5] As we have seen, Paul was his Greco-Roman name, Saul his Hebrew name. The shift at this point is because he was now moving into Gentile territory and would continue to be an apostle to the Gentiles throughout Acts. Gentiles like Sergius Paulus would not recognize him by his Jewish name but by this Roman name Paul (La., *Paulus*). It is striking, of course, that Paul had the same name as the proconsul.[6] The coincidence may have triggered Luke's mentioning it at this point, but the switch is entirely appropriate as Paul moves toward a primarily Gentile mission.

It has often been argued that the miracle-working Paul of Acts is entirely different from the Paul of the epistles. We must note once again that we are dealing with two types of literature—Luke's narrative history of Paul's mission and Paul's personal correspondence with his churches. As we have seen, Paul generally was reluctant to speak in terms of signs and spiritual experiences as a basis for his apostleship. That was done enough by his opponents, whom he considered to be false apostles. Paul did, on the other hand, refer to his manifesting the Spirit and power among his congregations in what seem to be references to miraculous deeds (Rom. 15:18–19; 1 Thess. 1:5; 1 Cor. 2:4). He spoke to the Galatians of his having brought them the Spirit, and he mentioned the miracles which had occurred among them (Gal. 3:1–5). In 1 Corinthians 12:28 he listed "mighty works" (*dunameis*) among the gifts of the Spirit, the same word used in the Synoptic Gospels to designate Jesus' miracles.[7] In his epistles, Paul did not deny the working of miracles; he just did not wear such experiences on his sleeve.

PISIDIAN ANTIOCH (13:13–52)

Voyage to Perga (13:13). From Paphos, the trio of missionaries sailed the 175 miles to the coast of Pamphylia (southern Turkey today). The territories of Pamphylia and Lycia formed a single Roman province in Paul's day, which consisted of the land along the Mediterranean south of the Taurus mountain range. The three probably landed at Attalia, the port city of Perga, the capital of the province, which lay twelve miles inland. The Cestrus River connected Attalia with Perga but may not have been navigable the whole way in Paul's day. Acts doesn't mention the Christian missionaries witnessing in Perga. One wonders why. Ramsay suggested that Paul came down with malaria in the Pamphylian lowlands and was unable to do any work there.[8] That is speculative; Luke gives no reasons why. Neither does he explain why Mark abandoned the mission at this point and returned to Jerusalem. This development has prompted even more scholarly speculation.

For instance, it has been suggested that Mark was intimidated when it dawned on him how difficult the next leg of the journey would be across the rugged Taurus mountains to Pisidian Antioch.[9] Others have suggested that Paul made an abrupt change of plans, having originally intended to travel to Ephesus. When he decided on Pisidian Antioch instead, Mark's youthful enthusiasm for the whole project dampened, and he went home in protest.[10] Was Mark offended that Paul was taking an increasing leadership role in the mission and overshadowing his cousin Barnabas? Or did he have second thoughts about Paul's manner of witnessing to Gentiles like Sergius Paulus *outside* the context of the synagogue? He later wholeheartedly embraced Paul's outreach and served as his coworker (Col. 4:10). But was he at this point not wholly convinced of Paul's approach, like many of his fellow Christians in the Jerusalem church? We can only speculate. Luke provided no answers.

Arrival in Antioch (13:14–16a). Pisidian Antioch was one of the sixteen Antiochs founded by Seleucus I Nicator and named for his father. It was established some time around 300 B.C. It lay about 100 miles north of Perga, nestled in the mountains on a high plateau some 3,600 to 3,800 feet above sea level. Ramsay suggested that Paul took refuge there to escape the heat of the lowlands in order to recover from his supposed malarial attack. Sergius Paulus may have presented a more likely reason for Paul and Barnabas to make Antioch their next place of ministry. Inscriptions have been discovered at Antioch to various members of the Paullus family. One mentions a Sergia Paulla and dates shortly after Paul's visit there. It is possible that she was a daughter of the Cypriot governor and that he suggested that Paul witness in this area where he had family.[11] All of this is quite conjectural, of course, and has no firm basis in the biblical account. In any event, Paul needed no special excuse to go to Antioch. It was the major city of its region and an apt place to witness.

Originally known as "Antioch near Pisidia," it was actually in Phrygia on the border with Pisidia. Eventually, it was referred to simply as "Pisidian Antioch." According to Strabo, at the founding of Antioch, Seleucus settled a number of Greeks there whom he brought from Magnesia on the Maeander River (*Geography* 12.8.14). The city was made a free city by the Romans in 189 B.C. when Rome seized Asia Minor from the Seleucids. In 39 B.C. Marc Antony ceded Antioch to Amyntas, the king of Galatia. When Amyntas died in 25 B.C., his will granted all his territory to Rome. At that time Rome reorganized all of the Galatian king's territory into a new province of Galatia, which included in its borders Antioch and all the surrounding territory of Phrygia and Pisidia. In 6 B.C. Augustus made Antioch a Roman colony and renamed it *Colonia Caesarea Antiocheia*. Veterans from the fifth and seventh legions were settled there and constituted the citizens of the new colony. The Pisidian and Magnesian stock of the old city do not seem to have obtained citizenship before the second century.

The dominant religion of the Phrygian region was the worship of Cybele, the Mother Goddess, an ancient fertility deity associated with the cycle of the seasons. The patron god of Antioch was a male figure known as *Men*. Judging from Acts 13, there must have been a sizable Jewish community in Antioch. Josephus mentioned the transfer of several thousand Jews from Mesopotamia to Phrygia by the Seleucid king Antiochus III in the later third century B.C. (*Ant.* 12.147–149). The Jewish community in Antioch may have had its origin from that time.[12]

When Paul and Barnabas arrived in Antioch around 47–48 B.C., it was an impressive Roman colony. The heyday of its building program had recently occurred, from about 15 B.C. to A.D. 35. Much like its sister city of Syrian Antioch, its most impressive architectural wonder seems to have been its colonnaded main street. The two apostles probably sought out the Jewish quarter upon their arrival. It was the most likely place for two traveling Jews to find lodging. They were probably already known to the Jewish community when the Sabbath arrived. Paul's speaking in the synagogue was likely prearranged. Synagogue services consisted mainly of prayers and Scripture readings. Scripture generally included a reading from the Pentateuch and a reading from the prophets, sometimes with a third text linking the other two. When a qualified teacher was present, he was often asked to expound on the day's Scripture reading. This seems to have been the case with Paul.

Paul's sermon at Antioch (13:16b–41). Paul's address in the synagogue of Pisidian Antioch is one of six major "speeches" of Paul that occur in Acts. About one-third of the text of Acts consists of sermons or "speeches." Many of them are fairly short, but there are ten of some length. Of the ten, three are attributed to Peter (2:14–40; 3:12–26; 10:34–43). One, the longest of all, was delivered by Stephen (7:2–53). The other six came from Paul. Interestingly, there is a *single* major speech by Paul on each of his three missionary journeys, and each is to a different type of audience. On the *first* journey occurs the speech at Pisidian Antioch (13:16–41). It was to *Jews* and *God-fearers*. On the *second* journey, Paul's major address was to the *pagan* philosophers in Athens (17:22–31). On his *third* missionary journey, Paul's main sermon was to the *Christian* elders at Miletus (20:18–35). The other three Pauline addresses are mainly defenses of his ministry. All occurred after his arrest in Jerusalem and while he was a prisoner. One was to the Jewish mob in the temple square (22:1–21). A second was delivered before the Roman governor Felix (24:10–21). The final one was presented before King Agrippa (26:2–29).

A comparison of the Acts speeches reveals many similarities between them. The language and style are much the same throughout the ten. They are Luke's own account of the addresses. This is not to say that Luke did not have reliable information about the various occasions and what was actually said. The speeches are short, much shorter than the actual addresses would have been. It was not a day of stenographers and tape recorders. People depended on memory. Luke was probably present when several of Paul's speeches were made. He likely secured information from Paul and his companions as well. All of this is to say that the speeches in Acts are quite different both in content and in context from Paul's epistles. The Acts speeches are *Luke's* summaries of Paul's addresses. The speeches themselves are presented in very different contexts from Paul's epistles.

As one would expect, of all Paul's speeches in Acts, the one most like Paul's epistles is the address to the elders at Miletus. It is the *only* one delivered to a Christian audience. Paul's epistles, of course, were all written to Christians. The speech delivered in the synagogue at Pisidian Antioch really has no counterpart in the epistles. No epistle presents Paul's witness to a group of non-Christian Jews. It is not surprising, then, that the closest points of comparison are the speeches of Peter in Acts 2 and 3, which were to nonbelieving Jews. There are, however, significant affinities between Paul's synagogue address and his epistles, and we will note these as they occur.

Paul's sermon began with a very terse summary of Israel's history from the patriarchs to King David (13:16b–22). One is reminded of Stephen's speech, which likewise consisted of highlights from Israel's history. Paul's treatment was as tendentious as Stephen's. He chose events which pointed to God's gracious election of Israel—God's choice of the patriarchs, his deliverance of Israel from bondage, his conquest of the promised land for them, his granting their request for a king, his choice of David, and his promise to David. The entire emphasis was on God's selection of Israel and his deeds of mercy toward his elect people. Verses 23–25 link God's past deliverance of Israel to his present salvation in Jesus Christ. There are two linking figures. The first is David. God promised deliverance to his people through David, and this salvation has now taken place in David's descendant Jesus (v. 23). The second linking figure is John the Baptist, who served as forerunner of the Messiah (vv. 24–25). The reference to John connects Paul's speech both with the Gospel tradition (Luke 3:16) and with Peter's speech to Cornelius (Acts 10:37).

The key statement in Paul's entire sermon is found in verse 26: God's message of salvation in Jesus is sent "to us." Who does this "us" include? The verse makes it clear that it refers to *both* the Jews and the God-fearing Gentiles present in the synagogue at Antioch. Verses 27–31 give a summary of Jesus' passion: the joint responsibility of Pilate and the Jerusalem Jewish leadership for Jesus' condemnation, his death on "the tree," his burial, his resurrection, and the apostolic witness to the resurrection. Verses 29–31 are closely parallel to the resurrection tradition summarized by Paul in 1 Corinthians 15:3–7—even down to the detail that all was "according to the Scriptures."

Verses 22–27 offer some of the scriptural proofs that point to Christ as being the Messiah promised by God. Paul first used two Old Testament texts which were based on God's promises to David that he would establish him on an everlasting throne (2 Sam. 7:4–17). The first of the texts was Psalm 2:7, which designated the Messiah as Son of God, a text often quoted in the New Testament. The second text was Isaiah 55:3, which referred to the certainty of the eternal blessings promised to David. Paul used a final text (Ps. 16:10) to show that the promise of an eternal kingship was not realized in David because he died. It has, however, been realized in his descendant, Jesus the Messiah. (Peter likewise used this text in his sermon at Pentecost [Acts 2:25–31].) In his epistles Paul argued in similar fashion that the promises made to Israel were irrevocable and that they ultimately were realized in Jesus. This is the premise of his thought in Romans 9–11 and, for that matter, in all of Romans.

Paul's sermon ended with an invitation and a warning (verses 38–41). The invitation was to accept this salvation in Jesus Christ, which is described as "the forgiveness of sins" (v. 38).[13] More significant, Paul described this salvation as being "justified from everything you could not be justified from by the law of Moses" (v. 39). The phraseology is somewhat awkward, but the thought is perfectly Pauline. *Justification* was a favorite Pauline term for salvation. For him, to be "justified" meant to become acceptable to God. Paul frequently used this language in his epistles—in Romans, Galatians, and in Philippians. Paul was convinced that one could not be made right with God through performing works of the law—only through faith in God's gracious work of salvation in Christ. We will examine Paul's teaching on justification in more detail later in the context of the epistles. Suffice it at this point to note that Luke fully understood Paul when he noted this emphasis on justification being through Christ and not through the Mosaic Law.

Paul ended his invitation with a warning, quoting Habakkuk 1:5. The Old Testament prophet warned the nation to repent, or the destructive might of the Babylonian armies would descend upon them. In like fashion, Paul urged his hearers in the synagogue at Antioch to repent and respond to God's salvation in Christ. Invitation and warning are not incompatible. They belong together. To refuse the invitation is to lose the opportunity of salvation. Unfortunately, that seems to have come true very soon for many in the synagogue that day.[14]

The sermon's aftermath (13:42–52). The response to Paul's sermon was varied, but basically favorable. They asked him to come back on the next Sabbath to expound more of this new message (v. 42). Some, both Jews and "devout converts," evidently had the seeds of faith planted in them. They are said to have "followed" Paul and Barnabas (v. 43), which may imply that they had already started on the road to discipleship. The two missionaries urged them to continue down the path of God's grace. Things took a nasty turn, however, when the next Sabbath rolled around. "Almost the whole city" showed up at the synagogue (v. 44). This probably indicates that the Gentiles outnumbered the Jews. The God-fearers in the synagogue had evidently invited their friends, and they all accepted the invitation! The Jews responded angrily. They began to speak against Paul and Barnabas. The Greek literally says that they "blasphemed" them (v. 45). Why this sudden defamation when so shortly before they had responded so favorably to Paul's words? Luke describes it as "jealousy," but why the jealousy?

Seemingly, it was because the full implications of Paul's message now dawned on them. Paul had addressed the God-fearers throughout his sermon (vv. 16, 26), and the Gentiles were responding. Particularly were they responding to a message which promised them salvation based on faith in Christ rather than on works of the Mosaic Law (v. 39). Paul may not at this point have realized himself the full ramifications of such a statement. The synagogue had always had a means for accepting Gentiles into the people of God—through circumcision and embracing the Law of Moses.

Paul's message seemed to imply a different acceptance on God's part—an acceptance not based on provisions of law but solely on the basis of faith in Christ. The Gentiles of Antioch seem to have sensed this gracious good news, and they responded enthusiastically.

In response to the Jewish rejection, Paul and Barnabas "turned to the Gentiles" (v. 46). The decision was in part negative. The Antiochene Jews had rejected the message of salvation; they had proved themselves "unworthy" of eternal life. They had not heeded Paul's warning from Habakkuk 1:5. Positively, it meant reaching out to the Gentiles for Paul, and this, too, had scriptural warrant. Paul quoted Isaiah 49:6, a psalm of the Servant Messiah that described him as "a light for the Gentiles, that you may bring salvation to the ends of the earth" (v. 47). This is a key Old Testament text in Acts. It occurs at the beginning of the book (Acts 1:8) and toward the end (26:23). It reflects Paul's apocalyptic orientation. He knew from prophets like Isaiah that the evangelization of the nations was a major task for the messianic age. For their part, the Gentiles at Antioch were thrilled. They "honored" God's word; they gave God the glory for having included them in the messianic salvation. Many believed. God had prepared their hearts, appointing them for eternal life (v. 48).

We have a pattern here which will continue throughout Acts. On arriving in a new place, Paul always began his witness in the synagogue, when one was available. Strategically, it was a natural place to begin. Paul began with the Jews out of conviction, as well. Jews were God's chosen people; Paul never abandoned that conviction. He often said it himself—to the Jew first, and then to the Gentile, both in salvation and in judgment (Rom. 1:16; 2:9–10). Indeed, the failure of the bulk of the Jewish people to embrace Jesus was the most heart-breaking reality of Paul's ministry, and it never ceased to torture him (Rom. 9–11). It was only when he was excluded from the synagogue and no longer able to witness there that he would turn to a Gentile witness outside the synagogue. But in the next town, Paul would be back in the synagogue again. The seeming finality of Paul's turning to the Gentiles at Pisidian Antioch was not final at all. In Iconium, "as usual," he starts in the synagogue once again (Acts 14:1).

Often in Acts, when a situation of conflict has been resolved, there is a note about peace coming to the Christian community. That occurs here in verse 49; for a while the word of God flourished in the region—among the Gentiles, that is. The peace did not last long. The wrath of the synagogue did not cool, and they soon stirred up against the missionaries the women of high standing who were attached to the synagogue. These in turn were able to convince some of the male leadership in the city that Paul and Barnabas were a threat to the peace of their town. Evidently, in the Diaspora, the synagogue was especially attractive to Gentile women, and many became God-fearers.[15] Why the women God-fearers of Antioch turned against Paul is something of a mystery. Usually, like Lydia they were attracted to Paul's liberating message. Perhaps the women of Antioch had found a certain status in the synagogue which they felt was threatened when Paul opened the way to a more inclusive community of salvation. In any event, Paul and Barnabas were expelled from the city.

At this point, Paul chose not to invoke his Roman citizenship. It would surely have carried weight in the Roman colony. Instead, they moved on to the next village, following Jesus' direction by shaking the dust off their feet as a witness against the unbelieving Antiochenes (cp. Mark 6:11; Matt. 10:14–15; Luke 9:5; 10:11). They were not discouraged but filled with joy that they had been considered worthy to suffer for the Lord (cp. Acts 5:41).

ICONIUM (14:1–7)

The city. Paul and Barnabas set out on the main Roman road that ran east of Antioch, known as the "imperial road." The road ran southeast, connecting Antioch with another colony, Lystra, about one hundred miles distant. The two would eventually go there, but at this point, about thirty-five miles out of Antioch they took the road that forked slightly northward to Iconium. Unlike Antioch and Lystra, Iconium was not a Roman colony. It was eventually granted that status, but much later, around A.D. 135, by the emperor Hadrian. It was, however, a very ancient city. Like Damascus, it was one of the oldest continually occupied cities in the world. Settlements there have been traced to at least the third millenium B.C. It continues to be occupied today (modern Konya). It was particularly important during the period of the Ottoman Empire, when it served as the capital city of the Seljuk Turks. The Seljuks were tolerant of the Christians, and numerous Christian churches could be found in the area as recently as the early twentieth century.[16]

Iconium owed its antiquity to its strategic location. It stood on the main east-west trade route between Asia and Syria. Standing on a fertile plateau 3,370 feet above sea level, it was watered by streams from the surrounding mountains. The streams had no outlet and formed marshes around Iconium, making the area agriculturally productive in a part of the world which was otherwise quite arid. Sheep grazed on the nearby mountains, and Iconium had a thriving woolen industry. In his travel memoirs Marco Polo remarked about the superior quality of the wool carpets of Iconium.

Iconium was on the border of Phrygia and Lycaonia, with the former lying to the west and the latter to the east. It had come under Seleucid influence from the third century B.C., then under the kings of Galatia, and finally under the Romans. Like Antioch and Lystra, it was placed in the newly organized province of Galatia in 25 B.C. The emperor Claudius honored the city, and during his reign it was renamed *Claudiconium* for him.

Legends abound about Iconium. The most ancient goes back to Hittite times and claims that Iconium was the first city to be rebuilt after the great flood that destroyed the world. In Greek legend Iconium was the city where Perseus destroyed the Medusa. The name Iconium was even traced to this legend, the Greek word *eikon* (icon) meaning "image." This was taken as a reference to the face/image of the Medusa. Coins of Iconium from the Roman period depict Perseus standing, holding up the severed head of the Medusa.

In Paul's day Iconium was a prosperous market town. Like most cities of the region, it possessed an amalgam of religions. There were the gods of the Greco-Roman pantheon. There was a Jewish community. There were the local Phrygian and Lycaonian gods, particularly the Mother Goddess, who had a major shrine connected with the copper mines located near Iconium.

Initial witness (14:1–2). Paul and Barnabas pursued their usual pattern by beginning in the synagogue. It was the natural place to begin. The Jews and Gentile God-fearers would be steeped in the Old Testament and would be already prepared for Paul and Barnabas's message of messianic fulfillment. As at Antioch, they were at first received very favorably. Many believed, including both Jews and Gentiles. Unfortunately, the Antioch pattern was repeated in other ways as well. The Jews who did *not* believe poisoned the minds of the Gentiles in the synagogue and turned them aganst the missionaries. Verse 2 does not state explicitly that Paul and Barnabas were at this point excluded from the synagogue, but that seems to be implied. That is the usual pattern of Paul's ministry as depicted throughout Acts—beginning in the synagogue, excluded from there, continuing to witness to the Gentile populace outside the context of the synagogue, and then often being forced to leave the city altogether.

Continued ministry (14:3–4). The word *so* ("therefore") in verse 3 presents a problem. It seems to contradict the previous verse. The synagogue opposed the missionaries (v. 2), *so* they continued for a while (v. 3). Verse 4 follows verse 2 more naturally: the opposition led to the city being divided over the two missionaries. Some interpreters have thus suggested radical surgery on the text, either removing verse 3 by arguing that it is a gloss and not a part of the original text, or reversing the order of verses 2 and 3.[17] A simpler solution is to assume a breach with the synagogue after verse 2. The two missionaries were ejected from the synagogue but continued their witness in the city nonetheless. They were empowered by the Spirit, as the references to their "bold" message and "signs and wonders" attest (v. 3). The city was divided. This is a consistent pattern throughout Acts. The gospel characteristically divides; it is not an indifferent matter. One either accepts it, or one rejects; there is no in between. Note that verse 4 refers to Paul and Barnabas as "apostles." The word is used twice in this chapter to refer to the two missionaries (14:4 and 14:14). Elsewhere in Acts, Luke reserved the term exclusively for the twelve disciples. Luke may have shown his awareness of the broader usage here, or he may have seen Paul and Barnabas as "apostles" from the church of Antioch in Syria (that is, as representatives of Antioch, those "sent out" by that congregation).[18]

Leaving Iconium (14:5–7). Eventually Paul and Barnabas had to leave Iconium. The opposition seems to have consisted of a coalition much like the one which drove them from Pisidian Antioch. Jews and Gentiles allied against Paul and Barnabas and persuaded the city leadership that the two were a threat to the well-being of the city. They plotted to stone the two apostles. Getting wind of the plot, they fled to the Lycaonian cities of Lystra and Derbe and the surrounding countryside. Iconium was on the border of Phrygia and Lycaonia. The two apostles sought safety by crossing the border into Lycaonia. Verse 7 prepares for Paul's ministry in the Lycaonian cities of Lystra and Derbe. It is unclear how much they evangelized the surrounding countryside. Lycaonia was basically rural. Lystra and Derbe were the major settlements, and this seems to be where Paul and Barnabas focused their ministry.

LYSTRA AND DERBE (14:8–20)

Lystra. The site of Lystra was uncertain until the year 1885, when an archaeologist named Sterrett discovered an inscription at Zoldera near Khatyn-Serai. The inscription was engraved on a monument eight and one-half feet tall and commemorated the establishment of Lystra as a colony by Caesar Augustus in 6 B.C. The site is located about twenty-four miles south of Iconium and is around 3,800 feet above sea level. Ramsay described the site as a green oasis in the midst of an otherwise arid terrain. It was a small settlement, evidently established as a border colony for the quartering of troops to protect the main Roman routes that ran from Syria west to the province of Asia. It lay on the same Roman road as Pisidian Antioch, about one hundred miles distant. It seems to have had some relationship with Antioch. A third-century inscription found in Antioch commemorates a concordat established between it and the colony at Lystra. The permanent Roman presence was probably small in Lystra. Few Latin inscriptions have been found in the area. The main population probably consisted of native Lycaonians, as the account in Acts would indicate.[19] It was primarily a Gentile settlement. Paul found no synagogue there. He did locate one partially Jewish family, that of Timothy, a young man with a Gentile father and a Jewish mother, who had reared him in the Old Testament Scriptures (Acts 16:1; 2 Tim. 1:5). Since Paul usually sought out the Jewish community upon his arrival in a new town, it is possible he stayed with Timothy's family, who may have been the only Jewish presence in Lystra.

Healing of a lame man (14:8–10). Paul came upon a lame man in Lystra, much as Peter encountered a lame man at the Beautiful Gate of the temple in Jerusalem (Acts 3:2–10). Both had been born lame and had never walked. Paul evidently sensed a glimmer of faith in the man (v. 9). Perhaps Paul had been preaching, and the message of Christ had aroused some hope in the crippled man's heart. Paul commanded him to rise on his feet, and he did. That took some degree of faith. The man had never walked before, but he responded to Paul's word, made the effort, and walked! Luke says that he "jumped" about, the same word he used of the lame man healed at the Beautiful Gate (Acts 3:8), the same word the prophet Isaiah used when he predicted that in the age of the Messiah the lame would "leap as a deer" (Isa. 35:6). The western text of Acts adds that Paul healed the man "in the name of the Lord Jesus," which is always implicit in the healings accomplished through the apostles.

Acclaimed as "gods" (14:11–13). The Lystran pagans were astounded by the healing. In their native Lycaonian dialect they began to proclaim that the gods had come down to visit them. They probably understood Greek; the lame man did. He did not hesitate to respond to Paul's (Greek) command to rise. But because Paul and Barnabas could not understand Lycaonian, they allowed the whole confused scene to progress as far as it did. The crowd dubbed Paul the god Hermes, and Barnabas they designated Zeus. Zeus was the chief of the Greek Olympian gods. Hermes was his son and was considered to be the inventor of language, the god of communication, the spokesperson of the gods. Paul had evidently been doing most of the speaking; to the Lystrans he *had* to be Hermes. Barnabas could *only* be Zeus and no other. The Lycaonians had a local tradition about a visit from those particular two gods. The healing had convinced them that the pair of gods were making a return visit.

The legend is related in the *Metamorphoses* of Ovid (8.626–724). It involves a visit to the region by Zeus and Hermes who were disguised as two weary travelers. No one took them in except for an elderly couple named Philemon and Baucis, who, totally unaware of their identity, entertained the two travelers from their own meager provisions. They were rewarded lavishly for their generosity, but their inhospitable neighbors were destroyed by a flood. The legend is just one of many similar stories from Greek folklore where the gods are said to have come to earth in human disguise. In particular, the two gods Zeus and Hermes were often seen as the companions and protectors of travelers.[20] An inscription found near the site of Lystra is dedicated to Zeus and Hermes and testifies to the importance of that particular pair of gods in the area.[21]

94

In any event, the Lystrans were not about to let a visit from the gods pass them by. In particular, they did not want to experience the fate of the inhospitable neighbors of Philemon and Baucis. The priest of the local temple of Zeus joined the enthusiasm of the crowd and prepared a sacrifice to be offered to the two "gods." He brought garlands and bulls to be sacrificed at the "gates," which probably means the gates of the temple, which would be the usual place for sacrifices. We cannot be sure exactly where Paul and Barnabas were while all of this was going on or when what was actually transpiring first dawned on them, but when it did, they lost no time in attempting to extinguish the ardor of their would-be worshipers.

The protest of the apostles (14:14–18). The attempt to worship the apostles is found in a number of places in Acts. It is always strenuously resisted. For example, Peter assured the crowd in the temple square that the name of Jesus, not himself, had healed the lame man at the Beautiful Gate (3:12). Likewise, he rebuffed Cornelius's attempt to worship him, assuring the centurion that he was a mere man like himself (10:25–26). Paul and Barnabas did essentially the same thing at Lystra. They rushed into the crowd in order to demonstrate that they were human like every other person in the throng. They loudly insisted that they were mere humans. Only one person in all of Acts failed to object when the crowds professed his divinity—Herod Agrippa. The crowds called him a god; he did not deny it; as a result, he immediately died (Acts 12:22–23).

Paul used the opportunity to tell the crowd about the *real* God. In all of Acts, this is a first for Paul. Always before, his speeches had been either to Jews or Gentile God-fearers and proselytes who already knew God. At Lystra he was speaking strictly to pagans—to polytheists who worshiped idols and a plurality of divine beings like Zeus and Hermes. He could not share the message of Christ until he had first convinced them of basic monotheism—that there is only *one* God and no other. They could not understand the Son of God until they first knew God. Paul's words at Lystra are the *beginning* of a sermon and nothing more. The fervor of the crowd did not allow him to complete it. A fuller summary of an address to pagans is provided in Acts 17:22–31 in Paul's address before the Areopagus at Athens. The content of the Lystran address is much simpler. It was delivered to the simple "backwoods" folk of Lystra. The Areopagus address was delivered before the philosophers of Athens. But both began at the same place: to introduce the pagan listeners to the one creator God.

At Lystra, Paul began by urging his listeners to renounce their worthless idols and to embrace the living God, the maker of heaven and earth. We don't have any example of Paul's preaching to pagans in his epistles. In 1 Thessalonians, however, he reminded his Gentile readers how he had preached when he first came to them. He said that he urged them to turn from idols to the living God (1 Thess. 1:9), exactly the emphases with which he began at Lystra. Paul then told the Lystrans that in the past God allowed all nations to "go their own way" (v. 16). This is the theme of God's past forebearance with regard to human sin and ignorance, a theme found elsewhere in Paul (cp. Rom. 3:25). The implication is that now things have changed. With the coming of Christ, all people stand under God's judgment (cp. Acts 17:30). Of course, at Lystra, Paul was cut short and not allowed to introduce Christ.

Paul continued his brief sermon with an exposition of God's providence. As Creator, God is loving and kind, he emphasized. It is these acts of providence in nature which provide everyone with some "testimony" to God, even the pagans of Lystra. They may never before have been introduced to God, but they could know him through his works of nature—sun and rain, bountiful harvest and food to make their hearts rejoice. Paul got no further. The crowd became even more insistent in their attempt to sacrifice to the two missionaries. Perhaps it was Paul's words about food and bountiful crops. Perhaps that was the kind of God they longed for all along—the gods of Philemon and Baucis who rewarded their worshipers with full stomachs.

In Romans 1:18–20 Paul made a similar appeal to a natural knowledge of God through the created order. He stated that even pagans who have no direct revelation of God can know something of him through his works. In Romans, Paul used the argument to establish the responsibility of Gentiles for their sins. He argued that sin distorted the natural knowledge of God and led humans to worship the creation rather then the Creator whom it revealed. At Lystra Paul employed the same observation for an almost opposite reason—to lead the pagans to an awareness of God. They may never have heard of God before, but they knew him, through his providential works in nature.

The apostles are rejected (14:19–20). The account of Paul's ministry at Lystra is severely compressed. From the acclamation of the crowd, the scene quickly shifts to an attempt on his life. In between, there must have been a period of ministry, at least enough time for the band of disciples to have formed that is mentioned in verse 20. All in all, the pattern of Paul's Lystran experience was a familiar one—from initial acceptance to final rejection. This time there was no synagogue to incite the masses. Jews from Antioch and Iconium came and did so. Coming from Iconium is understandable. It was only a day's walk away. But Antioch? It lay one hundred miles distant. This may, however, not be as unlikely as it would appear on first glance. Lystra and Antioch were sister Roman colonies. They were on the same highway. They seem to have carried on considerable commerce between them. It is not at all implausible that through such contacts Paul's presence in Lystra may have become known to his former opponents in the synagogue of Pisidian Antioch. In any event, the opposition was more violent at Lystra. Note the escalation: they were expelled from Antioch, they were threatened with stoning at Iconium, Paul was actually stoned at Lystra. Paul was dragged out of the city and left for dead. Fortunately, the hand of the Lord was with him. He survived the ordeal, and the Christians of the city led him back into town. He could not stay; the danger was too great. Next day he and Barnabas left for Derbe.

Why did the crowd that had hailed Barnabas and Paul as gods turn against them? Perhaps for the same reason that the crowd who shouted "hosanna" on Jesus' entry into Jerusalem so quickly shifted to "crucify him." Neither Jesus nor Paul met the expectations of the crowd. When the Lystran pagans realized that Paul and Barnabas were not gods who would shower them with gifts, they turned against them. Of course, not everyone did so. A nucleus of believers was established in every city. Lystra was no exception. It had its disciples as well.

Derbe (14:20b–21a). The site of Derbe is not at all certain. The most widely accepted location today is considerably farther from Lystra than earlier estimates. It is a place known as Kerti Huyuk, which is about sixty miles southeast of ancient Lystra. In Paul's day it was outside the borders of Roman Galatia, in the territory of King Antiochus IV of Commagene.[22] Little is known about Derbe. The town was evidently honored by Claudius. A few coins have been found inscribed to *Claudio-Derbe*. Luke seems to have had little specific information about Paul's ministry in Derbe. He only mentions that it was quite successful and that many converts were made there. Paul revisited the city on his second missionary journey (Acts 16:1), and a Christian from Derbe named Gaius seems to have been among Paul's entourage on his last visit to Jerusalem (Acts 20:4).

RETURN TO ANTIOCH (14:21–28)

Revisiting the churches (14:21b–25). Paul and Barnabas could have continued on south from Derbe along the route that led through the Cilician Gates to Paul's hometown of Tarsus. It would have been just over one hundred miles, a trip of no more than a week by foot. Instead they chose the far more arduous task of retracing their steps, revisiting each of the cities where work had been established. Paul considered the nurture of his congregations a top priority. The churches of Lystra, Iconium, and Derbe may have been in particular need of his reassurance since he had left them so abruptly and under such trying circumstances. Paul encouraged each of the congregations, urging them to continue true to the faith. His was no easy gospel. He told them that suffering often accompanies discipleship. Paul was himself the prime example. They had all witnessed how he had been persecuted and driven from their cities. He told them to expect the same. In 2 Timothy 3:11 Paul referred to these very persecutions which he suffered in Antioch, Lystra, and Iconium. In his other epistles he often spoke of the many hardships he endured as a missionary (1 Cor. 4:10–13; 2 Cor. 4:7–12; 6:3–10; 11:23–29). Paul was also concerned that his churches would have good leadership during his absence. He and Barnabas seem to have handpicked elders for the congregations. Elsewhere in Acts various congregations were directed to choose their own leaders (e.g. 6:1–6), but here in the founding stages of these churches, the apostles seem to have taken the initiative. They appointed "elders" in the pattern of the Jewish synagogues and the Jerusalem Christian church.

Feeling confident about the new congregations, Paul and Barnabas returned to Perga from which they had set out. This time they witnessed in the city for a while before descending to the port of Attalia, where they caught a ship for the return voyage to Syrian Antioch.

Back in Antioch (14:26–28). Verse 26 rounds off the account of the first missionary journey. The mention of completing the "work" forms an *inclusio* (a bracketing frame) with Acts 13:2, where the Holy Spirit called Paul and Barnabas and set them apart for "the work." At Antioch, their sponsoring church, they did what missionaries continue to do on their return home; they gave a report about their successful mission. Particularly did they emphasize the exceptional response of the Gentiles. Antioch had already reached out to Gentiles, but verse 27 implies that the door to the Gentiles had been opened even more widely on this mission. In what sense was this true? Was it the mission *outside* the synagogues that was new? That had probably already occurred at Syrian Antioch. Had Paul initiated a new strategy where Gentiles were accepted into the church without going the route of Jewish proselyte procedure? Had the principle been established that Gentiles could become Christians without first becoming Jewish proselytes? Surely it had—whether first at Antioch or whether later on Paul and Barnabas's missionary journey. The principle had been established, and it soon precipitated a major conference in Jerusalem over the issue (Acts 15; Gal. 2).

Two Related Questions

Our consideration of Paul's first missionary journey raises two issues related to that endeavor. The first has to do with Paul's missionary method. Was there a recurring pattern to Paul's missionary strategy? How did he envision his mission, and how did he carry it out? The second question relates to the territory in which Paul and Barnabas carried out this first mission. Is it correct to call the mainland churches "Galatian"? In particular, are Antioch, Lystra, and Iconium the churches to which Paul wrote his Galatian epistle?

Paul's Missionary Method

It is questionable whether Paul had a preconceived "grand design" for his mission. Both the scope and the method of his work probably evolved over time, growing out of his actual missionary experience. In both Acts and his epistles, however, several patterns emerge.

The area and extent of Paul's mission. Paul seems to have confined his work primarily to the part of the world controlled by Rome. All the areas where Acts and the epistles show him working were either within Roman provinces or in areas ruled by Roman client kings—Arabia, Syria-Cilicia, Cyprus, Galatia, Asia, Macedonia, Achaia, Italy. His plan to do further work in Spain (Rom. 15:24) still confined him to the Roman world. He does not seem to have entertained the idea of penetrating beyond Roman borders into such places as northern Europe or eastward to India and beyond. Early Christian legends abound of various apostles evangelizing such areas—Thomas to India and China, Matthias to Germany, Andrew to Scotland, and the like. But Paul restricted his work to the Roman world, and not all of that. He evidently never witnessed in Egypt or any of north Africa, for instance. He was surely wise to limit his work to the Roman domain. He enjoyed the advantages of his own Roman citizenship in those areas, and the Roman military control and superior road system afforded him security and freedom of movement he would not have experienced elsewhere. If he had any territorial "strategy," it would have been an "east to west" pattern, for that is the direction in which he progressed—Syria and Cilicia, the near eastern provinces of Galatia and Asia, Greece, Italy, Spain.[23]

We may not know the full extent of Paul's missionary work. Acts gives a selective account of his work. We know from his letters that he established a witness in areas never mentioned in Acts—the churches of the Lycus Valley in Asia, for example, Colosse and Laodicea. Acts does not mention them, but they were a product of Paul's mission. In Romans 15:19 Paul spoke of having preached the gospel fully all the way from Jerusalem to Illyricum. Illyricum was north of Macedonia on the Adriatic coast. Acts relates no work of Paul there. Luke was obviously selective in his treatment of Paul's missionary activity. And what of his activity *after* the end of Acts? If he was released from Roman imprisonment, where did he work? Did he go to Spain as he intended? The Pastoral Epistles mention work on Crete and at Nicopolis. Did he work in those places? Did he revisit his former fields? We will consider these questions in the final chapters of this book.

A pioneer missionary. Paul was in every sense a "pioneer" missionary. He wanted to cover as much of the world with the gospel as quickly as he could. This desire was related to his conviction that the age of the Messiah had dawned. The evangelization of the Gentiles was seen by many Jews as a major task of the messianic age. Paul saw himself involved in God's call to preach as far and wide and to as many as he could until the "full number" of the Gentiles had responded to God's grace in Christ (Rom. 11:25). Paul knew that he was one among many who had been called to the missionary task. It was thus his principle to break new ground only, *never* to work himself in an area already evangelized by others (2 Cor. 10:13–16; Rom. 15:20). And when he had established work in a new area, it was his principle to move on to new fields where the gospel had not yet been taken. One of the most remarkable statements Paul ever made was when in Romans 15:23 he spoke of no longer having any room for work "in these regions." The "regions" he was talking about covered Jerusalem to Illyricum (Rom. 15:19), a total land mass of over three hundred thousand square miles.[24] Obviously, Paul had not preached to every person or even to every village in the area, but mission churches had been established, and workers were there to continue the witness. For Paul the pioneer, the Gentile apostle, it was time to move on—to Spain and points west (Rom. 15:24).

The place of witness. Acts depicts Paul as consistently beginning his witness in each new place in the synagogue, when there was one present. This seems to be borne out in Paul's epistles. For example, in 2 Corinthians 11:24 he referred to the five times he had received a scourging at the hands of the Jews. The "forty-less-one" lashes were the customary disciplinary procedure of the Jewish synagogues. The synagogue was a natural place for Paul to begin. As a Jew, he would have instant entree there. There would probably also be God-fearers there, Gentiles who would already have some preparation in the Scriptures and in the worship of God. Paul probably did not do much "street preaching." That was a method pretty much confined to the Sophists and mendicant Cynics, people from whom Paul would have wanted to distance himself.[25]

Much of his witness probably took place in private homes where the Christians gathered, like the homes of Lydia (Acts 16:40) and Philemon (Philem. 2). Paul also may have witnessed in the context of the workshop as he pursued his tent-making trade. Homes were often connected with shops. Paul thus may have lodged, witnessed, and worked all in the same place when he took up with Aquila and Priscilla at Corinth (Acts 18:3).

Paul worked primarily out of the large population centers. His ministry was mainly urban. The picture of Paul the itinerant missionary hurrying all over the countryside is a false one. It is even somewhat misleading to speak of his missionary "journeys." The label "journey" best fits the first mission, as Paul traveled from Cyprus to Perga, Antioch, Iconium, Lystra, Derbe, and back. But even then, Paul probably spent some time in each place, sufficient time to establish well-rooted churches. And, what is more significant, he worked in the largest and most populous towns of the region. During his second mission period, Paul spent as much as half his time in a single city, Corinth. The third mission was really an Ephesian ministry. *Most* of this was spent in Ephesus, up to three years in all. Paul's strategy seems to have been to establish himself in the largest cities of a region and to work out from there. Coworkers like Timothy and Epaphras worked with him, evangelizing the surrounding territory and establishing churches. It is probably in this way that the churches of Colosse, Laodicea, and Hierapolis were established. They were up the river from Ephesus and were probably started by Paul's coworker Epaphras during the course of Paul's three-year ministry in Ephesus.

Paul's continuing nurture of his churches. Paul was often torn between his urgent call to establish new work and his concern for the well-being of the congregations he had already founded. In 2 Corinthians 11:28 he spoke of the constant pressure of his anxiety for his churches. His letters are ample testimony to his care for them. One way he could continue to nurture them, even when far away, was through correspondence. And write them he did. The thirteen letters we have are probably only a sample of his total correspondence with his churches. Paul mentioned others which are now evidently lost—an earlier letter to Corinth (1 Cor. 5:9), apparently a previous letter to Philippi (Phil. 3:1), and a lost Laodicean epistle (Col. 4:16).

Letters aren't the only way Paul maintained contact with his congregations. He revisited them whenever possible. For example, Acts mentions at least three times when Paul revisited the churches of his first missionary journey—at the end of the journey (14:21–23), at the outset of the second mission (16:1–5), and at the beginning of his third missionary period (18:23). Acts 14:21–23 is particularly instructive, as it shows Paul's concern for the nurture of his congregations—instructing them in the faith, encouraging them in the face of persecution, and establishing suitable leadership.[26] The coworkers whom Paul so often mentioned in his epistles were key figures in his ongoing ministry to the churches. They ministered to the congregations themselves and maintained communication between the apostle and his churches.

NORTH OR SOUTH GALATIA?

Are the churches which Paul established on his first missionary journey the same churches to which he addressed his Galatian epistle? Many scholars answer that question in the affirmative and about as many in the negative. The former would note, quite correctly, that Pisidian Antioch, Iconium, and Lystra were all located in the official Roman province of Galatia in Paul's day. The others would counter that nowhere in the course of the first missionary journey (Acts 13–14) does Luke refer to "Galatia," but to other territorial designations—Pamphylia, Pisidia, Phrygia, Lycaonia. They argue that neither Luke nor Paul in his epistle consider *this* area as Galatia. How did this division between scholars over Galatia come about? To understand it, one must begin with a sketch about Galatian history.[27]

History of the term Galatia. Around 278 B.C. a group of marauding Gauls progressed eastward from central Europe, crossing the Hellespont into Asia. They settled in central Asia Minor, establishing Ancyra as their capital (the same as Ankara in modern Turkey). For a while the borders of their kingdom extended as far south as Phrygia, but eventually (around 240 B.C.) the king of Pergamum stemmed their expansion and confined them to an area in northcentral Asia Minor that centered around the cities of Tavium, Pessinus, and Ancyra. Their realm became known as "Galatia," named after the Gauls who had settled there. In 121 B.C., Galatia came under Roman influence, the Galatian king becoming a Roman client monarch. In 36 B.C. the administration of Galatia was given by Rome to King Amyntas of Pisidia. Before his death Amyntas acquired additional territories in the region, including portions of Cilicia. Upon his death in 25 B.C., Amyntas willed all of his kingdom to Rome. Rome took Amyntas's expanded Galatian kingdom, added some additional territories to it, and organized the whole as the official province of Galatia. The new Galatian province included the former kingdom of Galatia, Pisidia, Isauria, and parts of Lycaonia, Phrygia, Paphlagonia, and Pontus. All of the mainland churches of Paul's first missionary journey were thus in the Galatian province, with the possible exception of Derbe. But Acts 13 and 14 are evidence that one could talk about this area without ever mentioning "Galatia." There seems to have still been a "popular" usage which reserved the term *Galatia* exclusively for the old northern kingdom of Galatia around Pessinus and Ancyra. Many scholars argue that this "north Galatia" is the Galatia of Paul's epistle. Others argue that Paul wrote the epistle to the "south Galatian" churches of the expanded Roman province of Galatia which Paul established on his first missionary journey. What is the evidence for each position?

The extra-biblical evidence. The idea that Galatians was written to the "south Galatian" churches of Paul's first missionary journey is a relatively "modern" theory. It seems to have first been suggested by Johann J. Schmidt in 1748. It was picked up and popularized in the nineteenth century by several French scholars, including George Perrot (1867) and Ernest Renan (1869). The theory really came into its own in the latter part of the nineteenth century when it was strongly championed by the influential British scholar Sir William Ramsay. Ramsay spent years of research in the area of Paul's first missionary journey. He discovered that most of the official Roman inscriptions dating from Paul's time referred to the Roman governor as the governor of "Galatia." The inscriptional evidence is not unambiguous, however. Some honorary inscriptions have been found which designate the governor as being over "Galatia, Pontus, Paphlagonia, Pisidia, Phrygia, and Lycaonia," thus listing all the former territories that comprised the new province of Galatia.[28]

The literary evidence is even more ambiguous than the inscriptions. Some Roman historians like Pliny and Tacitus referred to the southern area by its official name of the province of Galatia. Popular writers like Lucian and Memnon, however, used the term *Galatia* only for "ethnic" Galatia, the old northern area around Pessinus and Ancyra, the territory of the "Gauls."

This was the usage of all the early Christian writers. No Christian writer before the eighteenth century seems to have seen Galatians as having been addressed to the "south Galatian" area of Paul's first missionary journey. All place the Galatian churches in the "north Galatian" area of the old kingdom of the Gauls. Such evidence would be almost conclusive against the south Galatian view were it not for the fact that the Roman province of Galatia was short-lived. The province of Galatia was reorganized once again in the mid-second century. The southern territories were placed in a separate province known as the "Three Eparchies." The province of Galatia was accordingly reduced to about the size of the old Galatian kingdom, that is, the area around Tavium, Pessinus, and Ancyra. All the Christian writers who wrote about the Galatian epistle wrote *after* the time of the reorganization and thus would only have been aware of the Galatia of their own time, which was "northern Galatia." All in all, then, the extrabiblical evidence is ambiguous. Does the New Testament help us at all to decide between north and south Galatia?

The New Testament evidence. The term *Galatia* only occurs two times in the Book of Acts. First, it appears at the outset of Paul's second missionary journey. Paul had revisited the churches of Derbe and Lystra (16:1–5) and then is depicted as traveling through Phrygia and the Galatian region (16:6). Paul was headed west into the province of Asia, but the Spirit prevented him, and he started north toward Mysia and Bithynia, eventually being diverted to Troas on the Asian coast (16:6–9). Advocates of both views claim verse 6 as support. South Galatian advocates argue that one should take the terms *Phrygia* and *Galatia* together and see Paul as traveling from Lystra through the Phrygian portion of Galatia on his way to Asia. They argue that his diversion northward would not have taken him as far east as the old north Galatian cities. North Galatian advocates maintain that the most natural reading of Acts

16:1–9 would see a sequential itinerary. Paul began by revisiting the cities of his first journey (vv. 1–5). Leaving Antioch, he started west toward Asia. Prevented by the Holy Spirit from entering Asia, he proceeded north, going through Phrygia and eventually into northern Galatia around Pessinus. Paul would have stopped there and established the Galatian churches at that time. Luke did not elaborate on the work in Acts.

On the other hand, Luke never used the term *Galatia* for Paul's work on the first missionary journey. He *did* use the term one more time—in Acts 18:23, at the outset of the *third* mission. The verse is very compressed: "After spending some time in Antioch, Paul set out from there and traveled from place to place throughout the region of Galatia and Phrygia, strengthening all the disciples." What does "from place to place" refer to? What does "Galatia" entail? South Galatian advocates see Paul revisiting the churches of the first missionary journey (the "Galatian-Phrygian region") before turning west to Ephesus. Defenders of the north Galatian view generally argue that Paul took a more northerly route, a main Roman highway that led through northern Galatia westward through Phrygia and eventually on to Ephesus on the coast of Asia. Obviously, the evidence of Acts is inconclusive. The balance does seem to tip toward north Galatia in that Luke never used the term *Galatia* during Paul's first missionary journey. He reserved it for the second and third journeys, which may indicate that that was when and where (north Galatia) the Galatian churches were established.

The Galatian epistle does not settle the issue either. It is addressed to "the churches in Galatia" (1:2). But Galatia in what sense—ethnically (the "Gauls" of the northern territory) or provincially (people of the Roman province of Galatia)? It has been argued that Paul always used the official Roman provincial nomenclature—Macedonia, Achaia, Asia. That seems to hold true most of the time, but not always. For instance, he always referred to Judea as "Judea" (Rom. 15:31; 2 Cor. 1:16; Gal. 1:22; 1 Thess. 2:14), but Judea was not a province; it was an entity within the province of Syria. His references to Macedonia are no help, since the Roman province of Macedonia and the ancient territory of Macedonia were one and the same. Also, when Paul referred to Achaia, the designation seems to have referred primarily to the Peloponnesus, the ancient Achaian territory, and not to the much larger Roman Province of Achaia.

Paul used the term *Galatians* one more time in the epistle: when he referred to his readers as "foolish Galatians" (3:1). "Galatians" in what sense? In the ethnic sense, or in the official Roman provincial sense? Who would have responded to the term *Galatian* in Paul's day—those who came from the ancient territory of the Gauls, or those who found themselves within the borders of the expansive Roman province? Would people of Antioch have preferred to be called "Galatian" or "Pisidian"? Would Lystrans respond to "Lycaonian" or "Galatian"? Perhaps it isn't an altogether fair analogy to ask if natives of Scotland would prefer to be called "Britons" or "Scots," but it *is* something of the same.

There are two other places in the New Testament where the term *Galatia* occurs. First Peter 1:1 obviously refers to the official province of Galatia, but that says nothing for Luke or Paul's usage. Second Timothy 4:10 speaks of Crescens going to Galatia, but that is no help, since we have no idea to what part of Galatia he went. If anything, 2 Timothy supports Luke's usage in referring to the specific cities of Paul's first missionary journey rather than to the province in which they were located (2 Tim. 3:11).

In my opinion, the evidence seems to tip in the direction of the north Galatian view.[29] We will treat the establishment of the Galatian churches in the context of the second missionary journey. It must be admitted freely that this means Acts gives no account of Paul's work in Galatia. But Luke didn't elaborate on other work as well, like that at Colosse or Illyricum. On the other hand, if one holds strictly to Luke's own usage, he doesn't seem to have considered the churches of the first missionary journey as Galatian; he reserved that term for Paul's second missionary period.

NOTES

1. M. F. Unger, "Archaeology and Paul's Tour of Cyprus," *Bibliotheca Sacra* 117 (1960): 229–233.
2. D. W. J. Gill, "Paul's Travels Through Cyprus (Acts 13:4–12)," *Tyndale Bulletin* 46 (2, 1995): 219–228.
3. For the characterization of Bar-Jesus, I am indebted to H. J. Klauck, "With Paul in Paphos and Lystra: Magic and Paganism in the Acts of the Apostles," *Neotestamentica* 28 (1, 1994): 93–108.
4. For an example, see *Ant.* 20.142–143, which tells of a Cypriot Jewish sorcerer who aided Felix in seducing Drusilla away from her husband. It is unlikely this is the same Cypriot sorcerer as Bar-Jesus.
5. The only exceptions are in his personal testimony in the temple square (22:7) and before Agrippa (26:14), where Paul refers to the words that Jesus spoke at his conversion.
6. Inscriptions have been found which mention a Sergius Paulus (or Paullus)—at Pisidian Antioch, at Soli on northern Cyprus, and at Rome. There are problems with all of them, however, in attempting any linkage with the Sergius Paulus of Acts. See F. F. Bruce, "Chronological Questions in Acts," *Bulletin of the John Ryland's Library* 68 (2, 1986): 279–280.
7. See G. H. Twelftree, "Signs, Wonders, Miracles," in *Dictionary of Paul and His Letters*, ed. G. F. Hawthorne and R. P. Martin (Downers Grove, Ill.: InterVarsity, 1993), 875–877.
8. W. M. Ramsay, *St. Paul the Traveller and Roman Citizen* (London: Hodder and Stoughton, 1897), 93.
9. A. T. Robertson, *Epochs in the Life of Paul* (New York: Scribner's, 1909), 109–110.
10. J. T. Pennell, "Acts xiii.13," *Expository Times* 44 (1932–1933): 476; R. Hughes, "Acts xii.13," *Expository Times* 45 (1933–1934): 44–45.
11. S. Mitchell, "Antioch of Pisidia," *Anchor Bible Dictionary*, ed. D. N. Freedman (New York: Doubleday, 1992), I:264–265.
12. W. M. Ramsay, *The Cities of St. Paul: Their Influence on His Life and Thought* (London: Hodder and Stoughton, 1907), 247–296.
13. It is sometimes argued that salvation in terms of forgiveness is alien to Paul's thought, but surely it is the foundation of his doctrine of justification (obtaining right standing with God). Also, note his explicit references to forgiveness in passages like Romans 4:7; Colossians 1:14; and Ephesians 1:7.
14. Paul's sermon at Antioch is a prime example of the sermons to Jews in Acts which C. H. Dodd saw as the basic form of the early Christian *kerygma* (preaching). It consisted of a summary of the passion events, of Old Testament prophecies pointing to Christ, and of an appeal. See J. B. Polhill, "Kerygma and Didache," *Dictionary of the Later New Testament and its Developments*, ed. R. P. Martin and P. H. Davids (Downers Grove, Ill.: InterVarsity, 1997), 626–629.
15. Josephus (*War* 2. 561) claimed that numerous Gentile women in Damascus attended the synagogue, and the Roman satirist Juvenal (*Satire* 6. 542) complained of how the Roman women were becoming "addicted" to the Jewish religion.

16. For a description of ancient Iconium, see M. F. Unger, "Archaeology and Paul's Visit to Iconium, Lystra and Derbe," *Bibliotheca Sacra* 118 (1961): 107–112. See Also Ramsay, *Cities of St. Paul*, 317–370.

17. For a summary of the different solutions and an even more radical proposal (placing 14:3 in the middle of 13:48), see J. H. Michael, "The Original Position of Acts xv.3," *Expository Times* 40 (1929–1930): 514–516.

18. See the previous discussion of "apostle" in chapter 3, pp. 60–61.

19. For more on Lystra, see Ramsay, *Cities of St. Paul*, 407–419.

20. L. H. Martin, "Gods or Ambassadors of God? Barnabas and Paul in Lystra," *New Testament Studies* 41 (1995): 152–156.

21. W. M. Calder, "Zeus and Hermes at Lystra," *Expositor*, series 7, 10 (1910): 1–6. For the possibility that Zeus and Hermes were the hellenized form of two original Hittite weather gods, see C. Breytenbach, "Zeus und der lebendige Gott: Anmerkungen zu Apostelgeschichte 14.11–17," *New Testament Studies* 39 (1993): 396–413.

22. G. Ogg, "Derbe," *New Testament Studies* 9 (1962–1963): 367–370. See also B. van Elderen, "Some Archaeological Observations on Paul's First Missionary Journey," in *Apostolic History and the Gospel*, ed. W. W. Gasque and R. P. Martin (Grand Rapids: Eerdmans, 1970), 156–161.

23. P. Bowers, "Paul and Religious Propaganda in the First Century," *Novum Testamentum* 22 (4, 1980): 316–323.

24. J. Knox, *Chapters in a Life of Paul* (Nashville: Abingdon, 1950), 106–107.

25. S. K. Stowers, "Social Status, Public Speaking and Private Teaching: The Circumstances of Paul's Preaching Activity," *Novum Testamentum* 26 (1, 1984): 59–82.

26. D. F. Detwiler, "Paul's Approach to the Great Commission in Acts 14:21–23," *Bibliotheca Sacra* 152 (1, 1995): 33–41. See also P. Bowers, "Fulfilling the Gospel: The Scope of the Pauline Mission," *Journal of the Evangelical Theological Society* 30 (2, 1987): 185–198.

27. The following discussion is largely based on my article entitled "Galatia Revisited: The Life-Setting of the Epistle," *Review and Expositor* 69 (4, 1972): 437–443.

28. See W. M. Ramsay, *The Church in the Roman Empire* (New York: G. P. Putnam's Sons, 1893), 13–15.

29. The south Galatian hypothesis continues to have many able advocates. For a well-argued defense, see C. Breytenbach, *Paulus und Barnabas in der Provinz Galatien. Studien zu Apostelgeschichte 13f; 16:6, 18:23 und den Adressaten des Galaterbriefes*, Arbeiten zur Geschichte des antiken Judentums und des Urchristentums, 38 (Leiden: Brill, 1996).

SUGGESTED FURTHER READING

THE FIRST MISSIONARY JOURNEY

Bruce, F. F. *Paul: Apostle of the Heart Set Free*. Grand Rapids: Eerdmans, 1977, pp. 160–172.

Polhill, John B. *Acts*. New American Commentary. Nashville: Broadman, 1992, pp. 287–320.

Ramsay, William M. *The Cities of St. Paul*. London: Hodder and Stoughton, 1907, pp. 247–419.

PAUL'S MISSIONARY STRATEGY

Bowers, W. Paul. "Mission." In *Dictionary of Paul and His Letters*. Ed. G. F. Hawthorne and R. P. Martin. Downers Grove, Ill.: InterVarsity, 1993, pp. 608–619.

O'Brien, P. T. *Gospel and Mission in the Writings of St. Paul*. Grand Rapids: Baker, 1993.

THE NORTH/SOUTH GALATIAN QUESTION

Hansen, G. W. "Galatians, Letter to the." In *Dictionary of Paul and His Letters*, pp. 323–326.

Polhill, J. B. "Galatia Revisited, The Life-Setting of the Epistle," *Review and Expositor* 69 (4, 1972): 437–443.

6

PAUL DEFENDS HIS GENTILE MISSION

$\mathcal{T}$he Antioch mission to Gentiles had been a resounding success. The church there had taken on its own identity—not just a movement within Judaism, but a separate community of "Christians" (Acts 11:26). It is not clear to what extent the Antioch church had separated from the Jewish synagogues. They may have followed the pattern of the Christians in Jerusalem, having their own separate gatherings in homes but continuing to take an active part in the worship of the Jewish community. The Antioch Christians may originally have expected their Gentile converts to follow Jewish proselyte procedure, undergoing circumcision and agreeing to live by the Jewish law. At some point this changed, perhaps under the influence of Paul, perhaps earlier. In any event, Paul and Barnabas had certainly had to witness outside the context of the synagogue on their first missionary journey. Their "turning to the Gentiles" probably involved more than the ethnic composition of their new witness. It involved the *manner* of Gentile inclusion as well. No longer bound to the synagogue protocol regarding proselytes and God-fearers, Paul seems to have abandoned circumcision and the restrictive aspects of the Jewish law as requirements for Gentile converts. Particularly would this have been likely in places like Lystra, where there was no synagogue.

Paul and Barnabas were not alone with respect to the Gentile outreach. Peter may well have come to similar conclusions about requirements for Gentiles in his own experience with the centurion Cornelius (Acts 10:1–11:18). At that time God led Peter to see that no one should be deemed impure or unclean (10:28) and that in Christ God was accepting people "from every nation" (10:35). The coming of the Holy Spirit upon Cornelius and his family and friends convinced Peter that God had accepted them. Peter had them baptized, but there is no indication they were circumcised (10:47–48). Peter had no qualms in dining with the new Gentile converts. But a group of Jerusalem Christians had major problems with his so doing (11:3). Luke called them "those of the circumcision," which probably means those who insisted that all Christians be circumcised, including Gentiles. They represented a conservative Jewish Christian viewpoint that considered Christianity to be a movement *within Judaism*. In their view, Gentile converts to Christ had to undergo the same requirements that proselytes to Judaism had always had to follow—circumcision and complete observance of the Jewish law. The group that opposed Peter in

Jerusalem had to acquiesce when they heard his testimony of how Cornelius and his companions had received the gift of the Spirit (11:15–18). But the issue was not settled. Perhaps they considered Peter's experience with Cornelius as a unique, isolated episode. They do not seem to have considered it as the final word on how Gentiles should be received into the Christian fold. They would raise the question again—at Antioch.

CONFLICT AT ANTIOCH

Paul and Barnabas had not insisted that Gentile converts be circumcised, and evidently the Antioch Christians agreed with them. As more and more Gentiles responded to the Christian message, another related problem began to develop—the question of table fellowship. How could Jewish Christians participate in meals prepared by Gentile Christians without being exposed to ritual defilement? How could they eat with Gentiles and still be "kosher." Both problems came to a head at Antioch. Both resulted from the strong criticism of Christians who came from Jerusalem. Luke tells of their insistence that the Gentiles should be circumcised (Acts 15:1–2a). In what is probably an account of the same occasion, Paul focuses on their criticism of Jewish Christians eating with Gentile Christians (Gal. 2:11–14).

CONVERSION REQUIREMENTS FOR GENTILES (ACTS 15:1–2A)

In the fifteenth chapter of Acts, Luke told of a major conference in Jerusalem which dealt with the issues surrounding Gentile converts. The first two verses set the context. "Certain people" came from Judea to Antioch and started to teach the Christians there that they must be circumcised in order to be saved. They were almost certainly Christians, probably representing the same group whom Luke describes in verse 5 of the same chapter as "believers who belonged to the party of the Pharisees." In turn, they were probably some of the same people of the "circumcised believers" who had criticized Peter over his dealings with Cornelius (Acts 11:2). Their position was logical. They considered Christianity as a sect of Judaism. The apostles were all Jews. With few exceptions, the converts in Jerusalem, both "Hebrews" and "Hellenists," were Jews. Jesus was himself a Jew, the Messiah promised *to Israel*. They saw Christians as the true "way" within Israel, but definitely *within Israel*. What distinguished Christians from other Israelites was their belief in Jesus as Messiah. But in all other respects they were still Jews. From ancient times, they argued, Judaism had provided for Gentile converts. They were to become proselytes, which involved circumcision and submission to the full provisions of the Mosaic law. This was regular procedure. Any Pharisee would have argued this. It is no surprise that these Christians of a Pharisaic orientation insisted on the provisions of the law for Gentile proselytes (15:5).

Paul and Barnabas saw it differently and came into a sharp debate with them (v. 2a). The Christian Pharisaic position was tolerable for limited Gentile conversions. There had always been the occasional convert to Judaism. Some of these in turn became Christians, like Nicolas, a proselyte from Antioch (Acts 6:6). But such conversions to Judaism seem to have been few and far between. To insist that Gentiles undergo Jewish proselyte procedure was to insist that one had to become a Jew first in order to be a Christian. To do so would have *guaranteed* that Christianity would remain a sect within Judaism and never have any real impact on Gentiles. Paul knew this. He was convinced that God was reaching out to the Gentiles in Jesus Christ.

He also knew that such restrictive provisions of the Torah as circumcision and the food laws would in effect close the door to most Gentiles. Such provisions had always served to maintain Jewish identity. Should the Christians have insisted upon them, it would have ensured that Christianity would stay a strictly Jewish movement with little impact on the Gentile world.

Largely restricted to Jews in the Roman world, circumcision was a mark of Jewish exclusivism. It was both misunderstood and ridiculed by Gentiles. Like the Greeks, Romans tended to idealize the human body and considered circumcision a revolting mutilation of the flesh. The practice was the frequent butt of Gentile jokes. For example, the first-century Roman satirist Martial told the story about a comic actor who wore a sheath over his sex organ. Everyone assumed this was to serve as a check from sexual overindulgence, which might impair his voice. Such proved not to be the case. One day on the exercise ground the sheath fell off: "Behold, he was circumcised," to his chagrin and to everyone else's amusement.[1] Jewish distinctives were seen as sheer superstition by the Greeks and Romans. Particularly singled out was the Jewish insistence on three things: circumcision, their strict Sabbath observance, and their food laws. Gentiles found the Jewish refusal to eat pork especially incomprehensible.

All of this is to say that the very laws which preserved Jewish identity were the ones found most offensive by the Gentiles. To have insisted on such provisions for Gentile converts was tantamount to requiring them to leave their homes and move to the Jewish quarter of town. As A. D. Nock observed, it was hard to keep oneself covered in a public bath house.[2] Evidently, very early in his mission Paul abandoned such requirements for his Gentile converts. His own conversion had convinced him that Christ was central and that Christ was for Gentiles as well as for Jews. He could not allow such Jewish distinctives to subvert the mission to the Gentiles. But Paul was also concerned about the mission to the Jews. He acknowledged that there was a problem from the Jewish Christian perspective, and he willingly agreed to go to Jerusalem to settle the matter.

TABLE FELLOWSHIP (GAL. 2:11–18)

In Galatians 2:11–14 Paul spoke of an occasion when he had to oppose Peter "to his face." Peter had been eating with the Gentiles at Antioch but withdrew when he was challenged by some people "from James." The passage *follows* Paul's account of the conference in Jerusalem where the Gentile mission was at issue. It is quite possible that the incident actually *preceded* the Jerusalem Conference and was in fact its cause.[3] Nothing in the Greek text of Galatians 2:11 would necessitate that the incident should follow the events of verses 1–10. Paul simply stated, "When Peter came to Antioch, I opposed him." In the first two chapters of Galatians Paul argued his *independence* of the apostles in Jerusalem. He began his argument by showing how few his visits to Jerusalem had been, how brief they were, and how independently motivated. This argument runs from Galatians 1:13 through 2:10. Verse 11 of chapter 2 begins a new argument: not only was he not "instructed" by the Jerusalem apostles; on one occasion he even opposed the leading apostle Peter to his face, in front of everyone. This was Paul's "crowning" argument. He saved it for last.[4]

After Paul and Barnabas returned from their first missionary journey, the Gentile Christian community of Antioch must have flourished, evidently to the point where Jewish Christians were invited to share in fellowship meals in the homes of Gentile

Christians. Of course, there would be no problem for Gentile Christians to participate in a meal prepared by Jewish Christians. The latter would prepare the meal in a proper "kosher" fashion in accordance with the the food laws. It was only when Jews were invited to Gentile meals that problems occurred. This seems to have happened at Antioch. Peter at first had no problem with this arrangement. He had eaten with Gentiles before at the home of Cornelius, and God had showed him on that occasion that he should call no food—or person—unclean. So Peter joined the Gentile Christian table fellowship at Antioch.

But things changed when persons came "from James." Under pressure from them, Peter withdrew from the table, fearing those of "the circumcision group" (Gal. 2:12). The "circumcision group" could refer simply to Jews. More likely it refers to the conservative Jewish Christian group who insisted that Gentile converts should be circumcised and live by the Jewish law, the same people who confronted Peter over Cornelius (Acts 11:2), the same group that Acts describes as insisting on circumcision of Gentile converts (Acts 15:2, 5). They were the conservative Jewish Christians of Jerusalem who insisted that Jewish Christians should be faithful in all respects to the Jewish law and that Gentile Christians should convert to Judaism and keep the law as well.

In what sense did they represent James? James was the brother of Jesus. He had become head of the Jerusalem elders after the apostles had begun to leave the city on mission (cp. Acts 12:17). He continued on as leader of the Jerusalem church. From Acts 21:18–25 it is clear that James maintained a stance of strict fidelity to the Jewish law in order to witness effectively to the Jewish community. Later Christian tradition bears out this reputation. The early church historian Eusebius quotes sources which represent James as being the most law-abiding of all the Jews, known as the "just and pious" one, the "pillar" of the Jewish people. It was said that he prayed so often on his knees in the temple that he wore callouses on his knees and thus was given the nickname "camel-kneed" (Eusebius, *Ecclesiastical History*, 2.23).

These traditions have obviously been embellished over the years but probably go back to a reliable memory that James had been faithful to the Jewish law. He was faithful for the same reason that Paul lived as a Jew when among Jews—in order to win them (1 Cor. 9:20). It was likely this concern which brought the people from James to Antioch. The law-free stance of the Antioch Gentiles presented enough of a problem to James's mission to the Jews. But when Jewish Christians like Peter and Barnabas disregarded the food laws, that presented a real threat. A reputation for playing fast and loose with the law could do real damage to the mission to the Jews. James would not have endorsed the insistence on Gentile circumcision that some were calling for; his subsequent stance on the matter in Jerusalem makes that quite clear. He would, however, have had real concern about the matter of table fellowship. He was the one who ultimately developed the strategy for dealing with the problem.

We are used to looking at the Antioch incident from a "Gentile perspective," that is, from Paul's viewpoint. We should, however, be fair to James, Peter, and Barnabas for their sensitivity to the *Jewish* mission. Just as Paul would never have made any real inroads on the Gentile community had he insisted on circumcision, so the Jerusalem Christians would never have reached the Jews with the gospel had they been seen as rejecting the Torah. And Jews did place great emphasis on the food laws. They were central in maintaining Jewish identity and preserving the purity of the land. The rabbinic scholar Jacob Neusner estimates that of the 341 rabbinical rulings which are related to the Pharisees, some 229 (67 percent) involve food laws.[5] Particularly acute was the problem of eating with Gentiles. Gentiles were considered unclean. Not only did they eat unclean foods, they did not maintain themselves in a state of ritual purity. Jews seem to have avoided invitations to eat with Gentiles.

Jubilees 22:16 may be an extreme statement, but it reflects the sentiments of many Jews in Paul's day: "Separate yourself from the Gentiles, and do not eat with them, and do not perform deeds like theirs, and do not become associates of theirs, because their deeds are defiled, and all of their ways are contaminated, and despicable, and abominable." Gentile writers as well indicate that Jews usually did not dine with Gentiles. For instance, the Roman historian Tacitus stated that Jews generally ate "separately" (*History*, 5.5). Peter, James, and Barnabas do not seem to have personally borne this disdain toward Gentiles, but they witnessed to a people who often did.

Paul, of course, could only see Peter and Barnabas's stance as hypocritical. They had eaten with Gentiles; now they withdrew. Things would have been better had they never eaten with the Gentiles in the first place. "You are a Jew, yet you live like a Gentile and not like a Jew. How is it, then, that you force Gentiles to follow Jewish customs?" (v. 14). By withdrawing from table fellowship, Peter was in effect telling the Gentiles that they would have to live by the Jewish food laws. But Peter had already disregarded those same food laws himself by eating with the Gentiles. In so doing, he had tacitly admitted that they weren't important for Christian fellowship. His stance was totally inconsistent, and it was on that basis that Paul challenged him.

It is not clear in Galatians 2 where Paul's words to Peter at Antioch end and where Paul begins to address the Galatians directly. Possibly Paul's words to Peter end at verse 14, or at verse 15, as many scholars maintain. It is also quite possible that verses 16–18 continue Paul's rebuke of Peter at Antioch. If so, Paul's line of thought would have run something like this: Your behavior, Peter, would indicate that the Gentiles are still sinners, and we Jews cannot mingle with them (v. 15). But, the truth of the matter is that neither of us, Jew or Gentile, is right with God ("justified") through "observing the law." We are only made right through "faith in Christ" (v. 16). This, of course, is Paul's teaching on "justification by faith," and we will deal with this at length in the chapter on Romans. Suffice it at this point to note that "justification" means to become acceptable to God and is a manner of talking about salvation. Paul is stating here that salvation is either through "works of the law," or it is through faith in Christ.

Since Peter agreed with Paul that salvation is through Christ, then he had to admit that we have been made right with God through Christ. We are no longer "sinners." Through Christ, we are "righteous," acceptable to God. But by withdrawing from table fellowship with the Gentile Christians, Peter was treating them as if they were still "Gentile sinners," since they were not right by the measuring stick of the Jewish law. Further, Paul argued, if we have sought our salvation in Christ and then are *still* found to be sinners (and *not* right with God), then Christ has become an agent not of salvation but of sin (v. 17).[6] In essence, that was how Peter was treating the Gentiles—like sinners, as if they had not been made right with God through Christ. He was in effect denying salvation by Christ and affirming salvation by the Jewish law. But Peter didn't agree with this position any more than Paul did. He, too, had put all that behind him. He, Paul, and the Gentiles had all died to the law and now lived in Christ (vv. 19–20). But Peter's treating the Gentiles like sinners had denied all of that as if the law still had validity. What, then, did Paul mean in these verses by "works of the law"? The context makes it clear—things like circumcision and food laws.[7] These were the real offense of the law for Paul, the elements of Jewish exclusivism which the law represented. This was why it could never be a basis for salvation for the apostle to the Gentiles.

A number of scholars maintain that the Antioch incident marked a permanent breach between Paul on the one hand and Peter, Barnabas, and the church at Antioch on the other.[8] One can only hold this view by considering this incident as occurring *after* the Jerusalem Conference. Even then, it goes against the evidence of Acts, which shows Paul as being sponsored throughout the period of his three missions by the congregation at Antioch (cp. Acts 18:23). Likewise, Paul's epistles reflect his continuing efforts to maintain cordial relations with Peter (1 Cor. 1:12; 3:22) and Barnabas (1 Cor. 9:6; Col. 4:10).[9] Of course, if one views this incident as *precipitating* the Jerusalem Conference, as is here being argued, the Antioch incident was a creative moment in the life of the early church. It focused the issues arising from the Gentile mission—requirements for Gentile converts and a basis for fellowship between Jewish and Gentile Christians. Peter and Barnabas would be on Paul's side at the Jerusalem Conference—Barnabas attesting to God's presence in their mission to the Gentiles, and Peter defending Paul's law-free gospel for the Gentiles. Paul's presence at the conference is perhaps the most significant of all. He did not *have* to go. He went at God's leading and of his own volition. Perhaps he, too, came to see something of Peter's point in yielding to the people from James. He, too, was concerned for the *total* mission of the church and for its unity. It had become clear at Antioch that there were problems. The Jerusalem Conference was convened to address them.

THE JERUSALEM CONFERENCE

We have argued that Galatians 2:1–10 and Acts 15:2b–35 refer to the same event, a conference in Jerusalem which was primarily precipitated by the success of Paul's Gentile mission. There were two main questions to consider: (1) what requirements should be placed on Gentile converts? and (2) what basis could be established for enabling fellowship between Jewish and Gentile Christians, especially participation in meals together?

There are admittedly problems with seeing Galatians 2 and Acts 15 as referring to the same occasion. Galatians speaks of a private meeting between Paul and the Jerusalem leaders, Acts of a larger assembly. In Galatians, Titus accompanies Paul and Barnabas. He is not mentioned in Acts. In Galatians, Paul is requested to "remember the poor"; Acts is silent on this. On the other hand, there are matters in Acts which are not present in Paul's Galatian account—the speeches of Peter and James, the "apostolic decrees." Still, there are significant similarities between the two, which seem to outweigh the differences. Both accounts deal with a conference in Jerusalem over Paul's Gentile mission, with the issue of circumcision arising in each. For the most part, the same persons are central in both accounts—Paul and Barnabas, Peter and James. Finally, both arrive at the same central solution—acknowledgement of the legitimacy of Paul's mission to the Gentiles.[10]

PAUL'S ACCOUNT (GAL. 2:1–10)

Paul says that he went to Jerusalem "fourteen years later," that is, fourteen years after his previous visit to Jerusalem or about sixteen or seventeen years after his conversion. The date would have been around A.D. 48. Paul took with him Barnabas and Titus. Titus is not mentioned in Acts as accompanying Paul to the conference. For that matter, Titus is not mentioned in Acts at all. Apart from the epistle addressed to him and a brief reference in 2 Timothy 4:10, Titus is only mentioned elsewhere in the New Testament in Paul's second letter to the Corinthians. He is indeed quite prominent in that epistle, having served as Paul's representative with the Corinthians in a time of very strained relations between the church and the apostle. We have no idea when or where Titus joined Paul. He must have been an early Gentile convert. Tradition has him coming from Antioch, but that is uncertain and probably was based on Galatians 2:1–3.[11]

Paul says that he went to Jerusalem in response to a "revelation" (Gal. 2:2). Attempts to tie this to a specific incident in Paul's life, such as his temple vision (Acts 22:17–21), are futile. Paul's main concern in Galatians was to make it clear to the Galatians that he was not "summoned" to Jerusalem but went of his own volition. His whole gospel was "by revelation" (Gal. 1:16). He was not commissioned by the Jerusalem church but was called by Christ to be the apostle to the Gentiles. In fact, it was his concern to have his Gentile calling acknowledged by the Jerusalem leaders that led him to Jerusalem on this particular occasion.

Paul's main concern was that his Gentile mission would not be "in vain" (v. 2). How would it be "in vain"? It would be in vain if the "circumcision party" had its way and succeeded in making Jewish proselytes of all Paul's Gentile converts. That would just about kill the entire endeavor. This is why Paul brought up the issue of Titus's circumcision at this point. Titus was not "compelled" to be circumcised (v. 3). The statement is totally ambiguous. Was Paul stating flatly that Titus was not circumcised? Or was he saying that he *was* circumcised but was not *forced* to be? Did Titus submit to circumcision of his own volition?[12] Did Paul at this early stage in his missionary career allow Titus's circumcision in a momentary yielding to the pressure of the Judaizing group in Jerusalem?[13] It seems unlikely that Paul would have brought up the whole embarrassing situation in his Galatian epistle were Titus actually circumcised. Paul was endeavoring to persuade the Galatians *not* to be circumcised. He brought Titus into the picture because he was *not* circumcised, as an example to the Galatians that *they* as well not submit to the rite as the Judaizers were urging them to do.

This seems to be what the reference to the false brothers in verse 4 was all about. They were probably some of the Pharisaic Christians, the circumcisers who had confronted Peter over the conversion of Cornelius and who had insisted on circumcising the Gentile Christians at Antioch. Paul would not grant them any legitimacy at all; they were *false* brothers, *spies* who had *sneaked in* trying to rob others of their freedom. Verses 4 through 6 are extremely disjointed in the Greek text. Paul was so choked with rage at the circumcisers that he almost lost his train of thought. The NIV seems to preserve the thrust of Paul's argument. He wished to lay his mission before the Jerusalem leaders. All was going well in his private meeting with the leaders. Then the false brothers slipped in. *They* brought up the question of circumcision. *They* insisted that Paul's Gentile converts should be circumcised. *They* wanted to take the freedom out of Paul's law-free gospel. Paul did not yield to their pressure for a moment. Neither did the Jerusalem leaders.

Verses 7 and 8 spell out the agreement reached in Jerusalem. A division of territory was worked out, so to speak, although the agreement was probably more ethnographical than geographical. Peter was to continue his ministry to the Jews, just as Christ had called him to do. Paul was acknowledged as the minister to the Gentiles. Paul had received what he had come to Jerusalem for in the first place—acknowledgement of his Gentile apostolate, *on his terms*: nothing was added to his gospel for the Gentiles.[14]

Some have suggested that verses 7 and 8 may be an official extract from the Jerusalem meeting. It is interesting that Paul refers to Peter as "Peter" in these two verses—and only in these two verses. Elsewhere in Galatians (and also in his other epistles) Paul calls him "Cephas." It is argued that Paul characteristically called him by his Aramaic name Cephas but that in these two verses, the "official Jerusalem record," he used the more familiar "Peter."[15] In any event, verse 9 reiterates the agreement. The "pillar apostles" in Jerusalem gave Paul and Barnabas the "right hand of fellowship," acknowledging the legitimacy of Paul's divine call as apostle to the Gentiles.

One cannot help but note Paul's reticence in referring to the Jerusalem leadership throughout this passage. Four times he refers to them as those who were "reputed to be" or "seemed to be" of importance (vv. 2, 6a, 6b, and 9). The Greek word is *dokeō*, a word which often implies skepticism. Paul used the same word in Galatians 6:3 to describe someone who "thinks" he is something when in reality he is nothing. Paul obviously had an eye to those at Galatia who were holding up the Jerusalem apostles as models—apostles to the Jews, apostles to the circumcision. Paul did not want to grant them undue status; there were those among his Galatian Gentile converts who were already doing so.[16]

There was *one* provision the Jerusalem leadership requested. They asked that Paul and Barnabas continue to "remember the poor." This was no burden for Paul. He and Barnabas had already brought such a collection to Jerusalem in the past (Acts 11:28–30). Paul was "eager" to do so again. It would in fact be his consuming passion at the end of his third mission. It would be not only a provision for the needy but even more an expression of unity between Paul's Gentile churches and the Jewish Christian churches of Judea.[17]

LUKE'S ACCOUNT (ACTS 15:2B–35)

In Galatians Paul insisted that he went to Jerusalem of his own accord, "in response to a revelation." Luke says that the Antioch church "appointed" Paul and Barnabas and "some other believers" to go to Jerusalem to consult with the apostles and elders there about the issue of Gentile circumcision (15:2b). Galatians and Acts are in agreement that the initiative for the meeting lay with Paul and/or Antioch, not with the Jerusalem church. It wasn't a question of Jerusalem calling Paul on the carpet. It was a concern for the recognition of the Gentile mission and the unity of the church's *total* mission—to Gentiles *and* to Jews—that prompted the consultation in Jerusalem.

Verses 3–4 are something of a digression. They relate how Paul and Barnabas reported the success of their mission in the churches along the way on the long journey (250 miles) from Antioch to Jerusalem. The apostles visited the Christian communities that had been established earlier—the churches of Phoenicia, founded by the Hellenists (Acts 11:19), and those in Samaria, first evangelized by Philip (Acts 8:4–25). Arriving in Jerusalem, they gave their mission report there as well (Acts 15:4). The Lord's presence in their work was very important to their success in Jerusalem. It was hard for anyone to object in the face of God's obvious blessing of Paul and Barnabas's work. The circumcision party had found it hard to object about Peter's witness to Cornelius with the evidence of the Spirit's having descended upon them (11:18). They also found it difficult to protest in Jerusalem with the obvious presence of God in the work of Paul and Barnabas. But that did not prevent their raising the issue. As at Antioch, they stated their firm position that Gentile converts must undergo full proselyte procedure, including circumcision and observance of the Mosaic Law (15:5).

Luke describes this Judaizing group within the Jerusalem church as those "who belonged to the party of the Pharisees." Evidently a number of Pharisees joined the Christian movement. Paul was himself a Pharisee become Christian. Throughout Acts Pharisees often appear in a positive light. Sometimes they were the defenders of the Christians against the Jewish officials, who were usually Sadducees. The Pharisee Gamaliel, for example, warded off the execution of the apostles in the meeting of the Sanhedrin (Acts 5:33–39), and the Pharisees on the Sanhedrin later sided with Paul against the Sadducees (Acts 23:6–10). The latter incident is particularly instructive. The Pharisees defended Paul because they shared his belief that God would raise the dead in the end time, a doctrine which the Sadducees rejected. Pharisees shared other views with the Christians, like the hope in a coming Messiah. It is not surprising that many eventually embraced Christ as Messiah. As Pharisees, however, they would have continued to observe the Torah in the strictest terms. And the Torah provided that Gentile converts should be circumcised and take the law on their own shoulders. No one understood these believers from the Pharisees better than Paul. He had been one himself.

The Acts account gives every appearance of a more or less public or "plenary" session, with all the apostles and elders present. There may well have been a more private meeting between Paul and the Jerusalem "pillars," as is indicated by Galatians. We will attempt no harmonization but will take each account on its own terms. The version in Acts falls into four main parts: the speech of Peter (vv. 6–11), the speech of James (vv. 12–21), the final agreement drawn up in an official document (vv. 22–29), and the informing of the Syrian and Cilician churches of the agreement (vv. 30–35).

The speech of Peter (15:6–11). The position of the Pharisaic believers provoked considerable debate over the issue of Gentile acceptance (v. 6). But it was Peter who seems to have spoken the decisive word. Peter referred back to his experience with the Gentile God-fearer Cornelius (Acts 10:1–11:18). At that time God had shown Peter through the vision of the sheet filled with animals that no *person* is unclean in God's eyes. God led Peter to share the gospel with Cornelius and his friends. God sent his Holy Spirit upon Cornelius and the Gentiles gathered with him. Peter told the assembly that the experience of the Spirit was "just as" it had been with "us" (v. 8), a clear reference to Pentecost. God "made no distinction between us and them, for he purified their hearts by faith." Who could deny the Gentile Pentecost? Who could reject the work of the Spirit? Probably some of the same Pharisaic Christians who were now insisting on circumcision of Paul's Gentile converts had been among those who confronted Peter after his acceptance of Cornelius (11:3). They had not been able to deny the work of the Spirit in the instance of Cornelius (11:18). Peter was reminding them of that occasion and stating that things had not changed. God's acceptance of Cornelius was not an exception; it was the *rule*. Neither circumcision nor keeping of the law counted but the "cleansing of their hearts by faith."

Peter's position was clear: do not put the yoke of the law on the Gentiles (v. 10). He was thinking of the law particularly in its ceremonial aspects—circumcision and the food laws, the sort of Jewish distinctives that had already caused the rift between Jewish and Gentile Christians at Antioch. But what did Peter mean by speaking of the law as "a yoke that neither we nor our fathers have been able to bear" (v. 10)? He was using a term which the Jews often used to describe the Torah—not as a burden but as a yoke which bound them to God's will.[18] On the other hand, such provisions of the law as the intricate rules of purity *were* more than most Jews could bear. Those who observed them *in toto* were probably few; the average Jew probably didn't even attempt it. If Jews found difficulties with the law, how much more would this be true of Gentiles? Many of the ritual provisions of the law would virtually exclude them from the larger Gentile community if they lived by them. Peter was certainly not advocating the abandonment of the law *for Jewish Christians*. The law represented God's covenant with Israel. Its ritual aspects were a part of the Jewish heritage. The law was central to their identity as a people. But the law held no such meaning for Gentiles. Further, it was not a basis for salvation, anyway—for Gentile *or* for Jew.

Peter's final statement was his most striking: "We believe it is through the grace of our Lord Jesus that we are saved, just as they are" (v. 11). The bottom line is that in Christ Jew and Gentile are on an equal footing. Neither is saved by law; both are saved by grace. Peter's words sounded strikingly like Paul's words of rebuke to him at Antioch. Salvation is by faith and not by law (vv. 9–10; cp. Gal. 2:16). Jew and Gentile alike are saved solely by God's grace (v. 11; cp. Gal. 2:21). Peter seems to have learned his lesson well at Antioch. The incident may have supplied him with the words for his defense of Paul at the Jerusalem Conference.

The speech of James (vv. 12–21). Paul and Barnabas were the next to speak (v. 12). They did not offer any defense of their position or any polemic against the circumcisers. They only bore their witness to the "signs and wonders" God had worked among the Gentiles through them. In Acts, the expression "signs and wonders" is shorthand for the work of the Spirit. Just as the coming of the Spirit upon Cornelius and his friends marked their acceptance by God (Acts 11:17–18), so the Spirit's movement in the lives of the Gentiles in the course of Paul and Barnabas's mission was a certain sign that God was accepting them as well—and he was doing so without circumcision or any other strings attached.

The main speakers at the Jerusalem Conference each added their own distinct contribution to the discussion. Paul and Barnabas attested to God's presence in their mission to the Gentiles. That established the basic evidence that in Christ God was accepting the Gentiles as part of his people. Peter established the basic principle that Gentiles should remain Gentiles when they converted to Christianity. They should not have to be circumcised or live by the Jewish law. In short, they should not have to become Jews in order to be Christians. Thus, Peter dealt with the first issue that had been raised in the conflict at Antioch—the question of requirements for Gentile converts. His answer: no stipulations, only faith in Christ. James dealt with the second issue that had surfaced at Antioch, the problem of social contact between Jewish and Gentile Christians. He offered a solution that called for certain minimum observations on the part of the Gentiles that would facilitate fellowship between the two groups of Christians.

The main two leadership groups in Jerusalem were the apostles and the elders. They comprised the deliberative body at the Jerusalem Conference (vv. 6, 22). Peter was the leading apostle; James the ruling elder. Appropriately, each served as spokesperson for his group. James was in basic agreement with Peter. He acknowledged the legitimacy of Peter's experience with Cornelius. He saw it as clear evidence that God was now taking for himself a people from among the Gentiles (v. 14). He then offered scriptural proof to undergird this observation. James quoted Amos 9:11–12, which speaks of God's eschatological restoration of his people. The prophet stated that David's house would be rebuilt, that the true remnant would seek the Lord, and that the Gentiles would be included in God's people. James presented the text as a prophecy of the Messiah. He saw it as particularly appropriate to the current circumstances, because it alluded to the inclusion of the Gentiles. It furnished a scriptural basis for what was now occurring—God's inclusion of the Gentiles among the people of Christ Messiah. Verse 19 is very terse, but basically it means the same thing as Peter's words in verse 10: Gentiles should be presented with no difficulties—no need for circumcision and the law (cp. v. 28). The leading apostle and the leading elder were in agreement on the first issue.

James now presented a suggested solution to the second issue, the problem of table fellowship between Jewish and Gentile Christians. He suggested that the Gentiles be requested to abstain from four things: (1) from food polluted by idols (lit., "from the abominations of idols"), (2) from sexual immorality, (3) from strangled meat, and (4) from blood (v. 20). Of the four, three relate to food. "Strangled meat" and "blood" are virtually the same thing—meat which has not had the blood drained from it. Gentiles loved their "red meat," but Jewish food laws required that the blood of the animal be drained from meat before consumption. Strangled meat would be that from which no blood had been drained. (Animals were strangled precisely to preserve the blood in the meat.) The only "nonfood" item of the four was sexual immorality. It is even possible that *this* prohibition was primarily intended in a ritual sense, as forbidding the "defiling" sexual relationships condemned in the Old Testament (such things as bestiality and incest).[19] The source for these prohibitions is often discussed. They are sometimes traced to the "Noachic" commands, seven rules required of resident aliens in Israel designed to facilitate their interaction with Jews and prevent their polluting the land. The Noachic rules are found in the later rabbinic literature. The four suggested by James may be an early form of the Noachic provisions. One need go no further than the Holiness Code of the Old Testament, however. All four of the prohibitions suggested by James are found in Leviticus 17 and 18.

The four "decrees" are found extensively in various configurations in later Christianity, but usually with more of a moral than a ritual application. The first tendency in this direction occurs in the textual tradition of Acts. One manuscript of Acts (codex Beza) omits "strangled meat," adds the negative form of the golden rule, and has "idolatry" rather than "food polluted by idols." It thus ends up with four *moral* prohibitions: against idolatry, immorality, "blood" (viewed as "murder"), and doing something to someone you would not wish done to yourself.[20]

The later moralistic version of the decrees reflects a time when the church had become primarily Gentile. The problem of Jewish and Gentile relationships no longer existed, and the original ritual necessity for the decrees was no longer understood.

After suggesting the four ritual provisions, James concluded his speech by noting that from early times there had been a Jewish presence "in every city" where the law of Moses was preached and read on every Sabbath (v. 21). Just how this statement connects with the decrees is uncertain. Perhaps James meant that the suggestions he was making were really something neither burdensome nor surprising for Gentiles who had contact with the synagogues. Resident aliens in Israel and God-fearers in the Diaspora synagogues would be familiar with the law of Moses and the sort of ritual provision found there which provided a basis for interaction between Jews and Gentiles.

The official document (15:22–29). The whole assembly quickly concurred with James's recommendation. The circumcision party were probably not happy, but there was little they could do. They were outsmarted and perhaps not even a part of the deliberations. They did not give up, however. They would continue to ravage Paul's churches for years to come. The apostles and elders, however, were of one mind with James. They would not burden the Gentiles with circumcision and Torah, but they would follow James's suggestions for enabling fellowship. To make the matter official, they determined to address a formal letter to the Gentile congregations of Antioch, Syria, and Cilicia. They appointed official delegates to deliver the letter.

The two delegates who were chosen were Judas Barsabbas and Silas. We know nothing more of Judas than his role in this incident. Much more is known of Silas. Silas is a shortened form of the name Silvanus. Silas/Silvanus replaced Barnabas as Paul's partner on his second missionary journey. He is mentioned frequently in Acts in the course of that mission. Paul mentions him several times in his epistles (1 Thess. 1:1; 2 Thess. 1:1; 2 Cor. 1:19). Acts 16:37 implies that he, like Paul, was a Roman citizen. It is interesting to note how Barnabas was originally sent to Antioch in an official capacity by the Jerusalem church (Acts 11:22). He eventually became Paul's traveling companion. Likewise, Silas was an official representative of the Jerusalem congregation. He, too, became Paul's missionary partner. In this respect, Paul maintained a close, if not an official, relationship with the Jerusalem church.

The official letter composed by the Jerusalem congregation has all the marks of a formal Greek letter—much more formal than Paul's own epistles.[21] It begins with a salutation, which denotes the apostles and elders as the senders and the Gentile brothers of Antioch, Syria, and Cilicia as the recipients. Then comes the word *greetings* (Gk. *chairein*), the usual word of salutation in a Greek letter, as customary as our word *dear* (v. 23). The body of the letter follows. Here for the first time we learn that the "men from Judea" (v. 1) who had stirred up the circumcision controversy at Antioch were not official representatives of Jerusalem. In fact, the apostles and elders reflected a degree of annoyance with them (v. 24). Verses 26 and 27 designate the official representatives of the church. In a sense Paul and Barnabas are included, as participants in the conference and representatives of Antioch. The two Jerusalem delegates Judas and Silas are then introduced. Verse 27 accurately expresses the custom with ancient letters. Letters were often designed more to introduce the bearers than to give a full communication. The bearers were the real communicators of the intended message. The letter was written to commend their trustworthiness. Judas and Silas would inform the congregations in person of the full procedures that went on in Jerusalem; the letter offers only a sketch.

Verse 28 is the first time in the chapter to state unequivocally that Gentiles would be subject to no other requirements than the four "decrees." Verse 29 proceeds to outline the four with one minor variation from James's list in verse 20. It speaks of "food sacrificed to idols," which is somewhat less ambiguous than James's "polluted by idols." The polite tone of the letter should be noted. Verse 28 literally speaks of "necessary things," not "decrees." Verse 29 says that the Gentiles will "do well" if they observe these things. They are not given as an imposition laid on the Gentiles (the "yoke" which Peter urged against) so much as a *modus vivendi*, a provision for social interaction between Jewish and Gentile Christians. The issue of table fellowship was no small thing. It was in the context of the fellowship meal that Christians observed the Lord's Supper. Table fellowship symbolized the unity of the faith of the early church around its one Lord. There was give-and-take at the Jerusalem Conference. The Jerusalem leaders granted Paul the legitimacy of his law-free Gentile mission. The decrees requested the Gentiles to adjust to Jewish-Christian scruples to the degree that table fellowship would be possible.

Informing the churches (15:30–35). The narrative of the Jerusalem Conference is rounded off by verses 30–35. This concluding section centers wholly around Antioch. The letter was addressed to the churches of Syria and Cilicia as well. Antioch was the capital of Syria. The Syrian churches were probably closely connected to Antioch, probably its missions. Judas and Silas may have shared the letter and the decrees with the churches throughout Syria. Later Paul and Silas would travel to Cilicia, at which time they introduced the congregations to the decrees (15:41; 16:4). This raises the question of when the Cilician churches originated. Were they the product of Antioch's witness or of Paul during his "silent years"? Either is possible, or perhaps both.

It is often noted that Paul does not seem to refer to the decrees in his epistles. One natural reason is that they were primarily directed to the local churches of Syria and Cilicia, not those of Paul's wider mission.[22] Another factor is that table fellowship would not have been a problem in primarily Gentile churches. Many of Paul's congregations were almost exclusively Gentile. On the other hand, Paul sometimes did take a position in his letters which echoed the sentiments if not the actual letter of the decrees. His position on sexual morality in 1 Corinthians 5 may reflect the decrees, as well as his words about idol meat in 1 Corinthians 8–10. The latter particularly reflects the spirit of the decrees. A believer is to refuse to eat meat when it causes offense to others. This reflects the same social setting of a shared meal that the decrees addressed.

RESULTS OF THE JERUSALEM CONFERENCE

It would be hard to overestimate the importance of the Jerusalem Conference for Paul's subsequent mission. For one thing, Paul was recognized as the apostle to the Gentiles. He was encouraged by the Jerusalem leaders to continue in his effort to reach the Gentiles for Christ. Even more significantly, the basis of Gentile acceptance was established. Paul's principle of "faith in Christ alone" was acknowledged. Gentiles would be required neither to be circumcised nor to live by the Torah. This constituted a major concession on the part of the Jerusalem church. They had nothing to gain by it; they only stood to lose. It was a radical step and would not please the Jewish community. Acts 21:17–21 confirms the sort of difficulty this "law free" reputation of Paul's mission presented for the Jerusalem Christian witness to the Jews.

At the Jerusalem Conference Paul received the "right hand of fellowship" from the Jerusalem "pillars" (Gal. 2:9). This was important to Paul. It was his concern for his Gentile mission that led him to the Jerusalem meeting in the first place. He wanted recognition for his mission; he did not wish to have run "in vain" (Gal. 2:2). Paul continued to cherish and to nurture his relationship with the Jerusalem church. Acts pictures him as "going up" to Jerusalem at the end of every mission. He took Barnabas and Silas as his missionary partners; they both represented the Jerusalem church. He pictured his ministry as beginning *in Jerusalem* and spreading as far as Illyricum (Rom. 15:19). And at the end of his mission in the east he gave himself almost obsessively to gathering a collection for the saints in Jerusalem. He risked his life to take it, but it represented the very center of his missionary vision—the unity of Gentile and Jew in Jesus Christ.

NOTES

1. Martial, *Epigrams*, 7.82.
2. A. D. Nock, *St. Paul* (New York: Harper and Brothers, 1937), 104.
3. Those scholars who argue that the Jerusalem Conference of Galatians 2:1–10 took place in connection with the famine visit of Acts 11:28–30 usually also place the incident of Galatians 2:11–14 before Acts 15, which they see as a later second Jerusalem meeting over circumcision. For example, see F. F. Bruce, *Paul: Apostle of the Heart Set Free* (Grand Rapids: Eerdmans, 1977), 173–177.
4. Luedemann sees Acts 15 and Galatians 2:1–10 as referring to the same meeting, but he also sees the incident of Galatians 2:11–14 as *preceding* the conference. He argues from the canons of ancient rhetoric that it is Paul's closing argument, the "rhetorical cause" for the Jerusalem Conference. See Gerd Luedemann, *Paul: Apostle to the Gentiles. Studies in Chronology* (Philadelphia: Fortress, 1984), 75–77. The same position is taken by J. D. Hester, "The Use and Influence of Rhetoric in Galatians 2:1–14," *Theologische Zeitschrift* 42 (1986): 386–408. To see the incident as *following* the conference of Acts 15 would indicate that the "decrees" did not settle the issue of table fellowship at all. Many scholars, however, place the incident soon after the Jerusalem Conference. For example, see A. T. Robertson, *Epochs in the Life of Paul* (New York: Scribners, 1909), 134–136. Others would place the incident much later—at the end of the second missionary journey, in a time of rising Jewish zealotism: e.g., B. Reicke, "Der geschichtliche Hintergrund des Apostelkonzils und der Antiochia-Episode, Gal. 2:1–14," in *Studia Paulina in Honorem Johannes de Zwaan Septuagenarii* (Haarlem, Netherlands: De Erven F. Bohn, 1953), 172–187.
5. J. Neusner, *From Politics to Piety: The Emergence of Pharisaic Judaism* (Englewood Cliffs, N.J.: Prentice-Hall, 1973), 86.
6. J. D. G. Dunn, "The Incident at Antioch (Gal. 2:11–18)," *Journal for the Study of the New Testament* 18 (1983): 36.
7. J. D. G. Dunn, "The New Perspective on Paul," *Bulletin of the John Rylands Library* 65 (1983): 95–122. Dunn believes that Paul's doctrine of justification by faith first dawned on him in this encounter with Peter at Antioch.
8. For example, B. W. Bacon, "Peter's Triumph at Antioch," *Journal of Religion* 9 (1929): 204–223.
9. W. Schmithals, *Paul and James, Studies in Biblical Theology*, 46 (Naperville, Ill.: Alec R. Allenson, 1965), 74–78.
10. For a full defense for equating Galatians 2 and Acts 15, see R. Stein, "Jerusalem," *Dictionary of Paul and His Letters*, ed. G. F. Hawthorne and R. P. Martin (Downers Grove, Ill.: InterVarsity, 1993), 465–468. For the unique position that Galatians 2 is referring to the event attributed to Peter in Acts 11:1–18, see P. J. Achtemeier, "An Elusive Unity: Paul, Acts and the Early Church," *Catholic Biblical Quarterly* 48 (1986): 1–26. Achtemeier pre-

sents the same view in his book, *The Quest for Unity in the New Testament Church* (Philadelphia: Fortress, 1987).

11. R. Riesner, *Paul's Early Period: Chronology, Mission Strategy, Theology*, trans. D. Stott (Grand Rapids: Eerdmans, 1998), 269.

12. Titus voluntarily submitted to circumcision, according to O. Linton, "The Third Aspect: A Neglected Point of View," *Studia Theologica* 3 (1949): 79–95.

13. R. A. Martin, *Studies in the Life and Ministry of the Early Paul and Related Issues* (Lewiston, N.Y.: Mellen Biblical Press, 1993), 162–175.

14. B. H. McLean, "Galatians 2.7–9 and the Recognition of Paul's Apostolic Status at the Jerusalem Conference. A Critique of G. Luedemann's Solution," *New Testament Studies* 37 (1991): 67–76.

15. G. Klein, "Galater 2.6–9 und die Geschichte der Jerusalemer Urgemeinde," *Zeitschrift für Theologie und Kirche* 57 (1960) 283–284. In a provocative article, B. Ehrman has argued that Peter and Cephas are in fact two different people: "Cephas and Peter," *Journal of Biblical Literature* 109 (1990): 463–474.

16. "Paul and the 'Pillar' Apostles," in *Studia Paulina*, 1–19.

17. J. P. Sampley argues that the Jerusalem agreement was a formal partnership (a *consensus societas*) in the Roman legal sense—that the right hand of fellowship sealed the agreement (v. 9) and the collection was an outward manifestation of the partnership (v. 10): *Pauline Partnership in Christ: Christian Community and Commitment in the Light of Roman Law* (Philadelphia: Fortress, 1980): 21–41.

18. Cp. Mishnah, *Aboth* 3.5. Jesus also used the metaphor of a yoke in a positive sense (Matt. 11:29f.). See J. Nolland, "A Fresh Look at Acts 15:10," *New Testament Studies* 27 (1980): 105–115.

19. For the ritual understanding of the decrees, see M. Simon, "The Apostolic Decree and its Setting in the Ancient Church," *Bulletin of the John Rylands Library* 52 (1970): 437–460.

20. For a discussion of the later Christian use of the decrees, see F. F. Bruce, *Apostle of the Heart Set Free*, 185–186.

21. We will return to this subject in the next chapter, where we will examine the elements of Greek letters in some detail. At this point it might be noted that the letter in Acts 15 ends with the formal Greek closing *errōsthe* ("farewell"). It is the only letter in the New Testament with this formal Greek closing, although a number of manuscripts add it at the end of Acts 23:30.

22. A. S. Geyser, "Paul, the Apostolic Decree and the Liberals in Corinth," *Studia Paulina*, 124–138.

SUGGESTED FURTHER READING

Barrett, C. K. "Paul and the 'Pillar' Apostles." In *Studia Paulina in Honorem Johannis de Zwaan Septuagenarii*. Haarlem, Netherlands: De Erven F. Bohn, 1953, pp. 1–19.

Dunn, James D. G. "The Incident at Antioch (Gal. 2:11–18)." *Journal for the Study of the New Testament*. 18 (1983): 3–57.

Dunn, James D. G. "The New Perspective on Paul." *Bulletin of the John Rylands Library*. 65 (1983): 95–122.

Fitzmyer, Joseph A. *The Acts of the Apostles*. Anchor Bible. New York: Doubleday, 1998, pp. 494–537.

George, Timothy. *Galatians*. The New American Commentary. Nashville: Broadman and Holman, 1994, pp. 134–202.

Sampley, J. Paul. *Pauline Partnership in Christ: Christian Community and Commitment in Light of Roman Law*. Philadelphia: Fortress, 1980.

Simon, Marcel. "The Apostolic Decree and Its Setting in the Ancient Church." *Bulletin of the John Rylands Library* 52 (1970): 437–460.

Stein, Robert. "Jerusalem." *Dictionary of Paul and His Letters*. Ed. G. F. Hawthorne and R. P. Martin. Downers Grove, Ill.: InterVarsity, 1993, pp. 465–468.

7

~☙~

PAUL THE LETTER WRITER

$\mathcal{T}$he next chapter will be the first to introduce an epistle of Paul. It may prove helpful at this point to take an overview of his letters as a whole. In particular, we will examine them in the light of the epistolary conventions of Paul's day.

THE NATURE OF PAUL'S LETTERS

PRIVATE AND LITERARY LETTERS

Thirteen books of the New Testament bear the name of Paul as writer. All are in letter form. What sort of letters are they? Are they "literary" letters, designed for a general readership, or are they "private" letters, intended only for the individuals to whom they were addressed? In Paul's day there was a long tradition of producing letters for public consumption. Though often addressed to individuals, the address was largely a fictional device. They were not destined for individuals so much as for the public. Aristotle produced literary epistles of this sort, as did Epicurus. Perhaps the best known are the "moral epistles" (*Epistulae Morales*) of Seneca, a contemporary of Paul. For centuries these literary epistles were regarded as the prototype of Paul's letters. They were the main Greco-Roman letters that had been preserved. Literature tends to be kept over time; private correspondence rarely is.

In the nineteenth century, archaeologists uncovered large hordes of ancient papyri in Egypt. Among their discoveries were hundreds of letters, many dating from the first and second centuries A.D. They were private correspondence. Some were letters of introduction and recommendation. Some dealt with business matters. Some were family correspondence—for example, a husband expressing his concern to his pregnant wife, a son writing home for money, and the like. Around the turn of the twentieth century, Adolf Deissmann, a recognized expert in the papyri, argued that Paul's letters belonged to the same category as these private papyrus letters and should not be grouped with the literary epistles. They dealt with specific problems in individual churches and were not intended for public consumption.[1] Deissmann's work was well received and was a necessary correction to previous views.[2] Today, however, most scholars would maintain that Paul's letters are not exactly like the private papyrus letters of Egypt. They are somewhere between the papyri and the rhetorically polished literary epistles of a Seneca. They are for the most part longer than the papyri and shorter than the literary epistles.

More significantly, Paul always wrote in his role as an "apostle." That is, his communications to his churches carried with them his authority as an apostle and served as a substitute for his personal presence.[3] A. D. Nock suggested that Paul's letters were a new type of epistle, that of the "encyclical," which became a pattern for later bishops and popes in addressing their churches.[4] Though intended for specific congregations, Paul's letters always had an eye on the larger Christian community. Thus, he addressed his first letter to Corinth to both the church at Corinth and to "all those everywhere who call on the name of our Lord Jesus Christ" (1 Cor. 1:2). As an apostle of Christ Jesus, Paul's words to the specific needs at Corinth would be applicable in similar circumstances to Christians anywhere. Even Philemon, which is the most "private" of all Paul's letters, was addressed not just to the slave owner but to the *whole church* that met in his home (v. 2). In short, Paul's letters were both "occasional" (written for specific congregations) and general (carrying the apostle's authority for all who might read them).[5]

THE READING OF PAUL'S LETTERS

Unlike the private papyrus letters, Paul's letters were intended to be read aloud to his congregations. There were two reasons for this. First, they were intended for the entire congregation and addressed to them. Second, the literacy rate was low in Paul's day; most people in his churches probably could not read.[6] The oral presentation of his letters was a necessity. Colossians 4:16 reflects the practice: "After this letter has been read to you, see that it is also read in the church of the Laodiceans and that you in turn read the letter from Laodicea." The verse also bears out the "encyclical" nature of Paul's letters; churches were encouraged to exchange Paul's correspondence among one another. Incidentally, the Colossian passage also reminds us that we do not have all of Paul's correspondence today. The letter to the Laodiceans has evidently been lost.

Since Paul's letters were intended to be read aloud, he utilized a number of "traditional" materials in his letters, like hymns and confessions of faith. These were memorable and easy to retain in an oral culture. Thus, his epistles are filled with benedictions (1 Thess. 5:28) and doxologies (Rom. 9:5; 11:36; 16:25–27). He may have used many hymns from the worship of the churches. Many scholars would see Philippians 2:6–11 as a hymn to Christ. The same is maintained for Colossians 1:15–20 and Ephesians 1:3–14, both of which praise God's eternal purposes that have been fulfilled in Christ. This is the very stuff of hymns, and both passages have poetic characteristics, as one would expect with liturgical materials. To this day, hymns are often used in illiterate cultures as a major vehicle for transmitting the teachings of the faith. This was probably true in Paul's churches as well.[7]

Found throughout Paul's letters are confessions of faith, such as "God is one" (1 Cor. 8:6; Rom. 3:30; Eph. 4:6) and "Jesus is Lord" (Rom. 10:9; 1 Cor. 12:3). Paul's recitation of the liturgy of the Lord's Supper in 1 Corinthians 11:23–26 would probably already have been committed to memory by many of the Corinthians, as would the traditional statement of the Lord's death and resurrection in 1 Corinthians 15:3–7.[8] Scholars are just now beginning to appreciate the significance of the oral culture in which Paul ministered. His epistles belong to that culture, designed not so much to be read as to be heard. His teachings were presented in a form that could be easily committed to memory. No wonder his letters are filled with traditional materials and utilize traditional forms that would be easy to retain.

TYPES OF PAUL'S LETTERS

There were many types of Greek letters, and Paul's letters exhibit characteristics of a number of them. For instance, a common Greek letter was the epistle of friendship. Although none of Paul's letters could be typed exclusively as a friendship letter, there are individual passages within his letters which resemble the genre. For example, when in Philippians he spoke of "longing" for them (1:7–8) and when he bade them to join him in his feelings of joy (2:17–18), he was employing phrases common to the friendship letter. Another type of Greek letter was the letter of praise and blame (the *epideictic* letter). Again, no entire Pauline letter fits this category, but the apostle often employed elements of these letters, such as his frequent praise of his churches as he thanked God for them (Rom. 1:8; 1 Thess. 1:3; 2 Thess. 1:3–4). The Greek philosophers often produced *protreptic* letters, letters which exhorted readers to convert to their particular philosophy. Many portions of Romans reflect the protreptic form. Also very common among the Greek philosophers was the *paraenetic* letter, which presented moral teachings in traditional forms. All of Paul's letters contain elements of paraenesis. Just one example is Paul's offering himself as a model for his churches to emulate (Phil. 3:17). This was a common motif in paraenetic letters.[9]

One of the most common letters of all, particularly among the papyri, was the letter of recommendation. These letters were usually carried by the person being recommended and served to introduce them to the recipient, who was often an acquaintance of the recommender/sender. The recipient was urged to receive the bearer, or provide him lodging, or perhaps help him find employment, and the like. Paul's letter to Philemon has been described as a letter of recommendation. Many of his epistles contain short recommendations. The most obvious is the recommendation of Phoebe in Romans 16:1–2. It has all the elements of a Greek commendatory letter. Paul introduced her, identified her, and asked the recipients to receive her and give her assistance as needed. Other examples are Paul's urging the Thessalonians to accept their leaders (1 Thess. 5:12–13a), his appealing to the Corinthians to give due recognition to Stephanas, Achaicus, and Fortunatus (1 Cor. 16:17–18), and his commendation of Epaphroditus to the Philippians (Phil. 2:29–30).[10]

LETTER FORM

Paul's letters followed the typical form of the Greek private letter. This consisted of three main parts: the introduction, the body, and the conclusion. Some would expand the parts to four, considering the thanksgiving as a separate entity. It will be included as a part of the introduction in the following discussion.

THE INTRODUCTION

Greek letters opened with a standard form, consisting of the *sender*, to the *recipient*, followed by the word *greeting*. There were often just three terms, as in the following example: *Demetrius to Stephanas, greeting* (Gk., *chairein*). Sometimes the sender expanded on his own name in order to identify himself or herself more fully. Sometimes the recipient's name was expanded with identifying terms and titles. Particularly was this true of official correspondence, where extensive titles were often listed for both sender and recipient. Paul regularly expanded on his name, usually identifying himself as an apostle of Jesus Christ and often referring to his divine call-ing. In the Thessalonian letters, which are probably his two earliest extant epistles, he did not refer to his apostolic status or give any expansion on his name. He did, however, list two cosenders along with himself—Silvanus (Silas) and Timothy. First Corinthians is a good example of Paul's typical introduction of himself: "Paul, called to be an apostle of Christ Jesus by the will of God" (1:1). When Paul departed from this pattern, there was usually a reason. For instance, in Galatians Paul expanded on the description of his calling: "Paul, an apostle—sent not from men nor by man, but by Jesus Christ and God the father"(1:1). Paul's apostolic status was at stake in Gala-tia. At the very outset of the letter, he made it clear from whom he received his com-missioning—from God and not from men.

Galatians exhibits the shortest of Paul's designations for his recipients: "to the churches in Galatia" (1:2). Often he made further reference to his recipients as "saints": "to all in Rome who are loved by God and called to be saints" (Rom. 1:7). Sometimes he gave a "secondary" recipient, as in 1 Corinthians, where he referred to "all those everywhere who call on the name of our Lord Jesus Christ" (1:2), or in Philippians, where he singled out the overseers and deacons of the church (1:1), or in Philemon, where he addressed Apphia, Archippus, and the church that met in Philemon's home (v. 2). Of course, the three Pastoral Epistles are more like the typ-ical private Greek papyri in their introductions since they were addressed to individ-uals. Still, Paul expanded on the recipient's name in all three instances, referring to both Timothy and Titus as his "son."

After designating the sender and the recipient, Greek letters customarily followed immediately with the word *chairein*, or "greetings." This customary greeting is found in three New Testament letters: in the letter from the apostles and elders drawn up at the Jerusalem Conference (Acts 15:23), in the letter of the Roman tribune Lysias to the governor Felix (Acts 23:26), and in the salutation of the epistle of James (1:1). It was never used by Paul. Instead, Paul used a greeting that consisted of the two words *grace* and *peace*. The simplest form ("grace and peace to you") appears in 1 Thessalonians 1:1. Paul expanded the formula in 2 Thessalonians 1:2: "Grace and peace to you from God the Father and the Lord Jesus Christ." This is the basic form of his greetings in most of his epistles (Romans, 1 Corinthians, 2 Corinthians, Gala-tians, Ephesians, Philippians, Philemon, and Titus). The greeting in Colossians lacks the words "and the Lord Jesus Christ," and the two letters to Timothy add the word "mercy"—"grace, mercy and peace."

Paul's epistolary greeting of "grace and peace" seems to have been original with him. It drew from both the Greek and the Hebrew traditions. "Grace" was actually a pun on the customary Greek greeting term, *chairein*. The Greek word *grace* (*charis*) is very close in sound to *chairein*. Paul seems to have substituted this reminder of God's unmerited favor in Christ Jesus for the usual greeting word. "Grace" was infi-nitely more appropriate in greeting fellow Christians. Paul then included the addi-tional word "peace," which derived from the Hebrew tradition of greeting with the word *shalom*, "may God's peace (*shalom*) be with you."[11]

In Greek letters, the word of greeting was often followed by a wish for health and/or a brief formula of supplication to the gods for the good fortune of the recipi-ent. Sometimes the sender mentioned that he was bearing the recipient in mem-ory.[12] All of this is quite reminiscent of Paul's letters, where he too often offered a prayer on behalf of his readers and stated how he held them fondly in his memory whenever he mentioned them in his prayers (Phil. 1:3–4). In Paul's epistles, these elements of prayer and memory are a part of the thanksgiving that regularly follows the salutation. They occur in all of Paul's epistles except for Galatians, 2 Corinthians, and Titus. Sometimes a thanksgiving is found in the papyrus letters, but generally it is a thanksgiving to the gods for delivering the *sender* from some difficulty.[13] Paul customarily thanked God for his *congregations*, for the divine grace that had been at work among them, for their faith and love and growth. Often the thanksgiving introduces the body of the letter by looking ahead to some of the letter's main concerns. The thanksgiving of 1 Corinthians is a good example (1 Cor. 1:4–9). Paul thanked God for having enriched the Corinthians in speech and in knowledge (v. 5) and for having blessed them with every spiritual gift (v. 7). Knowledge and spiritual gifts were major problems at Corinth, and a great deal of 1 Corinthians is devoted to them: knowledge and wisdom (chaps. 1–4), spiritual gifts (chaps. 12–14).

THE BODY

One of the most difficult matters in analyzing the structure of a Pauline letter is to determine where the actual body of the epistle begins. A number of transitional formulae have been isolated, where Paul seemed to move from one topic to another. These are sometimes helpful in determining where the actual body begins. One of Paul's common transitional phrases is: "I appeal to you" (Greek, *parakaleō*). Paul used this word in 1 Corinthians 1:10, where it does indeed seem to mark the transition from the thanksgiving to the body of the epistle. Another transitional phrase that Paul often employed was "I want you to know," or "I do not want you to be unaware." Paul used this formula at Romans 1:13; Galatians 1:11; and Philippians 1:12. Quite possibly the body of these letters should be seen as beginning at these points.[14] It should, however, be observed that these formulae are found *throughout* Paul's letters. They may indeed mark the transition from thanksgiving to body, but they also mark transitions from one issue to another *within* the body itself.[15]

There are other transitional phrases that Paul liked to employ in moving from one thought to another: expressions of joy ("I rejoice greatly . . . that," Phil. 4:10; Philem. 7), statements of amazement ("I am astonished that," Gal. 1:6), reminders of what his readers already should know ("as we have already said," "for you have heard," Gal. 1:9; 1:13f.). Another common type of formula is Paul's statement of *confidence* that his readers have or will do the right thing (Gal. 5:1; Rom. 15:24; 2 Cor. 9:2). One often finds these same kinds of expressions in the papyrus letters.

The actual content of the letter depends on the specific occasion which Paul was addressing and thus usually varies widely from letter to letter.[16] There are, however, certain features which recur throughout the various letters. Many of Paul's letters deal with his travel plans, expressing such things as his desire to visit the congregation, his reasons for delay in coming, and the like. These are particularly prominent in 1 Corinthians, where Paul was evidently being criticized for his failure to visit them (1 Cor. 4:14–21; 16:5–12) and in Romans, which church Paul was preparing to visit for the first time (Rom. 1:8–13; 15:14–33). Paul was apprehensive about an approaching third visit to the troublesome Corinthian congregation (2 Cor. 12:14–13:13). Prison kept him from visiting his beloved Philippians, but he sent Timothy as his dearest personal representative (Phil. 2:19–24). Philemon was also written from prison. Paul told Philemon to prepare a guest room, because he hoped to have his prayers for release answered soon (Philem. 22).

Sometimes Paul's references were more to his past relationships with a congregation than with his future plans. Such was the case with the Galatians (Gal. 4:12–20). Particularly instructive was his long statement to the Thessalonians about how he longed to see them but had been prevented. Timothy made up for what he himself lacked in personal presence (1 Thess. 2:17–3:11). Paul's many references to his travel plans were a means of maintaining a personal presence with his congregations, through his written communication and through representatives like Timothy who bore the letters.[17]

Another type of material found in the body of all Paul's epistles (with the exception of Philemon) was *paraenesis*, the extensive ethical advice which Paul sent his congregations. Such moral instruction is commonly found in the literary epistles of the Greek philosophers. Some of the most common forms of paraenesis have already been introduced in chapter 1 of this book, such as the virtue and vice lists and the household codes. Usually this kind of moral teaching is found toward the end of Paul's epistles (Rom. 12:1–15:13; Gal. 5:1–6:10; 1 Thess. 4:1–5:22; Col. 3:1–4:6). In Ephesians it constitutes the entire second half of the epistle (Eph. 4–6). It is woven throughout Philippians, 1 Corinthians, and 2 Corinthians. Paul's paraenesis is traditional moral instruction, drawn from the Old Testament, the teachings of Jesus, and the best moral traditions of the day. Often in the ethical sections of his letters, Paul presented himself as a model to be emulated. The epistolary paraenesis was the sort of teaching he shared with his congregations when present with them. The amount of space Paul devoted to ethical instruction in his letters is testimony to the importance he placed on the moral aspect of the Christian life.

THE CONCLUSION

The Greek papyrus letters usually closed in rather conventional fashion. Sometimes there was a note about the writing of the letter, whether written by a secretary or by the sender himself. Sometimes there was an exchange of greetings *to* other persons in the vicinity of the recipient or *from* other persons in the vicinity of the sender. Often a brief note was appended, wishing health for the recipient and giving a word of farewell. The farewells were particularly stereotypical. The most common was the Greek word *errōsthe*. It is the usual concluding word of a first-century Greek letter but is found in the New Testament only once, at the close of the letter from the apostles and elders in Jerusalem that outlined the "decrees" (Acts 15:29). Paul generally ended his epistles as he began them, with a well-wishing that grace would abide on the recipients: "the grace of our Lord Jesus Christ be with you" (1 Thess. 5:28). Most of Paul's epistles end with this phrase (2 Thess. 3:18; 1 Cor. 16:23; Gal. 6:18; Eph. 6:24 [with variations]; Phil. 4:23; Philem. 25). The shorter form "grace be with you" is found in Colossians 4:18; 1 Timothy 6:21; 2 Timothy 4:22; and Titus 3:15. A longer trinitarian variation appears in 2 Corinthians 13:14: "May the grace of the Lord Jesus Christ, and the love of God, and the fellowship of the Holy Spirit be with you all."

Three epistles include an additional doxology in the conclusion. All are formal doxologies to God and end with a final "amen" (Rom. 16:25–27; Phil. 4:20; and 2 Tim. 4:18).[18] Other doxologies occur internally in some epistles, rounding off sections (cp. Rom. 9:5; 11:33–36; 2 Cor. 11:31; Eph. 3:20–21). Some scholars would argue that the doxologies mark conclusions of letters and are seams where letters have been pieced together. This is unlikely.

Paul's letters often have a note near the end stating that this part of the letter is being written by Paul—in his *own* hand (1 Cor. 16:21; Col. 4:18; Gal. 6:11; 2 Thess. 3:17; Philem. 19). This was a common practice often found in papyri that were mainly written by a secretary. At the end of the letter the sender would append a note that he was writing these concluding words himself. It is obvious that he was, because the concluding words are written in a different hand. Unlike the papyri, we don't have Paul's "autographs" and thus cannot see the different styles of handwriting (the secretary's and Paul's). We will discuss Paul's use of secretaries later in the chapter. These notes about writing in his own hand probably reflect that he used a secretary. The note in 2 Thessalonians 3:17 is particularly significant. Paul emphasized that this was *his* handwriting style. Earlier in the epistle he indicated that false letters were being circulated which claimed to have come from him (2 Thess. 2:2). Paul concluded the letter in his own hand; he wanted no mistake about the genuineness of *this* letter.

A number of times at the close of an epistle Paul asked the congregation to pray for him (Rom. 15:30–33; 1 Thess. 5:25; Col. 4:3; Eph. 6:19–20). Sometimes he bade them to greet one another with a "holy kiss" (1 Cor. 16:20; 2 Cor. 13:12; 1 Thess. 5:26; Rom. 16:16). This probably reflects the actual practice of Paul's churches when they assembled for worship. It also witnesses to the fact that the setting for the epistles was an oral presentation to the gathered congregation.

A final item commonly found in Paul's epistles was the exchange of greetings. Sometimes these are quite short, exchanging greetings with "all the saints," or "all the brothers," or "everyone with me" (1 Cor. 16:20; 2 Cor. 13:13; Phil. 4:21; Titus 3:15). Sometimes they are much more extensive, listing a number of individual names (2 Tim. 4:19–21; Col. 4:10–15). By far the most remarkable is the long list in Romans 16:3–24. Exchange of greetings was a common practice in the epistolary conventions of Paul's day. In a day when long-distance communication was severely limited, people would not fail to send notes to friends when they found someone traveling to their city.

SENDING LETTERS

Sending letters was not always easy in Paul's day. It often involved the use of an amanuensis or secretary to write down the communication. There was no postal service. The Roman government had a system of couriers for official communications, but this was not available to the public. One usually had to depend on other means, such as channels of commerce or people who were traveling to a destination where one had friends or acquaintances.

SECRETARIES

The use of secretaries is amply evidenced in the papyri. They were a professional class of scribes, sometimes called *amanuenses*. They earned their living through their writing skills, which the general public often lacked. When illiterate persons wished to write letters, they would secure assistance of a secretary. Usually such letters were brief. Papyrus leaves were expensive, and the scribe had to be paid. To this day one can find professional scribes with their typewriters positioned in the streets of North Africa, ready to prepare a letter or document for anyone who needs secretarial assistance. The papyri often carry a note at the end of the letter indicating that the sender was illiterate or "slow of writing," which indicates that a secretary had prepared it.

Not only did the illiterate employ secretaries, but the upper classes and educated as well. Public officials often hired secretaries to assist in the preparation of documents. Secretaries were essential in maintaining records and sending communications for business interests. Individuals of means who maintained an extensive correspondence would also use secretaries to assist them. The involvement of the secretary in the actual content of the letter varied. The secretary could write the letter down at the dictation of the sender, word for word. This was the slowest method. The fastest was when the secretary was instructed to write such and such a type of letter to someone. In such instances, the actual content of the letter was pretty much up to the secretary, though the letter would follow the customary form for that type of letter. Official documents and business letters were often composed in this fashion, where the general form and content of the letter was essentially predetermined. There was, however, a third degree of secretarial involvement. The secretary would be carefully instructed as to the full contents of the letter, would probably take down notes, but would then be left to draft the final form of the letter. The use of secretaries was never a careless matter. The sender was *always* responsible for the actual contents of the letter. No matter what the degree of secretarial involvement, literate senders would normally check out the work of their scribes.

The question is sometimes raised whether secretaries could take down "shorthand" in Paul's day. Cicero is known to have developed a system of Latin shorthand for his own scribes, and it is quite possible that a form of Greek shorthand existed in Paul's time, but we have no certain evidence for it. Even Cicero's method was not widespread. A person had to go to a school for special training. It does not seem to have been available to the average scribe.[19]

Paul used secretaries. The most direct evidence for this occurs in Romans 16:22, where Tertius identified himself as the one who "wrote down" the epistle. Less obvious pointers to Paul's use of a secretary are the instances where he noted at the end of the letter that he was writing "in [his] own hand." This practice of the sender writing the concluding lines of a letter is often found in the papyri. It is quite obvious; the handwriting style changes in the last lines. Of course, we cannot check Paul's epistles for this, since we have none of the autographs. In Galatians 6:11, Paul remarked that he was writing in "large letters" in his own hand. Some see this as evidence that Paul's eyesight was not good and suggest that this might be why Paul used scribal assistance in the first place. The other instances where Paul appended a note about writing in his own hand are 1 Corinthians 16:21; Colossians 4:18; 2 Thessalonians 3:17; and Philemon 19. With the possible exception of Philemon, these references probably indicate that all but these concluding lines of the letter were written by a secretary. Paul may have written *all* of Philemon. Paul's reference to writing in his own hand occurs in the body and not the conclusion of that epistle and functions not as a signature but as a formally signed I.O.U. that he would personally reimburse Philemon for anything owed him by the runaway slave Onesimus.

Some scholars believe that Paul's *usual* practice was to use a secretary. This may be indicated by 2 Thessalonians 3:17, where Paul spoke of his handwritten note as "the distinguishing mark in *all* my letters."[20] The degree of secretarial involvement in Paul's letters would be hard to assess. Perhaps he dictated them. Perhaps he outlined the contents for his assistant. If the latter was his practice, it would render invalid all the arguments from vocabulary and style that are often used in questions of Pauline authorship. If the style of one epistle differs from that of another, it could be explained simply as the involvement of different secretaries in the two epistles.

COSENDERS

Paul mentioned a cosender in the salutation of eight of his letters. In six of them he mentioned Timothy alongside himself (in 1 and 2 Thessalonians, Silvanus/Silas as well as Timothy). In 1 Corinthians 1:1, Paul spoke of Sosthenes as cosender, who was perhaps the synagogue ruler mentioned in Acts 18:17. In Galatians 1:2 Paul listed "all the brothers with me" as cosenders. The role of the cosender is anything but clear. Some have suggested that they are the secretaries to whom Paul dictated the letters. Obviously the listing of "all the brothers" in Galatians puts a strain on that interpretation. Others have suggested that the cosenders were the actual bearers of the letter and that the listing of their name was to introduce them to the community and to commend their reliability.[21] This view likewise has problems. For example, Timothy is listed as cosender of Colossians, but Tychicus seems to have carried the letter to Colossae (Col. 4:7–9). Likewise, Timothy was the cosender of Philippians, but Epaphroditus seems to have delivered the letter to Philippi (Phil. 2:25–30). One should note the important role of the deliverers. They were an "extension" of Paul's letters. They elaborated on the letters and filled in the details about Paul's circumstances for the congregations. In a real sense they were a substitute for Paul's personal presence, and Paul often went out of his way to commend them to the churches. They do not, however, seem to have been the same as cosenders.

What, then, was the role of the cosenders? Some have suggested that they must have had some voice in the actual contents of the letter.[22] One can see how this might have been the case with letters like 1 and 2 Thessalonians, where Paul listed Silas and Timothy as cosenders. The pair had worked with Paul in the establishment of the church, and Timothy had continued to minister there on a subsequent occasion (1 Thess. 3:2). If the two did not contribute anything to the actual contents of the letter, they at least were one with Paul in their concern for the congregation. Cosenders seem to have been primarily Paul's coworkers who had worked closely with the congregations addressed. They were truly joint senders of the letters. Mentioning them was not perfunctory. They shared with Paul in the concerns of the letter.

FORGERIES AND PSEUDEPIGRAPHA

Writing in someone else's name was not unheard of in Paul's day. Indeed, Paul indicates in 2 Thessalonians 2:2 that spurious letters may have been circulating which claimed to have been written by him. That is probably why he emphasized at the end of the letter that he was writing with his own distinguishing mark (3:17). It was *his* signature, indicating that the letter was his and not a forgery. Identification of the sender could present a real problem in the ancient world. When someone could not write and had to employ a secretary, there was no distinguishing personal handwriting to identify them. How could one be sure the letter was really from *that* person? A convention often found in the papyrus letters was for the secretary to give a distinguishing physical mark to identify the sender: "This letter is being sent by so-

and-so, who has a heart-shaped birthmark on his right cheek." Paul picked up his pen and appended his personal signature; that was *his* mark.

The practice of writing in Paul's name continued after his lifetime. For instance, some time in the third or fourth century, someone put together a patchwork of phrases from Paul's genuine epistles and circulated it as the "Epistle to the Laodiceans." It was evidently written out of the misguided desire to supply the missing epistle which Paul had mentioned in Colossians 4:16. It was recognized almost immediately as a forgery, and scholars like Jerome warned against it. On a totally different level is the question whether some of the canonical epistles that bear Paul's name might actually not have been written by Paul but rather by a later disciple of Paul. It has often been maintained that some of the epistles are pseudonymous, that is, written by another under Paul's name. The main epistles in question are 2 Thessalonians, Colossians, Ephesians, and the three Pastoral Epistles. There are many differing viewpoints as to which ones are genuine and which are not. For instance, many scholars would only reject the Pastoral Epistles, and some would argue that even those are not wholly pseudepigraphical but pieced together from genuine fragments of Paul's correspondence.

Obviously, we will need to examine the question of authenticity separately for each epistle or group of epistles in the chapter that treats it. At this point we only wish to clarify the position to be followed in this book. We will consider as genuinely Pauline the thirteen epistles in the New Testament that bear Paul's name. This excludes the book of Hebrews, which does not bear any author's name and has little in common with any Pauline epistle.[23] The student should always be aware of the Pauline canon with which an author works. The author will usually state her or his position early in the work as to which books are considered genuinely Pauline. The subsequent treatment of Paul's thought will be influenced by the books with which the author works. Obviously, an assessment of Paul's thought that excludes Colossians, Ephesians, and the Pastorals from consideration will differ significantly from one that includes them.

THE COLLECTING OF PAUL'S LETTERS

How did a group of epistles that were written to individual congregations and persons come to be put together and eventually to find their way into the New Testament canon? This is a question that has long preoccupied scholarship—that of the formation of the *Pauline corpus*. Another related question is that of the *integrity* of the individual epistles. Did Paul write all the epistles in exactly the form we have them, or do some of them exhibit the marks of editorial activity?

THE PAULINE CORPUS

Around the turn of the twentieth century Adolf Harnack proposed the theory that Paul's epistles were at some point gathered together and placed in a collection. He believed that after Paul's death the letters were preserved by the individual congregations to whom they were written. Around the end of the first century, someone sought them out and gathered them into a collection. He suggested Corinth as the possible origination point for the collection (or "corpus") of Paul's letters. Originally there were ten epistles in the collection. The earliest writers who used Paul's epistles and the earliest lists of his letters do not seem to have been aware of the three Pastoral Epistles. They were only added later, in the course of the second century.[24]

Other scholars offered alternative theories of how Paul's epistles came to be assembled. It was suggested, for instance, that from the first the churches exchanged Paul's letters and formed their own collections. In the early second century there was an effort to consolidate these collections and to form a uniform edition. It is indeed striking that when Paul's epistles began to be used by early Christian writers or to be included in official lists of Scripture, the epistles do not appear singly but usually in a group (at first the group of ten) as if from the start they were known only in *collected form.*

The most popular theory of the Pauline corpus in this country was that proposed by Edgar Goodspeed. Goodspeed suggested that the corpus was assembled around A.D. 90 after the publication of Acts, which stimulated people's interest in Paul. A disciple of Paul then set out to gather all the available letters of Paul. He then assembled the collection of epistles for publication and distribution to the churches. Goodspeed argued that the person who gathered the epistles together wrote Ephesians as an introductory essay ("frontispiece" was Goodspeed's word). Ephesians was put together from the choice passages of Paul's epistles, he argued. He also suggested the possibility that the compiler of the corpus was Onesimus, Philemon's runaway slave. (An Onesimus was bishop of Ephesus around the turn of the century when Ignatius addressed an epistle to that church.) Goodspeed's theory was at bottom much like that of Harnack—a collection of ten letters, gathered from Paul's churches, first assembled toward the end of the first century. Goodspeed developed his theory of the Pauline corpus more thoroughly than Harnack. Above all, he tied it to a suggestion about the origin of the Ephesian epistle, which is still quite popular today. We will return to it in the chapter on Ephesians.

In recent years there has been a revival of interest in the formation of the Pauline corpus. Building on Harnack's theory of a collection made in Corinth around the end of the first century, W. Schmithals suggested that the original collection consisted of seven epistles, all of which had a strongly anti-Gnostic thrust. Not many scholars were won over either by Schmithals's "Gnostic key" to the Pauline epistles or to his view of the corpus.[25] More recently David Trobisch has argued that the Pauline corpus was formed in stages. The earliest form of the collection was assembled by Paul himself. It consisted of four epistles, all of which grapple with the problem of Paul's relationship to the Jerusalem Christian community and all of which treat the collection: Romans, Galatians, and 1 and 2 Corinthians. According to Trobisch, Paul assembled this letter collection in Corinth as he prepared to go to Jerusalem with his monetary collection for the saints.[26]

It can readily be seen that no scholarly consensus exists as to what was the original impetus for assembling Paul's letters.[27] One thing is certain, however: by the last half of the second century, the collection of thirteen Pauline epistles was in wide use throughout all branches of the Christian church, in the east and in the west. The same was true of the four Gospels. Together they formed the nucleus of the Christian canon. The total shape of the canon would take another two centuries to finalize, but the Gospels and Pauline epistles were firmly in place almost within a century of Paul's death.

THE INTEGRITY OF THE EPISTLES

The theory of the Pauline corpus assumes editorial activity in assembling the letters. This raises the question of whether editorial work has taken place on the individual epistles as well. Many scholars feel that this is the case. Particularly has it been argued that many of Paul's epistles are composite. It has been maintained, for instance, that the last chapter of Romans is a fragment of a letter originally sent to Ephesus. Some see Philippians as a composite of three letters, or 1 Corinthians as a composite of two, or 2 Corinthians as pieced together from four or more letters. We will consider these issues in the contexts of the individual letters. At this point we only wish to introduce the subject. Such issues are referred to as questions of "integrity," which ask, Is the canonical form of the letter "integral" (is it a whole?) or is it a composite of more than one part?

PLACING OF THE EPISTLES

One final matter needs to be addressed before we proceed to consider Galatians in the next chapter. For the most part, in the chapters that follow we will seek to treat the epistles in the general period of Paul's career when they were *written;* we will weave the narrative of Paul's ministry together with his epistles. This will not always be the case, however, and that for several reasons. First, the chronology of Paul's epistles is often quite tenuous. For example, some scholars see Galatians as the first of Paul's extant epistles, written before the second missionary journey. Others place it late in the third mission period. Philippians is dated variously, depending on where one sees Paul as being imprisoned: Ephesus (A.D. 55–56), Caesarea (58–60), or Rome (60–62). There is little room for rigidity on such matters. The letters aren't dated, and the content of the letters often lends little help in placing them. A second consideration is the fact that the letters are usually tied to the situation in the congregations to whom they were addressed. It is often helpful to view the letter in the context of the narrative in Acts which describes the establishment of the congregation. In actual fact, the letter may have been written years later. Therefore, in several instances we have decided to deal with the letters in the context of the establishment of the congregations rather than in their actual chronological sequence. This is the case with the first three epistles that we will treat.

Galatians is discussed first, in the context of the early second missionary period, when we would argue that Paul established the Galatian churches. The actual epistle we would place during Paul's third mission period, perhaps written from Ephesus. Philippians is treated second, in the context of the congregation's founding. In actual fact, the letter was written much later, as noted above. The Thessalonian letters will likewise be considered in connection with the founding of the church. This is the least radical departure from the actual chronology, as the letters were probably written soon after the establishment of the congregation and still during the course of Paul's second mission.

NOTES

1. A. Deissmann, *Bible Studies*, trans. A. Grieve (Edinburgh: T. and T. Clark, 1901), 3–59; Deissmann, *Paul, A Study in Social and Religious History*, trans. W. E. Wilson (New York: George H. Doran, 1926), 3–19.

2. Even some of Deissmann's contemporaries, like W. M. Ramsay, accused him of overstating his case. See Ramsay, *The Teaching of St. Paul in Terms of the Present Day* (London: Hodder and Stoughton, 1913), 412–447.

3. J. L. White, "St. Paul and the Apostolic Letter Tradition," *Catholic Biblical Quarterly* 45 (3, 1983): 433–444.

4. A. D. Nock, *St. Paul* (New York: Harper and Brothers, 1937), 146.

5. L. Hartman, "On Reading Others' Letters," *Harvard Theological Review* 79 (1986): 137–146.

6. J. Dewey, "Textuality in an Oral Culture: A Survey of the Pauline Traditions," *Semeia* 65 (1994): 37–65.

7. For a discussion of Paul's use of hymns, see A. M. Hunter, *Paul and His Predecessors* (London: SCM Press, 1961), 36–44.

8. For a summary of liturgical materials in Paul's letters, see D. Aune, "Early Christian Letters and Homilies," in *The New Testament in its Literary Environment*, Library of Early Christianity, ed. Wayne Meeks (Philadelphia: Westminster, 1987), 193–194.

9. For a full taxonomy of Greek letters with many examples, see S. K. Stowers, *Letter Writing in Greco-Roman Antiquity*, Library of Early Christianity, ed. W. Meeks (Philadelphia: Westminster, 1986).

10. C. H. Kim, *Form and Structure of the Familiar Greek Letter of Recommendation*, SBL Dissertation Series, 4 (Missoula, Mont.: University of Montana, 1972).

11. J. M. Lieu, "'Grace to You, and Peace': The Apostolic Greeting," *Bulletin of the John Rylands Library* 68 (1985): 161–178.

12. W. G. Doty, *Letters in Primitive Christianity* (Philadelphia: Fortress, 1973), 30–31.

13. P. Arzt, "The 'Epistolary Introductory Thanksgiving' in the Papyri and in Paul," *Novum Testamentum* 36 (1994): 29–46.

14. J. L. White, "Introductory Formulae in the Body of the Pauline Letter," *Journal of Biblical Literature* 90 (1971): 91–97.

15. T. L. Mullins, "Formulas in New Testament Epistles," *Journal of Biblical Literature* 91 (1972): 380–390.

16. There are striking similarities between some letters—1 Thessalonians and 2 Thessalonians, Ephesians and Colossians, 1 Timothy and Titus. These will be considered in the chapters which introduce these epistles.

17. R. W. Funk, "The Apostolic Parousia: Form and Significance," in *Christian History and Interpretation: Studies Presented to John Knox*, ed. W. R. Farmer, C. F. D. Moule, and R. R. Niebuhr (Cambridge: Cambridge University Press, 1967), 249–268.

18. The doxologies of Romans are a notorious problem of textual criticism. Some manuscripts of Romans include the grace benediction at 16:24; others lack the verse. The long doxology of 16:25–27 is lacking in many manuscripts. This difficult problem will be treated in the chapter on Romans.

19. E. R. Richards, *The Secretary in the Letters of Paul*, Wissenschaftliche Untersuchungen zum Neuen Testament (Tübingen: Mohr-Siebeck, 1991), 26–43.

20. R. N. Longenecker, "Ancient Amanuenses and the Pauline Epistles," in *New Dimensions in New Testament Study*, ed. R. N. Longenecker and M. C. Tenney (Grand Rapids: Zondervan, 1974), 281–297.

21. Doty, *Letters in Primitive Christianity*, 30.

22. J. Murphy-O'Connor has suggested for 1 Corinthians that the cosender Sosthenes was the coauthor of the epistle and that his voice can be heard whenever Paul addressed the Corinthians in the first person plural (rather than the singular): *Paul the Letter-Writer: His World, His Options, His Skills* (Collegeville, Minn.: Liturgical Press, 1995), 16–34.

23. From an early period there were those who claimed Paul wrote Hebrews, usually because they were seeking an "apostolic" author for the treatise. Just as many of the early fathers denied that Paul wrote it. The tradition of Pauline authorship of Hebrews eventually found its way into the notes of the *Textus Receptus* and the King James translation. These notes sometimes reflect questionable traditions and in no sense are a part of the text of the New Testament itself.

24. A good summary of the various "corpus" theories is provided by Murphy-O'Connor, *Paul the Letter-Writer*, 114–118.

25. W. Schmithals, *Paul and the Gnostics* (Nashville: Abingdon, 1972), 239–274.
26. D. Trobisch, *Paul's Letter Collection: Tracing the Origins* (Minneapolis: Fortress, 1994). Murphy-O'Connor builds on Trobisch, seeing Paul's first collection in Corinth (Trobisch's four epistles), which was added to a second collection assembled around Thessalonica (Thessalonians, the Prison Epistles), to which eventually the Pastorals were added at Ephesus: *Paul the Letter-Writer*, 118–130.
27. H. Gamble notes that the varying textual traditions for Paul's letters (such as the doxologies in Romans) should warn us against seeing an early standard form for the epistles which the corpus theory assumes: "The Redaction of the Pauline Letters and the Formation of the Pauline Corpus," *Journal of Biblical Literature* 94 (1975): 403–418.

SUGGESTED FURTHER READING

Aune, David. "Early Christian Letters and Homilies." *The New Testament in Its Literary Environment.* Library of Early Christianity. Ed. Wayne Meeks. Philadelphia: Westminster, 1987, pp. 183–225.

Deissmann, Adolf. *Bible Studies.* Trans. Alexander Grieve. Edinburgh: T. and T. Clark, 1901, pp. 3–59.

Doty, William G. *Letters in Primitive Christianity.* Philadelphia: Fortress, 1973.

Kim, Chan-Hie. *Form and Structure of the Familiar Greek Letter of Recommendation.* SBL Dissertation Series, 4. Missoula, Mont.: University of Montana, 1972.

Longenecker, Richard N. "Ancient Amanuenses and the Pauline Epistles." In *New Dimensions in New Testament Study.* Ed. Richard N. Longenecker and M. C. Tenney. Grand Rapids: Zondervan, 1974, pp. 281–297.

Murphy-O'Connor, Jerome. *Paul the Letter-Writer: His World, His Options, His Skills.* Collegeville, Minn.: Liturgical Press, 1995.

Richards, E. Randolph. *The Secretary in the Letters of Paul.* Wissenschaftliche Untersuchungen zum Neuen Testament. Zweite Reihe, 42. Tübingen: Mohr-Siebeck, 1991.

Stowers, Stanley K. *Letter Writing in Greco-Roman Antiquity.* Library of Early Christianity, Ed. Wayne Meeks. Philadelphia: Westminster, 1986.

White, John L. *The Form and Function of the Body of the Greek Letter.* SBL Dissertation Series, 2. Missoula, Mont.: Scholars Press, 1972.

8

⁓ঌঌ⁓

"FOOLISH GALATIANS"

$\mathcal{T}$he first mention of "Galatia" in the Book of Acts occurs in the context of Paul's second major mission (Acts 15:36–18:22). With his mission to the Gentiles formally recognized at the Jerusalem Conference, Paul now pursued it in earnest in this second major endeavor. Over a period of four years, he carried the gospel across an ever-expanding frontier—into northern Galatia, to the Troad of Asia, into the cities of Macedonia, and to the Achaian cities of Athens and Corinth. Paul spent nearly half the period in Corinth. The first half was spent primarily in Galatia and Macedonia, with the establishment of churches in Galatia, Philippi, and Thessalonica. This chapter and the next two are devoted to Paul's work in these places and the letters which he wrote to the churches there. We actually have no extant letters of Paul from this two-year period. The letters to Galatia, Philippi, and Thessalonica all came later, but they will be considered here in connection with the establishment of the congregations.

ESTABLISHING THE GALATIAN CHURCHES

Assuming a "north Galatian" location for Paul's Galatian congregations, they would have been established early in his second missionary period. As was his pattern, Paul started from Antioch, choosing a coworker to accompany him (Acts 15:36–40). He then revisited the churches of his first mission. At Derbe he took on Timothy as an additional partner in the work (Acts 16:1–5). He evidently originally planned to continue westward to the cities of the Asian coast, such as Ephesus, but was diverted by the Spirit. The detour took him northward through the Galatian territory (Acts 16:6).

DEPARTURE FROM ANTIOCH (ACTS 15:36–41)

The Jerusalem Conference had recently been completed. The "decrees" had been delivered to Antioch by Judas and Silas (Acts 15:30–35). Paul's Gentile mission had been formally recognized by the apostles and elders at Jerusalem, and it had been agreed that Gentile converts would not have to be circumcised or to live by the Jewish law. Paul was ready to return to the work. He asked Barnabas to accompany him. It was especially appropriate, since Paul intended to revisit the churches which the two of them established on the first mission.

Unfortunately, a contention ensued between Paul and Barnabas. Barnabas wanted to take again his cousin John Mark. Although Mark had dropped out on the first mission, Barnabas wanted to give him a second chance. Paul, however, was of no mind to take a "quitter." The disagreement was so sharp that the two missionaries parted ways. One wonders if there weren't more to the problem for Paul to have been so adamantly opposed to Mark. Had Mark differed with Paul's accepting Gentile converts without circumcision? Even Barnabas had allowed himself to be pressured into "hypocrisy" by the strict "Torah party" of the Jerusalem church (Gal. 2:13). These are ultimately unanswerable questions, since Luke chose not to delve more deeply into the basis of the disagreement. What he *did* make clear was that Mark was not abandoned. Ever the "Son of Encouragement," Barnabas took his young cousin as his partner on a mission to Cyprus. That way, all the churches of their first mission were revisited and strengthened. Paul returned to Lystra, Derbe, Iconium, and Antioch, and Barnabas revisited the congregations of Cyprus.

Barnabas, of course, "rescued" young Mark. Paul's rejection could have been devastating had Barnabas not expressed *his* confidence in Mark. Paul would later have reason to be grateful for Barnabas's support of Mark. Mark eventually reconciled with Paul and became one of his trusted coworkers (Col. 4:10; Philem. 24; 2 Tim. 4:11). Mark also worked with Peter (1 Pet. 5:13). Reliable early tradition has it that Mark recorded Peter's testimony to Jesus in his Gospel, the first of the Gospels to be written. Of Barnabas's continued ministry we have no further record in the New Testament. Paul commended his unselfish service in 1 Corinthians 9:6. A sixth-century writing, the so-called Acts of Barnabas, claims that he continued to minister on Cyprus, where he died a martyr's death, being burned at the stake outside Salamis.[1] The tradition is not reliable and tells us more about sixth-century Christianity than Barnabas.

Paul chose Silas to be his new partner in mission. Silas had been one of the two official delegates chosen by the leadership of the Jerusalem church to deliver the decrees (15:22, 27, 32). Barnabas had also once been an official representative of the church in Jerusalem (Acts 11:22). Perhaps Paul deliberately chose those who had "Jerusalem connections" as his partners. This would be a means of maintaining good relationships with the Jewish-Christian mother church. Like Mark, Silas later became associated with Peter. He served as Peter's secretary in the writing of 1 Peter (1 Pet. 5:12).

Paul's mission continued to be formally supported by the church of Antioch. The phrase "commended by the brothers to the grace of the Lord" (15:40) is equivalent to the "commissioning" given Paul and Barnabas on the first mission (13:3). Paul and Silas started north from Antioch en route to the churches of the first mission. The main road would have taken them along the coast from Alexandria and Issus into the western Cilician plain, where they would have crossed the Pyramus River at Mopsuestia. From there they would have traveled to Adana, to Tarsus, and from there through the Cilician Gates northward in the Taurus mountains to Derbe.[2] Along the way they "strengthened the churches." As so often with the selective account of Acts, we have no record of the establishment of the churches of northern Syria and Cilicia. They were probably established by the Antiochene Christians and by Paul during his silent years. The Jerusalem church's letter had been addressed to the churches of "Syria and Cilicia" (15:23). Presumably Paul and Silas shared the letter with those congregations, particularly since Silas had been designated as an official delegate to administer it.

REVISITING THE CHURCHES OF PAUL'S FIRST MISSION (ACTS 16:1–5)

Paul revisited his churches in the reverse direction of the order in which they had been established, going this time from east to west. He reached Derbe first and from there proceeded the more than sixty miles to Lystra. At Lystra he found Timothy, whom Luke identifies as a "disciple." He was presumably a convert from Paul's first mission. Timothy's mother is called a "believer." She also was probably converted during Paul's initial work in Lystra. In his second letter to Timothy, Paul spoke of the genuine faith in God exemplified in Timothy's grandmother Lois and his mother Eunice (2 Tim. 1:5). Evidently that genuine Jewish piety had prepared them for receiving Paul's good news about Jesus the Messiah.

Paul wanted to take Timothy along as a coworker, and the Christians of both Lystra and nearby Iconium gave favorable reports about him. There was one problem, however. Timothy was half-Jewish, his mother being a Jewess and his father a Greek. Timothy was uncircumcised. According to the Mishnah, a child born of mixed parentage was considered a Jew when the mother was Jewish.[3] Because of this, Paul had Timothy circumcised. Luke adds that it was because the Jews of the area knew that his father was a Greek. That is, they knew of his mixed parentage and probably were aware of his uncircumcised state. Surely this was the key. Paul circumcised Timothy because the young man was by Jewish law considered a Jew and because he did not wish to put any obstacle in the way of the witness to Jews.

Some have argued that Paul would *never* have circumcised Timothy. They point to such passages as Galatians 5:6 and 6:15, where Paul insisted that circumcision meant nothing, and to Galatians 2:3, where he rejected the circumcision of the Gentile Titus. Paul had fought—and won—the battle in Jerusalem for a *circumcision-free* Gentile mission. So, it is said, he would never have reneged and allowed Timothy's circumcision because of Jewish pressure. He did not *still* preach circumcision himself (Gal. 5:11). The point, however, is that Timothy was *by Jewish definition* a Jew and *not* a Gentile. There is no evidence that Paul ever disavowed circumcision *for Jews*. As a Jew, he remained loyal to the Jewish law himself (1 Cor. 9:20). The circumcision of Timothy was essential if Paul was to continue his practice of beginning his witness in the synagogue. Sometimes 1 Corinthians 7:18–19 is brought into the discussion, where Paul told everyone to remain in the state in which they were called—circumcised should stay circumcised, uncircumcised should remain without circumcision. But that is *precisely* the point: for Paul the term *circumcision* was equivalent to "Jewish," and the term *uncircumcision* to "Gentile." Jews were not to become Gentiles when they became Christians, and Gentiles were not to become Jews. But Timothy *was* a Jew. He belonged to "the circumcision." So, Paul had him circumcised.

Timothy may have been set aside formally for his Christian ministry. First Timothy 1:18 speaks of prophecies that were once made concerning his special calling. In 2 Timothy 1:6 Paul spoke of how he had laid hands on Timothy, and in 1 Timothy 4:14 he mentioned how the elders had done the same. Likewise, in 1 Timothy 6:12 he spoke of Timothy's confession that was delivered in the presence of many witnesses. All of this sounds very much like a special setting apart of Timothy for his ministry. This might well have taken place at Lystra when the brothers from there and from Iconium "spoke well" of him (v. 2).

Timothy may have filled a role in Paul's entourage much like that occupied by Mark at the beginning of the first mission. Unlike Mark, however, Timothy seems never to have slackened in his devotion to Paul's work. He was with Paul throughout his second and third periods of missionary activity (Acts 17:14–15; 18:5; 19:22; 20:4), and Paul mentioned him frequently in his letters. Two were addressed to Timothy, and he is listed as cosender in six others (2 Corinthians, Philippians, Colossians, 1 Thessalonians, 2 Thessalonians, Philemon). Paul called him his fellow worker in the gospel (Rom. 16:21; 1 Cor. 16:10). He reminded the Corinthians of how Timothy had joined him and Silas in first presenting them with the gospel (2 Cor. 1:19). He had served as Paul's personal representative to Thessalonica (1 Thess. 3:2). In every respect he was like a "son" to Paul (1 Cor. 4:17; 1 Tim. 1:2; 2 Tim. 1:2; Phil. 2:22). In fact, Paul said, he had no other coworker who possessed such a selfless devotion to the cause of Christ (Phil. 2:19–21).[4]

From Lystra Paul, Silas, and Timothy "traveled from town to town" (16:4). Presumably they followed the route of Paul's first missionary journey, from Lystra to Iconium and from there to Pisidian Antioch. They are said to have delivered the decrees from the Jerusalem leaders. They were not *required* to do so. These churches were outside the territory of Syria and Cilicia to which the letter was addressed. However, there had been Jewish converts in towns like Iconium and Pisidian Antioch along with the Gentile converts. Since the decrees were primarily designed to enable table fellowship, they would have been very appropriate to "mixed" congregations such as these. When Paul left the area of his first journey and established the churches of northern Galatia, they seem to have been primarily Gentile in composition. The decrees would have been less relevant there. In any event, there is no more mention of Paul and Silas sharing them after 16:4. The final verse of the paragraph is a typical Lukan summary statement. Paul's visits to his former congregations strengthened them, and they flourished (v. 5). Luke's summaries usually served as transitions. The narrative now moves on to the next stage in Paul's mission.

THE GALATIAN "DETOUR" (ACTS 16:6; GAL. 4:12–20)

After revisiting the churches of his first mission, Paul evidently intended to proceed westward into the province of Asia. He was probably headed for the cities of the Aegean coast, especially Ephesus. Luke says, however, that he was prevented by the Holy Spirit from carrying through on this plan. He evidently then started northward, which he would have to do to reach Bithynia, which seems to have been his new destination (v. 7). Luke describes Paul as traveling "throughout the region of Phrygia and Galatia." If he started northward from Pisidian Antioch, his route would have taken him through the area where Phrygia overlapped the northern portion of Galatia. This would have been somewhere around Pessinus, the westernmost of the cities of the ancient Galatian kingdom. It may well be that Paul stopped in "northern" Galatia and established churches there. Luke does not mention his doing so, but, as we have seen, Luke was often selective in his coverage of Paul's work.

In Galatians 4:12–20 Paul spoke of the occasion when he first shared the gospel with the Galatians. He said that it was because of an illness that he stopped in Galatia. The reference is of interest in determining Paul's "thorn in the flesh." Evidently, it was the sort of malady that could have provoked the Galatians's scorn. Instead, they welcomed him as if he had been "an angel of God," almost as if he had been "Christ Jesus himself" (v. 14). Paul may have been talking metaphorically when he reminded the Galatians how they would have ripped out their own eyes and given them to him (v. 15). It is also possible that his illness in some respect involved his eyes. The most important concern for our present consideration, however, is that on this founding visit to Galatia the apostle was very gladly received. Paul reminded the Galatians of the warmth of their relationship. In fact, Galatians 4:12–20 is permeated with the language of friendship. Paul used it to bring the Galatians away from the false gospel that was threatening them and back to the original gospel they had heard him preach on that first visit.

The northern portion of the Roman province of Galatia consisted of the ancient kingdom of the Gauls, which centered around the three settlements of Pessinus, Tavium, and Ancyra. Caesar Augustus had set up three administrative regions around these three ancient cities. Apart from them, the area was primarily rural and sparsely settled. The countryside was hilly and rather bleak, snow-covered in winter, hot and dusty in the summer. The natives of Galatia were primarily the ancient Celtic stock that had migrated from Gaul, rude and somewhat belligerent in temperament.[5] The Galatians of Paul's epistle seem to have been primarily Gentiles, having once served the pagan gods who by nature "are not gods" (Gal. 4:8).

Ancyra was the most prominent of the Galatian cities, lying at the intersection of the main north–south and east–west trade routes. Augustus had built a marble temple there as a center of the imperial cult. Paul would more likely have stopped further east at Pessinus. Pessinus was famous as a center of the cult of Cybele, the Mother Goddess, an ancient fertility deity. The temple of Artemis at Ephesus was dedicated to this same ancient Phrygian deity. The cult of Cybele was noted for its ecstatic worship. It was presided over by the Galli, a group of eunuch priests who emasculated themselves in a state of ecstatic frenzy. It may well be that the practices of Cybele worship prepared the way for the later fascination of the Galatians with circumcision.

OCCASION FOR THE GALATIAN EPISTLE

There is little scholarly consensus on most issues involving the setting of the Galatian epistle—when it was written, where to, from where, and why. No serious doubts have been raised about Paul being the author, but that is where the agreement ends. The most important issue for understanding the message of the epistle is to determine who were Paul's opponents at Galatia.

TIME AND PLACE

Some scholars maintain that Galatians is Paul's earliest extant epistle. They believe that Paul wrote it from Antioch before the Jerusalem Conference and before the second missionary journey.[6] In our chronology, this would be around A.D. 48. This view necessitates a "south Galatian" destination for the epistle. One can, however, hold to a south Galatian destination for Galatians and still maintain that it was written at a later date. For example, B. W. Robinson believed that Paul addressed the letter to the south Galatian churches founded on his first missionary journey, but he also argued that Paul wrote the letter later, after he returned to Antioch at the *end* of his second mission (that is, around A.D. 52).[7]

There are good reasons for dating Galatians during the period of Paul's third mission. The epistles which have the most in common with Galatians were written during the course of his third mission. Especially noteworthy are 2 Corinthians, in which Paul fought the same sort of Judaizing battle as in Galatians, and Romans, in which Paul's treatment of justification by faith resembles the Galatian epistle. Because of these similarities, A. T. Robertson placed Galatians *between* 2 Corinthians and Romans, maintaining that Paul wrote it during his last visit to Corinth (Acts 20:2–3). The date would be late fall of A.D. 56 or early in A.D. 57.[8] A plausible case could also be made for Paul's writing Galatians in Ephesus, early in the period of his three-year ministry in that city, around A.D. 53.[9] Pessinus was to the east of Ephesus, on a main road and not that far away. It is easy to envision one of Paul's coworkers traveling that road to inform the apostle about the troubling developments in Galatia. One can also picture Paul dictating a hasty, angry letter to the "foolish" Galatians and dispatching it at once.

THE OPPOSITION TO PAUL'S GOSPEL

Determining the opposition in Galatia is not an easy task. Paul was writing at a distance and was evidently informed by others of the Galatian situation. He may not have been fully aware of all that was transpiring himself. Still, he said enough in the letter to give us an idea of some elements of the Galatian problem. Somebody was disturbing the Galatians, throwing them into confusion (1:7; 5:10). Paul never named the person or persons who were doing this. He always referred to them with the indefinite pronoun; they were only "somebodies," whom Paul really considered to be "nobodies" (6:3). Neither did Paul ever say whether these disturbers came from inside or outside of the congregation.

Paul did give some particulars about their teaching. They were evidently maintaining that the Galatians, who were Gentiles, should be circumcised (Gal. 5:2; 6:12). They also were encouraging them to maintain a special worship calendar—days, months, seasons, and years (4:10). Paul gave no other particulars about their system except to judge it as being a form of slavery (5:1). He considered the Galatian attraction to these disturbing new teachings as a form of apostasy; they were deserting Christ (1:6). He accused the teachers of wanting to escape persecution (6:12). He considered them to be opposing him personally by seeking to steal the loyalty of the Galatians away from him (4:17). In fact, they seem to have brought Paul's apostolic status into question, accusing him of being subordinate to the Jerusalem apostles (1:15–2:9) and of receiving his gospel "from men" (1:1; 11–12). They may even have argued that Paul advocated circumcision himself (5:11).

Paul was absolutely livid. He was angry with the Galatians for so quickly deserting the true gospel for a perversion (1:6). They were stupid; they were abandoning the Spirit for the flesh (3:1–5). They were alienating themselves from Christ, falling away from the way of grace into the way of law (5:2–4). He was angry with the disturbers for proclaiming such a perversion of the gospel. He implied that their "other gospel" was a path straight to hell (1:9) and that they would pay the penalty for their false teaching at the last judgment (5:10). He accused them of being wicked sorcerers who had bewitched the Galatians (3:1).[10] He said that they possessed an inflated self-esteem (6:3). He implied that they were morally depraved, accusing them of wishing to glory in the flesh of the Galatians (6:13). (Paul had just maintained in 5:17 that flesh and Spirit were in total conflict with each other.) The teachers were an evil leavening influence, poised to defile the entire loaf (5:9). Paul was so angry with these purveyors of the gospel of circumcision that he expressed his wish that they would finish the job and castrate themselves (5:12).

What is one to make of these statements? What was going on at Galatia? One must bear in mind that in Paul's day people often vilified their opponents, painting them in the starkest hues possible.[11] One should allow for some conventional rhetoric on Paul's part. One should also bear in mind the extreme difficulty of reading someone else's mail. In Galatians, we have a letter written by Paul in response to problems of which he had been informed by others. He did not address the false teachers directly. We have his warning about them to the Galatians. So we have to "mirror read" the position of the opponents from what Paul says to the Galatians.[12] We have only one side of the conversation. It is tricky business, and the widely differing scholarly opinions about the Galatian crisis testify to the difficulty of the task.

IDENTIFICATION OF THE OPPONENTS

Judaizers. The Galatian troublemakers have traditionally been identified as *Judaizers.* Their insistence that the Galatians be circumcised sounds very much like the "believers" from "the party of the Pharisees" at the Jerusalem Conference (Acts 15:5). Their emphasis on calendrical matters also fits those who would have the Galatians adopt Jewish ways. "Days" would correspond to Sabbaths, "months" to the Jewish observance of the New Moon each month, "seasons" to the annual festivals of Judaism, and "years" to sabbatical years (Gal. 4:10). Just how much of the Jewish law they insisted upon the Galatians adopting is not clear. Paul's insistence that to adopt one part of the law meant that one was submitting to the whole law may have come as a surprise to the Galatians (Gal. 5:3). The Judaizers may have only insisted on certain external marks of the covenant, like keeping the calendar and being circumcised.[13] It is more likely that they represented the strict Jewish Christian viewpoint. They insisted that Christians were Jews and that all Gentile Christians consequently must convert to Judaism in order to be followers of Christ the Messiah. They insisted on Gentiles being circumcised and living by the letter of the Torah. In short, they were either ignorant of or they ignored the decisions reached at the Jerusalem Conference.

We know that this sort of strict Jewish Christianity continued to exist long after Paul in small enclaves like those known as Ebionites. They observed a strict Torah-centered worship, which seems to have subordinated the Messiah to the Torah.[14] What was unique to the Pauline period was their effort to reach Gentiles. In their later existence they were strictly confined to Jews.

We would thus differ with those who see the Judaizers as having formal connections with the apostles and elders at Jerusalem. They were a group who did not accept the agreement worked out between Paul and the "pillar" apostles at Jerusalem (Gal. 2:9). Just where they came from and why they felt the urgency to circumcise Paul's converts we do not know. It has been suggested that the growing influence of zealotic Jews in the last two decades before the Jewish War put pressure on the Jewish Christians to conform more faithfully to the Torah. This is seen as explaining their efforts to circumcise the Gentile converts and to have them fulfill sufficient externals of the Torah to give the appearance of being faithful proselytes to Judaism. This is also seen as what Paul was referring to when he said that their efforts to circumcise the Gentiles were done "to avoid being persecuted" (Gal. 6:12).[15]

Evidently they claimed to be the true representatives of the apostles. It is otherwise hard to account for Paul's insistence on the *independence* of his apostolic commission in Galatians 1:11–2:13.[16] They also probably made extensive use of the Old Testament in urging circumcision for the Galatians. It is quite likely that the Scriptures used by Paul in Galatians 3 and 4 were originally used by the Judaizers to support their argument that only the circumcised are heirs of God's promises to Abraham. They sought to convince the Galatians that they could not be a part of God's people without circumcision. Paul felt otherwise: for him, Gentile Christians could not share in God's covenant if they *were* circumcised.

Gentile Judaizers. A minority viewpoint argues that the Galatian Judaizers were neither Jewish Christians nor outsiders. Instead, they are seen as *Gentile* members of the Galatian congregation whose study of the Old Testament led them to believe that they should be circumcised if they were to be a part of God's covenant people.

This understanding was strongly advocated by Johannes Munck.[17] He argued that Paul had shared with the Galatians a very positive picture of Jerusalem and the Jewish Christian leadership there. He did not even raise the issue of circumcision with them. After Paul's departure, their study of the Scripture led them to question whether they should adopt circumcision and aspects of the law. Like new converts today, they sought a higher holiness. Galatians 6:13 is a key in Munck's argument. He sees it as referring to members *presently within* the Galatian congregation who were being circumcised and seeking to have the others follow their precedent. They were not Judaizing Jewish Christians, who would have been obedient to the whole Torah. They were instead Gentile members of the Galatian congregation who had embraced only some elements of Torah practice. This is why Paul insisted throughout the letter that they must keep *all* the law if they were going to pursue any part of it (Gal. 3:10; 5:3). The problem with Munck's view is the first part of the letter, where Paul defended his apostolate and insisted on his *independence* from the Jewish Christian leadership. His recollection of the conflict at Antioch (Gal. 2:11–17) does not point to an issue of Gentile "Judaizing" but of fellow Jewish Christians doing so. Paul's debate throughout Galatians is with fellow Jews, between the Jew Paul and the Judaizing Jewish Christians.[18]

Two fronts. Another position with limited advocacy argues that Paul was having to fight on two fronts at Galatia. Those who hold this viewpoint usually see Judaizers as constituting one of the fronts. But they see Paul as also fighting another, opposite tendency in the Galatian church. This is sometimes labeled "antinomian," or "libertine," or "spiritualist/enthusiast," or "Gnostic."[19] Whatever label is used, the basis of this view is Paul's extensive treatment of ethics and the Spirit in 5:13–6:10. It is felt that this reflects an opposite problem to the legalism being imposed by the Judaizers, a problem of antinomian behavior and the abuse of freedom. In their words, Paul was having to fight two conflicting tendencies, tendencies that have plagued the church throughout its history—legalism and libertinism.

No one would deny that Paul faced this proverbial ethical dilemma in his churches. The question is whether there was an actual group at Galatia with a Gnostic or hyper-spiritualist agenda, with a "theology" of their own. In recent years, it has become less popular to argue that Paul fought on two distinct fronts in the Epistle to the Galatians. Some, however, *would* argue that the legalistic and spiritualist elements in Galatians can be traced to a single "Gnostic" front.

Gnostics. Before examining the viewpoint that Paul's opponents at Galatia were "Gnostics," it might prove helpful to give a brief sketch of what is meant by "Gnosticism." Classically, the term *Gnosticism* has been used to refer to certain early Christian heresies that are discussed in church fathers like Irenaeus, Origen, and Epiphanius. There were many different systems associated with various teachers like Simon, Basilides, and Valentinus. Coming to prominence in the mid-second century, Gnostic sects attracted many members and presented a real threat to the church. In modern scholarship, Gnosticism is often defined in much broader terms, including not only Christian but also non-Christian groups.[20] A Gnostic library was discovered in 1945 at Nag Hammadi in Upper Egypt. It consisted of some fifty-one separate treatises—some Gnostic Christian, some non-Christian Gnostic, and some not Gnostic at all. Though the writings themselves date from a later period, some scholars have argued that some are pre-Christian in origin. A debate has raged over whether it is proper to speak of "pre-Christian Gnosticism," particularly over whether there was a pre-Christian "redeemer myth."[21] For our purposes, we will use the term *Gnosticism* in the sense of the church fathers; that is, as a Christian heresy. Our attention will be confined solely to Gnosticism's influence, if any, on the Pauline writings.

The term *Gnosticism* casts a wide net and includes many diverse systems, even when restricted to the Christian groups. All Gnostics, however, held certain views in common. All believed in a cosmological dualism of matter and spirit. For the Gnostic, there were only these two basic realities; everything that exists is either spirit or matter. They usually gave an ethical value to the two; matter is evil, spirit is good. Gnostics invariably saw humans as dualistic, consisting of eternal spirit trapped in a material body. All Gnostic systems generally had a myth to explain how this human predicament came about. The individual myths differed from system to system but usually started with an original eternal spirit world, sometimes called the "fullness" (Gk., *plērōma*). Then came some sort of fall, with emanations of spirit falling out of the spirit world into lower spheres. Gnostics usually had an elaborate cosmology of multiple spheres marking various degrees of fallenness. At the top, in the highest heaven, was the *plērōma*, the realm of pure spirit. At the bottom, in the lowest heaven, resided the most fallen of the spirits which emanated from the spirit world. This was the *demiurge*, or creator. The *demiurge* created the material world, including humans. Only the most fallen, evil spirit could create the material world since matter itself was seen as evil. But trapped within the human creature is a fragment of the eternal spirit, a fragment whose real home is in the *plērōma*, the world of perfect spiritual unity. The human's destiny, then, is to escape the bondage of the body and return as spirit to one's home in the highest spirit world.

Gnostics often described humans as being "asleep," unaware of their real home and eternal destiny. Humans are awakened from their sleep of ignorance when they are fully informed of who they are, where they belong, and how to get there. This saving knowledge is called *gnōsis* (Greek for "knowledge"). Hence the term *Gnosticism*—salvation by knowledge. The saving knowledge is brought by a "redeemer" figure, a savior who descends from the *plērōma*. In the earlier Gnostic systems, Christ becomes a redeemer figure, bringing the saving knowledge. Early Gnostic writings like the Gospel of Thomas include many esoteric teachings which purport to be the saving knowledge brought by Jesus. (Many sayings are very much like the sayings found in our four Gospels; others are heavily "Gnosticized"; while others are wholly

Gnostic with no resemblance to the Gospel tradition.) These early Gnostic systems had a "docetic" Christology—that is, they rejected the incarnation, seeing Christ as purely spirit. The redeemer had to remain spirit; he could not be contaminated with evil matter.

The Gnostics also had no place for the atonement. The earliest systems were adoptionist, seeing the eternal Christ as "possessing" the man Jesus and departing before the death on the cross. Later systems did not mention the cross at all; salvation was strictly by the knowledge which the redeemer brought, not by his death on a cross.

When people become fully informed of the saving knowledge, they are "perfected," and at death their spirit separates from the body and ascends to the *plērōma*. Human spirits who do not possess the saving *gnōsis* are destined for endless reincarnations in matter until they are finally awakened by the saving knowledge. Among the Gnostics, ethics could go in one of two directions. They were often ascetics. Assuming that matter is evil, they made every effort to withdraw from it. They were often celibate, vegetarian, abstainers from strong drink, withdrawn from society into their own little conventicles. Other Gnostic groups went the opposite direction, drawing the opposite conclusion from the same premise that matter is evil. Since they were enlightened Gnostics, fully spiritual and risen above the level of matter, they could flaunt their freedom and do as they wished. Matter no longer had any control over them. The church fathers, probably for polemical reasons, labeled most Gnostics as libertines. The Gnostic writings which we have uncovered, however, would indicate that most Gnostics probably fell more in the ascetic camp.

We have provided this lengthy discussion of Gnosticism not because it is all that important to the Galatian problem, but because it has a way of coming up in discussions of the background of nearly every Pauline epistle. As for Galatians, only a few scholars advocate a Gnostic problem for the epistle. Most prominent among those who do is Walther Schmithals.[22] Schmithals has a reputation for seeing Gnosticism as the key to unlocking every Pauline mystery. Galatians is no exception. Schmithals argued that Paul contended in Galatia with a *Jewish Christian Gnosticism*. He was thus able to combine the legalistic and spiritual elements of the two-front theories into a single front. The difficulty with this is that we have no sources whatever for a Jewish Christian Gnosticism. Schmithals "constructed" such a group from heterodox Christian writings of the second century and later and from remarks made about Gnostics by the church fathers. He then "discovered" this form of the heresy in the Pauline writings, a virtual *tour de force* of circular reasoning. The crucial consideration is that there is really no evidence whatsoever of any Gnostic viewpoints in Paul's Galatian opponents.[23] Schmithals pointed to the emphasis on Spirit and freedom in Galatians, but one need not go beyond apocalyptic Judaism or Paul's own theology to find these emphases.

A STUDY OUTLINE OF GALATIANS

In his commentary on Galatians, Hans Dieter Betz made a major contribution not only to the study of Galatians but also New Testament study in general when he structured the epistle according to the canons of Greek rhetorical theory.[24] He classified the epistle as an "apologetic" letter, a type of forensic (judicial) rhetoric. Using the categories of such a rhetorical presentation, he delineated Galatians 1:6–11 as the *exordium*, the initial appeal to the Galatians as Paul presented his case. Betz saw

Galatians 1:12–2:14 as corresponding to the *narratio*, in which the main issues are set forth. The next element is the *propositio*, the main argument or thesis (2:15–21). The proofs supporting the argument constitute the *probatio* (3:1–4:31). Finally, Betz designated 5:1–6:10 as the *exhortatio* (or *paraenesis*). Betz admitted that he had trouble fitting this primarily hortatory section in his scheme. Others have differed with Betz over the category of the Galatian rhetoric, arguing that the epistle has more in common with deliberative (legislative) rhetoric than with forensic rhetoric.[25] Still, the study of Galatians in the light of ancient rhetorical convention is proving fruitful, and our own debt to these studies will be apparent in our summary of the epistle.

Rhetorical outlines run the risk of forcing the text to fit the theory. In the outline that follows, a more thematic approach is taken, organizing the epistle around its emphasis on freedom. Galatians has often been called a "charter of freedom."[26] Of twenty-nine occurrences of the word *freedom* in Paul's epistles, twelve occur in Galatians. The Galatians had once been enslaved to the gods and superstitions of pagan religion. They had found freedom in Christ. Paul did not want them to surrender that freedom for a new slavery to the law.

I. Introduction (1:1–9)
   A. Address (vv. 1–5)
   B. Occasion (vv. 6–9)
II. The Freedom of Paul's Apostleship (1:10–2:21)
   A. The Gospel That Is Not from Humans (1:10–17)
      1. It is not "people-pleasing" (v. 10)
      2. It did not come from humans (vv. 11–12)
      3. It came through conversion (vv. 13–14)
      4. It came through election (vv. 15–17)
   B. The Independence of Paul's Apostleship (1:18–2:10)
      1. Independent of Jerusalem at the outset (1:18–24)
      2. Independent at the Jerusalem Conference (2:1–10)
   C. The Testing of Paul's Gospel (2:11–21)
      1. The confrontation at Antioch (vv. 11–13)
      2. The argument against legalism (vv. 14–19)
      3. The new being in Christ (vv. 20–21)
III. Appeal for the Galatians to Return to Freedom (3:1–4:31)
   A. Appeal from the Galatians' Experience (3:1–5)
   B. Appeal from the Scriptures (3:6–14)
      1. Abraham's faith (vv. 6–9)
      2. The law's curse (vv. 10–14)
   C. Appeal Based on the Limitations of the Law (3:15–25)
      1. It does not abrogate the covenant with Abraham (vv. 15–18)
      2. It was given through intermediaries (vv. 19–20)
      3. It consigns all things to sin (vv. 21–22)
      4. It is at best a custodian in our minority (vv. 23–25)
   D. Appeal to Be the True Children of God (3:26–4:11)
      1. The new basis of becoming God's children—in Christ (3:26–29)
      2. Not slaves, but free children (4:1–7)
      3. The threat of relapse into slavery (4:8–11)
   E. Appeal Based on Personal Friendship (4:12–20)
   F. Concluding Appeal from Scripture (4:21–31)

HIGHLIGHTS OF GALATIANS

THE ADDRESS (1:1–5)

In several respects Paul departed from his customary salutation in Galatians. First, there is the emphatic statement that he received his apostleship from God and not from man. Paul often noted that he was called as an apostle by the will of God, but the negative statement that it was *not from man* is striking. It prepares for his argument that in no way was he dependent on the Jerusalem apostles. A second unique emphasis is that of Christ's giving himself to deliver us from "the present evil age" (v. 4). That Christ's death *alone* is the source of our salvation is an emphasis that runs throughout Galatians. That Christ delivers us from the present evil age and places us in a new creation (6:15) provides a cosmic framework for the entire epistle.[27] A third observation is that Paul omitted his customary thanksgiving and prayer for the Galatians. He was too upset with them to include it.

THE OCCASION (1:6–9)

This paragraph sets forth the occasion which prompted Paul to write the epistle. "Some people" (indefinite) were throwing the Galatians into confusion, attempting to pervert the gospel (v. 7). And the Galatians were following their lead! Employing military language, Paul said that they were "deserting" their calling in Christ (v. 6). Paul often used the word *calling* to refer to one's being called into the body of Christ, that is, to one's Christian commitment. Here at the outset he stated what really had him concerned about the Galatians; they were abandoning their original Christian calling for a false gospel. They were turning away from grace (5:4). Paul continued by emphasizing that there is only one gospel, and that is the gospel he had preached to them. Paul used emphatic language. Let anyone, even an angel, go to hell, if they preached a different gospel, because there *is* no other gospel, only false gospels. Paul was not swearing when he consigned the purveyors of a false gospel to perdition. He was convinced that they were headed exactly for that destination if they didn't mend their ways.

THE FREEDOM OF PAUL'S APOSTLESHIP (1:10–2:19)

This "autobiographical" section of Galatians has already been treated extensively in previous chapters. At this point we will only note how it lends itself to the overall argument of Galatians. Obviously Paul was concerned to establish the independence of his gospel. It came directly from God. He was called from his mother's womb. It was neither his own doing nor that of any other person (1:13–17). He was not indoctrinated by the Jerusalem apostles but visited them only briefly three years after his conversion. He insisted that this was the "gospel truth" (1:18–20). The other side of the picture, of course, is that he *did* go on his own initiative to Jerusalem to meet with Peter and James.[28] He *was* concerned that his ministry would receive the recognition of the wider Christian community. The same was true of his second visit to Jerusalem. He went of his own free will, by revelation (2:2). Exactly what he meant by "revelation" is uncertain. Whatever it referred to, it indicated that he was not "summoned" to Jerusalem. God directed his paths. Still, he did not want to "run in vain"; he wanted the recognition of the Jerusalem leadership.

The main question is, Why did Paul consider it necessary to provide this long autobiographical emphasis on the independence of his apostolate? The usual answer is that the Judaizers were forcing him to it. They were either accusing him of being no apostle at all, or, what is more likely, of being inferior in status and subordinate to the Jerusalem apostles. The Jerusalem apostles, they might have said, advocated a gospel that included circumcision. Paul's gospel didn't. Thus, Paul's was a false gospel. He had abandoned circumcision to "please men" (1:10). To this Paul responded by maintaining his independence of the Jerusalem apostles, even his readiness to confront them when they were clearly in the wrong (2:11–13).

There is another possibility. Paul may not have been responding to charges from Judaizers at all. He may have introduced the autobiographical section to provide a model for the Galatians. Those who were introducing circumcision in Galatia were threatening to enslave the Galatians with the false gospel of Torah. But Paul had been converted on the Damascus road to a gospel of freedom, and he had never turned back to the old enslavement, either with the apostles in Jerusalem, or with Peter in Antioch. Peter may have wavered because of the pressure from the people of James, but not Paul. Paul thus held himself up as a model of freedom and urged the Galatians to follow his example (cp. 4:12).[29]

THE NEW BEING IN CHRIST (2:20–21)

Betz sees 2:15–21 as the "proposition," the main argument or thesis of the epistle. It combines two major Pauline metaphors for salvation. First he used the law-court language of justification: we have become acceptable to God not by observing the law but by placing our faith in Christ Jesus (v. 16). But then Paul moved to a second picture, which in actual fact was his most frequent language for describing salvation: we have been crucified with Christ (v. 20). Paul often spoke of salvation in terms of our dying with Christ, dying to the old way of life, dying to the law (v. 19). Paul conceived of salvation in terms of "power spheres" or "dominions." Before Christ we lived "in the flesh," under the power of the present evil age (1:4), under the dominion of law, of sin, and of death. In Christ we died to the old dominion and were raised to the new existence of righteousness, of life, and of the Spirit. No longer do we live in the old humanity; we live in the new humanity in Christ, and Christ lives in us.[30]

Galatians 2:20 is considered a classic expression of Pauline "mysticism": "I have been crucified with Christ and I no longer live, but Christ lives in me." What exactly did Paul mean by Christ "living in me"? Scholars of the history-of-religions school like Bousset and Reitzenstein saw the phrase "in Christ" as evidence that Paul believed in a hellenistic type of mysticism in which the mystic was seen as being absorbed into the being of the divinity. But there are significant differences between hellenistic mysticism and Paul's concept of being in Christ. In Greek mysticism, the mystic initiated the contact with the divinity through mystic contemplation, seeking to be caught up into the being of the god. In Paul's "mysticism," union with Christ does not swallow one's personal identity.[31] Adolf Deissmann thus suggested that Paul's mysticism was of a different type, not personal striving for the beatific vision but a "reacting" sort of mystical possession in which one responds to the prior action of God's Spirit in one's life. It was a *real* possession of the believer by Christ. Deissmann described it as "quasi-physical," living in the element of Christ just as one lives in the air that is breathed. In Deissmann's view of Pauline mysticism, the believer's identity is never lost in the union with Christ, and living in Christ is seen as virtually synonymous with being filled with the Spirit.[32]

Albert Schweitzer pointed to the *eschatological* basis of Pauline mysticism. To be "in Christ" is to be incorporated into the people of the Messiah. Schweitzer saw this in both individual and corporate terms. Like Deissmann, he advocated an actual physical indwelling and saw this union with Christ as taking place through participation in baptism and the Lord's Supper.[33] Many contemporary scholars would agree with Schweitzer's eschatological understanding of Paul's "mysticism." They also would agree with his corporate emphasis. To be "in Christ" is to belong to the people of the Messiah, to be incorporated into the church, the new humanity.[34]

It is now generally agreed that Paul probably had no set "in Christ" formula. He used other expressions like "with Christ," "through Christ," and "of Christ" to express the same reality of the believer's union with Christ. Scholars also recognize that Paul used the actual phrase "in Christ" in various ways. Particularly did he employ it in soteriological terms; God's saving purposes are brought about in the believer through/in Christ Jesus.[35] Paul used the language of being in/with/of/through Christ in a variety of contexts which embrace the totality of the Christian experience: salvation through the death and resurrection of Christ, incorporation into the church/body of Christ, empowerment for the Christian ethical life, participation in the new creation.[36] To be "in Christ" is to belong to the new humanity of the "Second Adam."[37] The concept of being in Christ is pervasive in Galatians. It is found in the new community of "oneness" in Christ Jesus (3:28), in the idea of being sons of God through the one true Son (4:6), in the reality of living by the power of the Spirit (5:16), in belonging to the new creation (6:15). There is no fuller expression for the totality of the Christian life than Paul's language of incorporation into Christ.

APPEAL FROM THE EXPERIENCE OF THE GALATIANS (3:1–5)

In chapters 3 and 4 Paul employed several lines of argument in his attempt to refute the Judaizing error. First he appealed to the initial conversion experience of the Galatians. They responded in faith when Paul first brought them the message of the crucified Christ. This was sufficient. They received the Spirit as evidence of their acceptance into Christ, and they continued to observe the Spirit's power in their midst (v. 5).[38] We do not know what sort of suffering (v. 4) they had experienced—whether from the Gentile populace or the Jewish synagogue—but Paul's point is clear: their initial faith was strong enough that they were willing to suffer for it. But now, under the influence of the Judaizers, they were adding works of the law. For Paul the two were antithetical. It was *either* law *or* Spirit; it could not be both. The contrast continues throughout the letter.

APPEAL FROM THE SCRIPTURES (3:6–14)

Paul continued his argument by citing six Old Testament texts. His choice of Scripture was probably in large part dictated by the Scriptures the Judaizers had been using. They had probably used a text like Genesis 17:10–14 to argue that the Galatians would be cut off from God's people if they did not keep the covenant of circumcision which God had made with Abraham. Paul responded with Genesis 15:6 to argue that Abraham's standing with God was not based on circumcision or any other work but solely on faith. He then pointed to the promise which God made with Abraham that he would bless all the nations of the world through him (Gen. 12:3; 18:18). Paul then connected the two texts to argue that God's promise to bless the nations would be fulfilled through the kind of *faith* which Abraham exhibited.

The Judaizers probably cited Deuteronomy 27:26 to argue that those who did not abide by the Torah were under a curse.[39] Paul turned the text back on them by arguing that the opposite was the case—that in effect the law placed those who would live by it under a curse, since they were obligated to fulfill it in every respect, an impossible task (cp. Gal. 5:3).[40] Paul's fourth citation was Habakkuk 2:4. It was *his* text.[41] He chose it because it connected righteousness with faith: "The righteous will live by faith." He then paired it with Leviticus 18:5, which linked living and doing, to argue that faith and law are antithetical. One lives either by faith or by the "doing" of the law, one or the other. But right standing with God can only come by faith, as Habakkuk 2:4 makes clear.

Paul's concluding text in this section was Deuteronomy 21:23: "Cursed is everyone who is hung on a tree." Christ died on the tree of the cross. He became a curse for those who lived under the curse of the law. Born under the law (Gal. 4:4), he took the curse of the law upon himself. It is an argument very much like that of 2 Corinthians 5:21: he who knew not sin became sin for us.[42] The Jews, of course, were those who lived under the "curse" of the law. Christ's death removed the law's curse and opened up the way of salvation for Jews and Gentiles alike.[43] It is with this thought that Paul ended in verse 14. Note the emphasis on the "promise of the Spirit." Paul began his scriptural argument by speaking of the promise God made to Abraham that the nations/Gentiles would be blessed in him (v. 8). Now he equated the fulfillment of the promise with the gift of the Spirit. He began the chapter by contrasting Spirit and law. He then showed how the law brings a curse, a curse that Christ removed. Christ brought the Spirit. The Spirit is the primary evidence that Jew and Gentile have experienced the promise of salvation in Jesus Christ.[44]

APPEAL BASED ON THE LIMITATIONS OF THE LAW (3:15–25)

In verse 15 Paul introduced an argument from human analogy: no one can take away from a ratified will. In the same way God's faith-covenant with Abraham is inviolable. The law, which was given 430 years later to Moses, can in no way abrogate God's prior covenant with Abraham. To make it even more explicit, Paul then referred to the promise of blessing to Abraham's offspring in Genesis 12:7. Noting that the noun *offspring* is singular in that passage, Paul argued that the promise applied to *one* person only, and that person is Christ the Messiah. For all intents and purposes, Paul separated law from covenant altogether.[45] God's *only* true covenant is the covenant of promise to Abraham which includes both Jew and Gentile. That covenant of promise is fulfilled in Christ and in Christ alone.

Paul pointed out how the law was inferior in other ways as well. For one thing, it was given by angels through an intermediary. Paul was probably drawing from the Jewish tradition that the law was administered to Moses through the agency of angels. The tradition undoubtedly arose to enhance the holiness of the law, but Paul used it to argue its inferiority. He noted that a mediator implies more than one party. But God is one. God thus cannot have two covenants—a covenant of promise and a covenant of law. There can only be the one covenant, and that is the single covenant for *all* people which the one God made with Abraham.[46]

Paul may have realized at this point that his polemic against the Judaizers was leading him to a wholly negative assessment of the law. So he provided two reasons for God having given the law. First, it placed all the world under the judgment of sin (vv. 21–22). It set the limits and established culpability. Second, the law served as a guardian. Paul used the word "pedagogue" (vv. 24–25). Pedagogues were household slaves who served as custodians of children between the ages of six and sixteen. They were protectors and disciplinarians, keeping the children under restraint.[47] So the law served a positive function of keeping those subject to it in check. But pedagogues are for children, not for the mature.

APPEAL TO BE THE TRUE CHILDREN OF GOD (3:26–4:11)

Paul felt that by placing themselves under the law the Galatians were surrendering the freedom which they had found in Christ. They were submitting to the old covenant of the law, which was *no* covenant, and they were surrendering the covenant of promise. But God is one, and he has given only the one covenant for all, Jew and Gentile alike. All who have been baptized into Christ are fully mature, free sons and daughters of God through faith. They are "in Christ," a part of the new creation where the old human distinctions of race, status, and sex no longer have a place.[48] There is one God and one new humanity in Christ. The Jewish law could not serve as a basis for the new humanity. Its ritual demands separated people rather than uniting them. Faith in Christ unites; it fulfills the promises to Abraham (v. 29).

In Galatians 4:1–7 Paul returned to the same basic point he had made before about the law being a custodian or pedagogue. He changed his metaphor to that of a child who is an heir and under a trusteeship until the time of full majority. For the Jew the law played the role of guardian. The child was tied to the trustee, unable to touch the inheritance and scarcely any better off than a slave. In verse 3 Paul probably intended to extend the metaphor to the Gentiles. Before they knew Christ, in the time of *their* minority, they were slaves also—to the "basic principles of the world." Paul probably had in mind the superstition and fatalism of their former Gentile religion.[49] In any event, Jews and Gentiles alike were no longer children but had come into their full inheritance in Jesus Christ. Born under the law, Christ had borne its curse himself and redeemed those under the law (cp. 3:13). Those who belong to him, the true Son, themselves become children of God. They are no longer slaves, but children of God, joint heirs with Christ. The context of verse 6 is probably worship. The Spirit inspires the believer to cry "Abba," the intimate family word for "father," which Jesus taught his disciples to use when addressing their heavenly father. Once again the major contrast is prominent: the law means slavery, the Spirit marks sonship.

The Galatians were in danger of falling back into their former slavery. Before Christ came to them they most likely had worshiped the religion of nature, like the cult of Cybele with its emphasis on the turning seasons. Bound to the fatalism of an endless cycle of seasons and to the fear of nature's forces, they were enslaved by their belief in powers which were in reality no gods at all. By submitting to the law they were falling back into the same kind of slavery—bound to rules, no longer free. They had found freedom in Christ, but now they were about to revert to slavery. Paul worried about them. His appeal now took on a more anguished, personal tone (4:11).

APPEAL BASED ON PERSONAL FRIENDSHIP (4:12–20)

This section has already been treated at the beginning of this chapter. In it Paul appealed to the time when an illness forced him to stop in Galatia and first take the gospel there. Commentators often refer to it as a digression. It is anything but a digression. It is a strong personal appeal. In ancient rhetoric, personal appeal was one of the strongest means of persuasion available. Paul began by pleading for the Galatians to follow his own example (v. 12). He had set it before them in 1:10–2:21; it was an example of *freedom in Christ*. Then he reminded them of the relationship of trust and devotion that they had enjoyed between them in the past. He asked them why it should have changed (vv. 13–16). Finally, he warned them about the bad motives of the Judaizers (vv. 17–18) and assured them of his own genuine concern for them (vv. 19–20). He used a striking metaphor. He would gladly suffer the pains of childbirth if he could birth the Galatians to Christ once more!

CONCLUDING APPEAL FROM SCRIPTURE (4:21–31)

Paul returned to Scripture in his final argument against the Judaizers. This time he offered a striking "allegory" about Sarah and Hagar. Paul may have developed it because the same text was being used by the Judaizers.[50] It is easy to see what they could have argued from it. They would have pointed out that Abraham had two sons, Ishmael by the slave Hagar, and Isaac by his wife Sarah. God's chosen people descended from Isaac, while Gentiles descended from Ishmael. They would have urged the Galatians to join the true heirs of Abraham, the line of Isaac, by submitting to the law and circumcision.

Whether responding to an interpretation of the Judaizers or not, Paul turned the story on its head. He equated the Sinaitic law covenant with Hagar because it represented slavery. He then further equated Hagar with the earthly Jerusalem, because its inhabitants the Jews stood enslaved to the Torah. The free children, the true descendants of Abraham, are the children of the promise. Their covenant corresponds to the heavenly Jerusalem. No Jew could have fathomed Paul's equation of Hagar with Sinai and Jerusalem, but Paul was not speaking to Jews. He was speaking to Gentiles who were inclining to the Torah. His contrast for them was plain. They were free sons of the promise that God had made with Abraham. Did they want to submit to the slavery of Torah? Paul's real purpose in employing the allegory is probably most evident in his quotation of Genesis 21:10 in verse 30: "Get rid of the slave woman and her son." That is precisely what Paul wished the Galatians to do to the Judaizers with their enslaving message.

CONDUCT IN SERVITUDE AND CONDUCT IN FREEDOM (5:1–26)

Galatians 5:1–6:10 should probably not be viewed as a "paraenetic addendum" only loosely connected to the main argument of Galatians. Ethics may have been at the very heart of the Galatian problem. The Galatians may have been turning to the legalism of the Judaizers out of a felt need for a guide in their daily living. In this section Paul attempted to persuade them that the law really wouldn't help them attain the lifestyle they desired. It was an ethic of the "flesh," doomed to failure.[51] There was a higher ethic for the free children of God, an ethic lived in the Spirit. The theme for the section is set in 5:1. It is actually the theme of the entire epistle: Christ has called us to freedom; do not submit to a "yoke of slavery," which the Judaizers' appeal to the law would be.

Galatians 5:2–12 is the most direct assault on the Judaizers in the entire epistle. For the Galatians to be circumcised would render their faith in Christ meaningless (v. 2). They would have opted for the law rather than the Spirit. The Galatians may have seen the Judaizers' requirements as an addendum. Paul wanted them to realize that it was all or nothing. To submit to the law was to live by all of it (v. 3). To submit to the law was to live under the dominion of the law and not under the grace of Christ (v. 4). It was an either/or for Paul: to fall into the law-way was to fall out of the grace-way. There is only one means of obtaining "righteousness" (right standing) with God—through faith in Christ (v. 5). Faith in Christ knows no ethnic boundaries, no circumcised Jew or uncircumcised Gentile (v. 6). All are one in Christ Jesus (3:28). But to rely on Torah is to live by such boundaries. Paul's statement about "love" being what really counts was not just a passing reference. There seems to have been a real problem of fellowship in the Galatian community (cp. 5:13–15). In verses 7–12 Paul turned his guns directly on the Judaizers. He accused them of leading the Galatians away from the truth (v. 7). They were like leaven at Passover, rendering the whole lump of dough useless (v. 9). But they would get what was coming to them—on judgment day if not sooner (v. 10). If Paul had his way, they would let the knife slip and lop off the whole member (v. 12). This is all very clear language. What is not clear is what Paul meant when he insisted in verse 11 that he was no longer circumcising. Were some claiming that he was? Had the Judaizers argued that Paul still recognized the practice of circumcision for Gentiles? If so, Paul wanted to set the record straight.

In Galatians 5:13–15 Paul addressed the need for responsible expression of freedom within the Christian fellowship. He may have been alluding to an actual situation in the congregation of which he had been informed. The present tense of the verbs in verse 15 would indicate that this was the case. Paul's gospel of freedom sometimes led to misunderstanding. Freedom could be abused on both an individual and a social level. Individually, it could be viewed as a license for indulging the appetites. Corporately, it could result in one's trampling on the rights of others. The best antidote to the latter is love. People who love do not abuse their freedom in their relationships with others (v. 13). What did Paul mean by "law" in verse 14? Did he mean the Torah? He clearly did in Romans 13:8–10, when he spoke of love "fulfilling" the entire law. In Galatians Paul may not have meant the Torah.[52] He was too put out with the Judaizers to say anything really positive about the law. He may have meant something like the "law of Christ" (6:2), referring to Jesus' summation of the law as love for God and love for one's fellow human being (Mark 12:30–31). In a similar context, where Christians were using their sense of freedom in the Spirit to lord it over one another, Paul called upon love as the gift that unites rather than divides (1 Cor. 13).

Galatians 5:16–26 is probably the most familiar part of the epistle, with its lists of fleshly works and spiritual fruit. Verses 16–18 set the context with their sharp antithesis between flesh and Spirit. It is a dualism, but not the cosmological dualism of Gnosticism which views flesh as matter and thus inherently evil. Rather, it is an ethical and an eschatological dualism. To live by the "flesh" is to live by the spirit of the world, of the "present evil age" (1:4). To live by the Spirit is to live "in Christ," in the new creation (6:15). Note how law is a part of Paul's antithesis (v. 18). Law belongs to the old age, not to the new creation in Christ. It cannot be the basis of conduct for those who are in Christ. They are not directed by law but by the Spirit of Christ.

Paul often employed lists of vices to be avoided and virtues to be pursued. They were a standard form of ethical teaching in his day. The lists are representative, not exhaustive. They are sometimes rather stereotypical but also are often adjusted to the specific situations in the congregations Paul was addressing. This seems to be the case with the lists in Galatians. There was obviously conflict within the fellowship, so it comes as no surprise that many of the vices and virtues are of a social nature.

There are fifteen vices. Paul called them "works" (*erga*) of the flesh, the same word that he used in describing the works (*erga*) of the law (2:16). The vices can be grouped into four categories: Three are sexual (immorality, impurity, debauchery), two deal with false worship (idolatry, witchcraft), eight relate to interpersonal relationships (hatred, discord, jealousy, rage, selfish ambition, dissensions, factions, envy), and two deal with sins of personal excess (drunkenness, orgies). Since interpersonal relationships were a problem at Galatia, Paul weighted the list in that direction.

The same holds true for the virtues. Paul called them "fruits." They are not "works" pursued but gifts granted by God's Spirit. There are only nine of these, and all but the last one (*self-control*) have a social dimension. *Love* has already been given pride of place earlier in the chapter (5:5, 13–14). *Joy* is the joy of belonging to the new humanity in Christ. *Peace* comes from living under the shelter of God and within his people. *Patience* is forebearance, holding back when others get under your skin. *Kindness* and *goodness* are active words, expressing kind deeds and acts of charity to others. *Faithfulness* is fidelity in one's relationship with God and with others. *Gentleness* is not being arrogant or selfish but considering others as more important than oneself (Phil. 2:3).[53] Paul added that against such "there is no law." He probably also meant that the law is not effective in creating such qualities. It takes the Spirit. These "fruits" are a mark of membership in the new humanity. They characterize those who have died and risen with Christ, burying the old person with its selfish desires.

Verse 26 returns to the theme of getting along with one another. Evidently there was considerable conflict within the Galatian fellowship. One wonders how much the Judaizing controversy contributed to this.

FREE TO SERVE (6:1–10)

Galatians 6:1–5 should probably be viewed in the context of 5:16 and 5:26. Paul was still dealing with the problems of selfishness and strife within the fellowship. He urged the Galatians to restore the erring brother or sister gently and not censoriously (v. 1). Verses 3 and 4 should be taken in the same vein. One should regard oneself realistically and examine oneself in order to be able to share the burdens of others. In the end, however, each will be responsible for his or her own load. There is probably a note of judgment implicit in verse 5. Verse 6 is something of a surprise. Was providing for teachers a problem in the Galatian congregation? The principle is sound and in accordance with the teachings of Jesus (1 Cor. 9:14), but one wonders what prompted it. The saying about sowing and reaping also should be taken in the context of 5:13–15. Some had been sowing discord, biting and devouring others. Paul urged them to sow the seeds of peace and love so that they might reap the harvest of the Spirit's fruit in their fellowship.

CONCLUSION (6:11–18)

Verse 11 would indicate that Paul used an amanuensis in writing Galatians. Whether or not the "large letters" indicate a problem of eyesight one can only speculate about. Paul did not exchange any of his customary greetings. Instead, he took a final shot at the Judaizers and gave a final appeal to follow his own example. In so doing, he ended the letter with some of the main traits of a classical Greek *peroration* (final summation in a rhetorical argument). He criticized his opponents (vv. 12–13). He held up himself as an example (vv. 14–16), especially seeking to evoke the sympathy of the Galatians as he reminded them of how he bore in his body the marks of suffering for Christ (v. 17). To the very end of the letter Paul held his ground against the Judaizers. There was no room for the niceties of epistolary convention—no greetings, no travel plans, no word about his present circumstances—just a narrow focus from the beginning of the letter to the end on Paul's gospel of freedom. The Galatians were about to exchange it for a new bondage to the law. Paul relentlessly called them back to the freedom of the Spirit which they once knew when the apostle first opened the gospel to them.

NOTES

1. D. Smith, *The Life and Letters of St. Paul* (New York: George H. Doran, n.d.), 118.

2. W. M. Ramsay, "Paul's Road from Cilicia to Iconium," *Pauline and Other Studies in Early Christian History* (New York: A. C. Armstrong and Son, 1906), 273–298.

3. Mishnah *Qiddushin* 3.12. See S. Belkin, "The Problem of Paul's Background," *Journal of Biblical Literature* 54 (1935): 41–60. Some would argue that the Mishnaic evidence is too late (A.D. 200) to maintain that the matrilineal law was in effect in Paul's day; e.g. S. J. D. Cohen, "Was Timothy Jewish (Acts 16:1–3)? Patristic Exegesis, Rabbinic Law, and Matrilineal Descent," *Journal of Biblical Literature* 105 (1986): 251–268.

4. See J. P. Alexander, "The Character of Timothy," *Expository Times* 25 (1913–1914): 277–285.

5. For a good description of the Galatian temperament, see J. Murphy-O'Connor, *Paul, A Critical Life* (Oxford: Clarendon, 1996), 185–191.

6. This view usually equates the Jerusalem visit of Galatians 2:1–10 with the "famine visit" of Acts 11:28–30 and argues that the Acts 15 conference had not yet taken place. W. M.

Ramsay strongly advocated this view: *The Teaching of Paul in Terms of the Present Day* (London: Hodder and Stoughton, 1913), 383–403.

7. B. W. Robinson, *The Life of Paul* (Chicago: University of Chicago Press, 1918), 144–147.

8. A. T. Robertson, *Epochs in the Life of Paul* (New York: Scribner's, 1909), 200–205.

9. Murphy-O'Connor, *Paul, A Critical Life*, 185.

10. J. Neyrey points out that this was not mere name calling on Paul's part but an actual charge of working under Satanic influence: "Bewitched in Galatia: Paul and Cultural Anthropology," *Catholic Biblical Quarterly* 50 (1988): 72–100.

11. A. du Toit, "Vilification as a Pragmatic Device in Early Christian Epistolography," *Biblica* 75 (1994): 403–413.

12. J. M. G. Barclay, "Mirror-Reading a Polemical Letter: Galatians as a Test Case," *Journal for the Study of the New Testament* 31 (1987): 73–93.

13. J. C. Beker, *Paul the Apostle: The Triumph of God in Life and Thought* (Philadelphia: Fortress, 1980), 42–44.

14. J. L. Martyn, "A Law-Observant Mission to Gentiles: The Background of Galatians," *Scottish Journal of Theology* 38 (1985): 307–324.

15. R. Jewett, "The Agitators and the Galatian Congregation, *New Testament Studies* 17 (1970–1971): 198–212.

16. If one takes the Jerusalem Conference seriously, it is difficult to agree with Howard that the Judaizers were not antagonistic to Paul but saw him as representing their own viewpoint, even to the extent of circumcising Gentile converts: G. Howard, *Paul: Crisis in Galatia, A Study in Early Christian Theology*, 2nd ed. (Cambridge: Cambridge University Press, 1990).

17. J. Munck, *Paul and the Salvation of Mankind* (Richmond: John Knox, 1959), 87–133. A similar view is taken by L. Gaston, *Paul and the Torah* (Vancouver: University of British Columbia Press, 1987).

18. J. D. G. Dunn, "Echoes of Intra-Jewish Polemic in Paul's Letter to the Galatians," *Journal of Biblical Literature* 112 (1993):459–477.

19. A two-front theory was popularized in this country by J. H. Ropes, *The Singular Problem of the Epistle to the Galatians* (Cambridge, Mass.: Harvard University Press, 1929).

20. For the "existentialist" treatment of Gnosticism, which defines it more as a way of viewing reality than as a phenomenon of church history, see H. Jonas, *The Gnostic Religion*, 2nd ed. (Boston: Beacon Press, 1963).

21. There is no real evidence for a pre-Christian redeemer myth. See E. M. Yamauchi, *Pre-Christian Gnosticism: A Survey of the Proposed Evidences* (Grand Rapids: Eerdmans, 1973). For a good introduction to Gnosticism, see R. M. Wilson, *The Gnostic Problem* (London: A. R. Mowbray, 1958).

22. W. Schmithals, *Paul and the Gnostics*, trans. J. E. Steely (Nashville: Abingdon, 1972), 13–64.

23. R. M. Wilson, "Gnostics—in Galatia?" *Studia Evangelica*, Vol. IV, Part I: *The New Testament Scriptures*, ed. F. L. Cross. Texte und Untersuchungen, 102 (Berlin: Akademie Verlag, 1968), 358–367.

24. H. D. Betz, *Galatians: A Commentary on Paul's Letter to the Churches in Galatia* (Philadelphia: Fortress, 1979). For a summary of his outline, see H. D. Betz, "The Literary Composition and Function of Paul's Letter to the Galatians," *New Testament Studies* 21 (1975): 353–379.

25. R. G. Hall, "The Rhetorical Outline for Galatians: A Reconsideration," *Journal of Biblical Literature* 106 (1987): 277–287. A third analysis suggests that Galatians 1:10–2:21 should be considered *epideictic* rhetoric: G. Lyons, *Pauline Autobiography: Toward a New Understanding*, SBL Dissertation Series, 73 (Atlanta: Scholars, 1985). The fact that scholars can't even agree on the type of rhetoric is a warning against rigid rhetorical analysis. Paul

was probably familiar with certain rhetorical conventions of his day, and it is helpful to look for these. That he was trained in rhetoric or followed its strict canons is dubious.

26. B. W. Robinson, *The Life of Paul*, 147; D. Guthrie, *The Apostles* (Grand Rapids: Zondervan, 1975), 115–128.

27. B. R. Gaventa, "The Singularity of the Gospel," *Pauline Theology, Part I: Thessalonians, Philippians, Galatians, Philemon*, ed. J. M. Bassler (Minneapolis: Fortress, 1994), 147–159.

28. Paul lived in a group-oriented culture in which acceptance by the larger community was imperative. See B. J. Malina and J. H. Neyrey, *Portraits of Paul: An Archaeology of Ancient Personality* (Louisville: Westminster John Knox, 1996), 34–51.

29. G. Lyons, *Pauline Autobiography*, 125–176. A similar view is expressed by B. R. Gaventa, "Galatians 1 and 2: Autobiography as Paradigm," *Novum Testamentum* 28 (1986): 309–326.

30. R. C. Tannehill, *Dying and Rising with Christ: A Study in Pauline Theology* (Berlin: Toepelmann, 1967), 55–61.

31. A. Wikenhauser, *Pauline Mysticism: Christ in the Mystical Teaching of St. Paul* (New York: Herder, 1960), 183–242.

32. A. Deissmann, *Paul: A Study in Social and Religious History*, trans. W. E. Wilson (New York: George H. Doran, 1926), 135–157. C. K. Barrett criticized Deissmann's virtual equation of Christ with the Spirit. He distinguished between the *objective* event of being incorporated into the new age "in Christ" and the *subjective* experiencing of the power of the new age through the indwelling of the Spirit: *Paul, An Introduction to His Thought* (Louisville: Westminster John Knox, 1994), 134.

33. A. Schweitzer, *The Mysticism of Paul the Apostle*, trans. W. Montgomery (New York: Macmillan, 1931).

34. For example, see E. P. Sanders, *Paul and Palestinian Judaism* (Philadelphia: Fortress, 1977), 453–472, and N. T. Wright, *The Climax of the Covenant* (Minneapolis: Fortress, 1992), 41–49.

35. M. A. Seifrid, "In Christ," in *Dictionary of Paul and His Letters*, ed. G. F. Hawthorne and R. P. Martin (Downers Grove, Ill.: InterVarsity, 1993), 433–436. See also A. J. M. Wedderburn, "Some Observations on Paul's Use of the Phrases 'in Christ' and 'with Christ,'" *Journal for the Study of the New Testament* 25 (1985): 83–97.

36. J. D. G. Dunn, *The Theology of Paul the Apostle* (Grand Rapids: Eerdmans, 1998), 390–412.

37. W. D. Davies, *Paul and Rabbinic Judaism* (London: S.P.C.K., 1958), 86–110.

38. D. J. Lull notes that Paul connects the receiving of the Spirit with the Galatians' response of faith in the gospel and not with their baptism: *The Spirit in Galatia: Paul's Interpretation of the Promise of Divine Power*, SBL Dissertation Series, 49 (Chico, Calif.: Scholars, 1980), 54–74.

39. N. H. Young, "Who's Cursed—and Why? (Galatians 3:10–14)," *Journal of Biblical Literature* 117 (1998): 79–92.

40. T. R. Schreiner, "Is Perfect Obedience to the Law Possible? A Re-Examination of Galatians 3:10," *Journal of the Evangelical Theological Society* 27 (1984): 151–160.

41. E. P. Sanders, *Paul, the Law, and the Jewish People* (Minneapolis: Fortress, 1983), 17–27.

42. F. F. Bruce, "The Curse of the Law," in *Paul and Paulinism: Essays in Honour of C. K. Barrett*, ed. M. D. Hooker and S. G. Wilson (London: S.P.C.K., 1982), 27–35.

43. T. L. Donaldson, "The 'Curse of the Law' and the Inclusion of the Gentiles: Galatians 3.13–14," *New Testament Studies* 32 (1986): 94–112.

44. G. D. Fee, *God's Empowering Presence: The Holy Spirit in the Letters of Paul* (Peabody, Mass.: Hendrickson, 1994), 395.

45. J. L. Martyn, "Events in Galatia," in *Pauline Theology*, Vol. I, ed. Bassler, 171–174.

46. N. T. Wright, *The Climax of the Covenant*, 171–172.

47. See N. H. Young, "*Paidagogos*: The Social Setting of a Pauline Metaphor," *Novum Testamentum* 29 (1987): 150–176; D. Lull, "'The Law Was Our Pedagogue,': A Study in Galatians 3:19–25," *Journal of Biblical Literature* 105 (1986): 481–498; R. N. Longenecker, "The Pedagogical Nature of the Law in Galatians 3:19–4:7," *Journal of the Evangelical Theological Society* 25 (1982): 53–61.

48. For the possible background of Galatians 3:28 in a dominical saying, see D. R. MacDonald, *There is No Male and Female: The Fate of a Dominical Saying in Paul and Gnosticism*, Harvard Dissertations in Religion (Philadelphia: Fortress, 1987). For a possible Cynic background to the saying, see F. G. Downing, "A Cynic Preparation for Paul's Gospel for Jew and Greek, Slave and Free, Male and Female," *New Testament Studies* 42 (1996): 454–462.

49. In verses 3 and 9 Paul employed the word *stoicheia*, the exact meaning of which is debated. It could refer to "rudimentary/elementary principles" (ABC's): D. R. Bundrick, "Ta Stoicheia Tou Kosmou (Gal. 4:3)," *Journal of the Evangelical Theological Society* 34 (1991): 353–364. It often meant the basic compositional "elements" of the world—earth, air, fire, and water: E. Schweizer, "Slaves of the Elements and Worshipers of Angels: Gal. 4:3, 9 and Col. 2:8, 18, 20," *Journal of Biblical Literature* 107 (1988): 455–468. Or it could refer to the spiritual powers which the Greeks believed controlled the universe: D. G. Reid, "Elements/Elemental Spirits of the World," *Dictionary of Paul and His Letters*, 229–233.

50. C. K. Barrett, *Essays on Paul* (Philadelphia: Westminster, 1982), 154–170. See also P. Borgen, "Some Hebrew and Pagan Features in Philo's and Paul's Interpretation of Hagar and Ishmael," in *The New Testament and Hellenistic Judaism*, ed. P. Borgen and S. Giversen (Peabody, Mass.: Hendrickson, 1997).

51. W. Russell, "Who Were Paul's Opponents in Galatia?" *Bibliotheca Sacra* 147 (1990): 329–350.

52. J. L. Martyn, *Theological Issues in the Letters of Paul*, 235–249.

53. The discussion of the virtues and vices is largely drawn from G. Fee, *God's Empowering Presence*, 427–458.

SELECTED COMMENTARIES

BASED ON GREEK TEXT

Betz, Hans Dieter. *Galatians*. Hermeneia. Philadelphia: Fortress, 1979.

Bruce, F. F. *The Epistle to the Galatians: A Commentary on the Greek Text*. The New International Greek Testament Commentary. Grand Rapids: Eerdmans, 1982.

Burton, Ernest D. *A Critical and Exegetical Commentary on the Epistle to the Galatians*. International Critical Commentary. Edinburgh: T. and T. Clark, 1921.

Lightfoot, Joseph B. *The Epistle of Paul to the Galatians*. New York: Macmillan, 1868.

Longenecker, Richard N. *Galatians*. Word Biblical Commentary. Dallas, Tex.: Word, 1990.

BASED ON ENGLISH TEXT

Cole, R. Allan. *The Letter of Paul to the Galatians, An Introduction and Commentary*. 2nd edition. Tyndale New Testament Commentary. Grand Rapids: Eerdmans, 1989.

Cousar, Charles B. *Galatians: A Bible Commentary for Teaching and Preaching*. Interpretation. Atlanta: John Knox, 1982.

Dunn, James D. G. *The Epistle to the Galatians*. Black's New Testament Commentary. Peabody, Mass.: Hendrickson, 1993.

Fung, Ronald Y. K. *The Epistle to the Galatians*. New International Commentary on the New Testament. Grand Rapids: Eerdmans, 1988.

George, Timothy. *Galatians*. New American Commentary. Nashville: Broadman and Holman, 1994.

Guthrie, Donald. *Galatians*. New Century Bible. London: Thomas Nelson, 1969.

Hansen, G. Walter. *Galatians*. InterVarsity Press New Testament Commentary. Downers Grove, Ill.: InterVarsity, 1994.

Luhrmann, Dieter. *Galatians*. Continental Commentary Series. Minneapolis: Fortress, 1992.

Martyn, J. Louis. *Galatians*. Anchor Bible. New York: Doubleday, 1998.

Matera, Frank J. *Galatians*. Sacra Pagina. Collegeville, Minn.: Liturgical Press, 1992.

McKnight, Scot. *Galatians*. NIV Application Commentary. Grand Rapids: Zondervan, 1995.

Morris, Leon. *Galatians, Paul's Charter of Freedom*. Downers Grove, Ill.: InterVarsity, 1996.

Williams, Sam K. *Galatians*. Abingdon New Testament Commentaries. Nashville: Abingdon, 1997.

Witherington, Ben, III. *Grace in Galatia. A Commentary on St. Paul's Letter to the Galatians*. Grand Rapids: Eerdmans, 1998.

Ziesler, J. *The Epistle to the Galatians*. Epworth Commentaries. London: Epworth, 1992.

9

~✦~

PHILIPPIANS: PARTNERSHIP IN THE GOSPEL

$\mathcal{P}$hilippians has been called Paul's "epistle of joy." The theme of joy pervades the entire epistle (1:4, 18, 25; 2:2, 17–18; 3:1; 4:1, 10). The affectionate tone of the epistle indicates that Paul had a particularly warm relationship with the Philippian Christians. They were notably supportive of his mission. They formed a "partnership in the gospel" which started from the very "first day" (Phil. 1:5).

Paul established the congregation at Philippi on his second mission. Located at the eastern extremity of Macedonia, Philippi was his first church on European soil. His witness there was a major breakthrough—not in a geographical sense, since Philippi was quite close to Asia. Neither was it all that different culturally, since the cities of Asia were thoroughly hellenistic and under Roman dominion. But Philippi was a new part of the world for Paul—the west, the land of the Greeks, the home of Alexander the Great. Paul continued his westward movement as he expanded his witness into areas "where Christ was not known" (Rom. 15:20).

Among Paul's letters, Philippians is dated as variously as is Galatians. Some scholars would place it as early as A.D. 52. Others would put it a full decade later. Without prejudice to the time when Paul wrote the epistle, it will be discussed in *this* chapter. Many details in the letter are illuminated by the Acts account of Paul's establishing the congregation, making it advantageous to consider the two in conjunction.

ESTABLISHMENT OF THE CHURCH (ACTS 16:6–40)

Having left Galatia, Paul started northward toward Bithynia. Bithynia was a Roman province that bordered the Black Sea. Towns with significant populations were located there. Since the Holy Spirit kept Paul from traveling west to the Asian coast, he probably now had set his sight on these Bithynian communities. But again the "Spirit of Jesus" prevented his going there (v. 8). Paul's subsequent route is not clear. Mysia was not a province but a section in the northern portion of the province of Asia. Paul perhaps went from Galatia to Dorylaeum, which was close to the Mysian and Bithynian borders. His plans may have been thwarted somewhere in that area. From there, his route is totally uncertain. There were no major highways in the area. He would have been forced to use back roads. In any event, he headed for the coast, where he stopped at the populous city of Troas. His *route* is insignificant. What *is* important is the strong emphasis on the Spirit's leading. The Spirit prevented Paul from work in Asia (Ephesus) and in Bithynia. Perplexed, he headed westward to the closest major settlement—Troas. He was obviously being "led," but he wasn't sure where.

THE "MACEDONIAN CALL" (ACTS 16:6–11)

Troas. Our sources on Troas are limited. Strabo mentioned the town in the thirteenth book of his *Geography*. He devoted the major part of the book to a discussion of the Troad, especially ancient Troy, but only half a paragraph to Troas. However, he called it "one of the notable cities of the world" (*Geography* 13.1.26). The Troad was the whole land area east of the Hellespont (Dardanelles), the narrow strait which separated Asia from Thrace (eastern Europe). Ancient Troy was located at the southern entrance of the Hellespont. Troas was located ten miles farther south on the Aegean coast.

A settlement at Troas was begun by Alexander the Great. His successor Antigonus continued the project. The most significant development of the town was by Lysimachus, another of Alexander's successors, who had assumed rule over Thrace and the surrounding region. Defeating Antigonus in a coalition with Seleucus, Lysimachus extended his rule into Asia Minor. One of his major projects was Troas, which he developed extensively beginning around 300 B.C. He renamed it *Alexandria Troas* in honor of Alexander the Great. He conferred on it the status of a free city. The city around 190 B.C. came into the hands of the kings of Pergamum who eventually willed the region to Rome. Augustus gave the city the status of a Roman colony, naming it *Colonia Augusta Troas.* In Paul's day it was known simply as *Troas.*

Troas was an impressive city in Paul's time. Strabo states that Lysimachus built a wall around the city which had a circumference of five miles. The shores of the Troad provide no natural harbors. Troas, however, had a fine artificial harbor. Indeed, it was probably for this purpose that Troas was developed in the first place. It was the *only* good harbor in the area of the Troad. It provided a natural shelter for ships awaiting favorable winds for sailing through the Hellespont. It also furnished a convenient connection with Neapolis for land travel between the east and westward travel toward Rome on the Egnatian Way.[1] Paul followed the latter route himself.

Troas is prominent in the New Testament. In addition to Acts 16:8–11, Luke related Paul's visiting Troas at the end of his third mission, at which time he raised the young man Eutychus (Acts 20:5–12). The latter incident indicates that a church had already been established at Troas. The "Macedonian call" seems so "immediate" in Acts 16:9–10 that it is unlikely Paul established work in Troas at that time. In 2 Corinthians 2:12 Paul related the events that occurred to him after he concluded his three-year ministry in Ephesus. He said that he went to Troas and found an "open door" for witness there. He probably established the church there at that time. (Acts 20:5–12 dates about half a year later, after Paul had traveled on to Corinth and back.) A final mention of Troas is found in 2 Timothy 4:13, where Paul asked Timothy to bring the cloak and writings which he had left behind at Troas. This verse seems to indicate that Paul revisited the churches of the east after release from his first Roman imprisonment.[2]

The call (Acts 16:9–10). Verse 9 tells how Paul had a vision of a man of Macedonia calling him to come and witness there. The fact of a vision connects with the emphasis on the Spirit's preventing Paul from working in Asia and Bithynia. The ministry in Macedonia was a new frontier for Christian mission. Consistently in Acts new frontiers are never of human contrivance; they are always by divine direction. Note the implicit trinitarian emphasis in this section: Paul is led by the *Holy Spirit* (v. 6), the Spirit is identified as that of *Jesus* (v. 7), and the entire experience is summarized as being the call of *God* (v. 10).

Paul and his companions departed at once for Macedonia. There were evidently four of them now—Paul, Silas, Timothy, and Luke. Luke is never mentioned by name in Acts. But Luke indicated his presence by speaking in the first person plural. This happens for the first time in Acts 16:10, "*We* got ready . . . concluding that God called *us*." Luke does not indicate *how* he became connected with Paul. Some have suggested that Paul had the need of a physician at Troas and first met Luke in that connection.[3] Others have suggested that Luke was a native of Philippi and was the "Macedonian" who entreated Paul to come and witness in his own region.[4]

It is possible that Luke was a native of Philippi[5] but not likely that he was the "man of Macedonia" of Paul's vision. Luke himself makes it clear that Paul was led by a vision from God and not through a natural human encounter.

The journey (Acts 16:11). The trip from Troas to Neapolis was a common itinerary. In Paul's day it seems to have been the *usual* route for travelers who were headed west by land along the Egnatian Way. The island of Samothrace, halfway on the Troas to Neapolis run, was clearly visible from both places with its five-thousand-foot peak. Under favorable conditions, it was reached in a single day and was the usual stopping place for the night. Evidently the winds and the weather were good. The trip took one day to Samothrace, and after the night there, another day to Neapolis (modern Kavala). Prevailing winds could make a major difference. Later, when making the same journey in reverse, the trip took Paul five days (Acts 20:6).

THE CITY OF PHILIPPI (ACTS 16:12A)

Paul and his three companions landed at Neapolis and traveled the ten miles up to Philippi. Luke described Philippi as "a city of the first portion of Macedonia." In Paul's day, Macedonia was a single administrative entity with Thessalonica as capital. In earlier times, Macedonia had been divided into four districts, with Philippi in the "first" or easternmost division. Whatever Luke meant by "first city," Philippi was the leading city in far eastern Macedonia. Luke also described it as a "colony." It was indeed a Roman colony and had been so for nearly a century when Paul first visited the city around A.D. 49.

The region around Philippi had been settled from ancient times by native Thracians who worked the extensive silver, gold, and copper mines in the region. The mineral deposits were concentrated in the Pangaion mountain range just to the north of the city. Evidently people from the island of Thassos also worked the mines. (Thassos was just off the coast of Thrace, not far from Neapolis.) The Thassians established a settlement at the future site of Philippi around 360 B.C. Having difficulty in warding off the Thracians, in 356 B.C. they appealed for assistance to Philip, the Macedonian king. Seizing the opportunity, Philip established a major city on the site, partly as a line of defense against the Thracians and partly to capitalize on the mineral riches himself. He renamed the city after himself. He was the first great Macedonian leader but is overshadowed by the reputation of his famous son Alexander the Great.

Although Roman control of Macedonia began in 168 B.C., Philippi became closely associated with Rome in 42 B.C., when it was the site of the last great battle of the republican war. The imperial forces that defended the assassinated Caesar (under Antony, Octavian, and Lepidus) were pitted against the pro-republican forces led by Brutus and Cassius. The battle was fought on the "Plains of Philippi" southwest of the city. The victorious troops of Antony and Octavian rewarded Philippi by giving it the status of a colony and renaming it for their victory there: *Colonia Victrix Philippensium*. They settled veterans of the battle there as the colony's nucleus of citizens. Later, after his defeat of Antony at the battle of Actium in 31 B.C., Octavian (later Caesar Augustus) added a number of veterans from Antony's forces to the population of Philippi. He renamed it for his daughter: *Colonia Julia Philippensis*.

The administrative district covered by the colony of Philippi was extensive, embracing some seven hundred square miles from Mt. Pangaion in the north to Neapolis in the south. Like all Greek cities, Philippi was dominated by a hill, its *acropolis*. The original settlement lay at the foot of the acropolis. The later city expanded southward. The Via Egnatia ran through the center of the Roman colony. South of the road the ruins are predominantly Roman—temples to the Roman gods, a shrine for the imperial cult. The most extensive building programs for the city took place *after* Paul, in the second century. Still, Philippi was an impressive and very *Roman* community in Paul's day.[6]

THE FOUNDATIONAL MINISTRY (16:12B–40)

Luke described Paul's establishment of the Philippian Christian community in Acts 16:12–40. His account consists of four episodes, each centering around a main character or group of characters. Luke's episodic style gives the impression of a rapid succession of events and a short stay in the city. In actual fact, Paul's stay probably lasted some time, long enough for a very strong work to be established.[7]

Lydia (vv. 12b–15). Paul and his coworkers sought out the local synagogue in accordance with his usual pattern of beginning his witness in a place. Evidently there was none at Philippi, probably because there was not a large enough Jewish community there. What the four missionaries *did* find was a site outside the city that had been established as a place of prayer (v. 13). It was beside a river. Though synagogues were often located near water to facilitate purification rites, this does not seem to have been one. It was attended only by a group of women. In the Diaspora, Gentile women were often attracted to Judaism, becoming "God-fearers." Lydia is described as being a God-fearer ("worshiper of God," v. 14). This may have been the composition of the Philippian prayer group—a circle of devout Gentile women who had been led to put their faith in God. It is altogether possible that Lydia was the initial and driving force behind the group. She may have come to her faith in God back home in the synagogues of Thyatira. If so, she was a missionary already before Paul met her.

As so often with God-fearers, Lydia's heart was already prepared to hear Paul's message of how God was fully accepting her in Jesus Christ. She responded in faith to God's moving in her heart and was baptized. Her whole household was baptized with her. Their following her in baptism is a witness to the vibrancy of her own faith and the trust she inspired within them.[8] The household baptism reminds us that the earliest church met in homes. It is not incidental that Lydia prevailed on the four missionaries to stay in her home. Her home became the "home base" of the Philippian church (16:40).

Lydia is described as a "dealer in purple cloth" and as having come from the city of Thyatira (v. 14). Thyatira was a city within the region of Lydia, which was a part of the Roman province of Asia. "Lydia" was probably not her given name but what she was known by in Philippi, "The Lydian woman." The purple dye of the Lydian region was well-known, being praised as far back as Homer (*Iliad* 4.141–142). It was made from the juice of the madder root. Goods dyed in purple were quite expensive. Lydia was probably an agent for the purple goods which were woven and dyed in her native region. She was undoubtedly a woman of means. She sold expensive goods, had her own house, and evidently had servants. One cannot help but think that Lydia was a major player in the Philippian church's pattern of supporting Paul financially. One is also impressed with the extensive role that women played in the Philippian church, both in the evidence of Acts and of the epistle.[9]

The slave girl (vv. 16–24). The second episode in Acts relating to Paul's Philippian ministry was his exorcism of a possessed slave girl. The girl was evidently seen as a valuable piece of property, since multiple owners held shares in her (v. 19). Luke described her as having a spirit of a python (v. 16; KJV, "spirit of divination"). The python was a mythical symbol of Apollo, the god who presided over the Delphic oracle. The oracle at Delphi was the most venerated shrine in all of Greece. A priestess sat there on a three-legged stool over what was reputed to be the very center of the earth. In a state of artificially induced inspiration, she was reputed to make amazing predictions of the future. Thus, those who possessed powers of prediction were described as possessing the spirit of the Pythic Apollo. The Greeks put great store by such "psychic" powers, and undoubtedly some paid handsomely to hear this girl's predictions. The girl's powers led her to see into the truth of Paul's message, and she began hailing him as a proclaimer of the "Most High God" and of the "way to be saved." Although all of this was certainly true, the possessed girl was scarcely a genuine witness to Christ, and her words were open to serious misunderstanding by pagans.[10] Exasperated as the girl continued to follow him around with her unsolicited testimony, Paul finally exorcised the demon in the name of Jesus. The demon vanished, and with it the girl's psychic powers—also the financial benefits to her masters.

In Acts, money is often a "root of all evil," whether it be Ananias and Sapphira (5:2), Simon Magus (8:20), or the silversmiths of Ephesus (19:24–28). No longer possessed either by an alien spiritual force or by unscrupulous human profiteers, the girl was truly free for the first time in her life. But freedom means little to people who use others like things, and the owners dragged Paul and Silas off to the magistrates. The scene is filled with local color. It is a Roman colony, a little island of Rome in the Macedonian sea—complete with Roman magistrates, Roman police, and Roman law.[11] The irony, of course, is that the law enforcers become the lawbreakers by flogging the two Roman citizens Paul and Silas without a proper hearing. The charges brought by the owners should not be missed (vv. 20–21). There was nothing illegal with being a Jew; so the first charge had no substance. "Throwing [the] city into an uproar" was little more than rhetorical hyberbole, and the officials knew it meant nothing. The charge that got their attention was "advocating customs unlawful for us Romans." It, too, was nebulous, but it was the type of appeal to patriotic sentiments that was bound to evoke a response of indignation in the populace of the proud Roman colony.

Paul and Silas were stripped and beaten with Roman rods (cp. 2 Cor. 11:25). This is probably the incident of suffering and insult at Philippi which Paul mentioned to the Thessalonians (1 Thess. 2:2). Publicly flogged and humiliated, Paul and Silas were turned over to the town jailer, who secured their feet in the stocks of the inner prison. He was commanded to "guard them carefully," which probably meant literally "with your life."

The jailer (vv. 25–34). The story of the Philippian jailer is familiar, and we will note just a few details. The jailer was at the opposite end of the social spectrum from Lydia. Under Roman government, some civil servants were actually of the slave class—slaves to the city, so to speak. This *may* have been true of the Philippian jailer. The detail that Paul and Silas were singing in the midst of their adversity might have some application to Paul's Philippian epistle. Singing was surely a major means of witness for early Christians. Even here the other prisoners are said to have been listening to their testimony in song. It should come as no surprise if Paul occasionally used hymnic material in his epistles, as some believe is the case with Philippians 2:6–11.

When the earthquake came and the fetters fell, the two prisoners did not run.[12] For them, their witness was more important than their physical safety. This was a lesson Paul emphasized in his Philippian letter. The question of the jailer, "What must I do to be saved?" has often been noted as a *double entendre.* The word *salvation* in Greek means "deliverance." The deliverance can be either physical or spiritual. It is possible that the jailer was asking about his own physical deliverance. As a jailer, his life was on the line. If he lost a prisoner, he could pay with his own life (cp. Acts 12:19). But the jailer's words about salvation occur *after* Paul had assured him that all were accounted for, *after* he had brought Paul and Silas out, *after* any threat to his own life was past. So his words take on the deeper, more spiritual meaning. We do not know how much of Paul's message he was acquainted with at this point, but his words were those of an earnest inquirer. He had just witnessed the power of Paul's Savior, and he wanted a share in that salvation.

Paul's response to the jailer was Paul's consistent message: salvation rests on one thing and only one thing—*faith,* belief and trust in the Lord Jesus. There were temples to many "lords" at Philippi—Isis, Diana, Minerva, Jupiter, Caesar. But only one Lord can truly save, the Lord Jesus Christ. In this account the procedure with "household baptisms" is clear. First, Paul shared the gospel with them all (v. 32). All came to faith in Christ (v. 34). All were baptized (v. 33). Note the radical reversal in the jailer's relationship with Paul and Silas. First, he washed their wounds (v. 33). Earlier he had showed no such concern, evidently securing them in the stocks with the gashes from their flogging still undressed. Of course, he received a "washing," too, the washing of a renewed life that baptism symbolizes. Then he prepared a meal for the two. They were now brothers in Christ.

The magistrates (vv. 35–40). Just why the magistrates changed their minds so quickly we can't be sure. Perhaps the earthquake of the night convinced them that Paul and Silas's God was a deity not to be taken lightly.[13] Whatever the reason, they ordered the release of the two. But then Paul informed the officers sent to release them that they were Roman citizens. That changed everything, particularly in a town like Philippi that prided itself on its colony status. They had abused their own kind, treating them like ordinary provincials. Why Paul pulled this information so belatedly remains a mystery. Perhaps the commotion had been so great the day before that nobody had heard them; perhaps no one believed them. The latter was unlikely. One dared not lie about citizenship; the penalties were too great.

The other question, of course, is why Paul would simply not go in peace as directed. Why did he make such a big issue out of the matter? He certainly was in the right. His rights as a Roman citizen had been abused. The magistrates could get in serious trouble for such abuse. Paul was surely concerned for the young Christian movement and its reputation. He had been imprisoned *as a Christian,* but he had been in the right. He wanted no adverse legal precedents floating around to officials elsewhere. He wanted to set the record straight. He wanted it known that he—and his Christian gospel—had been exonerated at Philippi and had received a formal apology from the magistrates. In his letter to them, Paul reminded the Philippians of the suffering and abuse they had seen him undergo (1:29–30). He urged them not to cower before their opponents but to stand firm in the gospel (1:27–28). He may well have been thinking of this incident. Paul had served as a model of strength and courage in the face of opposition. He urged the Philippians to do the same.

The account in Acts of Paul's initial work in Philippi ends where it began—with Lydia (v. 40). The church held its meetings in her home. She was certainly a pillar, perhaps *the* pillar of the Philippian congregation. She may well be the one behind the strong support and loving concern that the Philippian congregation shared with Paul throughout his missionary work.

THE PHILIPPIAN EPISTLE

Several aspects of Philippians draw particular attention from current scholarship. Few today would question the Pauline authorship of the epistle, although there were those in the nineteenth century who did so.[14] The issues most debated today revolve around the place from which Paul wrote the epistle, whether the letter as we have it is an integral whole or a composite of several letters, and the identification of the opponents in chapter 3. Especially prominent in recent work are questions regarding the occasion for the epistle and its literary nature.

PAUL'S PLACE OF IMPRISONMENT

Paul wrote Philippians from prison—at least the first chapter of the epistle, where he repeatedly referred to his "chains" (1:7, 13–14, 17). Thus, scholars have grouped it together with other of Paul's epistles which were written from confinement and have designated them the "Prison Epistles." The group consists of Colossians, Philemon, Ephesians, and Philippians. The category of Prison Epistles can be misleading, however, as it implies that the four somehow "belong together." Colossians, Philemon, and Ephesians certainly do belong together. The language, content, and persons mentioned in these three letters link them and indicate that they were written at the same time. There is no such linkage with Philippians, however, and nothing that would necessitate it having been written during the same imprisonment as the other three. Because of this, scholars differ widely over where and when to place Paul's writing of the letter.

The traditional view, which was that of the earliest church fathers, places the epistle during Paul's house arrest in Rome as he awaited trial before Caesar (Acts 28:30–31). The date would be around A.D. 60–62. Several references within the epistle seem to link it with Rome. In Philippians 1:13, for instance, Paul spoke of witnessing to the whole "palace" or "palace guard." He used the Greek word *praetorium*, which was a term used also of the emperor's elite personal troops—the Praetorian Guard. The most natural place to find the emperor's palace guard would be where the palace was located—Rome. This is not as certain as appears on the surface, however. Detachments of the imperial Praetorian Guard were located throughout the empire. In fact, if *praetorium* is taken in its broad sense, a palace guard could be found anywhere a palace was located. But Paul also referred to "Caesar's household" in Philippians 4:22. In Paul's day a reference to a person's "household" often referred to the servants, and that is surely the meaning here. One would expect to find Caesar's household servants where his house was located—in Rome. But again, the term is more ambiguous than it appears. "Caesar's household" was a term applied to civil servants who served in the imperial administration. "Caesar's household" was the imperial bureaucracy and was to be found wherever the Roman presence had established itself. Of course, other things might indicate a Roman imprisonment as the setting for Philippians. The uncertainty of his trial outcome is indicated in several places, which would fit well Paul's anxiety as he awaited the hearing before Caesar (cp. 1:21–26; 2:17).

But Paul was uncertain in the face of an impending trial elsewhere as well—at Caesarea. Paul made his appeal to Caesar during his two-year confinement in Caesarea. He appealed to Caesar precisely because he feared the governor Festus would take him to Jerusalem for trial, a scenario likely to end in his death (Acts 25:6–12). Many scholars would thus place Philippians in Caesarea. The detail about the Praetorian Guard (Phil. 1:13) fits Caesarea perfectly, because Paul was confined in that city within "Herod's praetorium" (NIV, "palace," Acts 23:35). Other details in the Philippian letter would suit a Caesarean origin. Philippians 1:7 may refer to Paul already having made a "first defense." This was true at Caesarea, where Paul made an initial defense before Governor Felix. Also Paul felt confident of release when he wrote Philippians (cp. 1:25; 2:24), a prospect some think would be more likely before Felix or Festus in Caesarea than before Nero in Rome.[15] If written from Caesarea, Philippians would date betwen A.D. 57 and A.D. 59.

Many would argue for Paul writing Philippians during an *Ephesian* imprisonment. There is no reference to an Ephesian imprisonment of Paul, either in Acts or in Paul's epistles. There is "room" for one, however. In 2 Corinthians 11:23 Paul spoke of "frequent" imprisonments, but at the time he wrote 2 Corinthians, we have explicit reference in Acts to only one—that at Philippi. There *had* to be others—but neither Luke nor Paul spoke directly of any. In 1 Corinthians 15:32 Paul mentioned his having "fought wild beasts in Ephesus," which could be a metaphorical expression for a very trying time, such as an imprisonment. In 2 Corinthians 1:8–10 Paul mentioned a "deadly peril" in Asia (Ephesus), when he despaired even of life itself. That statement could be linked to his ambivalence over life or death in Philippians 1:20–26. It is possible that Paul was confined by the Asiarchs of Ephesus in a sort of protective custody during the time of the riot provoked by the silversmiths (Acts 19:28–31). There *is* a ruin on the site of ancient Ephesus, a tower known locally as "the prison of Paul." The tower is too late to be associated with Paul, but at least is testimony to a local tradition of the apostle's having been imprisoned in the city.

There are several things which make the Ephesian hypothesis quite attractive for Philippians. First, there is the extensive travel implied in the letter. Paul talked of

Epaphroditus having come to him and having become ill. News of this reached Philippi. Word came back to Paul that the Philippians were distressed over Epaphroditus's illness. Now Paul was sending Epaphroditus back with this letter (Phil. 2:25–28). Paul planned to send Timothy to Philippi somewhat later and hoped to come soon himself (Phil. 2:23–24). All told this implies a minimum of six trips, which is much easier to picture between Ephesus and Philippi (one hundred miles) than Rome and Philippi (eight hundred miles).[16] A second consideration is that Paul referred to Judaizers in the third chapter of Philippians, a problem which he addressed primarily in the correspondence of his third (primarily Ephesian) mission (Galatians, 2 Corinthians, Romans). Likewise, the language of "righteousness" in Philippians 3:7–10 has much in common with Romans and Galatians.

Finally, Paul spoke in Philippians 4:10–15 of the Philippians having revived their concern for him by sending him a gift. If Paul were in Ephesus, the gift would have come no more than five years after their earlier gifts. If in Rome, it would have been more than ten years, a long time for the church to wait on sending support. If one postulates an Ephesian origin for Philippians, the date would be some time between A.D. 52–55, within five years of the establishment of the church.

One other possibility has been mentioned—a Corinthian imprisonment during the course of Paul's second mission, around A.D. 50, before he appeared before Gallio.[17] This view has few advocates. The other three all have strong defenders. It can be seen that persuasive cases can be made for each. This writer finds it difficult to choose between these options; if pressed, the balance seems to tilt more toward the Ephesian hypothesis.[18]

ONE EPISTLE OR THREE?

In the early nineteenth century a few scholars began to question whether our present Philippians might not be a composite of two or more letters from Paul to Philippi.[19] The usual view was to see the epistle as composed of two letters. Philippians 3:2–4:1 was seen as a separate polemical fragment inserted into the other letter. Many recent scholars likewise maintain the composite nature of Philippians. Usually they see the present Philippians as composed of fragments from three separate letters.

A typical example is that of Pheme Perkins. She sees fragments from three letters written in the following order: (1) 4:10–20, Paul's thanks for the Philippian gift, (2) a personal letter of Paul detailing his present circumstances and the disposition of his case (1:1–3:1 + 4:2–7[8–9]), and (3) a separate fragment warning against Judaizing preachers (3:2–4:1).[20] Other reconstructions follow the same general pattern: a thank-you note (4:10–20), a polemical fragment (3:2–4:1), and a personal and/or "unity" letter (the rest of the letter). There are differences of detail, especially on where to start the polemical fragment (at 3:1b or 3:2?), or where to stop the polemical fragment (at 4:1 or 4:3?), and which letter to put the conclusion with (4:21–23).

The reasons for seeing the letter as composite often start with the remark of the second-century Christian writer Polycarp. In his letter to the Philippians, he spoke of the "letters" (plural) which Paul had written them. Polycarp may have based this on Philippians 3:1, where Paul spoke of writing the same things "again" to the Philippians. Most would agree that Polycarp simply opens up the possibility of a composite letter. The more significant arguments for partition are based on internal considerations. For instance, it is pointed out that Paul usually reserved for the *end* of his letters the sort of personal remarks that one finds in 2:19–30. The next verse (3:1) is seen as a concluding type of statement and is translated "in conclusion, farewell in the Lord." The Greek allows for this, since the word *rejoice* is the characteristic word of greeting one often finds in the salutations and conclusions of Greek letters (*chairete*). It is so used in 2 Corinthians 13:11 where it is also used in conjunction with "finally." The phrase "good-bye in the Lord," however, is strange and would be unique for Paul.

Further arguments for partition point to "breaks" indicated by the benedictions at 4:9 and 4:20, which are seen as marking conclusions to letters. It is also maintained that Paul would not have reserved his "thank-you" for the end of the letter but would have put it up front (hence the arguments that it was originally a separate note of thanks). But putting thanks first seems more a convention of modern rather than ancient letters, and Paul often included doxologies and benedictions within the *bodies* of his letters.

There are strong reasons for seeing the letter as a unity. The same themes run throughout *all parts* of the letter. Particularly is this true of the emphasis on joy and rejoicing. The theme of suffering permeates the letter (1:29; 2:17; 3:10) as do emphases on humility (2:2, 7; 3:3, 8) and struggling for progress in the Christian life (2:12–14; 3:12–16). As David Garland has pointed out, the motif of Christian "citizenship" forms an *inclusio* at 1:27 and 3:20, which links the so-called "polemical fragment" integrally to the entire letter.[21] The thank-you does not come only at the end of the letter. It is already implicit in Paul's thanksgiving to God for the Philippian partnership in the gospel at the letter's beginning (1:5). The epistle is best understood when taken as a unified whole.

THE "OPPONENTS" OF CHAPTER 3

One of the main reasons for partitioning Philippians has been the feeling that chapter 3 fits badly with the rest of the letter. Even for those who maintain the unity of the letter, the third chapter is often seen as a digression. It is viewed as being Paul's warning against outsiders who presented a potential threat to the Philippian church. In recent research the chapter has often been viewed more from the perspective of epideictic rhetoric, presenting a negative example of those who set their minds on earthly things as opposed to Paul, who presented himself as one who had not yet arrived but still pressed toward the heavenly goal. There is much to be said for this latter approach. It ties the chapter to the rest of the letter. Still, Paul's words are at points quite specific and seem to carry a note of warning as well as holding up an example. It is even possible that some of Paul's warnings addressed problems which were already latent at Philippi and perhaps to some extent behind its problems of unity.

In chapter 3 Paul seems to have addressed two kinds of error explicitly. First, there were the Judaizers. They are singled out in verses 2 and 3. Paul called them "dogs," "evil workers," and "mutilators." "Dogs" was an epithet used by Jews with reference to Gentiles. Ironically, Paul reversed the charge. "Workers" may have been a term used positively by the Judaizers to refer to their own missionary workers. Paul reversed it also, with the qualifier that their work was "evil." His most telling term reminds one of Galatians 5:12. They were "mutilators." He used the Greek word *katatomē* (lit. "cutting down") as a pun on the word *peritomē* ("cutting around" = circumcision). He was obviously directing himself against Judaizers, as in Galatians. He

167

insisted that Gentile Christians like the Philippians were the "true circumcision," those whose *hearts* were circumcised, those who worshiped in Spirit and boasted in Christ rather than in the flesh. Paul's following pedigree of his own former excellence in Jewish ways was almost surely directed against Judaizers. There is general agreement on this, but there the agreement stops.

At the end of the chapter, in verses 18–19, Paul seems to have focused on an opposite, libertine aberration. He spoke of those who were "enemies of the cross," whose stomach was their god, who gloried in their shameful behavior, whose minds were set on earthly things. These sound much like libertines, with the emphasis on the belly and the flesh. But could they possibly be the same group as the Judaizers of verses 2 and 3? Many scholars think they are. The "stomach" is seen as Paul's slur against their food laws, the "shame" in which they glory is seen as their fleshly circumcision.[22]

Others also see Paul as fighting a single group in Philippians 3 but see the opponents as having a more Gnostic orientation. Predictably, Schmithals argues that they were Jewish Christian Gnostics. They insisted on circumcision, but their behavior was typically libertine Gnostic. Schmithals also argues that Paul was alluding to their denial of the resurrection in verses 10–11 and to their claim of spiritual perfection (to having "arrived") in verses 12–15. As Gnostics they had no place for atonement in their theology; they were thus "enemies of the cross" (v. 18).[23]

A number of scholars maintain that Paul was warning the Philippians about two distinct groups. All would see the Judaizers as one of the groups. They would describe the others, the group of verses 18–19 as Gnostics, or spiritualists, or perfectionists, or libertines, or antinomians.[24] Perhaps the variety of designations is a warning that we simply do not have enough information in Philippians to pinpoint the group's identity. Neither do we know whether or to what extent the Philippians themselves may have been drawn into some of the tendencies treated in chapter 3. They are all perennial problems which still continue to plague the church.

THE OCCASION FOR PHILIPPIANS

Why did Paul write Philippians? The *immediate* occasion for the letter was Epaphroditus's return to Philippi (Phil. 2:25–30). Epaphroditus was a Philippian who had come to Paul in prison with a monetary gift (Phil. 4:14–19). In the process of administering the gift he had become gravely ill. The Philippians had heard about it, and Paul knew of their concern. Upon Epaphroditus's recovery Paul was eager to send him home to relieve the Philippian anxiety about him. Paul "accompanied" Epaphroditus by means of the letter which he sent with him, the Philippian epistle.

With the possible exception of Philemon, Philippians contains the most material dealing with Paul's own personal circumstances. Recent works have rightly described it as being a "friendship" letter. It has many of the characteristics of the "family" letters found among the hellenistic papyri.[25] But it has even more in common with the more literary friendship letters such as Seneca's letters to Lucilius, letters from an experienced friend to another, often offering counsel and guidance. The Philippian emphases on mutual affection, sharing, equality, and longing to be in the other's presence are all conventions of the friendship genre. Even the emphasis on common enemies in chapter 3 is not unusual for this type of letter.[26]

Half the epistle involves the personal relationship between the apostle and his congregation. In 1:12–26 Paul spoke of his current situation in prison. He returned to his own circumstances in 2:17–18 and in 2:19–24 spoke of his plans to send Timothy and to come himself as soon as possible. He continued his personal note by speaking of Epaphroditus in 2:25–30. Even chapter 3 is intensely personal as Paul held himself up as a model for the Philippians to emulate. He had given up all for Christ. He pressed toward the goal, but he had not himself yet arrived. Finally, in 4:10–23 he returned to his relationship with the Philippians, thanking them for their gift and exchanging final greetings with them.

The rest of Philippians deals with Paul's concerns about the Philippians. There is a strong emphasis throughout on the unity of the fellowship. Paul called on them to stand firm in their faith despite all opposition, to be one in concern and in purpose, following the self-denying example of Christ, working toward their salvation, shining together as blameless children of God in a wicked world (1:27–2:18). For whatever its seemingly polemical note, the ultimate thrust of chapter 3 is that like Paul the Philippians should leave the rubbish of their former lives behind and press toward full maturity in their heavenly citizenship. The emphasis on unity becomes explicit in 4:2–3, where Paul called on two female leaders in the church to come to an agreement in the Lord. There can be no doubt that Paul was concerned about the unity of the Philippian Christians.[27] There were differences among the fellowship. As with the "opponents" of chapter 3, we can only speculate about specific details. Whatever the difference, Paul's antidote, his formula for unity, is timeless and ultimately situationless. It is as applicable to Christian life today as to Philippi in Paul's day.

A STUDY OUTLINE OF PHILIPPIANS

I. Epistolary Introduction (1:1–11)
   A. Address and Salutation (vv. 1–2)
   B. Thanksgiving and Prayer (vv. 3–11)
      1. Thanksgiving for their partnership in the gospel (vv. 3–7)
      2. Petition for their abundance in Christ (vv. 8–11)
II. The Advance of the Gospel (1:12–26)
   A. Advance Through Paul's Imprisonment (vv. 12–14)
   B. Advance Despite the Unworthiness of the Proclaimer (vv. 15–18)
   C. Advance Through Life or Death (vv. 19–26)
III. A Partnership Worthy of the Gospel (1:27–2:30)
   A. Partnership in Suffering (1:27–30)
   B. Partnership of Mind and Purpose (2:1–11)
      1. With minds set on one another (vv. 1–4)
      2. With minds set on the mind of Christ (vv. 5–11)
   C. Partnership of Witness and Joy (2:12–18)
      1. Working out their own salvation (vv. 12–13)
      2. Shining as lights in the world (vv. 14–16)
      3. Rejoicing in the Lord (vv. 17–18)
   D. Partnership of Concern (2:19–30)
      1. Timothy's concern for the Philippians (vv. 19–24)
      2. Their concern for Epaphroditus (vv. 25–30)
IV. Twin Obstacles in the Christian Path (3:1–4:1)
   A. A False Confidence in the Flesh (3:1–11)
      1. Circumcision, true and false (vv. 1–3)

HIGHLIGHTS OF PHILIPPIANS

INTRODUCTION (1:1–11)

Like his early letters to the Thessalonians and his very personal note to Philemon, Paul did not "pull rank" on the Philippians by referring to himself as an "apostle;" he identified himself and his cosender Timothy simply as "servants" ("slaves") of Christ. His secondary greeting to the "overseers" ("bishops") and "deacons" perhaps reflects the particular leadership structure of the Philippian congregation. The Philippians may have developed it themselves, based more on the pattern of Roman associations and Roman family structure than the "elder" system of the Jewish synagogues.[28]

Paul's thanksgiving and prayer in Philippians (vv. 3–11) is a good example of how he often used this formal opening section to introduce the major topics to be discussed later in the body of the letter. *Joy* (v. 4) is a major theme of the epistle (*joy* in 1:25; 2:2, 29; 4:1; *rejoice* in 1:18; 2:17–18; 2:28; 3:1; 4:4, 10). Paul dealt at length with the Philippian *partnership/fellowship* in the gospel (v. 5; cp. 2:1; 3:10; 4:14–15).[29] The *advance* and *defense* of the gospel is a major concern throughout the epistle (vv. 7; 1:12, 16, 27; 2:22; 4:3, 15). In verse 7 Paul spoke of how he had *set his mind* (NIV, "feel this way") on the Philippians. Throughout the epistle Paul stressed the importance of having the right *mind-set*, a mind-set of mutual concern and unity in Christ (2:2, 5; 3:15, 19; 4:2, 10). In his prayer Paul twice reminded the Philippians of the future judgment, the *day of Christ* (vv. 6, 10). Perhaps this was because there were some at Philippi who thought they had already "arrived" (cp. 3:12–15), who had a deficient view of the future life in Christ (3:10–11, 20–21).

THE ADVANCE OF THE GOSPEL (1:12–26)

The body of the letter begins at verse 12 with a common Pauline transitional formula, "I want you to know." Paul began with this lengthy initial section that informed the Philippians about his current status in prison. Basically, he said three things. First, he insisted that his imprisonment was not a defeat but an opportunity for witness (vv. 12–14). There may have been some at Philippi with a triumphalist gospel for whom his imprisonment was an embarrassment. Second, Paul said that the gospel was being freely preached where he was, even if the motives of some witnesses were not the very best (vv. 15–18). This is a difficult principle to grasp, because sometimes a selfish or insincere witness can do real damage to the gospel, but it is a reminder that the gospel bears its own power and ultimately does not depend on the worthiness of the bearer. Paul's third personal note to the Philippians (vv. 19–26) related how in prison he had wrestled with the question of life or death and had in his mind worked through the alternatives. His outcome ultimately lay in God's hands and was not his to choose. He felt some confidence that the prayers of the Philippians and the prospect of further ministry would lead to his deliverance. But for Paul himself, whichever way his case might go presented a joyful prospect. Release meant further service for Christ; condemnation meant going to be with Christ. To live was to live *in Christ*; to die was to *be with Christ* (v. 21).

With regard to verse 23, it is sometimes maintained that Paul's view of the afterlife developed over time from an earlier position which saw the believer as being resurrected from the dead at the Lord's second coming. Philippians is seen as representing a later stage of thinking, when Paul saw himself as going to be with the Lord immediately upon death. We will return to this question later when we examine the eschatology of 1 Thessalonians, 1 Corinthians, and 2 Corinthians. It is probably best to avoid developmental theories for Paul's eschatology but to see an abiding tension between the reality of a final resurrection and the firm conviction that the believer is *never* absent from the Lord. Perhaps ultimately it is a mystery that our finite minds cannot comprehend, the tension between creaturely time-boundedness and eternity.

A PARTNERSHIP WORTHY OF THE GOSPEL (1:27–2:30)

From the initial consideration of his own affairs, Paul moved to those of the Philippians in 1:27–2:30. The section falls into four main parts. Paul's major concern about the Philippians is expressed in 1:27–30—that they remain firm in their commitment to Christ. Paul then appealed to the church to become united in mind, to be subservient to one another as Christ himself set the pattern of self-giving (2:1–11). Paul continued the theme of unity in 2:12–18, pointing to its importance for their witness. Finally, 2:19–30 focused on the prospective visits of Timothy, himself, and Epaphroditus.

Rhetorical analysis of Philippians has consistently seen 1:27–30 as the *narratio*, the setting of the main argument of the epistle. Paul urged the Philippians to "stand firm" in their witness. His concern for their unity first becomes explicit in verse 27. They are to stand *together*, "in one spirit." The Roman setting of the epistle is reflected in Paul's urging them to conduct themselves in a manner worthy of the gospel. For "conduct yourselves," he used a Greek word which means to "live as a citizen." He returned to the same language in 3:20, where he spoke of the Philippians's heavenly "citizenship." It is not likely that many of the Philippians held the coveted Roman citizenship. But as a Roman colony the city was governed by its nucleus of voting Roman citizens, and the Philippians knew the importance of citizenship. We do not know who opposed the Philippians (v. 28). It may have been the officials, or even the general populace of the colony, who could not understand the Christian refusal to participate in the official imperial cult. The Philippians had seen Paul suffer at the hands of the magistrates. Paul urged them to be willing to do the same in *their* witness (vv. 29–30). Paul tied his appeal for unity closely to this appeal that the Philippians be willing to suffer for Christ. It is very possible that local persecution of Christians was in some manner connected with the disunity within the fellowship.

Philippians 2:1–11 is a strong appeal to the unity of the church. Paul began by listing qualities that make for unity in a congregation—mutual encouragement, comfort, fellowship, tenderness, compassion (v. 1). In verses 2–4 he set forth various evidences of unity in the Spirit: like-mindedness, loving one another, sharing a common purpose, putting the concerns of others over one's personal concerns. Considering others before oneself is the real key to Christian fellowship, and Paul illustrated this quality with the example of Christ (vv. 5–11). Many see 2:6–11 as a pre-Pauline hymn which Paul incorporated into the text of his letter. It is the most "discussed" passage of Philippians and will be treated separately in the next section.

After his appeal to Christ's example of "self-emptying," in 2:12–13 Paul urged the Philippians to "work out" their own salvation with fear and trembling. Although Christians must individually work out the full implications of their commitment to Christ, in the context of Philippians Paul was concerned more about the "salvation" of the congregation. They were to work out their differences. God would work *in* them to accomplish this if they allowed him to do so. Then, when they were truly united and had laid aside all their petty squabbling, they would shine forth as "stars in the universe." The Roman political state often used light imagery with reference to itself. Officials were seen as "luminaries." Its coins sometimes depicted stars with radiating lines of light symbolizing the enlightening power of the government. Paul urged the Philippians to be witnesses to Christ, to be the *real* lights shining amidst the perversions of the imperial government with its false claims to deity.[30]

Verses 19–30 have already been treated above in the discussion of the occasion for the epistle. This section deals with the travel plans of Paul, Timothy, and Epaphroditus. Why did Paul place them at *this* point? He may have wanted to hold these Christians up as an example of the kind of "self-emptying" that he was seeking from the Philippians. He emphasized that Timothy was unlike any of the other workers in placing his own personal interests in a secondary position to the concerns of Christ (vv. 20–21). He pointed out how Epaphroditus had risked his life, almost dying in order to fulfill the Philippians' own ministry to Paul (v. 30). Paul wanted the Philippians to become of one mind. He knew that this could only happen when they were willing to surrender their own self-concerns in concern for others, as had been the case with Timothy, Epaphroditus . . . *and Christ.*

THE "CHRIST-HYMN" OF PHILIPPIANS 2:5–11

No portion of Philippians has received more scholarly attention than the Christological "hymn" of 2:6–11. It has been discussed from every conceivable angle. Can it accurately be described as a "hymn"? If it is a hymn, what is its structure? What is its background? How should it be translated? There is disagreement about nearly every line. Even the introductory verse is debated (v. 5). The verse literally runs: "Have this mind-set among you, which also is in Christ Jesus." The verb has to be supplied in the relative clause. It can be taken in two ways: "Have the mind-set that befits someone who belongs to Christ," or, "Have the mind-set that is exemplified by Christ." In the context, the latter seems the more likely. Paul wanted the Philippians to follow the *example* of Christ.[31]

Most contemporary scholars view Philippians 2:6–11 as a hymn or at least as being based on confessional materials. There have been attempts to outline its hymnic structure but little agreement among the reconstructions. One scholar suggests a hymn of six stanzas with three lines each, another a three-stanza hymn of four lines each, another a four-stanza hymn of three lines, and so forth.[32] The lack of agreement warns against tidy reconstructions of a carefully structured hymn. It would be sounder to argue that Paul incorporated materials from the liturgy and confessions of the church. It is also quite possible that Paul was himself the "liturgist" and composed this beautiful piece *ad hoc* to fit the Philippian situation.[33]

Various backgrounds have been suggested for Philippians 2:6–11. Many see a reference to Adam in the idea of "grasping" for equality with God (v. 6).[34] Others see an allusion to Isaiah's Servant of the Lord in verse 7.[35] Still others see the dominant background in the concept of the preexistent wisdom of God of the Jewish wisdom tradition.[36] Finally, there are those who see the descent and ascent of the Gnostic redeemer as forming the conceptual background of the Philippian hymn.[37] This latter is most unlikely, but the Adamic, servant, and wisdom backgrounds are quite possible, perhaps even a mix of them, as they are not mutually exclusive.

Several terms in the hymn are much discussed, such as the word in verse 6 translated by the NIV as "something to be grasped." The Greek word behind the translation is *harpagmos*. The word can be taken either actively (something to be "seized, snatched") or passively (something to be "held on to, tightly grasped"). Taken in the active sense, the statement would imply that Jesus did not possess equality with God and did not attempt to snatch it for himself. A passive sense would call for Jesus being equal with God but not clinging to his equality. (The translation "grasp" is deliberately ambiguous, allowing for either meaning.) A third possibility is that the expression may mean something that is available and at one's disposal. Taken this way, verse 6 would mean that Jesus had his equality with God fully at his disposal but he did not take advantage of it.[38] Instead, he "made himself nothing" (v. 7). The Greek literally says he "emptied" himself (Gk., *kenoō*).

This language of "emptying" has led to "kenotic" theology, which maintains that in some sense Jesus "emptied" himself of his divine "equality" in his incarnation. The question then becomes what he emptied himself of—his divine attributes, his glory? Such a question misses the point. "Emptying himself" means that Christ "poured himself out," sacrificed himself for others, making himself "nothing." It isn't that he forfeited any of his divinity but that he completely gave of himself.

How should the term *nature of a servant* be understood (v. 7)? The word translated *nature* is the Greek word *morphē* ("form") and is the same word used in verse 6 of Jesus' sharing God's "nature/form." It means to share the very character and being of something or someone. The word translated *servant* is literally *slave*. Jesus took on the being of a *slave*. The references to his being in human "likeness" and "appearance" do not mean that he did not become fully human but point to the fact that he was not fully describable in human terms. Though fully human and sharing humanity's likeness, he was *more than* human; he retained his divine nature as well.

The rest of verse 8 is less difficult. Jesus' "humbling" himself is exactly what Paul wanted the Philippians to do, using the same word for humility as in verse 3. Obedience is the key. Jesus, the second Adam, was obedient to God's purposes (cp. Rom. 5:19). He was obedient even to the point of his ignominious death by crucifixion. "Therefore, God exalted him to the highest place" (v. 9). Paul used a "double superlative," the Greek word for "exalt" ("lift to the highest place") with the prefix "super" added. God "super-exalted" Jesus. Paul probably only intended a very strong superlative: because of his obedience, God highly exalted Jesus. It is also possible that he meant that God exalted him to an even higher position than he had in his preexistence. If this is so, the "higher status" would be his status as Lord. In his preexistence he shared the full being of God. But only in his risen, exalted state has he come to

173

be worshiped as "Lord." The climax of the hymn is the early Christian confession, "Jesus Christ is Lord." In Roman colonies throughout the empire, the emperor cult revered Caesar as "Lord." For Christians there is only one Lord, Jesus Christ, who is one with God and shares God's Lordship.

Whether Philippians 2:6–11 is "pre-Pauline" or not will likely be discussed for a long time to come. Even if it originated with Paul himself, it attests to a very high Christology at a very early date, the early 50s by our dating of Philippians. Already by then all the elements of the church's basic Christological confession were already present: Christ's preexistence, his oneness with God, his being sent into the world, his incarnation, his exaltation to God's right hand, his primary title of "Lord."

TWIN OBSTACLES IN THE CHRISTIAN PATH (3:1–4:1)

The questions regarding literary unity and Paul's opponents have already been discussed and will not be repeated here. Likewise, earlier chapters have dealt with Paul's "Jewish pedigree" in verses 4–6. We will focus on three passages where Paul directs himself to the Philippians: 3:7–11; 3:12–16; and 3:20–4:1.

In 3:7–11 Paul discussed his loss and his gain. He really had lost a great deal by normal human standards when he embraced Christ—his status as a rising star in Pharisaic circles, perhaps even family ties. What had he gained? He had gained suffering, poverty, imprisonment, recalcitrant converts. No, he had gained Christ Jesus as his Lord. Everything else faded in comparison to Christ, everything he once treasured now seemed to be mere rubbish, material for the dung heap. Why was Christ so precious to Paul? Because in Christ and in him alone Paul had found his acceptance with God. Verse 9 provides a very tight summary of a central concept in Paul's understanding of salvation, the concept of *righteousness by faith*. Paul used the language of righteousness in various ways.[39] The Greek root for *righteous* means measuring up to a standard or norm, being "right." It was often used in legal contexts in the sense of measuring up to the standard of the law. The Greek word *righteousness* (*dikaiosunē*) was used in the Septuagint to translate the Hebrew word that described God's "righteousness" (*zedekah*). When applied to God, the word expressed both God's justice and his faithfulness. In the Old Testament it is especially used in the context of God's covenants with Israel. God is considered "righteous" because he is faithful to his covenant, faithful to his promises. The idea of God's righteousness, understood in the sense of his covenant loyalty, thus came to have a primary sense of God's desire to fulfill his promises to his people and is thus virtually synonymous with God's *salvation*.

When Paul spoke of our righteousness before God, he seems to have seen this both in legal and in covenantal terms. Human righteousness before God means acceptability to God, being accepted as "right" by God. The word is often translated *justification*, but the basic meaning is *being right with God*. In Philippians 3:9 Paul contrasted two ways of seeking to be right with God. First, there was his own way. That way was based on law. By keeping the law, Paul was relying on his own effort to establish his acceptance with God. That way was doomed to failure. The other way was to accept God's own acceptance of him. Through faith in Christ, God had accepted Paul as "righteous." For Paul, this status of acceptance/righteousness with God could only come as a gift, could only be conferred on humans out of God's own righteousness and was solely available through God's "righteousness-making" act—the death and resurrection of Christ. It thus can only come by faith in Christ.

The new status of righteousness is not a "legal fiction." God *does* accept us as righteous while we are still sinners, but he also transforms us and gives us his Spirit so that we might truly grow toward the full measurement of God's righteous standards. The covenantal context of righteousness is never far for Paul. It is not by accident that Paul discussed righteousness in the context of Judaizing in Philippians 3. As is the case in Galatians, Paul thought in terms of two covenants: the covenant of the law and the covenant of promise. The covenant of law could never grant acceptability before God. Only the covenant of promise could, the covenant based on faith in Christ. This "righteousness" was available not just to those who possessed the Torah but to all who professed their faith in Christ, including the Gentiles of Philippi.

Note how in 3:10–11 Paul quickly shifted from the language of justification/righteousness to the language of dying and rising with Christ, just as he did in Galatians 2:15–21. They are two ways of describing the same reality—finding acceptability with God, becoming one with Christ by dying and rising with him. But note how Paul spoke of resurrection here in terms of the *future*. There may have been some at Philippi who considered their Christian experience as already complete. Paul wanted to set them straight. Salvation is an ongoing process. It is not perfected in the present but always awaits the future as long as we are still in this life. Paul had certainly not "arrived" himself. In 3:12–14 he used the metaphor of a foot race to illustrate how he was always striving toward the full realization of his potential in Christ, losing no ground by glancing back, but always straining toward the goal of his heavenly calling in Christ. Note the noncompetitive nature of the content. Paul depicted himself as running against himself, striving for his *own prize*. Paul was concerned about the Philippians and their disunity; he urged them not to lose ground in the race (v. 16).

Paul concluded his words about legalism, libertinism, and perfectionism in 3:20–4:1 with an exhortation to the Philippians to realize their full potential as citizens of a heavenly dominion. The reference to citizenship harks back to 1:27 and Paul's first words to the Philippians that they stand firm in the faith (cp. 4:1). Events at Philippi seemed to be intimidating them. Paul reminded them that a secure, more glorious citizenship awaited them in the future if they held on to what they already had in Christ.

MATTERS PERSONAL AND CONGREGATIONAL (4:2–23)

In 4:2–3 Paul became more explicit in his appeal for unity, singling out two women in the congregation. They may have been leaders of house churches. They were active in Christian witness. Paul described them as "contending" together with him in the gospel. Paul and Luke alike depict the major role that women played in the church at Philippi. We do not know anything more about Clement or the identity of Paul's "loyal yokefellow," though Luke has often been suggested.

Philippians 4:4–7 is a characteristic paraenetic section coming toward the close of the letter. It is, however, closely associated with the rest of the epistle. The note of joy runs through the entire letter (v. 4). The Philippians needed to be more accepting and patient with one another in order to realize their full unity (v. 5). And there was anxiety in their midst as they worried about opposition from outside (1:28–29); God would bring them peace (vv. 6–7). Verses 8–9 provide a traditional hellenistic virtue list and a final appeal for the Philippians to follow Paul's example (cp. 3:17). Throughout the epistle Paul had appealed to his example—to his willingness to suffer for Christ, to his readiness to surrender everything in order to be found in Christ.

In verses 10–20 Paul thanked the Philippians for the gift sent by Epaphroditus. He expressed his gratitude with some hesitancy, especially in verses 11–13, where he spoke of his self-sufficiency in Christ. There may have been some debate within the church over providing funds for Paul's work, or Paul may simply have held up his own example of contentment in Christ as a pattern for the Philippians to follow themselves. In any event, the Philippians seem to have been particularly generous in their financial support of Paul's work. There were the first gifts sent when he was at Thessalonica (4:16), gifts when he established work at Corinth (2 Cor. 11:8–9), and now the gift brought by Epaphroditus (4:18). Later, when Paul gathered his collection for Jerusalem, the "Macedonians" stood out as a shining example for their generosity (2 Cor. 8:1–5). The pocketbook is often the best gauge of the heart. Both the tone of the Philippian epistle and the congregation's support of his work attest that the heart of the Philippians was with Paul.

NOTES

1. For a comprehensive treatment of archaeology in the Troad, see J. M. Cook, *The Troad: An Archaeological and Topographical Study* (Oxford: Clarendon, 1973). For Troas, see C. J. Hemer, "Alexandria Troas," *Tyndale Bulletin* 26 (1975): 79–112 and E. M. Yamauchi, "Troas," in *The Anchor Dictionary of the Bible*, ed. D. N. Freedman (New York: Doubleday, 1992), VI: 666–667.

2. Some scholars would see the haste in leaving his things behind as indicative that Paul was arrested in Troas before being taken to Rome for his second imprisonment there. Ignatius, under arrest and being taken to Rome (via Neapolis and the Via Egnatia) wrote three of his letters while awaiting a ship at Troas (*Philadelphians* 11, *Smyrneans* 12, *Polycarp* 8).

3. Conybeare and Howson, *The Life and Epistles of St. Paul* (Hartford, Conn.: S. S. Scranton, 1902), 244.

4. W. M. Ramsay, *St. Paul the Traveller and Roman Citizen* (London: Hodder and Stoughton, 1897), 200–205.

5. It is perhaps significant that the "we" narrative stops at Philippi in Acts 16 and only resumes when Paul sailed from *Philippi* (Acts 20:5–6), perhaps indicating Luke had remained at Philippi for all the intervening period.

6. For a full treatment of Philippi, see H. L. Hendrix, "Philippi," *Anchor Dictionary of the Bible*, V: 313–317.

7. J. Murphy-O'Connor argues that the sort of charges brought against Paul by the magistrates imply an extensive period of preaching on his part: *Paul, a Critical Life* (Oxford: Clarendon, 1996), 215.

8. Some scholars argue that "household" baptisms imply the baptism of infants, but there is no New Testament evidence for any baptism other than believer's baptism. See G. R. Beasley-Murray, *Baptism in the New Testament* (Exeter: Paternoster, 1972), 312–320.

9. W. D. Thomas, "The Place of Women in the Church at Philippi," *Expository Times* 83 (1972): 117–120.

10. All of the terms she used were also used with reference to the pagan gods or the emperor ("Most High God," "Savior"). See P. R. Trebilco, "Paul and Silas—'Servants of the Most High God' (Acts 16:16–18)," *Journal for the Study of the New Testament* 36 (1989): 51–73.

11. See the discussion under "Roman Government" in chapter 1.

12. The Western Text of Acts answers the inevitable question about the other prisoners, noting at verse 30 that they were resecured by the jailer before he departed with Paul and Silas.

13. Robertson, *Epochs in the Life of Paul* (New York: Scribner's, 1909), 152.

14. Particularly F. C. Baur, who argued that only those epistles which reflect a *strong* Judaizing controversy are authentically Pauline. By this criterion, he considered Paul as author of only four: Galatians, Romans, 1 Corinthians, and 2 Corinthians.

15. For a full presentation of the arguments for Caesarea, see G. F. Hawthorne, "Philippians, Letter to the," *Dictionary of Paul and His Letters*, ed. G. F. Hawthorne and R. P. Martin (Downers Grove, Ill.: InterVarsity, 1993), 710–711.

16. A. Deissmann strongly defended the Ephesian origin of the Prison Epistles and particularly pressed the travel argument: "Zur Ephesinischen Gefangenschaft des Apostels Paulus," in *Anatolian Studies* (Manchester: Manchester University Press, 1923), 121–127. See also W. Michaelis, "The Trial of St. Paul at Ephesus," *Journal of Theological Studies* 29 (1928): 368–375.

17. S. Dockx, "Lieu et date de l'épître aux Philippiens," *Revue Biblique* 80 (1973): 230–246.

18. This is basically the position of Carson, Moo, and Morris, *An Introduction to the New Testament* (Grand Rapids: Zondervan, 1992), 321. The most thorough presentation of the Ephesian hypothesis is that of G. S. Duncan, *St. Paul's Ephesian Ministry* (London, 1929).

19. V. Koperski, "The Early History of the Dissection of Philippians," *Journal of Theological Studies* 44 (1993): 599–603.

20. P. Perkins, "Philippians: Theology for the Heavenly Politeuma," in *Pauline Theology, Vol. I: Thessalonians, Philippians, Galatians, Philemon*, ed. J. M. Bassler (Minneapolis: Fortress, 1994), 89–90.

21. D. Garland, "The Composition and Unity of Philippians, Some Neglected Literary Factors," *Novum Testamentum* 27 (1985): 141–173. Recent rhetorical studies have tended to confirm Garland's thesis that chapter 3 consists of epideictic rhetoric by means of negative example and that it is an integral part of the argument of the entire letter. See D. F. Watson, "A Rhetorical Analysis of Philippians and its Implications for the Unity Question," *Novum Testamentum* 30 (1988): 57–88.

22. C. K. Barrett, *Paul, An Introduction to His Thought* (Louisville: Westminster John Knox, 1994), 39–41. M. Tellbe believes that the Judaizing originated *within* the Philippian church by those who wanted to identify with the Jews in order to obtain their exemptions from the imperial cult and thus avoid suffering: "The Sociological Factors Behind Philippians 3:1–11 and the Conflict at Philippi," *Journal for the Study of the New Testament* 55 (1994): 97–121.

23. W. Schmithals, *Paul and the Gnostics*, trans. J. E. Steely (Nashville: Abingdon, 1972). H. Koester also argues for a single Gnostic Jewish Christian front but does not see them as libertines but as legalists. Like Barrett, he sees Paul as using irony in verses 18–19 for food laws and circumcision: H. Koester, "The Purpose of the Polemic of a Pauline Fragment (Philippians III)," *New Testament Studies* 8 (1961–1962): 317–332.

24. Typical is D. Guthrie, who speaks of Judaizers and "perfectionists": *The Apostles* (Grand Rapids: Zondervan, 1975), 299–301. R. Jewett sees three groups in chapter 3—Judaizers, libertines, and Gentile perfectionists (3:10–17): "The Agitators and the Galatian Congregation," *New Testament Studies* 17 (1970–1971): 198–212.

25. L. Alexander, "Hellenistic Letter-Forms and the Structure of Philippians," *Journal for the Study of the New Testament* 37 (1989): 87–101.

26. S. K. Stowers, "Friends and Enemies in the Politics of Heaven: Reading Theology in Philippians," in *Pauline Theology, Vol. I*, ed. Bassler, 105–121.

27. Recent dissertations have highlighted the emphasis on unity in Philippians. See D. Peterlin, *Paul's Letter to the Philippians in the Light of Disunity in the Church* (Leiden: Brill, 1995); T. C. Geoffrion, *The Rhetorical Purpose and the Political and Military Character of Philippians: A Call to Stand Firm* (Lewiston, N.Y.: Mellen Biblical Press, 1993).

28. J. Reumann, "Contributions of the Philippian Community to Paul and to Earliest Christianity," *New Testament Studies* 39 (1993): 446–450.

29. J. P. Sampley believes that Paul developed a formal pact with the Philippians along the lines of Roman *consensual societas*. He sees this reflected in the pervasive language of fellowship (*koinonia*) and agreement (*phronein*): *Pauline Partnership in Christ: Christian Community and Commitment in the Light of Roman Law* (Philadelphia: Fortress, 1980), 51–77.

30. D. Georgi, *Theocracy in Paul's Praxis and Theology*, trans. D. E. Green (Minneapolis: Fortress, 1991), 72–78.

31. This "ethical example" understanding is flatly rejected by some interpreters such as G. Bornkamm, *Early Christian Experience*, trans. P. L. Hammer (New York: Harper and Row, 1969), 112–122.

32. For a comprehensive treatment of research in all aspects of the Philippian hymn, see R. P. Martin, *Carmen Christi: Philippians ii.5–11 in Recent Interpretation and in the Setting of Early Christian Worship* (Cambridge: University Press, 1967).

33. G. D. Fee, *Paul's Letter to the Philippians*. The New International Commentary on the New Testament (Grand Rapids: Eerdmans, 1995), 43–46.

34. J. D. G. Dunn argues for the Adamic background and sees it as referring to the earthly Jesus, not to his preexistence: *Christology in the Making: A New Testament Inquiry into the Origins of the Doctrine of the Incarnation* (Philadelphia: Westminster, 1980), 1114–1121. N. T. Wright also sees an Adamic background but sees it as applying to the *preexistent* Christ: *The Climax of the Covenant: Christ and the Law in Pauline Theology* (Minneapolis: Fortress, 1992), 56–98.

35. Suggested by Jeremias, the servant background is also emphasized by C. F. D. Moule, "Further Reflections on Philippians 2:5–11," in *Apostolic History and the Gospel*, ed. Gasque and Martin (Grand Rapids: Eerdmans, 1970), 264–276.

36. B. Witherington III, *Paul's Narrative Thought World: The Tapestry of Tragedy and Triumph* (Louisville: Westminster John Knox, 1994), 94–105. C. A. Wanamaker suggests a *Son of God* Christological background: "Philippians 2:6–11: Son of God or Adamic Christology?" *New Testament Studies* 33 (1987): 179–193.

37. E. Käsemann, "A Critical Analysis of Philippians 2:5–11," *Journal for Theology and the Church* 5 (1950): 45–88.

38. R. W. Hoover, "The Harpagmos Enigma: A Philological Solution," *Harvard Theological Review* 64 (1971): 95–119.

39. Paul's teaching on the righteousness of God is a major topic in contemporary Pauline studies. For good summaries of the discussion, see K. L. Onesti and M. T. Brauch, "Righteousness, Righteousness of God," in *Dictionary of Paul and His Letters*, 827–837; M. L. Soards, "The Righteousness of God in the Writings of the Apostle Paul," *Biblical Theology Bulletin* 15 (1985): 104–109.

SELECTED COMMENTARIES

BASED ON THE GREEK TEXT

Hawthorne, Gerald F. *Philippians*. Word Biblical Commentary. Waco, Tex.: Word, 1983.

Lightfoot, J. B. *St. Paul's Epistle to the Philippians*. London: Macmillan, 1873; Grand Rapids: Zondervan, 1974.

O'Brien, Peter T. *The Epistle to the Philippians. A Commentary on the Greek Text*. New International Greek Testament Commentary. Grand Rapids: Eerdmans, 1991.

Vincent, Marvin R. *The Epistles to the Philippians and to Philemon*. The International Critical Commentary. Edinburgh: T. and T. Clark, 1897.

BASED ON ENGLISH TEXT

Barth, Karl. *The Epistle to the Philippians*. Trans. J. W. Leitch. Richmond: John Knox, 1962.

Beare, F. W. *The Epistle to the Philippians*. Harper's New Testament Commentaries. New York: Harper, 1959.

Bockmuehl, Markus. *The Epistle to the Philippians*. Black's New Testament Commentary. Peabody, Mass.: Hendrickson, 1998.

Bruce, F. F. *Philippians*. New International Biblical Commentary. Peabody, Mass.: Hendrickson, 1989.

Craddock, Fred B. *Philippians*. Interpretation. Atlanta: Knox, 1985.

Fee, Gordon D. *Paul's Letter to the Philippians*. New International Commentary on the New Testament. Grand Rapids: Eerdmans, 1995.

Marshall, I. Howard. *The Epistle to the Philippians*. Epworth Commentaries. London: Epworth, 1992.

Martin, Ralph P. *The Epistle of Paul to the Philippians*. Tyndale New Testament Commentaries. Grand Rapids: Eerdmans, 1959.

Martin, Ralph P. *Philippians*. New Century Bible. Grand Rapids: Eerdmans, 1976.

Melick, Richard R. Jr. *Philippians, Colossians, Philemon*. New American Commentary. Nashville: Broadman, 1991.

Michael, J. Hugh. *The Epistle of Paul to the Philippians*. Moffatt New Testament Commentary. London: Hodder and Stoughton, 1928.

Silva, Moises. *Philippians*. Wycliffe Exegetical Commentary. Chicago: Moody, 1988.

Silva, Moises. *Philippians*. Baker Exegetical Commentary on the New Testament. Grand Rapids: Baker, 1992.

Thielman, Frank. *Philippians*. NIV Application Commentary. Grand Rapids: Zondervan, 1995.

10

⟨≈⟩

THESSALONICA: HOPE IN THE LORD

*P*aul's Thessalonian epistles both deal at length with questions related to the *parousia* (second coming) of Christ. The Thessalonians seem to have had serious questions in this area. The two letters look at Jesus' return from very different perspectives. First Thessalonians is quite pastoral. In the letter Paul sought to comfort and assure the Thessalonians about Jesus' coming. In 2 Thessalonians he was less patient. Some were spreading the false word to the church that the day of the Lord had already occurred, and Paul addressed the problem more forcefully.

The Thessalonian epistles are the earliest extant Pauline epistles. Paul established the Thessalonian church during his second mission, after leaving Philippi. The time was around A.D. 50. The two epistles were written in close proximity to the founding of the church, perhaps within six months from Paul's departure from the city. The two seem to have been written close together. They are strikingly similar in both language and content.

The first part of this chapter will treat Paul's establishing the work in Thessalonica and the period of his ministry immediately following, including his work in nearby Berea and his flight to Athens. It is possible that Paul wrote his first Thessalonian letter from Athens. The remainder of the chapter will introduce the Thessalonian correspondence.

ESTABLISHMENT OF THE CHURCH AT THESSALONICA

We have two accounts of Paul's founding the Christian community at Thessalonica. The first is Luke's account in Acts 17:1–9. Acts 17:10–15 tells of the work at Berea, and Acts 17:16 of Paul's arrival in Athens. The same period of missionary activity is covered by Paul's own account in 1 Thessalonians 1–3. The Lukan and Pauline versions are quite distinct. They supplement one another and will be examined separately.

THESSALONICA (ACTS 17:1)

After leaving Philippi, Paul, Silas, and Timothy proceeded along the Egnatian Way toward Thessalonica. A journey of approximately one hundred Roman miles, it took them through the towns of Amphipolis (thirty-two miles from Philippi) and Apollonia (thirty-one miles from Amphipolis, thirty-eight miles from Thessalonica). Amphipolis was a large town. In previous years it had been the capital of the first division of Macedonia. But Paul did not stop to witness there. He headed for Thessalonica. With a population of sixty-five thousand to one hundred thousand, it was the largest city of Macedonia.[1]

Thessalonica was an important commercial center located on major land and sea routes. The Egnatian Way ran through the center of town. The city had grown up around the best natural harbor of Macedonia. The ancient town of Therme had been located there. In 315 B.C., Cassander organized Therme and a number of surrounding towns into his new capital. Cassander had been one of Alexander's generals. He succeeded him as king of Macedonia. He renamed his new capital *Thessalonica* for his wife, who was also Alexander's half-sister. In the second century B.C., Macedonia allied against Rome and was defeated at the battle of Pydna (168 B.C.). The victorious Roman general Aemilius Paullus organized all of Macedonia into four administrative districts with Thessalonica as capital of the second.

In 146 B.C. Macedonia was made a Roman senatorial province with Thessalonica as capital. The city befriended Julius Caesar and subsequently Octavian and Antony at the time of the republican war. It was rewarded for its loyalty in 42 B.C. by being granted the status of a free city, a status that was reconfirmed by Octavian in 31 B.C. In A.D. 15 Octavian (now "Augustus") removed Macedonia from senatorial provincial status and placed it directly under his own rule (imperial provincial status) because of Macedonian unrest over the heavy provincial taxes. (Unlike senatorial provinces, imperial provinces were under the direct control of the emperor and had one or more legions stationed within them.) In A.D. 44 the emperor Claudius removed the legions, returning Macedonia to its former senatorial provincial status.

The significance of all this is that Thessalonica's fortunes were very closely tied to Rome. From the time of Augustus, a temple had been established there to the veneration of Julius Caesar. By Paul's day a cult had been established in Thessalonica for the worship of the goddess Roma.[2] Thessalonica was never made a Roman colony but remained a free Greek city. This meant that the local Greeks maintained their own legislative and governing prerogatives, were exempt from the provincial taxes, had their own rights of coinage, and had no Roman troops within their borders. The city's Greek government is reflected in the names of the local officials whom Luke mentioned in Acts 17:6, 8. He called them *politarchs* (NIV, "city officials"), a local term that only seems to have been used in Macedonia. The name has been found on some seventy inscriptions in Macedonia, twenty-eight of them from Thessalonica alone. The number of politarchs at any one time seems to have varied, but Thessalonica appears to have had five in Paul's day. They were the main public officials, responsible for maintaining records, keeping the peace, convening the town council, and maintaining good relations with the Roman provincial officials.[3]

PAUL'S RELATIONSHIP WITH THE THESSALONIANS ACCORDING TO ACTS 17:2–16

Establishing the church (17:2–4). Upon arrival in Thessalonica, Paul began in the synagogue, as was his custom. For three Sabbaths he "reasoned" with them from the Old Testament Scriptures, seeking to demonstrate that Jesus was the expected Messiah. Luke gave no details, but probably Paul employed such texts as those used by Peter in his sermon at Pentecost (Acts 2:16–35), by himself at Pisidian Antioch (Acts 13:16–41), and perhaps the servant passages which Philip shared with the

Ethiopian eunuch (Acts 8:30–35). As was generally the case, the members of the synagogue eventually turned on Paul but not before he had made many converts. Three categories of converts are mentioned: "some" Jews, "a large number" of God-fearing Greeks, and a sizable number of prominent Greek women (v. 4). Many such Gentile women, like Lydia, seem to have been attracted to the Diaspora synagogues.

The breach with the synagogue is indicated in Acts 17:5–9 by the account of the Jews stirring up a mob against Paul. The breach probably occurred a considerable time before the mob incident. Luke's reference to three Sabbaths (17:2) most likely refers to Paul's initial period of witness in Thessalonica, which occurred in the synagogue. Paul must have continued on in Thessalonica for some time after separating from the synagogue. An extensive period of ministry in Thessalonica is indicated by the Philippians sending him aid there "again and again" (Phil. 4:16) and by his having to support himself in Thessalonica with his own hands (1 Thess. 2:9; 2 Thess. 3:8).

The mob (17:5–6a). Eventually the Jewish opposition *did* force Paul to leave Thessalonica, a pattern all too familiar from Paul's first missionary journey. This time the Jews did not act alone. They incited the Gentile population against the Christians. Specifically, they enlisted some "bad characters from the marketplace." This riffraff succeeded in provoking a full-scale riot. The mob rushed to the house of a certain Jason, who was evidently a Christian with whom Paul and Silas had been staying. Not finding the missionaries, they dragged Jason and some of his fellow Christians off to the politarchs.

The charges (17:6b–8). Much as at Philippi, there were multiple charges but only one that would have raised the alarm of the magistrates. This was the charge that the Christians were "defying Caesar's decrees" by proclaiming that there was another king. Roman emperors were very nervous about their job security. Tiberius and Augustus had both issued decrees against persons who made any predictions pertaining to the person of the emperor. Everyone was expected to take an oath of loyalty to the emperor. When viewed superficially, the Christian message about Christ the King could be seen as seditious; it had been so taken in the case of Jesus (cp. John 19:12). The politarchs of Thessalonica found themselves much in the situation of Pilate with Jesus. On the one hand, the charges were unsubstantiated. On the other, there was an angry mob and a politically sensitive accusation. They seem to have arrived at a solution which they probably viewed as a reasonable compromise. No one suffered any physical harm and the peace was preserved.

Jason (v. 9). The politarchs had Jason "post bond" and then dismissed the Christians. Luke did not specify the terms of the bond. The larger narrative would suggest that Jason was asked to guarantee that there would be no further disturbances to the peace. It may have specified that Paul and Silas were to leave the city. Jason's role in the incident is significant. He seems to have been a Christian of considerable social standing. The church apparently met in his house. He was its patron. It is possible that his house was an urban *insula*, an apartment with a workshop on the ground floor and living quarters in the upper floors. If so, Paul may have worked in Jason's workshop and slept in his living quarters above.[4] It would have been the location for Christian assembling and witness after the expulsion from the synagogue.

Ministry in Berea (17:10–16). The Thessalonian Christians sent Paul and Silas out of the city under cover of night, evidently because they were still being sought by their persecutors. We are not told of Timothy's whereabouts at the time. He was later present with Paul and Silas in Berea (v. 14). Berea was southwest of Thessalonica about fifty miles. It was not located on the Egnatian Way but somewhat off the beaten path at the foot of Mt. Bermion in the Olympian mountain range. In the second century B.C. it had been capital of one of the four divisions of Macedonia and was still a sizable city in Paul's day.

At Berea Paul continued his procedure of preaching first in the synagogues. Luke provided no time references; so it is not clear how long Paul spent in the city. The Jews of Berea are described as being "more noble" ("refined") than those of Thessalonica. Not just on Sabbaths, but *daily* they joined Paul in study of the Scriptures to confirm the truth of his claim that Jesus was the Messiah. The same three groups responded as at Thessalonica (v. 12; cp. v. 4), only this time "many" of the *Jews* came to faith in Christ.

Paul's ministry in Berea was curtailed by the coming of Jews from Thessalonica. As at Thessalonica, they stirred up the "crowds" against the Christian missionaries. Nothing is said about the Berean Jews being involved. The "crowds" seem to have been the Gentile populace. The picture is thus very much like that of Thessalonica; the Jews as the instigators, the Gentile populace as the bulk of the mob. The text of Acts 17:14 is somewhat uncertain, and the meaning of the best reading is unclear. It says that Paul went as far as the coast. This could mean either that he went to Athens by sea or along the coastal land route. Whichever means of travel he took, he arrived there alone, having left Timothy and Silas behind in Berea (v. 14). At Athens Paul sent instructions back to Timothy and Silas that they were to join him there as soon as possible (vv. 15–16). It is unclear why they did not accompany him to Athens. They may have been working elsewhere in the vicinity when the mob arose and forced Paul's hasty departure from Berea.

PAUL'S RELATIONSHIP TO THESSALONICA ACCORDING TO 1 THESSALONIANS 1–3

Half of 1 Thessalonians is devoted to Paul's relationship with the church (chaps. 1–3). Paul reminded the Thessalonians of his coming to them and establishing the church (1:4–2:16). He also told them of his worry about them after his departure and of the events leading up to the writing of the epistle (2:17–3:10). There are significant differences between Paul's account in 1 Thessalonians 1–3 and Luke's account in Acts 17:1–16. Some would see them as irreconcilable contradictions. We would maintain that the two accounts are complementary rather than contradictory.

Paul's first preaching (1:4–2:16). Paul reminded the Thessalonians of how he had come to them after having been insulted and made to suffer at Philippi (2:1–2; cp. Acts 16:16–24). He spoke of how he came with deep conviction and in the demonstrable power of the Holy Spirit (1:5; cp. 1 Cor. 2:4; Gal. 3:3). In 1:9–10 Paul summarized his initial preaching at Thessalonica. It is clear from 1 Thessalonians that the church consisted mainly of Gentiles. Paul's first preaching to them is an example of his gospel for Gentiles. They were called upon to turn from dead idols to the one true and living God.[5] They were informed of the resurrection of Christ, of the Parousia hope, and of the coming judgment. In verse 10, Paul mentioned Christ's parousia for the first time in the epistle. It would continue to have a prominent place throughout the entire letter (cp. 2:19; 3:13; 4:13; 5:2, 23).

In 1 Thessalonians 2:3–12 Paul reminded the Thessalonians of how he had sought to model selfless ministry and genuine pastoral concern when he was with them. His motives were pure. He did not seek to please people; he did not flatter; he showed no greed. He provided gentle, loving care for the Thessalonians, like a mother caring for her children (2:7). Paul continued his family metaphors in verses 11–12, where he spoke of how he had also been a father to them, instructing them in the Christian life through words of comfort and encouragement. He did not want to be a burden to them; so he supported himself with his own manual labor (2:9; cp. 2 Thess. 3:8).

Paul's ministry in Thessalonica was not easy. He experienced strong opposition (2:2). The Thessalonians likewise had come to share in these same sufferings (1:6, 2:14–16). Just who the persecutors were is unclear from Paul's comments. He described them as "your own countrymen" and likened them to the Jews of Judea who persecuted the churches there (2:14). "Your own countrymen" seems to be more a political than a racial designation and could embrace both Jews and Gentiles, as in Acts 17:5–9. In any event, the Thessalonian endurance in the face of persecution had become well known and served as an example for Christians throughout Macedonia and Achaia (1:7). They were more than an example, however. Paul indicated that they had become active participants in the Christian mission themselves (1:8; cp. 4:10).

Paul's relationship with the Thessalonians after leaving them (2:17–3:10). At 2:17–20 Paul shifted from the events of his founding visit to his concern for the Thessalonians after being forced to leave them. He stated that he had attempted "again and again" to come see them, but had always been hindered by "Satan." One wonders what Paul meant by this satanic hindrance. In early Christianity "Satan" was sometimes employed as deliberately veiled language for Rome. One wonders if the charge of sedition and Jason's bond may not have formed the satanic barrier to Paul's returning to Thessalonica.

In 3:1–5 Paul continued to inform the Thessalonians of his intense desire to see them. He was worried about them, especially about how they were bearing up under the persecutions they were bound to be experiencing. He told of how he had sent Timothy as his personal envoy, to make up for his absence, to bring him back a personal report about his beloved Thessalonians. The sending of Timothy is perhaps the most serious of the supposed conflicts between Acts and Thessalonians. It will be remembered that Acts left Timothy and Silas in Berea when Paul went to Athens (17:14–16). Acts does not mention the pair rejoining Paul until Paul's arrival in Corinth (Acts 18:5). But in 1 Thessalonians 3:1–2, Paul stated that he sent Timothy *from Athens.* The accounts are not irreconcilable. Timothy's travels may have been more extensive than either Acts or 1 Thessalonians may indicate. The two together may furnish the whole picture.

First Thessalonians 3:6–10 rounds out Paul's recapitulation of the events that preceded his writing of the epistle. Timothy came back from Thessalonica with good news: the Thessalonians were still faithful to Paul and firm in the faith. Overcome with relief and joy, Paul wrote 1 Thessalonians. He was perhaps still in Athens when he sent the epistle, quite possibly again through the agency of Timothy. The first three chapters of 1 Thessalonians fit the genre of a "friendship" letter. What Paul could not express in personal presence he attempted through his letter. His strongest desire, of course, was to see them in person, and that request became the opening petition of a prayer for the Thessalonians as he concluded this personal portion of the epistle (3:11).

INTRODUCTION TO THE THESSALONIAN LETTERS

Several issues have occupied the attention of recent research in the Thessalonian epistles. A matter of particular prominence has been the situation of the church—its racial and social composition, its religious background, and the nature of the persecution it faced. Also much discussed is the integrity of the two letters, especially whether 1 Thessalonians 2:13–16 might be an interpolation. Closely related is the debate over the authenticity of 2 Thessalonians and the occasion for that epistle. A final area of research has been the genre of the epistles.

SOCIAL COMPOSITION OF THE CHURCH

The Thessalonian church seems to have been primarily Gentile in composition. This is indicated by Paul's summary of his initial preaching in 1 Thessalonians 1:9–10, which is aimed at Gentiles, urging them to abandon their idols and embrace the one true God. Likewise, the emphasis on sexual purity would point toward those with a pagan background (4:3–8). The church seems to have been somewhat mixed socially, having wealthier members like Jason and the noble women (Acts 17:4) together with a significant number from the working class and urban poor. Those tempted to idleness (2 Thess. 3:11) may have come from the ranks of the latter.[6]

The Thessalonians probably experienced considerable social disruption when they were converted. They needed to be integrated into a new community. This would explain Paul's extensive use of "family" language in 1 Thessalonians. The word *brother* occurs eighteen times in the letter, proportionately the heaviest density for any Pauline epistle. Paul described himself with a striking variety of family terms. He depicted himself as being gentle like a *mother* (2:7); he encouraged them like a *father* (2:11). They were his *children* (2:7, 11). Separation from them was like being *orphaned* (NIV, "torn away," 2:17). First Thessalonians is permeated with the language of encouragement and comfort, even in the hortatory sections of the epistle (cp. 4:18; 5:11). It is in every respect a pastoral epistle through which Paul sought to integrate the Thessalonians into their new Christian family.[7]

The need for pastoral care was the more urgent because the Thessalonians were facing intense persecution (1 Thess. 1:6; 2:14; 3:3–4; 2 Thess. 1:4–6). The nature of the persecution is debated. The account in Acts indicates that Paul's persecution in Thessalonica was at the hands of a Gentile mob that had been incited by Jews (Acts 17:5–9). First Thessalonians seems to point to the local Gentiles as the main persecutors of the Thessalonians, especially 2:14, which speaks of "your own countrymen." The "countrymen" may have included Jews, as is possibly indicated by the strong anti-Jewish polemic that follows in 2:15–16.

What was the basis of the persecution? Robert Jewett has suggested that it might be linked to the ancient Thessalonian cult of the Cabiri. A local religion that venerated a slain hero, it was historically associated with the working classes. Its symbol, for instance, was a hammer. In the first century the Cabirus cult was appropriated by the aristocracy and made into an official civil religion. This left the working class feeling abandoned. The resulting vacuum made Christianity particularly attractive to them. The eschatological aspect of the Christian message was especially appealing with its promise of social redress. In Jewett's view, this "millenarian" aspect of Thessalonian Christianity was seen as revolutionary by the authorities and provoked the persecution.[8] One does not need to postulate a millenarian movement to account for the persecution of the Thessalonian Christians. The local emperor cult would itself have furnished sufficient basis for the persecution of the Christians. Thessalonica prided itself on its close relationship with Rome.[9] The cult of Caesar was initiated there very early, during the time of Augustus. There are Thessalonian coins from that period which depict Julius Ceasar, designating him as *divus* ("divine"). The Acts account may actually mute the seriousness with which the Thessalonian politarchs took the Christian threat to their Roman connections. The local persecution made Paul's pastoral care to the new Christian family all the more urgent.

INTEGRITY OF THE EPISTLES

A scholarly minority have argued that the present form of 1 Thessalonians is a composite of two letters. This is usually based on the observation that the epistle has a second thanksgiving at 1 Thessalonians 2:13. It is argued that thanksgivings occur normally at the beginning of Paul's letters, thus indicating the introduction of an epistle at 2:13. According to this view, 1 Thessalonians 2:13–4:1(or 4:2) is a fragment of a separate letter inserted into 1 Thessalonians. The fragment deals primarily with Paul's relief over the good report brought by Timothy. It is usually seen as written *after* the remainder of 1 Thessalonians.[10]

Most interpreters maintain the integrity of 1 Thessalonians. A significant number, however, argue that 1 Thessalonians 2:13–16 is an interpolation. This is based primarily on its strong polemic against the Jews, which is viewed as being unlikely for Paul, who never gave up on his fellow Jews (cp. Rom. 9–11).[11] On the other hand, one must remember that Jews incited the mob at Thessalonica and "drove [Paul] out" (v. 15; cp. Acts 17:5–9). Also, 1 Thessalonians 2:14–16 is not directed against Jews in general but against the Jewish *persecutors* of the Christians.[12]

Very few scholars argue against the integrity of 2 Thessalonians. One of the few who has is Walther Schmithals, who argued that our present two Thessalonian letters are a composite of four originally separate letters. In his view, Paul's *first* letter to Thessalonica consisted of 2 Thessalonians 1:1–12 plus 3:6–16 and was primarily a warning against false teachers and idleness. It was followed by a *second* letter in which Paul had to defend himself against Gnostics in the church (1 Thess. 1:1–2:12 + 4:2–5:28). In a *third* letter, Paul countered the Gnostic claim that the day of the Lord had arrived (2 Thess. 2:13–14 + 2:1–12 + 2:15–3:3). A *fourth* and final letter expressed Paul's relief that the situation had been resolved (1 Thess. 2:13–4:1). Schmithals based his reconstruction on the assumption that Paul was contending with Gnostics at Thessalonica.[13] Hardly anyone has been convinced that Paul fought Gnostics in 1 Thessalonians, although a number who deny the Pauline authorship of 2 Thessalonians would see Gnosticism as the target of that epistle.

AUTHORSHIP OF 2 THESSALONIANS

A number of contemporary scholars argue that 2 Thessalonians was not written by Paul. Generally it is argued that a disciple of Paul wrote the letter in the latter part of the first century during a time when Christians were experiencing severe persecution. Arguments against Paul having written 2 Thessalonians run along several lines. First, the close similarity between 1 and 2 Thessalonians is noted. Fully a third of the actual phraseology of 2 Thessalonians is paralleled in 1 Thessalonians. Even unusual structural details are identical, such as the occurrence of a second thanksgiving (1 Thess. 2:13; 2 Thess. 2:13). This is seen to be slavish imitation by a later writer. It is also noted that the two epistles deal with the same themes—persecution, the Parousia of Christ, and the problem of idleness. Yet they deal with this in different ways.

First Thessalonians *encourages* the hope in the Lord's return; 2 Thessalonians stresses the *delay* of the Parousia. The tone of 1 Thessalonians is warm and pastoral; 2 Thessalonians is harsh and judgmental. Second Thessalonians 2:1–2 and 3:17 deal with the issue of forgeries. This is seen as a "diversionary tactic" on the part of the imitator. It is also argued that the emphasis on holding to the teachings that have been passed down is more indicative of the sense of tradition of a later age than of Paul (2:15; 3:6). Some would argue that the problems of a realized eschatology (2:1–2) and of disorder in the church (3:6–15) reflect the problems of the later church, perhaps an early form of Gnosticism. Finally, it is argued that the writer of 2 Thessalonians does not "encourage"; rather, he "commands" (3:6, 10, 12). The pastoral Paul of 1 Thessalonians has given way to the authoritarian voice of his 2 Thessalonian imitator.[14]

In support of Pauline authorship, it is argued that the language and style of the letter are thoroughly Pauline, even in the two-thirds of 2 Thessalonians that does not parallel the first epistle. The similarities are easily accounted for if Paul wrote the two in close proximity.[15] The patristic evidence unanimously favors Pauline authorship; no early canonical list of Paul's epistles omits 2 Thessalonians or questions Paul's having written it. Perhaps the key issue is the occasion for the epistle, especially the controversial eschatological section (2:1–12). When the later church fought eschatological enthusiasm or Gnosticism, it never seems to have incorporated the sort of apocalyptic schematic that one finds in these verses. They are more easily accounted for on the assumption of Pauline authorship than otherwise.

THE OCCASION FOR THE EPISTLES

The occasion for 1 Thessalonians has already been treated for the most part under the earlier discussion of 1 Thessalonians 1–3. Timothy had been sent by Paul from Athens as his personal envoy to Thessalonica. Timothy had returned to Paul, perhaps still at Athens, with a good report about the loyalty and steadfastness of the Thessalonians (3:1–10). Joyful at the good news, Paul wrote 1 Thessalonians, probably sending it back by Timothy. Timothy had brought him fresh news about the situation in the church. The church was still experiencing persecution, and Paul sought to encourage and fortify them. Also, Timothy may have reported about problems within the fellowship of a sexual nature, and Paul addressed that issue as well (4:3–8). It is possible that the Thessalonians had sent Paul a letter by way of Timothy. In three places (4:9; 4:13; 5:1) Paul used a set phrase "now concerning" (Gk., *peri de*), which may indicate points at which he was picking up questions they had raised. Two of the questions concerned the return of Christ (4:13; 5:1). Evidently, some members of the congregation had died, and there was concern about their involvement in the Lord's return. Paul dealt with the issue at some length, assuring them that both the dead and the living would participate fully in the Parousia and encouraging them to be alert and prepared for that event (4:13–5:11).

There is considerably more divergence of opinion about the occasion for 2 Thessalonians. Even among those who believe that Paul wrote it, there are major differences. A number of scholars maintain that Paul wrote 2 Thessalonians *before* 1 Thessalonians. They base this on several observations. First, it is argued that the note of persecution is much stronger in 2 Thessalonians (cp. 1:4–10) while the persecution seems to be past in 1 Thessalonians. Second, it is noted that Paul seemed to be learning about the problems of idleness for the first time in 2 Thessalonians 3:11–12, whereas they are not treated as something new in 1 Thessalonians 5:14. A final argument claims that the eschatology in 2 Thessalonians is closer to Jewish apocalyptic and hence more primitive than that of 1 Thessalonians.[16] Others would explain the differing eschatological treatment of the epistles on the basis of Paul's having written the two letters to two different groups. On this theory, they would have been written at the same time, with 2 Thessalonians going to another Christian group than the main Thessalonian congregation—to a Jewish minority at Thessalonica (Harnack), or to the church of Berea (Goguel), or to Philippi (E. Schweizer).[17]

There is no canonical reason 2 Thessalonians could not have been the earlier epistle. Writings were arranged in the canon according to length and not according to chronological considerations. There *are*, however, good reasons for seeing 2 Thessalonians as coming *after* 1 Thessalonians.

Second Thessalonians 2:15 refers to a letter Paul had previously written the Thessalonians. The most natural assumption is that the letter was 1 Thessalonians. It is also easier to account for the austerity, the tone, and the different eschatological emphasis of 2 Thessalonians on the assumption it was subsequent to 1 Thessalonians. Paul's treatment of the Parousia in 1 Thessalonians led some in the church to conclude that the Parousia had already come. Along with the eschatological excitement the tendency increased for some to be indolent and generally disruptive. The fervor of the apocalyptic group may have heightened the uneasiness of outsiders about the Christians and led to stronger persecution. Learning of these new developments, Paul, now located in Corinth, wrote 2 Thessalonians. He assured the suffering Thessalonians by reminding them that God would vindicate them over their persecutors (1:5–10). He introduced an apocalyptic program about the events of the end time that had *not yet occurred* in an effort to counter those who argued that it had already arrived (2:1–12).[18] Realizing the severity of the problems created by the indolent and disruptive members, he urged the others to shun them if they failed to contribute their fair share (3:6–15). It was probably a matter of months, perhaps only weeks after the writing of the first letter, some time around the end of A.D. 50 or the beginning of A.D. 51.

We do not know what effect the letter had on the Thessalonians. We *do* know that the church continued to be supportive of Paul's mission. Two Thessalonians accompanied Paul to Jerusalem with his later collection for the saints, Secundus and Aristarchus (Acts 20:4). Aristarchus was with Paul when the apostle departed on his voyage to Rome to appear before Caesar (Acts 27:2).

THE GENRE OF THE THESSALONIAN EPISTLES

Recent literary analyses have looked at the Thessalonian epistles from two different perspectives, with much the same results. Some have analyzed them by the canons of ancient rhetoric. There is a general consensus that 1 Thessalonians fits the *epideictic* category of rhetoric with its emphasis on example and praise. Wanamaker outlines the epistle according to the divisions of formal rhetoric, just as Betz did for Galatians. In 2 Thessalonians Paul made less of an attempt to hold himself up as an example. He devoted less space to praise of the Thessalonians, and he was far more directive in seeking to change their behavior. Accordingly, Wanamaker places 2 Thessalonians in the category of deliberative rhetoric and outlines it accordingly.[19]

Others have categorized 1 Thessalonians according to its *epistolary* genre. Meeks and Malherbe describe it as a *paraenetic* letter, a basically hortatory letter which sought to aid the Thessalonians in their process of community building.[20] Paul sought to teach them by his own personal example. He used the language of friendship throughout the letter, and even his exhortations to follow a Christan lifestyle were marked by a strong note of encouragement and consolation. Some have noted the setting of the epistle in the community's experience of being persecuted. They would categorize the letter as one of *consolation*, with its strong emphasis on following Paul's example in remaining steadfast through persecution.[21]

It is probably wise to avoid rigid categorization of Paul's epistles. Examination of his letters through the lenses of ancient rhetorical devices and epistolary conventions has helped us focus on them in a new light. Paul adapted his epistles to fit the specific occasions he was addressing. This was certainly true of both Thessalonian epistles. Both were aimed at formation of the new Christians, consoling and encouraging them. Though the tone of the two is quite different, ultimately both were occupied with primarily pastoral concerns.

A STUDY OUTLINE OF 1 THESSALONIANS

I. Opening of the Letter (1:1–10)
    A. Salutation (v. 1)
    B. Thanksgiving (vv. 2–10)
II. Paul's Relationship with the Thessalonians (2:1–3:13)
    A. Paul's Initial Ministry in Thessalonica (2:1–2:16)
       1. His pastoral care (vv. 1–12)
       2. His thanksgiving for their steadfastness in persecution (vv. 13–16)
    B. Paul's Continuing Concern for the Thessalonians (2:17–3:13)
       1. His longing to see them (2:17–20)
       2. His joy over Timothy's good report about them (3:1–10)
       3. His prayer for them (3:11–13)
III. Paul's Pastoral Advice for the Thessalonians (4:1–5:22)
    A. Purity, Both Sexual and Social (4:1–8)
    B. Living the Quiet Life in Mutual Love (4:9–12)
    C. Taking Comfort in the Coming of the Lord (4:13–5:11)
       1. Assured about the dead in Christ (4:13–18)
       2. Ready for the Lord's return (5:1–11)
    D. Living in Peace with One Another (5:12–15)
    E. Heeding General Admonitions (5:16–22)
IV. Conclusion of the Letter (5:23–28)
    A. Prayer for Blamelessness at Christ's Coming (vv. 23–24)
    B. Exchange of Greetings, Reading the Letter (vv. 25–27)
    C. Grace Benediction (v. 28)

HIGHLIGHTS OF 1 THESSALONIANS

OPENING OF THE LETTER (1:1–10)

In both Thessalonian letters Paul listed Silas and Timothy as cosenders. This was appropriate, since both had worked with Paul when the church was first established. Timothy had continued to be Paul's personal representative with the church. Paul usually began his letters with the "grace and peace" benediction. In 1 Thessalonians "peace" also occurs at the end of the letter (5:23), thus bracketing Paul's concern throughout the letter for the peace and consolation of the persecuted Christian community.[22]

As was often the case, Paul's opening thanksgiving introduced themes that were prominent in the body of the letter. The triad of faith, love, and hope (v. 3) occurs again toward the letter's end (5:8), forming a bracket for the entire epistle, just like "peace." Paul listed "hope" last in both places, probably for emphasis, since the Thessalonian assurance in the Christian hope was one of the primary concerns of the letter. In verse 6 Paul spoke of how the Thessalonians had "imitated" him. Serving as a model for the young Christians was an emphasis Paul continued, especially in 2:1–12. The Thessalonians, of course, had imitated Paul in their suffering for Christ (vv. 4–6), and Paul would return to that theme later in the epistle (2:14–16; 3:3–4).[23] Likewise, he would have occasion to mention again the Thessalonian participation in the Christian mission in their own province and throughout the world (vv. 7–8; cp. 4:10). Finally, in verse 10, as Paul summarized his initial preaching to them, he concluded with a reference to Christ's return and the coming judgment, which became the *central emphasis* of the entire letter (4:13–5:11).

PAUL'S INITIAL MINISTRY IN THESSALONICA (2:1–16)

Paul's reference to the style of his ministering among the Thessalonians in 2:1–12 has often been seen as the apostle's reply to his critics. For example, Schmithals saw Paul responding in these verses to charges of his Gnostic opponents that he was weak and lacking in personal presence. It is more likely that Paul was holding himself up as an example, urging that the Thessalonians follow him in their own selflessness and devotion to others. Paul's use of family terms throughout this passage was also a means of solidifying his friendship with them. The passage is not a response to opponents but a good example of epideictic rhetoric.[24] Paul was also perhaps distancing himself from the type of popular philosopher of the day who preyed on the unsuspecting and gullible.[25]

In 2:9 Paul referred to his example of honest work. He toiled "night and day" so as not to burden anyone. Paul's tent making would have been considered demeaning to the upper classes in his day. As a Roman citizen Paul probably shared more of an upper- than lower-class perspective himself. He probably saw his work as demeaning (cp. 2 Cor. 11:7). But he also shared the philosopher's ideal that it was better to earn one's keep in degrading work than to be dependent on anyone.[26] He must keep himself free to preach the gospel with no strings attached (1 Cor. 9:15–18). The fact that Paul resorted to self-support at Thessalonica indicates that he spent some time there. It is also quite possible that his workshop was a place of witness for him. Philosophers like Socrates were known to have carried on discussions in the context of the workshop. Paul may well have engaged in active witness as he worked at his tents.[27]

PAUL'S CONTINUING CONCERN FOR THE THESSALONIANS (2:17–3:13)

With the exception of Romans, 1 Thessalonians has the longest section devoted to Paul's personal affairs of all his epistles.[28] In the lengthy treatment of his personal circumstances in Romans 15, Paul sought to introduce himself to the church. In 1 Thessalonians he was concerned with strengthening the Thessalonian commitment to Christ and with solidifying his own relationship with them. He sent Timothy as his own personal envoy, an extension of himself.[29] He wanted to return to Thessalonica, but "Satan" had hindered him (2:18). The best commentary on this whole section is the account of Paul's forced departure from Thessalonica in Acts 17:5–9. Paul left Thessalonica abruptly because of the threat of the mob and whatever terms the politarchs had laid down in connection with the bond paid by Jason. The latter may well have been the "satanic hindrance" to which Paul was alluding; it may be that he *could not* himself return to Thessalonica. Paul knew that the Christians left behind in Thessalonica would continue to experience local hostility. He was concerned for both their safety and their stability in the faith. He longed to hear from them. Unable to go himself, he sent Timothy as an extension of himself. Timothy returned to Paul with the best possible news: the Thessalonians continued firm in their commitment to Christ and their devotion to Paul.

PAUL'S PASTORAL ADVICE: PURITY (4:1–8)

The whole of 1 Thessalonians 4:1–5:22 is "paraenetic," that is, advice about the living of the Christian life. Paraenesis was a traditional form of Greek moral teaching and was often quite general in nature. In 1 Thessalonians Paul's paraenesis is mostly quite specific, closely related to actual circumstances in the life of the Thessalonian church. The sources for Paul's information were certainly Timothy and possibly a letter from the Thessalonians. The first two verses of chapter 4 introduce the whole paraenetic section. Note the encouraging pastoral manner with which Paul broached the subject. He reminded them of how he had instructed them in Christian living when with them and he *commended* them for their having heeded his teachings (4:1–2).

The first subject Paul addressed was sexual purity (4:3–8). Pagan and biblical morality were miles apart in the area of sexuality, and Paul frequently had to deal with matters of sexual behavior when addressing Gentile converts. There are several obscurities in the Greek of this passage, particularly the word translated in verse 4 as "body" by the NIV. As the NIV footnote indicates, the word can also be translated "wife." The Greek word behind these translations literally means "a vessel." If translated "wife," it would tie in with the reference to taking advantage of one's brother in verse 6. The meaning would be that one is to honor his own marriage and not covet the wife of his brother. The more likely meaning of "vessel," however, is "body," and in particular the male sex organ. Some of the pagan cults of Thessalonica made extensive use of the phallus in their symbolism. This was true of the Cabirus cult and of the worship of Dionysus to whom a temple was dedicated in Thessalonica.[30] Paul may have deliberately alluded specifically to the male member to remind the Thessalonians that for Christians its proper place was not in the excesses of the pagan cults but only within the sanctity of a solid Christian marital commitment.

PAUL'S PASTORAL ADVICE: LIVING THE QUIET LIFE (4:9–12)

In verse 9 Paul used the phrase "now about" (Gk., *peri de*), which may indicate that he was addressing an issue raised by the Thessalonians, perhaps through a letter or through Timothy. The question concerned "brotherly love" and may have specifically applied to the area of financial assistance. Paul spoke of how they already loved their fellow Christians throughout Macedonia (v. 10). This probably referred to monetary support. Paul urged them to continue in this worthy endeavor, but in verses 11–12 he "adjusted" his advice somewhat. Christian benevolence did not mean the support of those who were unwilling to work with their own hands. No able person was to be dependent on others.

A majority of the Thessalonians may have come from the impoverished working classes. (In 2 Corinthians 8:2, Paul spoke of the "extreme poverty" of the Macedonians.) During the imperial period, Rome often provided a grain dole to maintain peace among the masses, and some of the Thessalonians may have once benefited from the Roman welfare system. Very possibly the Thessalonian Christians lived in a close-knit community. They may have regularly shared a common table. The community may have depended especially on the largesse of wealthier members like Jason. But such benefactors were unable to support the entire community. They may have been the ones who raised the question with Paul. They wanted to know the limits of this "brotherly love." Paul's answer was that there is no limit to Christian compassion, but there is also no place for Christian parasites. Everyone was to bear his or her own share. His urging them to lead the "quiet life" and to "win the respect of outsiders" may indicate that some of those who were *not* doing their fair share had become socially disruptive in their indolence. Their disorderliness may have raised concern in the non-Christian community about whether this new group might not be a threat to the peace and security of the city.

PAUL'S PASTORAL ENCOURAGEMENT: THE DEAD IN CHRIST (4:13–18)

At 4:13 Paul began a long treatment of the return of the Lord, which extends to 5:11. Paul dealt with two separate aspects of the Parousia—the place of dead Christians in it (4:13–18), and its timing (5:1–11). Paul seemed again to be responding to a question raised by the Thessalonians: "now concerning (*peri de*) those who fall asleep." Apparently there was concern that those who had died would in some regard miss out on the Parousia of Jesus. It is not clear what prompted this concern. Scholars differ widely on the question. Some have suggested that a group of Gnostics or "charismatics" at Thessalonica were teaching a thoroughly realized eschatology which left no place for a resurrection. This perturbed the Thessalonians, who had heard Paul speak of the resurrection of the dead. Paul thus wrote these words to reassure them of the reality of resurrection.[31]

The problem with this view is that Paul did not polemicize against a realized eschatology in 1 Thessalonians. He addressed not an erroneous eschatology but a *deficient* eschatology. The easiest explanation for the Thessalonian misunderstanding is that Paul had not dealt with the place of dead Christians when he first preached in Thessalonica. Some have argued that Paul was so caught up in his own expectation of the Lord's imminent return that he had not even considered the possibility that some Christians might die before the Parousia.[32] It is more likely that Paul had not dealt at any length with the issue. He had emphasized the Lord's return; he *did* expect it soon. But some Christians had died after Paul's departure, and it raised a real concern with the Thessalonians about the place of the dead in the events of the end time. They may not have questioned the reality of an eventual resurrection. They may simply have worried that those who died might be left out of the immediate events surrounding Christ's return. Paul gave no details as to what those events might involve. His concern in 1 Thessalonians was not to provide instruction in eschatology but comfort for bereaving Christians.

Paul began by assuring the Thessalonians of the reality of the resurrection (vv. 13–14). Christians are not hopeless like pagans. The resurrection of Christ is the precursor of the resurrection of those who are in Christ. Paul described the dead as those who "fall asleep." This is a euphemism for death and not Paul's discussion of the condition of believers between death and resurrection.[33] Paul did not discuss that issue here. In verse 16 he described the dead simply as "the dead in Christ." What did Paul mean when he stated that God would "bring with Jesus those who have fallen asleep in him" (v. 14)? Probably he meant the same thing as in 2 Corinthians 4:14, where he spoke of God raising the dead with Christ and presenting them in his presence.[34]

Paul's main concern is expressed in verse 15. He assured the Thessalonians that the living would have no precedence over the dead at the coming of the Lord. He described this as a word from the Lord. Exactly what he had in mind is uncertain. There is no saying in the Gospels to this effect. Some have argued that Paul was referring to a revelation which he had personally received from the risen Lord. It is more likely he was referring to an actual teaching of Jesus, either one that is lost, or a tradition like John 11:25–26.[35]

In verses 16–17 Paul summarized the events that would occur at the Parousia. Christ would descend from heaven, accompanied by a "loud command," "the voice of the archangel," and "the trumpet call of God." In apocalyptic literature a divine command is often associated with theophanies and with the coming day of the Lord. The voice of an archangel likewise is connected to theophanies.[36] Paul did not specify the identity of the archangel. Michael has been suggested, the only archangel denoted by name as an archangel in the New Testament (Jude 9). Trumpets are a major item in apocalyptic literature. One need only recall the seven trumpets of Revelation 8–11. At the blast of the seventh trumpet, God sits down on his throne for his eternal reign (Rev. 11:15). In 1 Corinthians 15:52 Paul spoke of the blowing of this "last trumpet" as preceding the resurrection. Here also the dead are depicted as rising at the trumpet's sound. They rise "first." Then only do the living rise. Note that Paul included himself among the living— "we who are still alive" (v. 17). He expected the Parousia to occur during his own lifetime. Apparently, he saw the dead as being transformed when they rise from the grave (cp. 1 Cor. 15:51–52). One would assume that the living are likewise transformed as they rise in the clouds to meet the Lord.[37]

An interesting detail is that the clouds are connected with the *ascent* of believers into heaven rather than with the Lord's *descent*. The significant matter is that believers will meet the Lord in the air "and so will be with the Lord forever." Interpreters differ as to whether the believers should be seen as "meeting" the Lord in the air and then escorting him to earth, or whether they are to be seen as joined by the Lord in their own ascent into heaven.[38] Paul gave no details. He was not interested in detailing the apocalyptic drama but only in comforting the Thessalonians. Hence his last statement about the Parousia was that *all*, both the living and the resurrected, would meet the Lord at his coming and would "be with him forever." Paul emphasized the assurance of the believer's eternal existence in the presence of the Lord. He urged the Thessalonians to comfort one another with the same assurance (4:18).

PAUL'S PASTORAL ADVICE: READY FOR THE LORD'S COMING (5:1–11)

If 4:13–18 emphasizes the aspect of comfort for the believer in the Lord's return, 5:1–11 focuses on the aspect of judgment. For Paul Christ's Parousia and the day of the Lord were one and the same event, and a major aspect of the day of the Lord is the divine judgment of mankind.[39] Much like the Old Testament prophets, Paul warned that for those who were unprepared the day of the Lord would be darkness and not light. Evidently the Thessalonians had inquired about the *time* of the Parousia. Paul did not provide any timetable for them but simply repeated what he evidently had already taught them: the Lord's return would be sudden and unexpected, like a thief breaking into a house during the night. The image is a familiar one. Jesus used it in his "Parousia parables" to warn of the sudden return of the Master (Luke 12:39; Matt. 24:43). The image became a standard description in early Christianity for the unexpectedness with which the Parousia would take place and the need to stay alert (cp. 2 Pet. 3:10).

Paul had unbelievers in mind when he warned against a false sense of security. Destruction would come suddenly like labor pains in childbirth. The language is that of the Old Testament prophets. Jeremiah admonished Israel about its false sense of security (Jer. 6:14), warning them of the destruction facing them as God meted out his judgment. It would be sudden and painful like a woman in childbirth (Jer. 6:24; cp. Isa. 13:8). Jesus used the same image to depict the "messianic woes" of the final times (Mark 13:8, Matt. 24:8), but in Thessalonians the emphasis is on the suddenness and unexpectedness of the coming judgment. It is much like the parables of Jesus that warn of the need to be prepared for the master's return (Luke 12:42–46) and to be watchful while the bridegroom delays (Matt. 25:1–13). One wonders if Paul's warning might have had a specific group in mind. The Roman presence on which Thessalonica so much depended promised peace and security. In the light of the coming judgment, it was a false security, a claim for peace which ultimately was no peace at all.[40]

In verses 4–8 Paul assured the Thessalonians that they need not fear the coming of the Lord, because they were children of the light and not of the darkness. The image of the thief at night probably led him to this vivid contrast between those who belonged to the darkness and those who walked in the light. It was a common and widespread religious metaphor. For example, the Essenes of Qumran claimed to be the "sons of light," describing their enemies as "the sons of darkness." Paul employed a paraenetic complex, which he used in other places as well. He spoke of belonging to the light (v. 5), staying alert and awake (v. 6), avoiding drunkenness and revelry (v. 7), and putting on the armor that befits the children of light (v. 8). Exactly this same group of motifs occurs in Romans 13:11–14. The same complex is found in Ephesians, where it is most fully developed: the children of the light contrasted with children of darkness (Eph. 5:8–13), an appeal to wake from sleep to the light of Christ (Eph. 5:14), the need to avoid drunkenness (Eph. 5:18), and a call to put on the whole armor of God (Eph. 6:10–20).

The image of the divine armor is found in Isaiah 59:17 and in a more developed form in the Wisdom of Solomon 5:17–20. Paul developed it most fully in Ephesians. In Thessalonians he used the armor imagery to emphasize the three essential Christian virtues of faith, love, and hope. The triad also appears—in the same order—in 1:3. In 3:6 Paul spoke of how Timothy had brought him a report on the faith and love of the Thessalonian Christians. *Hope* was missing. Perhaps it was not omitted by accident. The Thessalonians were unsure about some aspects of the Christian hope. Now, having dealt with the Christian hope extensively in the epistle, Paul may have trusted that their armor was complete with the full Christian triad.

Verses 9–11 are Paul's final words of encouragement with regard to the Lord's coming. The Thessalonians were chosen for salvation (cp. 1:4); they need not fear the coming judgment (v. 9). Verses 10 and 11 round off Paul's discussion of the

Parousia. Verse 10 harks back to the reference to those who are "asleep" in the Lord (4:13) and Paul's assurance that whether dead or alive at the Lord's return all Christians would join him and be with him forever. Verse 11 parallels 4:18: Paul's purpose had been the same in both sections of his discussion about the Lord's return—to encourage the Thessalonians about the Christian hope. The form may have been that of traditional ethical teaching. The purpose was to comfort and strengthen the Thessalonians. It was a thoroughly pastoral concern.

Living in Peace with One Another, General Admonitions, Epistolary Conclusion (5:12–28)

The whole section 5:11–15 may relate to the problem of the "idle" addressed in verse 14. The word translated *idle* literally means "disorderly" and could refer to some in the church who, though dependent on the church, were doing their "own thing," neither following the leadership of the church nor bearing their own share in providing for the church's common life. The problem seems to have increased by the time Paul wrote 2 Thessalonians, and Paul addressed it in more severe terms there (2 Thess. 3:6–15).

Verses 16–22 are the sort of general paraenesis one often finds at the end of Paul's letters. The assorted sayings were probably not directed to any specific problems in the church. First Thessalonians has two benedictions, Paul's customary concluding "grace benediction" of verse 28 and the "peace benediction" of verse 23. Paul's praying that the Thessalonians would experience God's peace may link up with 5:3. The world has its many false promises of peace; only God brings true peace. Only God can "sanctify." To be sanctified means to be set apart. God had set the Thessalonians apart in Christ; he chose them (1:4). And he would remain true to his calling them; he would keep them as his own, blameless until the coming of Christ. Paul thus ended with a final assurance that they would share in Christ's Parousia.

A Study Outline of 2 Thessalonians

I. Introduction (1:1–12)
   A. Salutation (vv. 1–2)
   B. Thanksgiving and Prayer (vv. 3-12)
      1. Thanksgiving for Thessalonian steadfastness (vv. 3–4)
      2. God's judgment on their persecutors (vv. 5–10)
      3. Prayer that God will be glorified in the community (vv. 11–12)
II. Appeal Not to Be Shaken by False Reports (2:1–3:5)
   A. False Reports That the Day of the Lord Has Come (2:1–2)
   B. End-time Events Which Have *Not* Come (2:3–12)
   C. Thanksgiving for Their Election and Prayer to Stand Firm (2:13–17)
   D. Prayer for Mutual Empowerment (3:1–5)
III. Appeal to Shun the Disorderly (3:6–15)
   A. Shun the Disorderly (vv. 6, 14–15)
   B. Follow Paul's Example (vv. 7–9)
   C. Earn One's Own Keep (vv. 10–13)
IV. Conclusion to the Epistle (3:16–18)
   A. Prayer for God's Peace (v. 16)
   B. Paul's Autograph (v. 17)
   C. Grace Benediction (v. 18)

HIGHLIGHTS OF 2 THESSALONIANS

INTRODUCTION (1:1–12)

Paul's second letter to Thessalonica begins very much like the first. The first verse of the two epistles is identical except for the addition of the word *our* to "Father" in 2 Thessalonians. In the thanksgiving of 2 Thessalonians, Paul again commended the Thessalonians for their faith and love and referred to their experiencing persecution. The unique element in the thanksgiving of 2 Thessalonians is Paul's detailed treatment of God's judgment. The emphasis is on God's vindicating the Thessalonians by punishing their persecutors. Both the length and intensity with which Paul depicted the divine judgment would indicate that the persecution of the Thessalonians had intensified. The closest corresponding passage in 1 Thessalonians is 2:13–16, where Paul spoke of God's wrath upon the Jews who had persecuted Christians. Paul's prayer for the church was a regular feature in many of his epistles, and he included one at 1:11–12. There is no corresponding prayer in 1 Thessalonians. The second epistle is certainly no "slavish imitation" of the first, as some who question Paul's being its author have claimed.

APPEAL NOT TO BE SHAKEN BY FALSE REPORTS (2:1–3:5)

Paul's words about the Parousia in his first letter seem to have been distorted by some. They were proclaiming that "the day of the Lord has already come" (2:2). Paul urged the Thessalonians not to be unsettled by such a teaching, even if its proclaimers claimed a basis in prophecy or in a letter supposed to have come from Paul himself. It is not clear who this group was or what was the basis of their teaching. They may have possibly been some millenarians who were claiming that the end of the world was at the door. They may have been "super-spiritualists" who maintained that they were already perfected in the Spirit, had already "arrived," and had nothing further to await in the future. Whatever their teaching, they seem to have claimed Paul's backing for their views. The most likely explanation for Paul's reference to a letter purported to have come from him (v. 2) is that they were claiming that Paul's treatment of the Parousia in 1 Thessalonians supported their viewpoint. Paul replied that he had said no such thing, either by word of mouth or by letter. He then proceeded to set forth the proof that the day of the Lord had indeed not yet arrived.

Paul countered the false eschatology by presenting a mini-apocalypse of events which would precede the Lord's return. There would be a period of great "rebellion," and this would accompany the coming of the "man of lawlessness" (v. 3). Paul said that this lawless one was now being held back by a "restraining power" (vv. 6–7), but eventually the restraint would be removed, giving him full room to do his lawless work (v. 8). The "lawless one" would set himself up in God's temple and claim to be God himself (v. 4). He would parade as God, working all sorts of miraculous deeds but would actually be the incarnation of Satan himself (v. 9). He would lead many astray who had not followed the truth, and God would confirm them in their mass delusion. They would suffer condemnation for their wickedness (vv. 10–12). The lawless one would not prevail. He would be utterly destroyed by Christ at his coming (v. 8).

Paul's purpose in employing this apocalyptic language is clear. He wanted to assure the Thessalonians in the face of an unsettling eschatological teaching. He reminded them (v. 5) that certain events would take place before the return of Christ. Since these had obviously *not* yet occurred, the claim that the day of the Lord had arrived was patently false. In particular, Paul employed the figure of the Antichrist, a feature found both in Jewish apocalyptic thought and elsewhere in the New Testament. Paul never used the term *Antichrist*. In fact, the term is found in the New Testament only in the Johannine epistles (1 John 2:18, 22, 4:3; 2 John 7). There it refers to false teachers who were denying the incarnation of Christ. The idea of the Antichrist is also found in Revelation in the figure of the arrogant beast that sets itself up as God, performing many apparent miracles and leading the masses astray (Rev. 11:7, chps. 13 and 17). The basic concept is that the Antichrist is the antithesis of Christ, the incarnation of Satan. He is a figure of the last days who will delude the masses, pretending to be God, leading them in a mass rebellion against all religion and authority.

The figure of the Antichrist has roots in the Old Testament—in the king of Babylon, who aspired to be above God (Isa. 14:12–14), in the arrogance of the prince of Tyre who called himself God (Ezek. 28:2). It seems to have fully developed during the time of Antiochus Epiphanes, who in 167 B.C. sought to stamp out the worship of God and install the cult of Zeus in the Jerusalem temple (Dan. 11:31, 36–37; 1 Macc. 1:54; 2 Macc. 6:2). Antiochus's attempt to replace the worship of God with his own cult in the Holy Place of God's temple came to be designated as the "desolating sacrilege" or "abomination of desolation." Jesus used this image in his teaching on the events of the end time (Mark 13:14). In the same discourse he warned of false messiahs who would employ signs and wonders to lead people astray (Mark 13:22). Scarcely a decade before Paul wrote 2 Thessalonians, the Antichrist concept had experienced a fresh stimulus in the attempt of the emperor Caligula in A.D. 40 to set up his image in the Holy of Holies in Jerusalem, an attempt thwarted only by his timely assassination (Josephus, *War*, 2, 184–203; *Ant*. 18, 261–309).[41] Paul had taught the Thessalonians previously about this coming incarnation of evil and the mass rebellion he would organize (v. 5). Obviously, these events had not yet occurred, and Christ would not return until they *had* taken place; the day of the Lord had *not* yet arrived.

Paul also reminded the Thessalonians that they knew what was holding the man of lawlessness back (vv. 6–7). The Thessalonians may have known what Paul meant by this "restraining power" (v. 6) or "restraining person" (v. 7). Unfortunately, we don't. Obviously Paul was speaking of something or someone that was holding the "lawless one" back, keeping him in check and thus also delaying the events of the final times. The early church fathers suggested that the "restraining power" was the Roman presence, particularly the law and order that it maintained. This understanding was very much in keeping with Paul's teaching about the purpose of government in Romans 13:1–5. Paul may have kept the reference to Rome veiled so as not to raise the suspicions of the authorities by his reference to its eventually being "taken out of the way" (v. 7). A less common view, also traceable to the church fathers, suggests that *Paul's mission* was the restraining power. God would hold back the events of the end until the full number of the nations had been reached with the gospel.[42] This is an attractive possibility. Its main problem is that Paul expected to be alive at the Parousia (1 Thess. 4:17); he surely did not expect to be "taken out of the way" before Christ returned. Some have suggested that the restraining power might be Satan,[43] or God himself. Paul would probably have agreed with the latter. What or whoever the restrainer might be, God himself ultimately is in control of all history.

Second Thessalonians has no section corresponding to 1 Thessalonians 2:17–3:10, where Paul detailed his personal relationship with the church. It does, however, have a second thanksgiving (2:13–15), corresponding to 1 Thessalonians 2:13. Paul urged the Thessalonians to stand firm, holding to the teachings which he had brought them by "word of mouth" (when with them) and "by letter" (1 Thessalonians). The teaching he was most concerned with was that about the Lord's return. If the Thessalonians held to Paul's teaching on that subject, they would realize that the Parousia could not yet have come. Just as in the first epistle, Paul concluded this initial portion of the body of the letter with a benediction (2:16–17; cp. 1 Thess. 3:11–13). It is perhaps not by accident that Paul did not mention the Lord's return in the benediction of 2 Thessalonians as he had in the first epistle (1 Thess. 3:13). There was enough eschatological fervor in the church already without adding fuel to the fire.

APPEAL TO SHUN THE DISORDERLY (3:6–15)

In addition to the confusion over the Lord's return, the problem of disorderliness seems to have escalated at Thessalonica. In all probability the two were related. The disorderly group were likely the same as those who were claiming that the day of the Lord had arrived. Paul described them with a word that literally means "disorderly" (Gk., *ataktos*; 3:6, 7 11; cp. 1 Thess. 5:14). The NIV translates the word as *idle*, and idleness was surely part of their problem. Paul accused them of not doing their share in community support (vv. 7–10), of not abiding by his teachings (v. 6), and of being general "busybodies" (v. 11). Throughout Christian history, groups that emphasize the imminent return of the Lord have been known to abandon their livelihood and cease normal human activity. This could have happened in Thessalonica. Just exactly what their full agenda was we do not know. We *do* know that they were generally disruptive to community life. They had become a burden to the larger fellowship. They presented a bad image of the Christian community to outsiders (1 Thess. 4:11–12). They also probably were the eschatological enthusiasts whose speculations were unsettling the church.

It has been suggested recently that the disrupters came largely from the unemployed urban poor, who were dependent on the wealthier members of the congregation to provide for them.[44] This may well have been the pattern of household churches like that of Lydia and perhaps Jason, where the heads of the households served as patrons or benefactors for the church that met in their homes. Robert Jewett has suggested another possible organization for the congregational life of the working class. He postulated that they may have met in the urban *insulae*, the apartment complexes of the inner city where shops were located on the street level with crowded living spaces on the upper floors. He saw them as perhaps renting their own meeting space and gathering together daily to partake of their meals. This makes sense of Paul's instructions that those who did not work should not be permitted to eat (v. 10). Such a rule implies that the church had community control over such matters. It also implies that it was a shared enterprise, with all doing their part in support of the community life.[45] Paul perhaps worked in a shop below their meeting place. They would all have been familiar with his personal example of doing his part in the material support of himself and the community (vv. 7–9).

The problem obviously reached serious proportions as is indicated by Paul's bidding the rest of the congregation to shun the disorderly members (vv. 6, 14). In 2 John 10, the elder advised the members of his churches to avoid those who denied the incarnation. In Thessalonica the problems seem to have been more social than theological, but probably involved both dimensions. In any event, Paul's advice not to associate with them was primarily intended to shake them back to their senses and return them to the truth (vv. 14–15).

Like 1 Thessalonians, the second epistle has two concluding benedictions, a grace benediction (v. 18) and a "peace" benediction (v. 16). Also like 1 Thessalonians, Paul concluded the letter with his own personal autograph. In 1 Thessalonians he urged the congregation to pray for him, exchange a "holy kiss," and see that everyone heard the letter (5:25–27). In 2 Thessalonians Paul insisted that he was writing the final greeting in his "own hand," probably to authenticate its contents against those who were claiming he had said or written things which he had not (2:2).

NOTES

1. R. Riesner, *Paul's Early Period: Chronology, Mission Strategy, Theology*, trans. Doug Stott (Grand Rapids: Eerdmans, 1998), 337–341.

2. J. Murphy-O'Connor, *Paul, a Critical Life* (Oxford: Clarendon, 1996), 114–116.

3. G. H. R. Horsley, "The Politarchs," in *The Book of Acts in its First Century Setting*, Vol. 2: *Graeco-Roman Setting* (Grand Rapids: Eerdmans, 1994), 419–431.

4. A. J. Malherbe, *Paul and the Thessalonians. The Philosophic Tradition of Pastoral Care* (Philadelphia: Fortress, 1987), 5–33.

5. God is at the center of Paul's teaching in 1 Thessalonians. See R. F. Collins, "The Theology of Paul's First Letter to the Thessalonians," *Louvain Studies* 6 (1977): 315–337.

6. W. Meeks, *The First Urban Christians: The Social World of the Apostle Paul* (New Haven: Yale University Press, 1983), 173–174.

7. Malherbe, *Paul and the Thessalonians*, 34–60.

8. R. Jewett, *The Thessalonian Correspondence: Pauline Rhetoric and Millenarian Piety* (Philadelphia: Fortress, 1986).

9. K. P. Donfried, "The Cults of Thessalonica and the Thessalonian Correspondence," *New Testament Studies* 31 (1985): 336–356.

10. Murphy-O'Connor, *Paul, a Critical Life*, 110–111.

11. B. Pearson, "1 Thessalonians 2:13–16: A Deutero-Pauline Interpolation," *Harvard Theological Review* 64 (1971): 79–94. For the argument that the grammatical structure of 1 Thessalonians 2:13–16 does not accord with the remainder of the epistle, see D. Schmidt, "1 Thess. 2:13-16: Linguistic Evidence for an Interpolation, *Journal of Biblical Literature* 102 (1983): 269–279.

12. K. P. Donfried, "Paul and Judaism: 1 Thessalonians 2:13–16 as a Test Case," *Interpretation* 38 (1984): 242–253. For further arguments against interpolation, see J. W. Simpson, "The Problems Posed by 1 Thessalonians 2:15–16 and a Solution," *Horizons in Biblical Theology* 12 (1990): 42–72.

13. W. Schmithals, *Paul and the Gnostics*, trans. J. E. Steely (Nashville: Abingdon, 1972), 123–218.

14. J. C. Beker, *Heirs of Paul: Paul's Legacy in the New Testament and in the Church Today* (Minneapolis: Fortress, 1991), 72–74. See also J. A. Bailey, "Who Wrote II Thessalonians?" *New Testament Studies* 25 (1979): 131–145.

15. For a comprehensive discussion of the authorship debate and a thorough defense of Pauline authorship, see C. A. Wanamaker, *The Epistles to the Thessalonians. A Commentary on the Greek Text* (Grand Rapids: Eerdmans, 1990): 17–28.

16. R. W. Thurston, "The Relationship Between the Thessalonian Epistles," *Expository Times* 85 (1973): 52–56.

17. Bailey, "Who Wrote II Thessalonians?" 140–141.

18. Jewett argues that the millenarian enthusiasts were responsible for the "realized eschatology" at Thessalonica: "A Matrix of Grace: The Theology of 2 Thessalonians as a Pauline Letter," in *Pauline Theology, Vol. I: Thessalonians, Philippians, Galatians, Philemon* (Minneapolis: Fortress, 1994), 63–70. See also in the same volume the article by E. Krentz, who maintains the pseudonymity of 2 Thessalonians, arguing that its main theme is apocalyptic judgment, written to assure Christians who were experiencing severe persecution: "Through a Lens: Theology and Fidelity in 2 Thessalonians," 52–62.

19. Wanamaker, *The Epistles to the Thessalonians*, 49–51. See also S. Walton, "What Has Aristotle to Do with Paul? Rhetorical Criticism and 1 Thessalonians," *Tyndale Bulletin* 46 (1995): 229–250.

20. W. Meeks, *The Moral World of the First Christians*, Library of Early Christianity (Philadelphia: Westminster, 1986), 125–130; A. J. Malherbe, "Exhortation in 1 Thessalonians," *Novum Testamentum* 25 (1983): 238–256.

21. J. Chapa, "Is First Thessalonians a Letter of Consolation?" *New Testament Studies* 40 (1994): 150–160.

22. J. M. Bassler, "Peace in All Ways: Theology in the Thessalonian Letters," in *Pauline Theology, Vol. I*, 71–85.

23. J. L. Sumney, "Paul's 'Weakness': An Integral Part of His Conception of Apostleship," *Journal for the Study of the New Testament* 52 (1993): 71–91.

24. G. Lyons, *Pauline Autobiography: Toward a New Understanding*, SBL Dissertation Series, 73 (Atlanta: Scholars, 1985), 177–221.

25. A. J. Malherbe, "'Gentle as a Nurse': The Cynic Background of I Thess. ii," *Novum Testamentum* 12 (1970): 203–217.

26. R. F. Hock, "Paul's Tentmaking and the Problem of His Social Class," *Journal of Biblical Literature* 97 (1978): 555–564.

27. R. F. Hock, "The Workshop as a Social Setting for Paul's Missionary Preaching," *Catholic Biblical Quarterly* 41 (1979): 438–450.

28. I. H. Marshall, "Pauline Theology in the Thessalonian Correspondence," in *Paul and Paulinism: Essays in Honour of C. K. Barrett*, ed. Hooker and Wilson (London: S.P.C.K., 1982), 179.

29. M. M. Mitchell, "New Testament Envoys in the Context of Greco-Roman Diplomatic and Epistolary Conventions: The Example of Timothy and Titus," *Journal of Biblical Literature* 111 (1992): 641–662.

30. Riesner, *Paul's Early Period*, 373–375.

31. C. L. Mearns, "Early Eschatological Development in Paul: The Evidence of I and II Thessalonians," *New Testament Studies* 27 (1981): 137–157.

32. G. Luedemann, *Paul, Apostle to the Gentiles: Studies in Chronology*, trans. F. S. Jones (Philadelphia: Fortress, 1984), 201–238.

33. Paul never deals clearly with this issue, and it has been the basis of much discussion. Some argue that Paul believed in a *disembodied* "intermediate state" between death and resurrection: e.g., B. Lindars, "The Sound of the Trumpet: Paul and Eschatology," *Bulletin of the John Rylands Library* 67 (1985): 766–782. Others argue for an *embodied* intermediate state: D. E. H. Whiteley, *The Theology of St. Paul* (Philadelphia: Fortress, 1964), 233–273. Still others maintain that Paul had no view of an intermediate state but saw believers as rising immediately at death to be with the Lord: H. M. Shires, *The Eschatology of St. Paul in the Light of Modern Scholarship* (Philadelphia: Westminster, 1966), 77–102. Many would argue for a development in Paul's eschatology from the concept of resurrection at the Parousia in 1 Thessalonians to that of immediate transformation at death in 2 Corinthians: e.g., F. F. Bruce, *Paul: Apostle of the Heart Set Free* (Grand Rapids: Eerdmans, 1977), 300–313.

34. For a thorough exegesis of the passage, see J. Plevnik, *Paul and the Parousia: An Exegetical and Theological Investigation* (Peabody, Mass.: Hendrickson, 1997), 65–98.

35. R. H. Gundry, "The Hellenization of Dominical Tradition and Christianization of Jewish Tradition in the Eschatology of 1–2 Thessalonians," *New Testament Studies* 33 (1987): 161–178.

36. This whole section draws from Jewish apocalyptic. In apocalypses such as 4 Ezra, the resurrection of the dead and the rising of the living are simultaneous, as in 1 Thessalonians. See A. F. J. Klijn, "1 Thessalonians 4:13–18 and its Background in Apocalyptic Literature," in *Paul and Paulinism*, 67–73.

37. J. Gillman, "Signals of Transformation in 1 Thessalonians 4:13–18," *Catholic Biblical Quarterly* 47 (1985): 263–281.

38. W. D. Davies maintains that "being with the Lord forever" implies one has reached the final abode: *Paul and Rabbinic Judaism* (London: S.P.C.K., 1958), 296.

39. T. L. Howard, "The Literary Unity of 1 Thessalonians 4:13–5:11, *Grace Theological Journal* 9 (1988): 163–190.

40. D. Georgi, *Theocracy in Paul's Praxis and Theology*, trans. D. E. Green (Minneapolis: Fortress, 1991), 25–31.

41. For a full discussion of the Antichrist, see F. F. Bruce, *1 and 2 Thessalonians*, Word Biblical Commentary (Waco,Tex.: Word, 1982), 178–188.

42. J. Munck, *Paul and the Salvation of Mankind* (Richmond: John Knox, 1959), 36–52.

43. P. S. Dixon, "The Evil Restraint in 2 Thess. 2:6," *Journal of the Evangelical Theological Society* 33/34 (1990): 445–449.

44. R. Russell, "The Idle in 2 Thess. 3.6–12: An Eschatological or a Social Problem?" *New Testament Studies* 34 (1988): 105–119.

45. R. Jewett, "Tenement Churches and Communal Meals in the Early Church: The Implications of a Form-Critical Analysis of 2 Thessalonians 3:10," *Biblical Research* 38 (1993): 23–43.

SELECTED COMMENTARIES

BASED ON THE GREEK TEXT

Bruce, F. F. *1 and 2 Thessalonians*. Word Biblical Commentary. Waco, Tex: Word, 1982.

Frame, James Everett. *A Critical and Exegetical Commentary on the Epistles of St. Paul to the Thessalonians*. The International Critical Commentary. Edinburgh: T. & T. Clark, 1912.

Milligan, George. *St. Paul's Epistles to the Thessalonians*. London: Macmillan, 1908.

Wanamaker, Charles A. *The Epistles to the Thessalonians. A Commentary on the Greek Text*. The New International Greek Testament Commentary. Grand Rapids: Eerdmans, 1990.

BASED ON THE ENGLISH TEXT

Best, Ernest. *The First and Second Epistles to the Thessalonians*. Harper's New Testament Commentaries. New York: Harper and Row, 1972.

Gaventa, Beverly R. *1 and 2 Thessalonians*. Interpretation. Louisville: Westminster/John Knox, 1998.

Hiebert, D. Edmond. *The Thessalonian Epistles: A Call to Readiness*. Chicago: Moody, 1971.

Marshall, I. Howard. *1 and 2 Thessalonians*. The New Century Bible. Grand Rapids: Eerdmans, 1983.

Martin, D. Michael. *1, 2 Thessalonians*. New American Commentary. Nashville: Broadman and Holman, 1995.

Morris, Leon. *The First and Second Epistles to the Thessalonians*. Revised edition. The New International Commentary on the New Testament. Grand Rapids: Eerdmans, 1991.

Neil, William. *The Epistles of Paul to the Thessalonians*. The Moffatt New Testament Commentary. New York: Harper and Brothers, 1950.

Richard, Earl J. *First and Second Thessalonians*. Sacra Pagina. Collegeville, Minn.: Liturgical Press, 1995.

Thomas, Robert L. *1 and 2 Thessalonians. 1 and 2 Timothy. Titus*. Expositor's Bible Commentary. Minneapolis: Fortress Press, 1996.

Williams, David J. *1 and 2 Thessalonians*. New International Biblical Commentary. Peabody, Mass: Hendrickson, 1992.

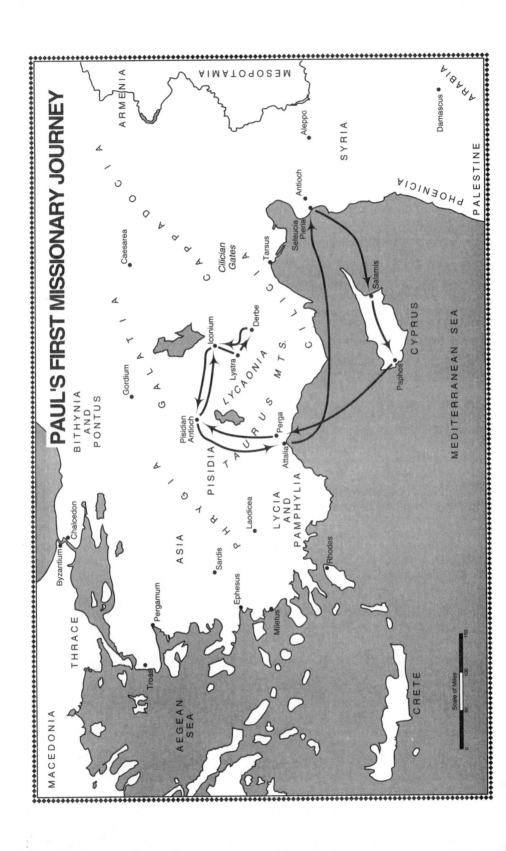

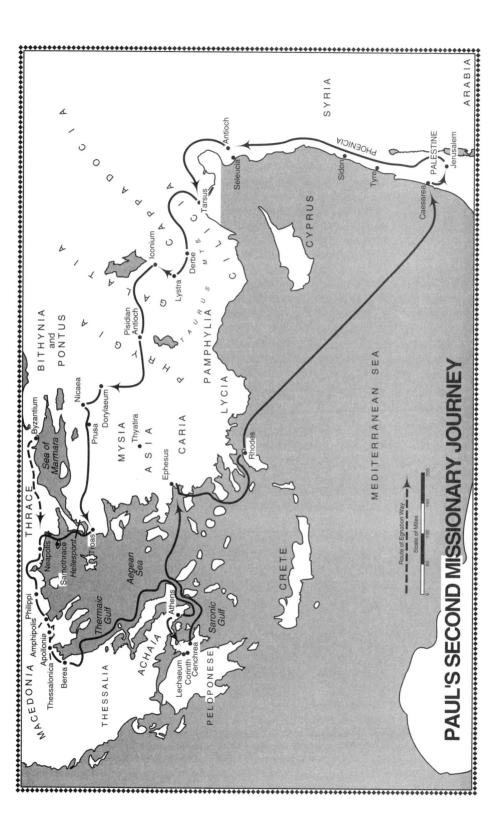

PAUL'S SECOND MISSIONARY JOURNEY

Route of Egnatian Way

Scale of Miles

0   50   100   150   200

ARABIA

SYRIA

PHOENICIA

PALESTINE

Jerusalem

Antioch

Seleucia

Sidon

Tyre

Caesarea

CYPRUS

Tarsus

CILICIA

TAURUS MTS.

Derbe

Lystra

Iconium

Pisidian
Antioch

CAPPADOCIA

GALATIA

PHRYGIA

PAMPHYLIA

LYCIA

Rhodes

MEDITERRANEAN SEA

CRETE

CARIA

Ephesus

ASIA

MYSIA

Thyatira

Prusa

Dorylaeum

Nicaea

BITHYNIA
and
PONTUS

Byzantium

Sea of
Marmara

THRACE

Neapolis

Samothrace

Hellespont

Troas

Aegean
Sea

Philippi

Amphipolis

Apollonia

Thessalonica

Berea

MACEDONIA

THESSALIA

Thermaic
Gulf

ACHAIA

Athens

Lechaeum

Corinth

Cenchrea

Saronic
Gulf

PELOPONESE

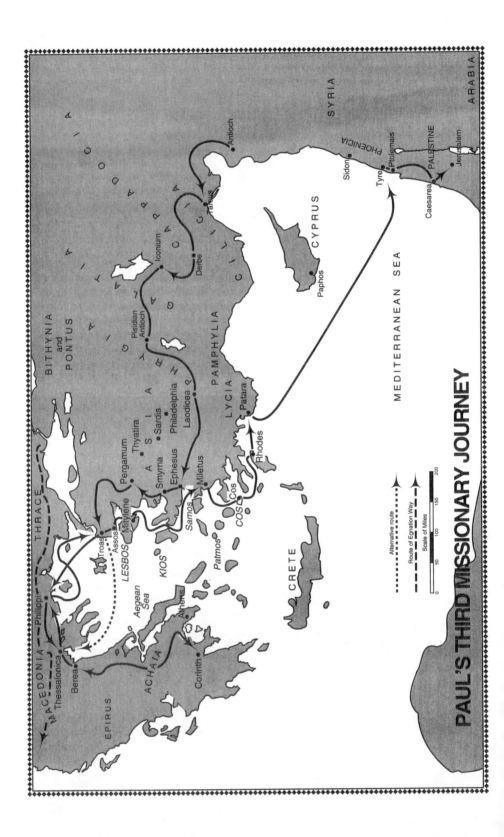

PAUL'S THIRD MISSIONARY JOURNEY

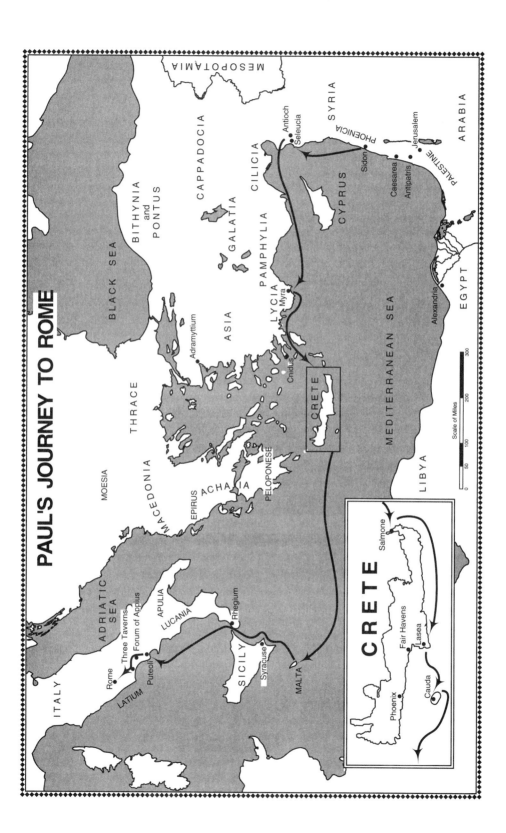

PAUL'S JOURNEY TO ROME

11

⁓ঞ⁓

PAUL'S URBAN MINISTRY
(ACTS 17:16–19:41)

*W*hen Paul left Berea for Athens, he entered a new Roman province, Achaia. Achaia was ancient Greece, the land of the great city-states—Athens, Sparta, Delphi, Corinth. Of these, Athens lay closest to Thessalonica, directly south on the Aegean coast. It was not a large city in Paul's day. Neither was it of any major political or commercial significance. It was still the most famous city of all Greece, the intellectual center of the world. Paul did not linger long in Athens. It evidently was not a prime location on his missionary agenda. It seems to have been only a stopping place as he awaited Timothy and Silas to join him (Acts 17:15–16).

Paul's destination was Corinth, a Roman colony and the administrative capital of Achaia. It was the largest city of Achaia, the commercial center of the province. After a short visit in Athens, Paul hastened to Corinth some fifty miles to the south. Corinth became his base of operations for the remainder of his second mission. He spent at least a year and six months there (Acts 18:11), probably half of the entire duration of his second mission.

When Paul had completed his initial work in Corinth, he returned to his sponsoring congregation at Syrian Antioch (Acts 18:22–23). On the journey home, he stopped in Ephesus, leaving Priscilla and Aquila there to set up work. He did not linger in Ephesus but promised to return (Acts 18:18–21). He did indeed return. Ephesus became the primary location for his third mission. He spent some three years in the city. It would be more accurate to call this period "Paul's Ephesian Ministry" than his "third missionary journey."

Assuming that the entire period of Paul's three missions covered about ten years, nearly half the time was spent in the two largest cities of all Asia and Greece, Corinth and Ephesus. Paul's missionary strategy was to go where the population was the densest. He set himself up in the urban centers and worked out from there.

This chapter covers the narrative of Acts 17:16–19:41, which is primarily Paul's ministry in Athens, Corinth, and Ephesus. This was an extensive letter-writing period for Paul. The two Thessalonian epistles were written early in the period, from Athens and/or Corinth during the course of Paul's second mission. Quite possibly Galatians and Philippians were written from Ephesus during Paul's third missionary period. First Corinthians was almost certainly written during the course of Paul's three-year stay in Ephesus. Second Corinthians was also penned during the course of the third mission, evidently soon after Paul had completed his three years in Ephesus and as he traveled by land to Corinth. Romans also belongs to Paul's third missionary period, probably written during the course of a final three-month stay in Corinth (Acts 20:1–3). Of these letters, Galatians, Philippians, and Thessalonians have already been introduced in chapters 8 through 10. Chapters 12 through 14 will examine the remaining three letters of Paul's third mission, the two Corinthian epistles and Romans. The present chapter will be confined to the Acts account and will provide a context for the epistles.

PAUL IN ATHENS (ACTS 17:16–34)

Paul seems not to have stayed long in Athens. It was primarily a stopping place as he awaited for Silas and Timothy to join him. First Thessalonians 3:1 indicates that Timothy came to Paul in Athens. We do not know about Silas; he may have been with Timothy or he may have continued on in Macedonia. Acts does not mention Timothy's coming to Athens, only his later coming with Silas to join Paul at Corinth (Acts 18:5). The most natural conjecture is that Paul sent Timothy from Athens to Thessalonica and that he returned to Paul with a good report, either at Athens or at Corinth. Upon Timothy's return, Paul wrote 1 Thessalonians (1 Thess. 3:1–10). Even if Timothy reported to Paul in Athens twice, we need not be talking about a long stay there—no more than a couple of months. When Paul's mind had been put at rest about Thessalonica and having at least established a witness in Athens, Paul was ready to move south to Corinth.

The Acts account of Paul's visit to Athens falls into three divisions. The first part treats his encounter with the Athenians in the agora (17:16–21). The second summarizes his speech at the Areopagus (17:22–31). The final portion relates the results of Paul's speech (17:32–34).

THE CITY OF ATHENS

The site of Athens was occupied at least as early as 2500 B.C. There is archaeological evidence that the acropolis was fortified around 1600 B.C. Athens flourished under the Mycenaean culture, until the invasion of the Dorian tribes. The Dorians initiated a period of general cultural deprivation, the so-called "dark ages" of early Greek civilization (eleventh to eighth centuries B.C.)[1] Athens came into prominence in the fifth century B.C., especially for its role in repelling the Persian invaders. It developed an extensive empire at this time, having virtual rule of the seas. In culture it enjoyed its "golden age." Its political power was diminished as a result of the Peloponnesian Wars with Sparta (431–404 B.C.), but its cultural ascendancy persisted. In the next century, Athens assumed a leadership role in the war of the Achaian cities against Philip of Macedonia. Although roundly defeated by Philip in the battle of Charonea (338 B.C.), Athens was allowed to retain its freedom. Philip's son Alexander was tutored by the Athenian philosopher Aristotle.

In the mid-second century B.C., the Greek city-states of Achaia came into conflict with the Romans. In resistance to Rome they formed the Achaian League. This alliance was defeated by the Roman general Mummius in 146 B.C. The victorious Romans seem to have first placed the cities of Achaia under the Macedonian provincial administration. At this time Athens was given the privileged status of a "free city." In 27 B.C. Achaia was made a separate province with the proconsular seat in Corinth.

Athens prospered under the Romans. Its free-city status was continued, and the city was often patronized by the Roman leaders. Julius Caesar began a new agora, which was extended by Augustus. The latter built new temples there to Ares and Demeter as well as an impressive Odeion (lecture and music hall). On the acropolis he built a temple to the goddess Roma next to the Parthenon. He initiated new athletic meets in honor of the imperial cult. In Paul's time, the emperor Claudius added the monumental flight of marble steps which leads up to the main entrance to the acropolis. Claudius seems to have been a special patron of Athens. Inscriptions have been found throughout the city which name him as "savior and benefactor."[2] Athens was not just patronized by the Romans. Every ruler in the empire seems to have wanted a memorial in the grand city. It was consequently a city of temples and monuments.

In Paul's day Athens was politically and commercially insignificant. Its voting population probably did not exceed five thousand. But it retained its reputation as the intellectual center of the world. In its golden age it produced dramatists like Sophocles, Euripides, and Aristophanes and philosophers such as Socrates, Plato, and Aristotle. Its schools of oratory were unsurpassed, and it produced the world's greatest sculptors. The golden age was long past by Paul's time, but Athens still retained its reputation for intellectual and cultural superiority. It was still *the* university town of the Roman Empire.

WITNESSING IN THE AGORA (17:16–21)

Acts 17:16–21 is viewed by scholars of the classics as the "most cultured" paragraph of the Bible. Luke employed all of his linguistic skills to make the agora come alive with the polite, inquisitive chatter of the Athenian intellectuals. The theme of Paul's entire Athenian sojourn is set in verse 16: Paul was distressed that the city was full of idols. Idols were not something new for Paul. Every Greco-Roman town was full of them. But Athens had more than its fair share. Patrons had furnished them on every corner. They were the traditional subject for the sculptor, and every aspiring artist longed to have his work on display in the city. There was a particularly heavy concentration of them in the northwest corner of the agora, where Paul would have first entered the city on coming from the direction of the sea. They were mainly "herms," stone pillars capped with the head of the god Hermes. Paul was thoroughly disgusted at the sight. It would furnish him the subject matter for his later sermon.

Luke describes Paul as witnessing to two groups in Athens, the Jews and the Gentiles. As per his usual custom, he preached in the synagogue on Sabbaths. His real focus, however, was in the agora where each day he would talk with "those who happened to be there." The agora is often translated "marketplace." Agoras were indeed the marketplaces of Greek towns, but they were much more than that. They were the civic center of the towns. Town meetings were often held there. Athletic events as well as cultural events like drama frequently took place in the agoras. The Athenian agora was a large rectangular area surrounded by four long colonnades called *stoas*. Originally the space between the stoas was open, but from the time of Augustus it was filled by various buildings, such as a temple to Ares and the Odeion (lecture/music hall). The agora of Athens was a gathering place for intellectuals. Zeno, the founder of Stoicism, regularly met with his disciples in one of the stoas, the Stoa

Poikile. His movement came to be known as "Stoicism" because it had met in the stoa.

Verse 18 mentions two groups of philosophers whom Paul encountered in the agora—Epicureans and Stoics. These were two of the main schools of his day. The Epicureans were established in 306 B.C. by Epicurus, who regularly met with his disciples in a place northwest of the city known as "the garden." The goal of the Epicurean was "detachment," a life lived as free from pain and stress as possible. Epicureans were basically materialists, believing in no life beyond this life. Stoics were pantheists. They believed that the divine principle in life (the *logos*) is to be found in all nature, including humans. They saw this spark of divinity as the cohesive rational principle that binds the entire universe together. For the Stoic, humans realize their fullest potential when they live by their inner *logos*/reason. It is this rational principle which links humans with the gods. Stoics believed that humans could discover ultimate truth for themselves. They maintained high ethical standards and emphasized self-sufficiency. They do not seem to have had a uniform view of the hereafter. At least some Stoics like Seneca seem to have believed in a survival of the soul after a separation from the body at death.[3]

Luke's account of Paul's encounter with the philosophers is filled with irony. The philosophers called Paul a "babbler" (v. 18). The Greek word behind the translation "babbler" is *spermologos*. It comes from the word for seed (*sperma*) and originally referred to birds in a barnyard pecking at random for seeds. It was often applied to low life who went after trash wagons picking up any scraps that might fall off. It thus came to be used metaphorically in intellectual circles for the plagiarist or dilettante who picked up random ideas but had no real idea how to use them correctly. The irony, of course, is that in this scene not Paul but the philosophers themselves are the real "seed pickers." They had little understanding of what Paul was talking about, but were dying to catch "the latest ideas" (v. 21). They knew Paul was proclaiming "foreign gods," but they weren't quite sure who they were. They figured out that Jesus must be a god, but they evidently decided that Paul's constant references to resurrection must refer to another divinity—the "Goddess Resurrection." The actual concept of a bodily resurrection was beyond their comprehension.

The philosophers wanted to hear more from Paul. They led him to the Areopagus (v. 19). The Greek is more ambiguous than the NIV would indicate. It says literally, "to the Areopagus," *not* "to a meeting of the Areopagus." The ambiguity is over whether "Areopagus" refers to a place (the "Hill of Ares") or to a judicial body ("the Council of the Areopagus"). Areopagus in Greek means literally "hill of Ares." (The Greek god Ares was the god of war, equivalent to the Roman god Mars; hence, "Mars Hill.") The Areopagus was both a hill and a court. It was a hill lying at the foot of the acropolis which had an elevation of around four hundred feet. From ancient times a court met on the hill. The court became known as the "Areopagus," because it met on the Hill of Ares. It seems to have originally been responsible for general matters of civic life such as education, public lectures, public morality, and religion. It is debated how much of its original power the Areopagus retained in Paul's period. Some see it as still being the primary judicial body of the city.[4] Others would see its responsibilities as more limited, perhaps primarily regulating visiting lecturers, religious teachers, and the like. There is also a question as to where it met in Paul's time. Evidence exists that it met in a building in the agora rather than on the hill of Ares.[5]

The main question is whether Paul appeared before the venerable court of the Areopagus or simply gave a public lecture on the Hill of Ares. Several factors perhaps indicate that Paul appeared before the court. For one thing, the question put to Paul, "May we know what this new teaching is that you are presenting?" (v. 19), is very much like the charges brought before Socrates when he was brought on trial before the Areopagus (Plato, *Apology* 24b). Luke may have noted the similarity and phrased the account accordingly. Second, Paul appeared regularly before the *main officials* of the cities that he visited—Philippi, Thessalonica, Corinth. Athens was probably no exception. Finally, one of the converts that Paul made was Dionysius, "a member of the Areopagus" (v. 34). Still, it was probably not a formal trial but an informal hearing, possibly open to the public. No deliberations were made, and Paul was free to go at will (v. 33).[6]

PAUL'S ADDRESS TO THE AREOPAGUS (17:22–31)

Paul's famous "unknown God" speech is probably the most discussed portion of the Book of Acts.[7] We will not attempt a full commentary on it here, just a summary of its main points. Though presented before the Athenian court, Paul's address is more a sermon than a defense speech. In the sermon Paul sought to confront the Athenian philosophers with the truth of the gospel. In so doing he attempted to build bridges with them by making points of contact with their own thought wherever possible. In particular he seems to have appealed to the Stoics. The thoroughly materialistic Epicureans would have found little in Paul's gospel that was congenial to their way of thinking. The main subject of Paul's sermon was the folly of idolatry. The sermon begins and ends on that note. It can be divided into five sections of two verses each.

The "unknown God" (17:22–23). Paul seemingly opened with an appeal to the goodwill of his hearers. He commended them on their being "very religious." The word he used was ambiguous. It could be taken in either a positive or a negative sense. It could mean "truly pious," or "superstitious." The Athenians seemed to have taken it in the good sense; Paul probably thought of it more in the negative sense.[8] The idols attested to a certain superficial but totally wrongheaded religiosity. Paul got their attention by referring to one particular altar which he had observed on first entering the city. It was inscribed "to an unknown god." No altar has as yet been discovered with that exact inscription, but ancient writers attest that altars existed that were dedicated "to unknown gods."[9] Jerome was aware of Athenian altars dedicated to "unknown gods" (plural) and suggested that Paul adapted his reference to the singular in the light of his monotheistic sermon (*Commentary on Titus* 1:12). The Athenians had surely provided such "anonymous" altars to keep from offending any god who might have been left out of their pantheon. They presented Paul with the perfect point of departure. There were gods everywhere in Athens. The city was literally groaning with idols that represented these gods. But the one god they did not know was the only God that counted. Paul said literally that the Athenians worshiped this one god "unknowingly" ("in ignorance"). Stoics, like those whom Paul addressed at the Areopagus, prided themselves on their rationality. The one thing they did not want to be accused of was ignorance. But Paul insisted they were guilty of precisely that—ignorance of the one true God.[10]

The Creator God (17:24–25). Paul began his exposition of the "unknown God" by referring to the thoroughly biblical concept of God as Creator. He basically made two points: (1) God is the maker of all that exists, and (2) God needs nothing from humanity. It follows that humans cannot provide God with anything through the works of their hands, such as idols or temples. The Greek philosophers would have found all this congenial to their own way of thinking. They, too, believed in a spiritual deity and not one served by hands. They, too, would have argued that divinity is complete within itself, totally without need. But they would not have understood Paul's concept of God as absolute Creator who stands above all that he creates. They were pantheists. For them, the divine is to be found *in* creation, not above it.

The providential God (17:26–27). Paul continued with his exposition of God as Creator. He pointed out how God had created humanity for two main purposes: (1) to inhabit the earth (v. 26), and (2) to seek him (v. 27). He spoke of how God had created all nations "from one man." Paul had Adam in mind. The Stoics would have resonated with the idea that all humanity derives from one man. They were strong believers in the brotherhood of humanity. They would also have found congenial the idea that God has provided the world so that people might "reach out for him and find him." Stoics believed that all humans possess an inner rational principle, a spark of divinity within. By reaching within, people can through their own striving discover divinity. Paul was not so certain about the ability of humans to discover God. He seemed at least to allow the hypothetical possibility of some revelation of God in the works of creation (cp. Rom. 1:18–20 and Acts 14:17), but he was thoroughly pessimistic about humans ever really coming to know God through their own striving.

The worship of God (17:28–29). Paul had no scriptural text for his sermon. The Old Testament would have carried little weight with the pagans of Athens. So Paul "took his text," so to speak, from a pagan philosopher. His first statement "in him we live and move and have our being" is probably not a quote.[11] Paul may have been alluding to the worthlessness of idolatry. Idols have no life. Idols can't move. Idols don't exist. Only God gives life, movement, and true being. Paul's "text" was "we are his offspring," a quote from the Stoic poet Aratus of Soli. Paul, of course, did not share the pantheism of the Stoics. He used the text to point to humans being created by God and to serve as a basis for his critique of idolatry in verse 29.

Paul arrived at his main argument in verse 29. If humans are God's offspring, they are made in *God's* image. But idolatry reverses the order. Idolatry makes God in *humanity's image.* This is not worship of God. It is worship of humanity! Thus, idolatry is the ultimate ignorance. It confuses the creature with the Creator.

The judgment of God (17:30–31). Paul now completed his sermon. He had presented the Athenians with the one, true, Creator God. He had established their guilt in failing to worship God, a guilt particularly manifest in their idolatry. Now he called them to repentance and decision. He noted that God had previously "overlooked" their ignorance of failing to acknowledge him (cp. Acts 14:16; Rom. 3:25). Now all had changed with the coming of Christ, "the man he has appointed" (v. 31). Paul spoke of two things in particular—the inevitable coming judgment, and the one who would conduct it, the one whom God had raised from the dead. Both ideas were incomprehensible to the Athenians. They had no concept of a final judgment, and the idea of a bodily resurrection from the dead made no sense to them.

THE RESULT OF PAUL'S ADDRESS (17:32–34)

There were three different responses to Paul's address. Some "sneered." Quite possibly these were the Epicureans. They believed neither in divine providence nor in any existence after death, spiritual or otherwise. To them judgment, resurrection, and eternity were meaningless. The Stoics were probably more open to Paul's message. They seem to have had at least some concept of a spiritual survival after death. They perhaps were those who wanted to hear Paul discuss the subject again. The third response was the most significant. At least one member of the venerable council came to faith in Christ, Dionysius the Areopagite (v. 34). Verse 34 is probably intended as a conclusion to Paul's entire Athenian mission, since verse 33 seems to conclude the Areopagus scene. Paul made "a few" (lit. "some") converts in Athens. Luke singled out two, a male (Dionysius) and a female (Damaris). Luke never failed to show the prominence of women in the churches of Paul (cp. 16:13–15; 17:4; 17:12).

It has sometimes been maintained that the theology of the Areopagus speech is in conflict with the theology of Paul's epistles. This conclusion is based on such observations as the absence of the cross in the Areopagus speech. The cross is indeed missing in the Areopagus address, but it is also missing in 1 Thessalonians 1:9–10, which is the one place in all Paul's epistles where Paul gave a summary of his initial message to Gentiles. Indeed, 1 Thessalonians 1:9–10 is almost an outline of the Areopagus speech: turning to God from idols, awaiting the Son who will deliver his own from judgment ("the coming wrath"), the resurrection from the dead. It is also said that the subject of the knowledge of God through creation is different in the Areopagus address from Paul's treatment in the Romans epistle (1:18–32). Actually, Paul made the same basic point in both: God can to some extent be known through the works of his creation. In Romans Paul used this observation to establish the guilt and responsibility of Gentiles before God. He argued that they distorted God's revelation, worshiping the creature rather than the Creator. Paul was more positive at the Areopagus, but even there he pointed to the folly of idolatry, which is to exchange the creature for the Creator (vv. 28–29).

Luke presented the Areopagus speech as the model of Paul's preaching to the pagan world. It is Luke's summary, based on the actual preaching of Paul. It shows how Paul sought to build bridges as he reached out to the philosophers of Athens. His sermon drew largely from the Old Testament but presented ideas compatible with the thought of the philosophers, especially the Stoics. Recognizing this, it has sometimes been argued that Paul's efforts before the Areopagus were a failure, a "disastrous blunder," as one interpreter put it.[12] Paul is said to have abandoned forever his attempt to reach the intellectuals and to have resolved to preach only the crucified Christ (1 Cor. 2:2). But Paul preached the dead and risen Christ in his Areopagus address (v. 31). It was at this point that he lost many of his audience. Paul knew there was no compromising on this central message of the gospel.

On the other hand, he did not fail to make all points of contact with his hearers that he legitimately could without compromising the gospel. His sermon is a model of missionary accomodation.[13] His sermon also was no failure. He won one of the thirty members of the venerable court, not an insignificant percentage. And Paul never abandoned his desire to probe the depths of the gospel, to seek a full understanding of his faith in Christ. His letters have challenged the best minds in every generation of Christians and will continue to do so. There may be anti-intellectual Christians; Paul was not one of them.

PAUL IN CORINTH (ACTS 18:1–22)

Paul spent at least half of his second mission in the city of Corinth. On his third mission he maintained a close relationship with the Corinthian Christians, writing at least four letters to them and visiting them twice during the period. Acts mentions only one of the visits, his final three-month stay in Corinth before departing for Jerusalem (Acts 20:1–3). The Acts account of his founding visit is also quite brief (Acts 18:1–17) but provides an essential background for understanding the Corinthian epistles. Corinth has been extensively excavated, and the archaeological findings have been useful in elucidating both the Acts account and Paul's letters to Corinth.[14]

THE CITY OF CORINTH

Location of the city. Corinth lies southwest of Athens about fifty miles, just south of the narrow isthmus which separates the southern portion of Greece (the Peloponnesus) from the mainland. The isthmus is only three and one-half miles across at its narrowest point, which provided ancient Corinth with two harbors. To the west was the harbor of Lechaion on the Corinthian Gulf, which reached into the Adriatic. On the east was the port of Cenchrea on the Saronic Gulf of the Aegean. Corinth thus had ready access to both east and west and was the *main* route between Rome and the east. The voyage around Cape Malea at the southern tip of the Peloponnesus was treacherous. Corinth provided an alternate route. From as far back as the sixth century B.C., the *diolkos* had been developed. This was a grooved pavement built across the narrowest point of the isthmus on which a cart was drawn, pulled by pack animals. Vessels were pulled up on the cart at one port and dragged across the isthmus to the other port. It is said that Alexander the Great considered digging a canal across the isthmus, and Nero actually began one. The project called for digging through a high cliff of sheer rock and proved impracticable until the advent of modern technology. One was finally completed in 1893.

Corinth itself lay on a plateau some two hundred feet above sea level. It was dominated by a single peak to the south. Known as the Acrocorinth (acropolis of Corinth), it was approximately 1,800 feet high. The area was blessed with natural springs, the largest of which, the Peirene, was located in the center of the city.

History of the city. Probably because of these springs, Corinth and its surrounding area was settled from ancient times, perhaps as far back as 3500 B.C. The name *Corinth* seems to have been used quite early and probably originally referred only to the Acrocorinth. In the *Iliad* Homer mentioned the city's participation in the Trojan wars and called it *Ephyra* (2.570; 13.664). Around 1000 B.C. Dorians invaded from the north, destroying the Mycenaean culture and initiating a period of diminished cultural achievement, just as in Athens. The Dorian period lasted around 350 years. During this time Corinth was ruled by a Dorian oligarchy known as the Bacchiadae. It gained some prominence among the Greek cities in this era. A shipbuilding industry flourished, and Corinthian colonies were established on Corfu and Syracuse. Corinth's renowned pottery dates from this period also. The Dorian oligarchy gave way to rule by a single man when the tyrant Cypselus seized control of the city in 657 B.C. Tyrants ruled until 585 B.C. when the last of them was overthrown and replaced with a democratic government. Corinth reached its "golden age" under one of the tyrants, Periander.

The fourth and fifth centuries B.C. were marked by wars and alliances as the various Greek city-states struggled among one another to gain ascendancy. The most famous of these was the Peloponnesian War (431–404 B.C.) in which Corinth allied with Sparta against Athens. The "Corinthian War" broke out in 395 B.C. and lasted until 386 B.C., this time seeing Corinth allied with Athens against Sparta. The wars took their toll, and in 338 B.C. all the cities of Achaia fell to the growing power of the Macedonian Kingdom under Philip.

In the third century B.C. the cities of Achaia formed a league, at first to throw off Macedonian rule and then to resist the growing influence of Rome in the region. In 196 B.C. Corinth assumed the leadership of the league. The league eventually found itself at war with Rome and was thoroughly defeated in 146 B.C. The victorious Roman general Mummius virtually razed the city. The men were massacred. The women and children were sold into slavery. Though the site seems to have continued to be occupied, the old city lay in virtual ruins for a century. Then, in 44 B.C. Julius Caesar decided to restore the city as a Roman colony. He settled a large number of freedmen there and named the new colony for himself: *Colonia Laus Julia Corinthiensis*.

The Roman city. When Paul visited Corinth, it was primarily a new city. The Romans had restored some of the old buildings that had not been completely gutted, such as the temple of Apollo and the south stoa. But basically it was a new city. Extensive building programs were carried on throughout the first two centuries A.D., particularly by Nero, Vespasian, and Hadrian. By the second century it was the finest city in all of Greece.[15] Particularly impressive was the agora, which was nearly six hundred feet long. It had two stoas. The south stoa ran nearly the length of the agora, dividing it in half. The southern half of the agora was about two meters higher than the north. The south stoa was the largest building of its kind anywhere. It ran five hundred feet long and had thirty-three shops. Many of the shops were establishments for eating and drinking. Each had a storage room in back with a well. The wells were connected with the spring of Peirene by underground channels. They served as a means of refrigeration for the shops. Just to the north of the south stoa, in the center of the agora, archaeologists discovered the *bema*, the judgment seat of the proconsul, where Paul appeared before Gallio.

During the Roman period Corinth was the undisputed political and commercial leader of the Greek cities. Its dual harbors made it one of the maritime powers of the world. Its pottery had a worldwide reputation. Its bronze was considered the finest to be had. It was also known for its wine and for a fruit that originated in the region and which was named for Corinth—the currant. Corinth was also known for its entertainment industry. It had three separate theaters: a music hall (Odeion) that seated three thousand, a theater for dramatic presentations and town meetings that seated eighteen thousand, and an amphitheater constructed by the Romans for gladiatorial shows.

Religion in Corinth. As one would expect in a port city like Corinth, almost every conceivable cult had found its way there. The city was laden with shrines to the Greek gods. The oldest building left standing after Mummius's destruction was the temple of Apollo with its Doric columns. It dated from the sixth century B.C. There was also a large statue of the god in the Peribolos (courtyard) of Apollo located near the Peirene spring. The temple of "Athena the Bridler" commemorated the myth of the goddess capturing the winged horse Pegasus. Pegasus became the symbol of the city and for centuries was depicted on its coins and those of its colonies. The Romans erected a number of temples after 44 B.C.—to Tyche (Fortune), Poseidon, Hermes, Jupiter. Augustus erected a temple dedicated to his sister Octavia. The Roman colonists also built a Pantheon in Corinth, a shrine to all the gods.

The older Greek cults persisted. Archaeologists discovered a spring connected with a secret tunnel and chamber, which seems to have been a cult center for Dionysus, the god of wine and revelry. On the Acrocorinth the temple of Aphrodite had been located from ancient times. Strabo said that it housed a thousand sacred prostitutes. That may have been true for former times but is doubtful for the Roman period. (That prostitution flourished in a port city like Corinth is beyond dispute.) Along the northern edge of the city, just within the walls, a temple to Asclepius was discovered. It was located next to a spring, with numerous channels leading from the spring into the building. Many clay replicas of body parts were found in the vicinity. Asclepius was the Greek god of healing. The replicas were representations of the particular ailing body parts which devotees brought to the god in seeking healing.

There were foreign gods in Corinth as well. In the region of the Acrocorinth, temples to the Egyptian gods Isis and Osiris have been found. At the foot of the mountain was a temple to Melicertes, the patron god of seafarers, a natural cult for a sailor's town. The interesting thing is that the Melicertes worship derived from Melkart, the main deity of Tyre. Of course, the religion of Israel had found its way to Corinth. Paul taught in the synagogue there. A stone lintel was discovered in the Lechaion road, just short of the entrance to the agora. It was inscribed, "the synagogue of the Jews." The style of writing indicates that it dates from the second century or later, but its location perhaps gives some idea of the general area where the synagogue was located in Paul's day.

Corinth also had its fair share of the popular moral religion of the day as propounded by peripatetic philosophers like the Cynics. Diogenes lived for many years in Corinth and was buried near the city gate on the Cenchrea road in a sacred grove known as the Craneum.

ESTABLISHMENT OF THE CORINTHIAN CHURCH (18:1–11)

Paul's arrival in Corinth (18:1–4). Paul probably traveled the fifty miles from Athens to Corinth by foot. It was an easy two-day journey. Arriving in Corinth, he met some kindred spirits, Priscilla and Aquila. They had three things in common: they were Jews, they were tent makers, and they were Christians. Luke did not say that the couple were already Christians when Paul arrived in Corinth, but that is the most natural assumption. Luke mentioned that the pair had come to Corinth after Claudius had ordered the Jews to leave Rome. The Roman historian Suetonius mentions Claudius's expulsion of the Jews from Rome, saying that it was at the instigation of "Chrestus."[16] "Chrestus" is almost surely a reference to Christ, and it is quite probable that the unrest in the synagogues of Rome was due to the arrival of the gospel there. The *Christian* Jews would have been Claudius's prime target. Also, in 1 Corinthians 16:15, Paul stated that the household of Stephanas were his first converts in Achaia. One would assume, then, that Aquila and Priscilla were Paul's first acquaintances in Corinth, but not his converts. They were already Christians when he met them.

Priscilla and Aquila became the primary "couple" among Paul's coworkers. They worked with him in Ephesus (Acts 18:19) as well as Corinth. The name Aquila means "eagle" in Latin. Luke said that he came from Pontus, which was in the Black Sea region, adjoining Bithynia. It is possible that Aquila was a freedman of the Acilius family, a prominent Roman patrician family. The name *Aquila* has been found as the name of freedmen in inscriptions. Interestingly, the name *Prisca/Priscilla* is a common name with the Acilius family.[17] Luke referred to her regularly by the diminutive form Priscilla ("little Prisca"). Paul always called her by her formal name Prisca. Both Luke and Paul usually refer to Prisca *before* Aquila—five out of seven times (Acts 18:18, 19, 26; Rom. 16:3; 2 Tim. 4:19).[18] This is not the usual Greco-Roman practice. The only reason to list the wife first would have been if she came from a prominent family or was better known than her husband. As a tent maker, Prisca probably did not come from prominent circles. It is more likely she was more conspicuous in her Christian involvement than her husband.

We have already seen Paul supporting himself at Thessalonica (1 Thess. 2:9; 2 Thess. 3:8). He also did so at Corinth (1 Cor. 4:12; 2 Cor. 11:7) and at Ephesus (Acts 20:34). Acts 18:3 is the only place where his trade is specified as that of a tent maker. No one is absolutely sure what this involved. The main question is the sort of material with which he worked. Did he work with *cilicium* (animal hair) or leather or linen? All of these materials were used in the manufacture of tents and awnings and the like. It is quite possible that tent makers like Prisca, Aquila, and Paul worked with various types of material and on many kinds of individual jobs.[19] Acts 18:1–3 indicates that Paul at first lodged with the two fellow artisans, most likely working in the shop below and sleeping in their quarters above the shop. Population density was very high in cities like Corinth. Quarters like those of Aquila and Priscilla were cramped. Typical dimensions of excavated city apartments (*insulae*) are from eight to fourteen feet in width by twelve to twenty-four feet in length as the *total* living area. Often ten to twenty persons would occupy a single room of this size.[20]

Paul likely was limited in his witness when he first arrived in Corinth. As usual he began in the synagogue, preaching to the Jews and Greek God-fearers there (v. 4). Typical work hours were long, and he was probably restricted to Sabbaths for his preaching. The workshop, of course, provided some opportunity for witness, but those who stopped by there would be limited in number.

Witness in Corinth (18:5–8). Paul was freed up considerably when Timothy and Silas arrived (v. 5). Timothy came from Thessalonica. Silas may have been working elsewhere in Macedonia, perhaps Philippi. That Paul was able to devote more time to preaching probably indicates that they brought him some material support. It may have come from Philippi (cp. Phil. 4:15–16), but it could just as well have come from Thessalonica (cp. 1 Thess. 4:10).[21] In any event, Paul was now able to give himself more completely to his ministry. The more intensive witness irritated some of the Jews, and Paul had to leave his base in the synagogue (v. 6). It was an oft-repeated scenario for Paul—beginning in the synagogue, encountering resistance, turning primarily to the Gentiles (cp. Acts 13:44–47; 19:8–9; 28:23–28). Paul's gesture of shaking out his garments was much like Jesus' recommendation to shake the dust off one's feet from an unreceptive village (Matt. 10:14). His remark that their blood was now on their own heads and not his was reminiscent of Ezekiel's words about the watchman over Israel (Ezek. 33:1–7). Like Ezekiel's watchman, Paul was to sound the trumpet heralding the good news about Jesus and also the warning of the coming judgment for those who failed to respond. Paul had been a herald to the synagogue at Corinth. He had faithfully discharged his task. *They* were now responsible for whatever response they made.

Paul did not go far. He moved next door into the house of a certain Titius Justus, who had evidently been attached to the synagogue as a God-fearer (v. 7). It is not clear whether Paul moved from the quarters of Priscilla and Aquila to the house of Titius Justus. The house of Justus certainly became the locale of Paul's preaching. Paul stayed in a home at Corinth several years later when he wrote Romans. He named Gaius as his host on that occasion (Rom. 16:23). Some have suggested that Gaius and Justus might have been the same person. Titius Justus looks very much like the nomen and cognomen of a Roman citizen. In that case, his full name would have been Gaius Titius Justus.[22] All of this is speculative. The main consideration is that Paul's ministry now centered on the Gentile community rather than the synagogue. Still, Paul's synagogue ministry had considerable success. There were probably other converts from among the God-fearers in addition to Justus. Even the household of the synagogue ruler Crispus had been baptized. In 1 Corinthians 1:14–16, Paul mentioned Crispus, Gaius, and the household of Stephanas as the only converts he personally baptized on his founding mission in Corinth.

All of these early converts seem to have been persons of some means. Crispus was a "synagogue ruler," which was an honorary position that often referred to patrons who supported the synagogue with their gifts. Gaius had his own household (Rom. 16:23). Stephanas also seems to have had his own house, and it is likely that Paul's reference to his "service" (*diakonia*) meant monetary support for the congregation (1 Cor. 16:15). Most significant of all was Erastus. In Romans 16:23, writing from Corinth, Paul sent greetings to the Roman Christians from Erastus, whom he identified as the "treasurer" (*oikonomos*) of the city. In the excavations of Corinth a portion of an inscription was found which was originally set in an area of pavement just south of the theater. It dates from between A.D. 50 and 100. The inscription notes that the pavement was installed and paid for by a person named Erastus during his tenure as an *aedile*. Aediles were the top-ranking magistrates at Corinth. "Treasurers" ranked just beneath them, and their position was considered a stepping-stone to that of aedile.[23] It is quite possible that the Erastus of the Corinthian church and the Erastus who financed the pavement were one and the same.

In 1 Corinthians 1:26 Paul reminded the Corinthians that "not many" of them were influential or of noble birth. "Not many" implies that *some* were—persons like Gaius, Crispus, Stephanas, and Erastus. It is interesting how each of Paul's churches seems to have begun with a nucleus of wealthier persons, such as Lydia at Philippi and Jason at Thessalonica. They may have primarily come from the God-fearers in the synagogues. They provided homes for meeting and probably other resources for the young congregations. They were decidedly a minority, as 1 Corinthians 1:26 implies. Paul's churches thus seem to have been of mixed composition, drawing from across the social spectrum. This did not proceed without its problems as we will see when we examine 1 Corinthians.

Encouragement in Corinth (18:9–11). Before he went to Corinth Paul probably spent no more than half a year in any one place. The pattern now changed. He spent more than eighteen months in Corinth (vv. 11, 18). Persecution had forced Paul to leave cities like Philippi, Thessalonica, and Berea. He may well have worried that the same would happen in Corinth. Already the pattern of resistance had begun in the synagogue (v. 6). His fears were allayed by a vision from the Lord. Paul had already experienced divine appearances that strengthened him and encouraged him in his ministry. These always occurred at critical junctures, like his original commission (9:10–18), and his Macedonian call (16:6–10). From the very start Paul had misgivings about witnessing in Corinth (1 Cor. 2:3). Encouraged by the Lord, Paul now continued in the city for a lengthy and fruitful ministry. The Lord assured him that no one would harm or hinder him in his witness. This subsequently proved to be true when an attempt was made to accuse Paul before the proconsul.

THE ACCUSATION BEFORE GALLIO (18:12–17)

Some time during Paul's ministry in Corinth some Jews attempted to have Paul condemned by the Roman proconsul Gallio. Proconsuls were the chief administrative officials in Roman senatorial provinces like Achaia. As the administrative capital of Achaia, the seat of the proconsul was located in Corinth. The proconsuls of Achaia generally were limited to one-year terms. Gallio's seems to have fallen in A.D. 51–52.[24] Gallio came from a distinguished Roman family. His brother was Seneca, the Stoic philosopher and tutor of Nero. He seems to have contracted an illness during his Achaian tenure which plagued him for the rest of his life. His political fortunes were very much tied up with those of his influential brother. The two of them died in A.D. 65, having come into the disfavor of Nero. Seneca described his brother as having an amiable disposition, a characteristic not particularly evident when the Jews made their accusation against Paul.

The judgment seat of the proconsul was known as the *bema*. It has been excavated, being located about midway in the agora, just north of the south stoa. The Jews made their accusation against Paul on a day when court was officially in session; Gallio had taken his seat on the bema. It seems to have been a spur-of-the-moment affair, without the usual legal preparations. The Jews suddenly descended upon Paul and hauled him before the proconsul. It was more like a mob than a trial, and this may have been what annoyed Gallio. The accusation against Paul was that he was "persuading the people to worship God in ways contrary to the law" (v. 13). It did not take Gallio long to determine that the god in question was the Jewish God and the law in question was Jewish religious law. It was not a matter of ordinary Roman law but was outside the bounds of Roman legal precedent (*extra ordinem*). In such instances it was left to the discretion of Roman officials to take up or to refuse the case.[25] Gallio chose the latter. Matters of Jewish religion were outside his jurisdiction; the Jews would have to handle such cases themselves (vv. 14–15). Rulings of proconsuls in matters not already covered by law established important precedents. Luke devoted so much space to this incident because it established the precedent that the main complaints against Christians had nothing to do with Roman law but were an internal matter of Jewish religion.

It is not clear who beat Sosthenes in front of the judgment seat or why (v. 17). Sosthenes is identified as the "synagogue ruler," evidently a successor of Crispus. The text simply says that "they all" turned on Sosthenes. Since the Jews are the main actors in verses 12–16, one would assume they were the ones who turned on Sosthenes. Why? Was he a ringleader in making the accusation, and were they venting their frustration on him? Had he taken up for Paul? Paul lists a "brother Sosthenes" as his coauthor in 1 Corinthians 1:1. Did the ruler of the synagogue follow in the footsteps of Crispus and become a Christian? It is also quite possible that "they all" refers to the Gentiles. Perhaps the incident gave them an opportunity to vent their own anti-Semitic feelings. Whatever the circumstances for the beating of Sosthenes, Gallio seems to have been thoroughly annoyed with the Jews; he turned a blind eye on the whole incident.

RETURN VOYAGE TO ANTIOCH (18:18–22)

When Paul had completed his time in Corinth, he decided to return to Syrian Antioch. He embarked from the port of Cenchrea. A church had evidently been established there. In his letter to the Romans Paul included a recommendation of Phoebe, a deacon of the Cenchrea church and perhaps also a patron ("helper of many," Rom. 16:1–2). Paul sailed east across the Aegean to Ephesus, a trip that modern steamers complete in a single night. He was accompanied by Priscilla and Aquila. Before leaving, he had his hair cut. Luke says that this was because of a vow he had taken. The reference to Paul's vow is laden with difficulties. The Greek is ambiguous; Aquila could have been the one who took the vow. That is unlikely. The vow was most probably a Nazirite vow (Num. 6:1–21). Such vows were usually completed in the temple in Jerusalem in a ceremony involving a burnt offering, the cutting of one's hair, and the throwing of the hair into the flames of the sacrifice (cp. Acts 21:20–24). Since Aquila did not go to Jerusalem, it is unlikely he took the vow. Those who took Nazirite vows did not cut their hair at all until the completion of the vow in the temple ceremony. Paul seems to have cut his hair before going to Jerusalem, which was most unusual. Usually one had a specific reason for taking such a solemn vow. Paul's reason is not given.

When they arrived in Ephesus, Paul left Prisca and Aquila in that city (v. 19). He hastened on to Palestine himself after putting in a brief appearance at the synagogue. Though asked to stay, he declined, promising to return as soon as possible (vv. 20–21). The reason for his haste may well have involved the need to complete his vow in Jerusalem. In any event, the stage was set for his third mission, which would center in Ephesus. It is interesting that Prisca and Aquila accompanied Paul to Ephesus. This may well have been by design. The couple seems to have prepared the way for Paul's ministry in Corinth, providing a Christian witness there before the apostle's arrival. Paul may have found this so advantageous that he asked them to do the groundwork of this ministry in Ephesus.

Paul set sail for Palestine. He landed at Caesarea, then "went up and greeted the church" (v. 22). This is almost surely a reference to the church of Jerusalem. In biblical language, one always "goes up" ("ascends") to the holy city. All three of Paul's missions followed the same pattern: they began in Syrian Antioch; they ended in Jerusalem. Having visited the Jerusalem church and probably having fulfilled his vow in the temple, Paul then "went down" to his sponsoring church of Antioch (v. 22b). The second mission was complete.

PAUL IN EPHESUS (ACTS 18:23–19:41)

Paul spent two-and-one-half to three years in Ephesus, the major part of his third mission. The groundwork for his Ephesian ministry was laid by others—Prisca, Aquila, and Apollos (18:24–28). The nineteenth chapter of Acts is devoted to Paul's work in Ephesus. It is an excellent example of Luke's "episodic style." Little detail is given about the actual progress of Paul's ministry in the city—just a few generalizing statements. The main part of the chapter relates four separate episodes from

Paul's three-year stay in the city: an encounter with some disciples of John the Baptist (vv. 1–7), the abortive attempt of some itinerant Jews to exorcise in Jesus' name (vv. 13–16), a massive burning of magical books as the result of Paul's preaching (vv. 17–20), and a riot instigated by the guild of silversmiths (vv. 23–41). In between the episodes are more general summaries of the course of Paul's ministry: his transfer from synagogue to lecture hall (vv. 8–10), his reputation as a healer (vv. 11–12), and his decision to minister in Rome (vv. 21–22). Paul's address to the elders at Miletus should also be taken into account (20:18–35), since in it Paul summarized his three-year witness in Ephesus.

THE CITY OF EPHESUS

The region of Ephesus was settled as early as the second millenium B.C., seemingly as a cult center for worship of the Anatolian Mother Goddess. The early cult seems to have been located in the open in a sacred grove. Some time around 1100–1050 B.C. the area was colonized by Ionian Greeks from Athens. They adapted the earlier cult to the Greek goddess Artemis. The Ephesian Artemis worship continued to have many traits of the older cult. Artemis remained a nature goddess, protector of life, insurer of fertility.

Around 560 B.C. Croesus, the king of Lydia, captured the Ephesian colony. He favored the Artemis cult, however, and contributed lavishly to the building of a temple for Artemis. The temple quickly became world-renowned for its splendor. In 546 B.C. Croesus's kingdom fell to Cyrus the Persian. For a while in the fifth century B.C., the Ephesians gained their independence from the Persians but were forced to join the Greek leagues during the period of wars between the city-states. Alexander the Great possessed the city in 334 B.C., and it was relocated and lavishly rebuilt by his successor Lysimachus.[26] By this time the old city had become landlocked by the silting of the Cayster River. Lysimachus moved the city farther west, restoring its natural access to the Aegean. This new hellenistic city prospered, even though occupied by a succession of rulers, including the Ptolemies and the Seleucids. The Seleucid king Antiochus the Great would have made Ephesus his capital but was defeated in 190 B.C. by the king of Pergamum with the assistance of the Romans. Ephesus remained under the dominion of Pergamum until 133 B.C. when its last king ceded his kingdom to Rome. Soon thereafter Asia was organized into a Roman province with Ephesus as its capital.

Ephesus flourished under the Romans, particularly from the time of Augustus. In Paul's day it was the largest and most powerful city in Asia. The city's harbor still seems to have been accessible in Paul's time. The main roads from the east converged in Ephesus. In fact, all the Roman milestones in Asia are calculated in the number of miles to Ephesus. The Romans carried on an extensive building program in the first two centuries A.D. In Paul's day there were several gymnasiums, two agoras, a medical school, an imposing city hall, numerous baths, and a stadium. Particularly impressive was the theater built into the foot of Mt. Pion, which overlooked the city. It had been recently enlarged when Paul arrived there and had a seating capacity of nearly 25,000. An impressive street 1,735 feet long led from the theater to the harbor. It was 35 feet wide and paved in marble, with colonnades 15 feet deep on both sides that provided stalls for shops. Ranking as the third-largest city of the empire, it is estimated that the population exceeded 250,000 in the first century.[27] The site of ancient Ephesus is no longer occupied and lies about 5 miles inland, due to silting of the River Cayster. It has been extensively excavated since the mid-nineteenth century.

PAUL'S EPHESIAN PRECURSORS (18:23–28)

Paul revisits his churches (Acts 18:23). Verse 23 gives a very tight summary of the outset of Paul's third mission period. Paul revisited the churches of "the region of Galatia and Phrygia." This probably included the churches of his first mission (Derbe, Lystra, Iconium, Pisidian Antioch) as well as the churches established in the northern portion of Galatia at the outset of his second mission. Paul likely covered the same territory as then (Acts 16:1–6). Paul was a pastor as well as a pioneer missionary. He ministered to his churches not only through letters and coworkers but in person as often as he could.

Apollos in Ephesus (Acts 18:24–26). Paul had left Priscilla and Aquila to carry on the witness in Ephesus until he could return (Acts 18:18–21). They seem to have worked exclusively out of the synagogue. They soon were joined there by Apollos. The background of Apollos is somewhat enigmatic. Luke described him as a Jew from Alexandria who was learned and had facility in the exposition of the Scriptures (v. 24). He seems to have been a Christian, for he had been instructed in the way of the Lord, and he taught "accurately" about Jesus (v. 25). He seems to have had one deficiency, however. He "knew only the baptism of John." It is not at all clear what that means. All sorts of suggestions have been offered to explain Apollos's Christian background, but none is wholly satisfying. Some see him as a disciple of John the Baptist like those whom Paul met when he first arrived in Ephesus (Acts 19:1–7). But those disciples do not seem to have known about Jesus; Apollos did. They do not seem to have experienced the Holy Spirit; Apollos is described as having great spiritual fervor (v. 25). They were rebaptized; it does not seem to have been necessary in the case of Apollos.[28] Whatever Apollos's deficiency, Prisca and Aquila took him aside and instructed him more adequately.

Apollos in Corinth (18:27–28). In Paul's epistles Apollos is closely connected with Corinth. Evidently, he went from Ephesus to that city (Achaia). The reference to "the brothers" in verse 27 indicates that a Christian community already existed in Ephesus by this time. It also illustrates how the early Christians followed the contemporary pattern of writing letters of recommendation to introduce their members to a new Christian community (cp. Rom. 16:1–2). Apollos is described as being particularly active in proving to the Corinthian Jews that Jesus was the Messiah.[29] But 1 Corinthians shows that Apollos had a pastoral role in the Christian congregation at Corinth as well. Some evidently attempted to pit Apollos against Paul (1 Cor. 1:12), but Paul insisted on their cooperative ministries (1 Cor. 4:6). He laid the foundation; Apollos built on it (1 Cor. 3:4–8). Evidently Apollos eventually returned to Ephesus. He seems to have been there when Paul wrote 1 Corinthians (cp. 1 Cor. 16:12).

PAUL'S EARLY EPHESIAN MINISTRY (19:1–22)

After revisiting his congregations in the province of Galatia, Paul went to Ephesus. Previously he had been prevented by the Holy Spirit from ministering there. It is not clear which route Paul took to Ephesus. Luke says that he went through the "upper regions" (NIV, "interior"). He may have taken the main Roman road that led through the Lycus Valley, where churches were later established at Colosse, Hierapolis, and Laodicea.

The disciples of John (19:1–7). On arriving at Ephesus, Paul encountered "some disciples." They seem to have been followers of John the Baptist. They had received John's baptism (v. 3) but were not aware of the coming of the Holy Spirit (v. 2). They also do not seem to have known about Jesus (v. 4). John himself contrasted his own water baptism that symbolized repentance with the coming baptism in the Spirit that the Messiah was to bring (Luke 3:16; Acts 1:5). These Ephesian disciples of John seem to have belonged to John's early messianic movement before Jesus appeared on the scene. They knew John's message of the coming Messiah but were unaware of Jesus' coming or of the outpouring of the Spirit at Pentecost. John had prepared them. Paul "completed" them with the good news about Jesus. They readily responded in faith, were baptized in the name of Jesus, and received the Spirit. Evidently baptizing groups like these that had been associated with John's movement continued to exist apart from the Christians. They were a major group for Christian evangelization. As Paul made clear to the twelve at Ephesus, true disciples of John must surely embrace Jesus, the "coming one" heralded by John (cp. Luke 7:18–23).[30]

Preaching in the synagogue and lecture hall (19:8–10). Priscilla, Aquila, and Apollos had already witnessed in the synagogue of Ephesus. Paul continued their testimony to Christ. He seems to have lasted longer in the Ephesian synagogue than elsewhere. He had to leave the Thessalonian synagogue after three weeks (17:2). He preached in that of Ephesus for three months. Still, the old pattern persisted. Opposition arose, even to the point where the Christian "way" was "publicly maligned." So, Paul left the synagogue and moved into the *scholē* of Tyrannus. Most translations translate the word *scholē* as "school" or "lecture hall." There is evidence that the word was also used of the guild halls where tradesmen met, and it is possible that Tyrannus was a fellow artisan and acquaintance of Paul. The Western Text of Acts notes that Paul spoke from the fifth to the tenth hour, that is, from 11:00 A.M. to 4:00 P.M. These were the hot hours of the day. In Asia the usual day began early. Workers tried to complete their tasks before noon. Paul may have worked at his trade himself in the early morning hours and then moved to the hall of Tyrannus when his working day ended in the noon heat. In the Miletus address, Paul spoke of how he had supported himself with his own labor while in Ephesus (20:34).

Archaeology has not yet uncovered the synagogue at Ephesus, and very few Jewish inscriptions have been found. On the other hand, Josephus spoke of a sizable Jewish community that existed in Ephesus from Seleucid times. He mentioned a number of special decrees that had been issued to preserve the Jewish rights to observe their ancestral customs (*Ant.* 14.223–227 and 262–264). The Ephesian church seems to have had a significant Jewish component. The witness in the synagogue lasted for a considerable period under Aquila, Prisca, Apollos, and then Paul. Paul took a number of "disciples" with him when he left the synagogue (v. 9). This probably included Jews and God-fearers. Throughout the account of Paul's ministry in Ephesus, Paul is said to have witnessed to both "Jews and Greeks" (19:10, 17; 20:21).[31]

Verse 10 is a very pithy summary of an extensive period of ministry for Paul. It speaks of Paul's continuing for two more years in Ephesus. Add this to the three months of verse 8 and "a little longer" in verse 22, and you end up with the three years or so given in Paul's Miletus address (20:31). Paul made Ephesus his headquarters during this period. His coworkers went out from Ephesus and established churches elsewhere in Asia—at Colosse, Hierapolis, Laodicea, indeed perhaps all seven of the churches addressed in Revelation 2–3. It was an extensive letter-writing period for Paul. First Corinthians was written from Ephesus and probably also an earlier letter mentioned in 1 Corinthians 5:9. Galatians and Philippians may have been written during Paul's Ephesian ministry, as we have already maintained. Some scholars would see *all* the Prison Epistles as being written from Ephesus. Paul also seems to have visited Corinth for a rather unhappy encounter during the course of the three-year Ephesian sojourn. In fact, he had extensive dealings with Corinth throughout this period, as reflected in the Corinthian letters. Luke mentions none of this in Acts. He is more concerned with depicting the gospel's triumphs in the city than giving a history of the Pauline mission there.

Paul's encounter with false religion in Ephesus (19:11–20). All of Acts 19:11–20 deals with the triumph of Paul's witness over the false piety that prevailed in the city. Verses 11–12 serve as a backdrop to the section. They relate the tremendous reputation which Paul came to have throughout the city for healings. People would carry off to the sick various items of apparel that had touched Paul's body—handkerchiefs or sweatbands, aprons or belts,[32] believing that the sick would be cured by this indirect contact with the apostle's person. One is reminded of the similar popular faith in Peter's shadow (Acts 5:15) or the touch of the hem of Jesus' garment (Mark 5:25–34; 6:56). The emphasis is all on God's power; Paul made no personal claims. The tradition sets the stage for the stories that follow. God's power was with *Paul*—not with the manipulations of the wandering exorcists (vv. 13–16) or with the gibberish of magical incantations (vv. 17–20).

The story of the sons of Sceva (vv. 13–16) is entertaining as well as edifying. It contains much irony and a touch of humor. We don't know of a Jewish high priest of the Jerusalem temple named Sceva. Josephus listed the names of the high priests up until the fall of Jerusalem in A.D. 70; none was named Sceva. He could have been from high priestly circles or from a rival cult. The significant thing is that the high priest was the only one allowed to invoke the ineffable name of Yahweh, and that only on the day of Atonement (Mishnah, *Yoma* 6:2). Exorcists like these seven itinerants used extensive incantations in their trade. Names of divine beings were considered particularly potent on the principle that a higher power is dominant over a lower power. The name of God would carry great power. Thus, the seven claimed a high priestly lineage with its prerogative to use the divine name. The same principle led them to invoke the name of Jesus in their attempted exorcism. They had seen Paul heal in Jesus' name and assumed the power was in the name. The power was indeed in the name and person of Jesus but not apart from the one who uttered the name. The demon made that clear. He knew the name of Jesus. He knew the Paul who invoked the name. He didn't know these would-be exorcists. The demoniac then fell upon the seven exorcists. In the melee they lost their clothes and fled the scene naked and humiliated. The point of the story is clear: there is nothing magical or manipulative about the Christian faith. There is tremendous power in the name of Christ, but not irregardless of its bearers.

The book burning of Ephesus (vv. 17–20) illustrates the same basic principle. Ephesus was famous for the so-called Ephesian "letters." These were six magical words which were evidently engraved on the image of Artemis in the temple. They were believed to carry great power. In the popular superstition of the first century, exotic words and incantations were seen to be potent. Collections of these were often written on papyrus leaves and sold for large sums. A number of such collections have been found in Egypt. They often consist of the names of foreign divinities. Hebrew names like "Yahweh Sabaoth" were particularly in vogue because of their exotic sound. Paul's preaching along with incidents like the unsuccessful exorcists made the Christians of Ephesus aware of the futility of their former superstition. They brought their books for a massive, but voluntary, book burning. It was a genuine sacrifice for them. The books were worth the wages for fifty thousand working days. They *could* have sold the valuable books. They preferred to sacrifice rather than to encourage others in the errors of magic.

Paul's plans for further ministry (19:21–22). Verse 21 is a turning point in the entire plot of Acts. Paul's itinerary for the rest of the book is outlined in this passage. After finishing in Ephesus, Paul would travel through Macedonia and Achaia and eventually to Jerusalem. Then he planned to go to Rome. This is exactly as it turned out, as is clear also from Paul's letters. Romans 15:22–33 is the best commentary on this passage. Acts does not mention the collection for Jerusalem, but the Roman epistle makes it clear that the collection for the saints was the reason for Paul's going to Jerusalem first before setting out for Rome. Paul did indeed go from Jerusalem to Rome but not exactly as originally planned. He went to Rome in chains.

Verse 22 mentions Paul sending Timothy and Erastus ahead of him into Macedonia while he delayed in Ephesus a little longer. The occasion may have been that outlined in 1 Corinthians 16, when Paul, writing from Ephesus, told the Corinthians that he was delaying his plans to visit them until after Pentecost (v. 8) but that he was sending Timothy on ahead of him (v. 10). Erastus may be the same as the treasurer of Corinth (Rom. 16:23). He may have been another; the name is not rare.

THE OPPOSITION OF THE EPHESIAN CRAFTSMEN (19:23–41)

The temple of Artemis was the pride of Ephesus. It was considered one of the seven architectural wonders of the ancient world. The first great temple had been built by King Croesus around 550 B.C. It was burned down in 356 B.C. by a madman named Herostratus, who said he did the deed so that his name would live in history. Unfortunately, he got his wish. Legend had it that Alexander the Great was born on the night of the temple's burning. One of Artemis's roles as a goddess was to assist in childbirth. As the story goes, Artemis was away participating in Alexander's birth, leaving her temple unprotected because she considered his birth more important than her own shrine.

The temple was soon rebuilt. When Lysimachus relocated the city, the temple was left on its original site, more than a mile from the new city. None of the temple stands today. Its foundations were not even known in modern times until located by the British archaeologist J. T. Wood in 1869. It was a massive structure. It stood on a platform 239 feet by 418 feet, the temple itself measuring 165 feet by 345 feet. It had 127 columns, each 60 feet in height. The altar was not discovered until 1965. It measured 32 meters by 22 meters and was shaped like a horseshoe. The building was covered with fine sculptures, many of them by Praxiteles and other famous artists. Both inside and out the temple was decorated in rich colors and gold leaf.

The image of Artemis stood in the area of the altar. It has not been found. A number of replicas have been located in various places. The image seems to have been in wood that had darkened with age, perhaps originally of cedar. The feet of the goddess were bound together like those of a mummy. The upper body was covered with twenty-four round objects which have been variously identified as planets, ostrich eggs, or breasts. The last seems the most likely, a reminder of the origins of the cult in the emphasis on fecundity of the Anatolian Mother Goddess. The altar was decorated with animals. Artemis was both goddess of the hunt and protector of the forest animals.

Artemis was a virgin goddess, and all sexual behavior was banned from the temple. Prior to the Roman period, self-emasculated priests presided over the cult, but this may have changed in later times. The young maidens who had a leading role in the processions of the Artemision were virgins. The Artemis cult emphasized the virginity of the goddess, but did not promote celibacy. Artemis was seen as the protector of maidens in their virginity but also as the one who prepared them for marriage and assisted in the birth of their children. The Artemision was the central festival of Artemis worship. It was held in the early spring and consisted of festivities that lasted a week, including dances and dramas enacting the mythology of the goddess. The culmination of the festival was a solemn processional in which the image of the goddess was carried more than a mile from the theater to the temple.

From time immemorial the temple had been designated as a place of refuge for fugitives. It continued to be so under the Roman emperors. Some of them even extended the area designated for refuge. The temple was also a major financial institution, accepting deposits and making loans. It was the largest banking center in Asia. In brief, the temple was central to the civic pride and commercial well-being of the city. In the episode with the silversmiths, Paul found himself accused of violating both these interests.

The accusation of Demetrius (19:23–27). The incident seems to have occurred toward the end of Paul's ministry in Ephesus. It may well have been around the time of the Artemision, when pilgrims came from all over the empire to participate in the festivities. The sales during that time could "make or break" those engaged in the production of replicas of the goddess and her temple. Demetrius was a leader in the local guild of silversmiths. Luke says that he made silver shrines of Artemis (replicas of the temple). Terra-cotta replicas of the temple have been found, and the temple appears on numerous silver coins, but no silver temple replicas have been found. Silver copies of the image of Artemis have also been discovered. One can thus imagine that Demetrius's business thrived, furnishing the pilgrims with souvenir shrines to take home or to present to the temple as votive offerings.

Evidently Paul's preaching had been having a negative effect on business. There is no evidence that Paul had made a direct attack on Artemis. The words of the town clerk denied that he had done so (v. 37). But Paul preached against magic and superstition (cp. vv. 17–20), and he never hesitated to point out the folly of idolatry, as he did before the Areopagus (Acts 17:29). He may not have directly denounced the worship of Artemis, but he certainly felt that the goddess was "nothing at all" (1 Cor. 8:4). So Demetrius was not altogether wrong in seeing Paul as being a threat to his business. Demetrius was a skilled demagogue. His real quarrel with Paul was the economic pinch he was feeling. That was a concern shared by his fellow craftsmen but would probably not have caused too much stir among the general populace. So Demetrius shifted the charge to a more volatile issue—civic pride. Paul, he said, was a threat to the reputation of the temple and its goddess and hence to the status of the city itself.

The riot incited by the craftsmen (19:28–34). The craftsmen picked up on Demetrius's appeal to civic pride. They rushed into the streets chanting in a sort of liturgy, "Great is Artemis of the Ephesians." The Ephesians were probably accustomed to this confession, and soon a crowd gathered, rallying to the chant. Most seemed not to have been fully aware of what was transpiring (v. 32), but enough was known that two of Paul's traveling companions were seized and dragged into the theater. The theater was fast filling up as the incessant chant to the goddess continued. Paul wanted to address the crowd but was prevented from entering the theater by his fellow Christians and some of the provincial officials (vv. 30–31). Luke called them by their official title of "Asiarch" (v. 31). It is not fully clear what their duties included, but they seem to have been associated with the temples dedicated to the emperors and to the goddess Roma. The office seems to have been largely honorary. The Asiarchs thus served as patrons of the imperial cult, one being appointed annually in each city where there was a temple to the emperors.[33] In Paul's day this included Ephesus, Smyrna, Pergamum, and Miletus. The significance of the Asiarchs to the narrative is that they were high-ranking officials of the Roman cult, and Paul the Roman citizen was on friendly terms with them. Whatever the reason for the riot, *they* certainly did not view Paul as a threat to the city.

The two Christians who served as Paul's substitutes were the Macedonians Gaius and Aristarchus. Artistarchus is probably the same as the Thessalonian who accompanied Paul to Jerusalem (Acts 20:4, 27:2). No Macedonian named Gaius is mentioned elsewhere in Acts.[34] Neither of the two plays any role in the story other than to associate the riot with the Pauline mission. Less clear is the part played by Alexander (v. 33). He seems to have been pushed forward by the Jews to make a defense, possibly in an attempt to dissociate the Jews from the Christians and thus deny any Jewish involvement in the riot. It has been recently argued that Alexander was a Jewish *Christian*.[35] Whoever Alexander was defending, however, the crowd gave him no opportunity to be heard. They did not want to hear from anyone who did not worship their goddess; so for two hours they drowned out all speakers with their cry, "Great is Artemis of the Ephesians."

The crowd dispersed by the town clerk (19:35–41). The chief official of Ephesus was the town clerk (Gk., *grammateus*). He presided over the full meetings of the citizens (the *ecclēsia*). He also was the presiding officer for meetings of the city magistrates and was the chief liaison between the city administration and the Roman provincial officials. The Ephesians were accustomed to seeing him in a presiding role, but it took even him some time to quiet the unruly crowd. He began by assuring them that the city was under no threat. The city's worldwide reputation was intact. Everyone everywhere knew that Ephesus was the "temple keeper" (*neōkoros*) of Artemis and of "the stone which fell from the sky" (v. 35). The latter seems to have been a meteorite. A meteorite associated with the worship of the Mother Goddess in Pessinus was carried to Rome in 204 B.C. No meteorite has been found at Ephesus, but it is possible that one was kept there, possibly dating back to the early stages of worship of the Anatolian Mother Goddess. There were at least thirty-three shrines to Artemis scattered throughout the Roman world. Ephesus was the acknowledged center of them all. It was believed that the goddess was born in the sacred grove where the Ephesian cult was first observed. Artemis was in no jeopardy, the clerk assured the crowd.

The clerk then proceeded to declare the innocence of the Christians (v. 37). Neither Gaius nor Aristarchus—nor for that matter Paul—had "robbed temples" or blasphemed the goddess. "Robbing temples" probably referred to robbing them of their reputation. Paul had surely preached his monotheistic message, which ultimately had profound implications for any other form of worship. But the Christians did not have a socially or politically disruptive agenda. The clerk thus declared the Christians innocent of the defamation charges advanced by the craftsmen.

The clerk's third line of argument was the most important consideration: the Ephesians were setting themselves up for a charge of unlawful assembly. The town assembly met in regularly scheduled meetings in the theater. Luke used the normal language for the assembly throughout this passage (*dēmos* in vv. 30, 33; *ecclēsia* in vv. 32, 39). The Romans would become very nervous whenever citizens gathered as a body at unauthorized times.[36] The filled theater looked much like such an unscheduled town meeting. If the Romans had any suspicions of an Ephesian riot (v. 40), they could strip the citizens of their rights of assembly altogether. Mob action was no way to handle a complaint. The clerk reminded them that they had legal channels, such as the regular court days of the proconsul and the scheduled legal meetings of the assembly (vv. 38–39). He urged Demetrius and his fellow craftsmen to follow these channels. Then he dismissed the assembly.

The Christians were exonerated through the intervention of the town clerk. There may have been lingering hostility toward them, however. Luke indicated that Paul departed the city soon after the incident (Acts 20:1). He may have been forced to leave for his own safety.

NOTES

1. S. E. Johnson, "Paul in Athens," *Lexington Theological Quarterly* 17 (1982): 37–43.

2. D. W. J. Gill, "Achaia," in *The Book of Acts in its First Century Setting*, Vol. 2: *Graeco-Roman Setting*, ed. D. W. J. Gill and C. Gempf (Grand Rapids: Eerdmans, 1994), 441–443.

3. N. C. Croy, "Hellenistic Philosophies and the Preaching of the Resurrection (Acts 17:18, 32)," *Novum Testamentum* 39 (1997): 21–39.

4. T. D. Barnes, "An Apostle on Trial," *Journal of Theological Studies*, n.s. 20 (1969): 407–419.

5. C. J. Hemer, "Paul at Athens: A Topographical Note," *New Testament Studies* 20 (1974): 341–350.

6. For an appearance before the Areopagus, see W. M. Ramsay, *St. Paul the Traveller and the Roman Citizen* (London: Hodder and Stoughton, 1897), 243–249. For it being a public lecture on the Hill of Ares, see W. G. Morrice, "Where did Paul Speak in Athens—on Mars' Hill or before the Court of the Areopagus? (Acts 17:19)," *Expository Times* 83 (1972): 377–378.

7. For a selective bibliography, see J. B. Polhill, *Acts*, New American Commentary (Nashville: Broadman, 1992), 369, fn. 75.

8. See H. A. Moellering, "Deisidaimonia, a Footnote to Acts 17:22," *Concordia Theological Monthly* 34 (1963): 466–471.

9. In his *Description of Greece*, Pausanias spoke of such altars being located on the road between Phalerum and Athens (1.1.4) and at Olympia (5.14.8). Philostratus spoke of one that was located in Athens (*Life of Apollonius*, 6.3.5). Diogenes Laertius spoke of "nameless altars" and suggested that they were provided to ensure against a god's feeling left out and venting his or her wrath on the city (*Lives of the Philosophers* 1.110–113).

10. H. Külling, "Zur Bedeutung des Agnostos Theos: Eine Exegese zu Apostelgeschichte 17, 22–23," *Theologische Zeitschrift* 36 (1980): 65–83.

11. A ninth-century Syriac commentary attributes the phrase to Epimenides of Crete, but this is dubious, as has been shown by M. Pohlenz, "Paulus und die Stoa," *Zeitschrift für die neutestamentliche Wissenschaft* 42 (1949): 101–105.

12. D. Smith, *The Life and Letters of St. Paul* (New York: George H. Doran, n.d.), 148–149.

13. J. Dupont, "Le discours à l'Aréopage (Ac. 17, 22–31), lieu de rencontre entre christianisme et hellénisme," *Biblica* 60 (1979): 535–536.

14. Due to an earthquake in 1858, the site of Corinth was abandoned, leaving it open for archaeologists. Excavation began in 1896 under the American School of Classical Studies. The following articles provide useful summaries of the Corinthian excavations: O. Broneer, "Corinth, Center of St. Paul's Missionary Work in Greece," *Biblical Archaeologist* 14 (1951): 78–96; W. A. McDonald, "Archaeology and St. Paul's Journeys in Greek Lands. Part III—Corinth," *Biblical Archaeologist* 5 (1942): 36–48; J. Murphy-O'Connor, "The Corinth that Paul Saw," *Biblical Archaeologist* 47 (1984): 147–159.

15. Descriptions of the cities can be found in the Greek geographers. Strabo describes the ancient city and the young new colony which he visited in 29 B.C.: *Geography*, 8.6.20–23. Pausanias describes the city as he saw it on his visit around A.D. 165: *Description of Greece*, 2.1–5.

16. Suetonius, *Claudius*, 25.4. Claudius's expulsion of the Jews is dated by Orosius at A.D. 49, thus setting that date as the earliest possible time of Paul's arrival in Corinth. See the discussion in chapter 4 on Pauline chronology.

17. J. Murphy-O'Connor notes that there is a Christian catacomb in Rome known as the catacomb of Priscilla. It is known to have originally belonged to the Acilius family. He is inclined to see both Priscilla and Aquila as freed slaves of that family. J. Murphy-O'Connor, "Prisca and Aquila," *Bible Review* 8 (1992): 40–51, 62.

18. Aquila precedes Prisca/Priscilla in Acts 18:2; 1 Cor. 16:19.

19. H. Szenat, What Did the ΣΚΗΝΟΠΟΙΟΣ Paul Produce?" *Neotestamentica* 27 (1993): 391–402.

20. J. Murphy-O'Connor, "Prisca and Aquila," 49–51.

21. Paul seems to have refused financial support when he was establishing a church but to have allowed them to assist him in his work elsewhere after he departed.

22. E. J. Goodspeed, "Gaius Titius Justus," *Journal of Biblical Literature* 69 (1950): 382–383.

23. H. J. Cadbury, "Erastus of Corinth," *Journal of Biblical Literature* 50 (1931): 42–58. See also D. W. J. Gill, "Erastus the Aedile," *Tyndale Bulletin* 40 (1989): 293–301. In the 1960s another Erastus inscription was discovered at Corinth but seems to date from the second century, thus referring to a subsequent official of the same name: A. D. Clarke, "Another Erastus Inscription," *Tyndale Bulletin* 42 (1991): 146–151. An Erastus is mentioned in Acts 19:22 as Paul's helper. Second Timothy 4:20 also refers to an Erastus who worked with Paul. It is uncertain whether either should be connected with the Corinthian official of Romans 16:23.

24. See the discussion of the Gallio inscription in chapter 4.

25. A. N. Sherwin-White, *Roman Society and Roman Law in the New Testament* (Oxford: Clarendon, 1963), 99–100.

26. For the history of the hellenistic city, see Strabo, *Geography*, 14.1.21–25.

27. For further reading on Ephesus, see R. E. Oster Jr., "Ephesus," *Anchor Bible Dictionary*, ed. D. N. Freedman (New York: Doubleday, 1992), II:542–549; W. M. Ramsay, *The Letters to the Seven Churches*, updated version, ed. M. W. Wilson (Peabody, Mass.: Hendrickson, 1994); M. M. Parvis, "Archaeology and St. Paul's Journeys in Greek lands, Part IV—Ephesus," *Biblical Archaeologist* 8 (1945): 62–73.

28. It has been recently suggested that Apollos was a disciple of Mark at Alexandria and that he knew the story of Jesus only as it began in Mark's Gospel, i.e. with the baptism of John. For this view, see R. Strelan, *Paul, Artemis and the Jews in Ephesus* (Berlin and New York: Walter de Gruyter, 1996), 215–223.

29. The same expression is used of *Paul's* proving Christ's messianic status to the Thessalonian Jews (Acts 17:3).
30. Baptizing sects who claimed John as their founder existed on into the fourth century. See C. H. H. Scobie, *John the Baptist* (Philadelphia: Fortress, 1964), 187–202.
31. The main thesis of R. Strelan (*Paul, Artemis, and the Jews in Ephesus*) is that the Ephesian church was small and primarily Jewish in membership.
32. It is not altogether clear what the rare Greek words refer to. See T. J. Leary, "The 'Aprons' of St. Paul—Acts 19:12," *Journal of Theological Studies* 41 (1990): 527–529. Ancients often believed in the curative power of bodily fluids such as sweat and spittle, and that may be the dynamic here.
33. F. V. Filson, "Ephesus and the New Testament," *Biblical Archaeologist* 8 (1945): 80.
34. The Gaius of Romans 16:23 was an Achaian, and the Gaius of Acts 20:4 was from Derbe in southern Galatia. Some manuscripts of Acts read *Douberos* (a Macedonian town) at Acts 20:4, evidently in an attempt to assimilate that Gaius to the Gaius of 19:29.
35. P. Lampe, "Acta 19 im Spiegel der ephesischen Inschriften," *Biblische Zeitschrift* 36 (1992): 59–76. R. F. Stoops has argued that the whole episode is based on a characteristic Diaspora Jewish apologetic that called upon officials to defend their rights when they could establish that their opponents were unruly and did not act according to the law: "Riot and Assembly: The Social Context of Acts 19:23–41," *Journal of Biblical Literature* 108 (1989): 73–91.
36. Ramsay pointed out that in the hellenistic period there were two types of assembly—regularly scheduled (ordinary) and nonscheduled (extraordinary). Only the regular assemblies could conduct business. The Romans seem to have eliminated the extraordinary meetings altogether. W. M. Ramsay, *Pauline and Other Studies in Early Christian History* (New York: A. C. Armstrong, 1906), 203–215.

SUGGESTED FURTHER READING

Bruce, F. F. *Paul: Apostle of the Heart Set Free*. Grand Rapids: Eerdmans, 1996, pp. 235–324.

Gaertner, Bertil. *The Areopagus Speech and Natural Revelation*. Uppsala: Gleerup, 1955.

Gempf, Conrad. "Athens, Paul at." *Dictionary of Paul and His Letters*. Ed. G. F. Hawthorne and R. P. Martin. Downers Grove, Ill.: InterVarsity, 1993, pp. 51–54.

Gill, David W. J. and Conrad Gempf, eds. *The Book of Acts in Its First-Century Setting*, Vol. 2: *Graeco-Roman Setting*. Grand Rapids: Eerdmans, 1994, pp. 105–118, 119–222, 291–376, 433–453.

Marshall, I. Howard. *Acts*. Tyndale New Testament Commentaries. Liecester, U.K.: InterVarsity, 1980, pp. 281–321.

Munck, Johannes. *The Acts of the Apostles*. The Anchor Bible. Garden City, N.Y.: Doubleday, 1967, pp. 168–197.

Murphy-O'Connor, Jerome. *St. Paul's Corinth: Texts and Archaeology*. Wilmington, Del.: Glazier, 1983.

Oster, Richard E. Jr. "Ephesus," in *Anchor Bible Dictionary*. Ed. D. N. Freedman. New York: Doubleday, 1992. Vol. II, 542–549.

Polhill, John B. *Acts*. New American Commentary. Nashville: Broadman, 1992, pp. 365–414.

Sherwin-White, A. N. *Roman Society and Roman Law in the New Testament*. Oxford: Clarendon, 1963, pp. 71–107.

Stambaugh, John E. and David L. Balch. *The New Testament in Its Social Environment*. Philadelphia: Westminster, 1986, pp. 107–167.

Stagg, Frank. *The Book of Acts: The Early Struggle for an Unhindered Gospel*. Nashville: Broadman, 1955, pp. 179–207.

Strelan, Rick. *Paul, Artemis, and the Jews in Ephesus*. New York: de Gruyter, 1996.

Tannehill, Robert. *The Narrative Unity of Luke-Acts*, Vol. 2: *The Acts of the Apostles*. Minneapolis: Fortress, 1990, pp. 210–244.

12

⁓❧⁓

1 CORINTHIANS: A CHURCH DIVIDED

$\mathcal{T}$oward the end of his third missionary period, Paul had extensive contact with the Corinthian church. One would never guess this from the account in Acts. Acts mentions only a final visit of Paul to Corinth after completion of his long Ephesian ministry and before his departure to Jerusalem with a collection for the saints (Acts 20:1–3). It is apparent from Paul's letters, however, that the apostle was quite involved with the Corinthians during the course of his third mission. Before the final visit mentioned in Acts 20:1–3, he wrote at least four letters to the Corinthians and made at least one additional visit to the city, which is not mentioned in Acts. It was a time of considerable stress for the Corinthians and for Paul. The church was divided, and some even challenged Paul's apostolic authority.

Of the four letters to Corinth, two were written from Ephesus—1 Corinthians and an earlier letter that Paul mentioned in 1 Corinthians 5:9–13. This "previous letter" is evidently lost. This chapter will deal with this period of Paul's Corinthian correspondence. It represents the early stages of the conflict between Paul and the Corinthians. After the writing of 1 Corinthians the relationship between the Corinthians and their apostle worsened, necessitating a brief visit of Paul to Corinth from Ephesus, during which he seems to have been personally assaulted by at least one person. Leaving in haste and frustration, he wrote an angry letter to the Corinthians, which is either lost or partially preserved in 2 Corinthians. In any event, 2 Corinthians records the events of this period of strained relationships. It will be the subject of the next chapter.

THE OCCASION AND PURPOSE OF 1 CORINTHIANS

Paul's third missionary period centered primarily in Ephesus, where he ministered for two-and-one-half to three years (Acts 19:1–20:1, 31). It was likely toward the end of this time, perhaps in the spring of A.D. 56, that Paul received news from Corinth which prompted his writing 1 Corinthians. He had written them a letter some time previously which had prompted some questions from the Corinthians. One of his reasons for writing 1 Corinthians was to clarify these matters.

THE PREVIOUS LETTER (1 COR. 5:9–13)

In the earlier letter Paul had told the Corinthians "not to associate with sexually immoral people" (5:9). In 1 Corinthians he proceeded to clarify himself. He did not mean that they were not to associate with the immoral *outside* the congregation. If that were the case, they would have to withdraw from the world altogether. Instead, he meant that they were not to associate with those who *claimed to be Christians* who had flagrantly immoral lifestyles. He had just recommended that they expel one such person from the congregation, a man living in an incestuous relationship (1 Cor. 5:1).

The "previous letter" mentioned in 1 Corinthians 5:9 is in all probability now lost. It has sometimes been argued that 2 Corinthians 6:14–7:1 is a portion of the previous letter. The passage deals with the issue of Christians associating with immoral people, and it breaks the context in which it appears. (2 Corinthians 6:13 and 7:2 fit together; 6:14–7:1 interrupts the flow of thought.) There are two main problems, however, with seeing 6:14–7:1 as a fragment of the letter mentioned in 1 Corinthians 5:9. The first is that the two references do not deal with the same sort of people. Second Corinthians 6:14–7:1 deals with *unbelievers*, while 1 Corinthians 5:9–13 treats immoral *Christians*. A second problem is accounting textually for the interpolation of 2 Corinthians 6:14–7:1 into its present place. There is no manuscript evidence that the passage was ever missing from the text of 2 Corinthians, and it would be hard to explain what would prompt a scribe to place a fragment in such an awkward place. It is more easily accounted for if one views 6:14–7:1 as a Pauline digression. Perhaps Paul took a break from writing the letter at 6:13. When resuming, the issue of Christian holiness was at the front of his mind, and he penned (or dictated) 6:14–7:1. Then he resumed his previous thought at 7:2 by repeating the concluding words of 6:13.[1]

Others would see the previous letter as imbedded in our present 1 Corinthians. These scholars view 1 Corinthians as a composite of two original letters, one of which would be the previous letter. Several scholars, such as J. Weiss, J. Héring, and W. Schmithals, have maintained this two-letter hypothesis. There is, however, little agreement between their individual reconstructions of the supposed letters. The basis of the two-letter hypothesis is the feeling that 1 Corinthians contains certain irreconcilable inconsistencies that could not possibly have been in the same letter. For instance, it is argued that Paul's travel plans are inconsistent in 1 Corinthians. First Corinthians 4:19 presupposes a quick coming to Corinth, while 16:5–9 seems to allow for a longer delay. The treatment of idol meat in chapters 8 and 10 is also seen to be inconsistent. In chapter 8 and in 10:23–11:1, Paul took a "tolerant" position toward meat that had been sacrificed to idols. The "strong" Christians with a clear conscience must abstain from it only when in the presence of a "weaker" Christian whom it might offend. In 10:1–22 he took a harder line: one should not participate at all in cultic meals (the "table of demons"). A final example is the argument that Paul's mention of women praying and prophesying in worship (1 Cor. 11:5) is contradicted by the command that they be silent in 14:34.

The solution offered for these alleged contradictions is to place the conflicting passages into different letters. The reconstruction of Schmithals will serve as an example. According to him, letter A (the "previous letter") consisted of 2 Corinthians 6:14–7:1; 1 Corinthians 6:12–20; 9:24–10:22; 11:2–34; 15; 16:13–24. Letter B (the response to the Corinthian letter to Paul) consisted of 1 Corinthians 1:1–6:11; 7:1–9:23; 10:23–11:1; 12:1–14:40; 16:1–12.[2] It can be readily seen that for every supposed inconsistency cited above, Schmithals resolves the problem by assigning the conflicting passages to different epistles.

The resolution of a few seeming inconsistencies by such partitioning raises more problems than it solves. The reconstructions differ radically from scholar to scholar. The inconsistencies are overblown. Paul could well have changed his travel plans between the writing of chapters 4 and 16. He probably composed the long letter over a number of days. The idol meat passages are not inconsistent but deal with different contexts, as do the passages which treat the activity of women in worship. Finally, the problems of compilation are enormous. There is really no evidence for scribes combining two letters in such a fashion, deleting introductions and endings, radically dividing up individual epistles. One can understand why few scholars have been attracted to compilation theories involving 1 Corinthians. Most assume the integrity of the epistle.

THE NEWS FROM CORINTH

Paul wrote 1 Corinthians from Ephesus, primarily to address questions and problems within the congregation which had come to his attention. He had three sources of information. One was the servants of a certain Chloe who informed Paul of serious divisions within the congregation (1:11–12). The Corinthians were treating their Christian leaders like the popular Greek sophists, pitting their favorite "wisdom teacher" against the others. Paul addressed the problem of the Corinthian wisdom speculation in chapters 1–4. Chloe's servants may also have informed Paul of the disunity and abuse of the Lord's Supper (11:17–22). We know nothing of Chloe. She may or may not have been a Christian. Some of her servants *were*, and they were Paul's informants. We do not know where they resided, whether they were Corinthians who had traveled to Ephesus or Ephesians who had visited Corinth. They probably represented the lower social strata of the congregation and felt particularly victimized by the disunity.

Paul's second source of information was a letter which the Corinthian congregation had composed and delivered to Paul, requesting clarification on a number of subjects relating to personal and congregational life. Paul referred explicitly to this letter in 1 Corinthians 7:1. Thereafter, when picking up on the questions raised in their letter he used a sort of shorthand, the phrase "now concerning" (Gk., *peri de*). The phrase occurs at the following points, where it likely designated their questions. These involved Christian celibacy (7:1), whether single Christians should marry (7:25), the consumption of meat that had been sacrificed to idols (8:1), spiritual gifts (12:1), Paul's collection for the saints (16:1), and when Apollos would visit them (16:12).

Paul's third source of information was an official delegation of three men who had come from Corinth to deliver the Corinthians' letter to Paul. They are mentioned in 16:17–18—Fortunatus, Achaicus, and Stephanas. Along with Chloe's people, they offered Paul verbal reports about the congregation. It was probably from these personal reports that Paul learned of the sexual problems treated in chapters 5 and 6, of the lawsuits among members (6:1–11), of the lack of decorum in worship (11:2–16), and of those who were denying the resurrection of believers (chap. 15).

The Corinthian problems were manifold, but in 1 Corinthians most of them involved conflict among the Corinthians themselves. Some seem to have advocated an ascetic ethic; others were more libertine. Some had no problem with consuming meat that had been sacrificed to idols; for others it was a real offense. Some boasted of their special spiritual gifts; others felt left out. Some "pigged out" at the Lord's Supper; others had barely enough to eat. Some sued their fellow Christians in the secular law courts. Some considered Paul their leader, others Apollos, still others Peter. Their conflict undoubtedly had its theological and philosophical dimensions, but it was social as well, human and petty, high on pride and low on love.

When Paul wrote 1 Corinthians, he was either unaware of the extent to which the conflict involved himself, or it had not yet turned on him. Probably the latter was the case. By the time of 2 Corinthians, Paul was painfully aware of the opposition in Corinth to his own leadership. But even in 1 Corinthians he seems to have been conscious of those who were questioning his leadership. How could it have been otherwise with those who were partial to Apollos or Peter rather than himself? His emphasis on his own humility in passages like 1 Corinthians 2:1–5 and 4:8–13 may imply his awareness that for some he did not cut a very impressive figure as an apostle. He referred explicitly to those who sat in judgment on him in 9:3 and rejected their assessment flatly in 4:3.

Finally, some specifically accused him of being fickle in his plans to visit them (1 Cor. 4:18–21). Paul's reference to this was expressed in anger and with a threat. It thus seems to have been a substantive accusation. Originally Paul had planned to visit them twice (2 Cor. 1:16). He had perhaps expressed this in his previous letter. But he had *not* come yet and was sending Timothy in his place (1 Cor. 4:17). At the writing of 1 Corinthians, he was delaying his visit even longer, as becomes clear in the final chapter (1 Cor. 16:5–9). Perhaps some of those who preferred other leaders were using Paul's delays against him, claiming that he really didn't love them, that he considered them a low priority, that he really shouldn't be considered their apostle. Clearly by the time of 2 Corinthians such things were being said about him (cp. 2 Cor. 11:7–12). Still, the criticism of Paul seems to have been somewhat muted at the writing of 1 Corinthians. The situation changed drastically by the time of 2 Corinthians.

PAUL'S CORINTHIAN OPPONENTS

The most debated issue in the interpretation of 1 Corinthians is the identification of Paul's "opponents," or the nature of the aberration he was addressing. Often the two Corinthian epistles are taken together in considering this question. That is a mistake. The problems differ in the two letters. In 1 Corinthians they are primarily within the congregation, consisting of its own problems of disunity. In 2 Corinthians, the conflict involved Paul much more directly. Even his congregational leadership was questioned. In 1 Corinthians, the problems in the congregation seem to have derived primarily from the Greco-Roman culture of the city. In 2 Corinthians the opposition to Paul has a decidedly Jewish stamp to it. It is thus best to take the two epistles separately when considering the Corinthian problems.

Most considerations of Paul's opponents in 1 Corinthians begin with 1 Corinthians 1:10–12, where Paul spoke of the various factions that had developed around himself, Apollos, and Cephas (Peter). Paul also spoke of a "Christ" faction. It is possible that he was being sarcastic, asking if in their zeal for human leaders any one claimed Christ. The grammatical structure of the phrase "I follow Christ" is identical to the others; so it is likely that there was an actual "Christ party" in the church along with the others. But what viewpoints would these factions have represented?[3]

The first to develop a comprehensive theory about the Corinthian factions seems to have been F. C. Baur, who in 1831 wrote an influential essay arguing that Paul's opponents in Corinth were Judaizers.[4] He maintained that there were two factions in Corinth. One was a Gentile Christian faction, advocating a Torah-free gospel, represented by Paul and Apollos. Opposed to them was the law-centered Judaizing gospel advocated by Peter. This "Cephas party" also went by the name "Christ party." Eventually Baur extended his theory to include the entire New Testament and to explain the whole history of first-century Christianity. He saw the period as being marked by a life-and-death conflict between Jewish Christianity (led by Peter) and Gentile Christianity (Paul). He placed the books of the New Testament in either the Judaizing camp or the Pauline, lawfree camp. If a book did not reflect this conflict, as is true of Acts, he placed it in the second century. If a Pauline epistle did not reflect a bitter Judaizing conflict, he argued that it could not have been written by Paul.

Baur's ambitious historical reconstruction was eventually discredited, not least because of the late date for his sources that were supposed to reflect the first-century conflict between Peter and Paul. He was surely wrong in his assessment of 1 Corinthians. There is really no evidence for Judaizing in the epistle. Even the question of idol meat seems to have been largely a Gentile problem in Corinth.[5] A Jewish dimension *is* present in the opposition to Paul reflected in 2 Corinthians, but that seems to have been a later development.

More recently, a Gnostic theory has been advanced as the "key" to unlocking Paul's opposition. The most consistent advocate of this position has been W. Schmithals. He argues that the Gnostics were the "Christ party," for they claimed to be embodiments of the spirit of Christ. He sees the references to *gnōsis* and *sophia* in the letter as evidence of a Gnostic opposition to Paul. According to Schmithals, they were Jewish Christian Gnostics, and Paul combatted them in both Corinthian epistles. They were libertine, held a docetic Christology, claimed to be spiritual, emphasized freedom, denied the resurrection and claimed to be apostles.[6] Very few have followed Schmithals in his hypothesis of a developed Gnosticism at Corinth. Most would agree with Wilson that full-blown Gnosticism with its redeemer myth and Gnostic Christology did not appear until the Christian heresies of the second century, although the roots are to be found in the first.[7] They prefer to speak of *gnōsis* rather than Gnosticism, of an "incipient" gnosticism, or pregnosticism, or protognosticism, or some such term. Usually they spell the word with a lower-case *g* to distinguish it from the second-century groups. The view is still quite popular that Paul contended with an early form of the kind of speculation that led to full-blown Gnosticism in the second century.[8] A growing trend is to avoid the term *Gnostic* altogether and to speak in terms of wisdom or realized eschatology, or hyperspiritualism, or something similar.

Some of the scholars who see one of the Corinthian factions as "hyperspiritualists" argue that they derived their views from Apollos, who brought to Corinth the sort of hellenistic Jewish wisdom speculation associated with Philo of Alexandria.[9] This view has the advantage of holding to a single opposition in the Corinthian letters, 1 Corinthians reflecting their wisdom speculation and 2 Corinthians their Jewish background.[10] A large number of scholars agree that some of the Corinthians had an overemphasis on the Spirit but are less specific in identifying the roots of the

Corinthian speculation. They possessed an "overrealized eschatology,"[11] which led them to such things as a denial of the resurrection and libertine behavior.

In an effort to bury forever the Judaizing emphasis advocated by those who still were influenced by "Baur's ghost," Johannes Munck argued that there were *no factions* in Corinth, just typical human bickering and preferences. He maintained that the Corinthians were overly influenced by their hellenistic milieu, adopting its views and customs, misunderstanding the gospel and Paul's teaching and overestimating their own capacity for wisdom and knowledge.[12] Munck probably overstated his case. The differences in Corinth went deeper than mere human bickerings. Part of the disunity was due to social diversity within the congregation, which influenced both ideas and ethics.[13] Part was due to the cosmopolitan nature of Corinth itself with all the alternative cultures and viewpoints that were "in the air" in the port city. Some of the Corinthians may have derived their ideas about superior wisdom and knowledge from the popular sophists who displayed their skills in the streets. They may have been influenced by the dualism of body and spirit maintained by the popular neoplatonic philosophy of the day. There was probably no one source nor one faction in the confusion of the Corinthians. Neither was there likely only one viewpoint in opposition to Paul in 1 Corinthians.[14]

A STUDY OUTLINE OF 1 CORINTHIANS

The following outline is in keeping with the time-honored procedure of dividing the epistle into two parts. The first part (chaps. 1–6) corresponds to the issues brought to Paul's attention through word of mouth by Chloe's servants and the three Corinthian delegates. The second major division (7:1–16:4) addresses the questions raised in the Corinthian letter. It should be noted at the outset that some of the matters discussed in this latter section may not have been raised in the Corinthian letter to Paul, such as the problems within the Christian assembly discussed in chapter 11. One could follow other equally suitable divisions according to the main content issues within the letter, such as matters relating to wisdom and unity in chapters 1–4, to sex in chapters 5–7, to idolatry in chapters 8–10, to worship in chapters 11–14, and to the resurrection in chapter 15.[15]

I. Introduction (1:1–9)
   A. Address (vv. 1–3)
   B. Prayer of Thanksgiving (vv. 4–9)
II. Bad News from Corinth (1:10–6:20)
   A. Worldly Wisdom and Divisions in the Community (1:10–4:21)
      1. The groups in the church (1:10–17)
      2. The gospel and worldly wisdom (1:18–3:23)
         (a) God's wisdom as foolishness (1:18–2:5)
         (b) The hiddenness of wisdom (2:6–16)
         (c) The true role of the minister (3:1–23)
      3. The Corinthians and their apostles (4:1–13)
      4. The Corinthians and their apostle: Paul's plans (4:14–21)
   B. An Incidence of Fornication (5:1–13)
   C. The Church and the World (6:1–20)
      1. The Christian and the law courts (vv. 1–11)
      2. The Christian and sexual freedom (vv. 12–20)

III. Answers to the Corinthians' Letter (7:1–16:4)
    A. Marriage and Related Questions (7:1–40)
        1. Sexual expression in marriage (vv. 1–7)
        2. Specific advice regarding marriage (vv. 8–16)
        3. The general rule of calling (vv. 17–24)
        4. Advice to virgins (vv. 25–38)
        5. A final word about widows (7:39–40)
    B. Freedom and Food Offered to Idols (8–11:1)
        1. The criteria of decision (8:1–13)
        2. True freedom is the freedom to limit oneself (9:1–27)
        3. The danger of idolatry (10:1–22)
        4. Idol meat and Christian freedom (10:23–11:1)
    C. The Christian Assembly (11:2–34)
        1. The covering of one's head in worship (vv. 2–16)
        2. Misuse of the Lord's Supper (vv. 17–34)
    D. Spiritual Gifts (12:1–14:40)
        1. The basic test: "Jesus is Lord" (12:1–3)
        2. Unity and diversity of gifts (12:4–31)
        3. The most excellent way (13:1–13)
        4. The proper expression of tongues and prophecy (14:1–40)
    E. The Resurrection (15:1–58)
        1. The tradition (vv. 1–11)
        2. The implications of the resurrection of Jesus (vv. 12–19)
        3. The events of the end (vv. 20–28)
        4. Arguments from a human viewpoint (vv. 29–34)
        5. Nature of the resurrection body (vv. 35–50)
        6. The moment of victory (vv. 51–58)
    F. The Collection (16:1–4)
IV. Conclusion (16:5–24)
    A. Personal Plans (vv. 5–9)
    B. Visits of Others (vv. 10–12)
    C. Concluding Exhortation to Love (vv. 13–14)
    D. Commendation of the Corinthian Leaders (vv. 15–18)
    E. Greetings and Concluding Benedictions (vv. 19–24)

HIGHLIGHTS OF 1 CORINTHIANS

INTRODUCTION (1:1–9)

In verse 1 Paul emphasized his divine call to apostleship. In his conflict with the Corinthians, Paul's apostolic status was challenged, as is particularly evident in 2 Corinthians. The Sosthenes mentioned in the first verse is quite possibly the Corinthian synagogue ruler of Acts 18:17, converted and now serving as Paul's coworker in Ephesus. Some scholars see the reference in verse 2 to "all those everywhere" as a later interpolation designed to make the letter applicable to all congregations. There is no textual evidence for deleting the phrase, and it fits in with Paul's view of the local church as a microcosm of the full body of Christ throughout the world.

Paul's formal prayer of thanksgiving (1:4–9) includes some of the main concerns of the epistle. Verse 5 speaks of the Corinthians having been "enriched" in all speech (*logos*) and knowledge (*gnōsis*). The "speech" may well be an allusion to the problem of tongues (chaps. 12–14), and "knowledge" to their pursuit of human wisdom(chaps. 1–4). Paul may have parodied their pride in being "enriched" in 4:8–13. Verse 7 clearly anticipates Paul's discussion of spiritual gifts (*charismata*) in chapters 12–14. Verse 8 is probably Paul's first attempt to counter the Corinthian "realized eschatology," by which some claimed to be fully perfected in the Spirit, completely "arrived." Paul reminded them of the "day of the Lord." There *is* a future for Christians. The Corinthians had *not* "already arrived," as some thought. Resurrection and judgment were yet to come.

WORLDLY WISDOM AND RIFT IN THE COMMUNITY (1:10–4:21)

Paul learned of the party spirit within the congregation from the servants of Chloe (1:11–12). The basic problem of the Corinthian "wisdom" was the disunity it created; every Corinthian had his or her own "favorite preacher." Paul responded to the problem in the first four chapters of his letter. He began by expressing his relief that he had baptized so few in Corinth himself. In the mysteries, the Greeks especially valued those who sponsored them in their initiations. Some of the Corinthians may have been extending this to Christian baptism. Paul reminded them that what counts is not the baptizer but baptism into the body of Christ, not the rite but the gospel that leads to the baptismal waters.

Paul considered the Corinthian espousal of their favorite teachers as the pursuit of human wisdom. He dealt with the problem in 1:18–3:23.[16] First, he argued the incompatibility of divine and human wisdom. By human standards God's wisdom is foolishness (1:18–2:5). The cross is the ultimate demonstration of this (1:18–25). By all standards of human wisdom, the cross is foolishness—folly to the Greek way of wisdom as well as to the Jewish way of divine manifestation by sign. But God's way of salvation is through the cross. The cross is thus the negation of all human attempts to know God. One can only know God by first being known by God and called by God in the wisdom and power of Christ and his atoning death (v. 24).

In 1:26–2:5 Paul appealed to the experience of the Corinthians as corroboration that God's power and wisdom are the denial of all human standards of wisdom and power. He first cited the Corinthians's conversion experience (1:26–31). Most of them were not wise or powerful or well-born by human standards, but God called *them* into the body of Christ.[17] Next, he reminded them of his own preaching when he first came to Corinth, the message to which they responded (2:1–5). He came in weakness and fear. He was not eloquent. He preached no "wisdom" other then the cross of Christ. He was unskilled in "persuasive words," but the Spirit was present, and their faith thus rested in God's power and not in Paul's ability or wisdom.[18]

In 2:6–16 Paul seemed to reverse himself, arguing that there *is* a wisdom for the mature. The passage is best taken as Paul's polemic against the human-centered wisdom pursued by the Corinthians. Mature wisdom is revealed wisdom. It does not come by human discovery but by revelation from God and through the inspiration of the Spirit of God. Only "spiritual people" like Paul, inspired by God's Spirit, can speak this wisdom, and only to those who are spiritually mature themselves.[19] Paul did not go into the content of this "hidden wisdom," and it is perhaps fruitless to speculate on it. His main purpose becomes clear in 3:1–4. He accused the Corinthians of being immature and still incapable of understanding the deeper spiritual truths. Their party spirit was itself evidence of their immaturity and lack of God's

Spirit. What a put-down of the arrogant Corinthians who were claiming to have been perfected in the Spirit![20]

In 3:5–23 Paul directly returned to the question begun at 1:10–12—the proper relationship of the Corinthians to their leaders. He used himself and Apollos as examples, since both had ministered in Corinth. He used two metaphors to illustrate how their ministries were complementary. Like a garden, Paul planted and Apollos watered. Like a building, Paul laid the foundation and others built on it. The essential thing is not the ministers, however, but the divine basis of their ministry. God gives the growth to the garden. Christ is the only true foundation for the church. A polemical tone is apparent in 3:11–15. Paul directed himself against other would-be teachers whom he considered to have performed an inferior ministry. Any attempt to identify them specifically is probably fruitless. More significant is what Paul meant by speaking of a minister's works being tested by fire. He was clearly referring to judgment day and seemed to imply that inferior works would be consumed by the fires of judgment. One's reward would be lost. The individual would be saved, however, since salvation is a matter of grace and not of works. Such a minister could probably not expect his Lord's commendation, "Well done, thou good and faithful servant."

Verses 16–17 deal with a different situation, one where a false ministry actually undermines the church, "the temple of God." Such a minister will not escape, not even with singed tail feathers. That one will be destroyed. Verses 18–23 complete Paul's treatment of the Corinthian parties, which began at 1:10. In verses 18–20 he returned to the theme of the foolishness of human wisdom when measured by God's standards (cp. 1:18–25). Verses 21–23 form an inclusion with 1:10–12 in their references to the Corinthian parties. Paul turned the matter around. The Corinthians did not belong to Paul or Apollos or Cephas; on the contrary, *all* the workers belonged *to them* as Christ's servants. The only "belonging" that counts is to belong to Christ, for only through him can one belong to God (v. 23).

The Corinthians and their apostles (4:1–13). This section continues Paul's attack against the human-centered Corinthian "wisdom." Paul did so under two main aspects. First came the judgments of the Corinthians, their human standards that sought to exalt one minister over another. Paul viewed their judgments as completely worthless. Only God's judgment is ultimately determinative for the value and validity of one's ministry (vv. 1–5). Second, Paul introduced an ironic argument. He pointed to the apostles like himself who were the spiritual leaders of the congregations. In striking contrast to the Corinthians, they had not yet "arrived," were hardly rich and reigning. On the contrary, they were weak and abused, cursed and persecuted, a sight for sore eyes, the scum of the earth (vv. 6–13). Here Paul began a theme which pervades 2 Corinthians: the mark of a true apostle is weakness and suffering. In the second Corinthian epistle he employed several similar lists of apostolic hardships (2 Cor. 4:7–12; 6:3–10; 11:23–29).

The phrase "Do not go beyond what is written" (1 Cor. 4:6) is something of an interpretive crux. It does not fit the context very well. Paul had made no particular appeal to any Scripture, unless he meant the texts from the prophets that he had quoted in chapters 1–3. Some have thus suggested that the text has been corrupted by a scribal error in which a marginal comment became incorporated into the main text.[21] By omitting the obscure phrase, the original text would then have read "that you may learn from us not [to] take pride in one man over against another." This makes ample sense in the context. If Paul *did* include the reference to Scripture, he may have been reacting to a slogan of the Corinthians. In their self-proclaimed "freedom" they may have claimed that they had risen "above and beyond the Scriptures." Paul responded that they had reached no such heights and had better *not* reach beyond what stood written. This, of course, is to read rather much between the lines and is almost as conjectural as the scribal gloss idea.[22]

Paul concluded this section of the epistle with a reference to his own travel plans (4:14–21). In all the epistle Paul is most on the defensive in this portion. As we have already noted, he seems to have been accused by some of not loving the Corinthians as evidenced by his failure to visit them. Paul reminded them that no matter how many leaders they might have, he alone was their "founding father" in Christ. He promised to send Timothy as his representative and to come himself as soon as possible. He warned them rather pointedly that his visit might not be altogether pleasant if some of them failed to overcome their arrogance and opposition.

AN INCIDENCE OF FORNICATION (5:1–6:20)

Chapters 5 and 6 are closely related around the theme of sexual immorality. Chapter 5 begins with a reference to sexual immorality (*porneia*, 5:1), and chapter 6 ends with an appeal to flee from such behavior (*porneia*, 6:18). The only problem with seeing the two chapters as a complete unity is the reference to lawsuits in 6:1–11. Of course, Paul gave no hint of what the lawsuit involved. It may have concerned some sexual offense, which would explain its position between the two sections relating to sexuality.[23]

Chapter 5 as a whole deals with an incidence of incest within the Christian fellowship. A man was evidently cohabiting with his stepmother, behavior which was forbidden by both Jewish and Roman law. Paul was especially concerned that some of the Corinthians were all puffed up about it ("proud"). The best explanation of their pride would be that they shared a dualistic viewpoint which claimed a spiritual perfection that rendered all physical norms irrelevant. The man was seen as being "super-spiritual" for his flaunting of the body; he had truly risen above the flesh. This, of course, was the kind of thought that lay behind later libertine Gnosticism.

Paul had already made up his mind in the matter. He instructed the Corinthians to assemble together and formally ban the man from the fellowship (5:1–5). Paul saw the action as being redemptive for the man. His real concern, however, was with the church.[24] Such flagrant abuse was an evil influence on the community. Paul may have written Corinthians around Passover, recalling the image of leaven penetrating the whole batch of dough and rendering it useless (vv. 6–8). Paul reminded the Corinthians of his previous letter and clarified that in it he had urged them not to associate with those who claimed to be Christians but led immoral lifestyles (vv. 9–11). That was the case with this incestuous individual. He was to be put out of the congregation to preserve the sanctity of the church (v. 13).[25]

THE CHURCH AND THE WORLD (6:1–20)

Chapter 5 concludes by calling on the church to judge itself, leaving God to judge the world (5:12–13). In 6:1–11 Paul continued his discussion of the Christian and judgment. If the Christian community had its own standard of holiness, it follows that worldly, secular judgment is not the domain for Christians. Paul's treatment of the Christians and the law courts falls into two parts. Verses 1–6 state the general premise that Christians should avoid secular law courts in their disputes with one another. In the Jewish theocracy, there was no separation between sacred and secular courts, and Paul implied that the same should pertain in the Christian community. Apocalyptic tradition held that the saints would participate in the last judgment, and Paul used this in a "lesser to greater" argument: if Christians are to judge angels, how much more should they be able to judge themselves. The Roman courts were often anything but "just," notorious for bribery, deferential toward the privileged classes. Christians would indeed be better off arbitrating their own disputes.[26] Verses 7–11 advance Paul's second, more radical reason for urging the Corinthians to avoid lawsuits in the secular courts: the very fact of such disputes was an admission of failure in the fellowship. In an atmosphere of genuine Christian love and selflessness, there should be no occasion for one member to bring legal action against another. Christians have been *washed* in the waters of baptism, *justified* of their sins and set right with God, *sanctified* ("set apart") by the Spirit of God (v. 11). There should thus be no place in their lives for the kind of sins listed in verses 9–10, no basis for wrongdoing toward one another. Ideally, Christians would completely forebear, having no disputes with one another and turning the other cheek when wronged.

In 6:12–20 Paul returned to the question of Christian sexual morality. He began by uttering what was probably a slogan of those Corinthians who were arguing their freedom in ethical matters—"everything is permissible for me." The Stoics would have agreed with the slogan. They would have agreed even more with Paul's response that he would not be mastered (enslaved) by anything (v. 12). Paul knew that one could become a slave to one's freedom. Whether it be sex or drugs or whatever, how often people become slaves to what they initially viewed as an exercise of their freedom! The Corinthians were probably also those who claimed that the stomach was made for food (v. 13)—hence, a license for gluttony. The corollary to their statement was that the genitals were made for sex. Paul would not buy into such a negative view of the body. In their dualistic world view the Corinthian superspiritualists considered the body an indifferent matter. It was destined to perish. They viewed only the spirit as eternal. Paul on the other hand held to a unity of body and spirit which would be raised at the last day (v. 14) and by implication would face the last judgment. He saw Christians as psychosomatic wholes who had become members of Christ's body and in whom the Holy Spirit dwelled. It was unholy and unthinkable for a Christian to join this body with a prostitute. Paul, of course, was thinking in terms of biblical morality in which marriage is the only God-ordained sexual relationship. Other relationships are unholy, a defilement of the body, the temple of God's Spirit (v. 19).

MARRIAGE AND RELATED QUESTIONS (7:1–40)

With 7:1 Paul turned to the Corinthian letter. He dealt first with their questions concerning marriage. He may have gone well beyond their questions in his lengthy discussion of marriage and singleness. Throughout chapter 7 his general advice was that a person should remain single whenever possible, but that marriage is also a holy state, and one should feel no guilt embracing it. In the course of the chapter it becomes clear that Paul's conviction of the imminent end of the world colored his view of marriage.

Sexual expression in marriage (7:1–7). Evidently some of the Corinthians were uttering the slogan, "It is good for a man not to marry" (lit., "not to touch a woman").[27] This ascetic strain in the church was in marked contrast to the men of chapter 6 who were going to prostitutes. In the first century, ascetic movements were widespread. For example, among the Jews, the Essenes, and the Therapeutae were ascetic. There was a temple of the Egyptian Isis cult in Corinth, a cult often associated with both male and female celibacy.[28] It is possible that asceticism was particularly appealing to the *women* of the Corinthian church as an expression of their freedom.[29] Married women were perhaps those who were withdrawing from sexual relations with their husbands in order to express their devotion (v. 5). The men going to prostitutes and the asceticism of 7:1–7 may be two sides of the same problem. Paul's advice in this situation is surprisingly "contemporary."

First, he urged marital partners to assume full responsibility for the sexual satisfaction of the other, wife for husband and husband for wife (v. 4). In the male-dominated first century this was remarkably egalitarian. Second, though Paul did not forbid sexual abstinence for devotional purposes, he urged that such practices be of limited duration and only by mutual consent (v. 5). Paul concluded by holding up his own single state as a model but granted that it was a gift (*charisma*) from God, a gift not possessed by every person (v. 7).[30]

Specific advice regarding marriage (7:8–16). Paul's general principle for the unmarried was that they remain single unless they were unable to control their sex drive, in which case they should marry (vv. 8–9). Married persons should not divorce, in accordance with Jesus' teaching on the subject (vv. 10–11). Paul allowed an exception to the no-divorce rule. In the case of a non-Christian partner *who wished to separate*, divorce was allowable. Otherwise, Christians should remain with unbelieving partners in the hope that they might eventually be saved (vv. 12–16). Paul noted that he had no tradition from Jesus on this matter (v. 12).

The general rule of calling (7:17–24). Paul laid down the general principle that the Corinthians should not seek a major change in their state of life but should remain as they were when God called them to be Christians. Jews (circumcised) should remain Jews, Gentiles (uncircumcised) should remain Gentiles. Slaves were to remain slaves. But if they were set free, they were to embrace their freedom and remain faithful to their calling in their new state as freedmen.[31] The general principle remained the same: one should not make a change in one's life circumstances a priority. In view of the approaching end time, one should be content with one's lot and make devotion to Christ the top priority.

Advice to virgins (7:25–38). Paul seemed to address the same people in verses 25–28 and 36–38. Both passages mention "virgins" (*parthenoi*). Probably Paul had engaged couples in mind.[32] Verse 25 addressed the virgin and verse 38 her fiancee. To both, Paul gave the same advice. They were better off if they remained single, but they committed no sin in marrying should that become necessary. In verses 29–31 Paul made explicit what has been implicit throughout chapter 7: the time is short; the world is passing away (v. 31). Those with family responsibilities would only experience increased stress in view of the impending tribulations. Verses 32–35 express another reason for remaining single: single persons are able to give undivided devotion to the affairs of the Lord.

Verses 36–38 are exceedingly difficult. The Greek is ambiguous and can be translated in different ways. Three interpretations have been advocated, each of which is followed in one or more major English translations. A view which dates from the patristic period sees the section as referring to a father who has a daughter who is about to pass her prime. The question is whether he should arrange for her marriage or keep her single (ASV). The NEB reflects a view which sees the couple living together in a celibate "spiritual marriage." The question is whether they should consummate the marriage physically. The practice of spiritual marriages is known to have existed in the second century church but has not been documented for Paul's time. It was eventually condemned by early church councils. The third and most widely held view of verses 36–38 sees the passage to be referring to engaged couples. It is reflected in the RSV and NIV.

A *final word about widows* (7:39–40). In verse 8 Paul advised widows to remain single. He returned to widows in the final two verses of the chapter. There he allowed that they were free to marry but still considered them better off remaining single. It is interesting how time and circumstances can alter one's opinion. When Paul wrote 1 Timothy 5:11–15 a decade or so later, the young widows of Ephesus were becoming idle and busybodies. Paul *urged* them to marry. (By that time he was also not as certain about the imminence of the end.)

FREEDOM AND FOOD OFFERED TO IDOLS (8:1–10:33)

Chapters 8–10 constitute an extended treatment of the issue of meat that had been sacrificed to idols. The issue is explicit in chapter 8 and in 10:14–11:1. It is implicit in the discussion of idolatry in 10:1–13. On the other hand, chapter 9 seems to deal with another issue altogether—Paul's right as an apostle to the material support of his congregations. The issue is closely related to the idol-meat question, however. Just as Paul had been willing to forego his apostolic "rights" for the sake of the gospel, so should the "strong" among the Corinthians for the sake of the larger Christian community be willing to suspend their right to eat idol meat.

In a Roman colony like Corinth one was quite likely to encounter idol meat in various contexts. One context was a cultic meal in a pagan temple, where meat was sacrificed and the participants dined on a portion of the meat *as an act of worship*. The temples were also used for social events, such as the meetings of various clubs and associations, marriages, and civic meetings. Large dining rooms for such purposes have been discovered at Corinth in the temples of Asclepius and Demeter.[33] Not all sacrificial meat was consumed in the sacred meals. Some was reserved for the priests. Other meat was served at social gatherings in the temple. Still other found its way to the local meat market. The seeming contradictions between Paul's words about the consumption of idol meat are best explained in light of these very different contexts.

Chapter 8 is best understood as relating to *social events held in the dining rooms of the temples*. Those of the upper classes would be those most likely to be invited to such events. Officials like Erastus could not have avoided attendance of civic meetings held in temples, which generally involved consumption of a meal. The more well-to-do Corinthians were probably the "strong," whom Paul addressed in chapter 8.[34] They had responded to Paul's monotheistic message and confessed the one true God. They had abandoned their former idolatry and polytheism. They now proceeded to use this "knowledge" (v. 1) to justify their continued consumption of sacrificial meat. If there is but one God, idols cannot be gods; they have no real existence (vv. 4–5). Paul agreed with their theology but modified it at two points. First, he introduced the principle of love. For the Christian, love is supreme; it governs all knowledge. To know God we must first be known by him. We know him through Christ. We know him through his love. He knew us before we knew him; he loved us first. So for Christians, love—not knowledge—is the governing principle.[35]

Second, Paul pointed out that though there is but one God there are still many "gods" and "lords" in the world. The gods of the pagan world dominated the imagination and lives of those who believed in them. For them they were existentially quite real. And for one who had once believed in them to be driven back into the old polytheism would be devastating indeed. Paul had these people in mind in verses 7–13. They were Gentiles—not Jews. They had once participated in the worship of idols and consumed the sacrificial meat, believing it truly represented communion with the pagan god (vv. 7–8).[36] They did not yet possess the full "knowledge" of the Corinthian "strong." Their consciences were still weak. For them a return to paganism was a real possibility. Should they see a fellow Christian eating in a pagan temple, they might be encouraged to do so themselves.[37] But for them it would not be an indifferent matter. They would see it as participation in an idol's cultic meal (vv. 9–10). That is, they would slip back into the old polytheism; Christ would become for them merely another god among many. The weak Christian's very status as a Christian would thus be at stake. Paul therefore urged the Corinthians of "strong" conviction not to consume idol meat in a context where a weaker Christian might observe them and be caused to stumble.[38]

In 10:23–11:1 Paul addressed a totally different context at the end of his discussion of meat offered to idols—that is, meat offered *outside the confines of the temples*. The Corinthian meat market probably did not distinguish between idol meat and meat from other sources.[39] Paul said that Christians with a clear conscience on the matter need not ask. They could eat whatever was presented in the market. The same pertained to an invitation to an unbeliever's home. One need not question whether idol meat was being served or not, not unless someone raised this issue. Then it became a matter of witness. A pagan might interpret the Christian's eating the meat as a condoning of idolatry.[40] In such a case Christians should abstain—for the sake of Christian witness. Paul was willing to forego his own rights for witness and the salvation of others. So should the Corinthians (10:32–11:1; cp. 9:12).[41]

In the first part of chapter 10 Paul warned the Corinthians about the *danger of falling into idolatry*. In 10:1–13 he issued his warning by employing a typology from the wilderness period of Israel's history. He argued that in a figurative sense Israel was "baptized" in the wilderness and provided with spiritual drink and food. Still, the Israelites slipped into idolatry, and many were destroyed. Paul was arguing that Israel's experience in many ways paralleled that of the Corinthians. He warned them against a false sense of security.[42] They needed to be very careful when participating in the temples. There was a clear line which must be drawn, a line between the indifferent matter of sacrificial meat and the sin of idolatry. He discussed the line in 10:14–22. It consisted of *actual participation in a cultic meal*. It was one thing to dine in a temple club room at the wedding feast of a neighbor. It was quite another to attend a cultic meal which worshiped a pagan god. Paul took a hard line on idolatry. Christians should flee the worship of idols in every case (v. 14). He cited the tradition of the Lord's Supper (vv. 15–17). It is a holy observance, an actual communion with Christ, a participation in his body—the body offered on the cross for our salvation *and* the body of believers who comprise his church. Paul still granted that idols were nothing, but the *worship* of idols acknowledges gods other than the Lord and so is a compromise on one's exclusive devotion to Christ. Paul may have condoned the eating of idol meat under neutral circumstances. He strictly forbade its consumption in the setting of idolatrous worship.

Chapter 9 is something of a diversion but is integral to Paul's argument. The Corinthians were claiming their freedom, their rights as Christians. Paul was probably the person who first taught them the basic principle of freedom in Christ. But in the church there is a limit to individual freedom—the limits of love and mutual concern. Paul never denied the "strong" group's right to partake of idol meat. He only urged them to forego those rights when exercise of them might cause a weaker brother or sister to stumble.[43] In chapter 9 Paul illustrated this principle by his own example. As an apostle, he had the "right" to be supported by the congregations he served (vv. 1–14). He had chosen not to claim this support, presumably because it might be a stumbling block for some in the congregation (vv. 15–18). Verses 19–24 express Paul's primary missionary strategy. He made himself a "slave to everyone, to win as many as possible" (v. 19). That is, he consistently subordinated himself to others for the sake of winning them to Christ. Verse 22 is especially significant. Paul was willing to become "weak" to the weak in order to win them. This was not compromise, but empathy. In like manner, he was urging the "strong" Corinthians to be sensitive to the weak for the sake of the gospel and the integrity of the Christian fellowship.

In 9:24–27 Paul employed athletic imagery to emphasize the need for discipline in the Christian life. Paul was perhaps looking back to his treatment of "rights" and urging the strong Corinthians to practice self-discipline in their concern for others. He was also perhaps looking forward to his discussion in chapter 10 of the danger of idolatry, warning the "strong" Corinthians that they may not be as strong as they thought. In any event, the Isthmian games were held regularly just outside Corinth. They were second in fame only to the Olympics. Paul's athletic example would surely have caught the attention of the Corinthians.[44]

THE CHRISTIAN ASSEMBLY (11:2–34)

In chapter 11 Paul dealt with two matters pertaining to Christian worship: the covering or uncovering of one's head (vv. 2–16), and the proper observance of the Lord's Supper (vv. 17–34). Paul introduced neither of them with the phrase "now concerning," which usually denotes questions from their letter to him. Probably both matters came to his attention by word of mouth, from Chloe's servants or the three Corinthian delegates.

The covering of one's head in worship (11:2–16). Perhaps no passage in 1 Corinthians is more obscure than this, as is evidenced by the vast diversity of interpretations in the scholarly literature. Paul's basic concern was the proper decorum in worship. For him, this meant that women should have their heads covered, men their heads uncovered.[45] What exactly was going on in worship at Corinth? Were the men worshiping with their heads covered?[46] Were the women worshiping with uncovered heads? How is one's head covering to be understood in the passage anyway—as a hood, a veil, one's hair?[47] In the balance, Paul seems to have devoted most attention to the women.[48] Most likely, the appearance of a few women in the congregation without head coverings or with their hair short prompted Paul's response in 1 Corinthians. One cannot be certain of the basis for their practice. Jewish women always wore veils in worship. A head covering was also normative for women in the Greek and Roman cults, but evidently some exceptions existed.[49]

Paul advanced four primary arguments for women covering their heads. One was the rabbinic argument based on Genesis 2 that women are the glory of their husbands. Paul concluded that the woman's glory should be reserved for the husband by being covered (vv. 3–9). Second, Paul argued that women should wear an "authority" on their head "because of the angels" (v. 10). The reference to "authority" is obscure but probably refers to the woman's authority to participate in worship by having the proper head covering (and thus acknowledging her husband's "authority").[50] The allusion to the "angels" is even more obscure and has led to all sorts of suggestions—the ministers of the congregation, the "sons of God" of Genesis 6 who mated with the daughters of men, the guardian angels who are present in divine worship,[51] or the angels who maintain world order (as in Rom. 13:1–7).[52] A third argument of Paul maintained that long hair was "natural" for women (vv. 13–15), and a final argument stated that this was the practice in all the churches (v. 16). This was likely the real basis of Paul's treatment. The women's behavior was against the social conventions of the day, was distressing to some and was disruptive of worship. There are strong hints in the passage of a more egalitarian stance on Paul's part—in the reference to the women praying and prophesying in worship (v. 5) and in his comment in verses 11–12 that from the perspective of birth man is wholly dependent on woman.

The misuse of the Lord's Supper (11:17–34). The second problem in corporate worship was more serious—the abuse of the Lord's Supper. Paul had no praises to sing them in that regard (v. 17). The situation reflected in verses 17–22 goes back to a time when the Lord's Supper was a part of a larger communal meal.[53] At Corinth some were stuffing themselves and getting drunk; others were not getting enough to eat and were being humiliated (v. 22). It was a division between rich and poor, the haves and the have-nots. The Corinthian congregation was socially diverse, but the scandal for Paul was that the Lord's Supper had become a stage for displaying this diversity. Instead of a time for expressing the unity of the body, it had become an occasion for dividing it.

One can see how this situation could have arisen in the house-church context of the Christian gatherings. The wealthier members, the patrons who furnished their homes for Christian gatherings, may also have provided the food for the community meal. It was a common practice in Roman culture for those who gave large banquets to invite their special friends early to a banquet and to serve them the choicest dishes in the *triclinium* (dining room). The *triclinium* was small, and most of the guests would dine on lesser fare in the larger *atrium* in the center of the home.[54] Something like this must have been happening at Corinth. Paul instructed those who were overindulging to do so at home before coming to the Christian gathering, where no such displays of social distinction were tolerable.[55]

In verses 23–26 Paul repeated the tradition of Jesus' words at the Last Supper. It is the oldest account of the words of institution in the New Testament, 1 Corinthians antedating the earliest of the Gospels by at least a decade. Paul introduced the tradition to emphasize that the supper was a remembrance of Christ and his atoning death. In desecrating the supper, the Corinthians were blaspheming the body of Christ in a double sense—failing to observe the unity of the body that is the church, and dishonoring Christ's own body, which was broken in his death on the cross. It was the latter sense that Paul stressed in his warning about judgment and the need for self-examination (vv. 27–32). Their abuse of the Lord's Supper was in effect to blaspheme Christ's death on their behalf. Paul saw the judgment as already working itself out in the sickness and death of some of the members. This is hard for us to comprehend today, but it reminds us of the very sacred character of the Lord's Supper and of the church which celebrates it. Neither is to be treated lightly.

SPIRITUAL GIFTS (12:1–14:40)

The telltale phrase "now about" occurs in 12:1, indicating that the Corinthian letter had asked Paul about the subject. From Paul's discussion in chapters 12–14, it seems that the gifts of the Spirit had created two main problems in the church: disunity between those who claimed the Spirit's endowment and those who felt left out, and disruption in worship because of the uncontrolled display of spiritual manifestations in that context. Paul responded to these problems by stating three main principles: (1) the *unity* in giftedness and *diversity* of gifts within the congregation (chap. 12), (2) the ruling principle of *love* (chap. 13), and (3) the importance that the *whole church be edified* (chap. 14).

The basic test: "Jesus is Lord" (12:1–3). Paul began by noting that ecstatic experience was not unique to Christianity. The Gentile Corinthians had experienced such phenomena in the pagan cults before their conversion (v. 2). But there was a difference, not in ecstatic manifestation so much as in content. Manifestations of the *Holy Spirit* will always be consistent with the basic Christian confession that "Jesus is Lord." A person, for instance, would never say "Jesus be cursed" through the Holy Spirit.[56]

Unity and diversity of gifts (12:4–31). Paul quickly shifted the discussion from the emphasis on the "gifted" to the "giver" by changing the vocabulary from "spiritual gifts" (*pneumatika*, 12:1), to "gifts of grace" (*charismata*, 12:4). *Pneuma* was the Corinthians's word; it emphasized *their receipt* of the Spirit. *Charisma* was Paul's word. It comes from the word "grace" (*charis*) and emphasizes *God's gift.*[57] In 1 Corinthians 12:4–31 Paul's main concern was to show that all Christians are gifted. There is no room for individualism and pride in a particular gift—all are from God and for the upbuilding of the whole church. Paul established this by three main approaches.

First, he emphasized the diversity of gifts (vv. 4–11). The Spirit gives gifts to all, but they differ. To illustrate this diversity, in verses 7–11 Paul provided a sample list of gifts, which moves from the more "rational" gifts of wisdom and knowledge to the more ecstatic gifts of tongues and their interpretation.

Second, Paul stressed the unity of these gifts within the body of Christ (vv. 12–26). In speaking of the church as a body, Paul used a common metaphor from the popular philosophy of his day, particularly Stoicism.[58] He applied the metaphor in various ways: the body is diverse, consisting not of one member but of many (vv. 14–18); the whole body cannot be equated with any one member (vv. 19–20); the members of the body are interdependent, each needing the others (v. 21); the weaker parts of the body are indispensable (vv. 22–25); and the body is a sympathetic whole (v. 26).

Third, Paul applied the body analogy to the church, providing a second sample list of the many and diverse gifts granted by God to the church (vv. 27–31). The breadth of the list indicates the comprehensive nature of the giftedness of the church members. The questions of verses 29–30 are constructed in a manner that expects a "no" answer. "Are all apostles?" No. "Do all work miracles?" No. All are not gifted alike, but all are gifted. And all the gifts are *God's gifts*, gifts of his grace, nothing in which individual Christians might pride themselves over others.

Verse 31 is a transitional verse. Paul began by urging the Corinthians to pursue the "greater gifts." What were they? Presumably the three that are enumerated at the beginning of the list in verse 28—apostles, prophets, teachers. All these are gifts of sharing the word. All Christians should aspire to be witnesses to the word. But there is another, still more perfect way, not a gift of the Spirit so much as a *fruit* of the Spirit (cp. Gal. 5:22), which is the quality, power, and motivation for all that the body of Christ is or hopes to be—*love*.

The most excellent way (chap. 13). It has often been argued that 1 Corinthians 13 is a separate piece, a hymn or piece of exalted prose written by Paul on an earlier occasion or by someone else and incorporated by the apostle at this point in his letter. It is more likely that Paul composed the piece as an integral part of the epistle. It is written in *his* style and fits the context admirably, not only of chapters 12 and 14, but of the whole letter.[59] The Corinthians abounded in many gifts. What they lacked was love (cp. 8:1–3).

Paul's encomium on love falls into three main sections.[60] It begins by enunciating the superiority of love (13:1–3). All the spiritual gifts are worthless if they are not expressed in love. This applies to tongues, knowledge, prophecy, and wonder-working faith, the very gifts so prized by the "Spirit people" of the Corinthian congregation. Paul's final example in verse 3 spoke either of giving one's body "to be burned" or giving it up "that one might boast." The variant translations are due to variant Greek texts with two words which sound very much alike in Greek: *kauthēsomai* (burn) and *kauchēsomai* (boast). Considering the context, perhaps "burn" is the more likely word. Even the ultimate sacrifice is worthless if unaccompanied by love.

Verses 4–7 speak of the work of love or qualities of love. Throughout the encomium Paul used the Greek word *agapē* in denoting love, that selfless sort of love exhibited by Christ in laying down his life for sinners. Most of the attributes ascribed to love in this section are negative, emphasizing the self-denying, self-emptying nature of *agapē*, which denies itself, does not envy, does not boast, is not self-seeking. These are the very traits that the Corinthians lacked. Their self-esteemed spiritual accomplishments made them proud and rude and disdainful of others. They lacked love.

Paul concluded by speaking of the endurance of love (13:8–13). The gifts the Corinthians so cherished would one day pass away, whether tongues, or knowledge, or prophecy. Paul was thinking eschatologically. The "perfect" (v. 10) is the life to come. When this life passes away and we enter that perfect realm where God is all in all (cp. 15:28), the gifts pertaining to this life will pass away also—prophecy, knowledge, tongues, and all the rest. Three things only will abide through eternity—*faith* made perfect, *hope* realized, and *love*. The last is the greatest, because it is the power by which heaven itself lives. It was ironic. With their realized eschatology, the superspiritualists of Corinth felt they had it all; the future held nothing more in store for them. The opposite was the case. Everything they *did* have would perish. The love they lacked would abide.

The proper expression of tongues and prophecy (chap. 14). At 14:1 Paul returned to the Corinthian term *spiritual gifts (pneumatika)* rather than his preferred "gifts of grace" *(charismata)*.[61] The Corinthians had asked Paul in their letter about the "spiritual gifts," and the content of chapter 14 would indicate that they understood these largely in terms of "tongues" (*glossōlalia*), an ecstatic, nonrational "Spirit language."[62] In chapter 14 Paul's immediate concern was for the Christian assembly, for which he demanded edification, instruction, and rational exhortation. One gets the impression that he viewed tongue speaking as a private, devotional matter, much like his own vision referred to in 2 Corinthians 12:1–6. He did not discourage the practice; he even admitted his own participation in tongues (14:18). He allowed it a place in Christian worship but only under strict regulation. Paul's discussion of tongues covers 1 Corinthians 14:1–33. It can be outlined in five main divisions.

(1) The superiority of prophecy to tongues (14:1–6). Paul pointed to the limitation of tongues in the setting of worship. Tongues edify primarily the speaker, not the congregation, since they are unintelligible. He argued the superiority of prophecy, since it is intelligible, offering instruction and guidance to the community.[63] Tongues can become edifying if an interpreter is present to express them in intelligible language.

(2) Analogies which point to the need for rational content (14:7–12). Using the analogies of music, the bugle call, and foreign languages, Paul pointed out the need for oral communicaton to be ordered and intelligible to the hearer.

(3) Paul's insistence on the rational element (14:13–19). For Paul, in the gathered Christian community the *edification* of all present was essential (v. 17). He viewed ecstatic manifestations like tongues as basically spiritual but not mental. Paul did not eschew the individual spiritual experience; he just insisted that *in worship* the experience must be communicated in rational, intelligible words that would benefit all present (v. 19).

(4) Tongues and the outsider (14:20–25). Just as the other Christians in the assembly are not edified by uninterpreted tongues, so the outsider will not be convicted and led to faith. He will see the tongues as chaos and madness. To speak rationally under the Spirit's inspiration as in prophecy will lead the visiting non-Christian to conviction of sin and confession of God. As in all the other arguments, Paul was concerned with the rational presentation of God's word in worship.

(5) Regulation of tongues and prophecy in worship (14:26–33). This section gives an insight into early Christian worship. It seems to have been a very "participatory" gathering with everyone contributing, often spontaneously. Obviously such an arrangement could get out of hand. Paul thus sought to regulate the more spontaneous contributions. First he appealed to the tongue speakers: they must be limited in number (three at most), must speak one at a time, and in the absence of an interpreter must keep quiet altogether (26–28). Even though Paul preferred prophecy, it too could become chaotic if all the prophets got inspired at the same time. So he insisted that they also should be limited to three at most and should speak one at a time. One should stop when the others received a revelation. Finally, they should be subject to the judgment of the other prophets (29–32). Paul saw the Spirit as God's gift to the *whole church*. There is no place for "independent spirits."

Paul dealt with an additional matter in verses 34–36, the silence of women in the church. The verses have provoked an extensive discussion. Paul acknowledged elsewhere in 1 Corinthians that women participated audibly in worship, both praying and prophesying (11:5). Many scholars have considered the conflict between the two passages to be so serious that they have argued verses 34–36 are a later interpolation into the text of 1 Corinthians. There is some weak textual basis for this, as

248

these verses are found in another place (after v. 40) in a small group of manuscripts.[64] (No manuscript, however, lacks them.) Paul must have enjoined silence under special circumstances in 14:34–36.

Numerous suggestions have been made: the women were chattering in church because they were accustomed to being off to themselves in the Jewish synagogue;[65] the women were self-proclaimed charismatic teachers who were teaching men (as in 1 Tim. 2:8–15);[66] Paul was forbidding the female prophets to participate in the judgment of the other prophets, since this would have placed them in an authoritative position over men.[67] These are but a sample of the many suggestions that have been made. All are guesswork.

In the light of 11:5, it is clear that Paul was not issuing a blanket prohibition of women speaking in worship. He had to be addressing some special circumstance. Judging from its position in chapter 14, it must have related somehow to the expression of the spiritual gifts. It is in the middle of the tongues/prophecy discussion. Paul summarized and concluded the discussion in the verses that follow (14:37–40).

THE RESURRECTION (CHAP. 15)

The question about the resurrection of the dead does not seem to have been raised by the Corinthians' letter (no *peri de* formula). It came to Paul by other means. Some in the church were evidently denying the resurrection of believers. On what basis is not clear. Paul himself may not have fully known why at this point. Perhaps they were the hyperspiritualist group, those who claimed to be already reigning (cp. 4:8). Influenced by neoplatonic dualism, they considered themselves already complete, spiritually perfected, awaiting only the separation of their soul from their bodies at death.[68] Their salvation awaited no future; they were already "perfected." In their scheme there was no place for a bodily resurrection. Paul responded to the word about their denial of the resurrection with a very comprehensive treatment. He covered all the bases, so to speak, giving the most comprehensive treatment of the resurrection of believers to be found in the New Testament.

First Paul appealed to the tradition of Christ's resurrection (15:1–11). It consisted of two parts: (1) the basic confession that Christ died, was buried, and rose on the third day (vv. 3–4), and (2) the tradition of those to whom the risen Lord had appeared, who could verify his resurrection (vv. 5–11). Paul included himself as the last witness. The Corinthians do not seem to have questioned Jesus' resurrection, only their own. For Paul, the two went together. If Jesus rose, so do those who are "in him." The basis of the resurrection of believers starts with Christ's resurrection.

Paul pointed out the implications of Jesus' resurrection for the believer's resurrection in verses 12–19. He employed a syllogism to argue the inseparability of Christ's resurrection from the believer's resurrection. If believers do not rise, then neither did Christ; the two are inseparable. Three things follow, however, if Christ did not rise: we are still in our sins, those who have already died have altogether perished, and we have hope only, the hope having no prospect of future realization.

In verses 20–28 Paul employed an apocalyptic schema which summarized the events of the end. Verses 21–22 emphasize again the inseparability of Christ and the believer by introducing the theme of the two Adams. Through the influence of platonism, later Judaism speculated that there was a perfect, unfallen heavenly Adam who preceded the earthly Adam. Paul reversed the order of the two Adams in the light of Christ. Just as we die in our sins because of our solidarity with the earthly

Adam, so we will live because of our belonging to Christ, the heavenly Adam.[69] Verses 23–28 give the order of the final events: Christ's resurrection as the "first-fruits," then the resurrection of believers, then the defeat by the Son of all powers opposing God, and then the Son's handing of the kingdom to the Father.[70] There is a "functional subordination" of Son to Father which underlines a strict monotheism: in the end God's reign will be uncontested.[71]

In verses 29–34 Paul used three "human" (*ad hominem*) arguments to advance the idea of the believer's resurrection. First he appealed to a practice that some may have actually been doing at Corinth—baptism for the dead.[72] Endless discussion has raged over what this entailed, but it seems to have been some sort of vicarious baptism, which Paul himself probably did not endorse. Paul only cited the practice as evidence for the resurrection. If the dead do not rise, how could a proxy baptism profit them anyway? Paul's second argument appealed to his own trials. Why undergo them if there is no future? Finally, he appealed to the Epicurean adage: if this life be all, why not live it in hedonistic abandon?

In verses 35–50 Paul discussed the nature of the resurrection body. Those at Corinth who were denying the resurrection probably held a Greek view of the survival of the *soul*. Paul, on the other hand, thought of personhood in terms of a psychosomatic whole. The future existence will not be as a naked spirit, he told them, but as an individual, transformed, spiritual body. In verses 35–41 he used seeds and animals and heavenly bodies to argue the infinite variety of bodies that exist. Particularly significant is his reference to a seed having to die first in order to take on its new body (v. 36)—a clear comparison with the resurrection body. Our mortal bodies must first die before they can be clothed with immortality. In verses 42–44 Paul discussed the nature of the resurrection body: it will be a transformed, spiritual body, a new order of existence, in continuity with but distinct from the mortal body. Drawing from a rabbinic midrash on Genesis 2:7, which spoke of the heavenly Adam as a "life-giving spirit," Paul once again employed the Adam speculation of Judaism to argue for the *spiritual* resurrection *body* of the believer (vv. 45–50).[73]

Verses 15:51–58 return to an apocalyptic schema of the events of the end that is reminiscent of 1 Thessalonians 4:15–18. When the last trumpet blows, the dead will rise and be clothed with immortality. The living, among whom Paul included himself (v. 52), will also be reclothed in their new spiritual bodies, and the last enemy, death, will die. The linkage of sin, law, and death in verse 56 is very Pauline; it will have to await our consideration of Romans 7. Verse 58 brings the whole discussion home. The real import of the resurrection hope is what we are doing *now*. All our labors in Christ are grounded in the resurrection hope, but until he comes what counts is *our labor*.

CONCLUSION (16:1–24)

A final major question raised by the Corinthians's letter was Paul's collection for the saints (1 Cor. 16:1–4). We will examine all the collection texts in a subsequent chapter. Most of the remainder of chapter 16 has either already been treated or will be in future chapters. Paul's next visit to Corinth did not turn out exactly as he planned in 16:5–9, and we will consider this in the next chapter. Timothy probably did go to Corinth (vv. 10–11) but came back with bad news, and that will occupy us also in the next chapter. The Corinthian letter may have asked when Apollos would visit them again (16:12). Paul's response that Apollos was unwilling to do so for the moment is enigmatic. After 1 Corinthians, Apollos drops out of view.

We have already considered 16:15–18. Stephanas was likely one of the wealthier Corinthians who furnished his home for the congregation and served as one of its patrons. The delegation of three (v. 17) were the bearers of the Corinthians' letter, and Paul gave them due recognition. First Corinthians concludes with many of the epistolary conventions characteristic of Paul's letters—the exchange of greetings, the holy kiss, the reference to writing the concluding words in his own hand, the grace benediction, the *agapē* wish. Worthy of note is the prayer for the Lord's return, which Paul wrote in the original Aramaic of the earliest Christians, transliterated into Greek (*marana tha*, "Come, Lord"). Some of the Corinthians had little concern for the future; they "had it all" now. Throughout the letter Paul reminded them of the future awaiting them as Christians. With the traditional Aramaic prayer, he gave a final reminder.

NOTES

1. J. B. Polhill, "Reconciliation at Corinth: 2 Corinthians 4–7," *Review and Expositor* 86 (1989): 354–356.

2. W. Schmithals, *Gnosticism in Corinth: An Investigation of the Letters to the Corinthians,* trans. J. E. Steely (Nashville: Abingdon, 1971), 90–96. For a very different reconstruction of the two letters, see J. Héring, *The First Epistle of St. Paul to the Corinthians,* trans. A. W. Heathcote and P. J. Allcock (London: Epworth, 1962), xi–xv.

3. For a comprehensive treatment of the various views regarding Paul's opponents, see J. J. Gunther, *St. Paul's Opponents and their Background* (Leiden: Brill, 1973).

4. F. C. Baur, "Die Christuspartie in der korinthischen Gemeinde," *Tübingen Zeitschrift für Theologie* 5 (1831): 61–206.

5. Among those who see a Jewish dimension to the problems in 1 Corinthians is C. K. Barrett. He sees the primary problem as an incipient Gnosticism but also sees Jewish perspectives among the "weak" with regard to idol meat and asceticism. See C. K. Barrett, *Essays on Paul* (Philadelphia: Westminster, 1982), 28–59.

6. W. Schmithals, *Gnosticism in Corinth,* 124–285.

7. R. McL. Wilson, "How Gnostic Were the Corinthians?" *New Testament Studies* 19 (1972–73): 65–74; *idem.,* "Gnosis at Corinth," in *Paul and Paulinism, Essays in Honour of C. K. Barrett,* ed. M. D. Hooker and S. G. Wilson (London: S.P.C.K., 1982), 102–114.

8. For examples, see M. L. Soards, *The Apostle Paul: An Introduction to His Writings and Teachings* (New York: Paulist, 1987), 74–75; J. W. Drane, *Paul, Libertine or Legalist: A Study of the Theology of the Major Pauline Epistles* (London: S.P.C.K., 1975). J. Painter contends that the Corinthians "gnosticised," being particularly influenced by the Greek mysteries: "Paul and the Pneumatikoi," in *Paul and Paulinism,* 237–250.

9. This is the view of R. Horsley, "Gnosis in Corinth: 1 Corinthians 8:1–6," *New Testament Studies* 27 (1980–81): 32–51. See also J. Murphy-O'Connor, *Paul, a Critical Life* (Oxford: Clarendon, 1996), 280–282. N. Hyldahl maintains the unlikely view that Apollos was not baptized and not considered a Christian by Paul: "Paul and Hellenistic Judaism in Corinth," in *The New Testament and Hellenistic Judaism,* ed. P. Borgen and S. Giversen (Peabody, Mass.: Hendrickson, 1997), 204–216.

10. B. Pearson also argues for a hellenistic background of the Corinthian spiritualists. In his view, they claimed to acquire the inbreathed Spirit by pursuing wisdom in accordance with their own distinctive exegesis of Genesis 2:7: B. A. Pearson, *The Pneumatikos-Psychikos Terminology in 1 Corinthians,* SBL Dissertation Series, #12 (Missoula, Mont.: Scholars, 1973).

11. C. H. Talbert, *Reading Corinthians: A Literary and Theological Commentary on 1 and 2 Corinthians* (New York: Crossroad, 1987), xxii.

12. J. Munck, *Paul and the Salvation of Mankind* (Richmond: Knox, 1959), 135–167.

13. For social factors in the Corinthian problem, see G. Theissen, *The Social Setting of Pauline Christianity*, ed. and trans. J. H. Schütz (Philadelphia: Fortress, 1982). For the idea that the Corinthian disharmony was a sort of civil strife, see L. L. Welborn, "On the Discord at Corinth: 1 Cor. 1–4 and Ancient Politics," *Journal of Biblical Literature* 106 (1987): 85–111.

14. W. Baird, *The Corinthian Church—A Biblical Approach to Urban Culture* (Nashville: Abingdon, 1964), 27.

15. This is roughly the division argued by K. Bailey, "The Structure of 1 Corinthians and Paul's Theological Method with Special Reference to 4:17," *Novum Testamentum* 25 (1983): 152–181.

16. Some scholars see Paul employing a homily in these chapters. For example, V. P. Branick traces a homily based on prophetic texts in 1:18–31; 2:6–16; 3:18–23: "Source and Redaction Analysis of 1 Corinthians 1–3," *Journal of Biblical Literature* 101 (1982): 251–269.

17. G. R. O'Day suggests that most of the Corinthians were well-to-do and Paul was urging them to take their security in their calling, not in their human status: "Jeremiah 9:22–23 and 1 Corinthians 1:26–31: A Study in Intertextuality," *Journal of Biblical Literature* 109 (1990): 259–267.

18. T. H. Lim, "Not in Persuasive Words of Wisdom, but in the Demonstration of the Spirit and Power," *Novum Testamentum* 29 (1987): 137–149. See also J. H. Schütz, *The Anatomy of Apostolic Authority* (Cambridge: University Press, 1975), 187–203.

19. E. E. Ellis, "'Wisdom' and 'Knowledge' in 1 Corinthians," *Tyndale Bulletin* 25 (1974): 82–98.

20. P. Lampe maintains that Paul used a rhetorical device that kept the application of the lesson of 1:18–2:16 hidden from the Corinthians until 3:1–4: "Theological Wisdom and the 'Word About the Cross': The Rhetorical Scheme in 1 Corinthians 1–4," *Interpretation* 44 (1990): 117–131.

21. First suggested by J. M. S. Baljon, it has been refined by J. Strugnell, "A Plea for Conjectural Emendation in the New Testament: With a Coda on 1 Cor. 4:6," *Catholic Biblical Quarterly* 36 (1974): 555–558.

22. A recent suggestion is that "what is written" refers not to the Old Testament but to possible written bylaws which the Corinthian church had adopted: J. C. Hanges, "1 Corinthians 4:6 and the Possibility of Written Bylaws in the Corinthian Church," *Journal of Biblical Literature* 117 (1998): 275–298.

23. W. Deming, "The Unity of 1 Corinthians 5–6," *Journal of Biblical Literature* 115 (1996): 289–312.

24. A. Y. Collins suggests that the man grounded his offensive behavior theologically, claiming it was "in Jesus' name": "The Function of 'Excommunication' in Paul," *Harvard Theological Review* 73 (1980): 251–263.

25. Recent sociological treatments of this passage emphasize how closely the control of the individual body is related to the purity concerns of the larger social body. See J. H. Neyrey, "Body Language in 1 Corinthians: The Use of Anthropological Models for Understanding Paul and His Opponents," *Semeia* 35 (1986) 129–170; G. Harris, "The Beginnings of Church Discipline: 1 Corinthians 5," *New Testament Studies* 37 (1991): 1–21.

26. B. W. Winter, "Civil Litigation in Secular Corinth and the Church: The Forensic Background to 1 Corinthians 6:1–8," *New Testament Studies* 37 (1991): 559–572.

27. J. C. Hurd Jr. *The Origin of 1 Corinthians* (London: S.P.C.K., 1965), 158–163.

28. R. E. Oster Jr., "Use, Misuse and Neglect of Archaeological Evidence in Some Modern Works on 1 Corinthians (1 Cor. 7:1–5; 8; 10; 11, 2–16; 12, 14–26)," *Zeitschrift für die neutestamentliche Wissenschaft* 83 (1992): 52–73.

29. M. Y. MacDonald, "Women Holy in Body and Spirit in the Social Setting of 1 Corinthians 7," *New Testament Studies* 36 (1990): 161–181.

30. W. Deming argues that 1 Corinthians 7 reflects the debate between Stoics and Cynics over marrriage: *Paul on Marriage and Celibacy: The Hellenistic Background of 1 Corinthians 7* (Cambridge: At the University Press, 1995).

31. S. S. Bartchy, **ΜΑΛΛΟΝ ΧΡΗΣΑΙ**: *First Century Slavery and 1 Corinthians 7:21*, SBL Dissertation Series 11 (Missoula, Mont.: Society of Biblical Literature, 1971).

32. J. K. Elliott, "Paul's Teaching on Marriage in 1 Corinthians: Some Problems Considered," *New Testament Studies* 19 (1973): 219–225.

33. Oster, "Use, Misuse and Neglect," 64–67.

34. Theissen, *The Social Setting,* 121–143.

35. N. T. Wright calls this "Christological monotheism": *The Climax of the Covenant* (Minneapolis: Fortress, 1992), 120–136.

36. J. Meggitt points out that there were cultic occasions when even the poor of the city would be provided with meat: "Meat Consumption and Social Conflict in Corinth," *Journal of Theological Studies* 45 (1994): 137–141.

37. The context pictured in chapter 8 is clearly the temple. See G. D. Fee, "Ειδωλοθυτα Once Again: An Interpretation of 1 Corinthians 8–10," *Biblica* 61 (1990): 172–197.

38. Paul seems to have been an exception in offering this "situational" view of idol meat. The early church as a whole seems to have consistently condemned its consumption, in keeping with the apostolic decrees. See J. C. Brunt, "Rejected, Ignored or Misunderstood? The Fate of Paul's Approach to the Problem of Food Offered to Idols in Early Christianity," *New Testament Studies* 31 (1985): 113–124.

39. On the Corinthian meat market (*macellum*) see H. J. Cadbury, "The Macellum of Corinth," *Journal of Biblical Literature* 53 (1934): 134–141; J. D. Gill, "The Meat Market of Corinth (1 Corinthians 10:25)," *Tyndale Bulletin* 43 (1992): 389–393.

40. B. Witherington distinguishes between the two Greek words used in chapter 8 (*eidolothuton*) and in 10:28 (*hierothuton*), arguing that the former is a technical term for full participation in idolatrous worship: "Not So Idle Thoughts about *Eidolothuton*," *Tyndale Bulletin* 44 (1993): 237–254.

41. P. T. O'Brien, *Gospel and Mission in the Writings of Paul* (Grand Rapids: Baker, 1993) 83–107.

42. This section is best viewed not as an attack on sacramentalism but a warning against idolatry: K-G. Sandelin, "Does Paul Argue Against Sacramentalism and Over-Confidence in 1 Cor 10, 1–14?" in *The New Testament and Hellenistic Judaism,* 165–182.

43. R. A. Horsley, "Consciousness and Freedom Among the Corinthians: 1 Corinthians 8–10," *Catholic Biblical Quarterly* 40 (1978): 574–589.

44. O. Broneer, "Paul and the Pagan Cults at Isthmia," *Harvard Theological Review* 64 (1971): 169–187.

45. A number of recent interpreters argue that both the men and the women were bucking custom, the men covering and the women uncovering their heads: cp. J. Murphy-O'Connor, "Sex and Logic in 1 Corinthians 11:12–16," *Catholic Biblical Quarterly* 42 (1980): 482–485; C. H. Talbert, *Reading Corinthians,* 68.

46. Among the Romans, priests and laymen alike often pulled their togas over their heads when praying or sacrificing: R. Oster, "When Men Wore Veils to Worship: The Historical Context of 1 Corinthians 11:4," *New Testament Studies* 34 (1988): 481–505.

47. "Covering" could refer to hair. W. J. Martin argued that the Corinthian women were shaving their heads, as was done in some Greek cults: "1 Corinthians 11:2–16, an Interpretation," in

Apostolic History and the Gospel, ed. Gasque and Martin (Grand Rapids: Eerdmans, 1970), 231–241.

48. A. Padgett suggests that the Corinthian *men* were responsible for the arguments of verses 4–7 while Paul advocated the more egalitarian stance of verses 10–16: "Paul on Women in the Church: The Contradictions of Coiffure in 1 Corinthians 11:2–16," *Journal for the Study of the New Testament* 20 (1984): 69–86.

49. The Isis cult, which had a temple in Corinth, granted women equal power with men and may have influenced the Christian women: J. E. Stambaugh and D. L. Balch, *The New Testament in Its Social Environment* (Philadelphia: Westminster, 1986), 159.

50. See M. Hooker, "Authority on Her Head: An Examination of 1 Corinthians 11:10," *New Testament Studies* 10 (1964): 410–416.

51. In the Qumran writings reference is made to angels who presided over the community's worship: J. A. Fitzmyer, "A Feature of Qumran Angelology and the Angels of 1 Cor. xi.10," *New Testament Studies* 4 (1957): 48–58.

52. G. B. Caird, "Paul and Women's Liberty," *Bulletin of the John Rylands Library* 54 (1972): 268–281.

53. G. Bornkamm, "Lord's Supper and Church in Paul," *Early Christian Experience,* trans. P. L. Hammer (New York: Harper and Row, 1969), 122–160. See also A. D. Nock, *St. Paul* (New York: Harper and Brothers, 1937), 186–195.

54. J. Murphy-O'Connor, "House Churches and the Eucharist," *Bible Today* 22 (1984): 32–38.

55. Theissen, *Social Setting,* 145–174.

56. Those who argue a Gnostic background for the Corinthian opponents see "Jesus be cursed" as representing a Gnostic denial of the fleshly Jesus and a docetic Christology that affirmed only a spiritual Christ.

57. D. L. Baker, "The Interpretation of 1 Corinthians 12–14," *Evangelical Quarterly* 46 (1974): 224–234.

58. A. E. Hill suggests that the clay body parts associated with the temple of Asclepius may have influenced Paul to use the body analogy: "The Temple of Asclepius: An Alternate Source for Paul's Body Theology," *Journal of Biblical Literature* 99 (1980): 437–439.

59. G. Bornkamm, "The More Excellent Way," in *Early Christian Experience,* 180–193.

60. For a rhetorical analysis of 1 Corinthians 13 as an encomium, see J. G. Sigountas, "The Genre of 1 Corinthians 13," *New Testament Studies* 40 (1994) 246–260; J. Smit, "The Genre of 1 Corinthians 13 in the Light of Ancient Rhetoric," *Novum Testamentum* 33 (1991): 193–216.

61. E. E. Ellis, "'Spiritual' Gifts in the Pauline Community," *New Testament Studies* 20 (1974) 128–144. See also T. Callan, "Prophecy and Ecstasy in Greco-Roman Religion and in 1 Corinthians," *Novum Testamentum* 27 (1985): 125–140.

62. For a comprehensive exposition of Paul's discussion of the gifts, see K. S. Hemphill, *Spiritual Gifts: Empowering the New Testament Church* (Nashville: Broadman, 1988).

63. For a general treatment of prophecy in 1 Corinthians and its wider biblical context, see W. A. Grudem, *The Gift of Prophecy in 1 Corinthians* (Washington, D.C.: University Press of America, 1982).

64. For example, G. D. Fee, *The First Epistle to the Corinthians,* New International Commentary on the New Testament (Grand Rapids: Eerdmans, 1987), 669–708.

65. J. S. Glen, *Pastoral Problems in First Corinthians* (Philadelphia: Westminster, 1964), 133–134.

66. R. P. Martin, *The Spirit and the Congregation: Studies in 1 Corinthians 12–15* (Grand Rapids: Eerdmans, 1984), 87.

67. Grudem, *Gift of Prophecy,* 250–255.

68. A. J. M. Wedderburn, "The Problem of the Denial of the Resurrection in 1 Corinthians xv," *Novum Testamentum* 23 (1981): 229–241.

69. R. Scroggs, *The Last Adam: A Study in Pauline Anthropology* (Philadelphia: Fortress, 1966), 82–89.

70. For a full exegesis of verses 23–28, see J. Plevnik, *Paul and the Parousia, An Exegetical and Theological Investigation* (Peabody, Mass.: Hendrickson, 1997), 145–169.

71. W. Schmithals, "The Pre-Pauline Tradition in 1 Corinthians 15:20–28," *Perspectives in Religious Studies* 20 (1993): 357–380.

72. For the Corinthian emphasis on death and the underworld, see R. E. DeMaris, "Corinthian Religion and Baptism for the Dead (1 Corinthians 15:29): Insights from Archaeology and Anthropology," *Journal of Biblical Literature* 114 (1995): 661–682.

73. J. D. G. Dunn, "1 Corinthians 15:45—Last Adam, Life-Giving Spirit," in *Christ and Spirit in the New Testament*, ed. Lindars and Smalley (Cambridge: University Press, 1973), 127–143.

SELECTED COMMENTARIES

BASED ON THE GREEK TEXT

Conzelmann, Hans. *A Commentary on the First Epistle to the Corinthians*. Trans. James W. Leitch. Hermeneia. Philadelphia: Fortress, 1975.

Ellicott, Charles J. *Commentary on St. Paul's First Epistle to the Corinthians*. Andover, Mass.: W. F. Draper, 1889.

Robertson, Archibald and Alfred Plummer. *A Critical and Exegetical Commentary on the First Epistle of St. Paul to the Corinthians*. International Critical Commentary. New York: Charles Scribner's Sons, 1916.

BASED ON THE ENGLISH TEXT

Barrett, C. K. *A Commentary on the First Epistle to the Corinthians*. Black's New Testament Commentaries. London: Adam and Charles Black, 1968.

Blomberg, Craig. *1 Corinthians*. NIV Application Commentary. Grand Rapids: Zondervan, 1994.

Dunn, James D. G. *1 Corinthians*. New Testament Guides. Sheffield, England: Sheffield Academic Press, 1996.

Fee, Gordon D. *The First Epistle to the Corinthians*. The New International Commentary on the New Testament. Grand Rapids: Eerdmans, 1987.

Hays, Richard B. *1 Corinthians*. Interpretation. Louisville: Westminster/John Knox, 1997.

Héring, Jean. *The First Epistle of Saint Paul to the Corinthians*. Trans. A. W. Heathcote and P. J. Allcock. London: Epworth, 1962.

Hodge, Charles. *An Exposition of the First Epistle to the Corinthians*. New York: Robert Carter and Brothers, 1882.

Kistemaker, S. J. *Exposition of the First Epistle to the Corinthians*. New Testament Commentary. Grand Rapids: Baker, 1993.

Moffatt, James. *The First Epistle of Paul to the Corinthians*. Moffatt Commentary on the New Testament. New York: Harper and Brothers, 1938.

Morris, Leon. *The First Epistle of Paul to the Corinthians*. Tyndale New Testament Commentaries. Grand Rapids: Eerdmans, 1958.

Watson, N. *The First Epistle to the Corinthians*. Epworth Commentaries. London: Epworth, 1992.

COMMENTARIES ON BOTH 1 AND 2 CORINTHIANS

Bruce, F. F. *1 and 2 Corinthians*. New Century Bible Commentary. Grand Rapids: Eerdmans, 1971.

Talbert, Charles H. *Reading Corinthians: A Literary and Theological Commentary on 1 and 2 Corinthians*. New York: Crossroad, 1987.

Thrall, Margaret E. *The First and Second Letters of Paul to the Corinthians*. The Cambridge Bible Commentary on the New English Bible. Cambridge: University Press, 1965.

Witherington, Ben. *Conflict and Community in Corinth: A Socio-Rhetorical Commentary on 1 and 2 Corinthians*. Grand Rapids: Eerdmans, 1995.

13

2 CORINTHIANS: TREASURE IN CLAY JARS

*I*n many ways 2 Corinthians is the most personal of Paul's letters. It was born of a very intense conflict that developed between the apostle and the church after the writing of 1 Corinthians. In the course of events Paul was personally attacked. The very legitimacy of his ministry was called into question. His leadership of the congregation was challenged.

Second Corinthians was written after the heat of the battle was over, after the majority of the congregation had reaffirmed Paul as their apostle. It reflects the pain and the heartache of the conflict as well as Paul's relief and joy that it had been resolved. But mainly it reflects Paul's sense of vindication for his ministry.[1] He had been true to his calling. He had borne the treasure of the gospel in his human weakness. God's glory became manifest through his own suffering and impotence. This was not a new dialectic for Paul. In 1 Corinthians he had emphasized that the divine power and wisdom are revealed in the seeming weakness and folly of the cross (1 Cor. 1:18–2:5). Now he had seen the lesson embodied in his own clash with the Corinthians. They had judged him by worldly standards, but he had remained true to the word of the cross. Second Corinthians is about power in weakness, about strength through suffering, about life through death, about triumph through seeming defeat. In short, it is about embodying the message of the cross.

INTRODUCTION TO 2 CORINTHIANS

Three matters are essential to understanding 2 Corinthians. First to be considered is Paul's relationship to the church. The epistle is filled with allusions to Paul's experiences with the Corinthians, and one must attempt some reconstruction of those events. Second, one's understanding of the letter will be affected about whether it is considered as a unity in its present form. No serious scholar questions Paul's having been the author of the epistle, but many argue that the present letter is a composite of fragments from two or more different letters to Corinth. Finally comes the question of the nature of Paul's opposition in 2 Corinthians. Who was responsible for the attack on his apostleship?

PAUL'S RELATIONSHIP WITH CORINTH

Paul's extensive interaction with the Corinthians during the course of his third (Ephesian) mission is not recounted in Acts. Second Corinthians deals extensively with Paul's relationship with the Corinthians during this period. One is forced to attempt some reconstruction of the full course of events.

Events following 1 Corinthians. According to 1 Corinthians 16:5–9, Paul evidently planned to visit Corinth soon, after he had first been to Macedonia. First Corinthians was possibly written around Easter, and Paul was delaying this trip until after Pentecost. He wanted to have plenty of time in Corinth, perhaps spending the winter there. In the same letter Paul indicated that Timothy would likely come to Corinth soon as his personal representative (1 Cor. 4:17, 16:10). Evidently Timothy made the planned trip but came back with a report that the situation at Corinth had deteriorated since the writing of 1 Corinthians.

The "painful visit." One would assume that Timothy brought back bad news to Paul at Ephesus, because the apostle seems to have made an abrupt, unplanned visit to Corinth himself. The visit is not mentioned in Acts but is implied in several places in 2 Corinthians. Second Corinthians 2:1 mentions a "painful visit" to Corinth. "Painful" hardly fits Paul's founding visit (Acts 18:1–18), the only visit to Corinth mentioned in the Acts narrative to this point. (Acts does mention a visit in 20:1–3, but that came later.) Paul, however, mentioned another, second visit to Corinth in 2 Corinthians 13:2, which seems to have been a "painful" time, when Paul issued stern warnings to the Corinthians. Likewise, 2 Corinthians 12:14 speaks of his coming a "third" time, which implies he had made a second visit. Paul probably sailed directly from Ephesus across the Aegean to the Corinthian port of Cenchrea.

According to 2 Corinthians 2:1–11, Paul seems to have been personally affronted by an individual within the congregation during the course of his second visit. The church evidently did not come to his defense at that time. The church's reticence to support Paul seems to have upset him as much if not more than the person's attack (2 Cor. 7:9–12). Who the individual was is not at all apparent. It has been suggested that it was the incestuous man of 1 Corinthians 5:1–5. Most interpreters feel that the person was more likely identified with the group that challenged Paul's apostolic status, whom he addressed in chapters 10–13.

The "epistle of tears." On his second visit Paul left Corinth in anger and frustration. Where he went is uncertain. He may have returned by sea directly to Ephesus. It is also possible he returned to Ephesus by the land route through Macedonia. It depends on how one interprets 2 Corinthians 1:15–16. There Paul said that he had planned to visit Corinth twice, going from Ephesus to Corinth to Macedonia and then back to Corinth a second time before finally departing for Judea. Obviously this was a change of plans from that outlined in 1 Corinthians 16:5–9.[2] It was clearly a plan for the *conclusion* of his third mission; from the second visit to Corinth he would sail to Judea. The painful visit seems to have been "unscheduled." Paul does not seem to have completed his work in Ephesus. Whether or not he *did* go on to Macedonia from Corinth, it is clear he did not return to Corinth at this time. Instead, he sent an epistle, an angry letter that sternly rebuked the Corinthians. He called upon the church to discipline the one who had confronted him (2:5–10). The letter was painful in every respect. Not only did Paul write it "with many tears" (2:4); it caused great sorrow among the Corinthians as well (2 Cor. 7:8–13). It evidently had the desired effect, as the Corinthians disciplined the offender and reaffirmed their devotion to Paul.

Two suggestions have attempted to identify the "epistle of tears." Some see it as being 1 Corinthians. First Corinthians, however, scarcely fits the description. There is no reason Paul would have wept upon writing 1 Corinthians, nor was the epistle written in a tone that would have evoked tears from the Corinthians. Another suggestion is that chapters 10–13 of 2 Corinthians are a fragment of the "sorrowful" epistle. These chapters reflect an undeniably harsher, more censorious tone than the preceding nine. The theory has its problems, however, and we will consider them in the next section. Perhaps the best conclusion is simply that the "epistle of tears" has been lost.

The letter was probably sent from Ephesus, perhaps in the summer of A.D. 56. Paul sent the letter in place of himself, to spare the Corinthians another painful visit (2 Cor. 2:1). By sending the letter Paul gave the Corinthians an opportunity to repent. It was delivered by Titus. Paul was exceedingly distraught about the Corinthian situation. He was not at all sure of his own welcome in the church. He dared not return to Corinth until he had received a report from Titus as to how the letter was received. Paul evidently issued an ultimatum that put everything on the line.

Good news from Titus. Having sent the angry letter by Titus, Paul concluded his mission in Ephesus and set out for Macedonia (cp. Acts 20:1). His route took him first to Alexandria Troas, the port city for sea traffic to Macedonia. According to 2 Corinthians 2:12, Paul found an "open door" at Troas, which probably means that he established the church there at that time. Despite this new opportunity for witness, Paul could find no peace of mind over the situation at Corinth (2 Cor. 2:13). Evidently he and Titus had prearranged their routes so that they would be sure to encounter one another as they traveled from opposite directions. Paul perhaps expected to meet Titus at Troas, but he did not come. It may have been running late in the sailing season. Paul may have caught the "last boat out" before bad weather cancelled all sailing for the fall and winter.

In some Christian community of Macedonia Paul finally met up with Titus. It could have been anywhere—Philippi, Thessalonica, Berea. Titus bore wonderful tidings. The letter had evidently had its desired effect, and the Corinthians had rallied to Paul. They had expressed their sorrow, they "longed for" Paul, they were concerned about him (2 Cor. 7:6–7, 13–16). Overjoyed, Paul now wrote his "letter of reconciliation" to the Corinthians. Scholars are divided over the extent of the letter. Some argue for the first seven, eight, or nine chapters of 2 Corinthians. Others see it as more restricted, consisting primarily of the "autobiographical" portions of 2 Corinthians (1:1–2:13 + 7:5–16). We would maintain that Paul wrote *all* of 2 Corinthians at this point.

Paul's final visit to Corinth. At this time Paul was very heavily occupied with a monetary collection for the Jerusalem Christians. He did not immediately go to Corinth but instead sent Titus ahead of him with 2 Corinthians, remaining behind to administer the collection.[3] Probably later in the fall of 56, Paul traveled to Corinth. Returning to his original travel plan of 1 Corinthians 16:6, he spent the three winter months there. This final Corinthian visit is mentioned in Acts 20:2–3a. Paul wrote Romans during this final Corinthian stay. In that epistle he spoke of Gaius's warm hospitality to him in Corinth on that occasion (Rom. 16:23). Evidently Paul continued to be reconciled with the Corinthians.

THE INTEGRITY OF 2 CORINTHIANS

No Pauline epistle has been subject to more elaborate partition theories than 2 Corinthians. Fragments from as many as six different epistles have been detected in our present 2 Corinthians. The main partition hypotheses revolve around the following passages.

2:14–7:4. A number of scholars would separate 2:14–7:4 out from 1:1–2:13 and 7:5–16. They argue that 2:13 and 7:5 connect together naturally, both dealing with Paul's waiting for the report from Titus. The section 2:14–7:4 is seen not only to break the flow of Paul's "travel account" but also to have an entirely different tone from 1:1–2:13 plus 7:5–16. The former (2:14–7:4) is seen as a polemical fragment aimed at Paul's opponents, while 1:1–2:13 plus 7:5–16 is seen as "the letter of reconciliation." Typically, 2:14–7:4 is viewed as having been written from Ephesus, between 1 Corinthians and Paul's "painful visit" to Corinth.[4]

There is undoubtedly a break between 2:13 and 7:5, but it is likely a break *intended by Paul* and not one introduced by a subsequent compiler. As Paul recounted his anxiety awaiting Titus in 2:13, he burst into a thanksgiving in 2:14 as he remembered the joyous news which Titus brought. Paul felt vindicated in his apostolic labors. It led him into a long digression on the nature of his apostleship, which occupied 2:14–7:4. The section is not so much polemical as it is apologetic. It is closely associated with 1:1–2:13 and 7:5–16. All of chapters 1–7 revolve around the themes of comfort and suffering. All deal with the nature of Paul's ministry in human weakness and divine power and how that ministry had been vindicated in the Corinthians' reaffirmation of him.

6:14–7:1. The section 6:14–7:1 is an even more striking break in context. In 6:13, Paul urged the Corinthians to open their hearts to him, and in 7:2 he again appealed to them to widen their hearts. The intervening verses (6:14–7:1) deal with an entirely different matter—the question of Christians being joined with unbelievers. The emphasis is on the separateness and purity of the Christian community. As we have seen, it is unlikely that this is a portion of the "previous letter" referred to in 1 Corinthians 5:9.[5] Many scholars would argue that this section is a pre-Pauline fragment that has been inserted into the text of 2 Corinthians. Particularly popular is the view that the fragment comes from early Jewish Christians influenced by Qumran.[6] One does not need to go beyond the Corinthian correspondence for the background to 6:14–7:1. The section is a repetition of Paul's warning against participation in idolatrous cults. Verse 16 is the center of the warning (cp. 1 Cor. 10:14, 21). Purity continued to be a problem in Corinth. Paul returned to the subject in 12:21.

Chapters 8 and 9. Both chapters 8 and 9 deal with Paul's collection for the Jerusalem Christians. In both chapters Paul appealed to the Corinthians to complete their commitment to the project. He did so from different angles. For example, in 8:1–5 he held the Macedonians up to the Corinthians as a model of generosity. In 9:1–5 he argued that he had held the Corinthians up as a model to the Macedonians. Some have felt that the treatments of the two chapters are too dissimilar to belong to the same letter. Some would see them as fragments from two entirely separate collection letters.[7] Others would argue that chapter 8 is a part of the letter of reconciliation but that chapter 9 comes from a separate collection letter.[8]

There is no reason chapters 8 and 9 should be separated from chapters 1–7. The reconciliation between congregation and apostle served as a basis for his renewed appeal that they demonstrate their reaffirmation of his ministry by participating in his collection for the Jerusalem saints. The two chapters are complementary. Together they present an extended appeal for Corinthian participation in the collection.

Chapters 10–13. The most popular partition theories for 2 Corinthians involve chapters 10–13. It is beyond question that the tone of these four chapters differs radically from that of chapters 1–9. The conciliatory note of the previous chapters is replaced by an angry, harsh, and often sarcastic denunciation of Paul's Corinthian opponents. It has thus been suggested that chapters 10–13 are a fragment of the "epistle of tears." This view was first suggested by A. Hausrath in 1870.[9] It was very popular in the early twentieth century,[10] and it still has strong defenders.[11] It has its problems, however. Perhaps the main one is that these chapters are all directed against a group of would-be apostles who opposed Paul, whereas the epistle of tears concerned the discipline of a single person. A more popular current view sees chapters 10–13 as the fragment of a letter *subsequent to* chapters 1–9.[12] In this view, Titus delivered the epistle of reconciliation (chaps. 1–9) to the Corinthians but returned to Paul in Macedonia with the report that the opposition was still very much alive. This prompted Paul's angry, sarcastic reply, of which 2 Corinthians 10–13 is a part.[13] This is seen as Paul's final communication with Corinth before his three-month visit there.

How can one account for the sharp change in tone between the first nine chapters and the last four and still maintain the unity of the epistle? Some have suggested that Paul may have received some news from Corinth in the interim between the writing of chapter 9 and chapter 10, news which made him realize that the problem of the opponents was still present in the congregation. Paul replied in anger without revising the earlier chapters. Others have noted that Paul spoke of the "majority" of the congregation rallying around him in 2 Corinthians 2:6. In this view, chapters 1–9 were intended for this majority, while chapters 10–13 were aimed at the minority who still opposed Paul's leadership.[14]

PAUL'S OPPOSITION AT CORINTH

The problems in 1 Corinthians were primarily internal to the congregation itself. Paul seems not to have been aware of any attack against himself apart from the general party spirit that prevailed. Everything had changed by the time he wrote 2 Corinthians. The conflict now focused on Paul himself. The new situation was evidently caused by outsiders who had recently come to Corinth (2 Cor. 11:4). Exactly who they were and what they taught has been the subject of much debate. What is clear is that they challenged Paul's leadership of the congregation. They questioned his right to be called an apostle, and in so doing gave welcome support to any latent opposition to Paul that already lurked in the congregation.

Nowhere in 2 Corinthians did Paul clearly delineate the views of these "outsiders." He made few direct accusations against them, but most of the content of chapters 10–13 is devoted to them and their attack on Paul. They evidently claimed some sort of apostolic status. Paul called them "false apostles" (11:13) and Satan's "servants" (11:14–15). He implied that they preached a "different gospel" and "another Jesus" from Paul's own message and that the Corinthians were all too eager to receive it (11:4). One is reminded of the similar situation at Galatia (Gal. 1:6–9). Paul referred to them sarcastically as "super-apostles" and noted how they took pride in their speaking abilities. They ran Paul down for his apparent lack of such skills (10:10; 11:5–6). They took pride in their own accomplishments, boasting "without limit," comparing themselves with one another by "worldly" standards (10:12–17; 11:12, 18). They boasted of their spirituality and their miraculous powers and charged Paul with being unspiritual and worldly (10:2–4; 12:12). They were evidently overbearing and highly authoritarian in establishing their control over the Corinthians (11:19–21a). They claimed a Jewish heritage and boasted about it (11:21b–22). They seem to have held Moses in particularly high esteem (3:7–18). They probably boasted of visionary experiences (12:1). They emphasized externally verifiable human credentials, making much of letters of recommendation which they brought with them (3:1–3). They demanded proof of Paul's claim to apostolic status (13:3). They evidently considered their receipt of payment from the Corinthians not only as a right but also as a necessary confirmation of their apostolic status (2:17; 11:7–11). They argued that Paul's refusal to accept remuneration was proof that he was not an apostle.

The emphasis on boasting and rivalry and on the miraculous remind one of the "spirit people" of 1 Corinthians. But the claim to apostolic status and the Jewish element are new to 2 Corinthians. The direct assault on Paul's leadership was also a new development. How are we to view these intruders on the Corinthian scene? A number of different configurations have been suggested, but these can be reduced to four main positions.

Judaizers. F. C. Baur argued that the opponents of both Corinthian letters were Judaizers who represented the Jerusalem apostles. Among contemporary scholars, C. K. Barrett is perhaps the most prominent exponent of this view. Barrett differs from Baur at a number of points. He sees the Jewish element as being minor in 1 Corinthians and the Judaizing problem as having been introduced later by outsiders. He sees the Judaizers as coming from Judea and representative of legalistic Jewish Christianity, but not as official representatives of the apostles.[15] He views them, however, as appealing to the Jerusalem apostles for their own legitimation. Barrett equates the "super-apostles" of 11:5 and 12:11 with the Jerusalem apostles, whom the Judaizers pitted against Paul.[16] A number of variations on the Judaizing hypothesis have been suggested.[17] Although they differ in detail, all see the opposition as coming from Palestinian Jewish Christianity and as legitimating their ministry by appealing in one way or another to the Jerusalem apostolate. The main disadvantage to the Judaizing view is the complete lack of evidence that Paul's Corinthian opponents insisted on the law or circumcision or any of the requirements advocated by the Judaizers as we know them from Galatians.

Gnostics. Although many contemporary interpreters see some sort of incipient Gnosticism as the main problem reflected in 1 Corinthians, few see Gnostics as the "super-apostles" opposing Paul in 2 Corinthians. An exception is W. Schmithals, who sees Paul as battling "Gnostic apostles" in both epistles.[18] As per his usual reconstruction, they were Jewish Christian Gnostics. They claimed to be apostles and embodiments of Christ (11:13). The "other Jesus" whom they preached (11:4) reflected their Gnostic docetism which denied the incarnation of the earthly Jesus. The main problem with Schmithals's "Gnostic key" is the lack of evidence that a first-century Jewish Christian Gnosticism ever existed. For 2 Corinthians there really is no evidence even for the kind of "pre-Gnosticism" of 1 Corinthians—no emphasis on ecstasy, no libertine behavior, no denial of the resurrection, and the like.

Hellenistic Jewish-Christian missionaries. A view originally associated with G. Bornkamm sees the outsiders of 2 Corinthians as hellenistic Jewish-Christian missionaries with roots in the Jewish apologetic tradition of the Diaspora synagogue. This view has a number of advocates. It has been most fully developed by D. Georgi.[19] According to Georgi, Paul's opponents were strongly influenced by Hellenism. They saw themselves as "divine men" (*theioi andres*) who were the embodiments of the divine Spirit as were Moses and Jesus before them. They emphasized Scripture interpretation, rhetorical skills, and miracle working. Like the Cynics, they insisted on pay, considering remuneration as a legitimation of their ministry. Their favorite self-designation was "servants/ministers" (*diakonoi*).[20] The main problem with this theory is again that of sources. Georgi's reconstruction of Diaspora Jewish apologetic is itself open to question as is his concept of the hellenistic "divine man," a theory which draws on sources from the second century and later.

"Pneumatics." In his book on Paul's opponents in 2 Corinthians, J. Sumney followed a suggestion first made by E. Käsemann. In this view, Paul's opponents were "pneumatics" (Spirit people) who claimed a Jewish background but were neither Judaizers nor had any Jerusalem connections.[21] This view accounts for the Jewish element in Paul's opposition as well as their emphasis on manifestations of the Spirit. The group is fairly undefined, however, and almost impossible to document.

It can readily be seen that the more specific one's attempt to define the Corinthian intruders, the more open to questioning it becomes. Perhaps it is best to paint Paul's opposition with broad strokes. They came from a Jewish background. They took pride in their rhetorical skills. They claimed to exhibit outward visible signs which validated that they were true apostles. They also maintained that Paul lacked these marks of an apostle. They may or may not have allied with the hyper-spiritualist group in Corinth with whom Paul had to contend in 1 Corinthians. To understand the message of 2 Corinthians, it is not necessary to be more specific than this. Paul's leadership was challenged by a group which claimed that one's apostolic status needed to be validated by external, verifiable signs, such as speaking ability, miracles, and "good references." Paul saw a different set of criteria as the real marks of an apostle—the marks of the cross.

A STUDY OUTLINE OF 2 CORINTHIANS

I. Paul's Ministry of Suffering (1:1–7:16)
   A. Introduction and Thanksgiving (1:1–11)
   B. Paul's Change in Travel Plans (1:12–2:4)
      1. In order to "spare" the Corinthians (1:12–14)
      2. In order to avoid another painful visit (2:1–4)
   C. Appeal for Milder Discipline of an Erring Brother (2:5–11)
   D. Paul's Apology for his Apostleship (2:12–7:4)
      1. Self-confidence in his divine commission (2:12–4:6)
         (a) Mention of Titus's coming (2:12–13)
         (b) The resulting reaffirmation of Paul's commission (2:14–17)
         (c) Paul's true recommendation—his people (3:1–3)
         (d) Paul's true qualification—the Spirit (3:4–18)
         (e) The honesty of Paul's witness to Christ (4:1–6)

2. Paul's sufferings as an apostle (4:7–5:10)
   (a) His many discouragements and trials (4:7–12)
   (b) The offsetting hope in the resurrection (4:13–5:10)
3. Paul's ministry of reconciliation (5:11–6:10)
   (a) The controlling love of Christ (5:11–15)
   (b) The message of reconciliation (5:16–21)
   (c) The service of suffering (6:1–10)
4. Paul's appeal to the congregation (6:11–13)
5. His warning against joining with unbelievers (6:14–7:1)
6. A renewed appeal to the congregation (7:2–4)
   E. Completion of the Prehistory of the Epistle (7:5–16)
II. The Collection (8:1–9:15)
   A. The Example of Macedonia (8:1–7)
   B. The Basis in Love (8:8–15)
   C. The Role of Titus and the Brothers (8:16–24)
   D. The Expectations of the Macedonians (9:1–5)
   E. The True Basis for Cheerful Giving (9:6–15)
III. Paul's Final Defense Against His Opponents (10:1–13:14)
   A. A New Warning (10:1–18)
      1. Paul's divine weapons (vv. 1–6)
      2. The strength of both his letters and his presence (vv. 7–12)
      3. His boast "in the Lord" (vv. 13–18)
   B. "Foolish" Self-Praise in Self-Defense (11:1–12:13)
      1. Paul and the "super-apostles" (11:1–6)
      2. Paul's refusal to accept support (11:7–11)
      3. The deceit of the false apostles (11:12–15)
      4. Paul's talk as a "fool" (11:16–21)
      5. Paul's grounds for boasting (11:22–12:10)
         (a) His Jewish pedigree (11:22)
         (b) His ministry of suffering (11:23–33)
         (c) His vision and his thorn in the flesh (12:1–10)
      6. Summary: The Corinthians should have read the "signs" (12:11–13)
   C. Paul's Plans for a Third Visit (12:14–13:10)
      1. Charges from the Corinthians against Paul (12:14–18)
      2. Paul's fear that he may have to reverse the charges (12:19–21)
      3. Exhortation to careful self-examination (13:1–10)
   D. Epistolary Conclusion (13:11–14)

HIGHLIGHTS OF 2 CORINTHIANS

INTRODUCTION (1:1–11)

In 2 Corinthians Paul's opening thanksgiving takes the form of a hymn of praise to God. Paul praised God for having comforted him. This set the theme for the entire epistle, which is *comfort in the midst of suffering,* a gospel which is *made perfect in weakness.* In verses 3–7 the word *comfort* occurs some ten times. Paul spoke of a fellowship of suffering and comfort. The afflictions Paul endured as an apostle were a participation in the sufferings of Christ, but Christ also brought him comfort. Through their own fellowship with Paul, the Corinthians participated in turn in the same experience of comfort in the midst of suffering.

In verses 8–11 Paul referred to a recent experience in Asia where he faced a peril so severe that he questioned whether he would live through it. What he referred to is uncertain. An imprisonment has been suggested, or perhaps a recurrence of a chronic illness. He might have had the incident with the Ephesian silversmiths in mind (Acts 19:23–41). In any event, the experience reminded him of his total dependence on God for his ministry (v. 9). This is a major theme throughout the epistle. The experience also reminded Paul of the importance of the Christian community, who participated in his ministry through their prayers (v. 11).

PAUL'S CHANGE IN TRAVEL PLANS (1:12–2:11)

In 1:12–14 Paul set forth the basis of his conduct as an apostle: he acted not in accordance with human wisdom but solely out of the grace of God. In this section Paul spoke of "boasting." The Corinthians could boast in Paul and Paul in the Corinthians, because Paul's witness and the Corinthian response were both rooted in God's grace. "Boasting" is a major theme of 2 Corinthians. Words for "boasting" occur some twenty-nine times in the epistle. Paul's opponents in Corinth evidently boasted a lot in their own accomplishments. Paul boasted in God alone.

As we have seen, Paul changed his travel plans several times. His opponents in Corinth used this against him, accusing him of being fickle (vv. 15–16). They probably also argued that it showed that he had little love and concern for the congregation. In 1:17–22 Paul responded to these accusations. He insisted that he was not inconsistent, speaking out of both sides of his mouth, saying both yes and no at the same time. Everything he did was based on his ministry for Christ and his devotion to the gospel of what God had done in Christ (v. 21). There is no equivocation in God's work in Christ, only a resounding "amen." In verse 20 Paul spoke of God's "glory" and in verse 22 of God's Spirit. He saw both as marks of the new covenant for which God had anointed him as a minister. He developed this theme at length in chapter 3.

In 1:23–2:4 Paul explained the reasons for his change of travel plans. He had not returned to Corinth after the painful visit in order to spare the Corinthians. He wanted to work *with* the Corinthians, not *over* them (v. 24). Later in the epistle he implied that his opponents had behaved far more autocratically toward them (11:20–21). Rather than risk another painful personal encounter, Paul chose to write a letter instead. The letter provided the Corinthians with an opportunity to repent and remedy the situation by their own actions.[22] Only the Corinthians themselves, the ones who had brought Paul grief in the first place, could now bring him relief and joy (v. 2); so he gave them time to recant.

The Corinthians seem to have responded positively to Paul's "epistle of tears" (2:5–11). They disciplined the individual who had opposed Paul. Paul's main concern all along had been not for himself but for the Corinthians and their fidelity to the gospel. Now that they had "proved themselves" (v. 9), Paul expressed concern for the individual and urged the church to act redemptively toward him. An unreconciled situation within the fellowship would only open the door for Satan (v. 11).

PAUL'S CONFIDENCE IN HIS DIVINE COMMISSION (2:12–4:6)

Paul recounted the events that followed his writing of the "epistle of tears"—the anxiety at Troas, the journey to Macedonia (2:12–13). He finally met up with Titus in Macedonia and received the good news that the Corinthians had rallied to him and his gospel (7:5–7). Paul did not relate these events at this point in his letter. The very thought of Titus's coming flooded his mind with the joy and relief he felt when Titus brought him the good news. He felt that his gospel had been vindicated. The thought led him to a long digression on the nature of his apostolic ministry, which occupied all of 2:14–7:4.

In 2:14–17 Paul described his ministry by using three pictures. First was that of a triumphal procession of a victorious Roman general (v. 14). Those who were led in such processions were usually the defeated who were being led to their *deaths*.[23] When Paul described God as leading him in triumph, he may have had this picture in mind. Only when he yielded to God was God able to use him. It was a ministry of the cross, in which life comes only through suffering and death. Paul's second picture was that of an odor which can exude either the fragrance of life or the stench of death (2:15–16). Paul was still probably thinking in terms of the cross and using the sacrificial imagery of the odor that rises from a burnt offering to God. The gospel of the cross has a double fragrance—rising to life for those who accept it, to death for those who refuse.[24] The final picture is that of peddlers (v. 17). Paul probably had in mind the false Corinthian apostles, who insisted on being paid for their ministry. Paul's was free of charge, and that was being used against him (cp. 11:7–15; 12:12–19). When Paul asked, "Who is equal to such a task?" he may have had the experience of Moses in mind (Exod. 4:10). Like Moses, Paul was not up to the task in and of himself, but he *was* sufficient for it when he surrendered himself and allowed God to lead him in triumph.

In 3:1–3 Paul spoke of his credentials. The Corinthian opponents may have carried letters of recommendation, perhaps even from the leadership in Jerusalem. Paul responded that the Corinthians themselves were *his* letter of recommendation. They were the fruit of his ministry and the proof that God had been working through him (cp. 1 Cor. 9:2). Verse 3 is transitional. Paul shifted from his treatment of written letters to a discussion of covenants, contrasting the old covenant of the law written on stone tables with the new covenant of the Spirit written on human hearts. Paul surely had Jeremiah's "new covenant" in mind (Jer. 31:31–34).

In 3:4–6 Paul returned to the theme of competence, of being equal to the task (cp. 2:16). Paul had no competence in himself, but God gave him the competence to be a minister of the new covenant, the covenant of the Spirit. Verse 6 has often been seen as a proof text for the sharp dichotomy between law and gospel: the written code leads to death, the Spirit to life. Paul's real contrast, however, was between the old covenant and the new covenant. The old covenant did not lead to life, not because of its own failure, but because of the people's failure, because of Israel's hardness of heart.[25]

In 3:7–18 Paul launched into an extensive exposition of Exodus 34:29–35, in which he compared Moses' ministry of the old covenant with his own ministry of the new. In the Exodus account Moses is shown to have reflected the radiant glory of God from his encounter on the mountain. He placed a veil over his face when approaching the people to protect them from the divine radiance, but he removed the veil when he entered the tabernacle in the presence of God. Paul used the Exodus story to argue three points.

First, he argued that if *glory* accompanied the old covenant, which brought death, how much more glorious must be the new covenant which brings life (vv. 7–11). Glory stands for God and especially for the revelation and knowledge of God. For Paul it is most fully revealed in the face of Christ (see 4:4–6).[26] Second, Paul applied the *veil* image to Israel, arguing that Israel had a veil over its face. Because of its hardness of heart it could not see God when the old covenant was read. Third, Paul built on the statement that when Moses turned to "the Lord" the veil was removed. In verse 16 Paul substituted the word *Spirit* for *Lord*. In this way he argued that when one turns to the *Spirit* the veil is removed.[27] Paul saw this as providing the Old Testament basis for the reality that in the new covenant one comes to a full experience of God. The veil is entirely removed. Through the Spirit believers are transformed into an ever-increasing reflection of the divine glory themselves.[28]

Having discussed the superiority of the new covenant which he administered, in 4:1–6 Paul returned to the subject of his personal ministry. Once again he emphasized that his apostleship depended on his fidelity to the gospel rather than upon any external criteria. His ministry was grounded in God's mercy (v. 1). He did not water down the gospel (v. 2). Christ was at the center of his preaching (vv. 5–6). In verses 3–4 Paul may have been responding to charges that his preaching was veiled. Did his opponents consider his preaching of the cross as his "veiled gospel"? It was indeed "foolish" from any human perspective and perhaps incomprehensible to the Corinthian intruders. Were they the ones blinded by the "god of this age" (that is, Satan)? Paul did not preach "this age." His preaching belonged to the "new creation." Verse 6 may be an allusion to Paul's conversion. It certainly is a reference to the "new creation" in Christ which Paul treated at greater length in 5:16–21.

Paul's Suffering as an Apostle (4:7–5:10)

Paul's ministry was paradoxical. By God's standards it was accompanied by glory. By human standards it was anything but glorious; it was marked by weakness and suffering. Paul highlighted that element in his ministry in 4:7–12. Verse 7 sets forth the basic concept: Paul bore about the treasure of the gospel in the fragile container of his human body. The ancients often hid treasures in earthen pots. Every now and then in the ancient Near East someone will uncover an ancient clay pot containing a horde of silver or even gold coins. Paul was all too aware of his human frailty. But God *used* him as a minister of the priceless gospel of Christ. Precisely because of his own weakness, Paul was aware that whatever was accomplished through him was not of his own doing but wholly due to God's grace (cp. 12:9–10).

In verses 8–9 Paul proceeded to list his trials as an apostle. It is not the only such list in the Corinthian correspondence. There are three others (1 Cor. 4:9–13; 2 Cor. 6:3–10; 11:23–29). Technically referred to as *peristasis* catalogs, they follow a form often found in ancient literature, particularly among the Stoics.[29] Stoics considered the ability to undergo many trials as a human virtue, a sign of detachment from the vicissitudes of life. Paul saw such tribulations as a sign of the cross that he preached.[30] Just as the sufferings of Christ led to resurrection and the promise of life for believers, so Paul saw his suffering as an apostle as an embodiment of the message of the cross, bringing life to those who responded.

Having dealt at length with the element of suffering and death in his ministry, Paul now turned in 4:13–5:10 to the other side of the picture: the assurance of resurrection and life. Quoting Psalm 116:10, which links faith with speaking, Paul showed how his faith in the resurrection lay behind his proclamation (vv. 13–15). This certainty was behind all the suffering which he was willing to endure in his ministry. His present difficulties were out of all proportion to the eternal glory that was yet to come (vv. 16–18). Here is where Paul differed most radically from the triumphalist theology of his Corinthian opponents. They reigned; Paul suffered. His theology of the cross taught him that the road to resurrection proceeds from the cross, that glory comes through suffering.

Paul was very sure of the resurrection hope, and he turned to it in 5:1–10. Of all Paul's discussions of the believer's resurrection, this one is surely the most debated. The main question concerns whether Paul's thoughts about the matter had advanced over his treatment in 1 Corinthians 15. Several things are clear. For one, he still thought in terms of a heavenly *body*. He used two metaphors for it, that of a building (v. 1), and that of a garment one puts on over the earthly body (vv. 2–3). He rejected altogether the idea of a naked soul (vv. 3–4).[31] He considered the Spirit to be our present guarantee that we will participate in the life to come (v. 5). He depicted two main alternatives for believers: we are either "at home in the body" or "at home with the Lord" (vv. 6–9). Finally, he reminded the Corinthians that we will all stand before Christ's judgment seat to give an account for what we have done in this life (v. 10). Perhaps Paul still had his eye on the Corinthians who denied the resurrection and felt that they had already arrived. Paul reminded them that not only will there be a future for us, but also there will be one in which we will be accountable for the present.

The question is whether Paul moved to a position that the believer goes to be with the Lord immediately upon death. Many interpreters see Paul making no advance in 2 Corinthians over his position in 1 Corinthians 15 and 1 Thessalonians 4. They see him still believing in a future bodily resurrection of the dead with some sort of intermediate state between.[32] Others feel that Paul's thought developed between 1 Corinthians 15 and 2 Corinthians 5, with Paul in the latter passage coming to the view that resurrection comes to the individual believer immediately upon death.[33] They see his near-death experience of 2 Corinthians 1:8–10 as leading him to this conclusion. Second Corinthians 4:14, however, seems to point to a *future* resurrection. The two views may not be as incompatible as we tend to make them. From the perspective of eternity, there is no past, present, or future—*no time* at all. Death *is* resurrection and entry into God's eternity.

PAUL'S MINISTRY OF RECONCILIATION (5:11–6:10)

Having discussed his commission as an apostle of the new covenant and the paradoxical nature of his ministry as one of suffering in the midst of hope, Paul now turned to the content of his ministry—the message of the reconciling love of Christ.

Paul spoke first of the motivation behind all his ministry, the love of Christ (5:11–13). His Corinthian opponents may have accused him of self-commendation (v. 12). He did not claim outwardly verifiable credentials like they did with their persuasive speech, their powerful deeds, and their letters of recommendation. Paul's cross-centered message of weakness and suffering may have seemed madness to them. But Paul was compelled by Christ's love (v. 14).

Verses 14–15 give a summary of Paul's gospel: Christ died for all people; "therefore all died." There is no limit to the efficacy of Christ's atonement. Potentially all have died to their sins and selves in Christ's sacrificial death. But each must appropriate Christ's work of salvation for himself or herself through personal commitment to Christ. Note that Paul described the new existence in Christ as "no longer living for oneself" (v. 15). One surrenders the old self-centered, sinful existence and embraces a new existence centered in Christ. This new being is the subject of verses 16–21.[34]

Verses 16–17 set forth two consequences of the new life in Christ. First, there is a new way of knowing (v. 16). Those in Christ no longer view anyone from the old human, worldly perspective. They neither think nor judge by human criteria like the Corinthian false apostles were doing as they compared their own accomplishments with Paul's and ruled him out. Those in Christ view others from the perspective of Christ's love, the self-denying love that led him to a cross. The second consequence is closely related. Those in Christ are a new creation (v. 17). This means that they will no longer live by the standards of the old creation. It means that they will look beyond the outward appearance of Paul's suffering and weakness to the treasure within. It means a new community reconciled to God and to one another.

In verses 18–21 the key word is *reconciliation*. It is a major Pauline concept used to express Christ's atoning work. It will be discussed at length in a subsequent chapter.[35] The basic idea of reconciliation is that of being brought into a relationship of mutual acceptance with God and with one another. In terms of our relationship with God, to be reconciled is to have the barrier of sin removed which separates us from a holy and righteous God. Christ removed that barrier through his death on the cross. This is probably how we are to understand verse 21. Christ removed the barrier of sin by being "made sin" in our place. On the cross, the entire load of human sin weighed on Christ's shoulders. He died in place of sinful humanity, bearing the full burden of sin in order that "we might become the righteousness of God." In Paul's usage, "righteousness" means acceptability to God, reconciliation to God. It is thus through the work of Christ on the cross that God has atoned for sinful humans, reconciling them to himself.

The main emphasis on reconciliation in 2 Corinthians 5 is that of Paul's ministry of reconciliation (v. 18). Those who have been reconciled to God in Christ become themselves ministers of God's reconciling love. Paul described this as being "ambassadors" for Christ (v. 20). An ambassador has a high rank, but the rank is totally derivative. The ambassador's message is that of the one who sent her or him. Christ's ambassadors bear his message of reconciling love. Paul may have been speaking from the heart in 2 Corinthians 5:16–21, as he had just experienced reconciliation himself with the Christians of Corinth.

Paul concluded his long discussion of his ministry by returning once again to its suffering nature (6:1–10). He was genuinely concerned about the Corinthians. If they followed the false gospel, the "other Jesus" of the "super-apostles," they would run the real danger of losing it all, of "receiving God's grace in vain" (v. 1). Paul called them to reaffirm their salvation (v. 2). He also called upon them to reaffirm his own ministry as he provided another long list of his apostolic hardships (vv. 3–10). This list is particularly neatly arranged, consisting of three categories of apostolic experience with nine items in each category. The first category lists external trials—beatings, imprisonments, and the like (vv. 4b–5). The second list provides positive traits which Paul needed in order to conduct his ministry—patience, purity, love, etc. (vv. 6–7). The final list consists of nine pairs of antithetical ways of viewing Paul's ministry (vv. 8–10). The contrast is that of the old human way of viewing things and the way of the new creation in Christ (5:16–17). By human standards, Paul's ministry merited neither honor nor fame, appeared deceptive, was that of a nobody, exhibited weakness and mortality, and seemed to be an unwarranted acceptance of constant punishment, grief, and poverty. By human standards it had little to commend it. For those who were able to see beyond the earthen jar to the treasure within, things appeared altogether different. The sorrow and sufferings of Paul's ministry pointed to God's grace and enhanced the treasure he bore.

PAUL'S APPEAL TO THE CONGREGATION (6:11–7:16)

Paul had completed his defense of his apostleship. Now he returned to his personal relationship with the Corinthians. He appealed to them to renew their hearts to him (6:11–13). As we have seen, Paul's appeal is interrupted by an abrupt shift in subject matter in 6:14–7:1, which focuses on the question of Christians consorting with unbelievers. The subject is hardly foreign to the Corinthian situation. Paul had already discussed the question of purity in 1 Corinthians 5 in the context of the incestuous man. He had advised the Corinthians *not* to resort to unbelieving judges in the law courts (1 Cor. 6:1–11). He told them to shun the pagan idol worship altogether (1 Cor. 10:14). The tone is even stricter in 2 Corinthians 6:14–7:1. Perhaps Paul felt the Corinthians were still accommodating too much to their pagan environment and needed even stronger medicine.

Paul renewed his appeal to the Corinthians in 7:2–4 and at 7:5 picked up on his personal history. He had broken this off at 2:13 when he introduced the long digression on his apostleship. Only with the arrival of Titus in Macedonia did Paul finally find peace. He returned to the language of comfort with which he had begun the epistle. Titus brought word that the Corinthians were truly sorry for what had happened to Paul and had renewed their concern for him. Paul was comforted; he was overjoyed (7:5–7).

Paul discussed the "sorrowful letter" at length in 7:8–12. He evidently had second thoughts for a moment after sending the letter. Now that he had seen how it had the desired effect, he was glad he had sent it. It had moved the Corinthians to "godly sorrow," to repentance, and to discipline of the wrongdoer. Paul spoke of the "injured party" in verse 12. It was probably himself. But Paul's relief was not so much over his own vindication as it was in the Corinthians' renewed zeal for his ministry. They had failed to support him when he was under attack on the occasion of the painful visit. Now they had done so and had proved their genuine innocence in the whole matter (v. 11).

Paul concluded the section by a reference to how Titus had been well received by the Corinthians (7:13–16). He had served as Paul's representative, and they had evidently received him with the dignity due the apostle himself. The note about Titus was not incidental. Paul was preparing them to receive Titus once again and to respect his mission. This time it was in connection with the collection for the Jerusalem saints.

THE COLLECTION (8:1–9:15)

At the end of his third mission Paul was preoccupied with a collection for the Jerusalem Christians. He dealt with the collection in every epistle written during this period—Galatians, 1 Corinthians, 2 Corinthians, and Romans. By far the most extensive treatment of the subject is that of 2 Corinthians. Paul seems to have encountered the most resistance to the collection from the Corinthians. The collection as a whole will be considered at length in chapter 15. At this point we will consider Paul's treatment only in broad outline.

Paul began by challenging the Corinthians with the example of the Macedonians, who had given sacrificially (8:1–7). He then held up the ultimate example of self-giving—Jesus, who became poor that we might be rich (8:8–9; cp. Phil. 2:6–11). He stated that the basis for Christians giving to one another should be equality, an example set with the equal portion of manna allotted to each Israelite in the wilderness (8:14–15). Paul then turned to details of the administration of the collection in Corinth by Titus and two other brothers (8:16–24). We will return to this passage later.

In 9:1–5 Paul returned to the example of giving among the Macedonians. This time he reversed his appeal, saying that he had boasted to the Macedonians about the Corinthian eagerness to give and didn't want them to let him down. The remainder of chapter 9 is devoted to a theology of giving. Paul began with an agricultural analogy drawn from Proverbs 22:8–9: whoever sows bountifully will reap bountifully (vv. 6–8). Such a person is a generous and cheerful giver. Again appealing to the Old Testament (Ps. 112:9), Paul pointed out that God is himself an example of generous giving (v. 9). In verse 10 Paul spoke of giving as a "harvest of your righteousness." In Pauline language, *righteousness* usually refers to being made right with God through Christ. In that sense, generous giving can be seen as a demonstration of one's right standing with God. Giving is also a means of expressing our thanksgiving to God (vv. 11–12), who has granted us the "indescribable gift" of salvation through Jesus Christ (v. 15). Finally, generous giving brings glory to God (vv. 13–14). It does so in three ways. First it confirms our confession in the gospel (v. 13a). Second, it demonstrates the integrity of the fellowship, the unity of God's people (v. 13b). Finally, it brings a response of prayerful gratitude from the recipients which redounds to the praise of God for his grace bestowed on the givers (v. 14).

A FINAL DEFENSE AGAINST PAUL'S OPPONENTS (10:1–12:13)

No one can deny the abrupt shift in tone at the beginning of chapter 10. Anger, warning, and sarcasm pervade the concluding four chapters of 2 Corinthians. We have seen how many argue that these chapters are a portion of the sorrowful letter written *before* chapters 1–9 or of a letter written *subsequent to* chapters 1–9. We would argue for the unity of the epistle. Whichever view one takes, it must be granted that these chapters are directed primarily against the intruders in Corinth and their claim to an apostolate rivaling that of Paul.

A new warning (chap. 10). In chapter 10 Paul focused on the charges of the Corinthian intruders against himself. They charged him with being "timid," with coming up short in his personal appearance (v. 2). They granted that his letters were weighty but saw his personal presence as weak and his speaking as "nothing" (v. 10). Paul, on the other hand, considered them to be judging by human standards, not by those of Christ. They compared themselves with one another (v. 12), not with Christ. Paul warned the Corinthians against being taken in by the worldly standards of the intruders. Paul could and would wage war against them, but not with worldly weapons (vv. 3–6). He would fight with the weapons of Christ which totally subvert all the standards of the world.[36] Paul's weapons were those of strength in weakness, of power manifest in the meekness and gentleness of Christ (v. 1). This had been Paul's argument with the Corinthians from the very first chapter of 1 Corinthians on. The word of the cross is God's "no" to all human estimations of wisdom and power. It is the divine word of power made strong in weakness, the kind of power that had been constantly manifested through the seeming weakness of Paul's apostolic ministry.

In 10:13–16 Paul spoke of how the intruders boasted "beyond limits." He probably meant that with special reference to their having "poached" on his field of ministry. Paul was the Corinthian apostle. He had taken the gospel to Corinth and was the spiritual leader of the church. Paul seemed to have viewed an apostle as one who took the gospel to a place where it had never been previously proclaimed (cp. Rom. 15:20). In that sense Paul was the Corinthians' apostle. Paul implied that he wanted the support of the Corinthians as he expanded his mission into new fields (vv. 15–16). He could not fathom why the Corinthians would allow these intruders to challenge his rightful leadership over them.

In chapter 10 Paul spoke a great deal about boasting. Throughout 2 Corinthians he spoke with seeming ambivalence about his boasting, sometimes commending himself (cp. 4:2; 6:4), sometimes denying self-commendation (3:1; 5:12). The key to this ambiguity is found in 10:12–18. Paul denied the sort of foolish human commendation that the intruders engaged in (v. 12). For Paul there was only one true basis for commendation for a Christian and that is the commendation of the Lord (v. 18). Paul's boasting was in God alone (v. 17; cp. Jer. 9:24).[37]

Paul and the "super-apostles" (11:1–21). In 11:1–6 Paul directed himself against the "super-apostles." Verse 4 implies that they were outsiders. They preached a perverted message—another Jesus, another gospel, another spirit. The Corinthians were coming close to adultery, for Paul had betrothed them to Christ in true and sincere devotion. Some have argued that the "super-apostles" of verse 5 are to be seen as the Jerusalem apostles, whom the Corinthian intruders were pitting against Paul. It is more likely that the intruders themselves were claiming apostolic status (cp. 11:13).

One of the prime charges against Paul was that he refused to take support from the Corinthians. Paul addressed that accusation in 11:7–12. It is clear from 1 Corinthians 9 that Paul voluntarily waived his right to support from the Corinthians in order to put no obstacle in the way of the gospel. This practice was now being used against him. He had allowed the Macedonians to send him a gift but refused support from the Corinthians. They argued that this showed he did not love them (v. 11). Much like the Cynic philosophers, the intruders may have argued that true apostles deserve their upkeep and that failure to accept support is an acknowledgement of one's unworthiness. Paul probably wanted to distance himself from any such association with the popular sophists.[38] Paul may also have been rejecting the patronage system of his day. Wealthy members of the congregation may have offered to support his ministry. His refusal to accept their patronage would have been a social insult. It also would have created a social indebtedness which Paul wanted to avoid so as not to compromise the gospel. In any event, Paul turned the support charge back on the super-apostles, accusing them of being mere "peddlers of the word" (2 Cor. 2:17).

272

Paul's most direct attack on the intruders is found in 11:12–15. He accused them of being false apostles, of masquerading as Christ's apostles. He likened them to Satan. He had already alluded to Satan in 11:3, where he expressed his fear that the Corinthians were being seduced like Eve. Now he directly accused them of being Satan's servants (v. 15).[39] Clearly for Paul it was not a matter of an alternative gospel but of a subversion of the very essence of the gospel itself, the substitution of a human system for the word of the cross.

In 11:1 Paul had ironically asked that the Corinthians allow him to play the fool for a moment. Now he returned to the theme of foolishness (11:16–21). The Corinthian intruders were following the wisdom of the world, a wisdom which is foolishness by God's standards. Since this sort of worldly boasting seemed to carry some conviction with the Corinthians, Paul begged permission to engage in a little of it himself. Evidently the Corinthian intruders were authoritarian, and the Corinthians had allowed them to exploit and insult them. Since the Corinthians were used to abuse, Paul felt it would not be too much to subject them to his own foolish boasting. Paul's words literally dripped with irony.[40]

Paul's boasting covered three main areas (11:22–12:13). First he boasted of his Jewishness (11:22). Obviously the super-apostles appealed to their Jewish roots. They had no edge on Paul in that regard: he was a Hebrew, an Israelite, a descendant of Abraham. Second, Paul turned to his accomplishments as an apostle (11:23–33). His Corinthian opponents would have pointed to their rhetorical skills, their miraculous deeds, their impressive letters of recommendation, their moments of triumph and acclaim. Paul instead spoke of his sufferings as an apostle. We have already seen him refer to his sufferings as a sign of his apostleship (4:7–12; 6:3–10). Paul was being far more than ironic as he compared himself to the super-apostles. His trials and human weakness were the very hallmark of his apostleship, the sign of God's divine power at work in him. Whatever he accomplished as an apostle, it was not of his own doing but solely due to God's grace at work in him.

Anyone who follows the list of Paul's travails in 11:23–33 is aware of how selective the Acts account is in depicting Paul's missionary experience. Most of the events recounted in these verses are not covered in Acts. For example, Paul spoke of many imprisonments. To this point in his ministry Acts mentions only one (Philippi). Paul was beaten with Roman rods at Philippi according to Acts; in 2 Corinthians Paul mentioned three such occasions. Acts relates none of the five synagogue floggings, nor any of the three shipwrecks during this period of Paul's ministry, nor the time adrift at sea. Paul was opposed by Jews, Gentiles, and false brothers (v. 26). The latter, like the intruders at Corinth, must have been the hardest for him to take. At the top of Paul's list was the daily pressure of concern for his scattered congregations, like Corinth itself (vv. 28–29). The incident in Damascus was the last item on Paul's list of apostolic calamities (vv. 30–33). Perhaps Paul saw it as illustrating the almost comic nature of his ministry from any human perspective. He had become a "spectacle to the whole universe" (1 Cor. 4:9).

Paul's third category of boasting was of his visionary experience some fourteen years previously (12:1–10). We have already discussed this at length in an earlier chapter.[41] Here we will only note how Paul used the incident in his polemic against the Corinthian super-apostles. Paul's opponents probably considered visionary experiences as essential, seeing them as signs of one's apostleship. Paul's vision was remarkable. He seems to have been caught up into the very presence of God. But

Paul considered it a very private experience and was somewhat embarrassed to speak of it. He referred to himself obliquely in the third person.

God had brought Paul down from the third heaven, however, by giving him the "thorn in the flesh."[42] Whether we see this as a persistent temptation, Paul's opponents, or as a chronic physical ailment, the function of the "thorn" would be the same. It was a reminder to Paul of his own inadequacy and weakness and his dependence upon God. The theme of power in weakness has run throughout 2 Corinthians. It actually begins in 1 Corinthians 1:18–2:5, where Paul spoke of the wisdom and power of the cross. The theme lies behind the picture of treasure in clay jars in 2 Corinthians 4:7–12 and Paul's catalogs of trials in 2 Corinthians 6:3–10 and 11:23–33. It reaches its climax in 2 Corinthians 12:7–10. Weakness was the *mark* of Paul's apostleship.[43] Through his own human frailty Paul could see the power of God's grace at work in his ministry, almost in spite of himself. It was a constant reminder of the cross, how out of weakness and death God brings resurrection and life. This is the theme that binds all of 2 Corinthians together. In response to the triumphalism of the super-apostles, Paul brought the word of the cross.

Paul concluded his "foolish boasting" by speaking directly to the Corinthians (12:11–13). He couldn't understand the attraction of the super-apostles for them. All the signs and wonders they could hope for were present during Paul's initial ministry with them—only not through Paul's accomplishment, rather through the Spirit at work among them (cp. 1 Cor. 2:4–5). The only thing Paul lacked was receiving support from them. With a final note of irony, he asked them to forgive him that injustice (v. 13).

PAUL'S PLANS FOR A THIRD VISIT (12:14–13:10)

Evidently some had accused Paul of deceit. They maintained that his refusal to take support was a cloak to cover up his greed in gathering the Jerusalem collection. They accused Titus and his companions of tricking them while administering the collection (12:14–18). Paul responded by assuring the Corinthians of his honest intentions in these matters and warning them that unless they straightened up *he* might be the one to bring charges as he came to them for a third visit (12:19–21). Throughout both letters Paul had expressed concern over the moral purity of the congregation. In both letters he had to deal with the factionalism and disunity within the congregation. He warned them to get right on both counts, or they might not find his forthcoming visit a pleasant one.

In 13:1–10 Paul continued to exhort the Corinthians in light of his forthcoming third visit. He did not want to experience again the kind of personal conflict that had marked the previous "painful" visit. He returned to the theme of weakness and power. He reminded them that the seeming weakness of the cross led to the power of the resurrection (vv. 3–4). This time he emphasized Christ's power to judge as he warned the Corinthians of their need to repent. A final time he returned to the theme as he expressed his hope that his own weakness as an apostle might lead to their strength in the faith (v. 9). This was Paul's greatest desire—the spiritual health of the church, even if he himself should seem in the end to have failed (v. 7).

Paul had laid it on the line with the Corinthians. He could easily have written them off. He had other, more loving congregations like Philippi. He could have rested content with them. Paul was, however, a minister of reconciliation, an ambassador for Christ. He never gave up on his difficult Corinthians. Surely his vision of the cross, of divine power perfected in human weakness, gave him the courage to persist through it all.

NOTES

1. L. Belleville classifies 2 Corinthians 1–7 as a "letter of apologetic self-commendation": "A Letter of Apologetic Self-Commendation: 2 Cor. 1:8–7:16," *Novum Testamentum* 3 (1989): 142–163.

2. For an alternative reconstruction to that given here, see J. M. Gilchrist, "Paul and the Corinthians—the Sequence of Letters and Visits," *Journal for the Study of the New Testament* 34 (1988): 47–69.

3. J. Murphy-O'Connor argues that at this point Paul traveled to Illyricum and established a mission there (cp. Rom. 15:19): *Paul, a Critical Life* (Oxford: Clarendon, 1996), 316–319.

4. Representative of this view is D. Georgi, *The Opponents of Paul in 2 Corinthians* (Philadelphia: Fortress, 1986; German original, 1964), 14–18.

5. See the discussion in chapter 12, pp. 231–232.

6. See J. Gnilka, "2 Cor 6:14–7:1 in the Light of the Qumran Texts and the Testaments of the Twelve Patriarchs," in *Paul and the Dead Sea Scrolls*, ed. Murphy-O'Connor and Charlesworth (New York: Crossroad, 1990), 48–68; J. A. Fitzmyer, "Qumran and the Interpolated Fragment in 2 Cor 6:14–7:1," *Catholic Biblical Quarterly* 23 (1961): 271–280.

7. M. L. Soards, *The Apostle Paul, An Introduction to His Writings and Teachings* (New York: Paulist, 1987), 89.

8. W. Schmithals, *Gnosticism in Corinth*, trans. J. Steely (Nashville: Abingdon, 1971), 96–101. For chapter 8 being inseparable from chapter 7, see N. A. Dahl, *Studies in Paul* (Minneapolis: Augsburg, 1977), 38–39.

9. A. Hausrath, *Der Vier-Capitel Brief des Paulus an de Corinther* (Heidelberg, 1870).

10. For example, D. Smith, *The Life and Letters of St. Paul* (New York: George H. Doran, n.d.), 327–341.

11. F. Watson, "2 Cor. x–xiii and Paul's Painful Letter to the Corinthians," *Journal of Theological Studies* 35 (1984): 324–346.

12. E.g., C. G. Kruse, *Paul, the Law, and Justification* (Peabody, Mass.: Hendrickson, 1997), 150–151.

13. A major argument for seeing 10–13 as subsequent to and separate from 1–9 is that 12:16ff. seems to *refer back* to the sending of Titus and the brothers, which is *yet to occur* in chapter 8: C. K. Barrett, "Titus," *Essays on Paul* (Philadelphia: Westminster, 1982), 116–131.

14. E.g., A. T. Robertson, *Epochs in the Life of Paul* (New York: Scribners, 1909), 199–200.

15. C. K. Barrett, *Paul, an Introduction to His Thought* (Louisville: Westminster John Knox, 1994), 33–38.

16. C. K. Barrett, "ΥΕΥΔΑΠΟΣΤΟΛΟΙ (2 Cor.11:13)" in *Essays on Paul*, 87–107. See also in the same volume "Paul's Opponents in 2 Corinthians" (pp. 60–86) and "Cephas and Corinth" (pp. 28–39). For a similar view, see M. E. Thrall, "Super-Apostles, Servants of Christ, and Servants of Satan," *Journal for the Study of the New Testament* 6 (1980): 42–57.

17. For example, P. W. Barnett argues that they were *charismatic* Jewish Christians from Palestine: "Opposition in Corinth," *Journal for the Study of the New Testament* 22 (1984): 3–17.

18. Schmithals, *Gnosticism in Corinth*.

19. Georgi, *The Opponents of Paul in 2 Corinthians*. See also J. H. Schütz, *Paul and the Anatomy of Apostolic Authority* (Cambridge: Cambridge University Press, 1975), 165–186.

20. He based this on Paul's application of the term to them in 2 Corinthians 11:15 and 11:23. G. Friedrich also saw them using the *diakonoi* designation and argued that they were the

same as the hellenist *diakonoi* of Acts 6:1ff.: "Die Gegner des Paulus im 2. Korinther-brief," in *Abraham Unser Vater*, ed. O. Betz et al. (Leiden: Brill, 1963), 181–215.

21. Käsemann argued that they *did* have Jerusalem connections. Sumney thinks not. See J. L. Sumney, *Identifying Paul's Opponents: The Question of Method in 2 Corinthians* (Sheffield, England: JSOT Press, 1990), 181–186.

22. W. L. Lane depicts Paul as following the pattern of a *rib*, a lawsuit of God against the Corinthians: "Covenant: The Key to Paul's Conflict with Corinth," *Tyndale Bulletin 33* (1982): 3–29.

23. S. J. Hafemann, *Suffering and Ministry in the Spirit: Paul's Defense of His Ministry in II Corinthians 2:14–3:3* (Grand Rapids: Eerdmans, 1990), 35–49.

24. T. W. Manson pointed out that the rabbis saw the Torah as having a similar dual func-tion of leading either to life or death: "2 Cor. 2:14–17: Suggestions Toward an Exegesis," *Studia Paulina*, ed. Sevenster and Van Unnik (Haarlem, Netherlands: De Erven F. Bohn, 1953), 155–162.

25. For a full treatment of 2 Corinthians 3:4–18, see S. J. Hafemann, *Paul, Moses and the His-tory of Israel: The Letter/Spirit Contrast and the Argument from Scripture in 2 Corinthians 3* (Peabody, Mass.: Hendrickson, 1996).

26. J. A. Fitzmyer, "Glory Reflected on the Face of Christ (2 Cor 3:7–4:6) and a Palestinian Jewish Motif," *Theological Studies 42* (1981): 630–644.

27. J. D. G. Dunn, "2 Corinthians III.17—'The Lord Is the Spirit,'" *Journal of Theological Studies 21* (1970): 309–320.

28. N. T. Wright points out that it is in the face of fellow Christians that we see the reflec-tion of the divine glory: *The Climax of the Covenant: Christ and the Law in Pauline Theology* (Minneapolis: Fortress, 1992), 175–192.

29. J. T. Fitzgerald, *Cracks in an Earthen Vessel: An Examination of the Catalogues of Hardships in the Corinthian Correspondence*, SBL Dissertation Series, 99 (Atlanta: Scholars, 1988).

30. N. Willert, "The Catalogues of Hardships in the Pauline Correspondence: Background and Function," in *The New Testament and Hellenistic Judaism*, ed. Borgen and Giversen (Peabody, Mass.: Hendrickson, 1997), 217–243.

31. J. N. Sevenster, "Some Remarks on the GUMNOS in II Cor. v. 3," in *Studia Paulina*, 202–214.

32. P. Barnett, *The Message of 2 Corinthians: Power in Weakness*, The Bible Speaks Today (Downers Grove, Ill.: InterVarsity, 1988), 96–102.

33. M. J. Harris, "2 Corinthians 5:1–10: Watershed in Paul's Eschatology?" *Tyndale Bulletin 22* (1971): 32–57. See also G. M. M. Pelser, "Resurrection and Eschatology in Paul's Let-ters," *Neotestamentica 20* (1986): 37–46.

34. For a full exegesis of 2 Corinthians 5:14–21, see W. H. Gloer, *An Exegetical and Theolog-ical Study of Paul's Understanding of New Creation and Reconciliation in 2 Cor. 5:14–21* (Lewiston, N.Y.: Mellen Biblical Press, 1996).

35. See chapter 18, pp. 366–367.

36. A. J. Dewey, "A Matter of Honor: A Social-Historical Analysis of 2 Corinthians 10," *Harvard Theological Review 78* (1985): 209–217. For the use of "stronghold" imagery among the Stoics, see A. J. Malherbe, *Paul and the Popular Philosophers* (Minneapolis: For-tress, 1989), 91–119.

37. S. Hafemann, "'Self-Commendation' and Apostolic Legitimacy in 2 Corinthians: A Pauline Dialectic?" *New Testament Studies 36* (1990): 66–88.

38. H. D. Betz argues that Paul followed the Socratic tradition in dissociating himself from the ways of the popular sophists: *Der Apostel Paulus und die sokratische Tradition* (Tübin-gen: Mohr/Siebeck, 1972). G. Theissen argues that the Corinthian intruders followed the charismatic tradition of Jesus and his disciples, who were itinerant and dependent on others for support: *The Social Setting of Pauline Christianity*, ed. and trans. J. H. Schütz (Philadelphia: Fortress, 1982), 44–46.

39. J. Neyrey maintained that Paul was not just name-calling but actually accusing the intruders of witchcraft: *Paul in Other Words: A Cultural Reading of His Letters* (Louisville: Westminster John Knox, 1990), 207–217.

40. A. B. Spencer, *Paul's Literary Style: A Stylistic and Historical Comparison of II Corinthians 11:16–12:13, Romans 8:9–39, and Philippians 3:2–4:13* (Jackson, Miss.: Evangelical Theological Society, 1984), 204–205. See Also C. Forbes, "Comparison, Self-Praise and Irony: Paul's Boasting and the Conventions of Hellenistic Rhetoric," *New Testament Studies* 32 (1986): 1–30.

41. Chapter 4, pp. 67–69.

42. This is discussed in chapter 2, pp. 40–41.

43. D. A. Black, *Paul, Apostle of Weakness: Astheneia and its Cognates in the Pauline Literature* (New York: Peter Lang, 1984), pp. 129–172. See also G. G. O'Collins, "Power Made Perfect in Weakness: 2 Cor 12:9–10," *Catholic Biblical Quarterly* 33 (1971): 528–537.

SELECTED COMMENTARIES

BASED ON THE GREEK TEXT

Bultmann, Rudolf. *The Second Letter to the Corinthians*. Trans. Roy A. Harrisville. Minneapolis: Augsburg, 1985.

Martin, Ralph P. *2 Corinthians*. Word Biblical Commentary. Waco, Tex.: Word, 1986.

Plummer, Alfred. *A Critical and Exegetical Commentary on the Second Epistle of St. Paul to the Corinthians*. International Critical Commentary. New York: Scribner's, 1915.

Thrall, Margaret E. *A Critical and Exegetical Commentary on the Second Epistle to the Corinthians. Vol. 1: Introduction and Commentary on II Corinthians 1–7*. International Critical Commentary, New Series. Edinburgh: T. and T. Clark, 1994.

BASED ON THE ENGLISH TEXT

Barnett, Paul. *The Second Epistle to the Corinthians*. New International Commentary on the New Testament. Grand Rapids: Eerdmans, 1997. See also his more popular treatment, *The Message of 2 Corinthians*. Downers, Grove, Ill.: InterVarsity, 1988.

Barrett, C. K. *A Commentary on the Second Epistle to the Corinthians*. Harper's New Testament Commentaries. New York: Harper and Row, 1973.

Belleville, L. L. *2 Corinthians*. IVP New Testament Commentary. Downers Grove, Ill.: InterVarsity, 1996.

Best, Ernest. *Second Corinthians*. Interpretation. Atlanta: John Knox, 1987.

Danker, Frederick W. *II Corinthians*. Augsburg Commentary on the New Testament. Minneapolis: Augsburg, 1989.

Furnish, Victor Paul. *II Corinthians*. The Anchor Bible. Garden City, N.Y.: Doubleday, 1984.

Héring, Jean. *The Second Epistle of Saint Paul to the Corinthians*. Trans. A. W. Heathcote and P. J. Allcock. London: Epworth, 1967.

Kreitzer, Larry J. *2 Corinthians*. New Testament Guides. Sheffield, England: Sheffield Academic Press, 1996.

Scott, James M. *2 Corinthians*. The New International Bible Commentary. Peabody, Mass.: Hendrickson, 1998.

Strachan, R. H. *Second Corinthians*. Moffatt Commentary. New York: Harper, 1935.

Tasker, R. V. G. *The Second Epistle of Paul to the Corinthians*. Tyndale New Testament Commentaries. Grand Rapids: Eerdmans, 1958.

Watson, N. *The Second Epistle to the Corinthians*. Epworth Commentaries. London: Epworth, 1993.

14

～❦～

ROMANS: THE JEW FIRST
AND ALSO THE GREEK

*P*aul was nearing the end of his third mission. He had completed with the Macedonians most of his arrangements for his Jerusalem collection. He had evidently worked out his problems with the Corinthians sufficiently that he now felt free to go there. It was probably the winter of 56–57 when he spent three months in Corinth (Acts 20:2–3). He was preoccupied with the collection for Jerusalem, but he took time during this period to dictate a lengthy letter to the Christians of Rome. His secretary was Tertius, who may have been a servant of Gaius, the Corinthian with whom Paul was staying (Rom. 16:22–23).

Paul planned to visit Rome, and the letter was designed to prepare his way. He addressed the Christians there with considerable diplomacy. It was not a church which he had established, and he could not presume upon their acceptance. Paul's letter was lengthy. It dealt with many diverse matters: God's means of salvation, the nature of the Christian life, the place of Jews and Gentiles in salvation history. As one would expect for a community which Paul had never visited, his comments often appear to be quite general. As a result, the letter has often been viewed as a "compendium of Christian doctrine," as Melanchthon described it. Yet Romans is scarcely Paul's systematic theology. Much is missing in Romans. One has to turn to other epistles for Paul's views on major doctrines like eschatology and Christology. Still, Paul dealt at length with central themes of his gospel and in a more detached and nonpolemical fashion than was often the case with his other epistles. One must ask, Why this particular letter to this particular Christian community? Such questions of occasion and purpose dominate the current scholarly discussion of Romans. Closely related is the consideration of the composition of the Roman church. A final cluster of issues is more literary in nature, involving the integrity of the epistle and its genre. In the following discussion we will consider these matters first before turning to a treatment of the actual text of Romans, which comprises the bulk of the chapter.

INTRODUCTION TO ROMANS

THE CHURCH OF ROME

No one seriously questions Paul's having written Romans. There is also a scholarly consensus that the bulk of the epistle was addressed to the Christians of Rome. But this raises the question as to how Christianity reached the capital city of the empire. Neither Acts nor Paul's epistles gives direct answers to that query.

Christianity in Rome. There is no doubt that Christianity reached Rome prior to Paul's arrival there. The Roman epistle itself testifies to a Christian community existing there around A.D. 57. The Book of Acts speaks of Roman Christians coming forth to greet Paul upon his arrival in their region some three years later (Acts 28:15). Less direct evidence is provided by Suetonius's reference to the expulsion of the Jews from Rome under Claudius (*Life of Claudius* 25.4). Suetonius said that the expulsion was provoked by Jewish riots that were instigated by "Chrestus." "Chrestus" is most likely a reference to Christ (Lat. "Christus"). The situation was probably provoked by the Christian gospel having arrived in the synagogues of the city.

But *how* did the gospel reach Rome? Roman Catholic tradition claims that Peter founded the Roman church. That Peter later ministered in Rome is likely. He seems to have been in Rome when he wrote 1 Peter (1 Pet. 5:13). The tradition that he was martyred in Rome under Nero is also probable.[1] He does not, however, seem to have preceded Paul to Rome. Paul had a personal policy not to infringe upon a mission territory established by another apostle (2 Cor. 10:15–16). In Romans, he implied that he was *not* violating this principle (Rom. 15:20). Roman Christianity thus does not seem to have owed its origin to an apostle. It is more likely that Christian laity were the first to witness in the city. It may have been pilgrims returning from Pentecost (Acts 2:10), or military personnel like Cornelius (Acts 10:1), or business people like Priscilla and Aquila. The latter couple probably did not take the gospel *to* Rome. They seem to have taken it *from* Rome to Corinth (Acts 18:2–3) and later to Ephesus (Acts 18:26). They are prime examples of how early Christian laity shared the gospel wherever they went, and this is likely how Christianity first reached the capital city.

Composition of the Roman church. Was the church at Rome composed primarily of Gentiles or of Jews, or was it a mixture of both? In answering this question, one should first observe that Paul never referred to "the church" of Rome. Instead, he addressed the letter to "all in Rome who are loved by God and called to be saints" (Rom. 1:7). Likely, there were a number of house-churches in Rome, not a single congregation, and the individual communities may have varied in ethnic composition. Paul wrote a general letter addressed to them all.

Some statements within Romans seem to have been addressed primarily to Gentiles. For example, Paul spoke of his witness among Gentiles in 1:5 and in 1:13 seems to have included his addressees in that group. In the eleventh chapter he clearly rebuked Gentiles for any superiority they may have felt over the Jews with respect to their election in Christ (11:13, 28, 31).[2]

On the other hand, Romans is preoccupied with *Jewish* issues, such as the role of the Torah and the place of the Jews in salvation history. The attention to such matters would be almost incomprehensible in a letter written primarily to Gentiles. Also, Paul greeted several Jews in the sixteenth chapter—Priscilla and Aquila (16:3), Andronicus and Junia (16:7), and Herodion (16:11). The most likely conclusion is that there were Jews among the Christians of Rome.³ There was an extensive Jewish community in Rome in the mid-first century, numbering as many as fifty thousand persons.⁴ Suetonius's reference to Claudius's expulsion of the Jews seems to link the Christians with that Jewish community.

The Roman Christian community thus seems to have been of mixed composition. They may have been segregated into separate house-churches. Some tension between the two groups may be indicated by Paul's treatment of the "weak" and the "strong" in Romans 14:1–15:13. Many contemporary interpreters would see the Jew/Gentile disunity as Paul's *main* concern in the letter.

PAUL'S PURPOSES IN WRITING

Paul's stated reasons. Why did Paul write the Roman epistle? He provided explicit reasons at the beginning and end of the letter. In 1:8–15 he explained that he had for a long time wished to come to Rome but had been prevented. He had wanted to share a "spiritual gift" with them (vv. 11–12). Note how carefully Paul phrased himself, emphasizing *mutual* encouragement. Rome was *not* "his" church, and he did not wish to appear presumptuous. Verse 13 is more direct: Paul wanted to have some "harvest" among the Romans, as he had experienced among the "other" Gentiles. Paul was not just coming for a visit. He wished to "preach the gospel" in Rome (v. 15). Rome evidently had no apostle. Was Paul implicitly volunteering to assume that role?

Toward the conclusion of the epistle Paul was more explicit about both his purposes for visiting the Roman Christians and his immediate plans (15:14–19). In a lengthy defense of his ministry, Paul explained that it was the concern for the Gentile mission that had prevented him from coming to Rome earlier (15:14–22). He was still quite diplomatic, explaining why he had been so bold as to address the Romans so forthrightly in the letter (15:14–16). He was aware that Rome was not his turf (15:20). But now he had completed his mission in the east—all the way from Jerusalem to Illyricum (the Adriatic Coast). He wanted to begin a new mission where the gospel had never yet been taken—Spain. He wanted Rome's support in that venture (15:24). He may well have wanted Rome to serve as his "mother church" for the mission in the west, just as Antioch had supported him in his eastern mission. He explained why he was *still* delaying his visit to them. He needed first to go to Jerusalem in person with his collection for the saints. Only after completing that ministry would he venture on to Rome and his Spanish mission (15:25–29). Paul added one further purpose in writing the Romans. He knew that the Jerusalem undertaking was fraught with danger, so he solicited the prayers of the Romans for his safe completion of that ministry (15:30–33).

Paul desired to share his gospel in Rome. He wanted Roman support for his proposed Spanish mission. These were his expressed purposes for writing the letter. That much is clear. But why the lengthy exposition of 1:16–15:13? Why the particular issues taken up in those chapters? Scholars are divided over that question. Some feel that Paul addressed mainly concerns which were currently preoccupying him in his personal circumstances. Others feel that he was primarily addressing the situation of the Christians in Rome.

Paul's personal circumstances. Those who emphasize Paul's own situation feel that he probably had little personal knowledge about circumstances in the Roman church. So he shared his gospel with the Romans, but primarily in terms of matters which were currently concerning him. They see Paul as focusing on his anticipated journey *to Jerusalem* and the defense he knew he would have to give there. Some see him as preparing a defense of his entire missionary enterprise, a sort of "last will and testament."[5] Others see Paul as soliciting Roman support for his collection; Romans is a draft of his forthcoming Jerusalem speech in defense of that undertaking.[6] Another variation views Paul as preparing a defense in Jerusalem against those who are accusing him of antinomianism.[7] Common to all these is that they view Paul as being more focused on his forthcoming trip to Jerusalem than on the Roman community.

The situation in the Roman church. F. C. Baur was one of the first to argue that Romans should be seen not as a theological treatise but as an occasional letter addressing specific problems in the Roman church. Consistent with his understanding of first-century Christianity, he saw Paul as combating a Torah-centered Jewish Christianity in Rome.[8] Few today would follow Baur's Judaizing view, but many argue that Romans *as a whole* is addressed to problems within the church. Most see these as related to tensions between the Jewish and Gentile segments of the church. Each group was "boasting" of its superior position over the other.[9] Some would go so far as to see the church divided into five or more distinct congregations, each with its own particular viewpoint and with Paul addressing these separately in various parts of his letter.[10] One reconstruction of the Roman conflict builds on Claudius's expulsion of the Jews in A.D. 49. This view argues that when the edict was rescinded upon Claudius's death five years later, returning Jewish Christians found that the Gentile Christian community had flourished in their absence and now held a dominant position. Paul was concerned to counter the resulting Gentile feelings of superiority.[11]

A combination of purposes. Many would see Paul as writing both out of his own personal concerns and to address problems within the Roman congregation. They maintain that Paul was primarily concerned with his own proposed mission to Spain, but he needed the support of a *unified* Roman church. Paul would likely have been aware of the affairs of the Roman church. Rome was not that remote from Corinth; a courier could travel between the two cities in the space of a week.[12] Paul was also concerned about his forthcoming Jerusalem visit, and he earnestly sought the prayers of the Roman Christians in that regard. One could thus summarize the purposes of Romans around the three destinations on which Paul had his eye: the defense he would need to make in *Jerusalem*, the need for unity in the church of *Rome*, and the proposal of a mission to *Spain*.[13]

SOME LITERARY ISSUES

The question of chapter 16. Very few scholars have propounded elaborate partition theories for Romans. More common is the argument that various passages have been interpolated into the original text of the epistle. Particularly has this been argued for 16:17–20, which is seen to have a polemical thrust out of keeping with the rest of Romans.[14]

Many, however, argue that the last chapter of Romans is a fragment of an epistle originally sent to Ephesus. This view is closely related to the textual history of Romans, particularly the concluding doxology (16:25–27). The doxology is found in various places in the different manuscript traditions and in various combinations with the "short doxology" (16:24). The problem is complex, involving at least six major variants. For our purposes, the significant observation is that the doxology occurs at the end of chapter 14 in some manuscripts and at the end of chapter 15 in another. Since doxologies usually come at the *end* of epistles, this could be viewed as evidence for editions of Romans ending with chapter 14 or 15. There is good additional evidence in the early fathers as well as some Old Latin versions for a text ending with chapter 14. In all probability this was an "expurgated text" of Marcion. Marcion was an anti-Semitic heretic of the mid-second century who eliminated everything Jewish from his canon of Scripture, including the entire Old Testament. He probably was offended by Paul's advice in Romans 14 and 15 that the "strong" (Gentile Christians) should be tolerant of the "weak" (Jewish Christians). Thus, he eliminated these chapters from his text. This, however, will not explain the reading which places the doxology at the end of chapter 15. This is only attested in one manuscript but a very important one, papyrus 46, our earliest witness to the text of Romans. Many scholars have used this to support their argument that the Roman epistle ends with chapter 15 and that chapter 16 is a fragment of an epistle to Ephesus.

The Ephesian hypothesis was very popular in the early twentieth century.[15] It was supported by a number of arguments, such as that the long list of greetings (twenty-six persons) would be likely only for a church Paul knew well, like Ephesus, not one he had never before visited. It was further observed that the first convert in Asia (16:5) would more likely be in Ephesus than in Rome, and that Aquila and Priscilla were located in Ephesus when last mentioned in Acts (18:26; cp. Rom. 16:3). The recommendation of Phoebe (16:1–2) is seen to be more likely for a church Paul knew, and the polemical note in 16:17–20 is viewed as fitting the Asian situation better than Rome.[16] T. W. Manson developed the fragment theory still further, arguing that Paul put out two editions of Romans—the epistle to Rome (chaps. 1–15) and a second sent to Ephesus (including chap. 16).[17]

The current scholarly consensus is moving back to seeing chapter 16 as an integral part of Paul's letter to Rome. It has been observed that many of the names in Romans 16 have been attested as common regional names in Roman inscriptions but have not been found at Ephesus.[18] Letters of recommendation did not presume familiarity but were based on the *prestige* of the recommender. The "first convert . . . in Asia" would scarcely need to be identified as such in his own Ephesian congregation but would probably not be known as first convert to the Roman Christian community. Priscilla and Aquila may well have returned to Rome, perhaps to prepare the way for Paul, perhaps solely because they *could* after Claudius's death. There probably *was* a good reason for such a long list of greetings in Romans 16. It was almost surely to gain support. Paul wanted to establish a base in Rome for his mission to Spain. He curried all the favor he could with that end in mind.

The literary nature of Romans. Romans has sometimes been characterized as a diatribe in the style of the popular Cynic and Stoic philosophers. There is no question that Paul used methods of teaching in common with the popular philosophers, such as his frequent use of rhetorical questions. Recent studies, however, have questioned whether it is accurate to speak of a "diatribe" genre at all.[19]

As with most of Paul's epistles, Romans has been examined in the categories of ancient rhetoric. Those who have done so are in general agreement that the epistle has most in common with epideictic (demonstrative) rhetoric.[20] It has, however, proved difficult to fit all parts of the epistle into the divisions of the ancient rhetorical handbooks. Other suggestions have been made. For instance, the epistle has been described as a "letter essay," that is, a summary of a larger work.[21] Another suggestion is that it follows the pattern of a *logos protreptikos*, that is, an exhortation designed to attract someone to a particular way of life.[22] Still another describes Romans as an *ambassadorial letter* designed to prepare Paul's way as God's ambassador on his Spanish mission.[23] Surely one literary category of which Romans partakes is the common letter of recommendation—not just that of Phoebe in 16:1–2, but Paul's own. Much of the letter is devoted to presenting himself and his mission to the Romans and to thus preparing the way for his coming.

A STUDY OUTLINE OF ROMANS

Apart from the introduction (1:1–17) and conclusion (15:14–16:27), Romans falls into four main parts. The first part deals with the righteousness of God as manifested in Christ (1:18–4:25). Chapter 5 is a transitional chapter. It is sometimes placed with chapters 1–4, as it still deals with the subject of God's gracious work in Christ. It also looks forward to Paul's description of the new life lived by those who are in Christ, which is the subject of chapters 6–8. We have chosen to place it with the latter division (5:1–8:39). The third section of the epistle deals with Israel's place in the new people of God in Christ (9:1–11:36). The final section treats the practical day-to-day life of those who belong to God in Christ (12:1–15:13).

I. Introduction to the Epistle (1:1–17)
   A. Salutation (vv. 1–7)
   B. Thanksgiving (vv. 8–15)
   C. Theme: The Righteousness of God (vv. 16–17)
II. The Old and the New Righteousness (1:18–4:25)
   A. The Old Righteousness (1:18–3:20)
      1. Failure of the Gentile to obtain righteousness (1:18–32)
      2. Failure of the Jew to obtain righteousness (2:1–3:20)
         (a) The impartiality of God (2:1–16)
         (b) The exclusion of boasting (2:17–29)
         (c) The advantage of the Jew (3:1–20)
   B. The New Righteousness (3:21–4:25)
      1. Right standing with God through faith in Christ (3:21–31)
      2. Faith and the example of Abraham (4:1–25)
III. The New Life in Christ (5:1–8:39)
   A. A New Life Through Christ (5:1–21)
      1. Marked by peace and reconciliation with God (vv. 1–11)
      2. Enabled by solidarity with Christ, the "Second Adam" (vv. 12–21)
   B. The New Life in Christ as Death to Sin (6:1–7:6)
      1. The symbolism of baptism (6:1–14)
      2. The analogy of slavery (6:15–23)
      3. The analogy of marriage (7:1–6)
   C. The Ways of Death and Life Contrasted (7:7–8:39)
      1. The way of law leads to death (7:7–25)
      2. The way of the Spirit leads to life and glory (8:1–39)
         (a) Through the Spirit, freedom from sin and death (vv. 1–11)
         (b) Through the Spirit, certainty of inheritance (vv. 12–17)
         (c) Through the Spirit, assurance of perfect redemption (vv. 18–30)

      (d) Concluding hymn of praise: "No separation" (vv. 31–39)

IV. Israel and God's Plan of Salvation (9:1–11:36)
    A. Paul's Agony Over His People (9:1–5)
    B. God's Freedom in Election (9:6–29)
    C. The Cause of Israel's Rejection (9:30–10:21)
       1. Pursuit of the wrong righteousness (9:30–10:13)
       2. Responsibility for rejecting the gospel (10:14–21)
    D. The Temporary Nature of the Rejection (11:1–36)
       1. A remnant of Israel abides (vv. 1–10)
       2. Israel's rejection leads to Gentile election (vv. 11–24)
       3. Israel's election is irrevocable (vv. 25–36)

V. Practical Advice for Christian Living (12:1–15:13)
    A. The Duties of Christians (12:1–13:14)
       1. To one another (12:1–16)
       2. To those outside the community of faith (12:17–13:10)
       3. The eschatological basis for all Christian relationships (13:11–14)
    B. The Strong and the Weak in the Congregation (14:1–15:13)
       1. The problem described (14:1–12)
       2. The solution prescribed (14:13–23)
       3. Living harmoniously in the example of Christ (15:1–13)

VI. Personal Conclusion to the Letter (15:14–16:27)
    A. Paul's Travel Plans (15:14–33)
    B. Commendation of Phoebe (16:1–2)
    C. Exchange of Greetings (16:3–16)
    D. Warning Against False Teachers (16:17–20)
    E. Greetings from Paul's Associates (16:21–23)
    F. Concluding Doxology (16:25–27)

HIGHLIGHTS OF ROMANS

INTRODUCTION (1:1–17)

Paul was writing to a church that had no apostle, a church over which he was not himself an apostle. Therefore he expounded at some length on his call to be an apostle to the Gentiles (vv. 1–2, 5–6). He introduced a summary of the gospel about Christ (vv. 3–4). It was not Paul's usual gospel of the preexistent Christ (cp. Phil. 2:5–11). Instead it spoke of Christ's human, messianic status. Paul may have employed a Jewish-Christian confession here in order to appeal to the Jewish elements in the Roman congregation. Paul's thanksgivings usually alluded to major concerns within the letter.[24] The thanksgiving of Romans relates his desire to visit the Roman Christians (1:8–15). Perhaps this is a clue to his overall purposes. Since there were many Gentiles in the Roman church, they were in a sense within his circle, since he was the apostle to the Gentiles (vv. 13–15).

Verses 16–17 set the theme for the entire epistle. Paul was not ashamed of the gospel, for it represented the very power of God himself.[25] The power of God (v. 16) and the righteousness of God (v. 17) are virtually synonymous in this context. Both relate to God's salvation of believers. Paul stated that this salvation was "first for the Jew, then for the Gentile." This is a subtheme of the entire epistle—God's impartiality in dealing with both Jews and Gentiles. The *main* theme is God himself and his righteousness.[26] The focus is particularly on God's righteousness in terms of his covenant, his faithfulness to his promises.[27] Paul said that the righteousness of God is revealed "from faith to faith." He may have meant by this "from first to last," as the NIV translates. He may have meant something more profound: from *God's* faith, understood in terms of his faithfulness, to *my* faith, which God evokes in me.[28] Paul saw Habakkuk 2:4 as the major Old Testament text supporting his contention that the real basis of acceptance with God is our faith and trust in Jesus Christ (cp. Gal. 3:11). The Scripture text presents a rough outline of the chapters that follow in Romans: "The one who is righteous by faith (chaps. 1–4) will live (chaps. 5–8)."

THE OLD AND THE NEW RIGHTEOUSNESS (1:18–4:25)

Overview. The opening section of the epistle establishes that there is only one means of acceptance with a righteous God—through faith in God's own provision of Christ's atoning death (3:21–31). All other attempts at securing divine acceptance are doomed to failure, whether it be that of the Gentile (1:18–32) or that of the Jew (2:1–3:20). The example of Abraham corroborates that God's acceptance of Jew and Gentile alike can come only through faith (4:1–25).

Failure of the Gentile to obtain righteousness (1:18–32). Paul began by establishing the responsibility of the Gentiles for their sin. He spoke in terms of God's wrath (*orgē*). The "revealing" of God's wrath in verse 18 is parallel with the "revealing" of his righteousness in verse 17. God's wrath is an expression of his righteousness. Since he is holy and righteous, God cannot condone sin; he *must* judge it. But God's righteousness has two sides: his *judgment* is most powerfully expressed through his *mercy*. That is the lesson of the cross (3:21–31).

Gentiles are responsible for their sin because God reveals something of himself in his creation (vv. 19–20). But the Gentiles have distorted God's revelation, falling into idolatry, worshiping the creation itself rather than its Creator (vv. 21–25). Idolatry leads to human perversion. Focusing on the creation rather than the Creator, people begin to worship themselves, to become beasts like the creaturely images they fashion. Their sexual relations are perverted into same-sex passion (vv. 26–27). Their social relationships are perverted into all sorts of antisocial attitudes and activities (vv. 28–31). Paul described this in terms of God "giving them over" (vv. 24, 26, 28).[29] Not only is God's wrath expressed in future judgment; it is also manifested in God's allowing sin to take its natural, destructive course in *this* life. All without exception are included in God's condemnation, both those who participate in such actions and those who condone them by their silent consent (v. 32).

God's impartiality (2:1–16). Many interpreters would see this first part of chapter 2 as addressed against self-righteousness in general, but it seems to be particularly appropriate to the Jewish sense of moral rightness over against the pagan world. The basic point to 2:1–16 is that God judges all people impartially on the basis of *what they are*; their *conduct*, not their privilege, is the sole criterion of God's judgment. One cannot escape judgment by judging others, by appealing to how much worse their behavior is than one's own. Such judgment of others leads one away from the necessary self-examination and repentance for one's own sins and results in God's inevitable judgment (vv. 1–5). Paul's main concern comes out in verses 6–11: just like his saving righteousness (1:17), God's judging righteousness comes without discrimination to all alike, Gentile *and* Jew. Perhaps in Rome both Jewish and Gentile

Christians felt they had some edge over each other in God's election. Not so, said Paul. In light of both their sin and the cross, they were on level ground.

Verses 6–12 present a problem. Did Paul sneak a "works-righteousness" in the back door when he stated that God would judge all alike on the basis of their works? His main purpose is clear. He wanted to show that the Jew has no edge on the Gentile by merely possessing the law. God will accept those who fulfill the demands of the law, whether they know the law (Jews) or whether they are ignorant of the law as such (Gentiles). Paul, of course, believed that *no one* in fact fulfills the law (3:9, 23). He was not speaking merely hypothetically here.[30] God *will* accept the person who faithfully accomplishes the demands of the law. *One*, in fact, *did*—Jesus Christ. And it is only through belonging to him that anyone can become acceptable to God.

The exclusion of boasting (2:17–29). Paul now turned to the two central elements in his contemporary Judaism—the law (Torah) and the covenant (circumcision). Jews could claim no edge over the Gentiles by possessing the Torah, he maintained (vv. 17–24). They had to fulfill its provisions, which they in fact did not do. Paul may have been speaking of actual known examples of stealing, adultery, and sacrilege among Jewish leaders. He more likely was echoing the prophetic critique of Israel—that they were robbing God of the honor due him, that they were adulterers through compromising the faith, that they desecrated God's holiness with purely external worship. The law is not an advantage; it is a *responsibility*, for it bears witness to God. When the people of the law fail to keep the law, it brings dishonor to God (v. 24).

Circumcision was the external sign of belonging to the covenant people of God. By its very nature, it made the covenant exclusive. Not only did it eliminate Gentiles from the covenant; it forced women into a situation where they could only be in the covenant by proxy, as it were. In verses 25–29 Paul argued that mere membership in the covenant would not ensure membership in God's people. Not the external circumcision of the foreskin but the internal circumcision of the heart is what counts with God. Here again Paul echoed the language of the prophets; God seeks the circumcised heart of humility (Deut. 10:16) and repentance (Jer. 4:4). In this passage Paul radically "denationalized" election. The true Jew is not the one of circumcised flesh but the one who gives evidence of election by showing the right heart-attitude toward God (v. 29).

The Jew's advantage is really no advantage (3:1–20). What Paul had just said about the law and the covenant being internal and not external had profound implications for Jewish election. Was Paul implying that the Jews were no longer the people of God, that their election had been abrogated, that God had reneged on his promises? These are the questions Paul sought to answer in 3:1–8. His treatment consists of a series of rhetorical questions raised by a Jewish protester. Paul's answers are anything but clear. He began by saying that the Jew had great advantages (v. 2). He ended by saying that the Jew was really no better off in the light of the universality of human sin (v. 9). Paul *answered* the question about God's righteousness: God remains true to his promises despite human failure (v. 6). Paul did *not*, however, answer the question about the continuing validity of God's covenant with Israel. He eventually returned to that subject in chapters 9–11.

Verses 9–20 are a conclusion to the entire discussion of 1:18–3:8. Neither Gentile nor Jew has any room for boasting. Neither has obtained acceptance with God—not the Gentile through idolatrous worship nor the Jew through Torah and membership in the covenant. All are alike "under sin" (v. 9). Verses 10–18 establish this assertion with scriptural proofs, a long catena of Old Testament texts that point to human sinfulness. Paul applied the texts to "those who are under the law" in verses 19–20. He referred to the Old Testament in very broad terms as "the law," even though none of the texts are from the books of the law strictly speaking. He obviously had Israel in mind. The Scripture was *their* law, and it established that they along with the Gentiles were sinners, and thus "unrighteous," unacceptable to God. Throughout Romans Paul wrestled with the role of the law. The reference to the law bringing consciousness of sin is not directly pertinent to his immediate discussion. It is, however, part of the larger issue. The law has a place in making one aware of sin; it cannot, however, make one right with God.[31] Paul returned to the subject of the law's role in chapter 7.

Right standing with God through faith in Christ (3:21–31). Romans 3:21–31 has often been considered the center of Paul's argument in Romans. Whether that is the case or not, it is certainly the center of his argument in 1:18–4:25. What humans could not do for themselves God has done for them in Jesus Christ. All have sinned and become unacceptable to a holy and righteous God (v. 23). The basic concept is "rightness." "Rightness" words occur some seven times in verses 21–26. This is obscured in English translations, which render them with other words like "justice" (= "rightness") or "just" (= "right") or "justify" (= "make right"). Behind all these terms is the basic meaning that God is "right/just." He alone establishes all standards of rightness. Human sin is not right. It is unrighteous, intolerable to a righteous God. Sin thus renders us unacceptable to God. We of ourselves cannot deal adequately with sin. This has been Paul's argument throughout 1:18–3:20. But now he showed that God has in Jesus Christ provided the means for removal of our sin and our establishment as being right and acceptable in his eyes. God's making us righteous through Christ is called in English theological terminology "justification" (= "righteousness," "being rendered right").

The new status of being acceptable/right with God comes through *faith* in Jesus Christ (v. 22). Many contemporary exegetes would prefer to translate this "through the faith *of* Jesus Christ," understanding faith as Christ's faithfulness and obedience to God's purposes.[32] Certainly the obedience of Christ is central in his death on the cross (cp. Phil. 2:8), but the appropriation of Christ's work in the faith of the believer is also central and is the main point of Romans 4. Believers are made right with God ("justified") solely through God's *grace* (v. 24). Grace (Gk., *charis*) refers to God's free, unmerited gift. This gracious gift of God is further described as *redemption*. Redemption is a slave-market term and refers to liberation. In this case the liberation is from the penalty of sin and its power in our lives. The removal of sin is described in verse 25 in terms of God's "sacrifice of atonement." The word Paul used (Gk., *hilastērion*) has been variously translated as "propitiation," "expiation," or "sacrifice of atonement." It is the same word that was used in the Greek Old Testament to render the "mercy seat" where the sacrificial blood was poured in Israel's worship on the day of atonement. Just as the mercy seat was the place where Israel sought God's forgiveness of their sins, so Christ is the means of obtaining God's forgiveness of *our* sins.[33] We are "atoned," "made one," made acceptable to God through the blood of Christ. "Blood" is Pauline shorthand for the death of Christ, but Paul understood that death as a sacrifice.

The death of Christ was the great dividing line of history. God no longer "forebears" human sinfulness (v. 25b). He dealt with it decisively in Christ, showing himself to be *just* (taking sin seriously) and *justifier* (providing people a means to be set right from sin and for relationship with himself, v. 26).

In verses 27–31 Paul returned to the subject of the law. He had in mind the Jews and their pride in their privileged relationship with God as epitomized in the law. Paul emphasized that the Jews had no grounds for boasting in the law, since salvation is solely through faith in Christ (vv. 27–28). He pointed out why it *had* to be so. If God is one, as the Jews confessed daily in the *shema* (Deut. 6:4), then he has to be God of *all*, Jew *and* Gentile. The means of becoming right with God must then be truly inclusive, truly monotheistic (vv. 29–30).[34] The law separates peoples; faith in Christ unites them. In verse 31 Paul stated that the way of faith "upheld" the law. In verse 21 he spoke of the law and the prophets testifying to the new righteousness based on faith. Probably in both passages he had the Scripture in mind. He now turned to the Scripture about Abraham to show how the Old Testament testifies to the priority of faith.

The example of Abraham verifies the new way of faith (4:1–25). Paul first turned to Genesis 15:6 and Psalm 32:1–2 to establish that for Abraham faith rather than law was the basis of his being accepted by God (vv. 1–8). In both passages Paul built his argument on a word that means "reckon, account, or credit."[35] Genesis 15:6 states that Abraham had faith in God, and God "accounted/credited" this to him as "righteousness" (as a basis of acceptance). Paul argued that to be freely credited with something implies that it is received as a gift and not as something earned. Abraham thus obtained God's acceptance solely on the basis of his faith and trust in God, not through any work. Paul then appealed to Psalm 32:1–2, where the same word is used in connection with God's not counting/reckoning sins. Paul saw this as additional evidence for God's forgiving and accepting persons apart from works of the law.

Verses 9–15 carry Paul's argument a step further. God accepted Abraham on the basis of faith (Gen. 15:6) *before* he established the covenant of circumcision with him (Gen. 17:19–24). Abraham was thus accepted on the basis of faith while still uncircumcised, making him father of all those whom God accepted on the basis of faith, whether uncircumcised Gentiles or circumcised Jews. Paul did not wish to eliminate the Jews from election but only to show that in the light of Christ both Jews and Gentiles were included on an equal basis.

Verses 16–25 cap off the application to the Gentiles. Paul appealed to two additional Old Testament texts. Genesis 17:5 (v. 17) records God's promise to Abraham that he would be the father of "many nations." Now the word *Gentiles* (Gk., *ethnē*) meant to the Jew "all the nations other than Israel." As the father of many nations, Abraham was the father of all the Gentiles. Genesis 15:5 (v. 18) spoke of how Abraham's offspring would be as numerous as the stars of heaven. Paul then argued that this showed how Abraham had faith in God to bring life out of death. Both Abraham and Sarah were old and as good as dead as far as childbearing was concerned. But Abraham believed God's promise that he would have many descendants, and God honored his faith, accepting him as righteous. Thus, Paul implied, the very *content* of Abraham's faith links him with those who have faith in Christ. Both share the resurrection faith that God can bring life out of death. Verse 25 ends with what was quite likely an early Christian confession of faith: Christ died that our sins might be forgiven; he was raised that we might live in the full acceptance of God (justification).

THE NEW BEING IN CHRIST (5:1–8:39)

Overview. This section deals with the fruits of the new relationship with God which have come about through Jesus Christ. Paul began to list these benefits in 5:1–11. Then, 5:12–21 seems to shift back to the theme of chapters 1–4, the old "Adamic" life in sin, the new life brought about by Jesus Christ. The section is transitional, for it looks ahead to the description of the new life in Christ in chapters 6–8. Paul had been hard on the Torah in chapters 1–4. He had opened himself up to charges that he was antinomian and that he completely disparaged the law of God. In chapter 6 he addressed the charge of antinomianism, and in chapter 7 he focused on the place of the law. In chapter 8 he showed the real basis of the Christian life: not law, but Spirit.

Peace, joy, and reconciliation with God (5:1–11). Verses 1–11 begin to enumerate the benefits of the new life in Christ, a discussion which Paul returned to and treated more fully in chapter 8. Having been justified (made right) with God, we now have peace and access to him through Christ (vv. 1–2). This is the language of reconciliation (cp. vv. 10–11). We will discuss Paul's concept of reconciliation at length in the chapter on Ephesians. Paul also spoke of the joy of salvation which carries us through the tribulations of this life in full confidence (hope) of the glory to come. In the light of this hope, our troubles only serve to make us persevere the more. Perseverance produces proven character, and that in turn strengthens our hope. This hope is not an empty hope; the Spirit assures us of the certainty of the life to come. Above all, we are assured of God's love for us, love demonstrated in Christ's dying for us while we were still sinners (vv. 6–8).[36] Perhaps no portion of Romans states more clearly the "forensic" (legal) nature of our acceptance in Christ. God accepts us in spite of our sinfulness. He declares us innocent of our sin when we are in fact guilty. It is not that he takes sin lightly. Far from it. He gave up his only Son to die for our sin. And the "righteousness" God grants us is not a legal fiction either. He grants us his Spirit to enable us to grow into the full measure of his standards, his "righteousness." *All* of chapters 6–8 deal with this subject.

Solidarity with Christ, the "Second Adam" (5:12–21). This section is not a digression. It focuses on the reality of the old life of sin and the new life in Christ from a salvation-historical and corporate perspective. As such, it is parallel to 1:18–4:25. Paul built on the Adam–Christ typology which he had already employed in 1 Corinthians 15.

Verses 12–14 focus on humanity's corporate solidarity with Adam. Adam represents all humanity. With Adam's sin began all human sinfulness, and with sin came death. Paul saw a real connection between sin and death. The inevitable consequence of sin is death, both spiritual and physical (cp. 6:23). The only way to life is to share in the resurrection life of Christ. Verse 12 surely speaks of "original sin" but not in the Augustinian sense of a transmission through the male sperm. Rather, it expresses that all humans inevitably share in Adam's sin. On the other hand, each person is ultimately individually responsible.[37] Paul also connected sin with law. He argued that sin is more fully accountable where law is present, for law establishes the rules and boundaries. But he granted that sin was surely in the world between Adam and Moses (when the law came), because death reigned over all during that time

(vv. 13–14). (Paul had already argued in 1:18–32 that Gentiles without the law are responsible for their sin.) The conclusion is simple: from Adam on, all humanity, those with and those without the law, have been bound up in the sin of Adam.

Fortunately, that is not the whole story. There are now two humanities—humanity in Adam and humanity in Christ, the "second Adam."[38] Verses 15–21 contrast the two. Through the disobedience of Adam came condemnation and death. Through the obedience of Christ came righteousness and life, full acceptance with God. Paul came close to a "universalism" in this passage. He clearly stated the universal membership of all humanity in the sinful Adamic existence. In his contrast with Adam, he spoke of Christ's obedience as bringing life for *all* people (v. 18). This all-inclusiveness is, however, at best conditional. Christ's atoning work is efficacious for the salvation of all but nonetheless must be appropriated in faith by each individual. Paul was convinced of the ultimate triumph of the work of Christ. No matter how bad the sinfulness of Adamic humanity, it cannot eclipse the grace of Christ, which abounds to life eternal (vv. 20–21).

The new life in Christ as death to sin (6:1–7:6). Paul's insistence that salvation is by grace and not by works raises the ethical question acutely. Why not sin in order that grace might abound (6:1)? This is the antinomian's response to grace. Paul emphatically rejected it, using three analogies to establish that right living is a necessary accompaniment of the justified life. The first is that of Christian baptism (6:1–14). This is Paul's fullest treatment of baptism. He described it here as dying and rising with Christ. Scholars debate where Paul derived the ideas. It is unlikely he got it from the Greek mysteries, as some have maintained.[39] More likely it developed along with his closely related ideas of the new creation in Christ (2 Cor. 5:14–21) and Christ as the second Adam (Rom. 5:12–21).[40]

In any event, Paul was not presenting a theology of baptism here. He used the picture of baptism to portray how the Christian has buried the old life by participating in Christ's death and has been raised to a new life (v. 4). It was more than a picture for Paul. He saw the believer as participating in the death of Christ. Believers do not die in the baptismal waters; they die with Christ in his actual death on the cross. Paul stopped short of saying that believers have shared in Christ's resurrection. That is a future event (v. 5). Believers are not yet perfected this side of the general resurrection. They still live in a sinful world and are constantly being pulled into its ways. That is why Paul exhorts the Romans in verses 11–14 not to allow sin to take rule in their bodies. They belong to Christ and must strive to live like those who have been brought from death to life in him.

Paul's second analogy is developed in 6:15–23. It is that of slavery. One can be either a slave of sin or a slave of God's righteousness. It is strictly either/or. One cannot be a slave to two masters at the same time. One is either "in Adam" or "in Christ." Paul developed a paradox. He maintained that when we were slaves of sin we were not really free to do right; we just *could not*. Now that we are in Christ, we are slaves to righteousness and really are not free to sin. It is a major Pauline paradox. Christians are truly most free when they enslave themselves to Christ.

Paul's third analogy is the most difficult—the analogy of marriage (7:1–6). Paul's main point was that marriage establishes legal bonds. When death ends the marriage, the legal encumbrances are dissolved. Since as Christians we have died to sin, we are now free from sin and free to marry righteousness. Like the other two analogies, Paul wanted to make a simple point: the Christian life is a life of righteousness in the moral as well as legal sense. Not only have we been accepted as right by God, but we must grow in "rightness," grow into God's standard of righteousness. We have died to sin and are alive in Christ to God's righteousness. The third analogy becomes somewhat confused with Paul's introduction of the law into the picture. Paul believed that sin and law and death are bound closely together. When we die to sin, we also die to the law-centered way of living. Verse 6 is the key. For the Christian, the Spirit, not the law, is the source of morality. Paul returned to this theme in chapter 8, but first he treated the pressing question of the law and its purposes.

The way of the law leads to death (7:7–25). For the Jew, the law (Torah) represented God's covenant with Israel. It accompanied God's gracious election of them as his people. But Paul had been very hard on the law up to this point in Romans. He had argued strenuously that one could not be saved through observing the provisions of the law. He connected the law with sin and death. For the Jewish Christian community of Rome, as for Jews in general, Paul's stance must have presented real problems. If the law is an expression of God's covenant, was God reneging on his promises? Paul had already begun to discuss this problem in 3:1–10. It had two main aspects: (1) the nature and purpose of the law, and (2) the abiding validity of God's election of Israel. Paul addressed the latter issue in 9–11. He turned to the first issue in 7:7; 25.

Paul's treatment of the law falls into two main sections, 7:7–12 and 7:13–25. The first section deals with the law's role in human sinfulness (7:7–12). Paul began by emphatically denying that the law is itself sinful (v. 7). To the contrary, the law represents God's will and as such is "holy, righteous, and good" (v. 12). Humanity's problem is not God's law, but sin, rebellion against the law. Law, however, contributes to sin. First, it reveals sin as sin. It sets the standard and makes us aware when we transgress it (v. 7). Second, law serves as a catalyst for sin; the prohibition increases the desire (v. 8). Finally, the law establishes responsibility. The law sets forth God's norm, thus making someone accountable for transgressing it (vv. 9–11; cp. 5:13). Verses 7–11 are all written in the first person singular. Who did Paul intend with this "I"? Probably not himself; Paul never lived without the law. The passage probably draws from the story of Adam and Eve's temptation in paradise.[41]

The second part of Paul's treatment deals with the inadequacy of the law to deal with sin (7:13–25). Paul continued in the "I" style, but this time in the *present* rather than the past tense. The law did not produce death, Paul said. Sin was the culprit. The law merely brought sin into the open, exposing it for what it really is (v. 13). There follows the classic description of the "I" who is divided between willing and doing, the "fleshly" individual who knows what is right but cannot do what is right because sin perverts his or her best intentions. Throughout this section of Romans, Paul spoke in strongly dualistic terms, of life and death, sin and righteousness, flesh and Spirit. Unlike the Gnostics, however, Paul's dualism was *ethical*, not metaphysical. He did not view human flesh as inherently evil. The evil body is not the physical body; it is the body yielded to sin, the old "Adamic" body. The same body can be righteous and good when yielded to God's Spirit. But Paul's main point was that this sinful self *cannot* do what is right. The law can inform the conscience. It can produce the willing, but it cannot produce the "doing." The presence of sin renders it ineffective.

Who is the "I" who experiences this ethical frustration of willing but not doing? Was Paul referring to his own pre-Christian experience of wrestling with the Torah?

Not likely. The pre-Christian Paul seems to have viewed himself as "faultless" with respect to doing the law (cp. Phil. 3:6). Of course, the *Christian* Paul, looking back on his former life, may have seen it all quite differently.[42] Was Paul perhaps referring to Jews in general and to the failure of their law-centered life? There is little evidence in the Jewish literature that Paul's contemporaries experienced such frustration between willing and doing the law. Paul may have been referring to Christians; Christians alone would be fully aware of the pull in their life between God's standards and their continuing failure to measure up.[43] Verse 25 seems to point in this direction: in this life, short of the resurrection we are not yet perfected and are still a slave to sin's law, but in our inmost self we belong not to sin but to God. We are "in Christ," no longer "in Adam."

In the end, one may not really have to choose between the various alternatives. Paul may have been expressing the experience of everyone, Jew or Gentile, Christian or non-Christian, who seeks to lead a life that measures up to God's standards.[44] Such persons are doomed to failure when left to their own resources, their own desiring and willing. Sin is too powerful a force.[45] Only one thing can deliver them from the bondage to sin and its inevitable consequence of death. "Thanks be to God . . . . Therefore, there is now no condemnation for those who are in Christ Jesus" (7:25; 8:1). One must move right through the chapter divisions. Paul had none in his original letter. The divisions and numbers of the biblical text were added by later scribes and editors, and they made a major blunder in dividing Romans 7 and 8. The answer to the cry of despair in 7:24 is the affirmation of salvation in Christ in 8:1. The answer to the sinful self's futility in fulfilling the law in 7:14–25 is the gift of the Spirit in chapter 8.

The way of the Spirit brings life (8:1–39). Chapter 8 concludes Paul's treatment of the new life in Christ. The main emphasis of the chapter is *assurance through the Spirit.* The Holy Spirit is the believer's assurance in the midst of the tribulations of this life that a perfect life will one day surely come. The chapter can be divided into four main sections.

Verses 1–11 deal with the questions raised in chapter 7. What the law could not do the Spirit has accomplished for us—freedom from sin and death. God provided the cure for sin himself by sending his Son in sin's own territory ("in the likeness of sinful man") as a sacrifice for sin. Not only did this secure the forgiveness of our sin; it also furnished us the power to deal with sin through the gift of the Spirit. Verse 4 affirms the "righteous requirements" of the law. In its moral aspects the law really does embody God's standards, and the Spirit enables us to live by them.[46] Verses 5–11 return to the theme of 6:1–7:6, the death of the Christian to the old sinful nature, this time described in terms of the indwelling Spirit. Manifestation of the Spirit is a necessary mark of the Christian (v. 9). True, the Christian still lives in a sinful world and a mortal body, but the Spirit provides the power to cope with sin's pull and the assurance of the immortal resurrection life to come (vv. 10–11).

Second, through the Spirit comes certainty that we are God's children (vv. 12–17). In our present life we appear to be no different from the rest of humanity. But in fact, we are God's children, joint heirs of God's kingdom through our relationship to God's true Son Jesus Christ. The Spirit gives us inner assurance of our new status of being heirs with Christ, leading us to affirm God as "Abba," our heavenly Father. Verse 17b is transitional to the next section. Even though we are heirs of God's kingdom, suffering often marks our lot in this life.

The third section deals with this tension between our future glory and the suffering of this present life: Through the Spirit comes assurance of the perfect redemption that is to come (vv. 18–30). Our present existence is not perfect. Even the created order witnesses to the present imperfection and eagerly awaits the future when the kingdom of God will come in power and God's true children will come into their inheritance (vv. 18–22). Here Paul shared the prophetic vision of a new heaven and a new earth and the realization that somehow even the nonhuman creation shares in the human tragedy. Modern ecological studies have demonstrated for us how very true this is. Of course, it is not only nature that waits. Christians also "groan," awaiting the full redemption to come, the exchange of the mortal body for the glorious resurrection body (vv. 22–23). The Spirit undergirds our hope, but it remains a hope and not a present reality (vv. 24–25). Verses 26–27 show how the Spirit undergirds our lives in our present imperfection and inadequacy. We don't even know how to pray, but the Spirit intercedes for us, speaking beyond human capacity on God's level, in God's manner, and in accordance with God's purposes.

Verses 28–30 conclude the discussion of the Spirit's assurances in the midst of life's imperfections by affirming the absolute steadfastness of God's eternal plans: God will surely bring to completion the fullness of the coming glory for which the Spirit is our present guarantee. Verse 28 is a debated text. It does not express a "naive optimism." In context it means that in spite of all of the imperfections, suffering, and adversity of *this* life, God's plans for his children will prevail, working toward their ultimate good in the full realization of God's kingdom. Verses 29–30 make basically the same point in more "predestinarian" language. Paul used a chain of past-tense verbs to emphasize the certainty of our salvation by pointing to the various stages of God's working in our lives. He *foreknew* us, knew us before all eternity. He *predestined* us for salvation before all time. We did not choose him; he *called* us. He *justified* us, accepting us as his own without any merit on our part. He *glorified* us, making us joint heirs with Christ in the life to come. Glorification is, of course, future, but Paul was so certain of it he spoke in the past tense as if it were an accomplished reality.

Paul's predestinarian language is always a way of expressing God's grace. It emphasizes that our relationship with God does not depend on our own doing but on God's. Our assurances rest in the purposes of God. Paul never eliminated human responsibility. Somehow the divine sovereignty and human response intertwine in the mystery of divine election.[47]

Romans 8 ends with a concluding hymn of praise to God's triumphant love in Christ (vv. 31–39). It serves as a fitting conclusion to all of Paul's message from Romans 1:16 on. Verses 31–34 develop the theme of "no condemnation" through a series of rhetorical questions. God has chosen us in his beloved Son, whom he gave up for our salvation. If God has so chosen us, who can possibly condemn us? Our relationship to God is secure. Verses 35–39 develop the theme of "no separation" of Christ from those whom he loves—no earthly calamities (vv. 35–36), no supraterrestrial forces (vv. 37–38), absolutely nothing can separate us from God's love in Christ Jesus.

ISRAEL AND GOD'S PLAN OF SALVATION (9:1–11:36)

Time was when Romans 9–11 was considered peripheral to the main argument of Romans. Today many would argue that these chapters are at the center of the book, that Paul's concern for Israel lies behind every portion of the letter.[48] Much of the current interest in Romans 9–11 grows out of the dialogue between Jews and Christians and the problem of anti-Semitism. Thus, many recent treatments of these chapters see Paul as directing himself more against Gentiles than toward Jews or as emphasizing throughout all three chapters the *inclusion* of the Jews, or even as maintaining the continuing validity of the old covenant with Israel *apart from* the covenant in Christ.[49] That Paul was concerned with Gentile feelings of superiority over the Jews is evident in chapter 11, but it is hard to avoid the conclusion that Paul's main concern was the failure of his Jewish contemporaries to respond to the gospel. Paul returned to the question of God's faithfulness to his promises to Israel which he had begun in 3:1–9. His treatment in chapters 9–11 grows directly out of his emphases on God's purposes in 8:28–30. God had chosen Israel. Had he backed down on those promises? The question concerned Gentiles as well as Jews. If God proved unfaithful to his promises to Israel, how could one be certain he would remain faithful to the promises in Christ? Nothing less than the righteousness of God was at stake, his covenant fidelity.

The rhetorical questions of the diatribe style are more numerous in these chapters than anywhere else in the epistle. The section is filled with Old Testament references, leading some scholars to believe that Paul may have employed a sermon which he had previously prepared. His argument falls into three main sections.[50] The first section establishes God's sovereign freedom to choose whom he will (9:6–29). The second deals with Israel's rejection of the gospel (9:30–10:21). The third affirms that Israel's rejection is only temporary (11:1–36). The opening five verses of chapter 9 introduce the issue. Paul agonized over Israel's failure to respond to the gospel. He could not understand it. All the divine promises were given to Israel. The Messiah himself came from Israel.[51] Paul would gladly have given himself for the salvation of his fellow Jews were that possible.

God's freedom in election (9:6–29). Paul's basic premise is stated in verse 6: God's word to Israel had *not* failed.[52] Paul did not fully resolve the tension between this statement and Israel's failure until chapter 11. He began his argument by noting that being an Israelite is not really a matter of physical descent, as is evident in the case of Isaac and Ishmael (vv. 7–9). Both descended from Abraham, but God chose only Isaac. The same freedom of God to make his own choice is exemplified in his favoring Jacob over Esau, contrary to the usual rights of the firstborn (vv. 10–13). Pharaoh furnishes another example of how God shows his mercy to some but not to others. God hardened Pharaoh's heart in order to show mercy to Israel (vv. 14–18). In chapter 11 Paul argued that God was doing exactly this *to Israel* in his own time in order to show mercy to the Gentiles. Paul concluded his argument with an example of a potter working with his clay (vv. 19–24). As creator of the vessels, the potter has complete control over their form and use. That is in his hands as creator. Paul showed his real concern with this image in verse 23. He wished to emphasize God's choice, his mercy. Paul turned to two further Old Testament texts to establish his main concerns. Hosea showed how God was now choosing a new people who had not formerly been among his people—the Gentiles (vv. 25–26). Isaiah spoke of God's remnant; this points to the present Israel who believed in Christ (vv. 27–28).[53]

The cause of Israel's rejection (9:30–10:21). In the second part of his argument, Paul made two main points: (1) Israel rejected Christ because it chose to follow the way of its law rather than the way of Christ (9:30–10:13), and (2) Israel was responsible for this situation because it had heard the gospel of God's grace in Christ (10:14–21). The form of this section is basically sermonic, built around a series of Old Testament texts. First, Paul showed how Israel had stumbled (9:30–33). The picture is that of a foot race.[54] The Gentiles did not enter the race but received the prize of God's acceptance anyway, through faith. The Jews raced but stumbled. Their pursuit of the law blinded them to the only true means of gaining righteousness (God's acceptance), that which is in Christ, and so Christ became for them a stumbling block. They failed to embrace him and kept on running after the law.

Israel pursued its own righteousness (10:1–4). Verse 3 is a classic exposition of why zeal for the law is unenlightened. It is self-striving, self-dependent, and not based on God's mercy. Paul had already shown in chapters 2–3 how it was doomed to fail. But what did Paul mean in 10:4 when he spoke of Christ as the "end of the law"? Did he mean that the law terminated with Christ, or did he mean that Christ is the final "end," the purpose and goal of the law.[55] The question is hotly debated and will be considered in the excursus on the law below. Whatever Paul meant by this enigmatic phrase, he was convinced the law was no means to righteousness. One finds acceptance with God in Christ alone. In verses 5–10 Paul used two texts to contrast the two ways of seeking righteousness. Leviticus 18:5 illustrates righteousness by law; one "lives" in the law and is bound to it exclusively. Deuteronomy 30:12–13 foreshadows the new, inward righteousness in Christ.[56] Verses 6–10 are a sermonic exposition of the Deuteronomy text, depicting the error of the self-striving quest to storm heaven to bring down the Messiah. In contrast is the way of righteousness through faith and trust, where the word is near, within the heart. Verses 11–13 express what was probably Paul's central problem with the Torah, its exclusiveness. In contrast, the gospel is without distinction for Jew and Gentile alike.

In 10:14–21 Paul argued that Israel was responsible for its failure to embrace Christ. Messengers had gone forth, the gospel had been preached, Israel had heard the gospel, but still it failed to respond in faith. Paul concluded with two Old Testament texts which should have prepared Israel for the Gentile response to the gospel. Deuteronomy 32:21 spoke of God's making Israel jealous through a people who lacked understanding. In the next chapter he developed this jealousy motif further. Isaiah 65:1 spoke of God revealing himself to those who did not seek him, as he was now doing with the Gentiles through Christ. Paul continued to the next verse, quoting Isaiah 65:2, which spoke of an obstinate and disobedient people. That was the other side of the coin—unbelieving Israel.

The temporary nature of Israel's rejection (11:1–36). Israel's rejection of the Messiah was neither total nor was it final. There *were* those who believed in Christ like Paul himself. They represented the same sort of faithful remnant whom Elijah encountered in his day. The remnant, of course, owed their status in Christ solely to God's grace, just like the Gentiles (vv. 5–6). There is an underside to grace, however. The rest of Israel failed to obtain the promises in Christ. Like Pharaoh, their hearts were hardened in blindness, deafness, and unbelief (vv. 7–10). What was to become of them? Here at last Paul came to something of a solution to the problem of Israel's "hardness." The unbelief of Israel, he stated, was only temporary. It had a purpose. God was using Israel's unbelief as an opportunity to bring salvation to the Gentiles. The success among the Gentiles would eventually provoke Israel to jealousy and response to the gospel (vv. 11–12). Paul was as much concerned with negative Gentile attitudes toward Jews as he was with Jewish criticism of his Gentile mission. So he reminded the Gentiles that a positive response of the Jews to the gospel was in their own interest. He implied that the final resurrection at the Lord's return depended on the Jews' turning to Christ (vv. 13–15).

Paul then employed an unusual analogy of grafting branches on an olive tree (17–24). His picture was of a domestic tree (Israel) having some of its branches removed in order to graft in branches from a wild tree (the Gentiles).[57] He argued that if the wild branches flourished in the root stock (as they had), how much easier would it be to graft the original domestic branches back in (v. 24). The lesson for the Gentiles was that Israel was indeed the main stock, God's people. Gentiles had no room to boast, and they needed to take care lest in their arrogance they be removed (vv. 20–21).

Paul concluded his argument in 11:25–36. God is indeed faithful to his promises. His call is irrevocable (v. 29). It had turned out in reverse of the normal Jewish apocalyptic expectation. The usual vision was that Israel would lead the Gentiles to the Messiah. Paul saw the reverse as taking place.[58] God was temporarily hardening Israel for the sake of the Gentile mission (v. 25). But through jealousy the Gentile successes would eventually lead the Jews to Christ. In the end "all Israel will be saved" (v. 26). Just what Paul meant by this is a matter of discussion. The most obvious meaning is that there would be a major turning of the Jews to the gospel before the Lord's return. In light of this conviction, Paul ended with a hymn of praise to the inscrutable ways of God's mercy, a mercy Paul felt assured would one day come upon his fellow Jews.

EXCURSUS: PAUL AND THE JEWISH LAW

Perhaps no aspect of Pauline thought is more discussed today than his attitude toward the law. This is in large part due to the work of E. P. Sanders, whose book of 1977 attacked the old consensus view that Paul contended with a Judaism oriented towards "works righteousness."[59] Sanders showed that most Jews in Paul's day did not see salvation in terms of earning merit through fulfillment of the law. Instead, they held to a "covenantal nomism," which saw the law as a part of God's covenant with Israel, a covenant based in grace and not demand. Keeping the law was not the means for entering the covenant. God established the covenant in his grace. The law was his means of maintaining the covenant. Equally influential has been the work of Krister Stendahl, who argued that Paul was not a tortured rabbi who had come to the end of his rope in his own effort to fulfill the law.[60] Stendahl saw Paul's thought as deriving more from his Gentile mission than his disillusionment with the law.

The work of Sanders, Stendahl, and others has brought about a major "paradigm shift" in the understanding of Paul, particularly his understanding of the law. For instance, James D. G. Dunn has maintained that Paul primarily attacked the ceremonial aspects of the law. These were those Jewish nationalistic elements of the law which served as "boundary markers" and separated Jews from Gentiles.[61] John Calvin himself made a distinction between the ceremonial and moral aspects of the law. Paul never explicitly made such a distinction, but his comments on the law often seem to imply as much.

Paul's statements about the law sometimes seem to contradict one another. As an example, Paul in Romans 3:20 stated that no one can be declared righteous by observing the law, whereas Romans 2:13 seems to state just the opposite. Such seeming conflicts have led Heikki Räisänen to declare Paul confused and hopelessly *con-*

tradictory, a muddled thinker and poor theologian.[62] Most have chosen not to go this route but have explained the tensions between Paul's statements on the law by other means. Many, such as Hans Hübner, have argued that Paul's thought on the law *developed* over time. Hübner, for instance, maintained that in Galatians Paul saw Christ as the absolute end of the law but that by the time of Romans he had modified his view to argue that Christ was only the end to legalism.[63] Beker is probably more on target by arguing that the differences are due to the *differing contexts* of the two epistles.[64]

Did Paul teach that Christ was the end of the law in the sense of its termination? A number of scholars argue that Paul considered the law ended and no longer valid for the believer. Among these are A. Schweitzer, E. Käsemann, and F. F. Bruce. Others argue that the law in its moral aspects continues to be valid for believers. Among these are C. E. B. Cranfield, R. N. Longenecker, and H. Conzelmann.[65] Many, in fact, would argue that Christ is the goal and fulfillment of the law.[66] The debate on Paul's view of the law is far from finished and promises to continue for a long time to come.[67]

PRACTICAL ADVICE FOR CHRISTIAN LIVING (12:1–15:13)

In chapter 12, Paul turned to practical advice about day-to-day Christian living. Paul often concluded his epistles with such hortatory (*paraenetic*) sections. This type of ethical instruction was common among the popular teachers of his day and usually was quite general in nature. But Paul's paraenetic treatment was often tied to the overall concerns of his letters. This is certainly the case with Romans. The "therefore" of 12:1 indicates that the advice to follow is based on what precedes in chapters 1–11. Indeed, many contemporary interpreters would see chapters 12–15 as addressed to actual problems within the Roman church of which Paul was aware. They would thus see these chapters as the key for understanding all of the epistle.[68]

Christ presented himself as a sacrifice for us. The proper and logical response to this divine act of grace is to sacrifice ourselves in sacred service to our Lord.[69] Paul used words in verses 1–2 which describe liturgical service, spiritual worship of God. Living *in* the world, we are not to live by its standards but to conduct ourselves with renewed minds, the minds of God's new creatures in Christ. This new being in Christ of verses 1–2 serves as the presupposition of all the exhortation that follows in 12:3 to 15:13.

Paul began by discussing relationships within the Christian congregation (12:3–16). One of his main considerations seems to have been to counter the pride and haughtiness of some over others within the congregation (vv. 3, 16).[70] This may reflect his concern for tensions between Jewish and Gentile groups in the Roman Christian fellowship. Paul employed the body analogy which he had developed previously in 1 Corinthians 12 (vv. 4–8). His list of the spiritual gifts is more general in Romans. (Tongues, for instance, were probably not an issue at Rome.) Just as in 1 Corinthians 13, Paul moved from the body analogy to the principle of love (vv. 9–10). He urged the Romans to "maintain the spiritual glow" (Moffatt translation of v. 11) and to share with one another through the active practice of Christian hospitality (v. 13). Early Christians freely provided for the needs of fellow Christians who visited their communities, particularly itinerant missionaries (cp. 3 John). Indeed, one of Paul's main purposes in writing Romans was to secure such hospitality for himself. Verse 14 is reminiscent of the teachings of Jesus (cp. Matt. 5:44). The theme reappears in verses 17–21. Christians are to live in genuine empathy and harmony with one another (vv. 15–16). This means putting aside all pride and arrogance. Conceited persons are incapable of empathy toward others.

In 12:17–13:10 Paul turned to the broader range of relationships outside the Christian community. The section falls into three main parts. First, Paul dealt with the issue of not repaying evil for evil (12:17–21). Echoing Jesus' teaching about loving one's enemies, he quoted Proverbs 25:21–22 to establish the principle of nonretaliation as a possible means to winning one's antagonists over. The desire for vengeance can be destructive. When people seek to repay evil with evil, they are dragged down to evil's level and always lose. One's persecutors might be within the Christian community. It is more likely, however, that Paul had his eye on outsiders.

Paul certainly broadened his focus beyond the Christian community in the second section, which dealt with the Christian's relationship to the state (13:1–7). Paul took a conservative stance. He pointed out that secular rulers are established by God and that to oppose them is thus to oppose God (vv. 1–2). The real purpose of government is to preserve the good and to punish wrong (vv. 3–4). Christians must thus be subject to them. Otherwise, they will incur God's wrath and suffer judgment, and they will violate their own consciences by transgressing what God has ordained (v. 5).[71] In concrete terms, this means that Christians should render respect to officials and pay their taxes and all other civil obligations. Some have suggested that Paul was addressing a concrete situation in Rome. There is evidence of unrest over heavy tax burdens in the city at this time.[72] Paul felt that Christians needed to be especially careful not to appear seditious. (Paul's judgment was on target, judging from what happened to the Roman Christians under Nero less than a decade after he wrote Romans.) Paul, of course, had in mind a government which actually functioned as instruments of God. He did not address a situation where the government had become demonic and actually opposed God, as John had to face in the time of Revelation. The latter's experience with the Roman government differed radically from Paul's.[73]

Paul's third section relates to love of one's neighbor (13:8–10). In this context the word neighbor probably reaches beyond the Christian community and includes conduct toward those outside. Jesus summarized the law in terms of love for God and love for one's neighbor (Matt. 22:40). Paul noted here that love can work no evil against one's fellow, and that is why it embraces all provisions of the law.[74] This section of Romans is a key passage in the current debate over Paul's understanding of the law. In it he seems to recognize the abiding validity of the provisions of the law while at the same time invoking a higher principle for fulfilling it.

Verses 11–14 establish the eschatological basis for all Christian relationships. Christians live in constant expectation of the Lord's return. The eschatological hope provided for Paul a basis for the present Christian life. Each day is to be lived soberly, expectantly. Walking in the light of the new day (the Lord's return), Christians should put behind them past deeds of darkness. Clothed in Christ, they are to remove the encumbrances of worldly ways. The best commentary on this passage is Ephesians 5:3–20, which shares most of its themes.

The strong and the weak in the Roman church (14:1–15:13). Most interpreters believe that Romans 14:1–15:13 reflects an actual situation within the Roman church,[75] although a minority would argue that it is only general paraenesis and not specific to Rome.[76] Much as in 1 Corinthians, Paul dealt with the problem in terms of the weak and the strong but with significant differences. In Corinth the stumbling block for the weak was meat that had been offered to idols. This does not seem to have been the case at Rome. The Roman weak are described with three characteristics: (1) they were vegetarian (14:2), (2) they observed a special day (14:5), and (3) they abstained from wine (14:21). Most feel that this points toward a Jewish Christian group. Vegetarianism, however, is hard to document for Jewish groups, although there were a number of Jewish sects (e.g., Therapeutae in Egypt) who abstained from alcoholic drink. Whoever the weak were, there seems to have been *mutual* condemnation between strong and weak at Rome. The strong haughtily disputed the reservations of the weak and looked down on them (vv. 1, 3). The weak responded by censuring those who had no scruples at all about what they ate (v. 3). Paul condemned both for their judgmental attitude, reminding them that the true basis for such matters was their relationship to the Lord, not to each other (vv. 4–6). Both groups stood on equal ground under the lordship of Christ (vv. 7–9). Rather than judging each other, they needed to worry more about how they would fare in *God's* judgment (vv. 10–12).

Paul provided the solution in 14:13–23. Although he had already told the weak to stop their censure, it was easier for the strong to yield than for the weak. For the strong, such observances as foods and worship days were *adiaphora* (indifferent issues); for the weak, they were a matter of conscience (v. 14). Thus, just as in 1 Corinthians, Paul urged the strong to give the weak no cause for stumbling (v. 13). Even though Paul agreed with the strong that nothing is unclean in itself, he insisted that love must be the ruling principle in relationships among Christians (cp. 12:9–10, 16). What really counts for the Christian are not indifferent matters like food and drink but the important things like righteousness, peace, joy in the Spirit, and upbuilding of one another (vv. 17–19).

In verses 20–21, Paul expressed the reason the strong should defer to the scruples of the weak. He was concerned about the actual damage to the faith of the weak. In verses 22–23 Paul gave a final word of advice to each group. He told the strong to keep their faith to themselves, probably meaning they were not to attempt to change the opinions of the weak in such a way as to risk their stumbling (v. 22). He advised the weak not to violate their own consciences (v. 23). Paul was speaking in a context of ethically neutral issues. He was not saying that each person should be a law unto himself or herself. He was saying that if an individual Christian has a conscience against a matter which others may condone that person should not go against her or his scruples, for that would be rebellion, and rebellion is sin.

In 15:1–13 Paul concluded his treatment of the divisions at Rome by urging the Romans to live in harmony in the example of Christ. He appealed to Christ as one who did not insist on his own rights (v. 3). He exhorted them to follow Christ's example by living in harmony and thus presenting a unified witness to the Lord Jesus Christ (vv. 5–6). In verses 7–13 it becomes apparent that the divisions in the church were between Jewish and Gentile groups. Paul reminded the Gentiles in the church that Christ came *to the Jews* to confirm the promises to the patriarchs. He reminded the Jews that Christ came as a *minister to the Gentiles*. He supported both these affirmations with Scriptures (Ps. 18:49; Deut. 32:43; Ps. 117:1; Isa. 11:10).

PERSONAL CONCLUSION TO THE LETTER (15:14–16:27)

We examined earlier in this chapter Paul's stated reasons for writing (15:14–33). We will return to this section in the next chapter in connection with Paul's collection for the saints in Jerusalem. One of Paul's reasons for writing Romans was to commend Phoebe (16:1–2). She may have been the bearer of the letter to Rome. Paul was undoubtedly known by reputation to the Romans, and his recommendation would have secured for her the hospitality and assistance of the church. Why Phoebe was traveling to Rome is unknown. She may have been a businessperson like Lydia. She probably was a person of some means, as she seems to have been a patron of the church at Cenchrea ("a great help to many people," v. 2).[77]

Romans 16:3–16 gives the longest list of greetings in any of Paul's letters. Several things are striking about it. One is the presence of Priscilla and Aquila in Rome (16:3–4). Where they risked their necks for Paul is uncertain. It could have been in Corinth or Ephesus. They had a way of following Paul around. This may not have been by chance. They were Paul's coworkers. They may have preceded him to Rome to prepare for his work there, perhaps even for his Spanish mission. The many names in the list reflect the mixed nature of Roman Christianity. Many are Jewish names or are identified by Paul as fellow Jews ("relatives")—Andronicus and Junia (v. 7), Herodion (v. 11), and, of course, Priscilla and Aquila (vv. 3–4). Particularly striking are the many women in Romans 16—Phoebe, Priscilla, Mary (v. 6), Tryphaena, Tryphosa, Persis (v. 12), the mother of Rufus (v. 13), Julia the sister of Nereus (v. 15). Junia should probably be listed (v. 7). The masculine form "Junias" is a recent innovation. The church fathers uniformly identified her as a female, and the KJV is almost surely correct in reading the feminine form of the name, "Junia." She was probably Adronicus's wife and with him was "outstanding among the apostles" (v. 7).[78]

Verses 17–20 come as something of an intrusion. It is a polemical note against those who created divisions with self-serving flattery and smooth talk. Scholars who see Romans as a fragment of an Ephesian letter see these verses as warning against the sort of Gnostic and libertine elements that eventually plagued the Asian church. Others argue that the verses are a later interpolation into the original text of Romans. The main subject of the verses is those who cause divisions, and that need not take us beyond Paul's concerns in 14:1–15:13.

In verses 21–23 Paul sent greetings from his coworkers. Tertius identified himself as Paul's amanuensis/secretary. Paul sent greetings on behalf of Gaius, with whom he was staying in Corinth and on behalf of Erastus, the "director of public works." These prominent men probably had acquaintances of means in Rome. One of Paul's concerns was to secure material support from the Romans for his Spanish mission. The protocol of including so many greetings was probably due in large part to that concern.

Verse 24 is omitted or bracketed in most modern translations. It is poorly attested among the ancient manuscripts, and is probably a later addition to Romans. It is redundant with the second, longer benediction of 16:25–27. As we have seen, the latter is found in various places in the manuscript tradition, but most likely it *was* a part of Paul's letter and came at its conclusion.

NOTES

1. See O. Cullmann, *Peter: Disciple, Apostle, Martyr* (Philadelphia: Westminster, 1962).
2. J. Munck believed the Roman Christians were almost exclusively Gentiles: *Paul and the Salvation of Mankind* (Richmond: John Knox, 1959), 201.

3. It is, however, most unlikely that the church was *predominantly* Jewish, as is maintained by W. Wiefel, "The Jewish Community in Ancient Rome and the Origins of Roman Christianity," in *The Romans Debate*, ed. K. P. Donfried, expanded ed. (Peabody, Mass.: Hendrickson, 1991), 85–101.

4. H. J. Leon, *The Jews of Ancient Rome*, updated ed. (Peabody, Mass.: Hendrickson, 1995), 229–238.

5. G. Bornkamm, "The Letter to Romans as Paul's Last Will and Testament," in *The Romans Debate*, 16–28.

6. J. Jervell, "The Letter to Jerusalem," in *The Romans Debate*, 53–64.

7. J. W. Drane, "Why Did Paul Write Romans?" in *Pauline Studies*, ed. Hagner and Harris (Grand Rapids: Eerdmans, 1980), 208–227.

8. A position also advocated by A. T. Robertson, *Epochs in the Life of Paul* (New York: Scribner's, 1909), 209–212. Against this view, see J. Munck, *Paul and the Salvation of Mankind*, 196–209.

9. W. S. Campbell, "The Rule of Faith in Romans 12:1–15:13: The Obligation of Humble Obedience to Christ as the Only Adequate Response to the Mercies of God," in *Pauline Theology, Vol. III: Romans*, ed. D. M. Hay and E. E. Johnson (Minneapolis: Fortress, 1995), 259–286. See also W. S. Campbell, "Romans III as a Key to the Structure and Thought of the Letter," in *The Romans Debate*, 251–264.

10. P. S. Minear, *The Obedience of Faith: The Purposes of Paul in the Epistle to the Romans*, Studies in Biblical Theology, series 2, #19 (London: SCM, 1971).

11. K. P. Donfried, "A Short Note on Romans 16," and "False Presuppositions in the Study of Romans," *The Romans Debate*, 44–52, 102–125.

12. R. Jewett, "Ecumenical Theology for the Sake of Mission," in *Pauline Theology, Vol. III*, 89–108. See also P. Stuhlmacher, "The Purpose of Romans," *The Romans Debate*, 231–242.

13. F. F. Bruce, "The Romans Debate—Continued," *The Romans Debate*, 175–194. For a similar view, see A. J. M. Wedderburn, *The Reasons for Romans* (Edinburgh: T. and T. Clark, 1988).

14. For a discussion of the various partition and interpolation theories, see Wedderburn, *Reasons for Romans*, 25–29 and L. E. Keck, "What Makes Romans Tick?" *Pauline Theology, Vol. III*, 7–16.

15. E.g., B. W. Robinson, *The Life of Paul* (Chicago: University of Chicago Press, 1918), 180.

16. W. Schmithals, *Paul and the Gnostics*, trans. J. E. Steeley (Nashville: Abingdon, 1962), 219–238.

17. T. W. Manson, "St. Paul's Letter to the Romans—And Others," *The Romans Debate*, 2–15.

18. Peter Lampe, "The Roman Christians of Romans 16," *The Romans Debate*, 216–230.

19. S. K. Stowers, *The Diatribe and Paul's Letter to the Romans*, SBL Dissertation Series 57 (Chico, Calif.: Scholars, 1981).

20. W. Wuellner, "Paul's Rhetoric of Argumentation in Romans: An Alternative to the Donfried-Karris Debate Over Romans"; R. Jewett, "Following the Argument of Romans," *The Romans Debate*, 128–146, 265–277.

21. M. L. Stirewalt Jr., "The Form and Function of the Greek Letter-Essay," *The Romans Debate*, 147–171.

22. D. E. Aune, "Romans as a *Logos Proptreptikos*," *The Romans Debate*, 278–296.

23. R. Jewett, "Romans as an Ambassadorial Letter," *Interpretation* 36 (1982): 5–20.

24. A major concern of Romans was the mutual acceptance of the Romans, and so Paul emphasized mutuality here. See M. J. Reid, "A Consideration of the Function of Rom 1:8–15 in Light of Greco-Roman Rhetoric," *Journal of the Evangelical Theological Society* 38 (1995): 181–191.

25. The power of one's deity was important in an honor-shame society like Paul's: H. Moxnes, "Honour and Righteousness in Romans," _Journal for the Study of the New Testament_ 32 (1988): 61–77.

26. L. Morris, "The Theme of Romans," _Apostolic History and the Gospel,_ ed. Gasque and Martin (Grand Rapids: Eerdmans, 1970), 249–263.

27. See the discussion of righteousness in chapter 9, pp. 174–175. See also S. K. Williams, "The 'Righteousness of God' in Romans," _Journal of Biblical Literature_ 99 (1980): 241–290.

28. Barth suggested this, and many recent interpreters have followed him. See D. A. Campbell, "Romans 1:17—A Crux Interpretum for the Πιστις Χριστου Debate," _Journal of Biblical Literature_ 113 (1994): 265–285; Brian Dodd, "Romans 1:17—A Crux Interpretum for the Πιστις Χριστου Debate?" _Journal of Biblical Literature_ 114 (1995): 470–473.

29. C. H. Dodd emphasized this present "working-out" of the divine wrath to the virtual exclusion of its manifestation in future judgment: _The Epistle of Paul to the Romans_ (New York: Harper, 1932), 22–24.

30. K. R. Snodgrass, "Justification by Grace—to the Doers: An Analysis of the Place of Romans 2 in the Theology of Paul," _New Testament Studies_ 32 (1986): 72–93.

31. T. R. Schreiner, "'Works of the Law' in Paul," _Novum Testamentum_ 33 (1991): 217–244.

32. L. T. Johnson, "Romans 3:21–26 and the Faith of Jesus," _Catholic Biblical Quarterly_ 44 (1982): 77–90; R. B. Hays, _The Faith of Jesus Christ_ (Chico, Calif.: Scholars, 1983). For the view that the faith is that of the believer, see A. J. Hultgren, "The _Pistis Christou_ Formulation in Paul," _Novum Testamentum_ 22 (1980): 249–263.

33. C. K. Barrett, _Paul: An Introduction to His Thought_ (Louisville: Westminster John Knox, 1994), 114–116.

34. See N. A. Dahl, "The One God of Jews and Gentiles," _Studies in Paul_ (Minneapolis: Augsburg, 1977), 178–191.

35. M. Crawford, "Abraham in Romans 4: The Father of All Who Believe," _New Testament Studies_ 41 (1995): 71–88. Romans 4 is far less polemical than Paul's treatment of Abraham in Galatians 3:6–9: T. H. Tobin, "What Shall We Say That Abraham Found? The Controversy Behind Romans 4," _Harvard Theological Review_ 88 (1995): 437–452.

36. According to M. Hengel, Christ's dying for us/for our sins is the single most important early Christian confessional statement: _The Atonement: The Origins of the Doctrine in the New Testament_ (Philadelphia: Fortress, 1981), 37. See also C. B. Cousar, _A Theology of the Cross: The Death of Jesus in the Pauline Letters_ (Minneapolis: Fortress, 1990).

37. For the interplay of determinism and individual responsibility, see A. J. M. Wedderburn, "The Theological Structure of Rom. V:12," _New Testament Studies_ 19 (1973): 339–352; R. Scroggs, _The Last Adam: A Study in Pauline Anthropology_ (Philadelphia: Fortress, 1966), 76–82. For the theological debate over original sin, see S. L. Johnson Jr., "Romans 5:12—an Exercise in Exegesis and Theology," in _New Dimensions in New Testament Study,_ ed. Longenecker and Tenney (Grand Rapids: Zondervan, 1974), 298–316.

38. H. Ridderbos calls the Adam–Christ typology a "fundamental structure" at the heart of Paul's theology: _Paul, an Outline of His Theology,_ trans. J. R. DeWitt (Grand Rapids: Eerdmans, 1975), 57–65.

39. G. Wagner argues _against_ a mystery religions background: _Pauline Baptism and the Pagan Mysteries,_ trans. J. P. Smith (Edinburgh: Oliver and Boyd, 1967). See also A. J. M. Wedderburn, "Hellenistic Christian Traditions in Romans 6?" _New Testament Studies_ 29 (1983): 337–355.

40. R. C. Tannehill, _Dying and Rising with Christ: A Study in Pauline Theology_ (Berlin: Toepelmann, 1967), 14–43. See also H. D. Betz, "Transferring a Ritual: Paul's Interpretation of Baptism in Romans 6," in _Paul in His Hellenistic Context,_ ed. T. Engberg-Pedersen (Minneapolis: Fortress, 1995), 84–118.

41. R. N. Longenecker, *Paul, Apostle of Liberty* (New York: Harper and Row, 1964), 86–97. D. J. Moo suggested that these verses refer to Israel's receipt of the law at Sinai: "Israel and Paul in Romans 7:7–12," *New Testament Studies* 32 (1986): 122–135.

42. For the view that Paul was referring to unredeemed persons as viewed from a Christian perspective, see G. Bornkamm, *Early Christian Experience*, trans. P. Hammer (New York: Harper and Row, 1969), 87–104; B. L. Martin, *Christ and the Law in Paul* (Leiden: Brill, 1989), 78–84; B. Witherington III, *Paul's Narrative Thought World* (Louisville: Westminster John Knox, 1994), 23–26.

43. M. A. Seifrid, "The Subject of Rom. 7:14–25," *Novum Testamentum* 34 (1992): 313–333; J. D. G. Dunn, "Rom. 7, 14–25 in the Theology of Paul," *Theologische Zeitschrift* 31 (1975): 257–273.

44. C. L. Mitton, "Romans VII Reconsidered," *Expository Times* 65 (1954): 78–81, 99–103, 132–135.

45. R. B. Sloan, "Paul and the Law: Why the Law Cannot Save," *Novum Testamentum* 33 (1991): 35–60.

46. See T. R. Schreiner, "The Abolition and Fulfillment of the Law in Paul," *Journal for the Study of the New Testament* 35 (1989): 47–74; S. R. Westerholm, "Letter and Spirit: The Foundation of Pauline Ethics," *New Testament Studies* 30 (1984): 229–248.

47. See D. A. Carson, *Divine Sovereignty and Human Responsibility* (Atlanta: John Knox, 1980).

48. J. Munck, *Christ and Israel: An Interpretation of Romans 9–11*, trans. I. Nixon (Philadelphia: Fortress, 1967); K. Stendahl, *Paul Among Jews and Gentiles and Other Essays* (Philadelphia: Fortress, 1976).

49. M. A. Getty, "Paul on the Covenants and the Future of Israel," *Biblical Theology Bulletin* 17 (1987): 92–99 [sees all three chapters as emphasizing the *inclusion* of the Jews]; L. Gaston, *Paul and the Torah* (Vancouver: University of British Columbia Press, 1987) [maintains the continuing validity of the old covenant apart from the new—the so-called "two covenants" view]. For a debate on this issue, see the two articles by Johnson and Moo in *Pauline Theology Vol. III*, 211–258.

50. C. K. Barrett, "Romans 9:30–10:21: Fall and Responsibility of Israel," in *Essays on Paul* (Philadelphia: Westminster, 1982), 132–153.

51. It is grammatically uncertain that Paul called Christ "God over all" in verse 5. It would be the only place where Paul called Christ God, but it appears to be the best attested early reading. See B. M. Metzger, "The Punctuation of Rom. 9:5," *Christ and Spirit in the New Testament*, ed. Lindars and Smalley (Cambridge: University Press, 1973), 95–112.

52. N. A. Dahl, *Studies in Paul*, 137–158.

53. The idea of the remnant shows that Paul had individuals and not just "corporate Israel" in mind throughout Romans 9–11. See T. R. Schreiner, "Does Romans 9 Teach Individual Election unto Salvation? Some Exegetical and Theological Reflections," *Journal of the Evangelical Theological Society* 36 (1993): 25–40.

54. See F. Thielman, *Paul and the Law: A Contextual Approach* (Downers Grove, Ill.: InterVarsity, 1994), 205–208. See by the same author *From Plight to Solution: A Jewish Framework for Understanding Paul's View of the Law in Galatians and Romans* (Leiden: Brill, 1989).

55. For Christ as the termination of the law, see C. G. Kruse, *Paul, the Law and Justification* (Peabody, Mass.: Hendrickson, 1997), 228–229. For Christ as the goal of the law, see C. E. B. Cranfield, "St. Paul and the Law," *Scottish Journal of Theology* 17 (1964): 43–68.

56. P. J. Bekken, "Paul's Use of Deut. 30:12–14 in Jewish Context: Some Observations," *The New Testament and Hellenistic Judaism*, ed. Borgen and Giversen (Peabody, Mass.: Hendrickson, 1997), 183–203.

57. Grafting wild branches onto an old olive tree was sometimes done to rejuvenate it. See W. M. Ramsay, "The Olive Tree and the Wild Olive," *Pauline and Other Studies in Early Christian History* (New York: A. C. Armstrong and Son, 1906), 219–250.

58. S. Kim, "The 'Mystery' of Rom. 11:25–26 Once More," *New Testament Studies* 43 (1997): 412–429.

59. E. P. Sanders, *Paul and Palestinian Judaism* (Philadelphia: Fortress, 1977). See also his *Paul, the Law, and the Jewish People* (Minneapolis: Fortress, 1983).

60. K. Stendahl, *Paul Among Jews and Gentiles*.

61. J. D. G. Dunn, "Works of the Law and the Curse of the Law (Galatians 3:10–14)," *New Testament Studies* 31 (1985): 523–542.

62. H. Räisänen, *Paul and the Law* (Philadelphia: Fortress, 1986).

63. H. Hübner, *Law in Paul's Thought* (Edinburgh: T. and T. Clark, 1984).

64. J. C. Beker, *Paul the Apostle: The Triumph of God in Life and Thought* (Philadelphia: Fortress, 1980), 37–108.

65. For an excellent summary of the differing views, see B. L. Martin, *Christ and the Law in Paul* (Leiden: Brill, 1989), 55–68.

66. For the "teleological" argument, see R. Badenas, *Christ the End of the Law: Romans 10:4 in Pauline Perspective* (Sheffield, England: JSOT Press, 1985).

67. For further bibliography, see J. M. G. Barclay, "Paul and the Law: Observations on Some Recent Debates," *Themelios* 12 (1986): 5–15; D. Moo, "Paul and the Law in the Last Ten Years," *Scottish Journal of Theology* 40 (1987): 287–307.

68. For example, see J. Moiser, "Rethinking Romans 12–15," *New Testament Studies* 36 (1990): 571–582.

69. Stendahl notes now Paul emphasizes *reason* as the basis of his ethic ("reasonable service," KJV, v. 1): *Final Account: Paul's Letter to the Romans* (Minneapolis: Fortress, 1993), 45–48.

70. H. Moxnes, "The Quest for Honor and the Unity of the Community in Romans 12 and in the Orations of Dio Chrysostom," *Paul in His Hellenistic Context*, 203–230.

71. R. H. Stein, "The Argument of Romans 13:1–7," *Novum Testamentum* 31 (1989): 325–343.

72. J. Friedrich, W. Pohlmann, and P. Stuhlmacher, "Zur historischen Situation und Intention von Rom. 13:1–7," *Zeitschrift für Theologie und Kirche* 73 (1976): 131–166.

73. E. Käsemann, "Principles of Interpretation of Romans 13," *New Testament Questions of Today*, trans. W. J. Montague (Philadelphia: Fortress, 1969), 196–216.

74. D. M. Smith, "The Love Command: John and Paul?" *Theology and Ethics in Paul and His Interpreters*, ed. E. H. Levering Jr., and J. L. Sumney (Nashville: Abingdon, 1996), 207–217; V. P. Furnish, *Theology and Ethics in Paul* (Nashville: Abingdon, 1968), 199–200; Furnish, *The Love Command in the New Testament* (Nashville: Abingdon, 1972).

75. F. Watson, "The Two Roman Congregations: Romans 14:1–15:13," in *The Romans Debate*, 203–215.

76. R. J. Karris, "Romans 14:1–15:13 and the Occasion of Romans," in *The Romans Debate*, 65–84.

77. C. F. Whelan, "Amici Pauli: The Role of Phoebe in the Early Church," *Journal for the Study of the New Testament* 49 (1993): 67–85.

78. R. S. Cervin, "A Note Regarding the Name 'Junia(s)' in Romans 16:7," *New Testament Studies* 40 (1994) 464–470; J. Thorley, "Junia, a Woman Apostle," *Novum Testamentum* 38 (1996): 18–29.

SELECTED COMMENTARIES

BASED ON THE GREEK TEXT

Cranfield, C. E. B. *A Critical and Exegetical Commentary on the Epistle to the Romans, Vol. I: Introduction and Commentary on Romans I–VIII; Vol. II: Commentary on Romans IX–XVI and Essays.* International Critical Commentary. Edinburgh: T. and T. Clark, 1975 and 1979.

Dunn, James D. G. *Romans.* 2 vols. Word Biblical Commentary. Dallas: Word, 1988.

Käsemann, Ernst. *Commentary on Romans.* Trans. and ed. G. W. Bromiley. Grand Rapids: Eerdmans, 1980.

Sanday, William and Arthur C. Headlam. *A Critical and Exegetical Commentary on the Epistle to the Romans.* Fifth edition. International Critical Commentary. Edinburgh: T. and T. Clark, 1908.

BASED ON THE ENGLISH TEXT

Achtemeier, Paul J. *Romans.* Interpretation. Atlanta: John Knox, 1985.

Barrett, C. K. *A Commentary on the Epistle to the Romans.* Second, revised edition. New York: Harper and Brothers, 1991.

Barth, Karl. *The Epistle to the Romans.* Trans. E. C. Hoskyns. London: Oxford, 1933.

Black, Matthew. *Romans.* New Century Bible. London: Marshall, Morgan and Scott, 1973.

Byrne, B. *Romans.* Sacra Pagina. Collegeville, Minn.: Liturgical Press, 1996.

Dodd, C. H. *The Epistle of Paul to the Romans.* Moffatt New Testament Commentary. New York: Harper and Brothers, 1932.

Edwards, J. R. *Romans.* New International Biblical Commentary. Peabody, Mass.: Hendrickson, 1992.

Fitzmyer, Joseph A. *Romans: A New Translation with Introduction and Commentary.* Anchor Bible. New York: Doubleday, 1993.

Grayston, K. *The Epistle to the Romans.* Epworth Commentaries. London: Epworth, 1997.

Harrisville, Roy A. *Romans.* Augsburg Commentary on the New Testament. Minneapolis: Augsburg, 1980.

Moo, Douglas J. *The Epistle to the Romans.* New International Commentary on the New Testament. Grand Rapids: Eerdmans, 1996.

Mounce, Robert H. *Romans.* The New American Commentary. Nashville: Broadman and Holman, 1995.

Nygren, Anders. *Commentary on Romans.* Trans. Carl C. Rasmussen. Philadelphia: Muhlenberg, 1949.

Schreiner, Thomas R. *Romans.* Baker Exegetical Commentary on the New Testament. Grand Rapids: Baker, 1998.

Stuhlmacher, Peter. *Paul's Letter to the Romans, A Commentary.* Trans. S. J. Hafemann. Louisville: Westminster John Knox, 1994.

Ziesler, J. *Romans.* TPI New Testament Commentaries. Philadelphia: Trinity Press International, 1989.

15

PAUL'S COLLECTION FOR JERUSALEM

*A*t the end of his third mission, Paul gathered a collection for the Jerusalem Christians from the Gentile churches which he had established in Asia and in Greece. He dealt with the collection in each of the letters that he wrote during this period of his ministry, Galatians, 1 and 2 Corinthians, and Romans. In the Roman epistle, Paul explained that he was delaying his trip to Rome and his mission to Spain in order first to deliver the collection to Jerusalem (15:25–29). The Book of Acts is strangely silent about Paul's collection. It deals at length with the journey to Jerusalem at the end of his third mission. Paul's own letters reveal that this journey was undertaken to deliver the collection. Acts shows how the journey was marked by warnings from Christians and Paul's own forebodings that danger awaited him in Jerusalem.

In Romans 15:30–32 Paul spoke of his fear of what might happen to him in Jerusalem and asked for the Roman Christians to pray on his behalf. He made two specific prayer requests: (1) that he would be delivered from the non-Christian Jews of Jerusalem, and (2) that his collection would be acceptable to the Christian community of the city. Because of the silence of Acts about Paul's collection, we cannot be sure how well it was received. The Acts account, however, confirms that Paul's forebodings were well-founded about the unbelieving Jews of Jerusalem. Paul *did* fall into their hands and escaped with his life only through the timely intervention of the Roman troops. Paul's desire to visit Rome was fulfilled, though not as he originally intended. He eventually went to Rome—not as a free missionary but as a prisoner.

This chapter deals with the collection and its aftermath. First, Paul's letters furnish the picture of the collection, how it was administered, its scope, its purposes. Then Acts furnishes the framework for the delivery of the collection and its results. We have outlined the treatment of Acts in three parts: (1) the journey to Jerusalem (20:3–21:16), (2) the temple mob and Paul's arrest (21:17–22:21), and (3) Paul's early Roman custody (22:22–24:27).

THE COLLECTION

The sole source for the collection is the Pauline correspondence. Paul mentioned the collection in all of the letters he wrote in the latter part of his third missionary period. We will consider them in the order in which they likely were written. This procedure should provide some sense of how the undertaking progressed over time.

GALATIANS 2:10

The idea of a collection for the Christians of Jerusalem first appears as the result of the prophet Agabus's prediction of a famine (Acts 11:27–30). In response, the church of Antioch gathered a relief offering for the Christians of Judea, which seems to have been particularly hard hit by the famine. Paul and Barnabas delivered the offering. The Antioch offering likely provides the background to Galatians 2:10. The context is the Jerusalem Conference (Gal. 2:1–9; Acts 15:1–29). There Paul's "law-free" Gentile mission was endorsed by the leading apostles in Jerusalem. At the conclusion of his account of the Jerusalem meeting in Galatians, Paul added that the apostles on that occasion asked him to "continue to remember the poor" (Gal. 2:10). The present tense ("continue to") implies that he had already been doing so, which is probably a reference to the Antioch relief offering. "The poor" refers to the Christians of Jerusalem. It was a term used in Judaism to refer to the humble, godly righteous people, who often were quite poor. They were known as the "pious poor." The term was taken over as a self-designation of the Jewish Christians.

Galatians 2:10 establishes the principle of the collection and Paul's commitment to it ("the very thing I was eager to do"). This remains true whether one dates Galatians early or late. If one dates the epistle during Paul's third mission, as we would do, the reference may be a gentle reminder to the Galatians of their own need to participate in the collection. In fact, there may be a less direct allusion to the offering in Galatians 6:6–10, where Paul urged the Galatians to share their material goods with one another, particularly with the teachers of the word. He used the analogy of sowing and reaping bountifully. He employed the same picture in 2 Corinthians 9:6 with specific reference to the collection for Jerusalem.[1] He may have had the collection in mind when he urged the Galatians to share freely with their fellow Christians.

1 CORINTHIANS 16:1–4

The first explicit directions about participating in the collection are found in 1 Corinthians 16:1–4. Paul referred to it as being for "the saints" (v. 1). Paul regularly called all Christians "saints," meaning those who have been "set apart" in Jesus Christ. Here he had in mind the "saints: in Jerusalem (v. 3; cp. Rom. 15:26). Paul mentioned that he had already given directions to the Christians in Galatia about the administration of the collection (v. 1). This is probably not a reference to the epistle to the Galatians, but some other communication Paul had with the Galatian Christians regarding the manner of assembling the offering.

Paul instructed the Corinthians to set aside money on the "first day" of each week. The first day of the Jewish week was Sunday, and this seems to be an early reference to Sunday being a day for Christian assembly. The picture is of the individual Corinthians bringing their contributions regularly to their Sunday gatherings and the church then setting the offering aside until Paul's arrival. Paul insisted that the offering was voluntary and only in proportion to the capacity of each person to contribute. Paul wanted the church to administer the collection; he did *not* want to have to supervise it himself. At this point he seems to have left it entirely up to the Corinthians. No representatives of Paul were sent to administer the gift.[2]

Verse 3 outlines the procedure for sending the collection to Jerusalem. The church was to select official representatives who would accompany the gift to Jerusalem. Since Paul was known to the Jerusalem leadership, he would write letters of recommendation introducing the delegates. At this point Paul was uncertain whether he would go himself. Obviously, if he did the delegates would not need commendatory letters (v. 4).

2 CORINTHIANS 8

The most extensive treatment of the collection is found in 2 Corinthians 8–9. Paul's discussion is so long and at points so seemingly redundant that many would argue the two chapters belong to different letters. Typical is H. D. Betz. He sees chapter 8 as addressed to Corinth; chapter 9 is a more general epistle addressed to all the churches of Achaia.[3] Though we would argue for the unity of 2 Corinthians, we have divided the two chapters here but solely for purposes of outlining.

The administration of the offering. Chapter 8 deals at length with the procedure for gathering the collection. Paul still referred to it as an offering for "the saints" (v. 4). He held up the Macedonians as an example (vv. 1–5). These churches (Philippi, Thessalonica, Berea) had given sacrificially, even begging Paul for the privilege of sharing in the collection (v. 4). Evidently Titus had begun the process of gathering the collection at Corinth (v. 6). Perhaps he was the bearer of 1 Corinthians and upon delivering the letter gave verbal instructions in addition to Paul's written directions. In any event, Titus was coming again to make final arrangements for the offering (v. 17). Paul was somewhere in Macedonia when he wrote 2 Corinthians and sent Titus to administer the collection. Paul had finished his Ephesian ministry, was winding up the collection in Macedonia, and soon would be coming to Corinth himself for his final three-month stay.

Paul had been occupied with the collection for at least a year. Indeed, Corinth had pledged its participation a year previously (v. 10; cp. 9:2). Titus was coming to Corinth with two other brothers to administer the collection. One was an official delegate chosen by the churches. Paul described him as being praised in all the churches for his gospel ministry (vv. 18–19). The reference is tantalizing, and many have attempted to identify this famous brother. Some have suggested Luke.[4] Others have postulated one of the two appointed by Jerusalem to share the apostolic decrees with the churches, Judas Barsabbas or Silas (Acts 15:22).[5] Frankly, there is nothing in the text of 2 Corinthians to assist in identifying him, nor is there any basis for determining the second brother whom Paul was sending (v. 22). Paul was being very cautious. He was sending Titus and the two brothers for a good reason—to establish multiple responsibility for the monetary gift and thereby maintain his own personal integrity in the matter. Paul did not want any basis for an accusation that he had misused funds (vv. 20–21). Evidently there were some people in Corinth who had already charged him with doing just that (2 Cor. 12:17–18). Paul's principle of multiple responsibility for church funds is still a sound practice for churches to follow.

Paul grounded his appeal for the Corinthian participation in three basic Christian principles of giving. The first is that of Christian service. Giving is a form of Christian ministry. Paul referred to the collection as a service or ministry (Gk., *diakonia*, vv. 4, 19). Second, the Lord Jesus himself set the pattern of giving for us. He did not cling to his divine riches but became poor for our sakes, that we might become rich as his joint heirs (v. 9). Paul may well have had Philippians 2:5–11 in mind. Third is the principle of equality. Christians should share with fellow Christians who are in need. Paul used the example of Israel's wilderness experience, where God allotted an equal portion of manna daily to each Israelite (vv. 13–15).[6] Paul may have had in mind the fact that the gospel had gone forth from Jerusalem, bringing spiritual blessings to Gentiles like the Corinthians. Now it was their turn to equalize matters with their material blessings for Jerusalem (Rom. 15:27).

2 CORINTHIANS 9

Paul did not provide any additional information in 2 Corinthians 9 about the administration of the collection. He mainly continued his appeal for the Corinthians to live up to their previous commitment to participate in the collection. He seems to have used a bit of "reverse psychology" in verses 1–5. In 8:1–5 he challenged the Corinthians with the example of Macedonia. In 9:1–5 he told the Corinthians that he had challenged the Macedonians with *their* readiness to give. He didn't want to be put to shame. If some Macedonians accompanied him to Corinth and found the Corinthians unwilling to give, Paul was sure to lose face. In 1 Corinthians 16:3 Paul spoke of how the churches were to appoint official delegates to represent them in carrying the offering to Jerusalem. The Macedonians who might accompany Paul to Corinth were possibly the delegates from the Macedonian churches (v. 4).

Most of chapter 9 is devoted to establishing a theological basis for giving. Paul grounded Christian giving in God's own righteousness (v. 9). As a gracious God who maintains his covenant love, God is "righteous," providing amply for his own. God's own righteousness is thus the basis of all our own righteousness (v. 10). The Jews often used the word *righteousness* to refer to the practice of charity ("alms"). Paul may have had this in mind. The collection was a monetary expression, an act of one's righteousness based in the righteousness of God. Paul also saw the collection as an expression of thanksgiving to God for his "indescribable gift" in Christ Jesus (v. 15). Verses 14–15 contain a play on words. In Greek the same word (*charis*) can be used to express either "grace" or "thanks." The same relationship occurs in the English language: *grat*itude is the proper response to *grace*.[7]

ROMANS 15:25–33

Paul wrote Romans during his final three-month stay in Corinth. He was winding up his ministry in the east, having preached all the way from Jerusalem to the Adriatic coast of Greece (v. 19). He was making the final arrangements for the collection. With the coming of spring and favorable weather for navigation, his plans were to sail straight for Jerusalem with the collection. Paul wanted to visit Rome. He wanted Rome to support him in a mission to Spain (vv. 23–24, 28–29). Paul explained to the Romans why he was still delaying his coming to them. He must first deliver the collection to the saints in Jerusalem (v. 25). It must have been very pressing for Paul. When he wrote 1 Corinthians a year or so earlier, he was not even sure he would accompany the church representatives with the gift. Now he was definitely going, even though it meant delaying his Spanish mission, even though it was at considerable personal risk.

Paul mentioned that Achaia and Macedonia had contributed to the collection (v. 26). One wonders why he failed to mention Galatia and Asia. From the composition of the delegation mentioned in Acts 20:4, they seem to have participated. Perhaps at the point when Paul wrote Romans from Corinth the Macedonians had already come and joined the Achaians in preparation for the collection journey. The Asians and Galatians may not yet have met up with them.

Paul requested the prayers of the Romans (vv. 30–32). He specifically requested two petitions. First, he asked for prayer that the collection would be acceptable to the Jerusalem Christians. Perhaps the fact that it might not be well received helped him make the decision to accompany the collection in person. Second, he prayed that he would be delivered from the unbelievers in Jerusalem. Paul was well aware of the danger that awaited him in Jerusalem. As things turned out, his forebodings were very well-grounded.

ACTS

Acts never explicitly mentions Paul's collection. It relates in great detail Paul's final journey to Jerusalem, the journey which we know from his letters was primarily undertaken to deliver the collection. Luke was certainly aware of early Christian charity. He told of the Antioch relief to Jerusalem, which seems to have provided the pattern for Paul's collection (Acts 11:27–30). He also spoke of the Jerusalem church's practice of extensive sharing, which may have contributed to the financial distress of the church (Acts 4:32–5:11). Acts is not totally silent about the collection. Acts 24:17 mentions Paul's having brought "gifts" and "offerings" to Jerusalem, which is probably a reference to the collection. It is, however, buried in a speech before the Roman governor. One would never guess from this vague reference that Paul had undertaken such an extensive offering from his Gentile churches for the Jewish Christians of Jerusalem. One could look for hints at the collection in Acts. For example, Paul's strong emphasis on giving in his Miletus address may echo his preoccupation with the gift (cp. 20:35).

Certainly the list of delegates in Acts 20:4 points to the collection. Why such a delegation at all? Paul never before took such a group with him when he returned to Jerusalem. One would have to postulate something like the collection to explain their presence. They represented a broad spectrum of Paul's churches. There were three from *Macedonia*, Sopater, Aristarchus, and Secundus. Gaius and Timothy represented *Galatia*. Tychicus and Trophimus were *Asians*. The only area not included was *Achaia*. Did Luke simply fail to mention the Achaians? Were they perhaps overlooked because they were "too obvious"? Titus has sometimes been suggested as the Achaian representative.[8] It is also striking that Philippi had no representative listed. Luke himself may have represented that congregation. The resumption of the "we" in Acts 20:5–6 seems to indicate that Luke joined the collection delegation at Philippi. In any event, Paul's large entourage on his journey to Jerusalem is best explained as being the official delegation from the churches which accompanied him with the collection (cp. 1 Cor. 16:3–4).

Why did Luke not mention the collection? The occurrence of the "we" would indicate that Luke accompanied Paul to Jerusalem and eventually on to Rome. He *had* to be aware of the collection.[9] Of course, the collection may have proved to be an embarrassment. Palestine in the late 50s was a hotbed of Jewish nationalism and anti-Roman sentiment, a situation which led to the war with Rome in less than a decade. A collection from Gentiles may have proved dangerous and thus unwelcome to Jewish Christians in such a political climate. It may have simply been refused, a failure which Luke chose not to narrate.[10] Some have suggested that the collection might have seemed to be some sort of peace offering and thus have run counter to

Luke's picture of a healthy relationship between Paul and the Jerusalem apostles.[11] One could respond to the latter observation by noting that Paul in his letters did not himself reflect an unhealthy relationship with the leadership in Jerusalem. The collection surely symbolized Christian unity but in a positive rather than a negative sense.

Another suggestion for Luke's silence focuses more on the Romans than the Jews. It has been argued that the Romans might have considered the collection an illegal levy, a form of taxation in competition with their own. Writing most likely *after* the fall of Jerusalem, when the Romans had already appropriated the Jewish temple tax in support of their own temples, Luke may have felt that the Romans would look askance at any remotely similar Christian levy. Thus, he chose not to write about it lest it create difficulty between the Christians and the Romans.[12] This theory is based on the assumption that Paul's collection was patterned after the Jewish temple tax, which is not likely. Paul's was a completely voluntary offering, not an assessment. It is unlikely the Romans would have viewed it otherwise. The most likely explanation for Luke's silence about the collection is simply that he chose to concentrate on other things that he wished to emphasize in his narrative. For instance, he wanted to emphasize how the *Spirit* led Paul to Jerusalem and eventually to Rome.[13] He might have considered the collection as a sidetrack from the main theological emphases he wished to draw upon.

THE REASONS FOR THE COLLECTION

Why did Paul undertake the collection? He had many reasons *not* to go. For one, the danger in Jerusalem was intense. It was a time of extreme patriotism. Paul's Gentile mission and lax attitude toward the Torah made him a renegade in the eyes of many Jews. The collection also meant a major delay in Paul's plans to begin a new mission in Spain. Paul was eager to enlist the Roman Christians in this enterprise. Rome was only a week's journey from Corinth, from which Paul departed with the collection. The trip to Jerusalem was a journey of several weeks in the opposite direction. Obviously the collection was very important to Paul. Why? Three main reasons have been suggested. They are not mutually exclusive. Paul's goals with the collection may have in part embraced all three.

Charity. The Jerusalem church seems to have often been in dire need. This was probably due to a combination of factors, such as the famines that plagued Palestine and the extensive charity of the Jerusalem church itself (cp. Acts 6:1). As Paul told the Romans (15:27), it was only right for the Gentile churches to share with the mother church to which they owed their very existence. But the delegates of the churches were sufficient to administer such a charity. Paul's letters of introduction would have been sufficient. Why did he feel the need to go *in person?*

The eschatological basis. Paul's concept of his Gentile mission was rooted in his conviction that Christ was the promised Messiah. As we have seen, the Gentile mission was in Jewish thought an accompaniment of the messianic age. The prophets pictured the Gentiles as streaming to Jerusalem in the end time (Isa. 2:3; Mic. 4:2). Paul surely shared this vision, and it lay at the heart of his own sense of calling as the apostle to the Gentiles. Other prophetic texts speak of the wealth of the nations flowing to Jerusalem in the final days (Isa. 60:5; 66:20). Building on this, some scholars have argued that Paul interpreted his collection in terms of this prophetic scheme, seeing the offering from the Gentiles as an act that would bring about the final events.[14] That Paul saw his Gentile mission in apocalyptic terms is likely. That he saw his collection as a culminating event that would precipitate the final times is not so probable. Paul seems to have settled in for a longer ministry. If he thought his collection would bring about the end, why did he concern himself with a mission to Spain?[15]

Christian unity. Throughout his ministry Paul maintained a close relationship with the church in Jerusalem. He visited the Jerusalem Christian community at the end of each missionary journey. He went to Jerusalem voluntarily to secure Jewish-Christian recognition of his ministry to the Gentiles (Gal. 2:1–10). Israel was the native covenantal stock into which Paul's Gentile converts were being grafted. Paul always viewed his Christian faith in terms of God's promises to Israel (cp. Rom. 11). That is why it was important for him to continue to win the approval of the Jewish Christian leadership in Jerusalem for his mission among the Gentiles. Now he was planning a new mission to Spain. One major reason to go to Jerusalem *at this time* was probably to secure recognition of that new undertaking. In any event, Paul's collection was a symbol of Christian unity—of Paul's uncircumcised Gentile converts sacrificing for the needs of their Jewish sisters and brothers in Christ. Paul had experienced severe conflict with the Judaizers at Galatia and Jewish "super-apostles" at Corinth. They were radicals. There is no indication that the Jerusalem Jewish Christian leadership sympathized with them. Still, the experience may have impressed on Paul's mind the importance of a unified people of God, Jew and Gentile in Christ. The collection became for him more than just a charitable act, though it was certainly that. It became a visible expression of the inclusive gospel that embraces all peoples in Christ Jesus. That was a cause Paul was willing to die for.

THE JOURNEY TO JERUSALEM (ACTS 20:3–21:16)

Acts may be silent about Paul's collection, but it is certainly not silent about the forebodings that Paul shared concerning his trip to Jerusalem. Luke related Paul's final Jerusalem journey at some length, noting how all along the way he was warned that suffering and imprisonment awaited him in the holy city. One is reminded of Jesus' similar journey to Jerusalem, of how he shared with his disciples that suffering and death awaited him there. Like Jesus, Paul was arrested in Jerusalem and taken before both Jewish and Roman officials, even the Jewish king. There were major differences, of course. Jesus was crucified in Jerusalem. Paul lived to bear witness to the risen Christ—before courts and kings and even the emperor himself.

FROM CORINTH TO TROAS (20:3–6)

Paul's original plan was to sail directly to Syria from Corinth. When he heard that some Jews were plotting to attack him, he changed his itinerary and went on land by way of Macedonia to Philippi. The two Asian delegates, Tychicus and Trophimus, evidently returned to Asia, perhaps to arrange for a ship. They were to rejoin the larger party at Troas. It was Passover. The group remained in Philippi for the days of unleavened bread, then sailed to Troas.

TROAS (20:7–12)

Alexandria Troas was the main connecting point between Macedonia and Asia. Paul had received his Macedonian call there (16:9–10) but does not seem to have established a church there until the latter part of his third mission (2 Cor. 2:12). The church was probably only months old when Paul and the collection delegation spent a week with them. The main part of the narrative is the story of Eutychus, a young man whose name meant "good fortune." We would call him Lucky.[16] It is a delightfully told story. The Christians were gathered to hear the apostle as he spoke in a crowded upper room long into the night. Many lamps consumed the oxygen, making the air stifling. Eutychus, perched in a window, sunk into a deep sleep and fell three stories to the ground below. Going down, Paul lifted him up and declared that his life was in him. Luke had clearly stated that the boy was dead (v. 9). We are to see this as a resurrection miracle. God restored the boy to life through Paul, just as Dorcas was raised through Peter (Acts 9:36–41). It was around Passover, the time when Christ rose from the dead. The restoration of Eutychus was for the Christians at Troas a living reminder that Christ is the resurrection and the life.

TROAS TO MILETUS (20:13–16)

The ship departed for Assos with Paul's traveling companions, but Paul stayed behind in Troas, probably to remain with the young church to the last possible minute. Next day he went to Assos by foot. The sea journey to Assos was twice the distance of the journey by foot. Joining the company at Assos, the ship put out to its next port of Mitylene on the island of Lesbos. The ship was probably a coasting vessel, which hung close to the coast and put in to port each night after the daytime winds had died down. The journey from Troas to Miletus seems to have taken five days. Their course took them close to Ephesus, but they did not put in there. They continued on to Miletus, where the boat docked. Paul sent for the leaders of the Ephesian church to come join him in Miletus. One wonders why he did not stop in Ephesus. Luke said that Paul was in a hurry to get to Jerusalem by Pentecost, but it would have involved less time had they docked in Ephesus. Miletus is thirty miles south of Ephesus by the shortest route. A messenger would have to be sent from Miletus to Ephesus to fetch the elders. Several days would have elapsed. Perhaps it was still not safe for Paul in Ephesus after the turmoil with the silversmiths. Perhaps Paul knew that it would be difficult for him to tear himself away from the Ephesian Christians. Maybe it was simply a matter of the ship's schedule. Paul had no control over where the ship would stop, and Miletus may have been a scheduled stopping place for several days.

MILETUS

In its heyday Miletus was the largest port on the Aegean coast of Asia. Lying at the mouth of the Maeander River, it had four natural harbors. Like Ephesus, these are today all silted in, and the ancient city lies some five miles inland. The site seems to have been occupied from prehistoric times. It was first settled as an outpost by Mycenean Greeks from Achaia (fourteenth century B.C.). Ionians occupied it in the twelfth century B.C. Under the Ionians, from the twelfth until the fifth century B.C., it was the greatest city of all Asia. The Persians conquered the region in the sixth century B.C., and in the fifth century B.C. Miletus led an unsuccessful revolt against them. The Persians destroyed the city, and though it was rebuilt, it never recovered its former prominence, being thereafter eclipsed by Ephesus. Still, in Paul's day it was a prosperous city, still possessing the finest harbor in the region. It had a population of perhaps sixty thousand. It boasted three separate agoras, a testimony to its prominence as a commercial center.[17]

PAUL'S ADDRESS AT MILETUS (20:17–38)

Paul's speech to the Ephesian church leaders is the third major Pauline address in Acts. There is a major speech for each of the three Pauline missions, and each is to a different audience. On his first mission, Paul spoke to the Jews and God-fearers at Pisidian Antioch (13:16–41). On the second mission, the speech was to the *pagan* philosophers of Athens (17:22–31). Here at Miletus at the end of his third mission Paul addressed the *Christian* leaders from Ephesus. Of all Paul's speeches in Acts, it is closest to Paul's own letters and is particularly reminiscent of the Pastoral Epistles. It has often been likened to a "farewell address."[18] It is certainly Paul's farewell to the Asian churches but is not a farewell in the "ultimate" sense; it does not presage his martyrdom.[19] As it turned out, it may not have been his final farewell to Asia. He may have returned to the region after release from his first Roman imprisonment. Paul's address to the elders can be outlined in four main divisions.

1. Paul's past example (20:18–21). Paul began by listing three characteristics of his three-year ministry in Ephesus: his humility (v. 19), his openness (v. 20), and his inclusiveness (v. 21). Paul preached to everybody, both Jews and Greeks alike (cp. 19:20).

2. Paul's future prospects (20:22–27). Paul turned to the future dangers that awaited him in Jerusalem. (Throughout his journey as narrated in 21:1–16, Christians along the way through the Spirit's inspiration warned him of the trials he would encounter in the holy city.) In verses 26–27 Paul drew from the image of the watchman in Ezekiel, which emphasizes that the watchman is only responsible for faithfully sounding the alarm. Paul had done that; he had been a faithful witness to God's word to all. He was thus innocent of anyone's life. Each was responsible for his own response. Verse 25 is the key verse in the whole speech. It prepares for Paul's tearful departure in verse 38, and for the ominous tone that pervades Paul's entire journey to Jerusalem.

3. Paul's warning of future heresies (20:28–31). Paul now appealed to the Ephesian leaders to take responsibility for their flock and to protect them from false teachers who would arise in the future to ravage them. Paul addressed the leaders as "overseers" (Gk., *episkopos*, sometimes translated "bishop"). In verse 17 Luke called them "elders." The two terms *bishop* and *elder* seem to be synonymous in New Testament usage. Throughout this section Paul described the leaders functionally as shepherds, employing the shepherd imagery of Ezekiel 34.[20] Verse 28 is the central verse in the section and stands at the center of the entire speech with its reference to God's purchasing his church with his own blood (or "with the blood of his own [son]"). It is the clearest reference to the blood atonement in the Book of Acts.[21]

4. Paul's blessing and final admonition (20:32–35). Paul concluded by admonishing the Ephesians about their relation to material goods. The only legacy that counts, he said, is one's divine inheritance (v. 32). Because of that, he never coveted anyone's silver or gold but worked with his own hands to support himself and his coworkers. Paul spoke of supporting himself in 1 Thessalonians and 1 Corinthians, but this is the only place where he spoke of supporting his assistants. The key lesson is embodied in the saying from Jesus, a saying not found in the Gospels: "It is more blessed to give than to receive" (v. 35). In a sense, this verse sets the theme of Paul's entire address. Paul had modeled a giving ministry in Ephesus, and he urged the Ephesian leaders to follow his example. At the center stood God's own sacrificial giving (v. 28).[22]

Epilogue. Verses 36–38 provide the conclusion to the Miletus scene. His speech concluded, it was time for Paul to depart. It was a sad scene with many hugs and even more tears. The Ephesians were grieved over Paul's words that they would not see him again. The tone thereby is set for the continuing journey to Jerusalem.

The word translated *accompanied* in verse 38 may imply more than that they simply accompanied Paul to the ship. It is a Greek word (*propempein*) which often is used in a semitechnical sense for furnishing provisions for someone's voyage. There were no ancient passenger vessels. One had to secure passage on a merchant vessel. One didn't eat at the captain's table. Travelers were responsible for their own meals. The Christian group at Miletus may well have sent Paul forth on the voyage with the provisions he and the collection delegation would need for their journey.

MILETUS TO JERUSALEM (21:1–16)

Tyre (21:1–6). Paul now set out for Jerusalem. His trip is narrated in some detail, as Luke continued to list each port where the ship put in for the night. Their coasting vessel eventually reached the port of Patara, where they secured passage in a larger, open-sea vessel bound for the Phoenician coast. Patara was about four hundred miles from Tyre by sea, and the journey could be made in five days under favorable conditions. The group spent a week with the Christians of Tyre, as their ship unloaded its cargo there. The Christian community of Tyre probably owed its existence to Hellenist Christian missionaries (cp. Acts 11:19). The Christians of Tyre through the Spirit urged Paul not to go to Jerusalem. This should not be viewed as a conflict with Paul's equally strong feeling that the Spirit was leading him to Jerusalem. The warnings of the Christians served to fortify Paul for the unpleasant experiences that awaited him in the city, but Paul was under conviction that God's will was for him to go (cp. 20:22–23). The fears of the Tyrian Christians serve to heighten the dramatic tension in the narrative as does the tearful departure on the shore (vv. 5–6).

Philip (21:7–9). Paul's group seems to have continued on in the same ship to its next port of call, Ptolemais. Ptolemais was an ancient settlement, the southernmost port of the Phoenician coast. It is mentioned in Judges 1:31, where it is called Acco. It was called Acre in the Crusader period and has returned in modern times to its ancient name of Acco. Paul visited briefly with the Christians there, staying only a day before journeying on the twenty-five miles to Caesarea. In Caesarea he stayed with Philip the evangelist. Philip seems to have settled in Caesarea after his encounter with the Ethiopian eunuch (Acts 8:40). We are told that Philip had four daughters with the gift of prophecy. Eusebius cited later traditions which associated Philip and his daughters with Heirapolis in the Lycus River Valley, an Asian church originally founded by Paul (Col. 4:13; Eusebius, *Eccl. Hist.* 3.31.2–5). In Acts 21, Philip's daughters do not prophesy. The Judean prophet Agabus does (cp. Acts 11:27–30).

Agabus (21:10–14). Agabus followed an Old Testament pattern of an "acted out" prophecy in which the prophet dramatically portrayed God's message for his people.[23] In this instance Agabus used Paul's "belt," the long band of cloth wrapped several times around his waist. The prophet bound himself hand and foot with the cloth and declared that the Jews of Jerusalem would bind Paul in like fashion and deliver him to the Gentiles. In this case, Agabus seemed to offer no option. This *would* happen to Paul, he predicted. The Christians present, including Luke ("we"), urged Paul not to go (v. 12). But Paul had resolved that he must go. If there had ever been any doubt whether he might be dissuaded from going, Paul now provided no option. He was ready even to die for Jesus in Jerusalem (v. 13). The Christians present conceded to Paul's resolve: "the Lord's will be done," they said (v. 14). Truly it was "Paul's Gethsemanie."[24] The comparison to Jesus could hardly be missed. Like his Lord, Paul was to be bound by the Jews and delivered to the Gentiles (cp. Matt. 20:18–19; Luke 18:32).

Mnason (21:15–16). Having remained with the Caesarean Christians for a number of days (v. 10), Paul set out with his delegation on the sixty-four mile trip to Jerusalem. Some Caesarean Christians led the way, putting them up with an "early disciple" named Mnason. *Mnason* is a Greek name, equivalent to Jason. He is said to have come from Cyprus. He was probably one of those Greek-speaking Christian "Hellenists" like his fellow Cypriot Barnabas. It is not clear whether Mnason lived in Jerusalem or whether his house was a stopping place on the journey between the two cities. The Western Text of Acts implies the latter. But if Mnason lived in Jerusalem, it would perhaps cast light on the following narrative. In that case Paul would not have stayed with the Jewish Christians of Jerusalem but with his fellow Greek-speaking Hellenist Christians.

THE TEMPLE MOB AND PAUL'S ARREST (ACTS 21:17–22:21)

Things turned out exactly as the Spirit had led Paul to anticipate. He was not delivered from the unbelievers in Judea (Rom. 15:31) but was assaulted by a Jewish mob in the temple area and taken into custody by the Romans.

THE CONCERN OF THE JERUSALEM CHRISTIAN ELDERS (21:17–26)

Verse 17 implies that Paul's collection was well received by the Jerusalem Christians. He was greeted "warmly." Still, Paul presented something of an embarrassment to the leaders of the Jewish Christian congregations. Paul's Gentile mission had given him a reputation for being antinomian, even for encouraging the *Jews* on his mission field not to live by the law. The elders called a meeting to consult with Paul on the matter, a meeting not unlike the Jerusalem Conference a decade or so earlier (Acts 15:1–31). It is undoubtedly significant that James referred back to that meeting by citing the "decrees" that had been agreed upon then (v. 25). In that conference the issue of Gentile obligation to the Torah had been settled. Now a *new* problem had arisen, that of the *Jewish* Christian minority in Paul's Gentile-dominated churches. There may have been a grain of truth in James's concern that the Jewish Christians in Paul's churches may have found it difficult to maintain the Jewish ceremonial laws in congregations that were primarily Gentile. Even should that have been the case, it would not have been at Paul's encouragement. Paul always urged the Jewish Christians to continue living by their Jewish customs (cp. 1 Cor. 7:18–20).

The problem was exacerbated for the Christian elders in Jerusalem by two factors. One was their own increasing success in reaching the Jews with the gospel. Thousands had been won to faith in Jesus Messiah, but they were messianic *Jews*; they were all "zealous for the law" (v. 20). The second problem was closely related—the rising Jewish nationalism that marked this period, the decade just prior to the outbreak of war between the Jews and Rome. Any whisper that Paul was encouraging Jewish infidelity to the Torah would be roundly censured. James himself seems to have been a model of faithfulness to the Jewish law, a strategy he probably followed in order to be as effective as possible in his outreach to his fellow Jews with the gospel.[25]

James and his fellow elders had come up with a solution whereby Paul could establish his faithfulness to the law. They asked him to underwrite the expenses of four Jewish Christians who were approaching the conclusion of a Nazarite vow they had taken (vv. 23–24). Those who took a Nazirite vow abstained from alcohol and let their hair grow during the entire period of the vow. At the vow's completion, they had their hair cut at the temple, offered a sacrifice there, and cast their shorn hair in the flames. The sacrifices were expensive, involving two lambs, a ram, and various grain and drink offerings for each Nazirite (Num. 6:14–15). Vows lasted at least thirty days, so it is not a question of Paul's joining in the vow, only of his paying the expenses of the four Nazirites. The purification which Paul underwent (v. 26) was probably a ritual cleansing that Jews often practiced when returning to the Holy Land from abroad, based on the principle for the removal of defilement established in Numbers 19:12. It called for a seven-day period of purification, which Paul seems to have undergone (v. 27). Nazirite vows were a somewhat extreme form of piety. Paul's participation was thus an apt way to express his continuing fidelity to Judaism, his still being "a Jew to the Jews" (1 Cor. 9:20).

THE RIOT IN THE TEMPLE AREA (21:27–36)

The agitators (vv. 27–29). One could hardly have established a more perfect setup to get Paul in trouble. He had been seen in town with the Ephesian collection delegate Trophimus by some Asian Jews who recognized them both (v. 29). They were probably Ephesians themselves who had come to Jerusalem as Pentecost pilgrims. Paul had appeared in the temple with the Nazirites to make a formal announcement of the ceremonies to take place a week later. Everyone thus knew exactly when Paul would be back in the temple. The Asians may have seized the opportunity to prepare a foment. In any event, when Paul did appear for the Nazirite ceremony, they stirred up a mob, leveling three incendiary accusations against Paul: he taught against the Jewish people, he spoke against the law, and he defiled the temple. The Asians may have actually imagined that Paul had brought his Gentile friend Trophimus into the sacred precincts. Even though it was untrue, the accusation alone was enough to provoke a riot.

Paul was charged with a serious offense from the Jewish perspective—defilement of the sanctuary. The Herodian temple consisted of a large outer courtyard. Known as the court of the Gentiles, it comprised the greater part of the temple precincts and was open to everyone. However, only Jews were allowed into the temple proper, which was located in the northern part of the temple area. At its entrance it was surrounded by a stone barrier about chest high, into which had been set warning stones at regular intervals. These stones bore an inscription which told non-Jews not to proceed any further on pain of death. In the last century or so, two of these stones have been found.[26]

The riot (vv. 30–32). The mob dragged Paul outside of the sacred enclosure so as not to defile the sanctuary with his blood. The gates were slammed shut, probably the beautiful Corinthian bronze gates that separated the court of the men of Israel from the court of the women. Word soon reached the commander of the Roman garrison in Jerusalem that a riot was occurring in the court of the Gentiles. The commander had the rank of a tribune, which meant that he had one thousand troops under him. His name was Claudius Lysias (23:26). The Romans quartered their troops in the tower of Antonia, a palatial structure built by Herod the Great at the northwest corner of the temple wall. It had four towers. The southeast tower was elevated over one hundred feet from the ground and overlooked the entire temple complex. A sentry there could see anything going on in the temple area below. A double staircase from Antonia led directly into the court of the Gentiles (Josephus, *War*, 5. 238–247). It thus did not take the Romans long to ascertain the trouble and get to the scene of the riot. Verse 32 says that Lysias took some "centurions" (NIV, "officers") and soldiers. Centurions commanded one hundred soldiers; so a considerable force was involved. At this show of power, the mob quickly dispersed. The whole scene was filled with irony. Paul had come to the temple to prove his Jewishness. It only resulted in the mob accusing him of being an enemy of the Jews.

The arrest (vv. 33–36). Lysias had no idea what had caused the disturbance. Obviously Paul was the center of attention. It was equally obvious that Paul would be torn to shreds if the tribune left him in the hands of the mob. So Lysias had Paul arrested. He had him bound with two chains, which may either mean chained by hand to a solider on each side, or bound both hand and foot. The latter would fit the prophecy of Agabus (21:11). The crowd was so unruly that Lysias could not determine the nature of their grievances against Paul. The crowd pressed so close against the troops that Paul had to be lifted up and carried up the stairs to Antonia. The crowd shouted, "Away with him" (v. 36), the same words the crowd shouted against Jesus (Luke 23:18; John 19:15).

PAUL'S REQUEST TO ADDRESS THE CROWD (21:37–40)

As they were entering the barracks, Paul politely asked the tribune if he might have a word with him. Lysias was somewhat taken aback, having no idea that Paul was a cultured person who could speak fluent Greek. Quite to the contrary, he had surmised that Paul was a revolutionary like the Egyptian Jew who had several years previously led an abortive revolt against the Romans. Josephus also mentioned this Egyptian Jew (*War* 2.261–263; *Ant.* 20.168–172). Josephus was prone to exaggeration. He said that the Egyptian persuaded some thirty thousand to follow him (cp. the four thousand of v. 38). Leading them to the Mount of Olives, he promised them that at his command the walls of Jerusalem would miraculously fall. Instead, Felix arrived with his troops and scattered the revolutionaries, killing some four hundred and arresting two hundred others. The Egyptian managed to escape, however. Lysias wondered if he had not returned in the person of Paul.

Paul may have been offended at Lysias's insinuation that he might be an uncultured Egyptian provincial. He replied that far from being a peasant he was a citizen of a prestigious city, the city of Tarsus in Cilicia. At this point he chose not to divulge his Roman citizenship. He would do that later, when needed (22:25). Paul then informed Lysias of his request; he would like to address the Jewish crowd. Lysias granted him permission to do so. He probably wanted himself to hear from Paul, perhaps to determine from his words to the crowd exactly what were the grievances. The crowd became silent when Paul addressed them. They were probably surprised by his addressing them in the language of Jerusalem. They probably expected him to be a Diaspora Greek speaker, not someone fluent in their own native tongue. With his first Aramaic word Paul was on his way toward establishing his point. He wanted to convince the crowd that their accusations were wrong, that in every respect he was a loyal Jew.

PAUL'S SPEECH BEFORE THE TEMPLE MOB (22:1–21)

Chapters 22–26 of Acts are filled with speeches, as Paul offered his defense in various settings. At the time of Paul's conversion, God had told Ananias that Paul would be his witness before Gentiles, kings, and the people of Israel (Acts 9:15). These words are fulfilled in this section of Acts, where the apostle is shown to have witnessed before the *people of Israel* (22:1–21), including its leaders (23:1–10), before the *Gentile* governors (24:10–21), and before the Jewish *king* (26:1–29). Ultimately he would witness before Caesar himself. His first testimony was to the Jewish mob from the steps of Antonia. His main purpose in this speech was to establish his Jewishness.

Paul's former zeal (vv. 1–5). Paul began his speech by addressing the Jewish crowd as "brothers and fathers," exactly as Stephen did in his defense (Acts 7:2). Their charges that Paul had violated both law and temple (21:28) were the same charges as those brought against Stephen (Acts 6:13). Paul referred to his complicity in Stephen's death at the end of this speech (v. 20). How ironic that the persecutor Paul who first appeared in Acts as Stephen's adversary (7:58) now had to defend himself against the very accusations that led to Stephen's martyrdom.

To establish his Jewish pedigree Paul employed a set Greek formula used to express someone's heritage—born, reared, educated. He was born in Tarsus and "brought up" in Jerusalem. Because the Greek word for "brought up" often refers to one's *early* upbringing, some have argued that Paul's family moved to Jerusalem when he was a small child.[27] It is more likely that Paul went to Jerusalem in his early teens to study Torah under Gamaliel. His pride in his Tarsian citizenship (21:39) would make little sense if he had scarcely lived there at all. One has to allow for Paul's rhetoric. He was seeking to establish his *ethos* (his good will) with the Jewish crowd.[28] He may have been born in the Diaspora, he urged, but the really formative influences on him were in Jerusalem, and he was thus thoroughly Jewish.

Paul next showed his former zeal for Judaism (vv. 4–5). He had been a persecutor of "the Way." Notice how even here Paul subtly began to press his gospel. He referred to his Christian faith as "the Way," the true way of God, *the* way within Judaism. Paul's reference to his days as persecutor set the stage for the total miracle that had happened in his life and turned him around. Paul now turned to that miracle, his encounter with Christ on the Damascus road.

The encounter on the Damascus road (vv. 6–11). Acts gives three detailed accounts of Paul's conversion, which closely parallel each other (9:1–19; 22:3–16; 26:4–18). We have examined the three already in the chapter on Paul's conversion and will not duplicate that treatment here.[29] The accounts of chapters 22 and 26 differ in some respects from chapter 9 because they are Paul's personal testimony of his experience, whereas chapter 9 is a third-person narrative of the event. The accounts also differ because of their *context*. In chapter 22 Paul was addressing Jews and seeking to establish his own loyalty to Judaism. It should come as no surprise that he emphasized Jewish elements in his conversion experience.

One of the unique emphases of Paul's conversion testimony in chapter 22 is the emphasis on light. Paul noted that his vision occurred at noon, when he was blinded by a bright light flashing from heaven (v. 6). This light was so brilliant it outshone the noonday sun. Paul noted how his companions *saw the light* of his vision (v. 9). (In 9:7 the emphasis is on their hearing the voice.) Finally, unique to chapter 22 is the emphasis on light being the source of Paul's blindness (v. 11). Light is often associated with an epiphany of God in the Old Testament. Paul wanted his Jewish audience to realize that he really did have a divine encounter on the Damascus road, that the reason why the persecutor had become the preacher was his encounter with the Messiah of Israel.

The role of Ananias (vv. 12–16). Paul treated Ananias in a unique way in chapter 22. He, of course, did not speak of God's appearance to Ananias, as Luke did; Ananias's vision was not a part of Paul's own personal experience which he was relating. In chapter 22 Paul emphasized that Ananias was a loyal *Jew*. (Luke pointed to his *Christian* discipleship in chap. 9). Paul did not even mention Ananias in his speech to the largely Gentile audience of chapter 26; he would have had little significance for them. But in the address to the *Jews*, Paul showed how Ananias was a devout observer of the Torah and well-respected by the Jews of Damascus (v. 12). Ananias's words to Paul were steeped in the language of the Old Testament with their references to "the God of our Fathers" and "the Righteous One" (v. 14). Ananias told Paul that he would be a witness "to all men" (v. 15). At this point the Jews in the temple yard did not realize that "all" included Gentiles.

The commission in the temple (vv. 17–21). The Jews charged Paul with violating the sanctity of the temple. In a sense Paul responded to that charge when he referred to his vision in the temple. People who go to the temple for prayer are hardly there to desecrate it. The vision seems to have occurred upon Paul's first visit to Jerusalem after his conversion. God told him to leave Jerusalem with haste (v. 18). At that time he witnessed to the Greek-speaking Jews of Jerusalem, and they indeed did not accept his testimony but attempted to kill him (9:29). Paul protested God's command for him to leave Jerusalem by pointing out that the Jews would know how he had been a zealous persecutor of the church. Surely this would make his message credible to them. No, God replied, he had other purposes for Paul. He was to go far away to the Gentiles (v. 21). In a sense this vision presaged a pattern Paul would continue to experience on the mission field. He would always begin his witness with the Jews, even as he had done in Jerusalem. Only when they rejected his testimony did he turn to the Gentiles (cp. 13:46; 18:6). The Jews in the temple yard had accused Paul of taking a Gentile into the sacred precincts. The mention of the Gentiles perhaps reminded them of this. It certainly was something they did not want to hear. Paul had spoken "one word too many"—Gentile.[30] The Jewish crowd raised their voices, drowning Paul out and curtailing his speech.

PAUL'S EARLY ROMAN CUSTODY (ACTS 22:22–24:27)

Paul was in Roman custody for the remainder of the period covered by Acts. He was first of all in the keeping of the tribune Lysias in Jerusalem, then under the Roman procurators Felix and Festus in Caesarea. Though confined by the Romans, Paul's real adversaries were the Jews. They were the ones who brought charges against Paul. Luke made it clear that the Romans found him guilty of nothing so far as their law was concerned. The real charges were matters of Jewish laws and convictions. The last thing Paul wanted was to be remanded to Jewish jurisdiction, however. That almost surely would mean death for him. Though the Romans were far from perfect, Paul still felt greater security in their hands. Ultimately, this became the basis for his appeal to Caesar.

THE ATTEMPTED SCOURGING (22:22–29)

The Jewish mob resumed its cry to do away with Paul. The literal meaning of their words called for "taking him out" (v. 22; cp. 21:36). Their body language of throwing dust and their garments in the air was an expression of rage and protest at what they saw as Paul's blasphemy. Lysias still did not have his answers. He still did not know why the Jewish crowd was venting all this hostility toward Paul. He thus prepared what was for the Romans a very cruel but standard means of examining someone suspected of a crime—the *flagellum*. The *flagellum* was a leather whip with metal balls or bits of metal attached to its ends, designed to tear into the flesh of the victim. It was usually effective in getting to the truth but was not to be applied to Roman citizens, particularly one who had not yet been formally charged.[31] Paul knew this, and he certainly did not relish being tortured with the *flagellum*. He asked the centurion who was administering his scourging if this was legal procedure in the case of a Roman citizen such as himself. The centurion immediately stopped the process and informed Lysias of Paul's citizenship.

Coming promptly, Lysias asked Paul about his citizenship, informing Paul how he had paid a considerable sum for his own citizenship. In former times, one could not purchase citizenship. It had to be conferred or secured through special services to the state. But in the time of Claudius, it evidently became possible to purchase Roman citizenship.[32] Lysias probably derived his name of Claudius from the emperor from whom he had purchased his citizen rights. Paul did not receive his citizenship in such a mundane fashion. He was *born* a Roman citizen (v. 28). This gave Paul considerably more status in the tribune's eyes, and he was literally terrified at the prospect of having almost scourged a Roman. He ordered the scourging process to cease and probably relieved Paul of all his shackles as well.[33]

PAUL BEFORE THE SANHEDRIN (22:30–23:11)

Frustrated in his attempts to determine what Paul was guilty of, Lysias now turned to the Sanhedrin for assistance. Obviously Paul had offended the Jews in some way. Perhaps the top Jewish judicial body could assist him in ascertaining the actual charges against Paul. It was not a trial, merely a hearing, with the Sanhedrin serving in an advisory capacity. Evidently Lysias gave Paul a large degree of freedom in his appearance before the Sanhedrin (v. 30). Paul seems to have had no guard, and it is even uncertain as to whether Lysias himself remained for the hearing.

Paul and Ananias (23:1–5). The high priest before whom Paul appeared was Ananias, the son of Nedebaeus, who served from A.D. 47 to 58. He was one of the very worst of the high priests, noted for his pro-Roman sentiments, his cruelty, and his greed. He even is said to have plundered the tithes which were designated for the impoverished common priests (Josephus, *Ant,* 20.205–213). Paul incurred his anger when he began the hearing by declaring that he had a clear conscience. Paul was declaring his innocence before God, which meant that the Jews who opposed him, like Ananias himself, had to be guilty. The high priest saw this as blasphemy, and ordered the bystanders to strike Paul on his blasphemous lips. Paul responded by calling him a "whitewashed wall," words reminiscent of Jesus, who called the Pharisees tombs that had been whitewashed to cover the dead bones within (Matt. 23:27).

Paul also told him "God will strike you" (v. 3). Paul's words were prophetic: a group of Jewish zealots assassinated Ananias at the outbreak of the war with Rome in A.D. 66 (Josephus, *War* 2.441–442).

When Paul was rebuked for insulting the high priest, he apologized, saying that he did not realize Ananias was the high priest (vv. 4–5) and quoting Exodus 22:28 to the effect that Israel's law demanded respect for its leaders. Paul may have been ironic, implying that Ananias had certainly not behaved as a high priest should in having him struck without cause. He may have been acknowledging respect for the high priestly office, if not the man who held it. He was surely showing that he was a faithful Jew who lived by the law.

The resurrection (vv. 6–10). Paul then proceeded to divide the Sanhedrin by shouting that the real basis for the accusations against him was his belief in the resurrection of the dead. The Sanhedrin was composed of a majority of Sadducees and a Pharisaic minority. Pharisees believed that when the Messiah came there would be a resurrection of the dead. The Sadducees did not believe in a resurrection. In a narrative aside (parenthetical remark), Luke said that they did not believe in angels or spirits either (v. 8). The Sadducees accepted the Pentateuch as their sole Scripture. The Spirit and angels appear in the Pentateuch; the Sadducees thus could not have rejected them as such. Perhaps what Luke meant was that the Sadducees did not believe that the Spirit speaks *through humans* or that people exist after death in an angelic or spiritual state (cp. Acts 12:15).[34]

In any event, Paul's mention of the resurrection provoked a heated discussion between the two parties, with the Pharisees siding with Paul. They called for following Gamaliel's advice, urging that he be left alone lest an angel or spirit was speaking through him (Acts 5:33–39). Paul's appeal to the resurrection certainly diverted attention from himself. It was more than a clever ploy, however. It was the *real issue*. The resurrection *of Jesus* was the main point of difference between Paul and *all* the members of the Sanhedrin, Pharisees as well as Sadducees. If they accepted the resurrection of Jesus, they would accept him as Messiah and confess the truth of Paul's gospel. It is not by accident that the resurrection is at the heart of *all* Paul's defense speeches in Acts 23–26. Jesus' resurrection was the main issue separating Paul from his fellow Jews.[35]

The debate in the Sanhedrin became so violent that Lysias had to intervene with his troops to keep Paul from being torn to shreds between the two factions. Safely back in the barracks, Paul had a vision from the Lord reassuring him that he need not fear despite all the turmoil he was experiencing in Jerusalem. He would be delivered to testify also in Rome (v. 11). From this point in Acts, the focus is on Paul's witness in Rome.

THE PLOT TO AMBUSH PAUL (23:12–22)

The plot hatched (vv. 12–15). Paul was still in Roman custody. His Jewish opponents were still thwarted in any attempt to get at him. A group of more than forty zealous Jews resorted to extreme measures. They placed themselves under a solemn vow before God that they would neither eat nor drink until they had killed Paul (v. 12). The vow was an "anathema," meaning that they invoked an eternal curse on themselves should they not fulfill the vow. They enlisted the Sanhedrin in their plot. The Sanhedrin was to request another hearing of Paul from Lysias. The assassins would lie in wait along the way between Antonia and the council chamber and ambush Paul.

Paul informed (vv. 16–23). Paul evidently had a sister living in Jerusalem. Her son caught wind of the plot. He is described as a "young man" (Gk., *neaniskos*, v. 18), probably in his late teens. Paul evidently had considerable freedom in his confinement, perhaps being held in the quarters of the Roman officers in Antonia. His nephew was able to gain quick access to him and inform him of the conspiracy. Paul called the centurion over and requested that the lad be taken to Lysias. The centurion did so promptly. Lysias took Paul's nephew aside, learned of the plot, and told him to tell no one that he had given this report. The whole incident is told in great detail. From the reader's perspective, it is told twice. This repetition, the extensive dialogue, and the confidentiality motif all heighten the suspense of the narrative.

PAUL SENT TO CAESAREA (23:23–25)

The escort (vv. 23–24). Lysias acted at once. He decided to remand Paul to the governor at Caesarea. He prepared an extensive force to accompany Paul. They were to leave immediately, that very night at nine. The force consisted of almost five hundred, including foot soldiers and cavalry, nearly half the entire Jerusalem garrison. If this seems extreme, it is testimony to the instability of the times. Revolutionary movements were commonplace. A group of forty zealous Jews was no insignificant force. From Lysias's perspective, they could provide the spark that could ignite a general riot in the city. Paul had too many enemies in Jerusalem. He was a threat to the security of the city. Lysias had probably already decided to deliver Paul to the governor in Caesarea. As a tribune, Lysias had no *imperium*, no authority to conduct trials; that lay solely in the governor's hands. The plot probably only served to expedite a decision the tribune had already made. As for the plotters, they were obviously unable to fulfill their vow. Under Jewish law, when a vow proved unfulfillable, those making it were released from its obligations (Mishnah, *Nedarim* 3:3).

The letter (vv. 25–30). It was standard practice for a Roman official to write a letter of dismissal when remanding a prisoner to another jurisdiction. In this case, Lysias was sending Paul to the provincial governor, who possessed the authority to try the case.[36] Lysias was being deferential when he addressed Felix as "excellency." The title technically could be borne only by those of equestrian rank (knights), and freedmen like Felix could not hold that rank. Lysias sought to present himself in the best possible light in his letter to his superior. He described his arrest of Paul in the temple court as his concern to protect a Roman citizen (v. 27), which is stretching the facts considerably. Lysias's most important word in the letter was his assertion that he had found Paul innocent and not deserving of death or even imprisonment (v. 29).

The trip to Caesarea (vv. 31–33). Jerusalem to Caesarea is just over sixty miles. The route the soldiers followed took them downhill to Antipatris, a military station thirty-five miles from Jerusalem. The most dangerous part of the route was from Jerusalem to Antipatris, and the foot soldiers evidently returned when they reached the latter destination. After resting at Antipatris, the next day the cavalry accompanied Paul the twenty-five miles across the Plain of Sharon to Caesarea.

Caesarea. Caesarea was the seat of the Roman government of Judea. It was an impressive Hellenistic city built by Herod the Great. It had been a small harbor town since the fourth century B.C. when a Sidonian king named Strato built a tower there to serve as a lighthouse and a harbor for trade with Egypt. Known as Strato's Tower, it continued to provide a port for small vessels under the Ptolemies and the Seleucids. After it had fallen into disrepair in the first century B.C., Herod chose it as the main site for a Judean harbor, rebuilding it on a grand scale. By constructing a large semicircular breakwater and a mole in the sea, he created a fine artificial harbor. Herod's city boasted a theater, a hippodrome, a temple to Augustus, a splendid palace for his own quarters, and extensive storage buildings for the commerce that regularly flowed through the harbor. In A.D. 6, when Roman procurators assumed jurisdiction over Judea, they made Caesarea the seat of the government. The governor resided in Herod's palace (*praetorium*). Some three thousand auxiliary troops were stationed in the area. The mint was located there. Quickly Caesarea outstripped Jerusalem as the commercial and political center of Judaea. Though it was primarily a Greek-style city with a heavily Gentile population, there was still a large Jewish community there, going back to Herodian times. Jews comprised perhaps as much as 50 percent of the population.[37]

Considerable tension existed between the Jewish and Gentile communities in the city. This came to a head during the time of Felix, when the Jewish elements of the city rose up against the Gentiles, demanding equal rights of citizenship. Felix intervened with his troops on the side of the Gentiles. His action only aggravated the conflict within the city, and he was removed from office for his mishandling of the situation. All of this occurred while Paul was imprisoned in Caesarea. The place of Paul's imprisonment is designated in Acts 23:35 as "Herod's palace" (praetorium). This was the governor's residence. Recent excavations have possibly located the ruins of this impressive residence on a promontory to the south of the harbor.[38]

In Caesarea (vv. 34–35). When Paul reached Caesarea, the governor inquired about his native province. When he ascertained that Paul was a Cilician, he realized that he came under his own jurisdiction. Cilicia was a part of the province of Syria, to which Judea also belonged. An imperial legate was the top-ranking official over Syria-Cilicia. The legate was the governor's immediate superior. He probably realized his superior would not want to handle this Judean matter, and so he decided to try Paul himself.

The governor was Felix. He served as procurator of Judaea from A.D. 52 to 59.[39] He was a freedman, as was his brother Pallas, who had considerable influence in the imperial court. Pallas was the key to Felix's success. The Roman historian Tacitus spoke of Felix's governing abilities with considerable disdain, saying that he "wielded the power of a king with all the instincts of a slave" (*Histories* 5. 9). Felix's royal aspirations are nowhere more evident then in his marriages. He married three princesses. The first was a granddaughter of Antony and Cleopatra. The third was Drusilla, the daughter of the Jewish king Agrippa I. Felix gained her by deception and when she was only sixteen (see comments on 24:24). He is said to have promised her "happiness," an obvious pun on his name, which in Latin means "happy."

THE TRIAL IN CAESAREA (24:1–23)

Luke presents only one formal trial of Paul before the Roman officials, the trial before Felix. It provides an excellent example of forensic rhetoric, with formal charges being leveled against Paul by the lawyer Tertullus (vv. 2–9) and Paul responding with his defense (vv. 10–21).[40]

The setting (v. 1). Lysias had already urged Paul's Jewish opponents to prepare a case against Paul to be presented before Felix (23:30). Five days had passed, and the Jewish delegation had arrived in Caesarea. It consisted of the high priest Ananias, some "elders" (probably Sanhedrin members) and the lawyer Tertullus. Tertullus may or may not have been a Jew. The important thing is that he was a professional lawyer (*rhētōr*) against whom Paul was more than able to hold his own.

Tertullus's accusation (vv. 2–9). Tertullus began his accusation with a standard rhetorical device designed to win the goodwill of the audience, known as the *captatio benevolentiae* (vv. 2–4). In this instance he appealed to the governor, noting the peace and reforms that had marked his administration. This might seem like a piece of blatant and undeserved flattery. Felix's procuratorship was not one of peace but of constant foment, as the governor put down with utmost cruelty one revolutionary movement after another. Still Tertullus's *captatio* was closely related to his purpose. He wanted to emphasize how Felix had maintained the peace and how Paul was a threat to that peace.[41]

In verses 5–8 Tertullus stated his charges against Paul. His main accusation was that Paul was a threat to the peace, a seditious fellow who had stirred up riots everywhere. This was the charge that would most get the attention of the Romans. The second charge was closely related. Paul was a ringleader of the Nazarene sect. Linked with the first charge, Tertullus implied that the Christians were dangerous revolutionaries. Felix knew better (v. 22). The third charge was that Paul had desecrated the temple. This was the most serious accusation. The Romans had granted the Jews capital jurisdiction in the single instance of temple desecration. Were this charge made to stick, the Romans would have turned Paul over to the Jews and almost certain death.[42]

Paul's defense (vv. 10–12). Paul began his defense with a brief *captatio* of his own, which appealed to the one really germane consideration—Felix's competence to judge the matter (v. 10). Paul then answered each of Tertullus's charges in turn. To the charge of sedition, Paul responded that he had been in Jerusalem only a short while (not long enough to organize a revolution), that he had come to worship, and that he had not himself stirred up any riots (vv. 11–13). He accepted the charge that he was a Christian (Nazarene). But, he preferred to call it the true "Way" for Judaism, not a mere sect of Judaism. Like all Jewish Christians, he believed the Scriptures, kept the law, and looked to the resurrection of the dead (vv. 14–16). To the charge of temple desecration, Paul answered that he went there to bring offerings and to worship, not to commit sacrilege. He had even submitted to ritual purification in the temple (vv. 17–18). Paul's most telling comment was that the very ones who had accused him of desecration were not present at Caesarea to charge him. Roman law required face-to-face confrontation with one's accusers (cp. 25:16). The prosecution had prepared a poor case; its primary witnesses were conspicuous by their absence.

In verses 20–21 Paul moved the case away from the prosecution's charges to his own charges. The real contention between the Jews and Paul involved his faith that Jesus was the promised Messiah. Paul pointed to the members of the Sanhedrin who had accompanied the Jewish delegation to Caesarea. They would be able to affirm what was apparent in Paul's hearing before them—that the real issue was the resurrection of the dead. Specifically, of course, it was Jesus' resurrection, which was the proof that he was the Messiah.

Felix's judgment (vv. 22–23). As procurator Felix had full powers to judge. It was at his discretion whether to hear a case or not. He determined the extent of the crime and the penalties. He could make an immediate judgment upon hearing a case, could delay his judgment, could release the prisoner or send the accused to another court.[43] In this instance Felix chose to delay. His stated reason was that he would wait for Lysias to come and report on the case. There is no evidence that Lysias ever did or that Felix ever attempted to hear Paul's case again. There were two other reasons Felix delayed his judgment. For one, he hoped to receive a bribe from Paul (v. 26). Second, he hoped to do the Jews "a favor" (v. 27). Felix's accurate knowledge of Christians probably convinced him that Paul had done no wrong by Roman law (v. 22). His only just decision on the evidence at hand would have been to release Paul. But this would have angered the Jewish leadership. Felix administered a Jewish territory. He did not want to antagonize the most powerful of his subjects. It was easier and safer to put the matter off and leave Paul in confinement.[44]

PAUL AND FELIX IN PRIVATE (24:24–27)

Paul probably continued to be held in the large Herodian palace in Caesarea. Felix placed him in a relaxed custody which gave him a degree of freedom and allowed friends to visit him and provide for his needs (v. 23). Among those who consulted Paul was the procurator himself, who came with his wife Drusilla. Their marriage had been scandalous. Drusilla was a daughter of Herod Agrippa I and sister of Agrippa II. The younger Agrippa had arranged for her marriage at age fourteen to Azizus, king of Emesa, a petty Syrian territory. Unhappy in her marriage, Felix took advantage of the situation to woo her through the assistance and trickery of a magician from Cyprus named Atomos (Josephus, *Ant.* 20.139–144). Drusilla may have been the one who encouraged Felix to visit with Paul, as the Western Text of Acts maintains. Whether that was so, Paul's message of righteousness, self-control, and divine judgment hit a little close to home, making Felix uncomfortable. He put Paul off (v. 25). He also put off Paul's release. Paul languished in his confinement for a full two years, until Nero relieved Felix of his office and replaced him with Porcius Festus. The time of Paul's Ceasarean imprisonment under Felix was around A.D. 57 to 59.

NOTES

1. L. W. Hurtado, "The Jerusalem Collection and the Book of Galatians," *Journal for the Study of the New Testament* 5 (1979): 46–62.
2. D. Georgi, *Remembering the Poor: The History of Paul's Collection for Jerusalem* (Nashville: Abingdon, 1992), 54–61.
3. H. D. Betz, *2 Corinthians 8 and 9: A Commentary on Two Administrative Letters of the Apostle Paul*, Hermeneia (Philadelphia: Fortress, 1985). Betz provided a rhetorical analysis of each epistle on pp. 38–41 and 88–90.
4. W. M. Ramsay, *St. Paul the Traveller and the Roman Citizen* (London: Hodder and Stoughton, 1897), 289.
5. K. F. Nickle, *The Collection: A Study in Paul's Strategy*, Studies in Biblical Theology 48 (London: SCM, 1966), 20–22.
6. Equality of citizens was a major ideal of Greek democracy. See Georgi, *Remembering the Poor*, 84–91.
7. For a fuller treatment of 2 Corinthians 9, see chapter 13, p. 271.
8. F. F. Bruce, *Paul: Apostle of the Heart Set Free* (Grand Rapids: Eerdmans, 1977), 339, fn. 5.

9. Unless, of course, one does not see the author of Acts as Paul's traveling companion. Then one could argue that the author was unaware of Paul's collection, as does C. Bowen, "Paul's Collection and the Book of Acts," *Journal of Biblical Literature* 42 (1923): 49–59.

10. A. J. Mattill, "The Purpose of Acts: Schneckenburger Reconsidered," in *Apostolic History and the Gospel*, ed. Gasque and Martin (Grand Rapids: Eerdmans, 1970), 116.

11. J. Knox, *Chapters in a Life of Paul* (Nashville: Abingdon, 1950), 71–72.

12. Nickle, *The Collection*, 148–150.

13. R. Tannehill, *The Narrative Unity of Luke-Acts, A Literary Interpretation*, Vol. 2: *The Acts of the Apostles* (Minneapolis: Fortress, 1990), 266.

14. J. Munck, *Paul and the Salvation of Mankind* (Richmond: John Knox, 1959), 301–308.

15. W. D. Davies, *The Gospel and the Land: Early Christianity and Jewish Territorial Doctrine* (Berkeley: University of California Press, 1974), 195–208.

16. For an interesting but unlikely parallel between Eutychus and Homer's Elpenor, see D. R. MacDonald, "Luke's Eutychus and Homer's Elpenor: Acts 20:7–12 and Odyssey 10–12," *Journal of Higher Criticism* 1 (1994): 5–24.

17. J. McRay, "Miletus," *The Anchor Bible Dictionary*, ed. D. N. Freedman (New York: Doubleday, 1992), IV:825–826.

18. J. Lambrecht, "Paul's Farewell-Address at Miletus (Acts 20:17–38) *Les Actes des Apôtres*, ed. J. Kremer (Gembloux: J. Duculot, 1979), 308–337.

19. For a rebuttal of the martyrdom view, see B. Witherington III, *The Acts of the Apostles: A Socio-Rhetorical Commentary* (Grand Rapids: Eerdmans, 1998), 618–620.

20. E. Lövestam, "Paul's Address at Miletus," *Studia Theologica* 41 (1987): 1–10.

21. C. F. D. Moule, "The Christology of Acts," *Studies in Luke-Acts*, ed. Keck and Martyn (Nashville: Abingdon, 1966), 171.

22. R. F. O'Toole, "What Role Does Jesus' Saying in Acts 20:35 Play in Paul's Address to the Ephesian Elders?" *Biblica* 75 (1994): 329–349.

23. For examples, see 1 Kings 11:29–31; Isaiah 8:1–4; 20:1–4; Jeremiah 13:1–11; 19:1–13; 27:1–22; Hosea 1:2.

24. H. Patsch, "Die Prophetie des Agabus," *Theologische Zeitschrift* 28 (1972): 228–232.

25. In relating James's death at the hands of the high priest Ananus, Josephus spoke of the high respect in which Torah-abiding Jews held him (*Ant*, 20.197–203). Eusebius recorded a more legendary account of James's martyrdom according to which he had the reputation of being the most righteous of all the Jews with respect to the Torah (*Eccl. Hist.* 2.23).

26. The first was discovered in 1871 and the second in 1935. See J. Polhill, *Acts*, New American Commentary (Nashville: Broadman, 1992), 452, fn. 16. According to Josephus, the Romans allowed the Jews to pass a death penalty solely for this one offense of temple desecration (*War* 6.124–26).

27. W. C. Van Unnik, "Tarsus or Jerusalem: The City of Paul's Youth," trans. G. Ogg, *Sparsa Collecta*, Part 1 (Leiden: Brill, 1973), 259–320.

28. B. J. Malina and J. H. Neyrey, *Portraits of Paul: An Archaeology of Ancient Personality* (Louisville: Westminster John Knox, 1996), 64–91.

29. See chapter 3, pp 44–51.

30. A. T. Robertson, *Epochs in the Life of Paul* (New York: Scribners, 1909), 231.

31. H. W. Tajra, *The Trial of St. Paul* (Tübingen: Mohr/Siebeck, 1989), 74.

32. Dio Cassius was highly critical of this procedure, saying that in Claudius's time one could buy citizenship with broken pieces of glass (*Roman History* lx.17:5–6).

33. B. Rapske, *The Book of Acts and Paul in Roman Custody*, vol. 3 of *The Book of Acts in Its First Century Setting* (Grand Rapids: Eerdmans, 1994), 145–149.

34. For the former suggestion, see B. J. Bamberger, "The Sadducees and the Belief in Angels," *Journal of Biblical Literature* 82 (1963): 433–435. For the latter, see D. Daube, "On Acts 23: Sadducees and Angels," *Journal of Biblical Literature* 109 (1990): 493–497.

35. R. J. Kepple, "The Hope of Israel, the Resurrection of the Dead and Jesus: A Study of Their Relationship in Acts with Particular Regard to the Understanding of Paul's Trial Defense," *Journal of the Evangelical Theological Society* 20 (1977): 231–241.

36. There is some question about Felix's Gentile (tribal) name. Was it Antonius Felix as designated by Tacitus (*Annals*, 12.54) or Claudius Felix, as given by Josephus (*Ant.* 20.137)? Felix was a freedman, either of Claudius, or of his mother Antonia. An inscription found in Israel in 1966 seems to tip the scale toward his being named for Claudius. See Bruce, *Apostle of the Heart Set Free*, 353, n. 54.

37. For a full discussion of Caesarea, see L. I. Levine, *Caesarea Under Roman Rule* (Leiden: Brill, 1975), 5–33.

38. B. Burrell, K. Gleason, and E. Netzer, "Uncovering Herod's Seaside Palace," *Biblical Archaeology Review* 19 (1993): 50–57, 76.

39. The Roman official over Judea seems to have been called "prefect" during some periods, "procurator" at other times. The latter term seems to have been used during the time of Felix and Festus. Luke used the more general term "governor" (*hēgemōn*) or "ruler."

40. For the heavy occurrence of legal language in this section of Acts, see A. A. Trites, "The Importance of Legal Scenes and Language in the Book of Acts," *Novum Testamentum* 16 (1974): 278–284.

41. B. Winter, "The Importance of the *Captatio Benevolentiae* in the Speeches of Tertullus and Paul in Acts 24:1–21," *Journal of Theological Studies* 42 (1991): 505–531.

42. There is a major textual problem involving verses 6b–7, where a longer western reading adds that the Jews would have tried Paul themselves had not Lysias intervened. On this reading, verse 8 would involve Felix examining Lysias, not Paul. The shorter reading, followed in the NIV (omitting v. 7), has better manuscript support.

43. Tajra, *The Trial of Paul*, 114–116.

44. Rapske, *The Book of Acts and Paul in Roman Custody*, 164–167.

SUGGESTED FURTHER READING

Betz, Hans Dieter. *2 Corinthians 8 and 9: A Commentary on Two Administrative Letters of the Apostle Paul*. Hermeneia. Philadelphia: Fortress, 1985.

Bruce, F. F. *The Acts of the Apostles: The Greek Text with Introduction and Commentary*. Third, revised and enlarged edition. Grand Rapids: Eerdmans, 1990, pp. 422–485.

Georgi, Dieter. *Remembering the Poor: The History of Paul's Collection for Jerusalem*. Nashville: Abingdon, 1992.

Levine, Lee I. *Caesarea Under Roman Rule*. Leiden: Brill, 1975, pp. 5–33.

Nickle, Keith F. *The Collection: A Study in Paul's Strategy*. Studies in Biblical Theology, 48. London: SCM, 1966.

Polhill, John B. *Acts*. New American Commentary. Nashville: Broadman, 1992, pp. 414–488.

Rapske, Brian. *The Book of Acts in Its First Century Setting*. Vol. 3: *Paul in Roman Custody*. Grand Rapids: Eerdmans, 1994, pp. 135–172.

Tajra, H. W. *The Trial of St. Paul: A Juridical Exegesis of the Second Half of the Acts of the Apostles*. Wissenschaftliche Untersuchungen zum Neuen Testament. 2. Reihe #35. Tübingen: Mohr/Siebeck, 1989, pp. 61–134.

Tannehill, Robert C. *The Narrative Unity of Luke-Acts: A Literary Interpretation*. Vol. 2: *The Acts of the Apostles*. Minneapolis: Fortress, 1990, pp. 245–304.

Witherington, Ben, III. *The Acts of the Apostles: A Socio-Rhetorical Commentary*. Grand Rapids: Eerdmans, 1998, pp. 600–717.

16

COLOSSE: A BIG SAVIOR
FOR A SMALL CHURCH

*P*aul was in continuous custody for a long period. Arrested in Jerusalem in the spring of A.D. 57, he was transferred to Caesarea and imprisoned there for more than two years. Having made an appeal to Caesar, he was transferred to Rome in the fall of 59. He was shipwrecked along with his guard and delayed from reaching Rome until spring of 60. In Rome Paul remained under house arrest for two years, awaiting his appearance before the emperor (Acts 28:30). The narrative of Acts ends at this point, but we can assume a minimum period of Roman custody for five years, between A.D. 57 and 62.

Sometime during this period Paul wrote three letters, Colossians, Philemon, and Ephesians. He seems to have written all three at the same time. There are internal links between them. The relationship between Ephesians and Colossians is particularly striking. One-third of the contents of Colossians is paralleled in Ephesians. Both epistles designate Tychicus as their bearer and do so in identical wording (Eph. 6:21–22; Col. 4:7–8). Colossians 4:9 adds that Onesimus accompanied Tychicus. This links it with the epistle to Philemon. Onesimus is mentioned in Philemon 10. He was evidently Philemon's slave, whom Paul was sending back to his master. Colossians and Philemon are also linked to one another by listing the same people as present with Paul at the time of writing: Epaphras, Mark, Aristarchus, Demas, and Luke (Philem. 23; Col. 4:10–14). Likewise, Paul addressed Archippus in both epistles (Philem. 2, Col. 4:17). Paul thus seems to have written the three letters on the same occasion. They were of three distinct types. Colossians follows Paul's usual pattern of a letter to a congregation or group of churches in a single community. Philemon is a private letter, intended primarily for the individual slave owner. Ephesians seems to have been a more general epistle, perhaps intended for circulation among all the Asian churches.

In this chapter we will focus on the two "Colossian" epistles. (Philemon seems to have lived in Colosse.) We have chosen to place the three "Lycus Valley epistles" at this point (chaps. 16–17), that is, between the Caesarean and Roman imprisonment, so as to leave open the question of whether Paul wrote them early or late during the period of his Roman custody. Also this will separate them from the later Pastoral Epistles, from which they differ markedly.

THE CHURCHES OF THE LYCUS VALLEY

Three "Pauline" churches were located in the valley of the Lycus River in the southwestern area of modern Turkey. One was Colosse, to which Paul addressed his epistle. The other two congregations are mentioned in the Colossian letter. They are Laodicea (Col. 2:1, 13, 16) and Hierapolis (Col. 4:13). The three churches were closely related, within a ten-mile radius of one another.

DESCRIPTION OF THE AREA

The Lycus River is a tributary of the Maeander River, running south and east of it. It is located in an area noted for its natural phenomena. Earthquakes are frequent in the area. Tacitus mentioned a major earthquake in A.D. 60/61 which devastated Laodicea (*Annals* 14.27.1). Eusebius told of the same earthquake but dated it after the burning of Rome (A.D. 64) and said that it leveled Colosse and Hierapolis as well.[1] The Lycus Valley could be designated the "Yellowstone of Asia." There are many thermal phenomena, such as steam vents. The cliffs around Hierapolis (modern Pamukkale) are covered with cascading white stalactites, which are created by calcium-laden hot springs. The formations are visible from twenty miles distance. Because of its striking natural phenomena, Hierapolis was from very early times a center of the native Phrygian worship of the Mother Goddess.

FOUNDING OF THE CHURCHES

Paul does not seem to have personally established the churches of the Lycus Valley. On his second missionary journey, his route through Phrygia and Galatia took him well north of the area to Mysia and then west to Alexandria Troas (Acts 16:6–7). It is possible that at the outset of his third mission Paul traveled through the Lycus Valley on his route through Phrygia to Ephesus (Acts 18:23). However, at Acts 19:1 Luke stated that Paul traveled through the "upper country" (RSV) to Ephesus. This seems to indicate that he took the main Roman highway that led from Pessinus to Sardis and then he went south to Ephesus.

Even had Paul gone through the Lycus Valley prior to writing Colossians, he does not seem to have stopped to establish churches there. Colossians itself testifies to Paul's not having personally founded them. Paul spoke of his having "heard" of their faith (Col. 1:4, 9). He indicated that neither they nor the Laodicean Christians had met him personally (Col. 2:1). The churches seem to have been established by Paul's coworker Epaphras (Col. 1:7), who was a native Colossian (Col. 4:12). Luke indicated that during Paul's ministry in Ephesus "all the Jews and Greeks who lived in the province of Asia heard the word of the Lord" (Acts 19:10). Paul followed his usual missionary strategy of establishing himself in a major city, with his coworkers fanning out into the countryside to establish churches in the wider region. The Lycus Valley churches were a product of Paul's Ephesian ministry. Epaphras served as Paul's coworker, establishing the churches there. Still, Paul considered them *his* churches. They were the product of his apostolic ministry. When difficulties arose in them, Epaphras turned to the apostle for guidance and assistance. Colossians is the product of that relationship.

THE THREE CHURCHES

Laodicea. Traveling from Ephesus, Laodicea was the first of the three churches one would have reached, being some ninety miles or so distant and just east of the point where the Lycus flows into the Maeander. It was strategically located on the south bank of the Lycus, on the main trade route that led from the cities of the Aegean coast east to Persia and Syria. It was a fairly new city, having been founded by the Seleucid king Antiochus II in 250 B.C. and named for his wife Laodice. (A minor town had existed there previously by the name of Rhoas.) Along with all the cities of Asia, Laodicea came under the kings of Pergamum in 190 B.C. and then under direct Roman rule in 133 B.C. when the last of the kings of Pergamum bequeathed his kingdom to Rome. In Paul's day, Laodicea was the most prominent city of the Lycus Valley. It was the *conventus*, the tax-gathering and judicial center for the whole administrative area, which consisted of twenty-seven towns, including Hierapolis and Colosse. It was prosperous, boasting a thriving industry in black woolen goods and a famous medical center. It was the banking center for the entire southeastern region of Asia.

Laodicea continued on as a prominent Christian center. One of the seven letters of Revelation was addressed to it (Rev. 3:14–22). In A.D. 363, an ecumenical council was held there, where fifty-nine canons were adopted for regulating the religion of the churches in Lydia and Phrygia. Among these were rules prohibiting Christians from living by the Jewish Sabbath laws and from worshiping angels. Clergy were forbidden to practice magic or astrology. Christians were not to participate in Jewish festivals or to receive unleavened bread from Judaizers. These rules are perhaps evidence that the Colossian problems were still alive and well in the area some three hundred years after Paul!

Hierapolis. Hierapolis was located on a terrace three hundred feet high on the northern side of the Lycus, six miles north of Laodicea and ten miles west of Colosse. People often visited the city to bathe in its hot springs, which were believed to possess curative qualities. Hierapolis was a center of the Great Mother cult in ancient times. There is evidence that mystery cults were established in this region in the Roman period. For instance, inscriptions found in the area attest the presence of the Egyptian cult of Serapis.

Though the area was settled and venerated from an ancient period, the city of Hierapolis was even newer than Laodicea, being founded by a king of Pergamum, Eumenes II, in the early second century B.C. It was a prosperous city in Paul's day and, like Laodicea, continued to be a Christian center. It was the seat of a bishop. The most famous of its bishops was Papias, whom Eusebius often quoted in his *Church History*. Tradition also has it that Philip the Evangelist and his prophesying daughters ministered and were buried in Hierapolis.

Colosse. Colosse had evidently known more illustrious days. Herodotus characterized it as a "great city" in the fifth century B.C. (*History* 7.30). In the first century B.C., Strabo listed it among the "small towns" of the region (*Geography*, 7.8.13). The site has never been excavated, and the visible ruins of the city are meager, consisting mainly of some ruins of the acropolis and a few seats of the amphitheater. Lightfoot described it as "without doubt . . . the least important church to which any epistle of St. Paul is addressed."[2]

The city was located in the southwest corner of Phrygia, on the southern bank of the Lycus, ten miles east of Laodicea. Its necropolis (cemetery) was positioned on the northern bank of the river. Very little is known of the city, since it has not been excavated, and the ancient writers scarcely mention it. Unlike Laodicea and Hierapolis, it had no prominence as a subsequent Christian center. Some coins have been discovered which seem to indicate that it survived at least into the third century. Otherwise one might assume it never recovered from the great earthquake of 60/61.

THE JEWISH POPULATION OF PHRYGIA

Since the problem at Colosse seems to have involved some Jewish elements, the extent of Jewish presence in the area is of importance. Evidently it was considerable. According to Josephus, Antiochus the Great settled two thousand Jewish families in Lydia and Phrygia (*Ant*, 12.147–153). In 62 B.C. Flaccus, a Roman official in Asia seized at Laodicea the funds which the Jewish community had gathered for the tax to support the temple in Jerusalem. Charges were brought against Flaccus for illegal seizure, and Cicero defended him in the case. Cicero says that the amount involved exceeded twenty pounds of gold (*Pro Flacco* 28.68). The annual temple tax was assessed at one-half shekel (two Greek drachmai) per male. Twenty pounds of gold would work out to more than eleven thousand Jewish males. As the *conventus*, Laodicea was probably the gathering point for the entire region. This demonstrates that a considerable Jewish community resided in Phrygia.

THE PLACE OF PAUL'S IMPRISONMENT

Where was Paul when he wrote the prison epistles? Three places have been suggested. The earliest is a proposed imprisonment of Paul in Ephesus, during his third mission, between A.D. 52 and 55. The next possibility would be Paul's two-year imprisonment in Caesarea, A.D. 57 to 59. Finally, Paul's first Roman imprisonment has long served as the "traditional" setting for the letters (A.D. 60–62).

EPHESUS

Many have argued that Paul wrote the four prison epistles from Ephesus. We have already discussed the issue in the chapter on Philippians and will not repeat ourselves here.[3] As argued there, it is probably best to separate Philippians from the other three in discussing the issue. Philippians has much in common with the letters of Paul's third mission (1 and 2 Corinthians, Galatians, Romans), and a good case can be made for placing it in Ephesus during this general period. Colossians and Ephesians, however, have very different emphases from the epistles of Paul's third mission and seem to reflect a later stage of Paul's thinking. The strongest argument for an Ephesian setting for the "Colossians group" is the short distance (one hundred miles) between Ephesus and the Lycus valley as opposed to the almost one thousand miles from Colosse to Caesarea and more than one thousand miles to Rome. Still, the very different theological emphases in Colossians and Ephesians (such as the view of the church, the "cosmic" Christology, and the emphasis on unity) find no real presence in the epistles of the third mission, which makes it most implausible that they were written at that time.

CAESAREA

Caesarea is the least advocated of the three possible settings for Colossians, Philemon, and Ephesians. Yet, when all is said and done, there is little reason these three could not have been written from Caesarea as easily as from Rome. It is simply a matter of earlier or later during Paul's Roman custody. Since Caesarea is often neglected as a possibility, it might prove useful to list some of the main reasons in favor of this view.

First is the Laodicean earthquake of A.D. 60/61. Tacitus's date seems to be accurate, not the later date given by Eusebius.[4] Colosse may well have been in ruins during the period of Paul's first Roman imprisonment. Another argument relates to Paul's manner of detention. In Caesarea he was under military custody in Herod's praetorium, thus perhaps to some extent held in bonds. Paul refers to his bonds in the Colossian group of epistles. In Rome, however, he enjoyed a more liberal house arrest and was not held so closely. Caesarea was probably more accessible to a runaway slave like Onesimus than Rome, particularly if he fled by foot. It was a land route all the way. Even if he could afford to book passage on a ship, it was a short land journey from Colosse south to Patara or Myra and then a voyage of a week or less to Caesarea, much quicker than a voyage to Rome. Then there is the matter of Paul's associates. In Colossians Paul mentioned as being with him Timothy, Luke, Aristarchus, and Tychicus. All of these accompanied Paul to Jerusalem with the collection (Acts 20:4–5). All may well have stayed on with him in Caesarea. In Ephesians Paul used the image of the wall (Eph. 2:14). In Caesarea the temple wall would still be much on his mind; it was the reason for his chains.[5] The same would be true for his emphasis on unity of Jew and Greek in Christ (Col. 3:11; Eph. 2:11–22). Concern for unity was behind the collection trip to Jerusalem; it was the reason he now lay in prison.

These arguments do not rule out a Roman imprisonment. They are only listed here to show how one can make an equally good case for Caesarea. Neither are the usual reasons *against* a Caesarean imprisonment compelling. For instance, it is said that when Paul asked Philemon to prepare a guest room for him (Philem. 22) he would have to have abandoned his desire to visit Rome if he were writing from Caesarea.[6] One must, however, assume Paul changed his plans in any event. As is clear in Romans, Paul's real desire in coming to Rome was to begin work eventually in *Spain*. If writing from Rome, he would have abandoned that plan as well if now he were planning to visit Philemon at Colosse.

ROME

A Roman imprisonment has the strong element of tradition behind it. It allows the fullest amount of time for the sort of syncretistic thought to develop at Colosse that Paul had to address in the epistle. It allows the longest time for the flowering of Paul's thought that one finds in Ephesians. Still, it must be remembered that we are dealing with a rather short span of time in any event, not more than five years total time for the entire Roman custody, certainly not enough for any major developmental theory. It is sometimes assumed that a runaway slave would automatically run to the anonymity of the capital city of the empire. This could, however, be a good argument *against* Rome. The city would perhaps be the first place a master would look for a fugitive slave. Then, too, as we will see, it is quite possible Onesimus sought Paul out, that he ran away from his master seeking Paul's protection. In that event, he would have gone wherever he knew Paul to be in prison—Ephesus, Caesarea, or Rome. We are back to square one again. On the balance, however, we are personally inclined to go with Caesarea for Colossians/Philemon and Ephesians.

THE AUTHORSHIP OF COLOSSIANS

A number of scholars have questioned the Pauline authorship of Colossians, beginning with F. C. Baur and his school, who argued that the Gnostic language of Colossians showed it was a product of second-century Christianity. Contemporary interpreters continue to question whether Paul wrote Colossians. Their questions are of four general types.

Historical questions. Few today would argue like Baur that the Gnostic-like language found in Colossians is impossible for the time of Paul. On the other hand, many see the cosmic Christology of Colossians as being alien to Paul. They see the picture of Paul in Colossians as being that of a hero and a martyr rather than Paul's own self-image.[7] The book is viewed as coming from a later generation, which emphasized doctrinal conformity, a this-worldly ethic, and fidelity to the traditions of the faith. These kinds of observation are largely based on what Paul said about himself and his ministry in such passages as Colossians 1:24–29. These should not be seen as hero worship but instead as the apostle's effort to introduce himself to a church that did not know him personally.

Stylistic arguments. In the late nineteenth century, the Pauline authorship of Colossians was questioned on the basis of the unique vocabulary of the epistle in comparison with the other "undisputed" Pauline epistles, like Romans, 1 and 2 Corinthians, and Galatians. It was noted that Colossians contains thirty-four words found nowhere else in the New Testament and an additional twenty-eight found in no other Pauline epistle. The obvious answer to this is the particular false teaching at Colosse. Paul used their words in combating their views. It has also been noted that the style of Colossians is different from that of the undisputed epistles—long sentences, lots of participles and relative clauses, for example. These characteristics can probably be explained on the basis of Paul's employing extensive confessional material from the worship of the church. As we have seen previously, stylistic arguments cannot be primary in considering matters of authorship. Paul is known to have used secretaries. Peculiarities of vocabulary may well be attributable to them. A number of scholars argue that Paul used a secretary for Colossians. In particular, Timothy has been suggested.[8]

Theological arguments. Among contemporary scholars the main reasons for rejecting Pauline authorship involve the theology of the epistle. For instance, the eschatology of the epistle is seen to be "realized" rather than future, the view of the church as universal rather than local. The cosmic view of Christ and the "bourgeois" ethic of the household order are considered to be alien to Paul. It is observed that some of the major Pauline doctrines like justification are totally missing in Colossians. Now, many of the alleged theological contradictions and omissions actually do have their parallels in the "undisputed" epistles—the church universal, the cosmic Christ, and the like. Admittedly, they are more fully developed in Colossians. The main reason for the differing emphases and omissions is surely the contextual factor. Paul's agenda was in large part dictated by the nature of the problem at Colosse itself.

The relationship to Ephesians. A final line of argument involves the close literary relationship between Colossians and Ephesians. A full third of the text of Colossians is paralleled in Ephesians. In 1838 a German scholar named Mayerhoff rejected Colossians on this basis, arguing that it was the product of a later Paulinist who used Ephesians as his base. Mayerhoff assumed Ephesians was a genuine Pauline epistle. A more complicated solution was proposed by H. J. Holtzmann in 1872. He maintained that Paul wrote an original shorter Colossian epistle, which is today lost. He argued that a later disciple of Paul interpolated into the original short Colossians passages from Paul's Ephesian epistle. What we now have, he said, is the interpolated edition of Colossians. Today few would use the parallels between Colossians and Ephesians to argue against the Pauline authorship of Colossians. It is generally recognized that Ephesians is the more developed work. Thus, many use the parallels to argue that Paul did not write Ephesians, that it was written by a later Paulinist using Colossians as a base (the reverse of Mayerhoff's theory). The simplest explanation is that neither epistle is a later copy using the other as a base. The close resemblance between the two is due to Paul's having written both at the same time and to different destinations—Colossians to a specific situation in a single congregation and Ephesians as a general epistle to a group of churches.[9]

For Pauline authorship. The unique characteristics of Colossians can be explained on the basis of the particular problem at Colosse which Paul was addressing in the epistle. Perhaps the strongest argument in favor of Colossian authenticity is its close relationship to Philemon. No one today questions Paul's having written Philemon. Colossians is closely tied to it. The same persons are addressed in the two epistles: Epaphras, Aristarchus, Mark, Luke, and Demas. Archippus is addressed in both. Onesimus, the slave of Philemon, is mentioned in Colossians, so it comes as no surprise that Colossians deals at length with the slave-master relationship. There is thus a natural link between the two epistles, not the sort a later pseudepigrapher would dream up. As John Knox put it, it is an "uninventable" relationship between two genuine letters of the apostle.[10]

THE PROBLEM AT COLOSSE

Paul's main purpose in writing Colossians was to put the Colossians on guard against those who propounded a false teaching. Most interpreters would see the teaching as already being present in the congregation. Paul described it as a deception based on fine-sounding rhetoric (2:4), as a "philosophy" that would lead them down the path of human systems as opposed to those based on Christ (2:8). Though there is general agreement that Paul was warning against a false teaching, which was already present, views differ widely over the precise identification of the teaching.

THE EVIDENCE OF THE BIBLICAL TEXT

Paul alluded to the teaching directly in Colossians 2:16–23. Those who were promoting it seem to have been harshly judgmental of those who did not concur with their practices (v. 16). They sought to "disqualify" them, serving as "umpires" who ruled them out of bounds for receiving the ultimate prize of salvation (v. 18). Their system seems to have had a number of Jewish elements. It emphasized the keeping of holy days. The three mentioned in verse 16 should probably be seen as the main types of Jewish holy days: the annual festivals, the monthly New Moons, and the weekly Sabbaths. The Colossian system seems to have had a strongly ascetic bent, carefully regulating food and drink (v. 16) and being steeped in purity regulations about what one could and could not touch or consume (v. 21). The ascetic severity to the body was seen as a form of piety, a demonstration of humility and devotion (v. 23). It is even possible that circumcision was a part of their ascetic regimen, seen not from the Judaizing perspective of a covenantal badge of membership but as an extreme form of devotion through self-mortification, a "stripping off" of the fleshly nature (v. 11).

Verse 18 is the key verse in the debate over the Colossian false teaching. It is notoriously difficult to translate. As we will see, the way one translates the verse is directly related to how one views the Colossian errorists. Most would agree on several characteristics indicated in verse 18. For one, humility seems to have been important to them, probably in the sense of bodily severity, as in verse 23. Likewise, visions seem to have played a role in their system (NIV, "what he has seen"). Paul considered them too filled with pride in their religious experiences ("puffed up"). He also referred to angels having a role in their worship. They either worshiped angels or based their own worship on the pattern of the angels' worship of God. As we shall see, this distinction becomes crucial in the various attempts to delineate the teaching.

A highly debated point is whether the Colossian teaching involved a doctrine of intermediary spiritual powers between God and humans. A number of seemingly technical terms for spiritual powers appear in Colossians. These do not appear in Paul's direct attack on the Colossian problem. In detecting them elsewhere one thus runs the risk of "mirror-reading," of finding too much "between the lines." Still, one is struck by the proliferation throughout the epistle of terms which refer to spiritual powers in the literature contemporary to Paul. This leads to the very real possibility that they played some part in the Colossian system. It is questionable, however, that the term *stoicheia* in verses 8 and 20 refers to spiritual powers, as has often been maintained.

The most common meaning of *stoicheia* in Paul's time was with reference to the basic elements of the world (earth, fire, air, and water). Paul may have simply been referring to the human earthbound nature of the false teaching when he used this term to describe it. On the other hand, the terms *powers* (*exousiai*) and *authorities* (*archai*) may have a cosmological reference (1:16; 2:10, 15). This is especially true of 2:15, which refers to Christ's victory over the demons in his death on the cross. Some would see the term *fullness* in 1:19 and 2:9 as referring to the sum totality of the spiritual world, a meaning which the term (*plērōma*) came to have in later Gnostic systems. It is questionable whether it had such a meaning in Paul's day. Paul used it to emphasize the completeness of Christ's divinity and the completeness of the believer's experience in Christ. Christians simply do not need to worry about powers and authorities or any earthly or heavenly forces, because they are filled with Christ. He is a complete Savior. In some sense the Colossian errorists did not see it that way. They felt that some additional observance was necessary to make their salvation complete.

SPECIFIC SUGGESTIONS

We will make no endeavor to outline all the attempts to delineate the teaching which threatened the Colossians but will only provide a few examples of some of the main types of suggestion.

The Hellenistic mysteries. Many scholars in the early twentieth century suggested that the Colossian teaching was influenced by the Greek mystery religions. This view was especially associated with Martin Dibelius, who suggested that the Colossians were embracing a native Phrygian cult of the elements, based in the *stoicheia*, who were seen as the spiritual powers that control the earthly elements. Dibelius argued that in 2:18 Paul used a technical term for entering upon the initiatory rites of a mystery religion (Gk., *embateuein*, translated by the NIV as "goes in great detail about").[11] There is, however, little evidence that the word had such a technical meaning, and few today would argue for a mystery background to the Colossian problem.

Gnosticism. Many see the Colossian problem as being influenced by some incipient form of Gnosticism. J. B. Lightfoot, for instance, argued that the Colossian teaching was a combination of Hellenistic Gnostic ideas with Jewish Essenism. Gunther Bornkamm took Colossians back to the roots of Gnosticism in the Iranian myth of a primal heavenly man whose body composed all the elements of the earth. He argued that the Colossian errorists sought assimilation to this primal heavenly body by veneration of the spirit powers (*stoicheia*). Paul responded that they were already complete in the *body of Christ.*[12] Bornkamm saw the Colossian system as based in a form of Jewish Gnosticism. Particularly influential in maintaining a Gnostic background has been Ernst Käsemann. He argued that the Christological hymn of Colossians 1:15–20 is a Christian adaptation of an original Gnostic hymn about the descent and ascent of the heavenly Redeemer. Most contemporary scholars who use the term *gnostic* to refer to the Colossian teaching do so with a "small g," seeing it as being in an early incipient form which had a gnostic-like cosmology but without the full metaphysical dualism and the docetic Christology of later Gnosticism. Many would agree with Bornkamm that the Colossian teaching grew out of a form of Jewish Gnosticism.

Hellenistic philosophy. Several interpreters take quite literally Paul's warnings against "fine-sounding arguments" (2:4) and "philosophy" (2:8). They see the main background to the Colossian problem as Hellenistic philosophy. The view has been suggested before. For instance, Calvin saw the Colossian problem as being rooted in Platonism. Eduard Schweizer has suggested that the Colossian preoccupation with ascetic rites has close affinities with Neo-Pythagoreanism, a first-century system which also advocated a rigid ascetic discipline in its attempt to rise above the strife-ridden plain of the earthly elements (*stoicheia*).[13] Recently Troy Martin has suggested that in Colossians Paul sought to assure the Colossians in the face of a criticism being leveled against their Christian faith by Cynic philosophers.[14] For the most part, however, the attempts to link the Colossian problem with Hellenistic philosophy have been limited in number.

Jewish. All of the above views see some degree of Greek influence in the Colossian problem. Others would see the background to the Colossian teaching as primarily Jewish. In fact, some would see the Colossian "opponents" as coming from the local synagogue. For example, James Dunn argues that it was local Jews who sought to "disqualify" the new Gentile Christian group in Colosse for their claims to being the people of the Messiah and members of God's covenant. The Gentiles did not keep the Sabbath or food laws; neither were they circumcised. For Dunn, it was not a matter of a Colossian false teaching at all but of a normal Jewish criticism of the Christian claims.[15]

Essenes. J. B. Lightfoot suggested that the Colossian problem was based on a blend of Gnostic "theosophic speculation" and Essenism. Writing long before the discoveries at Qumran, Lightfoot's knowledge of the Essenes was primarily based on the information in Josephus and Philo. Lightfoot saw links between the Colossian teaching and various aspects of Essene thought, such as their mystical bent, their philosophical characterization in Josephus and Philo, and their asceticism. More recent investigations have seen even closer ties with the Essenes on the basis of the Dead Sea Scrolls.[16] Most would grant that the Essenes of Palestine may not have penetrated to Asia, but they would see the Essenes as providing an example of the type of heterodox Judaism which may have influenced the Colossians.

Jewish mysticism. The most common contemporary view is that the Colossian errorists were influenced by the kind of Jewish mysticism that emphasized visions of the heavenly throne room, that is, *Merkabah* mysticism.[17] Fred Francis has advocated this view. He argues that the reference to "angel worship" in 2:18 refers to the experience of beholding a vision of angels worshiping in heaven. The Colossians sought to emulate this angelic mode of worship that they beheld in their visions. Their ascetic practices were standard preparation for experiencing visions in Jewish mysticism. The group felt that the mystical experience was in some sense necessary for a complete experience of salvation.[18] This view that the Colossian teaching involved Jewish mystical practice is perhaps the dominant view in the current discussion.[19]

Conclusions. In his book of 1973, John Gunther pointed to forty-four different reconstructions of the Colossian teaching.[20] If one were so inclined, one could probably greatly expand the list today. The great variety of views tends to make one despair of ever really uncovering the specific problem at Colosse. Many interpreters are thus content to describe it in the most general terms as a syncretistic blend of Jewish, Christian, and Hellenistic ideas.[21] Or, perhaps, as Morna Hooker has suggested, there may not have been a false teaching afoot at Colosse at all. Paul may simply have been warning the church in advance of the type of problems that *might* come, problems he had experienced in his other congregations.[22] Still, Paul's words in 2:16–23 are too specific and direct to conclude that Paul was simply warning the Colossians of possibilities that might come. He seems to have been addressing present realities.

Whatever one finally concludes about the specific problem at Colosse, several things seem to stand out. Some people at Colosse had an inadequate view of Christ. They felt the need to add to their worship and to their practice in order to ensure their full salvation. They also had an inadequate ethic. They focused on a sort of negative, fleshly self-denial, which Paul argued would in the end only aggravate the desires they were seeking to control. Their would-be piety led to serious social problems within the congregation, as some felt superior to others and sought to disqualify them from the faith. Paul saw a single solution to all these manifestations of the Colossian problem. The Colossians needed a greater grasp on their Savior, a tighter hold on their head. To the Colossian problem Paul responded with the most exalted presentation of Christ to be found in any of his epistles.

A STUDY OUTLINE OF COLOSSIANS

I. Introduction to the Epistle (1:1–2:3)
   A. Salutation (1:1–2)
   B. Paul's Thanksgiving for the Colossians (1:3–8)
      1. For their faith, hope, and love (vv. 3–5a)
      2. For their foundation in the word of truth (vv. 5b–8)
   C. Paul's Prayer for the Colossians (1:9–14)
      1. For wisdom, Christian deportment, and spiritual power (vv. 9–11)

        2. For their deliverance and share in the inheritance of the saints (vv. 12–14)
    D. Paul's Hymn to Christ (1:15–20)
        1. The first creation (vv. 15–17)
        2. The new creation (vv. 18–20)
    E. Paul's Personal Appeal to the Colossians (1:21–2:3)
        1. Their reconciliation (1:21–23)
        2. Paul's stewardship (1:24–2:3)
II. Attack on the False Teaching at Colosse (2:4–3:4)
    A. The Danger of Being Led Astray (2:4–8)
        1. The false teaching characterized (2:4, 8)
        2. The contrasting teaching of Christ (2:5–7)
    B. The Right View of the Person and Work of Christ (2:9–15)
        1. The correct understanding of Christ's person (vv. 9–10)
        2. The true meaning of baptism (vv. 11–13)
        3. The full understanding of Christ's atoning death (vv. 14–15)
    C. Direct Attack on the Colossian Error (2:16–19)
        1. Its asceticism, visionary emphasis, veneration of the wrong things (v. 16)
        2. These are but a shadow; the substance belongs to Christ (vv. 17–19)
    D. The Ultimate Response to the Error (2:20–3:4)
        1. Dying with Christ (2:20–23)
        2. Rising with Christ (3:1–4)
III. The Right Basis for Christian Conduct (3:5–4:6)
    A. "Put Off" the Old Person (3:5–11)
    B. "Put On" the New (3:12–17)
    C. "Be Subject" to One Another (3:18–4:1)
        1. Husbands and wives (3:18–19)
        2. Parents and children (3:20–21)
        3. Slaves and masters (3:22–4:1)
    D. "Watch and Pray" (4:2–6)
IV. Conclusion of the Epistle (4:7–18)
    A. The Bearer of the Letter (vv. 7–9)
    B. Greetings from Various Brothers (vv. 10–15)
    C. The Exchange with Laodicea (vv. 16–17)
    D. Concluding Benediction (v. 18)

HIGHLIGHTS OF COLOSSIANS

We will not treat all of Colossians here. Paul's attack on the false teaching in 2:16–20 has already been examined, and the personal greetings of chapter 4 have already been covered or will be in considering Philemon. In this section we will concentrate on the Christology of chapters 1 and 2 and the treatment of Christian ethics in 2:20–4:6.

INTRODUCTORY THANKSGIVING AND PRAYER (1:1–14)

Paul characteristically began his letters with a thanksgiving and prayer. Usually this section introduced themes which were central to the main message of his letter. This is the case with Colossians. Some of the Colossians were pursuing a teaching that Paul considered false and not centered in the gospel. In the thanksgiving and prayer, Paul reminded them of the *basics* of the Christian gospel. First, they already possessed the primary Christian virtues of *faith* in Christ, confident *hope* in the future life in Christ, and *love* expressed in active charity toward one another (vv. 3–5). Paul reminded them of how they had heard the full truth of the gospel from Epaphras and informed them that it was bearing fruit throughout the world (in contrast, perhaps, to their own localized teaching, vv. 6–8). Paul then prayed that they would have full knowledge, conduct pleasing to God, and strength to carry through on their commitment (vv. 9–11). This too may have been an implicit critique of the Colossian system, which was certainly occupied with knowledge of spiritual beings, with a concern for power, and with an ascetic ethic which Paul considered to be ineffective.

Paul concluded with a reminder of their experience in Christ (vv. 12–14). He used the language of transfer from one power sphere to another. They had been transported from the realm of darkness into the realm of light, from the power of sin into the dominion of God's beloved Son. They had been fully forgiven and fully redeemed. The Israelites described their deliverance from the Egyptian bondage in terms of "redemption." Like Israel, in Christ Christians have been "redeemed," set free from bondage to sin and given a lot among the saints. The term *lot* (*klēros*) is used in the Greek Old Testament for the allotments to the tribes in the promised land. Here Paul assured the Colossians of the certainty of their salvation, of their securing their lot among the people of God. They needed no further salvation. He then proceeded to describe their Savior, their all-sufficient Savior. They needed no further Savior, either (vv. 15–20).

THE "HYMN TO CHRIST" (1:15–20)

Most interpreters see Colossians 1:15–20 as being poetic in structure and drawing heavily from the worship language of the church. Many see it as being a pre-Pauline hymn, but there is nothing in it which could not have come from Paul himself. The important consideration is that the "hymn" is not a mere ornament but is closely related to the message of the epistle as a whole. It is one of the three great Christological confessions of the New Testament that sing the praises of Christ's role in creation (cp. John 1:1–4; Heb. 1:1–3). It also links up with statements of Paul in his other epistles that affirm the unity and equality of Christ and God (cp. 1 Cor. 8:6; Phil. 2:6–11).

The background to the conceptuality of this great Christological statement has often been discussed. For instance, Käsemann argued that it is a Christian adaptation of a Gnostic hymn that originally applied to the descent to earth of the heavenly Redeemer.[23] Few today would argue for a Gnostic background. There is a general consensus that the conceptuality of the hymn draws from Jewish wisdom theology, particularly the personification of divine wisdom that one finds in such passages as Proverbs 8:22–31, Sirach 24, and Wisdom of Solomon 7:25–26, where wisdom is pictured as active in creation and is called the very "image" of God.[24] It is not a question of wisdom producing Christian theology but of the wisdom theology providing conceptuality suitable to the Christian understanding of Christ.[25]

One reason for viewing Colossians 1:15–20 as a hymn is its structure. It falls into two natural stanzas. The first stanza (vv. 15–17) depicts Christ's role in the creation of the universe. The second stanza portrays Christ's role in the new creation, the church (vv. 18–20). The first half speaks of Christ as the "firstborn" of creation, the second of Christ as the "firstborn" from the dead.[26]

First stanza: Christ, by whom all things were created (vv. 15–17). Nowhere else did Paul pile up so many attributes in praise of the preexistent Christ. He called him the "image" of God, almost surely drawing from Genesis 1:26.[27] "Image" means the very essence and form of God himself. Christ alone is the true image of God (cp. 2 Cor. 4:4); we share in Christ's image when we belong to him (cp. 2 Cor. 3:18). Paul then referred to Christ as the "firstborn over all creation." An early Christian heresy known as Arianism appealed to this verse to argue that Christ was a created being, albeit the *first* of God's creation. That is obviously not the meaning in this context, where Christ is described as himself being active in creation (v. 16). The meaning is rather the Old Testament sense of having the rights and prestige which belong to the firstborn, the preeminence of the firstborn son (cp. Ps. 89:27).[28] "All things" were created by Christ (v. 16).

All things was a Stoic term (Gk., *ta panta*) which meant literally everything that exists, both animate and inanimate. Paul then proceeded to list some of the things created by Christ—thrones, powers, rulers, authorities. In Jewish apocalyptic literature these are the spiritual powers which rule over the highest heavens. Paul could well have had his eyes on the Colossian errorists, as if to say, "Why do you worry about other powers? Christ created them all, and you are secure in him. What can they do to you?" Not only were all things created *by* Christ; they were created *for* him as well (v. 16b). Literally, the Greek says that they were created "unto" (*eis*) him. In other words, Christ is not only the origin of creation. He is its goal as well—it is moving toward him. Verse 17 completes the picture. Christ is preexistent.[29] He existed "before all things." Also, all things "hold together" in him. He is the "cosmic glue" by whom all things cohere. Christ is thus at the center of creation in all respects—its originator, its sustainer, its goal.

Second stanza: Christ, the firstborn of the new creation (vv. 18–20). One must assume a gap between the two stanzas.[30] In the history of humanity, there is the stark reality of the fall. Humans did not fulfill God's purposes in the original creation. A new creation of redeemed humanity became necessary. The new creation came about in Christ. Stoics often described the world as a body. Here Christ is described as the head of the new world body, the new creation, the church (v. 18). The concept of Christ as the head of the body is an advance over Paul's body analogy as it appears in 1 Corinthians 12 and Romans 12. The church is not merely *like* a body; it *is* a body, a living organism, with Christ as its head. This theology of the church is elaborated further in Ephesians, and we will examine it in the next chapter. Christ is the head of the new creation by being "firstborn from . . . the dead," the "firstfruit" of the resurrection.[31] The new creation *is* the new humanity which shares in the resurrection of Christ.

Paul further described Christ as possessing all the "fullness" (*plērōma*) of God (v. 19). He probably did not mean this in the later Gnostic sense of the sum totality of the spirit world but in the sense of Christ being the image of God (v. 15). As such, he was uniquely equipped to serve as God's agent for the reconciliation of all things (v. 20). He set the reconciliation in motion through his death on the cross.[32] The picture is the same as the idea of all creation moving toward Christ as its goal. Literally, all things will one day be reconciled in Christ. He is creation's goal. There is a decided "universalism" in this concept, but it is not universal salvation so much as it is universal recognition of God's sovereignty.[33] When Christ's work is ultimately complete in his cosmos, every knee will bow and declare him Lord, and God will once again be all in all.

Significance of the hymn. Through the Christological hymn, Paul sought to bring the Colossians to a full confession of faith in Christ. Their view of the Savior was too small, or they would not have been letting people make them fret that they needed to do more or to have new experiences in order to fortify their salvation. The message is continually relevant, for there is always the temptation to "add" to our faith in Christ, to look for new experiences which will ensure our salvation.

Paul's message of the all-sufficient Christ is liberating. We only need to continue in our relationship to him, and he will sustain us. The realization that Christ is both Creator and Redeemer at the same time is also an important lesson. All life is of a single piece. The God who made us is the same God who loves us and gave himself to save us. Paul's picture of the cosmic Christ who created and sustains "all things" is a particularly relevant message for our own times, a time when human selfishness and arrogance could literally destroy all of God's creation.[34] If Christ stands at the center of creation, then we who acknowledge him as Lord should of all people be the most sensitive about the care and preservation of that creation. Finally, it is significant that Paul's great Christological statement is set in the form of a hymn, a confession of faith. It is often in our worship and our praise that we are brought closest to a full awareness of God and his greatness, something that the purely rational exercise of our theological endeavors could never do.[35]

PAUL'S PERSONAL APPEAL TO THE COLOSSIANS (1:21–2:19)

Reconciliation for the Colossians (1:21–23). Having presented the greatness of their Savior, Paul now assured the Colossians of the completeness of their salvation. He spoke in terms of reconciliation, a restored relation to God. God accomplished his reconciling work through the death of Jesus on the cross. Through the atoning death of Christ, the believer is rendered holy and blameless and acceptable to God. Paul emphasized that the Colossians must remain firmly rooted in this one true gospel and not moved in some new direction. He probably had in mind the Colossian false teaching.

Paul's ministry of the gospel (1:24–2:3). Paul pointed to his personal role in proclaiming this gospel of reconciliation in Christ. First he spoke of the suffering nature of his ministry (v. 24). Paul often spoke of the suffering which accompanied his ministry. What is unique about his statement here is that he saw the suffering as a "filling up . . . what is still lacking in regard to Christ's afflictions." Paul did not mean that in any sense Christ's atoning work is incomplete. What was lacking was the proclamation of the good news of that atoning work to all people. It was *that* ministry for which Paul suffered. The Colossians had not met Paul. Here he introduced himself as the apostle to the Gentiles. The center of his message was the open proclamation of the message that was formerly hidden: that in Jesus Christ God was including the Gentiles in his salvation. They too partake of the certain hope of eternal glory through Christ (v. 27). Paul's was a "democratic" gospel; it was for "everyone" (v. 28). Paul emphasized his constant struggle on behalf of his Gentile churches (1:29; 2:1). His goal was that they would become fully mature in knowledge and united in love (2:2–3).

Warning not to be led astray (2:4–8). Paul began his argument against the Colossian false teaching. He described it as "fine-sounding arguments," rhetorical flourish which on the surface seemed plausible and persuasive (v. 4). In reality, he said, they represented a strictly human philosophy based on earthly principles (v. 8). The false teachers were "deceivers," making prey of the Colossians, leading them down a false path. In contrast, the Colossians had received the real truth in Christ. They needed to remain fully rooted in the gospel and their basic faith in Christ (vv. 6–7).

The reliable teaching: the person and work of Christ (2:9–15). Before moving to the specific errors of the Colossian teaching, Paul once again focused on the completeness of the salvation in Christ. In terms reminiscent of the hymn of 1:15–20, he spoke of how the full being of God indwelt Christ. Paul's reference was not to the incarnation but to the completeness of Christ's divine nature. The important thing for the Colossians was that they partook of this completeness as Christ indwelt them; they needed nothing more nor did they need to fret about any fatalistic power or authority over them. Their Savior stood over all the powers.

Paul then turned to the Colossians' experience of baptism (vv. 11–12). He likened baptism to circumcision. He was not saying that baptism replaces circumcision as an initiatory rite, as some have maintained. Rather, he treated circumcision as a fleshly rite, an extreme form of self-mortification. Some of the Colossian errorists may actually have been undergoing the rite in their ascetic practice. Paul described baptism as a picture of Christ's far more effective treatment of the flesh than circumcision. It represents Christ's total stripping off of his body of flesh in his death on the cross. Just so, the believer totally buries the old person and rises to newness of life through dying and rising with Christ (cp. Rom. 6:1ff.). In dying and rising with Christ, the believer's salvation is complete. Nothing additional is needed.

Paul completed his reminder of the completeness of the salvation in Christ by pointing to Christ's total victory over the demonic powers in his death on the cross (vv. 13–15). Often called the "Christus Victor" theme, this understanding of Christ's atoning work emphasizes how he turned the tables on Satan. In what seemed to be their finest hour, the powers of evil led the Son of God to the cross. Instead of victory, it proved to be their ultimate defeat. Christ conquered sin and with it their claim against mankind. Through the resurrection he conquered sin's greatest power, death. He nailed sin's claim against mankind to the cross and triumphed forever over the satanic powers. Why should the Colossians concern themselves with any spiritual powers and authorities when they belonged to Christ who ruled them all?

THE RELIABLE BASE FOR CHRISTIAN LIVING (2:20–4:6)

The Colossian errorists emphasized the moral life. In particular, they practiced a strict asceticism through which they sought to maintain their purity before God. It was basically a negative way: don't touch this, don't eat that (v. 21; cp. v. 16). All of these regulations Paul considered to be merely human, as focusing on the "flesh" (the earthly self, the self apart from Christ). Paul considered them ineffective as a basis for genuine purity. On the surface, they seemed to reflect piety, but in reality they could not check the very passions they sought to control. The translation of verse 23 is notoriously difficult. A good case can be made for Paul's having said that the regulations of the false teaching actually *led to* sensual indulgence. By focusing on the passions in the effort to overcome them, one became consumed by them and ultimately mastered by them. A more effective manner of controlling one's conduct was needed. Paul provided that in 3:1–4.

Rising with Christ (3:1–4). Paul had emphasized that Christians have died to the old sinful, Adamic person by dying with Christ, as symbolized in the waters of baptism (2:11–12, 20). The corollary is that they have risen to a new life in the resurrection of Christ. Here Paul enunciated a basically "realized eschatology," emphasizing Christ's exaltation to God's right hand and the believer's new life being "hidden" with the risen Christ. To correct any misconception, he introduced the future coming of Christ in verse 4, when the believer's resurrection will take place. The final stage of salvation is thus future; the glory of the resurrection life awaits Christ's return. But Paul's main concern at this point was to emphasize the present experience of abiding in the risen Christ. Believers abide in Christ. They have buried the old person and are alive in the risen Christ. Their minds must thus be directed *above*, on the exalted Christ, not focused below on earthly things, like the Colossian ascetics were doing.

How does a person direct his or her vision *above?* The Spirit is not mentioned here, but in the overall treatment of Paul's epistles, the Spirit is the key. The Christian's present experience of Christ is through the Spirit, and the Spirit is the power of the Christian's ethical life (cp. Gal. 5:16–25; Rom. 8:3–8).[36] Paul's ethic is not peripheral to his theology. It grows out of it. Justification leads to sanctification. One whom God has declared righteous will actually grow in righteousness—not as a "work" but as a continuing experience of God's grace at work in one's life. Paul's epistles are filled with moral imperatives. Chapter 3 of Colossians is an excellent example. Paul began with the basic principle that Christians have died and risen with Christ and thus should set their focus on Christ above. He then fleshed out this principle with directions for many specific areas of Christian living (3:5–4:6). This has often been described as the "imperative" which derives from the "indicative." The Christian *is* (indicative) risen with Christ, hidden with Christ in God. Therefore, the Christian *should* (imperative) live out of this reality. Christians should actually live like those who in effect they are (those in whom Christ dwells).[37] Some would reduce Paul's ethic to general principles, especially that of love (cp. Rom. 13:8–10). Certainly, general principles are essential in Paul's ethic. He provided no systematized ethic to cover every area of life or every newly emerging eventuality. General Christian principles like love must guide the individual Christian when facing new ethical dilemmas. But Paul also gave a number of very specific ethical guidelines, as in Colossians 3. Paul never seems to have abandoned the moral aspects of the Old Testament law. He recognized that the law could not save, but he also realized that it set the standards of God's will. Paul was not a relativist. He believed that God established some absolutes.[38]

Putting off the old and putting on the new (3:5–17). In verses 5–11, Paul used the language of dying and rising with Christ. Christians have died to the old Adamic self. They should thus "kill" those sinful aspects of their former life. Paul employed a standard form of hellenistic moral teaching, the "vice" lists, which are often found in the writings of the Stoics. The list of verse 5 primarily deals with sins of purity—idolatry and sexual vices.[39] The list of verse 8 focuses on sins of speech, one of which, lying, is given special emphasis in verse 9. The language of taking off and putting on in verses 10–11 may reflect the early Christian practice of exchanging an old soiled garment for a clean new garment at baptism as a symbolic gesture. Those who have been baptized with Christ are a new creation. The old human distinctions and prejudices have no place (v. 11; cp. Gal. 3:27–28).

Verses 12–17 list the positive qualities that Christians are to "put on." Verse 12 employs a "virtue" list parallel to the vice lists of verses 5 and 8. All three lists have five members each. Christians are to be forgiving (v. 13) and loving (v. 14). Note how Paul's exhortation is always rooted theologically. Christians are to exemplify these positive qualities because they have been *called by* God (v. 12). They are to forgive because God has forgiven them (v. 13). Above all, Paul emphasized gratitude. The peace of Christ rules in the Christian's heart. For this Christians should express thanks (v. 15). One way of expressing thanks is through hymns of praise (v. 16). This verse and its Ephesian parallel are the most direct references in the New Testament to the use of music in the worship and instruction of the early church. "Spiritual songs" may refer to "improvisation," individuals offering spontaneous compositions under the Spirit's inspiration. Verse 17 offers a general principle for Christian ethical decision. Whatever Christians do, they should remember "who they are." They are Christ's, and all their behavior should be consistent with their bearing his name. They are saved by his grace, and all their living should be an expression of gratitude for their salvation.[40]

The household order (3:18–4:1). In 3:18–4:1 Paul employed a form of ethical teaching known as the "household order" (Ger. *Haustafeln*). It was widely used in the Hellenistic age and can be found as far back as Plato. The Stoics found it particularly useful, because they saw the household as the basis for the overall social order.[41] Paul used the form elsewhere, especially in the Pastoral Epistles.[42] The household order is directed to the members of a household, which in Paul's day consisted of three main sets of relationships: husbands and wives, parents and children, slaves and masters. In the Pastorals, the form is expanded to include relationships to the civil authorities and to fellow members within the "church family."

When one compares the Christian household codes with their Hellenistic counterparts, significant differences appear. In the latter, the "weight" of advice generally is placed on the subordinate members—wives, children, slaves. The Christian codes are more reciprocal and egalitarian. Wives are to subordinate themselves to their husbands, but husbands are to love their wives, which in the Christian context of Christ's self-giving love (*agapē*) is an ultimate subordination of one's self-concerns to those of the other. Children are to obey their parents, but parents are to discipline their children in a manner worthy of their obedience, one that does not dishearten the child. The main difference from the secular codes is that the Christian household orders are always rooted in the relationship to Christ. Wives are to submit "as is fitting in the Lord." It "pleases the Lord" when children obey their parents. All Christian ethics are grounded in the relationship to Christ.

The most striking characteristic about the Colossian code is the disproportionate treatment of the master-slave relationship. It is much longer than the other two combined. Slaves receive the most attention (3:22–24). They are to be totally obedient to their masters, to do the very best job (not just when watched), to work from the heart, and to work as serving the Lord and not humans. Masters receive briefer advice: they are to do what is fair and just, remembering that they too have a Master in heaven and will ultimately face his judgment (4:1). Verse 25 of chapter 3 may be deliberately sandwiched between the advice to slaves and that to masters, reminding both that God shows no favoritism and will judge slave and master alike by the same standards. Why this extended treatment of slaves and masters? Could it have had something to do with the return of the runaway slave Onesimus (4:9)?

A STUDY OUTLINE OF PHILEMON

I.   Salutation (1–3)
II. Thanksgiving (4–7)
III. Paul's Appeal on Behalf of Onesimus (8–16)
IV. Paul's Request from Philemon (17–22)
V.   Epistolary Conclusion (23–25)

HIGHLIGHTS OF PHILEMON

THE OCCASION

When Paul sent his epistle to Colosse, Tychicus was the bearer of the letter, and he was accompanied by Onesimus, whom Paul described as being "one of you" (i.e., a Colossian; Col. 4:9). Onesimus is mentioned in Paul's letter to Philemon (v. 10). There Paul said that he was sending him back to Philemon (v. 12). In Philemon 16 he described him as a slave. From the time of the earliest church fathers who commented on Philemon, it has been assumed that Onesimus was the fugitive slave of Philemon. Somewhere he had come across Paul in prison, and Paul had led him to Christ. Now in his new Christian status he was returning to his owner, and Paul's letter was an attempt to intercede on his behalf.[43]

This traditional understanding has recently been challenged on the basis that Paul would have been guilty of a serious breach of law had he harbored a fugitive slave. There were circumstances, however, when a slave might legally flee to a friend or acquaintance of his master in order to seek clemency in a particularly threatening altercation between himself and his master.[44] In such cases the slave would have to be restored to his master in some fashion, but at least with some advocacy from the one to whom he fled. In those instances, the one receiving the slave would have to have some status of special honor in relation to the slave's master. It is suggested that this was the situation with Onesimus. He deliberately fled to Paul, knowing the respect in which Paul was held by his master and seeking Paul's intercession on his behalf. He was now returning to his master with Paul's intercessory letter.

Another attempt to deal with the legal problems of Paul harboring a fugitive suggests that the slave Onesimus may have originally been sent to Paul to help him in prison as the personal representative of Philemon and the church in his household. Now that he had become a Christian, he was particularly valuable to Paul. Paul wanted him as his assistant on a permanent basis and preferred that he be set free for this purpose. Paul agreed to pay whatever obligations the slave might have owed in order to seal a formal contract remitting him to the apostle (v. 18).[45]

It has even been suggested that Onesimus was not Philemon's slave at all but rather his wayward brother. In this view, the reference to Onesimus being "more than" a brother in verse 16 is taken quite literally to mean that he was in fact Philemon's blood brother.[46] It seems more likely that "slave" should be viewed as the more literal term in verse 16. The traditional view still seems to account best for the overall content of the letter. Onesimus had fled from his master. He had been pretty "useless" to him (v. 11). He had perhaps taken some of his master's property when he fled (vv. 18–19). All this had radically changed when he found Paul and through the apostle was led to Christ (v. 10). Paul could not retain him. By law he belonged to Philemon, and so Paul returned him to his master but with a strong plea on his behalf.

OVERVIEW OF THE EPISTLE

Just exactly what did Paul want Philemon to do? Paul never directly answered this question, and it is strongly debated. An overview of the epistle can perhaps help in focusing the issues.

The thanksgiving (vv. 4–7). Paul appealed to Philemon's reputation for charity in the thanksgiving. He noted how Philemon's faith and love had been expressed in his sharing with his fellow Christians. There are close connections between the thanksgiving and the body of the letter. In verses 5 and 7 Paul referred to Philemon's *love* and then appealed to his love in verse 10. In verse 6 he spoke of Philemon's *good thing* (Gk., *agathon*) and used the same word with reference to his request of Philemon in verse 14 (NIV, "favor"). In verse 6 Paul also spoke of Philemon's *sharing*, and in verse 17 appealed to Philemon's "sharing" (NIV, "partnership") with him. In verse 7 Paul spoke of Philemon's having "refreshed the hearts of the saints," and in verse 20 he requested that Philemon "refresh" his own "heart." In short, in his thanksgiving Paul appealed to Philemon's generosity and Christian love. In the body of the letter he urged him to demonstrate those same qualities on behalf of Onesimus.[47]

Paul's appeal on behalf of Onesimus (vv. 8–16). Paul began his appeal by waiving his rights as an apostle and ambassador of Christ. He had the authority to command Philemon about what he should do, but instead he appealed to him on the basis of love (vv. 8–9). This was a strong appeal. In effect, Paul exerted his authority by refusing to use it. He then expressed the main concern of the letter: he was appealing on behalf of Onesimus. While in prison, Paul had led him to Christ and now considered him his child in Christ (v. 10). Paul played on the name *Onesimus*, which in Greek means "useful." Formerly he had been "useless" to Philemon. But now, a different person in Christ, he was "useful," both to Philemon and to Paul (v. 11). Paul would have liked to have kept him as his assistant, but he would not do anything without Philemon's consent (vv. 12–14). Paul implied that he wanted Philemon to do a "good thing" ("favor") in the matter; but did not specify what that good thing might be. Paul was particularly ambiguous in verses 15–16. It is clear he wanted Onesimus returned to assist himself, but he now spoke of Philemon's having him back "forever." Paul's main emphasis is unmistakable. The situation had changed radically with reference to Onesimus. He was no longer merely Philemon's slave. Now he was his brother in Christ.

Paul's request from Philemon (vv. 17–22). Paul concluded by stating his requests of Philemon. First, he wanted Philemon to accept Onesimus just like he would receive Paul himself (v. 17). Paul was willing to stand in for the slave and assume any debts he owed (v. 18). He gave Philemon his personal handwritten I.O.U. (v. 19). Not so subtly, he reminded Philemon that he owed himself to Paul. He meant, of course, his new Christian self. Paul may have actually led Philemon to Christ himself. It is more likely Paul was referring to his apostolic ministry through Epaphras. In verse 20 Paul picked up the pun on Onesimus once again. The word translated *benefit* is the same as the word *useful*. Paul wanted something beneficial/useful from Philemon. Did his pun imply he wanted "Useful" back to serve himself? Paul's appeal heightened with each succeeding line of the letter. He wanted Philemon to do "even more" than he had requested (v. 21). We are not sure what he was requesting in the first place. What could be "even more"?—freeing the slave? Perhaps the strongest pressure of all is in verse 22, a seemingly innocuous request that Philemon prepare him a guest room. Was Paul, however, really threatening to come in person to make sure that Philemon did the right thing in regard to Onesimus? We cannot be sure. It is clear that Paul wanted Philemon to treat Onesimus right, as a Christian brother and not merely as his slave. But exactly what the right treatment might have involved Paul never explicitly stated.

WHAT WAS PAUL'S REQUEST?

What did Paul want from Philemon? Did he want to have Onesimus back to assist himself? Was he asking Philemon to free the slave? Many interpreters think he was. They point to the many innuendoes throughout the letter which seem to look in that direction. Paul insisted that Onesimus's social status had completely turned around. No longer was he a slave. He was a brother in Christ, where the old social distinctions of slave and free no longer apply (cp. Col. 3:11).[48] Paul appealed to Philemon's reputation for charity, to his love, to his personal relationship with himself. He even used rather strong social pressure. The inclusion of Apphia, Archippus, and the whole house-church in the epistle's address probably indicates that Paul intended for Philemon to share the letter with the church.[49]

John Knox took the social context of Philemon to an extreme. Through a series of plausible conjectures he argued that the entire Colossian church was enlisted by Paul to bring pressure on Philemon to free Onesimus. First, Knox suggested that Philemon was not the slave owner. He was instead Paul's coworker (Philem. 1), his "associational missionary" for the churches of the Lycus Valley. The real slave owner was Archippus. He lived at Colosse. Philemon served as a sort of go-between, to carry Paul's letter about Onesimus to the slave owner, Archippus. When in Colossians 4:16 Paul asked the Colossians to read the letter from Laodicea, he was referring to the epistle to Philemon. When he then asked Archippus to "complete the work you have received in the Lord" (Col. 4:17), he was referring to the work of manumitting Onesimus. Paul made the matter a concern of the entire fellowship; he brought enormous social pressure to bear on the slave owner. Knox further observed that in the first decade of the second century, when Ignatius wrote a letter to the church at Ephesus, he identified its bishop as having the name of Onesimus. This may well indicate that the slave was not only freed but rose to high rank in the church.[50] Unfortunately, Knox's theory is based on too many "possibilities," each stacked upon the other. The first card in his deck is probably the most vulnerable—that Archippus was the slave owner. That removed, the whole stack collapses. One would like to follow his thinking that Paul took such a strong stance in favor of emancipation, but that was probably not the case.

It is not by accident that American slave owners in the early 1800s appealed to Philemon to justify their practice of slavery. Paul called for emancipation nowhere in the epistle, or anywhere else for that matter. That should come as no surprise. The whole economy of the Roman Empire was established on slavery. Abolition of slavery would have meant total economic chaos, and any group advocating it would have been considered countercultural and dangerous.[51]

Of course, slavery in the first century was for the most part quite different from the agricultural slavery of colonial America.[52] There was, to be sure, a harsh type of slavery—in the fields, in the mines, in the galleys. But the sort of slavery that One-simus experienced, the lot of a household slave, was often quite comfortable and even offered some advantages. This is why the poor often gave up their children into slavery in hope that it would provide them a better life. Sometimes people voluntarily became slaves to pay off their debts. Many slaves were highly skilled—accountants, teachers, physicians. They had great freedom of movement. It is estimated that over half of the slaves at any given time in the first century could eventually expect to be freed. Manumission was very common and was often to the owner's economic advantage. Many individuals preferred slave status to freedom because their lot was better as privileged slaves in wealthy households than it would be on their own. Still, slaves *were* another person's property. They had no legal rights of their own, could not enter into a legal marriage, could not own their own property. The desire of most slaves was to be free, and Paul urged slaves to seize the opportunity for freedom should it come their way (1 Cor. 7:21).

Yet, neither Paul nor any New Testament writer seems to have taken a stand advocating the abolition of slavery. Paul told Christians not to seek to change their social situation, and that included slaves (1 Cor. 7:21–22). The Colossian household order itself takes a very socially conservative stand with regard to slavery: Christian slaves are to be "good" slaves, altogether obedient and devoted to their masters (Col. 3:22–25). Paul did not change his advice in the Pastoral Epistles. In fact, he admonished slaves in 1 Timothy 6:2 against using their Christian status as an opportunity to show disrespect to their Christian masters. Evidently, by the second century Christians began to free their slaves, but even then there were limits. Ignatius, for instance, told Christian slaves *not* to ask the church to contribute the funds needed for their manumission (Ign., *Polycarp* 4:3).

There were several reasons early Christianity did not push the issue of emancipation. For one, Paul made it clear in 1 Corinthians 7 that the expectation of the Lord's near return made any changes in one's social status unnecessary. Further, Christianity was a small nascent movement fighting for its life. It did not have the power to effect a radical agenda of social transformation. It sought to adjust as much as possible to the social realities of the time. It eventually encountered enough opposition from the political powers as it was. Of course, there was more. Paul had his vision of a new creation where the discriminations of the old creation no longer held sway, not Jew and Greek in Christ, no male or female, no slave or free (Gal. 3:28; Col. 3:11). Christianity is no longer the small, struggling movement that it was in Paul's day. It has for a long time been a powerful force in the world. It is to its shame that it has as yet still not put Paul's vision fully into effect.

Paul simply never commanded Philemon to free Onesimus. He may have wanted to, but given his social context as the slave's master, it was solely Philemon's decision. Paul was deliberately ambiguous in his request.[53] We really cannot read between the lines. That there have been so many interpretations is itself evidence that we can't. Perhaps Philemon could. Perhaps he did read between the lines. Perhaps he did do "more than" Paul requested, and perhaps the later bishop of Ephesus really was the freedman of Philemon.

NOTES

1. J. B. Lightfoot, *Saint Paul's Epistles to the Colossians and to Philemon* (London: Macmillan, 1897), 38–39.

2. Ibid., 16.

3. See chapter 9, pp. 165–166.

4. B. Reicke, "The Historical Setting of Colossians," *Review and Expositor* 70 (1973): 429–438.

5. For pro-Caesarea arguments, see J. J. Gunther, *Paul: Messenger and Exile, A Study in the Chronology of His Life and Letters* (Valley Forge, Penn.: Judson, 1972), 91–107; B. Reicke, "Caesarea, Rome and the Captivity Epistles," in *Apostolic History and the Gospel*, ed. W. W. Gasque and R. P. Martin (Grand Rapids: Eerdmans, 1970), 277–282; E. L. Hicks, "Did St. Paul Write from Caesarea?" *The Interpreter* 6 (1909–1910): 241–253.

6. F. F. Bruce, *Paul: Apostle of the Heart Set Free* (Grand Rapids: Eerdmans, 1977), 360.

7. J. C. Beker, *Heirs of Paul: Paul's Legacy in the New Testament and in the Church Today* (Minneapolis: Fortress, 1991), 64–68.

8. E. Schweizer, *The Letter to the Colossians*, trans. A. Chester (Minneapolis: Augsburg, 1976), 15–24.

9. J. B. Polhill, "The Relationship Between Ephesians and Colossians," *Review and Expositor* 70 (1973): 439–450.

10. J. Knox, "Philemon and the Authenticity of Colossians," *Journal of Religion* 18 (1938): 144–160.

11. M. Dibelius, "The Isis Initiation in Apuleius and Related Initiatory Rites," *Conflict at Colossae: A Problem in the Interpretation of Early Christianity, illustrated by Selected Modern Studies*, ed. F. O. Francis and W. A. Meeks (Missoula, Mont: Society of Biblical Literature, 1975), 61–121.

12. G. Bornkamm, "The Heresy of Colossians," *Conflict at Colossae*, 123–145. M. Goulder argues that Gnosticism developed out of Judaism and that the Colossian problem reflects an early stage of the development, being between Judaism and the later full-blown Gnostic systems: M. Goulder, "Colossians and Barbelo," *New Testament Studies* 41 (1995): 601–619.

13. E. Schweizer, *The Letter to the Colossians*, 125–134.

14. T. W. Martin, *By Philosophy and Empty Deceit: Colossians as a Response to a Cynic Critique*, JSNT Supplement Series, 118 (Sheffield: JSOT Press, 1996). For the view that the Colossian teaching was a blend of Middle Platonic, Jewish, and Christian elements, see R. E. Demaris, *The Colossian Controversy*, JSNT Supplement Series, 96 (Sheffield: JSOT Press, 1994).

15. J. D. G. Dunn, "The Colossian Philosophy: A Confident Jewish Apologia," *Biblica* 76 (1995): 153–181.

16. J. B. Lightfoot, Colossians and Philemon, 71–111; S. Lyonnet, "St. Paul's Adversaries in Colossae," in *Conflict at Colossae*, 147–161.

17. See the previous discussion of Merkabah mysticism in chapter 4, p. 68.

18. F. O. Francis, "Humility and Angel Worship in Col. 2:18," *Conflict at Colossae*, 163–195.

19. For examples, see Craig Evans, "The Colossian Mystics," *Biblica* 63 (1982): 188–205; Christopher Rowland, "Apocalyptic Visions and the Exaltation of Christ in the Letter to the Colossians," *Journal for the Study of the New Testament* 19 (1983): 73–83; J. Sumney, "Those Who 'Pass Judgment': The Identity of the Opponents in Colossians," *Biblica* 74 (1993): 366–388; A J. Banstra, "Did the Colossian Errorists Need a Mediator?" *New Dimensions in New Testament Study*, ed. R. N. Longenecker and M. C. Tenney (Grand Rapids: Zondervan, 1974), 329–343.

20. J. J. Gunther, *St. Paul's Opponents and Their Background, Supplements to Novum Testamentum*, 35 (Leiden: Brill, 1973), 3–4.

21. H. W. House, "Heresies in the Colossian Church," *Bibliotheca Sacra* 149 (1992): 45–59.

22. M. D. Hooker, "Were There False Teachers in Colossae?" *Christ and Spirit in the New Testament*, ed. B. Lindars and S. S. Smalley (Cambridge: University Press, 1973), 315–331. For a similar view, see N. T. Wright, *The Epistles of Paul to the Colossians and to Philemon*, Tyndale New Testament Commentaries (Grand Rapids: Eerdmans, 1986), 23–30.

23. Ernst Käsemann, "A Primitive Christian Baptismal Liturgy," *Essays on New Testament Themes*, trans. W. J. Montague, Studies in Biblical Theology, 41 (Naperville, Ill.: Allenson, 1964), 149–168.

24. W. D. Davies, *Paul and Rabbinic Judaism* (London: S.P.C.K., 1958), 147–176.

25. M. Thrall argued that Paul's conversion convinced him of Christ's preexistence and led him eventually to apply the wisdom theology to Christ: "The Origin of Pauline Christology," *Apostolic History and the Gospel*, 304–316.

26. A more precise division would call for each stanza to begin with the "firstborn" statement. In such a division, stanza one would embrace verses 15–16 and stanza 2 verses 18b–20, with 17–18a as a transition linking the two sections. See F. F. Bruce, "Colossian Problems, Part 2: The 'Christ Hymn' of Colossians 1:15–20," *Bibliotheca Sacra* 141 (1984): 99–111.

27. N. T. Wright, *The Climax of the Covenant* (Minneapolis: Fortress, 1992), 99–119.

28. P. Beasley-Murray, "Colossians 1:15–20: An Early Christian Hymn Celebrating the Lordship of Christ," *Pauline Studies*, ed. D. A. Hagner and M. J. Harris (Grand Rapids: Eerdmans, 1970), 170–173.

29. J. D. G. Dunn maintains that the concept of wisdom as a personification of God is preexistent—not Christ: *The Theology of Paul the Apostle* (Grand Rapids: Eerdmans, 1998), 99–119. Against him L. L. Helyer argued that for Paul Christ was both personally preexistent and cosmic redeemer: "Cosmic Christology and Col. 1:15–20," *Journal of the Evangelical Theological Society* 37 (1994): 235–246.

30. B. Vawter, "The Colossian Hymn and the Principle of Redaction," *Catholic Biblical Quarterly* 33 (1971): 76.

31. H. Ridderbos notes that Paul probably started with the second stanza and then went to the first. Paul's theology of Christ began with his resurrection: *Paul, An Outline of His Theology*, trans. J. R. DeWitt (Grand Rapids: Eerdmans, 1975), 78–86.

32. Paul's concept of reconciliation is discussed in chapter 17.

33. B. Witherington, III, *Paul's Narrative Thought World* (Louisville: Westminster John Knox, 1994), 110.

34. M. Barth, "Christ and All Things," *Paul and Paulinism*, ed. Hooker and Wilson (London: S. P.C.K., 1982), 160–172.

35. E. Schweizer, *The Letter to the Colossians*, 82–88.

36. P. Perkins, "Paul and Ethics," *Interpretation* 38 (1984): 268–280.

37. V. P. Furnish, *Theology and Ethics in Paul* (Nashville: Abingdon, 1968), 214–216.

38. For a good summary of the main nineteenth- and twentieth-century currents in the study of Pauline ethics, see Furnish, Theology and Ethics in Paul, 242–279. Furnish took the discussion down to 1964. It has been updated from 1964 to 1994 by W. L. Willis, "Bibliography: Pauline Ethics, 1964–1994," *Theology and Ethics in Paul and His Interpreters: Essays in Honor of Victor Paul Furnish*, ed. E. H. Lovering and J. L. Sumney (Nashville: Abingdon, 1996), 306–318. For a collection of articles representing the major viewpoints in the discussion, see B. S. Rosner, ed., *Understanding Paul's Ethics: Twentieth-Century Approaches* (Grand Rapids: Eerdmans, 1995).

39. M. S. Enslin, *The Ethics of Paul* (Nashville: Abingdon, 1957), 143–145.

40. L. Hartman sees echoes of the Ten Commandments in 3:5–17 and in 3:18–4:1 as well: "Code and Context: A Few Reflections on the Paraenesis of Colossians 3:6–4:1," *Understanding Paul's Ethics*, 177–191.

41. J. E. Crouch, *The Origin and Intention of the Colossian Haustafeln* (Göttingen: Vandenhoeck und Ruprecht, 1972).

42. Ephesians 5:22–6:9; 1 Timothy 2:1–15; 5:1–2; 6:1–2; 6:17–19; Titus 2:1–3:8; cp. 1 Peter 2:13–3:7.

43. For a defense of the traditional view, see J. G. Nordling, "Onesimus Fugitivus: A Defense of the Runaway Slave Hypothesis in Philemon," *Journal for the Study of the New Testament* 41 (1991): 97–119.

44. This was first suggested by E. R. Goodenough, "Paul and Onesimus," *Harvard Theological Review* 22 (1929): 181–183. See also B. M. Rapske, "The Prisoner Paul in the Eyes of Onesimus," *New Testament Studies* 37 (1991): 187–203.

45. S. C. Winter, "Paul's Letter to Philemon," *New Testament Studies* 33 (1987): 1–15.

46. A. D. Callahan, "Paul's Epistle to Philemon: Toward an Alternative Argumentum," *Harvard Theological Review* 86 (1993): 357–376. See also Callahan's book, *Embassy of Onesimus: The Letter of Paul to Philemon, The New Testament in Context* (Valley Forge, Penn.: Trinity Press International, 1997).

47. For a helpful rhetorical analysis of Philemon, see F. F. Church, "Rhetorical Structure and Design in Paul's Letter to Philemon," *Harvard Theological Review* 71 (1978): 17–33. He divides the epistle into exordium (vv. 4–7), proof (vv. 8–16), and peroration (vv. 17–22).

48. N. R. Peterson, *Rediscovering Paul: Philemon and the Sociology of Paul's Narrative World* (Philadelphia: Fortress, 1985).

49. J. H. Elliott, "Philemon and House Churches," *Bible Today* 22 (1984): 145–150.

50. J. Knox, *Philemon Among the Letters of Paul*, rev. ed. (Nashville: Abingdon, 1959). See also L. Cope, "On Rethinking the Philemon-Colossians Connection," *Biblical Research* 30 (1985): 45–50.

51. P. V. Kea, "Paul's Letter to Philemon: A Short Analysis of its Values," *Perspectives in Religious Studies* 23 (1996): 223–232.

52. See C. Osiek, "Slavery in the New Testament World," *Bible Today* 22 (1984): 151–155.

53. J. M. G. Barclay, "Paul, Philemon and the Dilemma of Christian Slave-Ownership," *New Testament Studies* 37 (1991): 161–186.

SELECTED COMMENTARIES

BASED ON THE GREEK TEXT

Abbott, T. K. A Critical and Exegetical Commentary on the Epistles to the Ephesians and to the Colossians. International Critical Commentary. New York: Scribner's, 1897.

Dunn, James D. G. The Epistles to the Colossians and to Philemon. New International Greek Testament Commentary. Grand Rapids: Eerdmans, 1996.

Harris, Murray J. Colossians and Philemon. Exegetical Guide to the Greek New Testament. Grand Rapids: Eerdmans, 1991.

Lightfoot, J. B. Saint Paul's Epistles to the Colossians and to Philemon. Revised edition. London: Macmillan, 1897.

Lohse, Eduard. Colossians and Philemon. Trans. William R. Poehlmann and Robert J. Karris. Hermeneia. Philadelphia: Fortress, 1971.

Moule, C. F. D. The Epistles to Colossians and to Philemon. The Cambridge Greek New Testament Commentary. Cambridge: University Press, 1962.

O'Brien, Peter T. Colossians, Philemon. Word Biblical Commentary. Waco, TX: Word, 1982.

BASED ON THE ENGLISH TEXT

Barth, Markus and H. Blanke. Colossians: A New Translation with Introduction and Commentary. Trans. A. B. Beck. Anchor Bible. New York: Doubleday, 1994.

Garland, David. Colossians/Philemon. NIV Application Commentary. Grand Rapids: Zondervan, 1998.

Martin, Ralph P. *Colossians and Philemon*. The New Century Bible Commentary. Grand Rapids: Eerdmans, 1981.

Martin, Ralph P. *Colossians: The Church's Lord and the Christian's Liberty, An Expository Commentary*. Grand Rapids: Zondervan, 1972.

Pokorny, Petr. *Colossians, A Commentary*. Trans. Siegfried S. Schatzmann. Peabody, Mass.: Hendrickson, 1991.

Schweizer, Eduard. *The Letter to the Colossians*. Trans. Andrew Chester. Minneapolis: Augsburg, 1982.

Wall, R. W. *Colossians and Philemon*. IVP New Testament Commentary. Downers Grove, Ill.: InterVarsity, 1993.

Wright, N. T. *The Epistles of Paul to the Colossians and to Philemon*. Tyndale New Testament Commentaries. New series. Grand Rapids: Eerdmans, 1986.

Yates, R. *The Epistle to the Colossians*. Epworth Commentaries. London: Epworth, 1993.

COMPOSITE COMMENTARIES (ENGLISH TEXT) ON COLOSSIANS, PHILEMON, AND OTHER PRISON EPISTLES

Bruce, F. F. *The Epistle to the Colossians, to Philemon, and to the Ephesians*. New International Commentary. Grand Rapids: Eerdmans, 1984.

Caird, G. B. *Paul's Letters from Prison*. New Clarendon Bible. London: Oxford, 1976.

Houlden, J. L. *Paul's Letters from Prison*. Pelican New Testament Commentaries. Baltimore, Md.: Penguin Books, 1970.

Martin, Ralph P. *Ephesians, Colossians and Philemon*. Interpretation. Atlanta: Knox, 1991.

Melick, Richard R. *Philippians, Colossians, Philemon*. New American Commentary. Nashville: Broadman, 1991.

Patzia, Arthur G. *Colossians, Philemon and Ephesians*. A Good News Commentary. San Francisco: Harper and Row, 1984.

Patzia, Arthur G. *Ephesians, Colossians, Philemon*. New International Biblical Commentary. Peabody, Mass.: Hendrickson, 1990.

Scott, Ernest F. *Colossians, Philemon and Ephesians*. Moffatt New Testament Commentary. New York: Harper and Brothers, 1930.

Taylor, Walter F., Jr. and John H. P. Reumann. *Ephesians and Colossians*. Augsburg Commentary on the New Testament. Minneapolis: Augsburg: 1985.

17

⟐

EPHESIANS: THE UNITY OF THE SPIRIT

*W*hen Tychicus set out with Colossians and Philemon, he bore a third letter, which we know as the epistle to the Ephesians. Whether it was intended solely for Ephesus is often discussed. Whether it should even be called a letter has been questioned. Particularly, whether Paul wrote it or not has been debated.

The previous chapter dealt with the setting of Philemon, Colossians, and Ephesians. There it was maintained that all three letters were written by Paul, perhaps with some secretarial assistance. All were presented as being written from prison during the period of Paul's first Roman custody, either from Caesarea or Rome, between the years of A.D. 57 and 62. A number of scholars who would agree on this setting for Philemon and Colossians would challenge that it is applicable to Ephesians. They would argue that Ephesians does not derive from Paul's own lifetime but is the product of a later disciple of the apostle.

There is no doubt that Ephesians is unique among the Pauline epistles. It lacks the occasional nature of Paul's other epistles. It does not address any specific problems that would point to a particular congregation or group of congregations. It is written in a very lofty style, in the language of worship and praise. It has emphases that stand out among Paul's epistles, such as the church as the universal body of Christ, the reconciliation of all people into one new humanity in Christ, and the final unification of all creation in Christ. The germ of all these emphases can be found in Paul's other epistles, particularly in Colossians, but the extent with which they are emphasized in Ephesians is unparalleled elsewhere. Many feel that these unique qualities point to a later day and a different hand than Paul's.

THE LITERARY NATURE OF EPHESIANS

Ephesians claims to be an epistle of the apostle Paul. In the same language as Colossians, the salutation identifies the writer as Paul an apostle "by the will of God" (1:1). Chapter 3 gives an expanded introduction to Paul's apostolic ministry, emphasizing his special call to proclaim to the Gentiles how in Jesus Christ they were now being included in God's people. In 4:1 Paul is again identified as a prisoner for the Lord. Finally, the conclusion (6:21–22) refers to Tychicus as the bearer of the letter in wording which exactly parallels Colossians 4:7–8.

Apart from the salutation and the mention of Tychicus, the letter is almost wholly lacking in any references that would link it with a specific congregation. The majority of the ancient manuscripts designate Ephesus as the destination in the first verse, but other significant textual witnesses give no place-name. The usual greetings are completely lacking at the end, and in the body of the letter there is nothing which reflects the particular circumstances of the recipients. To whom, then, was Ephesians written? Should it even be called a letter?

THE EPHESIAN ADDRESS

Was Ephesians written to Ephesus? Would Paul have written such a general letter to a church where he had worked for nearly three years no more than five years previously, perhaps as recently as two years? Would he need to introduce himself and his ministry to his beloved Ephesians? In 3:2 he indicated that they may have "heard about" his ministry. Would the Ephesians know him only by hearsay?

The textual tradition of Ephesians seems to indicate that the words "in Ephesus" were not present in the original letter.[1] The reference to Ephesus is lacking in the three earliest manuscript witnesses to Ephesians—papyrus 46, and codexes Vaticanus and Sinaiticus. Early church fathers such as Jerome and Origen indicated that the words were lacking in their copies of Ephesians. It is thus quite possible that the original form of the letter lacked a place-name altogether and read something like "to the saints, who are also faithful in Christ Jesus." Later, as the Pauline letters were gathered together and widely circulated, the need for a place-name was felt.[2] At that time, Ephesus was added, probably because in some manner the letter was associated with that city, either as one of its original recipients or as the place from which it disseminated to the later churches.

It may be that some other congregation was the original recipient of the letter. When he drew up his canon in the mid-second century, Marcion seems to have designated Ephesians as "the epistle to the Laodiceans." Building on this, Harnack argued that Ephesians is actually the Laodicean letter to which Paul referred in Colossians 4:16.[3] It was later deleted from the text after Laodicea developed the bad reputation reflected in Revelation 3:15–19. This theory may help explain the text problem. It cannot, however, deal adequately with the very general nature of the epistle.

THE NATURE OF EPHESIANS

Many have suggested that Ephesians should not be considered a letter at all. Some maintain that it is a compendium of Pauline theology or a collection of the choice statements from Paul's epistles. The latter view was that of E. J. Goodspeed; it will be considered more fully below. Others would see Ephesians as the written equivalent of a sermon or homily adapted to letter form.[4] In particular it has been suggested that Ephesians is a homily drawing upon the baptismal liturgy of the church.[5]

Assuming Pauline authorship, the easiest explanation of the distinctives of Ephesians is to see it as a general epistle intended for circulation among the churches of Asia. On this theory, the original letter would have had no address. There are different explanations of the process. Some have suggested that there were multiple copies for the various congregations. The Ephesian designation in the textual tradition would have derived from the copy sent to Ephesus. Making multiple copies may be more of a modern than an ancient practice. Tychicus or another may have traveled from church to church sharing the letter. Churches may have then made their own copies of the encyclical. For instance, Ephesus may have made a copy for itself, thus explaining the later identification of the letter with that congregation. This "circular letter" hypothesis would account for many of the distinctive features of Ephesians: the general nature of its contents, its lack of personal greetings, the need of Paul to introduce himself to churches on the circuit which would not have met him, and the like.

AUTHOR AND PURPOSE

THE AUTHORSHIP DEBATE

Ephesians claims to be by the apostle Paul, and the earliest witnesses to the authorship of the letter all attribute it to Paul. Marcion (ca. A.D. 140) listed it among the Pauline letters in his canon of Scripture, designating it as "Laodiceans." In the last quarter of the second century, all who remarked on the epistle's author attributed it to Paul—Irenaeus, Tertullian, Clement of Alexandria, and the Muratorian Canon. In fact, no questions seem to have been raised about Pauline authorship before the eighteenth century, when the Englishman Edward Evanson declared Paul could not have written it. (Evanson also believed Paul did not write Colossians, Philemon, Philippians, and Romans!) Today many see Ephesians as not written by Paul, even some who would argue for his having written Colossians. In large part this is due to the close relationship between the two epistles. Ephesians is believed to be dependent on Colossians. There are other reasons for their denying Pauline authorship of Ephesians.[6] In general, four main lines of argument have been advanced.

1. Vocabulary and style. Like Colossians, Ephesians has a rather large number of distinctive words. Because of differences in the Greek manuscripts, the count differs from scholar to scholar. Generally speaking, there are around forty-two words in Ephesians found nowhere else in the New Testament and an additional thirty-nine not found in any other Pauline letter. This is not remarkable, however. Similar statistics can be produced for other Pauline epistles. For instance, Galatians, which is shorter than Ephesians, has forty-two words not found in any other Pauline epistle, as opposed to the thirty-nine in Ephesians.

More significant is the stylistic individuality of Ephesians. The epistle is full of long sentences that consist of chains of clauses loosely tied together. Ephesians 1:3–14 is an example. In Greek it is one long sentence. English translations invariably break it up into a number of short sentences. (It would otherwise be intolerable in English.)[7] Ephesians makes an excessive use of prepositions. There are 115 occurrences of the preposition "in" alone (Gk., *en*). The genitive case is overworked, especially in a descriptive sense. For example, Ephesians 4:13 speaks of "the measure *of* the stature *of* the fullness *of* Christ" (NKJV). The NIV translates this nonliterally in a less labored fashion: "the whole measure of the fullness of Christ." The style of Ephesians is pleonastic; that is, synonymns are piled one upon another. For instance, Ephesians 6:10 uses three words for power (*strength*, *might*, and *power*), all of which mean basically the same thing. Throughout Ephesians one encounters numerous parallel clauses: e.g., "excluded from citizenship in Israel and foreigners to the covenants of promise" (2:12). Both clauses say basically the same thing.

Most are in agreement today that this is a liturgical style. It is the type of exalted language used in worship. Paul often used such language in his other epistles. The difference is the frequency of the worship style in Ephesians. It is used to a degree unprecedented in the Pauline epistles. Is this impossible for Paul? Could it only have come from the later church? It is true that Christian literature of the second century made extensive use of liturgical materials, which links Ephesians with them. It has also been shown that the type of worship language used in Ephesians is much like that found in the Qumran literature. Both the scrolls and Ephesians reflect the Jewish liturgical tradition.[8] It comes down to a question of psychological probability. Is such a style impossible for Paul, or could the general nature of the Ephesian epistle have had something to do with its more labored style and its greater use of the language of worship? Paul had plenty of time in prison for reflection, which may have had something to do with the heavy style of Ephesians; he may have burned the midnight oil. He was writing to challenge churches that may never have met him. What better way to establish contact than to draw from the language of the church's worship, which they all would have held in common?

2. *The literary relationships of Ephesians.* Many have argued that Ephesians is the work of a later disciple of Paul who used Paul's other letters as a basis for the Ephesian epistle. Goodspeed in particular popularized this view, arguing that a full 88 percent of the contents of Ephesians is drawn from Paul's other epistles, especially from Colossians and Romans.[9] When one examines Goodspeed's non-Colossian parallels to Ephesians, however, they are neither verbal nor close. They show common thought, not literary parallels. They are more accountable as coming from Paul's own mind than from someone else using his letters.

By far the most common argument is that the author of Ephesians based his work on Colossians. It is noted that fully one-third of Colossians is paralleled in Ephesians.[10] Few of these are close verbal parallels. The most significant parallel is the reference to Tychicus as bearer of the letter in Colossians 4:7–8 and Ephesians 6:21–22, where twenty-nine consecutive words are parallel. There are other passages where five or more words are parallel, such as the body image in Colossians 2:19 and Ephesians 4:16, and the ethical language of putting on and putting off in Colossians 3:8–10 and Ephesians 4:22–24. Mostly the parallels are single words, short phrases, and similar conceptuality. Those who believe that one epistle is based on the other usually argue that Ephesians is the dependent work, seeing such things as the doctrines of reconciliation and of the church as being more developed in Ephesians.[11] It is also maintained that Ephesians often puts together into a single statement two ideas found separately in Colossians. It is argued that a later copyist would be more likely to put ideas together than to separate them; hence, Ephesians is seen as the later, dependent work.

The obvious rejoinder is that Paul himself would be the most likely candidate for using similar ideas and language in two different epistles written at the same time. That similar language is applied in different ways is due to the different purposes of the writings—one to combat a specific false teaching, the other as a more general expression of his concerns.

3. *Theological arguments.* Some have argued that the theology of Ephesians is not compatible with Paul's emphases elsewhere. For instance, the exclusive emphasis on the church universal is unique to Ephesians. The comparison of marriage with Christ's relationship to the church in Ephesians 5 is seen to be incompatible with Paul's more negative assessment in 1 Corinthians 7. The emphasis on the exalted Christ and the realized eschatology of Ephesians are viewed as being un-Pauline.

Again, it is a matter of emphasis. Ephesians presents in most fully developed form ideas already found in Paul's other epistles. For instance, Paul used the bride of Christ imagery in 2 Corinthians 11:2. Colossians also emphasizes the exalted Christ (cp. 3:1). Paul's eschatology is nowhere exclusively realized or future. It is a matter of balance. In Ephesians, the emphasis is on the present, but the future dimension is not absent. There is nothing in Ephesians which is not compatible with or a natural development of Paul's thought as found in his other epistles.

4. *Historical arguments.* A final line of argument is that Ephesians reflects a stage of early Christian history later than Paul's lifetime. It is argued that the church had become wholly Gentile. It had developed a strong sense of tradition (cp. 2:20; 3:5). The encyclical form of the letter is believed to belong to the age of the "general epistle," the latter part of the first century, not the time of Paul. The church is viewed as being under the threat of false teaching; Gnosticism is on the rise and with it the appeal to libertine behavior.[12] The church is concerned with its orthodoxy and unity in face of these threats. Käsemann in particular has advanced this view of Ephesians. He sees it as an example of "early catholicism."[13] One feels that these observations are a bit overdone. Ephesians reflects a very simple church organization, not the hierarchical successionism of a later age. There is not a hint of the docetism or dualism of later Gnosticism. Paul was indeed writing primarily to Gentile churches in Asia, much as he was to the Gentiles of Colosse. Much of the theological distinctiveness of the two epistles is not due to their belonging to a later age but to Paul's addressing the thinking and concerns of these predominantly Gentile churches.

THE PURPOSE OF EPHESIANS

At the heart of the problem of Ephesians is the question of its purpose. How does one account for this particular letter with this particular content, especially one as general and "situationless" as Ephesians seems to be? This is one of the strongest arguments against seeing the epistle as pseudonymous. One can understand why someone might write under the apostle's name in order to combat a false teaching, to appeal to Paul's authority in fighting heresy. But Ephesians is totally nonpolemical. There have been some attempts to uncover a polemical edge in Ephesians. It has been argued, for example, that Paul was fighting the same sort of visionaries that were threatening Colosse, but the evidence for this is lacking.[14] Some have argued for a Gnostic threat, but there really are no Gnostic distinctives apparent in Ephesians. The epistle simply has no polemical thrust.

Most present-day interpreters see a more pastoral purpose behind Ephesians. Dahl suggested that a disciple of Paul wrote the epistle to address two problems in the later Gentile churches of Asia. They were close to losing their roots, so he reminded them of their Old Testament Jewish heritage. Second, he provided them with a conventional morality that would assist them in surviving as a minority in a pagan culture.[15] Clinton Arnold has argued that Paul was the author and that he wrote to address the Christians' sense of lostness in an Asian culture dominated by a sense of enslavement to cosmic powers, magic, and fate.[16]

Ralph Martin suggested that Luke may have authored Ephesians. He traced the salvation-historical emphasis in Ephesians and its emphasis on unity back to the author of Luke-Acts.[17] Edgar Goodspeed likewise suggested an alternative author for Ephesians in the person of Onesimus, the slave of Philemon. Goodspeed proposed a plausible setting for Ephesians. He argued that it was composed as a "frontispiece" or preface to the published edition of the Pauline corpus of epistles. He believed that Paul's epistles were gathered into a group from the various churches he was known to have written. The epistles were then assembled into a body or "corpus" some time around A.D. 90, after the publication of Acts, which made people aware of Paul. According to Goodspeed, this assembling of the corpus took place in Ephesus. The compiler of the corpus put Ephesians together as a preface, basing it largely on the Colossian epistle and choice passages drawn from the other epistles. This introductory "sample" of Paul's thought was designed to stimulate interest in the rest of Paul's epistles that followed in the corpus. Goodspeed suggested, but did not insist, that Onesimus may have been the compiler of the corpus. He was bishop of Ephesus around that time and would be especially familiar with Colossians, which he used as his base. Also, this would explain how a short private letter like Philemon made it into the corpus.

Goodspeed's theory is intriguing but based on too many conjectures. As we have seen, his suggestion that Ephesians was based on passages selected from the Pauline corpus is not convincing. The supposed parallels are for the most part simply not there. What *is* there are reminiscences of Paul's letters. What more likely candidate to reflect these than Paul himself?

One can make a good case for a setting of Ephesians within Paul's own ministry. Many have seen the epistle as a pinnacle of his thought. Who was more likely to reach these heights than Paul himself? A major concern of the epistle is the unity of the church, specifically the union of Jew and Gentile in Christ. Paul wrote from Roman custody. The very reason for his imprisonment was his concern for the unity of the Christian movement. He brought the collection to Jerusalem as a tangible expression of the concern of his Gentile churches for their Jewish Christian brothers and sisters. He brought it at great personal risk, because it expressed the passion of his entire ministry—the oneness of Jew and Gentile in Christ. That concern ultimately led to his confinement. No longer could he bring offerings from his Gentile churches to Jerusalem. No longer could he express his concern for Christian unity in that way. He could express it in another way, however. He could relate it in his letters. That is what he did in Ephesians. It is probably not by chance that in the heart of his argument about Jewish and Gentile unity in Christ he used the symbolism of a wall (Eph. 2:14). Paul had experienced that barrier firsthand in the temple at Jerusalem, and it had cost him his freedom. But he knew that for those in Christ it no longer existed. There was one new people of God in Christ, a community without barriers. That vision lay behind Paul's collection. It lies behind the Ephesian epistle.

A STUDY OUTLINE OF EPHESIANS

Ephesians falls into two halves of three chapters each. The first half is the more "theological" portion of the epistle. In what could be described as an extended thanksgiving and prayer, Paul praised God for his mighty act of reconciliation in Jesus Christ and for granting him his own role in proclaiming it. The second half is paraenetic, exhorting the readers to be faithful to their Christian calling in all aspects of their life. The line between theology and ethics in Ephesians is not rigid. Even the paraenetic chapters are filled with theology.

OUTLINE OF THE EPISTLE

The Letter's Greeting (1:1–2)

I. Part I: The Mystery of God's Will—the Unity of All Things in Christ (1:3–3:21)

    A. Doxology: Praise to God for His Eternal Plan of Reconciling All Things (1:3–14)

        1. An eternal plan (vv. 3–4)

        2. Conceived in love through Christ (vv. 5–6)

        3. A love which brings redemption (vv. 7–8)

        4. A love with a cosmic scope (vv. 9–10)

        5. Guaranteed by the Spirit for Jew and Gentile alike (vv. 11–14)

    B. Prayer That the Readers Will Understand This Great Mystery (1:15–23)

        1. The depth of this mystery and wealth of their inheritance (vv. 15–19)

        2. The lordship of Christ over his body, the church (vv. 20–23)

    C. The Old Life and the New Life (2:1–22)

        1. Death and life (vv. 1–10)

            (a) Then: death in bondage to the spirits of this world (vv. 1–3)

            (b) Now: a new workmanship, saved by grace (vv. 4–10)

        2. Alienation and reconciliation (vv. 11–22)

            (a) Then: Gentile strangers to the covenants (vv. 11–12)

            (b) Now: one new people reconciled by Christ (vv. 13–18)

            (c) The church that embodies this new unity (vv. 19–22)

    D. The Apostle: His Commission and His Prayer (3:1–21)

        1. Paul's commission as a minister of this mystery to the Gentiles (vv. 1–13)

            (a) His personal role as a steward of the mystery (vv. 1–9)

            (b) The cosmic scope of the church's witness (vv. 10–13)

        2. Paul's prayer for his readers (vv. 14–21)

            (a) To comprehend the fullness of God's plan in Christ (vv. 14–19)

            (b) Concluding doxology: Glory to God in the church (vv. 20–21)

II. Part II: Living the Life of Those Who Have Been United in Christ (4:1–6:20)

    A. Promoting the Unity of the Church (4:1–16)

        1. Qualities that promote unity (vv. 1–3)

        2. A confession of faith that enhances unity (vv. 4–6)

        3. Gifts of ministry that serve unity (vv. 7–12)

        4. The goal of unity: full maturity of the body of Christ (vv. 13–16)

    B. Abandoning the Old Pagan Lifestyle (4:17–5:20)

        1. The old nature and the new (4:17–24)

        2. Sins of human nature that destroy unity (4:25–32)

        3. Imitating God and Christ (5:1–2)

        4. Abandoning impurity and walking in the light (5:3–14)

        5. Walking in the Spirit (5:15–20)

    C. Being Subject to One Another in Family Relationships (5:21–6:9)

        1. Wives and husbands to be as Christ and his church (5:21–33)

        2. Children reared in the discipline and instruction of the Lord (6:1–4)

        3. Slaves and masters to relate as those having the same heavenly Master (6:5–9)

      D. Fighting the Battle for Christ (6:10–20)
          1. The enemy (vv. 10–12)
          2. The armor (vv. 13–17)
          3. The power (prayer) (vv. 18–20)
 III. Conclusion to the Letter (6:21–24)

THEME OF THE EPISTLE

As stated earlier, the main theme of Ephesians is unity. The emphasis begins in chapter 1 and carries through to the last chapter of the epistle.[18] The scope of the unity is all-embracing, from the entire universe down to the lone individual. In fact, the theme is developed in precisely that descending order. It begins in chapter 1 with the widest possible perspective—God's eternal plan to unite everything in heaven and earth under the headship of Christ (1:10). In chapter 2 the focus is a bit narrower—not on the whole universe, but on humanity. In Christ God purposed to unite all peoples, Jew and Gentile, into a single new humanity (2:15). Chapter 3 continues that theme as it focuses on Paul's role in proclaiming the gospel that unites Jew and Gentile. The theme then moves to the next level, that of the unity of the church. In the midst of all mankind the church is the ultimate witness to the unity that God wills for all. The church is the focus of chapter 4.

The focus narrows still more in chapter 5, centering on families. The family is the basic social unit, and church families are only as strong and as unified as the individual families that comprise them. So in 5:22–6:4 attention is directed to the family. Families, of course, are made up of individuals. Families are thus only as strong as the individuals who belong to them, who must individually arm themselves for the struggle against the spirit forces of evil (6:10–20). With the spiritual forces of evil, we are back full circle with the concerns expressed in chapter 1—God's ultimate purpose of unifying all things in Christ, things seen and unseen, spiritual and tangible. God's purpose in Christ is to unite *all things*, and God's people, the church, are at the heart of that purpose. That is the main theme of Ephesians.

HIGHLIGHTS OF EPHESIANS

PRAISE FOR GOD'S ETERNAL PURPOSE IN CHRIST (1:3–14)

In place of the usual thanksgiving and prayer, Ephesians begins with a traditional Jewish *berakah*, a praise-hymn to God. The thanksgiving and prayer follow it in verses 15–23. Scholars debate whether verses 3–14 should technically be described as a hymn. The single long Greek sentence is certainly filled with the language of worship. It is trinitarian in structure. Verses 3–6 relate the work of the *Father*. Verses 7–12 set forth the work of the *Son*. Verses 13–14 treat the work of the *Spirit*. Each section ends with the same refrain: "to the praise of his glory" (vv. 6, 12, 14).[19] If not an actual hymn, Paul constructed it of liturgical materials and presented it in poetic form.

Verses 3–6 focus on the work of God the Father. He is praised for blessing us with every spiritual blessing "in the heavenly realms." The expression "heavenly realms" is a single word in Greek (*epouranioi*) and is unique to Ephesians. It occurs five times in Ephesians (1:3; 1:20; 2:6; 3:10; 6:12) and describes the world of supraterrestrial spiritual beings, the realm of astral powers. People in Paul's day worried that these beings could control their fate and destiny.[20] To be blessed in the heavenly places is to be caught up into God's own being, far above every power, totally secure in God. Verses 4–5 employ predestinarian language. Before all creation God chose us to be adopted as his children through Jesus Christ. The language of God's eternal choice reminds us that our salvation is not of our own doing but is totally of God's grace (v. 6). It also reminds us that God's redemptive work in Christ Jesus was not an after-thought, but was God's purpose for humanity from all eternity. Note the language of adoption. We are not by nature God's children. That relationship has been ruptured through human sin. We *become* God's children through belonging to the one who is truly God's beloved Son, Jesus Christ.

Verses 7–10 focus on Christ's role in God's eternal plan. Christ's work is described as redemption, liberation. From what are we liberated? We are freed from sin, both from its penalty and from its power over our lives. All of this took place through Christ's "blood," through his giving of his life for us on the cross. This was solely the work of God's lavish grace. This description of Christ's gracious, redeeming work through his death on the cross is reminiscent of Romans 3:21–25. Verses 9–10 look at the work of Christ from another angle, using the "cosmic" language distinctive of Colossians and Ephesians. What God intended in Christ was an eternal mystery. Now it has been revealed at the right time, in God's own time. In biblical language "mystery" refers to God's revelation of himself. In Christ God has revealed his ulti-mate purposes for creation. That purpose is nothing less than the "bringing together" (heading up) of all things in Christ (v. 10).[21] It is the same thought as the statement that all things were created "for" Christ (with Christ as the goal) in Colossians 1:16.

In a real sense, verse 10 is the thematic verse for all of Ephesians. The entire mes-sage of the epistle is the unity of all creation that God wills to bring about in Jesus Christ—a unity manifested in the coming together of Jew and Gentile in Christ, in the oneness of the body of Christ, in the bond of family relationships and in individ-uals armed against the evil powers that rebel against God and threaten all unity. The idea of summing up all things in Christ is very close to the idea of reconciliation of all things (cp. Col. 1:20).

Verses 11–14 bring the vision home to the readers. The passage focuses on how God has worked his eternal purposes among his people. Verses 11–12 begin with the Jews. In the early chapters of Ephesians, the pronouns *we* and *you* are a kind of short-hand for "we Jews" (Paul was a Jew) and "you Gentiles" (most of the readers of Ephe-sians were Gentiles). So Paul began with the Jews. Historically speaking, those who first believed in Christ were Jewish Christians like Paul himself. But now the Gen-tiles ("you") had been included in God's people because of the work of Christ (vv. 13–14). It is not by accident that Paul's reference to the "mystery" of bringing all things together in Christ (vv. 9–10) is followed immediately by the reference to the Gentiles being included along with the Jews among God's people (vv. 11–14). For Paul the ultimate mystery or revelation of God's purposes was that in Christ the Gentiles were included in his people (Eph. 3:6; Col. 1:26–27).

The Holy Spirit is a major actor in Ephesians. In verses 13 and 14 he appears for the first time. He is described as a "seal" (v. 13) and a "deposit" or "earnest" (v. 14). Both terms describe the Spirit's role in guaranteeing the Christian's eternal destiny in Christ. The Spirit is the down payment which guarantees full receipt of salvation in the future. The Spirit is the "seal" on a package which ensures that the contents inside have not been tampered with. In verse 14 *we* are the possession, and God is the possessor. The Spirit guarantees that in the final time God will take hold of us and possess us for his eternal kingdom.

THE BODY OF CHRIST (1:22–23; 2:19–22; 4:15–16)

The church is one of the main subjects of Ephesians. It is explicitly mentioned in every chapter but the last. It has often been observed that in Ephesians the church is consistently referred to in the "universal" sense, that is, as being comprised of all Christian believers everywhere. In his other epistles, Paul generally spoke of the church as a local congregation of believers. The broader sense is sometimes found in his other epistles, however. A good example is 1 Corinthians 1:2, where Paul addressed the church both in the local sense (Corinth) and in its fuller sense (all everywhere who call on Jesus).[22]

Paul used various metaphors to describe the church in Ephesians. In 1:22 he described it as a body, with Christ as its head. Paul also depicted it as a body in Romans 12 and in 1 Corinthians 12, primarily to set forth the diversity of the church's various members. The concept of Christ's headship of the body is new to Colossians (1:18) and Ephesians. By describing Christ as head of the church, Paul may have wanted to emphasize that the church derives from Christ: he is the source of the church's very being. He may likewise have wished to emphasize Christ's authority over the church. Paul also described the church as the "fullness" of Christ. The final phrase in verse 23 can be taken in one of two ways—either to mean that the church fills or completes Christ (cp. Col. 1:24), or to mean that Christ wholly fills the church (Col. 2:10). Some would opt for the first meaning and argue that the church is an "extension of the incarnation," the continuing actual bodily presence of Christ on earth. It is much more likely that Paul meant the latter sense: the church is wholly filled by Christ. It finds its fullness in him. But the church is *not* Christ. He always remains separate. As its head, he always stands over the church, and the church is responsible to him. The church cannot exist apart from its head; Christ can and does exist apart from his body. The church is the earthly manifestation of the people who belong to Christ; there can be no individual Christian apart from membership in the body of Christ.[23]

In 2:19–22 Paul used three metaphors to describe the church: political ("fellow citizens"), family ("members of God's household") and as a building. The building image is most fully developed. It starts with the foundation stone of the apostles and Christian prophets who proclaimed the word of Christ. Christ is described either as the "cornerstone" or "keystone" in verse 20. The Greek word was used with both of these meanings.[24] A strong case can be made for Paul referring to the keystone which holds an arch together. Roman arches had no mortar, being constructed of stones leaning inward on both sides with the keystone in the middle of the arch at its apex. Remove the keystone and the whole structure would topple, just as the church would crumble without Christ. Paul probably meant the cornerstone, however. The cornerstone was the first to be laid. It determined the direction of the whole building. The keystone depicts a basically static structure. The cornerstone metaphor allows for a growing building, which is implied in verse 21 where Paul spoke of the church "growing" (NIV, "rises") into a holy temple. The temple reference is a further development of the building metaphor. Early in the chapter Paul referred to the Jewish temple with its wall that barred Gentiles (2:14). In verse 22 he completed the picture. In Christ is a new temple, a temple without walls, a temple which God indwells through his Spirit. This temple is the church.

Paul referred to the church briefly in 3:10, but it is perhaps the most exalted picture of the church in all of Ephesians. It refers to the cosmic sweep of the church's witness. How do the rebellious spiritual powers know of God's eternal purposes that all things are to be brought together in Christ (1:10)? They know through the church. The unity of God's people which is (or *should be*) manifest in the church is God's greatest witness to his intention for unity of the entire created order. The picture is not of the church carrying on a witness to the powers. That is scarcely possible. Paul meant that just by *being* the one body of Jew and Gentile united in Christ the church would witness to God's eternal purpose for the unity of all.

In 4:15–16 Paul returned to the metaphor of the body. He depicted the church as a growing organism.[25] Each part is so fitted to the other that nourishment and sustenance flow from one part to the next. One can readily see the advance over 1 Corinthians 12, where the church is described as being like a body with a variety of interdependent members. In Ephesians, the church *is* a body, a real organism. Each part depends on the other for its health and growth. If one part fails, the other parts receive no nourishment, and the whole organism is likely to die.

All of 4:1–14 relates to the church. We will discuss the passage separately below. Likewise, the metaphor of the church as the bride of Christ in 5:22–33 will be discussed below in the context of the Ephesian household order.

THEN AND NOW: DEATH AND LIFE (2:1–10)

This section picks up the thought of 1:11–14, which spoke of the common destiny of Jew and Gentile in Christ. In verses 1–2 Paul reminded the Gentiles ("you") of their former life in sin. They were dead in their sins, living under the control of Satan, who is described as the "ruler of the kingdom of the air." In the cosmology of Ephesians, the spiritual powers live "in the air," in the "heavenly realms" (Eph. 6:12). Note the strong "realized eschatology." Those who are enslaved to sin will not just die the future eternal death; they are *already dead* in this life (v. 1). With the reference to "all of us" in verse 3, Paul included the Jews in his description of how all apart from Christ are enslaved to sin and under the just condemnation of God's wrath (cp. Rom. 1:18ff.).

Verses 4–7 depict the new life in Christ for both Jews and Gentiles. The emphasis is on God's mercy and grace. His work of salvation through Christ is described in terms of raising us up and seating us in the heavenly places in Christ. In 1:20–21 Paul spoke of God's having raised Christ from the dead and having seated him in the highest heaven at his own right hand, far above all spiritual powers that now exist or ever might exist. In 2:6 he stated that believers have been seated with Christ in this highest heaven and thus above the threat of any spiritual power. It was a comforting message in a pagan world that worried constantly about the threat of fate and hostile spiritual beings.

Verses 8–10 are a classic summary of Paul's teaching on salvation by grace alone. As often stated in his other epistles, salvation is solely an act of God's grace, a gift, totally unearned by human "works." All boasting is thus excluded. There are some unique emphases here. For one, salvation is described in the perfect tense ("you have been saved," v. 8), not in the future, as Paul usually did. Sometimes, however, Paul depicted salvation as so assured that he spoke of it in the past tense (cp. "glorified" in Rom. 8:30). The really unique element in Ephesians is the description of "works" of grace, the good works that are the fruit of the new life in Christ, works for which one can still claim no merit since God himself predestined them. Paul often wrestled with the ethical implications of salvation by grace. Nowhere is it worked out more succinctly than here.

Many who would deny that Paul wrote Ephesians argue that his doctrine of justification by faith is lacking in the epistle. It is. In fact, its absence is glaring in the present passage, where all the concepts are there—grace, faith, not by works, no boasting, God's gift. What is lacking is the word *justification* or any hint of legal terminology.[26] Instead Paul spoke in terms of being removed from the realm of darkness and raised to the heavenly places with Christ. It is the language of transferal of dominion from one lordship to another, from Satan to Christ, from the first Adam to the second. It is language often found in Paul's other epistles. The language of justification had most meaning in a Jewish context, where it was a question of salvation by Torah or salvation by Christ. The language of transferal from the hostile powers to the kingdom of God's beloved son would have had far more meaning to Gentiles, for whom Torah and covenant would have had little meaning.[27] Still, the essence of Paul's teaching was there. The act of deliverance is solely by God's grace—not due to any human effort.

THEN AND NOW: ALIENATION AND RECONCILIATION (2:11–22)

For Paul the unity between Jew and Gentile in Christ was the prime witness to the unity which God intended for all creation. In 2:11–22 he developed this theme from a salvation-historical perspective. Looked at from this vantage point, the Gentiles were formerly not among God's people. Now, in Christ all that has changed, and the Gentiles have equal access to God.

Verses 11–12 depict the former state of the Gentiles: they were the uncircumcised. Since circumcision was viewed as the external mark of membership in God's covenant people, this meant that Gentiles were outsiders. They were "foreigners," totally alienated from the people of God. They were "separate from Christ," that is, they had no share in the messianic salvation. Though they had many gods of their own, they were without the one and only true God. All that had changed with Jesus Christ. The Gentiles who were once so far from the divine promises, so without hope of salvation, now have "come near" in Christ. At verse 13 Paul alluded to the text of Isaiah 57:19, which spoke of peace coming both to those who were far off and those who were near. Paul developed a homily on this text in verses 14–18, quoting it explicitly in verse 17. In the context, the "near" were the original Jewish members of God's covenant people, the "far" were the Gentiles.[28]

Christ is described as the means of bringing peace between the alienated Jews and Gentiles. He destroyed the wall of hostility that separated them. Did Paul have a particular wall in mind? Some think he may have intended the wall of Gnostic speculation, which was believed to separate the spiritual world from the terrestrial world, However, there is nothing in the immediate context to indicate this sort of cosmological thought. Others have suggested Paul may have been thinking of the oral law, which the rabbis described as a "fence" around the Torah, but the rabbinic traditions would have had little meaning for the Gentile recipients of Ephesians. More likely is the suggestion that Paul was talking about the written Torah itself, whose provisions in many ways separated Jews from Gentiles. Verse 14 would indicate that this was indeed the dividing point Paul had in mind. But does the picture of the law as a "wall" have a more specific reference? If it does, the most likely candidate would be the stone barrier around the sanctuary in Jerusalem that warned Gentiles to proceed no farther.[29] Paul had been mobbed in the temple square under the false accusation that he had violated that sanction. It was the reason he now lay in Roman custody. Would Gentiles have known of the temple barrier? Probably. The temple was the most well-known landmark in Israel. Had they not already known of it, the Pauline coworker who circulated the epistle would surely have shared with them the story of Paul's arrest.

The real wall that separated Jew and Gentile was the Jewish law (v. 15). Paul particularly had in mind the ceremonial aspects of the law, like circumcision, the food regulations, and the strict Sabbath provisions. These set the Jews apart from others and were difficult for would-be proselytes to fulfill without having to leave the Gentile community altogether. Destroying the barrier, Christ made it possible for Jew and Gentile to come together, no longer as two distinct entities but as "one new person." Gentiles were no longer "far off" from the covenants of promise. In Christ they had come near (v. 17). They shared equal access to God through possessing the same Spirit (v. 18).

When Paul spoke of Christ's redemptive work as creating one new person out of the two (v. 15), it was an advance over the salvation-historical perspective of Romans 11. In Romans Paul spoke of the Gentiles being grafted into the root stock of Israel. Israel remained the original people of God, now redefined in light of Christ, now open to the inclusion of the Gentiles. In Ephesians 2, however, Paul seems to have developed his view. Now it became a matter of a new people, a new creation formed out of the two formerly separate peoples.

RECONCILIATION IN PAUL

In Ephesians 2:16 Paul spoke of Christ's death on the cross as the means of *reconciling* Jew and Gentile to God. Reconciliation is one of Paul's most important soteriological terms. Like justification, it speaks of how one becomes right with God through the atoning work of Christ. Rather than expressing this in legal terminology (justification), it does so in the language of human relationships. Reconciliation is the restoration of personal relationship between parties who have been alienated from one another. In the language of reconciliation, salvation is the removal of the barrier of human sin which separates us from God. With the removal of sin, relationship to God is once again made possible; we are given "access" to God (v. 18).

Paul spoke of Christ's work in terms of reconciliation in four of his epistles. The first reference occurs in Romans 5:10, where it depicts how the enmity to God created by human sinfulness has been removed through the death of Christ. In 2 Corinthians 5:18–20 Paul again spoke of God's reconciling work in Christ, this time combined with the language of justification ("not counting their trespasses against them"). What is most distinctive about 2 Corinthians is the reference to Paul's being an "ambassador" with a "message of reconciliation," calling others to be reconciled to God by responding to Christ. A third reference to reconciliation is found in Colossians 1:20, where Paul spoke of God's eternal purpose of reconciling "all things" to himself through Christ. This picture of "cosmic reconciliation" is very close to the image in Ephesians 1:10 of all things being "brought together" ("headed up") in Christ. The final reference is here in Ephesians 2:16, where Paul spoke of Jew and Gentile being *both* reconciled to God through the death of Christ.

Taking these four references together, several things stand out in Paul's understanding of reconciliation. First, people are seen as needing reconciliation to God. Human sin has created a barrier between them and God. Sin has alienated them from God. Thus, humans are wholly responsible for this state of enmity. Second, God himself initiates the work of reconciliation. The idea of the offended party being the one who initiates reconciliation was totally unique to Paul.[30] It is, of course, a way of expressing God's grace. Third, God's reconciling work took place in the cross of Jesus. It was through Christ's "blood" or by his "death" that God removed the enemy barrier of sin and restored us to right relationship to himself. (Here it is especially clear that reconciliation is an alternative expression along with justification for atonement.) A fourth emphasis is that the primary relationship to be restored is one's relationship to God; that is the key to the reconciliation of all other relationships. In Ephesians 2:16 both Jew and Gentile are described as being reconciled "*to God* in one body through the cross" (NKJV). The phrase "in one body" highlights a fifth emphasis of reconciliation; it embraces human relationships. The "peace" between Jews and Gentiles, their incorporation into one body in Christ, was enabled by their being both reconciled to God. There can be no real human reconciliation apart from a prior removal of the archetypal alienation from the Creator. Only when reconciled with God are we in a real position to be reconciled to one another. Paul would probably add that if we are truly reconciled to God we will seek reconciliation with one another.

A sixth emphasis in Paul's teaching on reconciliation is that of being ambassadors, as found in 2 Corinthians 5:20. Those who have been reconciled to God become proclaimers of reconciliation, calling others to the reconciling love of Christ. Finally, as Paul indicated in Colossians 1:20, the scope of reconciliation is cosmic. God wills nothing short of the reconciliation and unification of all the created order. This is not a far-fetched hyperbolic statement. It has strong implications for ecology. God desires nothing less than a completely harmonious and unified world as he created it to be. Those of us who have been reconciled to God in Christ should seek to be ministers of reconciliation on every level—among our fellow human beings and toward the natural order as well.

Paul probably sometimes found the language of justification perplexing to his Gentile converts. Not coming from a religious background steeped in law, they may not always have understood the forensic terminology of justification. Everyone knows the language of human relationships, of alienation and reconciliation. Paul probably found this an effective manner of communicating the message of God's redemptive work in Christ. For our world, with all its human barriers and human alienation, it still provides a particularly effective form in which to proclaim the gospel.

PAUL'S COMMISSION OF GOD'S MYSTERY (3:1–13)

In Ephesians 3:1–13 Paul introduced himself to those who might not have known him personally. If Ephesians was a circular letter, it is easy to understand that the epistle would have been read to many who really did not know much about the apostle. Paul emphasized his distinctive calling as the apostle to the Gentiles. He described his message of God's inclusion of the Gentiles as a great mystery which had formerly been hidden in the eternal purposes of God but which now had been revealed in Jesus Christ (vv. 3, 6, 9).[31] In Colossians 1:26–27 Paul likewise described the inclusion of the Gentiles as a mystery, and this may well be the "hidden wisdom" of God to which he referred in 1 Corinthians 2:7 (NKJV). At the beginning of Ephesians Paul described as a mystery God's eternal plan for bringing all things together in Christ (1:9–10). For Paul the realization of God's plan to unify all things in Christ had already begun in the unity of Jew and Gentile in the church. As we have already noted, he saw the church's unity as a powerful witness to God's purpose to unite all things in Christ, a witness of cosmic dimensions which extended even to the spiritual powers (3:10).

THE UNITY OF THE SPIRIT IN THE BOND OF PEACE (4:1–16)

Paul's emphasis on the unity of the church reached its peak in Ephesians 4:1–16. The section begins the paraenetic (hortatory) half of the epistle. Verses 1–6 are an appeal for the church to strive for unity. Verses 7–16 continue the appeal, reminding the church that they are to follow the leadership Christ has given them and to grow into the full stature of Christ.

Verses 1–3 set forth the qualities that produce unity. Christians are asked to lead a life "worthy of the calling." *Calling* refers to their initial commitment to Christ, their being called into his body. Members of the body are to be united, and unity is best accomplished by their exemplifying such selfless qualities as humility, gentleness, and patience. The key to the unity of the body is the presence of the Spirit. When the Spirit is present, the members of the body are knit together in peace with one another.

Verses 4–6 list the basic elements in the Christian confession that bind all Christians together in the body of Christ. For Greeks, triads were considered to be a particularly effective rhetorical device, especially for committing something to memory. Paul used the triad to a perfection in verses 4–6, employing three groups of three members each. First he listed *one body, one Spirit, one hope* (v. 4). The second group of three consisted of *one Lord, one faith, one baptism* (v. 5). The final triad consisted of three prepositions used to describe God: he is *over* all, *through* all, and *in* all. The second triad received the greatest emphasis by its central location. It is also the most perfectly formed. The Greek number one occurs in all three genders—masculine (*heis*), feminine (*mia*), and neuter (*hen*). The central triad employed one word of each gender: one Lord (*heis kurios*), one faith (*mia pistis*), and one baptism (*hen baptisma*). The use of the three genders would make the formula almost "unforgettable" for a person who spoke Greek. The three triads are also trinitarian in structure. Verse 4 centers on the *Spirit*. The Spirit is the indwelling power who unifies the *body* of Christ. The Spirit is the down payment and guarantee of the Christian *hope*. Verse 5 centers on the *Son*. He is Lord. By *faith* we confess him. By *baptism* we are joined to his body. Verse 6 focuses on *God*. God is *over, in* and *through* all things. He created all, and his eternal purpose is to unite all things to himself through Christ. God wills to be "all in all." All Christians can make this basic confession. They may differ in their individual expressions of the faith. This was certainly true of Jewish and Gentile Christians in Paul's day. Still, all Christians are one in their commitment to these central elements of the faith.

Verses 7–10 introduce a new note. Though the body of Christ is one, the unity is promoted through a diversity of individual gifts. The lesson is much like that of

1 Corinthians 12: the unity of the body expresses itself through the diversity of its individual members. Paul began by citing Psalm 68:18 as an Old Testament text that points to the reality of God's granting gifts to his people. In Paul's day the psalm was interpreted by the rabbis as a reference to Moses' ascending the mountain to receive the gift of the law from God. Paul applied it to Christ and his descent in the Spirit to grant gifts of ministry to the church. Verses 9 and 10 are Paul's interpretive comments. Paul argued that if the psalm spoke of an ascent, that implied a descent. Thus, the Christ who ascended to God's right hand is the same one who descended to grant gifts to his people. The reference to Christ's descent is not his descent to preach to the spirits in hell (cp. 1 Pet. 3:19–20); this context has nothing to do with that. The reference is rather to Christ's descent to earth in the Spirit to bring gifts to his church.[32]

The gifts are listed in verse 11. They are more limited and more formal than the gifts of 1 Corinthians, more of the order of the ministries within the church: apostles, prophets, evangelists, pastor-teachers. Apostles were the pioneer missionaries of the early church, who started new work, like Paul himself. Prophets were those like Agabus and Philip's daughters who under the inspiration of the Spirit spoke God's word to the church. The structure of the Greek suggests that pastors ("shepherds") and teachers really designate a single group of leaders of the flock who were primarily responsible for the teaching ministry. Verses 12–13 give the ultimate purpose of these various ministers whom God has granted to the church. These leaders are "to prepare God's people for works of service." The word translated *service* here is the word for ministry (*diakonia*). All the members of the body of Christ are to do the work of ministry. The church leaders are equippers. The entire body of Christ are the ministers. When all work together, the church progresses toward its goal of full maturity in Christ (v. 13). This is described as being fully unified, having full knowledge of Christ, and reaching the full measure of Christ's stature.

When one recalls Paul's picture of the church as a body with Christ as the head, the idea of growing into Christ's stature becomes clear. Paul was calling the church to be a body that fits its head. Its head is no less than Christ himself. A church body that is as full-grown as Christ its head is a tall order indeed! A church that is fully grown in Christ will be a mature fellowship, not showing youthful instability but with its convictions firmly in hand and its feet on the ground (v. 14). We cannot be sure whether Paul had some actual currents of false teaching in mind when he addressed these words to the churches of Asia. Whether he did or not, he had had enough previous experience with churches like Colosse to know that all Christians need to be firm in their conviction, stable against the contrary winds of doctrine which are sure to come.

Abandoning the Old Pagan Lifestyle (4:17–5:20)

At verse 17 Paul began the more traditional type of paraenesis. As in 2:1–3 he reminded his readers of their former pagan lifestyle and urged them to put it behind them for good (vv. 17–19). As in Colossians 3:5–17, he used the language of donning and doffing a garment to exhort them to live as Christians (vv. 21–24). He used both types of ethical appeal, reminding them of the specific body of Christian ethical teaching that they had been taught and also challenging them to live in accordance with their transformed nature in Christ. They were to become in their day-to-day

369

living what in effect they already were—those who had in Christ buried the old pagan self with its darkened, hardened heart.

In 4:25–5:2 Paul directed his attention to relationships within the body of Christ. Throughout 4:17–5:2 Paul's concern was not so much to condemn the outside world as to call Christians to purity and responsibility in their relationships with one another.[33] He focused on the sort of attitudes which can destroy the Christian fellowship, such as lying, anger, stealing, evil talk (vv. 25–29). Paul followed a basic hortatory structure that consisted of three parts—negative command, appeal to positive conduct, and the Christian basis for this. Verse 25 can serve as an example: "put off falsehood" (negative command), "speak the truth" (positive conduct), "we are members of one body" (basis of the appeal). Verses 31–32 follow the form of Hellenistic virtue and vice lists. They list as vices the attitudes which destroy the unity of the fellowship. The virtues of kindness, compassion, and forgiveness promote the unity of the body of Christ. Verse 30 is central. The Holy Spirit is the power behind the unity of the church. When Christians exemplify any of these acts and attitudes that destroy unity, they bring grief to the Spirit. They grieve God as well. God set the pattern in his self-sacrificing love through Jesus Christ. Christians are to imitate God's love (5:1–2). Through that self-denying spirit they will bring about the full unity of the body.

In 5:3–21 Paul employed a traditional form of paraenesis that is found in the contemporary Jewish literature, especially that of Qumran. In the Qumran literature, for instance, immorality, impurity, and greed are listed as the three cardinal sins, as they are in 5:3. The contrast of light and darkness is frequently found in the Dead Sea Scrolls. It is perhaps most familiar in the scroll known as The War Between the Sons of Light and the Sons of Darkness. The dualistic light-darkness contrast probably came into Jewish thought through the influence of Zoroastrianism during the exilic period. For Judaism, however, the dualism was not metaphysical nor was there seen to be any equality between darkness and light, evil and good. God is Creator, Satan is not coeternal with him. The dualism in Jewish thought was ethical. To walk in darkness is to walk by the "prince of the power of the air" (Eph. 2:2 NKJV). To walk in the light is to have one's life directed by God.

Some have argued that verses 8–14 are directed against a Gnostic libertinism. This is seen to be behind the mention of shameful deeds performed in secret (v. 12). Particularly is the little hymn of verse 14 seen to have a Gnostic background. The call to wake up is seen as the enlightenment that comes to those who are awakened from the sleep of ignorance to the knowledge of their true spiritual nature. All the ideas of verses 8–14, however, can be found in the Jewish literature. All, in fact, are found in the Qumran literature—the contrast of light and darkness, the call to expose the errors of one's sister or brother (v. 13), even the call to waken from the sleep and drunkenness of sin (v. 14).[34]

In verses 15–20 Paul concluded the general paraenesis with advice strongly reminiscent of Colossians: making most of the time (v. 16; Col. 4:5), expressing thanksgiving to God through singing (vv. 19–20; Col. 3:16–17). Distinctive to Ephesians is the warning against drunkenness (v. 18). It ties in with the emphasis on the spirit that runs throughout the epistle. As a Christian, one's joy is not expressed in the artificial stimuli of alcohol or other drugs but through the indwelling of the Spirit.

WIVES AND HUSBANDS ARE TO RELATE AS CHRIST AND HIS CHURCH (5:21–33)

The household order of Ephesians is closely parallel to that of Colossians. This is most true of the child-parent and slave-master relationships. As in Colossians, children are exhorted to obey their parents. Ephesians adds the biblical basis by quoting the commandment to honor one's parents (6:1–3). As in Colossians, fathers are urged not to discourage or provoke their children. Ephesians adds that they are responsible for the discipline and religious instruction of the children (6:4), a pattern in conformity to the structure of the Jewish household. The advice to slaves (6:5–8) is close to that of Colossians, but the advice to masters is extended somewhat (6:9). The reminder of God's impartiality in judgment is explicitly applied to the slave owners (cp. Col. 3:25), and they are warned not to threaten their slaves.

The most striking difference between the household orders of Colossians and Ephesians is the expansion of the advice to husbands and wives in the latter epistle. It covers only two verses in Colossians (3:18–19), twelve in Ephesians (5:22–33). The actual advice to husbands and wives goes little beyond what is said in Colossians. The main expansion is a treatment of Christ's union with the church, which is interwoven with the advice to husbands and wives. As we have seen, the theme of the church as Christ's body is a major theme of Ephesians. It reaches its pinnacle in this passage. In fact, the major focus of the passage is not on human marriage but on Christ's union with the church. Paul used the marriage relationship as an analogy to portray Christ's relationship to the church. The passage is thus a doctrinal exposition of Christ's union with the church, which uses the household order as a point of departure.

The heading for the entire household order of Ephesians appears in verse 21, where all Christians are called to submit to one another out of reverence for Christ. In fact, verse 22 contains no verb. It simply says "wives to your husbands." The verb "submit" comes from the general advice in verse 21 for all in the body of Christ to submit to each other. The submission of wives to their husbands is the first example of this mutual submission. The section 5:22–33 falls into four main parts: (1) verses 22–24 apply to wives; (2) verses 25–31 address husbands; (3) verse 32 is a first conclusion (applying to Christ and his church); (4) verse 33 is a second conclusion (applying to wives and husbands).

Exhortation to wives (vv. 22–24). The basic advice to wives is that they should "submit" to their husbands. *Submit* is perhaps too harsh a translation. *Submit* in modern English carries a connotation of giving in to arbitrary force. Nothing could be further from Paul's intention. He used a Greek word that related to the establishment of the social order. It meant to be subordinate to another, to be "ordered under" them. In 1 Corinthians 11:3 Paul spoke of the "headship" of husbands over their wives. This reflected the traditional household order in both Jewish and Greco-Roman families. Paul began his analogy with the reference to Christ as the head of the church in verse 23. He noted that Christ was head of the church because he was its Savior. Already the reality of the church's relationship to Christ was outstripping the human analogy that Paul was employing. In no sense is a husband the wife's Savior; only Christ is.

Advice to husbands (vv. 25–31). It looks like the advice to husbands has been greatly extended. Actually, it has not. Only two things in these verses apply to husbands: (1) they are to love their wives (vv. 25, 28), and (2) they are to care for and feed them (v. 29). Everything else in this section applies solely to Christ and the church. Christ sacrificed himself, giving himself completely for his church (v. 25). He also sanctified the church, washing it and adorning it that it might be presented pure and blameless before God. The reference to purity and blamelessness forms an inclusion with Ephesians 1:4, where at the very outset of the epistle Paul set forth God's eternal plan to have a people who were pure and blameless in his sight. The reference to washing in verse 26 may draw from the imagery of baptism, not in any sacramental sense, but as a picture of cleansing from sin. The background of the picture of Christ washing his church is the Old Testament picture of God betrothing Israel, cleansing her and adorning her in splendid garments as his bride (cp. Ezek. 16:8–14; Ps. 45:10–15). Paul had already used this picture of the betrothal of Christ and the church in 2 Corinthians 11:2.

Verses 28–30 introduce a new thought. If Christ is one with his body, the church, that means that he will care for it and nourish it. No one hates his or her own body. It follows that husbands will love their wives, because they are joined to them in a single body. Paul was looking ahead to verse 31, where he quoted Genesis 2:24 to depict the intimate one-flesh union between husband and wife, Christ and church. Jesus had quoted this same verse to emphasize the sanctity of marriage over against the rather low view of the union exemplified by his Pharisaic opponents (Matt. 19:5).

The section ends with two conclusions (vv. 32 and 33), both of which apply the lesson of Genesis 2:24 (quoted in v. 31). The first conclusion (v. 32) applies the text to the mystical union of Christ and the church. Paul called the union a *mystery*. Throughout the epistle he used the word *mystery* to refer to God's great purpose of uniting all things in Christ (1:9–10; 3:6). The unity of the church in Christ is an earthly manifestation of the union which God intends for all creation. It is a *total* union of church and Savior, a "one flesh" relationship. The second conclusion (v. 33) completes the household order. Because they are one flesh, husbands and wives depend upon one another. Husbands are to love their wives (selflessly, as Christ loved the church, v. 25). Wives are to respect their husbands. The appeal to the wives to respect (Gk., *phobeō*) their husbands connects with verse 21, where all Christians are urged to subordinate themselves to each other out of their respect (*phobos*) for Christ.[35]

The husband-wife household order has sometimes been distorted and misapplied to justify abuse in marital relationships. This is the exact opposite of its original intention. Written in a day when wives (and slaves) were often abused, the household order sought to rectify the social situation by invoking several basic principles which were rather unique to the culture. The first was that of *reciprocity*. Hellenistic moral teaching usually enjoined wives to be subordinate to their husbands. To bid husbands to love their wives selflessly, however, was unprecedented. Second was the principle of *order*. The household order had as its major purpose to maintain lines of order and responsibility within the household. The lack of order and agreed-upon responsibilities within a household can lead to its disintegration. A final principle is the *Christocentric* nature of the New Testament household orders. All Christian relationships are to be lived in the light of our primary relationship to Christ. There will be no abuse when husbands and wives manage their lives together out of their primary commitment to Christ.

The analogy between Christian marriage and Christ's union with the church is challenging from the perspective of both relationships. First, it is a challenge to the church. The church is to be *intimately* related to its Lord, as intimately as the closest of human relationships. Paul used sexual language in applying the one-flesh analogy. As the body of Christ, the church is to become one flesh, completely united, to the will of its head. On the other hand, the analogy makes a profound statement about the sanctity of marriage and the holiness of human sexuality. Of all human relationships, Paul chose marriage to depict Christ's union with his church. Just as our relationship with our Lord is holy, so should be our union with our spouses. It is a very high view of marriage indeed.

ARMING AGAINST THE POWERS THAT THREATEN UNITY (6:10–20)

Throughout Ephesians Paul used cosmological language, referring to the various spiritual powers that inhabited the heavenly places. The general first-century worldview conceived of a multilayered heavenly realm that was inhabited by various spirits. The view was common to most forms of religion, from the Greek mysteries to the Jewish apocalyptic writings. At the center of the Colossian false teaching seems to have been the belief in these intermediary spiritual powers between humans and God. Christians today often reduce their view of the spiritual realm to two single beings, Satan and the Holy Spirit.[36] Ephesians, however, speaks of the demonic consistently in the plural. Paul spoke of our struggle against a whole host of spiritual powers hostile to God—"rulers," "authorities," "powers" (v. 12). They are *not* human authorities, not "flesh and blood," but "spiritual forces of evil in the heavenly realm."[37] The word translated *powers* is literally *cosmocrators* (Gk., *kosmokratores*), a term used in Greek astrology for the highest powers, related to the sun god. Paul may have been punning when he said that these so-called sun gods were really powers of darkness (v. 12).[38]

Humans cannot contend against superior spiritual forces. Alone, they stand helpless against the schemes of Satan (v. 11). But armed with God's armor they can maintain their stance throughout the battle. Paul described the battle against the demonic powers as being a "struggle" (Gk., *palē*), a word which usually refers to a wrestling match. He may have intended that meaning, the picture being one of hand-to-hand combat, a wrestling match in armor, struggling to maintain one's stance and not be thrown to the ground.[39]

Paul's main image was that of donning the armor for the struggle against the satanic powers. The picture of God's armor goes back to Old Testament roots, where it depicts God being armed for battle (Isa. 59:17; cp. Wisdom of Solomon 5:17–18). Paul also drew from other passages in Isaiah for the picture of the messenger's feet shod with the good news of peace (Isa. 52:7) and of having one's loins girded with God's truth (Isa. 11:4–5). Paul's description of the Christian armor is much like the standard armor of a Roman foot soldier and would have been quite familiar to people throughout the Roman world. Paul elsewhere likened to warfare his own struggles as an apostle (cp. 2 Cor. 10:4). He spoke of himself and his colleagues as soldiers (Phil. 2:25; Philem. 2). Especially in the Pastoral Epistles, he used the language of Christians serving as soldiers (cp. 1 Tim. 6:12; 2 Tim. 2:4). He spoke of the Christian's armor of light in Romans 13:12, and in 1 Thessalonians 5:8 he described the familiar triad of faith, hope, and love in terms of armor. Particularly striking in Ephesians 6 is the mention of the two weapons of offense: the shoes which enable the carrying of the gospel, and the sword of God's Spirit, his convicting Word.[40]

Paul probably departed from the armor analogy when he moved to speak of prayer in verse 18, but prayer is probably a person's strongest defense against the assault of evil. Paul in particular asked his readers to pray for him that he might be bold in proclaiming the "mystery" of the gospel. Paul had come full circle in his epistle to the saints of Asia Minor. He had expounded the mystery of Christ's union with his church (5:32) and the mystery that in Christ the Gentiles were being included in God's people (3:3–6). It was probably in connection with the latter aspect of God's mystery that he requested prayer in 6:19–20. He wanted the freedom to proclaim it boldly.[41] The ultimate mystery, of course, was the eternal plan, formerly hidden in the counsel of God, now manifested in the gospel, that all things would one day be "brought together" in Christ (1:9–10). In a sense, Paul was in chains for his ministry of this mystery. He sought to demonstrate this unity through his Gentile collection for the Jerusalem saints. In the Ephesian epistle what he could no longer preach in person he proclaimed with his pen—the message of unity in Christ.

NOTES

1. For a defense of the "in Ephesus" reading, see D. A. Black, "The Peculiarities of Ephesians and the Ephesian Address," *Grace Theological Journal* 2 (1981): 59–73.
2. For the likelihood that "in Ephesus" was a later addition to the text and for a suggested textual history, see E. Best, "Ephesians 1:1 Again," in *Paul and Paulinism*, ed. M. D. Hooker and S. G. Wilson (London: S.P.C.K., 1982), 273–279. See also E. Best, "Recipients and Title of the Letter to the Ephesians: Why and When the Designation 'Ephesians,'" *Aufstieg und Niedergang der römischen Welt* II.25.4, 3247–3279.
3. For a Laodicean destination, see M. D. Goulder, "The Visionaries of Laodicea," *Journal for the Study of the New Testament* 43 (1991): 15–39. A. van Roon sees the epistle as being addressed to both Laodicea and Hierapolis: *The Authenticity of Ephesians*, trans. S. Prescod-Jokel (Leiden: Brill, 1974), 82–85.
4. A. T. Lincoln, *Ephesians*, Word Biblical Commentary (Dallas, Tex.: Word, 1990), xxxix.
5. J. C. Kirby, *Ephesians, Baptism and Pentecost: An Inquiry into the Structure and Purpose of the Epistle to the Ephesians* (Montreal: McGill University Press, 1968).
6. Massive five-hundred-page books have been written for and against the Pauline authorship of Ephesians. For a defense of Pauline authorship, see van Roon, *The Authenticity of Ephesians*; E. Percy, *Die Probleme der Kolosser-und Epheserbriefes* (Lund: Gleerup, 1946). For pseudonymity, see C. L. Mitton, *The Epistle to the Ephesians: Its Authorship, Origin and Purpose* (Oxford: Clarendon, 1951). For a briefer introduction to the arguments pro and con, see the articles by Sanders and Nineham in *Studies in Ephesians*, ed. F. L. Cross (London: A. R. Mowbray, 1956).
7. Such long sentences are characteristic of Greek rhetorical style. See C. J. Robbins, "The Composition of Eph 1:3–14," *Journal of Biblical Literature* 105 (1986): 677–687. Long periodic sentences are also characteristic of Greco-Roman honorific decrees: see H. Hendrix, "On the Form and Ethos of Ephesians," *Union Seminary Quarterly Review* 42 (1988): 3–15.
8. K. G. Kuhn, "The Epistle to the Ephesians in the Light of the Qumran Texts," in *Paul and the Dead Sea Scrolls*, ed. J. Murphy-O'Connor and J. H. Charlesworth (New York: Crossroad, 1990), 115–131. See in the same volume, F. Mussner, "Contributions Made by Qumran to the Understanding of the Epistle to the Ephesians," 159–178.
9. See Goodspeed's charts of "parallels" in *The Meaning of Ephesians* (Chicago: University of Chicago Press, 1933), 79–165.
10. See J. B. Polhill, "The Relationship Between Ephesians and Colossians," *Review and Expositor* 70 (1973): 439–450.

11. Some still argue like Holtzmann that Colossians is dependent on Ephesians. See J. Coutts, "The Relationship of Ephesians and Colossians," *New Testament Studies* 4 (1957–1958): 201–207. E. Best suggests that Colossians and Ephesians may have come from two different disciples of Paul, who "compared notes," as it were: "Who Used Whom? The Relationship of Ephesians and Colossians," *New Testament Studies* 43 (1997): 72–96.

12. For a good summary of the view that sees Gnosticism as the background to Ephesians, see N. A. Dahl, "Interpreting Ephesians: Then and Now," *Theology Digest* 25 (1977): 305–315. For a thorough rebuttal of the Gnostic background and for the argument that Ephesians is set wholly within hellenistic Jewish thought, see van Roon, *Authenticity of Ephesians*, 212–349.

13. E. Käsemann, "Paul and Early Catholicism," *New Testament Questions of Today*, trans. W. J. Montague (Philadelphia: Fortress, 1969), 237–250.

14. M. D. Goulder, "The Visionaries of Laodicea," 15–39.

15. N. A. Dahl, "Gentiles, Christians, and Israelites in the Epistle to the Ephesians," *Harvard Theological Review* 79 (1986): 31–39.

16. C. E. Arnold, *Ephesians: Power and Magic. The Concept of Power in Ephesians in Light of its Historical Setting* (Cambridge: Cambridge University Press, 1989), 167–172.

17. R. P. Martin, "An Epistle in Search of a Life-Setting," *Expository Times* 79 (1968): 297–302.

18. S. Hanson, *The Unity of the Church in the New Testament: Colossians and Ephesians* (Uppsala: Almqvist & Wiksells, 1946), 121–123.

19. For the hymnic structure, see J. Coutts, "Ephesians 1.3–14 and 1 Peter 1.3–12," *New Testament Studies* 3 (1956–1957): 115–127. J. T. Sanders argues *against* seeing vv. 3–14 as a hymn: "Hymnic Elements in Ephesians 1–3," *Zeitschrift für die neutestamentliche Wissenschaft* 56 (1965): 214–232.

20. Arnold, *Ephesians: Power and Magic*, 151–155.

21. J. McHugh, "A Reconsideration of Ephesians 1.10b in the Light of Irenaeus," in *Paul and Paulinism*, 302–309.

22. R. Banks, *Paul's Idea of Community: The Early House Churches in Their Historical Setting* (Grand Rapids: Eerdmans, 1980), 66–67.

23. See E. Käsemann, "The Theological Problem Presented by the Motif of the Body of Christ," *Perspectives on Paul* (Philadelphia: Fortress, 1971), 102–121.

24. For "cornerstone," see van Roon, *The Authenticity of Ephesians*, 353–363. For "keystone," see Hanson, *Unity of the Church in the New Testament*, 131–134.

25. For the body image, see E. Best, *One Body in Christ: A Study in the Relationship of the Church to Christ in the Epistles of the Apostle Paul* (London: S.P.C.K., 1955), 139–159.

26. A. T. Lincoln, "Ephesians 2:8–10: A Summary of Paul's Gospel?" *Catholic Biblical Quarterly* 45 (1983): 617–630.

27. Arnold, *Ephesians: Power and Magic*, 147–150.

28. P. Stuhlmacher, "'He is Our Peace' (Eph. 2:14). On the Exegesis and Significance of Eph. 2:14–18," *Reconciliation, Law and Righteousness: Essays in Biblical Theology* (Philadelphia: Fortress, 1986), 182–200.

29. M. Barth, *The Broken Wall: A Study of the Epistle to the Ephesians* (Valley Forge, Penn.: Judson, 1959), 39–51.

30. S. E. Porter and K. D. Clarke, "Canonical-Critical Perspective and the Relationship of Colossians and Ephesians," *Biblica* 78 (1997): 57–86.

31. See C. C. Caragounis, *The Ephesian Mysterion: Meaning and Context* (Lund: CWK Gleerup, 1977).

32. A. T. Lincoln, "The Use of the Old Testament in Ephesians," *Journal for the Study of the New Testament* 14 (1982): 18–25.

33. E. Best, "Ephesians: Two Types of Existence," *Interpretation* 47 (1993): 39–51.

34. K. G. Kuhn, "The Epistle to the Ephesians in the Light of the Qumran Texts," 120–131.

35. For a full treatment of this passage, see J. P. Sampley, "*And the Two Shall Become One Flesh.*" *A Study of the Traditions in Ephesians 5:21–33*, Society for the Study of the New Testament Monograph Series, 16 (Cambridge University Press, 1971).

36. We moderns have perhaps gone too far in reducing our sense of how much the demonic penetrates our existence. See J. S. Stewart, "On a Neglected Emphasis in New Testament Theology," *Scottish Journal of Theology* 4 (1951): 392–401.

37. W. Wink has written a trilogy of books that address the problem of the powers in modern life. All have been published by Fortress Press, Minneapolis: *Naming the Powers* (1984), *Unmasking the Powers* (1986), and *Engaging the Powers* (1992).

38. G. H. C. MacGregor, "Principalities and Powers: The Cosmic Background of Paul's Thought," *New Testament Studies* 1 (1954–1955): 17–28.

39. M. E. Gudorf, "The Use of Παλη in Ephesians 6:12," *Journal of Biblical Literature* 117 (1998): 331–335.

40. Paul did not often speak of the witness of individual Christians in his epistles. These references to sharing the gospel of peace and the word of God surely do imply such witness. See P. T. O'Brien, *Gospel and Mission in the Writings of Paul: An Exegetical and Theological Analysis* (Grand Rapids: Baker, 1993), 119–125.

41. R. A. Wild, "The Warrior and the Prisoner: Some Reflections on Ephesians 6:10–20," *Catholic Biblical Quarterly* 46 (1984): 284–298.

SELECTED COMMENTARIES

BASED ON THE GREEK TEXT

Abbott, T. K. *A Critical and Exegetical Commentary on the Epistles to the Ephesians and to the Colossians*. International Critical Commentary. Edinburgh: T. and T. Clark, 1897.

Best, Ernest. *Ephesians*. International Critical Commentary. New Series. Edinburgh: T and T Clark, 1999.

Eadie, John. *A Commentary on the Greek Text of the Epistle of Paul to the Ephesians*. London: Richard Griffin and Co., 1854.

Ellicott, Charles J. *A Critical and Grammatical Commentary on St. Paul's Epistle to the Ephesians*. London: John W. Parker and Son, 1859.

Lincoln, Andrew T. *Ephesians*. Word Biblical Commentary. Dallas, Tex.: Word, 1990.

Robinson, J. Armitage. *St. Paul's Epistle to the Ephesians*. Second edition. London: Macmillan, 1907.

Westcott, B. F. *Saint Paul's Epistle to the Ephesians: The Greek Text with Notes and Addenda*. Grand Rapids: Eerdmans, 1950 (reprint of 1906 edition).

BASED ON THE ENGLISH TEXT

Barth, Markus. *Ephesians*. The Anchor Bible. 2 vols. Garden City, N.Y.: Doubleday, 1974.

Best, Ernest. *Ephesians*. New Testament Guides. Sheffield, UK: JSOT Press, 1993.

Bruce, F. F. *The Epistle to the Ephesians: A Verse-by-Verse Exposition*. London: Pickering and Inglis, 1961.

Carver, William Owen. *The Glory of God in the Christian Calling: A Study of the Ephesian Epistle*. Nashville: Broadman, 1949.

Foulkes, Francis. *The Epistle of Paul to the Ephesians: An Introduction and Commentary*. Tyndale New Testament Commentaries. London: Tyndale, 1963.

Lock, Walter. *The Epistle to the Ephesians*. Westminster Commentaries. London: Methuen and Company, 1929.

Mitton, C. Leslie. *Ephesians*. New Century Bible. Greenwood, S.C.: Attic Press, 1976.

Perkins, Pheme. *Ephesians*. Abingdon New Testament Commentaries. Nashville: Abingdon, 1997.

Schnackenburg, Rudolf. *Ephesians, A Commentary*. Trans. H. Heron. Edinburgh: T. and T. Clark, 1991.

Snodgrass, Klyne. *Ephesians*. NIV Application Commentary. Grand Rapids: Zondervan, 1996.

Summers, Ray. *Ephesians: Pattern for Christian Living*. Nashville: Broadman, 1960.

Note: For composite commentaries that include both Ephesians and Colossians or other Prison Epistles, see the final section of the bibliography, on page 353, in chapter 16 (Colossians).

18

❧

"PREACHING BOLDLY IN ROME"

*P*aul's greatest desire was to witness in the capital city of Rome itself. Paul's epistles and Acts both make that clear.[1] Probably as long as Felix strung out his detention in Caesarea, Paul held some hope that the governor would eventually release him. Felix had virtually acknowledged Paul's innocence by not reconvening his trial and by giving him considerable freedom in his custody (Acts 24:23). But matters did not turn out that way. Paul did indeed eventually reach Rome—not as a free man but still in Roman custody, as the result of his appeal to Caesar.

Paul's lot quickly shifted when Felix was removed from office for mismanaging a dispute between the Jews and Gentiles of Caesarea. Rome sent a new governor Porcius Festus some time around A.D. 59.[2] After a short term of only two or three years, Festus died of an illness while still in office. We know very little about his administration. Josephus made only a brief mention of him. The few remarks that he did make about the governor are all quite positive. He praised Festus for ridding the countryside of terrorists and brigands (*Ant.* 20.182–188). The change in administration did not bode well for Paul, however. Often a new governor would release prisoners at the outset of his term, but Festus did not free Paul. Instead, he put him in even greater jeopardy. Like his predecessor, he perpetuated the injustices done to Paul for precisely the same reason—"to grant a favor to the Jews" (24:27). The one thing Paul did not want was to be remanded to Jewish jurisdiction. He knew that would mean almost certain death. When it became apparent early in Festus's term that the governor was intent on trying him in Jerusalem, Paul took refuge in the one recourse remaining to him as a Roman citizen: he appealed to the emperor (25:1–12).

The remainder of Acts is devoted to Paul's appeal. Acts 25:13–26:32 relates Festus's turning to the Jewish King Agrippa to help him draw up charges against Paul to send to Caesar. Acts 27:1–28:16 tells of Paul's long and perilous journey to the imperial city. The final verses of Acts find Paul in Rome under house guard, awaiting his hearing before the emperor (28:17–31).

PAUL'S APPEAL TO CAESAR (ACTS 25–26)

Shortly after arriving in Caesarea to assume his office, Festus went to Jerusalem to meet with the Jewish leadership (25:1–2). At that time the Jewish leaders asked him to grant them the "favor" of transferring Paul to their jurisdiction. Luke explained that they were planning a new ambush attempt against Paul (25:3). The governor was unaware of their plot and unknowingly served as Paul's protector by insisting that it would be more proper protocol to try Paul under Roman jurisdiction in his court at Caesarea (25:4–5).

PAUL'S APPEAL (25:6–12)

Upon his return to Caesarea, Festus promptly convened court to hear Paul's case. The Jews who came from Jerusalem accused Paul with basically the same charges that the Asian Jews had leveled against him in the temple yard (21:28) and Tertullus in the trial before Felix (24:5–6). One can ascertain their charges from Paul's defense in verse 8: that he spoke against the Jewish law, that he had defiled the temple, and that he was guilty of sedition against Rome. Festus must have quickly determined Paul's innocence of the last charge and become aware that the Jewish case against Paul primarily concerned their own religion. He decided that it would be best to try Paul before the Jews. So he asked Paul if he would be willing to go to Jerusalem for trial. He made clear that *he* would be the judge. It was a matter of consulting the Jewish leaders, *not* of turning Paul over to their jurisdiction. Paul did not find this reassuring. He remembered the ambush plot in Jerusalem. He was well aware that Festus wanted "to do the Jews a favor" (v. 9). *That* was the key issue. Just how far was the procurator willing to go in his "favors" to the Jewish leaders?

Paul had to halt the course of events. Legally he possessed a right as a Roman citizen that could do just that. He made a formal appeal to be tried before the emperor himself (vv. 10–11). The right of appeal was an ancient Roman citizen's right that allowed one to appeal for a trial before a jury of one's peers. In imperial times the jury was replaced by a trial before the emperor. Experts on Roman law are not in agreement as to exactly how the appeal law worked in Paul's day. Some argue that appeal (*appellatio*) only applied to an appeal *after* judgment by a magistrate.[3] Obviously that was not Paul's situation. Festus had not even leveled any charges. Others argue that there was another form of appeal (*provocatio*), an appeal *before* trial, which better fits Paul's case.[4]

In any event, all seem to agree that Paul had the right as a Roman citizen to choose his place of trial. In this instance, he chose not to be tried by the Jews but before the court of the emperor. It is also debated whether an appeal *had* to be honored in Paul's day. Could Festus have refused it? Evidently he could *not* in a case like Paul's, one not involving well-established legal precedent, one which the Romans called "extraordinary" (*extra ordinem*). It is another question whether Festus could have aborted the appeal process altogether by setting Paul free. Perhaps he could have. From all evidence, Festus would not have wanted to follow such a course, however. Paul was a troublesome prisoner. The Jewish leaders would have been antagonized if he were released. Festus was probably all too glad to send him to the higher court. After a brief consultation with his advisory council, he formally accepted Paul's appeal (v. 12).

FESTUS AND AGRIPPA (25:13–22)

Festus had a problem; he didn't know what charges to formulate against Paul. In order to remand Paul to Caesar, he needed to prepare a formal statement of the charges. He felt that Paul had broken no Roman laws, and he did not understand the religious charges that the Jews were bringing. Fortunately an opportunity presented itself for him to consult someone who knew both the Jewish and the Roman worlds well. The titular Jewish king, Agrippa II (A.D. 27–100) had come to Caesarea on a state visit to greet Festus on his accession. The king had little power, but considerable status. He was seventeen when his father Agrippa I died in A.D. 44 (Acts 12:20–23). The younger Agrippa had grown up in Rome and was favored by both Claudius and Nero. In A.D. 48 he was given the small kingdom of Chalcis upon the death of its king, who was Agrippa's uncle. In A.D. 53 Agrippa was granted the territories formerly ruled by Philip and Lysanias (cp. Luke 3:1), which included Abilene, Batanea, Traconitis, and Gaulinitis. In A.D. 56 Nero gave him some additional cities in the vicinity of Galilee, including Caesarea Philippi, which Agrippa made his capital. More important than his territories, Agrippa had been granted the formal title "king of the Jews" and was given the right to appoint the Jewish high priest.[5]

Agrippa was accompanied in Caesarea by his half sister Bernice. Bernice was one year younger than her brother. She had been married at age thirteen to her uncle, the king of Chalcis. When he died and Agrippa took over the kingdom, Bernice moved in with her brother and was his constant companion. There was considerable gossip about an incestuous relationship. In A.D. 63 Bernice married a Cilician king but did not live with him for long. In the 70s she accompanied Agrippa to Rome and soon became the mistress of Titus, the son of the emperor Vespasian and conqueror of Jerusalem. Titus would have married her, but marriage to a Jewess was not considered acceptable in Roman patrician circles. When Titus became emperor in A.D. 79, he had to abandon altogether his liaison with Bernice.

Festus explained Paul's situation to Agrippa (vv. 14–21). His account of events was somewhat slanted, as he placed himself in the best possible light. He noted how he had put the Jews off in their attempt to condemn Paul, insisting on the sort of face-to-face accusation that Roman justice demanded (vv. 15–16). He talked of how he had handled the matter with great dispatch (v. 17) and how he had wanted to try Paul in Jerusalem to get at the heart of the Jewish case against him (v. 20). He spoke not a word about his wanting to do the Jews a favor, only words that made himself appear as a paragon of Roman justice.[6] Agrippa responded that he would like to hear Paul himself. Ever a man of dispatch, Festus set the hearing for the next day (v. 22). It would in no sense be a trial but only a hearing to give Agrippa sufficient information to help Festus formulate the charges against Paul.

PAUL'S ADDRESS BEFORE AGRIPPA: THE SETTING (25:23–27)

In 25:23–27, Luke presented the setting for Paul's hearing before Agrippa. He emphasized the great pomp and ceremony of the occasion. It was a final fulfillment of God's words to Ananias about Paul in Acts 9:15 that the apostle would appear before Gentiles, kings, and the sons of Israel. In Acts 22–26 Paul appeared before the sons of Israel in the temple square and the Sanhedrin, before the Gentile governors Felix and Festus. Now he was appearing before the Jewish king. Ultimately, of course, he was to bear witness before the emperor. The high-ranking officers and leading men who attended the hearing (v. 23) probably were members of Festus's *concilium*, his advisory panel of military and civic officials.

In verses 24–27 Festus virtually repeated his words before Agrippa, stating that the main purpose for the hearing was to assist in formulating the charges. In verses

18–19 Festus told Agrippa that he had not found Paul guilty of any real crimes, only matters of Jewish belief, particularly about a dead man coming to life again. These are the two central emphases of Paul's appearance before Agrippa. The first was Paul's innocence. Festus affirmed it explicitly in 25:18, and Agrippa concurred in 26:32. The second was the resurrection. The Romans could not understand the idea of a resurrection. The Jews could not accept the resurrection of Jesus. But Jesus' resurrection meant life for them both. A main concern of Paul's speech was that both groups would discover the meaning of the resurrection.

PAUL'S ADDRESS BEFORE AGRIPPA: THE SPEECH (26:1–32)

Introduction (26:1–3). Agrippa granted Paul permission to speak (v. 1). Festus convened the hearing, making the introductory remarks, but Agrippa was the presiding officer over the whole proceeding. As the speech progressed, it became obvious that Paul's main presentation was directed to the Jewish king more than to the Gentiles who were present. His speech began in proper rhetorical form with a *captatio benevolentiae* that emphasized Agrippa's competence to hear the case (vv. 2–3).[7] Agrippa knew the Jewish customs, but he was in many respects more Roman than he was Jewish. It was his knowledge of both Jewish and Roman ways that made him particularly competent to hear Paul's case.

Paul's faithfulness to his Jewish heritage (26:4–11). Much as he had with the Jews in the temple yard (22:3), Paul began with Agrippa by emphasizing his strong Jewish background, how he had even lived in the strict code of the Pharisees. In earlier speeches Paul had emphasized the Jewish "hope" in the resurrection (cp. 23:6; 24:21). Throughout Acts, the hope of the Jews, the resurrection, and the Messiah are all of one piece. Jesus' resurrection is depicted as the proof of his messianic status. Jesus' coming as Messiah is presented as the fulfillment of Israel's hope, the fulfillment of God's promises to the nation. The resurrection was the central theme of Paul's speech before Agrippa. He mentioned it at the beginning (v. 8) and end (v. 23) of his testimony.

Just as he had done before the Jewish mob in the temple yard, Paul moved from his Jewish heritage to his role as persecutor of the Christians. In his epistles Paul spoke of how he had persecuted the church (1 Cor. 15:9; cp. Eph. 3:8). For him, his former role of persecutor was a reminder of how God in his grace had radically turned him around. For Agrippa and the Jews at the temple, it was evidence of Paul's zeal for Judaism. It was also a sign of God's power, that the former persecutor of Christ should now be his proclaimer. Paul's emphasis on his role as persecutor is stated more emphatically in the speech before Agrippa than anywhere else. Paul noted how he had dragged Christians from synagogues, how he tried to make them blaspheme the name of Jesus, how he even "cast [his] vote" for their death. The latter is probably meant metaphorically, as an expression of his total agreement in decisions to execute the Christians as had been the case with Stephen. Paul's Christian faith was no light thing. It was a radical about-face.

Paul's commission from Christ (26:12–18). The third conversion account in Acts differs in several significant respects from those of chapters 9 and 22. This is partly due to the different audiences. Before Agrippa and the Gentile audience at Caesarea, the role of the pious Jewish Christian Ananias was somewhat superfluous, so Paul omitted reference to him. On the other hand, Jesus' words about kicking against the goads (v. 14) echoed a familiar proverb often found in Gentile literature.[8] The Gentiles at the hearing would have readily understood what Jesus meant in his words to Paul: that it was useless to fight a divine imperative. Paul's persecuting zeal was like a mule kicking back at the goads; he was fighting God's will and was bound to come out the worse for it.

The most significant difference in this third conversion account is the way Paul's commission to be a witness to the Gentiles is telescoped into the Damascus road call. In chapters 9 and 22 the Gentile commission occurs subsequently to the appearance on the road to Damascus. In chapter 26 it is combined with the account of the appearance. In Paul's own mind the two were inseparable. His call to be a Christian was at the same time his call to be Christ's apostle to the Gentiles. Note the strong emphasis on light in Paul's testimony. The miracle of Christ's appearance was all light, brighter than the noonday sun (v. 13). Like the Isaianic servant, God called Paul to be a light to the nations/Gentiles (vv. 17–18; cp. Isa. 49:6). By his resurrection, Christ proclaims light to all, both Jew and Gentile (v. 23).

Paul's witness to Christ (26:19–23). Paul assured Agrippa that he had been obedient to his heavenly call. He preached Christ in Damascus, in Jerusalem and Judea, and to the Gentiles. In short, he personally fulfilled the full scope of Jesus' commission of Acts 1:8. Paul's summary of the message in verses 22–23 connects closely with the entire message of Luke-Acts. In the upper room, Jesus had opened the Scriptures to the disciples, showing from Moses and the prophets how the Messiah must suffer and rise and then preach salvation to all the people (Luke 24:44–48). Jesus was Messiah/Savior by virtue of his death and resurrection. That was the message Paul had proclaimed to Jews and Gentiles alike. Ironically, that message of light and life was the reason Paul now found himself in chains (v. 21).

Paul's appeal to Agrippa (26:24–29). Festus had already found Paul's idea of resurrection to be confusing (25:19). Paul's mention of the resurrection provoked his response. He accused Paul of ranting like a madman. It was a softened rebuke, however, for he blamed Paul's ranting on his great learning. At this point Paul chose not to engage with Festus. He simply denied his madness and then directed all his energy to Agrippa. Agrippa was a Jew. *He* knew what Paul was talking about. Resurrection, Messiah, the hope of Israel—Agrippa knew the significance of these realities. Paul shifted to a direct appeal to the king. He reminded him that the Christians were not a secretive group off in a corner hoarding their witness to themselves (v. 26).[9] They had shouted it from the rooftops. The king had surely heard it. Why did he not believe? The prophets proclaimed all that had come to pass in Christ. Did the king not believe the prophets?

Paul had put Agrippa on the spot. He surely did not want to deny the prophets. He was not ready to accept Paul's gospel, however. His response is not altogether clear. He seems to have either asked Paul if he was trying to make a Christian out of him in a short period of time *or* if he was attempting to do so with only a brief argument. Undaunted, Paul picked up on the king's words. Short time or long time, short argument or long argument—it made little difference to Paul. He wished for *all* to respond to the gospel by whatever means it took, small or great, kings or peasants. Verse 29 is the climax toward which all Paul's defense from chapter 22 on had been building. Paul had in none of the speeches really defended himself. What he most had attempted to do was to bear his witness to the risen Lord. His witness reached its peak before Agrippa. The Jews in the temple yard, the members of the Sanhedrin, the Roman governors, the Jewish kings—Paul called them all to find the light of the risen Lord. The invitation is implicit in all the speeches. Before Agrippa it came into the open.

Agrippa's response (26:30–32). Like Felix before him (24:25), Paul's pressure made the king a bit nervous. He rose to his feet and summarily curtailed the proceedings (v. 30). As they departed, king and governor alike professed Paul's innocence to one another (v. 31). Agrippa even declared that Paul could have been set free had he not made the appeal (v. 32). Probably he did not entirely mean that. Neither he nor Festus wanted to face the fallout with the Jewish leadership that Paul's release would provoke. It was easy for them to proclaim Paul's innocence to each other in private. In public was another story.

THE JOURNEY TO ROME (ACTS 27:1–28:16)
Paul's journey to Rome is one of the longest and most engaging narratives of Acts. It is considered one of the most reliable accounts for ancient techniques of navigation. Some scholars have even suggested that Luke simply took over an ancient account of a sea journey and adapted it to his own purposes by inserting the references to Paul.[10] This is not likely. The course of the voyage is precisely the route Paul would have followed and is accurate down to the smallest detail.[11]

Paul traveled extensively by sea. It has been estimated that the voyages involved in Paul's three missionary journeys alone would have covered more then three thousand miles.[12] There must have been other voyages as well, perhaps during his "silent years" in Syria and Cilicia or in the course of his long ministries in the cities of Corinth and Ephesus. In 2 Corinthians 11:25 Paul mentioned that he had been shipwrecked three times and had been adrift at sea for a day and a night. None of these is related in Acts. Judging from the literature, shipwreck was not all that uncommon in the ancient world. Josephus, for instance, spoke of a journey he made to Rome in his twenty-sixth year. His ship foundered in "the sea of Adria," and he was adrift on planks from the ship until rescued by a ship from Cyrene (*The Life* 15).

THE JOURNEY TO FAIR HAVENS (27:1–8)
Paul accompanied several other prisoners on the journey to Rome. They play no role in the story. They were all under the supervision of a centurion named Julius. He is described as belonging to the Imperial Regiment.[13] This was a term often applied to auxiliary troops, and auxiliary forces are known to have been stationed in Caesarea. Paul was accompanied by Luke and the Thessalonian Aristarchus. Aristarchus was a member of the collection embassy that went with Paul to Jerusalem (Acts 20:4). He was with Paul when he wrote Colossians from prison, either in Caesarea or Rome (Col. 4:10). Paul called Aristarchus his "fellow prisoner," probably referring to his companionship, not to a literal prisoner status. Luke included himself by his use of "we" throughout this narrative. Acts 27:1–28:16 is the longest sustained "we passage" in all of Acts.[14]

At Caesarea the group boarded a ship of Adramyttium, which was probably returning home. Adramyttium was a port on the Aegean coast of Asia, not far south of Troas. It is possible that Julius originally planned to go to Troas, make the short passage to Neapolis and pick up the land route to Rome via the Egnatian Way. More likely, the Adramyttian ship was the first available coasting vessel, and Julius all along intended to transfer to a larger ship bound for Rome. The brief stop in Sidon is significant. From early in the narrative, the centurion is shown to be kind and trusting of the apostle (v. 3). Here he allowed him to visit the Christian community of Sidon. Julius's trust of Paul plays a major role in the overall narrative.

As the late-summer winds were blowing out of the west, the ship was unable to put out into the open sea but had to hug close to the coastline under the lee of Cyprus (v. 4). Eventually it reached Myra in Lycia on the southern coast of Asia (v. 5). Myra was a major port for the grain traffic between Egypt and Rome. The prevailing westerly winds of summer made it virtually impossible to sail directly west from Alexandria to Italy. The usual route was to sail north to the southern Asian ports like Myra and then westward to the north of Crete and Malta and on to Sicily. This is the route Julius would have had in mind when he transferred at Myra to an Alexandrian ship bound for Rome (v. 6). The ship was one of the great grain transporters, probably under license to the emperor. The ships were enormous. In his book *The Ship*, Lucian told of an Alexandrian ship named the Isis that was blown off course and ended up in the Athenian port of Piraeus. It was 180 feet long, 45 feet wide, and had a hold with a depth of 43 1/2 feet.[15]

Paul's ship didn't fare much better than the Isis. The winds had become so heavy that it was unable to take the normal westerly course to the south of Rhodes. Instead, it held close to the Asian coast, only with difficulty reaching Cnidus at the southwestern tip of Asia (v. 7). The ship could not continue on the normal westerly course but had to sail in a southwesterly direction. This took it around Cape Salmone, a promontory on the northeastern coast of Crete. From there the ship sailed on the southern side of Crete until it came to a small harbor by the name of Fair Havens (v. 8). There is a settlement on the site today, still known by its ancient name of Fair Havens (*Limenas Kalous*). Paul's ship put in there.

THE DECISION TO SAIL ON (27:9–12)

It was getting late in the sailing season, already past the "Fast" (the Day of Atonement). The year was probably A.D. 59. In that year the Day of Atonement fell on October 5. From mid-September the Mediterranean was treacherous. After mid-November, it was closed to sea traffic. The crew of Paul's ship were faced with a dilemma. On the one hand, it was a dangerous time for sailing. On the other hand, Fair Havens was not a good place for a large grain ship to spend the winter. It was a small harbor, and it was open to the strong easterly winter winds. About forty nautical miles to the west was the far more suitable harbor of Phoenix. The ship only had to hug the coast of Crete, sailing around Cape Matala, which lay some six miles to the west of Fair Havens, and then sail northwesterly to Phoenix. Under favorable conditions, the voyage would only be a matter of a few hours at the most.

The owner of the ship and its pilot called a conference. Julius was invited for the consultation. It is an attestation of Paul's status that he was also invited and even given a voice in the deliberations. Paul's advice was that they not proceed any further but remain in Fair Havens. He warned that if they did proceed there would be loss of ship, cargo, and lives (v. 10). As it panned out, he was right about the ship and the cargo but not about the loss of life. At this point Paul was expressing his own premonition. He had no direct words from the Lord. That would change. At this point, Julius was more inclined to agree with the opinion of the seasoned mariners than with Paul. That would change also. In any event, the majority decided to make the break for Phoenix. Paul, however, had given his warning. In the form of ancient sea narratives, a warning like Paul's served a dramatic function. It meant, "Look out, storm clouds ahead!"[16]

THE STORM (27:13–20)

When a favorable south wind began to blow, the ship set out for Phoenix.[17] They sailed along the shoreline of Cape Matala. Suddenly the wind shifted. Crete has mountains that rise to a height of seven thousand feet. A violent northeast wind rushed down from the mountains and caught the ship. Unable to make headway, the crew gave in to the wind and allowed the ship to be carried along. Luke described the wind as being "typhonic" (*typhonikos*) and named it a "northeaster" (*euraquilo*). Today the dreaded Mediterranean storm is called the *gregale*. *Euraquilo* is a hybrid of the Greek word for east wind (*euros*) and the Latin word for north wind (*aquilo*). Until recent times, this rare form was unattested outside Acts 27. Now it has been discovered on an ancient mosaic in the town of Thugga in North Africa. The mosaic depicts a wind rose, showing the points of the compass. On it, the term *eruaquilo* occurs at exactly the right point, thirty degrees north of east.[18]

The storm blew the ship south some twenty-three miles to the small island of Cauda (modern Gozzo). Protected from the winds under the lee of the island, the sailors performed three functions to protect the ship. First, they raised the lifeboat and secured it (v. 16). Then they fastened the ship with ropes. The text says literally that they "undergirded" the ship (v. 17a). This could have referred to one of several different procedures. Sometimes cords were run *under* the ship. Sometimes, especially in warships, cords were extended *around* the ship. In both instances the procedure was designed to hold the timbers of the ship together. A third procedure was to "lower the equipment" (v. 17b). Just what the "equipment" refers to is uncertain. It could be the mainsail. More likely it was the drift anchor which would be let out from the stern to slow the drift of the ship (the NIV translates it as such). The main worry of the sailors was that the ship would be blown south by the northern wind onto the sandbars and shoals of the North African coast known as the Syrtis. This inhospitable coast had the reputation of being a graveyard of ships, being second in notoriety only to Sylla and Charybdis.

On the second day of the storm the sailors took further precautions. They began to throw things overboard (v. 18). Literally they are said to have performed "a jettisoning." Exactly what was jettisoned is not specified. It is usually assumed that it was the cargo, the load of grain. Judging from 27:38, not all the grain would have been thrown overboard on the second day of the storm. In fact, none of it may have been. It is possible that other material was jettisoned, perhaps some of the ship's tackle.[19] On the third day the ship's mainyard or spar was thrown overboard (v. 19). With crippled ship, they were adrift on a stormy sea. In a time before compasses, with no sun or stars they couldn't even determine where they were. As the days dragged on with the storm unabated, they began to give up "all hope of being saved" (v. 20). As we will see, the "salvation" word-family plays a major role in the narrative of Acts 27. Perhaps Luke intended a double entendre already in this first occurrence of the word. The pagan voyagers were despairing of ever being saved. They had someone aboard, however, whose God would save their lives and offer them an even greater salvation as well. As morale reached its lowest ebb, Paul's God appeared to offer hope and deliverance.

PAUL'S ASSURING VISION (27:21–26)

The voyagers had gone a long time without food (v. 21). It may be that they had lost their appetite in the storm-tossed seas. It also may be that they were unable to get to the food. They hadn't jettisoned all the grain; in fact, they may not have thrown any of it overboard. In all likelihood, however, they would have secured the grain as much as possible. Grain swells when wet. Swollen grain could burst the hold and sink the ship. With the storm still raging, they may have deliberately refrained from opening the hatch in order to keep the grain as dry as possible.[20]

In any event, morale was about gone. Paul rose to address the group. He had done so on an earlier occasion, and they hadn't heeded his advice. He reminded them of that (v. 21). Things were different now. Paul had more to back him now. He had a word from his Lord. He also had a different sort of message, not a warning but a word of hope and encouragement. An angel had appeared to Paul in a vision and informed him that he would indeed appear before Caesar to bear his witness. Paul had first conceived of his Roman witness in Ephesus (19:21). In a previous vision God had assured him that it would happen (23:11). Now for a final time he was given the same assurance. And because God would deliver Paul for his witness, so would he deliver all on board the ship. Their safety was tied up with Paul's. It is interesting to compare Paul's experience with Jonah's. Jonah too was caught on a ship in a raging storm. But Jonah's flight from God was the cause of the peril. Jonah's presence on the ship endangered everyone aboard. Only when he was thrown overboard was the ship delivered. Exactly the opposite was true of Paul. His *presence* assured the deliverance of all on board the ship.

THE PROSPECT OF LANDING (27:27–32)

The ship was still being driven by the storm. It had now drifted north into the "sea of Adria." This is not to be confused with the modern Adriatic Sea between Italy and Yugoslavia. In the ancient world that was known as the "Gulf of Adria." The Adriatic Sea was farther south, the northern Mediterranean between Malta, Italy, Greece, and Crete, including the Ionian Sea (Strabo, *Geography* 2.5.20). With no compass in the storm's darkness, the sailors would not have known where they were. It was around midnight of the fourteenth night that the sailors heard the breakers on the rocks off Point Koura at the northeastern corner of the island of Malta where their ship had drifted. They confirmed their suspicion by taking soundings—20 fathoms (120 feet), then 15 fathoms (90 feet). Now well aware of the rocks, they dropped four anchors from the stern to hold the ship until morning's light. Ancient ships often had multiple anchors. In this instance they were dropped from the stern rather than the bow so the ship would be headed toward shore when they attempted to beach it.

The sailors must have assessed the situation as being particularly dangerous, because they attempted to abandon ship and escape in the lifeboat (vv. 30–32). They lowered the lifeboat on the pretense that they were going to put an anchor out from the bow. Paul quickly saw through their ruse and pointed it out to Julius. This time the centurion lost no time in heeding Paul's advice. He had his men cut the cables to the lifeboat, and it drifted away. The action seems a bit extreme. The lifeboat would have been useful later in evacuating the ship. Perhaps Julius felt the sailors would try it again when he might not be looking. In any event, he realized the soundness of Paul's advice. Without the expertise of the mariners, it would be difficult for the passengers to make it safely to shore.

PAUL URGES ALL TO EAT (27:33–38)

For a second time Paul rose to address the whole party aboard ship. This time he urged all to partake of food for strength. After eating their fill, the grain was to be jettisoned in order to lighten the ship for beaching (v. 38). Paul explained to his fellow voyagers that they needed the food for their "salvation" (NIV, "to survive"). The salvation word-family occurs seven times in the journey narrative (27:20, 31, 34, 43, 44; 28:1, 4). In all instances it refers to the physical deliverance from the shipwreck. For Christians, however, it is a word with more spiritual overtones, and one wonders if Luke did not use it in a certain symbolic sense in this section.[21]

The same applies to Paul's words of blessing over the food in verse 35. The familiar pattern of taking bread, giving thanks, and breaking it is the same pattern found in the New Testament accounts of the Lord's Supper (cp. Luke 22:19; 1 Cor. 11:23f.). It is the pattern of blessing which Jesus followed in feeding the five thousand (Luke 9:16, pars.), and the pattern he followed when dining with his followers (e.g. Luke 24:30). Of course, it was the customary Jewish mode of giving thanks over a meal. Still, it is so associated with Jesus that one wonders if the meal on the ship did not have some special assurance of the Lord's presence for the Christians aboard. It was surely not a communion service, but perhaps it had the same sort of anticipatory, symbolic meaning that it had in the feeding of the five thousand, the Lord's promise that his table is open to all who will receive him. Combined with the "salvation" from the peril of the sea, the whole scene may be viewed from a Christian perspective as representing the Lord's ultimate deliverance that is open to all. Luke did not relate any direct witness of Paul to the pagans aboard the ship, or on Malta for that matter. One cannot imagine that Paul did not do so. Perhaps the symbolism of the "salvation" and the meal was Luke's way of pictorially presenting Paul's witness.[22]

Why did Luke wait until the end of the narrative to mention that there were 276 on board the ship (v. 37)? The number 276 is a "triangular number"; that is, it is the sum of all the numbers from 1 to 23. That is probably coincidental and means nothing. Luke probably wanted to emphasize the greatness of the deliverance. There was a large group on board, and "not a single hair" was lost. The number of passengers was not a large number for a grain vessel. Josephus spoke of 600 being on his voyage to Rome. He also spoke of only 80 being rescued. All on Paul's ship were delivered. And all were delivered because Paul was on board. As the angel said, their lives were "given" to him (v. 24).

THE DELIVERANCE OF ALL (27:39–44)

When morning came, the sailors attempted to beach the ship. Cutting the anchors, they lifted the small foresail, using it to steer the ship, and they headed for land.[23] Their attempt failed. Luke says that the ship ran into "a place of two seas" (v. 41, *diathalasson*). This could mean any number of things—a sandbar (as the NIV), a shoal, or perhaps a place where two currents come together.[24] Whatever the cause, the ship ran aground, the bow being stuck fast and the stern torn to pieces by the pounding surf. With it apparent that it would soon be "every man for himself," the soldiers worried lest the prisoners might escape. Concerned that they would themselves be held accountable for the prisoners, they decided to kill them (v. 42). As with the sailors, Julius again intervened and rescued the prisoners. Everyone reached land safely (vv. 43–44). Everyone could thank Paul. His presence was the key to their "salvation."[25]

THE WINTER ON MALTA (28:1–10)

The voyagers soon ascertained that they had landed on the island of Malta, just south of Sicily.[26] The sailors had no idea where the storm had taken them. Miraculously, they had drifted far to the west in easy access of Italy. Luke referred to the natives of the island as "barbarians" (NIV, "islanders," v. 2). To a Greek like Luke, this was not a prejudicial term. To a Greek, anyone speaking a language other than Greek was considered a "barbarian" (that is, someone whose speech sounded strange and foreign, like "bar, bar"). The native Maltese language seems to have been a form of Punic, going back to the time when Phoenicians occupied the island. Inscriptions indicate that in the first century Punic and Greek were the two main languages of the island, and the island seems to have been under the administration of a Roman procurator.

Luke was impressed by the Maltese and the kind hospitality they provided the shipwrecked strangers (v. 2). He told of how Paul was bitten by a viper and suffered no ill effects (vv. 3–5). Luke used a term that usually referred to a poisonous snake (*echidna*). The islanders expected Paul to die. They recalled popular stories like one told by the Romans of how a man had escaped from a shipwreck only to be killed by a poisonous snake while recovering on the beach.[27] When Paul did not die, the islanders concluded that the opposite must be true of Paul. He was no fugitive fleeing justice; he was a god. Paul must have quickly corrected their misunderstanding. He was not a god but one protected by his God, both from the shipwreck and the viper's bite.

Verses 7–10 tell in very summary fashion the three-month visit of the shipwrecked party on Malta. Two things are emphasized: the healings performed by Paul, and the hospitality of the Maltese. In particular, Paul healed the father of Publius, the chief official (*Prōtos*) of the island (v. 8). Inscriptions have been found on Malta verifying the use of *Prōtos* as an official title. Much as with Jesus' healing of Peter's mother-in-law, also of a fever, word soon got around, and the whole neighborhood began to bring their sick (cp. Mark 1:30–34). The Maltese showed their visitors extraordinary kindness: on their arrival (v. 2), during their stay (v. 7), and upon their departure, furnishing them with the food and supplies they would need for their journey (v. 10). Luke does not mention Paul's witnessing on the island. Paul surely must have done so. Generally in Acts healing and witnessing go together. Surely that happened on Malta. Maltese Christian tradition naturally insists that it did and that Paul was the one who brought Christianity to their island.

THE FINAL LEG TO ROME (28:11–16)

After three months on Malta, Paul's party set sail for Sicily. It was probably early in February, the earliest possible time for sailing. They had found passage on another Alexandrian grain vessel that had wintered on Malta. The ship is said to have had a masthead depicting the twin gods Castor and Pollux, who were the patron gods of sailors. The pair were also believed to be the enforcers of justice on the high seas.

Paul's sailing safely under their sign may be another small touch in the narrative to indicate his total innocence.[28]

The ship followed the normal route from Malta via Syracuse at the southeastern end of Sicily and then Rhegium at the tip of the boot of Italy. They stopped over in Rhegium for three days, probably awaiting favorable winds. When a southerly wind arose, they set sail through the Straits of Messina northward to Puteoli, making the 210-mile journey in a single day. Puteoli (modern Puzzuoli) was the ship's destination. In Paul's day it was the main port for the large grain ships, the Roman port of Ostia not having yet been enlarged sufficiently to accommodate them. Embarking at Puteoli, Paul found a Christian community, with whom Julius allowed Paul to stay for a week. It is unknown how Christianity first arrived in Puteoli. It may have been by means of Jewish Christian travelers witnessing in the synagogues there.[29]

After the week in Puteoli, Paul's group set out on foot for Rome. The route covered some 130 miles and took about 5 days. It went by the Via Campana north to Capua where it merged into the Appian Way. On the Appian Way they stopped at a market town named the Forum of Appius, located some 43 miles south of Rome. There they were met by a group of Christians who had come from Rome to greet them (v. 15). Word of Paul's arrival must have been sent to them early in his stay at Puteoli. Obviously Paul's Roman epistle had had its desired effect of introducing him to the Christians of the city. They were so eager to see him that they had traveled a two-day journey to intercept him on his way. In fact, after traveling another 10 miles on the Appian Way toward Rome, they met up with a second group of Roman Christians at the way station of Three Taverns. This group probably represented a separate Roman house-congregation from the earlier group. Paul was elated (v. 15b). His prayers had been answered. Despite his not being the apostle who brought the gospel to the Romans, despite the ignominy of his chains, still he had been warmly received by the Christians of Rome.

Verses 14b and 16 are somewhat redundant. Verse 16 relates Paul's actual arrival in the city of Rome itself. Verse 14b speaks of Paul's "coming to Rome" in the context of his encountering the Roman Christians more than forty miles south of the city. Perhaps Luke was looking at it from Paul's viewpoint. With the arrival of the Roman Christians to welcome the apostle, he surely felt that his intentions to visit the Roman congregations were already complete; he had at last made it to Rome.

Paul seems to have been granted even more freedom as a prisoner in Rome than he had experienced under Felix at Caesarea (Acts 24:23). He was allowed to live "by himself," with only a single soldier to guard him rather than the usual pair. Verse 30 specifies that Paul's lodging was private, provided at his own expense.[30]

PAUL'S WITNESS IN ROME (ACTS 28:17–31)

The Acts account of Paul's Roman custody comes as something of a surprise. One would expect to read of Paul's appearance before Caesar. We are told nothing of that—only that Paul was under house arrest for two years. Paul was the apostle to the Gentiles. One would expect a treatment of his ministry to the Gentiles of Rome. Instead, we are given a picture of his witness to the Jewish community of Rome. It is a surprise ending. However, when one considers the overall Acts narrative, it is one for which Luke has been preparing us all along. It falls into three scenes: (1) Paul's initial conversation with the Jewish leadership (vv. 17–22), (2) his witness to a larger group of Jews (vv. 23–28), and finally, (3) his witness in his rented quarters to "all" who came to him (vv. 30–31). Note how Paul's witness increases in an ever-widening circle in the three scenes.

PAUL'S FIRST MEETING WITH THE JEWS OF ROME (28:17–22)

The Jewish community of Rome in Paul's time was large, perhaps as many as fifty thousand people. They do not seem to have been confined to a single quarter but were scattered in small communities, mostly in the Transtiberian region of the city. The extensive Jewish catacombs in Rome have yielded references to at least eleven synagogues in the city in the second and third centuries. Perhaps as many as five of them were already in existence in Paul's day. For the most part, the Roman Jews were poor, though there seem to have been a few of means.[31] The political status of the Roman Jews varied from period to period. Julius Caesar granted them various freedoms—the right to hold their own religious gatherings, permission to collect the tax for the Jerusalem temple, exemption from military service. According to Philo, these rights were reconfirmed by Augustus (*Embassy to Gaius* 154).

But there were occasions when the rights were restricted, such as the time in A.D. 19 when Tiberius consigned four thousand young Jewish men to serve in the military in Sardinia. According to Tacitus, the rest of the Jews were at that time compelled to leave the city (*Annals* 2.85). Josephus related the same explusion. He attributed the cause of Tiberius's action to a group of four Jewish con artists who bilked a Roman patrician matron out of considerable funds (*Ant.* 18.81–84). Forty years later Claudius expelled the Jews from the city over the unrest in their communities provoked by "Chrestus" (Suetonius, *Claudius* 25.4). As we have seen, the latter incident probably resulted from the Christian gospel reaching the synagogues of the city and provoking controversy. All of which is to say that the Roman Jews would have been apprehensive over a fellow Jew like Paul who was about to appear before the emperor on charges leveled by the Jews of Palestine. Controversies within the Jewish community had not gone well for them with local officials in the past. They had no reason to believe it would be any different now.[32]

Paul was eager to meet with the Jews of Rome. He knew they would be apprehensive about his case when it came to their attention. He wanted to assure them that he wished no harm to the Roman Jewish community. He probably realized they could exert their influence against him before Caesar and wanted to curry their favor if possible. Most of all, as always, he wanted to share the gospel with them.

Paul's first meeting was with the Jewish leaders. He invited them to his quarters (v. 17). They had to come to him; he could not visit them. The leaders were probably the synagogue elders. In Rome the synagogues seem to have been administered by a council of elders called a *gerousia*. The elders were named *gerousiarchs*.[33] Paul wanted them to realize from the very start that his custody was undeserved. As he had done constantly in his previous defense speeches in Jerusalem and Caesarea (chaps. 22–26), he once again emphasized that he had done nothing contrary to Jewish laws or customs but was a loyal Jew in every respect. He proceeded to inform the Roman Jewish leaders of how he had been forced to appeal to the emperor because of the Jewish pressure on the Roman leaders (vv. 18–19). He insisted that the Romans had found him innocent, but he assured the Roman Jewish leaders that he had no intention of filing any counter suit against his fellow Jews (v. 19b). Paul concluded by centering on the real issue that had brought him to Rome—the "hope of Israel" (v. 20). It *was* the main issue that separated Paul from the rest of the Jews—his belief in Jesus' resurrection and his conviction that it proved that Jesus was the fulfillment of the Jewish messianic hope. All along this had been the central underlying issue in all Paul's trials (cp. 23:6; 24:15; 26:6–7).

Surprisingly, the Roman Jewish leaders responded that they had heard nothing about Paul nor received any letters from Judea concerning him (v. 21). Perhaps the winter hiatus on sailing had prevented any communication from Jerusalem. Perhaps they didn't have particularly close relationships with the Jerusalem leadership anyway. Perhaps they were being diplomatic with Paul. They surely must have known something about the Christians from the "Chrestus" controversy if from nothing else. But they wanted to know more (v. 22), and Paul was eager to share it with them.

PAUL'S WITNESS TO THE JEWS (28:23–28)

Paul's witness to the Jews of Pisidian Antioch (Acts 13:14–50) and his witness to the Roman Jews (Acts 28:17–28) form a frame around the entire ministry of Paul in Acts. One stands at the beginning of his missionary activity, the other at the end. They are strikingly similar. Both consist of two stages of witness, an initial limited witness followed by a subsequent witness to a much larger group. In both Paul's message proves to be divisive, some believing, others disbelieving. In both there is a turning to the Gentiles. In both the turning is explained in the light of a text from the prophet Isaiah. At Antioch, Isaiah 49:6 served as the scriptural base for Paul's proclaiming the light of Christ to the Gentiles (13:47). In Rome, Isaiah 6:9–10 was cited to establish the failure of the Jews to respond to the gospel, which served as Paul's basis for turning to the Gentiles (28:28). The pattern of Paul's beginning with the Jews and turning to the Gentiles is repeated constantly throughout Acts in city after city between Antioch and Rome. Rome is the last time it happens. The natural question is whether this time it was final. There is no reason to believe that it was. The failure of Israel as a whole to respond to the gospel was a fact which Paul experienced throughout his ministry and which he addressed in anguish in Romans 9–11. In Romans he did not abandon his hope in Israel's conversion, and there is no reason to believe he did so here with the Jews of Rome.

A larger group of Jews came to hear Paul on the second occasion, its size probably only limited by the confines of Paul's rented quarters. Paul preached to them all day, seeking to convince them from the books of the Law (Moses) and the prophets that Jesus was the promised Messiah. This was Paul's usual method of approaching Jews with the gospel, persuading them on the basis of the Scriptures. (Compare his witness in Berea in Acts 17:11 for an example.) The response to Paul's witness to the Roman Jews also followed a familiar pattern. Most were not persuaded, but there was a significant minority that believed (cp. Acts 13:43; 14:1; 17:4, 12; 18:8; 19:9).

Their house divided, the Jews began to leave Paul's quarters but not before Paul had placed on them one last word. He quoted Isaiah 6:9–10, where the prophet spoke of Israel's total lack of sensory perception as shown in their failure to respond to God's word. They had ears that should hear, eyes that should see, and hearts that should be able to feel and to will. But their hearts were hardened and could not feel, their ears were dull and could not hear, their eyes were blind and could not see. Otherwise, they would have turned and received God's deliverance. Paul had seen the same thing happen to the Jews of his generation. In fact, Isaiah 6:9–10 was a text which Jesus cited when referring to the failure of the Jews to respond to his teaching in parables (Matt. 13:14–15; Mark 4:12).

Paul quoted the same text in Romans 11:8 when speaking of the failure of his fellow Jews to embrace the gospel. In Romans, Paul clearly had not abandoned the hope that Israel would eventually respond. In Romans he spoke of how the gospel had come to the Gentiles because of Israel's failure to respond. Here Paul told the Roman Jews basically the same thing, that their failure to believe had led him to turn to the Gentiles (v. 28). Surely here too he held out the same hope that this would provoke the Jews to jealousy (cp. Rom. 11:11). His words to the Roman Jews were not words of rejection but of challenge.[34] Unfortunately, the Jews did not respond. Just as Romans 11, Acts ends on a tragic note, the reality that in his lifetime Paul did not see his fellow Jewish people embrace the gospel as he so longed to see them do.[35]

PAUL'S WITNESS TO ALL (ACTS 28:30–31)

The New Testament account of Paul's ministry ends abruptly in Acts 28:30–31 where we are told that he lived for two years at his own expense and that he preached Jesus and the kingdom of God quite freely to all who came to him.[36] It seems to us a strange way for the story to end. Ever since Paul's appeal before Festus we have been anticipating his appearance before the emperor. The sea narrative made clear that Paul's life was being preserved for this witness.[37] Instead, we are told nothing about that. The reference to two years only serves to heighten the impression of incompleteness. What happened after two years? Recent narrative studies of Acts have come to something of a consensus that Luke probably intended to end the story where he did and in the fashion he did. The emphasis is on the gospel and Paul's bold proclamation of it in the capital city of the empire. He was preaching to "all" (v. 30), both Jews and Gentiles. Despite Paul's chains, the gospel was "unshackled," and the apostle shared it freely with all who would hear (v. 31). Perhaps Luke intended to conclude Acts open-endedly, without closure, as if to say that the story was not over, that the bold witness must continue.

We, of course, would like to know what happened after two years. Did Paul appear before the emperor? Was he set free? Was he condemned? Many different answers have been given to these questions. It has often been suggested that Luke wrote Acts around A.D. 62, two years after Paul's arrival in Rome. The trial had not yet taken place, and Luke stopped the story at exactly the point that he wrote Acts.[38] The main problem with this view is that it dates Acts earlier than is likely.[39] Others have suggested that Luke intended to write a third volume in which he would relate the continuing story of Paul. This is based in part on the argument that the reference to the Gospel of Luke as the "first volume" (rather than the "former") in Acts 1:1 implies a series of more than two. This linguistic distinction, however, will not hold for Hellenistic Greek where the word *first* (*prōtos*) often refers to a series of only two members. More significantly, there is a vast difference between the manner with which Luke concluded his Gospel and the way he ended Acts. The Gospel of Luke comes to a full closure and summarizes the opening portion of Acts. The conclusion of Acts neither comes to closure nor summarizes any further events. It simply does not anticipate another story the way the Gospel does. A proposed third volume is most unlikely.

One of the most popular explanations for the abrupt ending of Acts argues from a supposed Roman statute of limitations of two years for a case pending trial. The assumption is that in cases such as Paul's the accusers were to appear for the trial within two years of the initial appeal. If they failed to do so, the case would be dismissed by default. It is argued that people of the first century who read Acts would be familiar with this law and would interpret Luke's reference as meaning that Paul did not come to trial within the legal time limit and thus was set free.[40] Unfortunately, the evidence upon which this view is based has either been misinterpreted or dates from a considerably later time.[41] There does not seem to have been such a statute of limitations in Paul's day, although the emperor Claudius is known to have put strong pressure on accusers to appear in court. If they delayed, however, it was not a question of freeing the accused but rather of penalizing the accusers.

Many have argued that Luke did not report Paul's trial because it did not go well. In their view, Paul would have been tried and executed, and Luke preferred to end Acts on the positive note of his bold witness in home incarceration rather than with a somber reference to his martyrdom.[42] As we will see in the final chapter of this book, the early tradition that Paul died a martyr's death in Rome has a strong claim to reliability. But these traditions place Paul's death alongside that of Peter, during the period of the Neronic persecution three or more years *after* the lapse of the two years mentioned in verse 31. This would make for a very long period of custody in Rome, five years or so at the least.

The possibility that Paul was released from this first Roman imprisonment is based on a very strong tradition. Some would see 2 Timothy 4:16–17 as referring to a first trial in Rome, in which Paul made a successful defense and was released ("delivered from the lion's mouth"). Several early Christian writings maintain Paul's release from his first imprisonment. First Clement spoke of Paul's witnessing to Spain ("the limits of the west") which implies his release (1 Clem. 5:5–7). Clement could possibly have only inferred Paul's western mission from Paul's reference to intending such a mission in Romans 15:24. In his *Church History* (2.22), Eusebius was more explicit, citing a tradition that had come to him according to which Paul was released and went forth on further mission, only to be placed under Roman arrest a second time and martyred under Nero. The evidence of Eusebius is late, coming some two centuries after the fact. Perhaps the strongest basis for seeing Paul as being released is the existence of the Pastoral Epistles. The personal references in the Pastorals are hard to fit into the account of Paul's ministry given in Acts. They are best explained on the assumption that Paul was released in Rome and that the events referred to in the Pastorals took place in his subsequent ministry. Of course, it is always possible that the Pastorals mention details from Paul's ministry which were not covered in Acts. Some would place these epistles during the first Roman imprisonment or even earlier in Paul's ministry. In our opinion, their being written after his first Roman imprisonment best accounts for their content, and we have accordingly placed them at this point in Paul's ministry.

NOTES

1. Romans 1:11–13; 15:23–24; 15:28–29; Acts 19:21; 23:11.

2. On the dating of Festus's term, see E. Schürer, *The History of the Jewish People in the Age of Jesus Christ (175 B.C.–A.D. 135)*, New English version rev. and ed. G. Vermes, F. Millar, and M. Black, vol. 1 (Edinburgh: T. and T. Clark, 1979), fn. 42, pp. 465–466.

3. P. Garnsey, "The *Lex Julia* and Appeal Under the Empire," *Journal of Roman Studies* 56 (1966): 167–189.

4. A. H. M. Jones, *Studies in Roman Law and Government* (Oxford University Press, 1960), 96–99. See also A. N. Sherwin-White, *Roman Society and Roman Law in the New Testament* (Oxford: Clarendon, 1963), 57–70.

5. For references to Agrippa and Bernice in Josephus and Tacitus, see J. Polhill, *Acts*, New American Commentary (Nashville: Broadman, 1992), fn. 139–141, p. 493.

6. See F. S. Spencer, *Acts*, Readings (Sheffield: Academic Press, 1997), 223–224.

7. Paul's speech mainly consists of a narration (*narratio*) of his experience (vv. 4–21). For a rhetorical analysis, see B. Witherington III, *The Acts of the Apostles: A Socio-Rhetorical Commentary* (Grand Rapids: Eerdmans, 1998), 737.

8. For instance, in Euripides, *Bacchae*, 794f; Aeschylus, *Agamemnon* 1624; Pindar, *Pythian Ode* 2, 173. It also appears in Psalms of Solomon 16:4.

9. For the background in Greek philosophy of the "not in a corner" image, see A. J. Malherbe, "'Not in a Corner': Early Christian Apologetic in Acts 26:26," *The Second Century* 5 (1985–1986): 193–210.

10. M. Dibelius, *Studies in the Acts of the Apostles* (London: SCM, 1956), 204–206.

11. This was established by the careful study of J. Smith, first published in 1848 and still perhaps the best source on Paul's voyage: *The Voyage and Shipwreck of St. Paul* (Grand Rapids: Baker [reprint], 1978). See also C. J. Hemer, "First Person Narrative in Acts 27–28," *Tyndale Bulletin* 36 (1985): 79–109.

12. E. Haenchen, *The Acts of the Apostles*, trans. B. Noble and G. Shinn (Philadelphia: Westminster, 1971), 702–703.

13. W. M. Ramsay argued that Julius was a *frumentarius*, an officer involved in administering the imperial grain supply: *St. Paul the Traveller and the Roman Citizen* (London: Hodder and Stoughton, 1897), 322–344. Sherwin-White observed that there is no evidence that grain officers were given the responsibility of transporting prisoners as early as Paul's time (*Roman Society and Roman Law*, 109).

14. V. K. Robbins has argued that the "we" is a literary device characteristic of sea narratives: "By Land and By Sea: The We-Passages and Ancient Sea Voyages," in *Perspectives on Luke-Acts*, ed. C. H. Talbert (Edinburgh: T. and T. Clark, 1978), 215–242. For a rebuttal, see the article by Hemer listed in note 11 above.

15. For a description of the grain ships, see N. Hirschfeld, "The Ship of St. Paul. Part I: Historical Background," *Biblical Archaeologist* 53 (1990): 25–30. See Also L. Casson, *Ships and Seamanship in the Ancient World* (Princeton University Press, 1971).

16. See S. M. Praeder, "Acts 27:1–28:16: Sea Voyages in Ancient Literature and the Theology of Luke-Acts," *Catholic Biblical Quarterly* 46 (1984): 689–691.

17. The ancient harbor of Phoenix is probably the same as the modern town by that name, *Phineka*. See R. M. Ogilvie, "Phoenix," *Journal of Theological Studies* 9 (1958): 308–314.

18. C. J. Hemer, "Euraquilo and Melita," *Journal of Theological Studies* 26 (1975): 110–111.

19. D. J. Clark suggests that they "attempted" on the second day to jettison the ship's mainyard, an operation they completed "by hand" on the third day: "What Went Overboard First?" *Bible Translator* 26 (1975): 144–146.

20. J. R. Madan, "The ΑΣΙΤΙΑ on St. Paul's Voyage: Acts xxvii," *Journal of Theological Studies* 4 (1904): 116–121.

21. R. C. Tannehill, *The Narrative Unity of Luke-Acts, A Literary Interpretation*, Vol. 2: *The Acts of the Apostles* (Minneapolis: Fortress, 1990), 334–337.

22. Note how Paul described the deliverance of the voyagers in the biblical language of divine protection: not a hair of their head would be lost. See 1 Samuel 14:45; 2 Samuel 14:11; 1 Kings 1:52; Matthew 10:30; Luke 12:7; 21:18.

23. Luke used the Latin name for the foresail (*artemōn*). The Roman grain vessels often had two large sails and the small *artemōn* on the bow, used for steering. See M. Fitzgerald, "The Ship of St. Paul. Part II: Comparative Archaeology," *Biblical Archaeologist* 53 (1990): 31–39.

24. See J. M. Gilchrist, "The Historicity of Paul's Shipwreck," *Journal for the Study of the New Testament* 61 (1996): 29–51.

25. G. B. Miles and G. Trompf argue that Paul's deliverance from the peril at sea would be seen by pagans as proof of his innocence: "Luke and Antiphon: The Theology of Acts 27–28 in the Light of Pagan Beliefs about Divine Retribution, Pollution and Shipwreck," *Harvard Theological Review* 69 (1976): 259–267.

26. Because of the reference to the Sea of Adria in 27:27, sporadic attempts have been made to place Malta in the modern Adriatic, particularly on the island of Mljet off the Yugoslavian coast near Dubrovnik. See A. Acworth, "Where Was Paul Shipwrecked? A Reexamination of the Evidence," *Journal of Theological Studies*, 24 (1973): 190–193; O. F. A. Meinardus, "St. Paul Shipwrecked in Dalmatia," *Biblical Archaeologist* 39 (1976): 145–147. For a rebuttal, see C. J. Hemer, "Euraquilo and Melita."

27. *Palatine Anthology*, 7.290. The rabbinic writings relate similar stories. See L. H. Silberman, "Paul's Viper, Acts 28:3–6," *Forum* 8 (1992): 247–253.

28. D. Ladouceur, "Hellenistic Preconceptions of Shipwreck and Pollution as a Context for Acts 27–28," *Harvard Theological Review* 73 (1980): 435–449.

29. Josephus referred to the Jewish community of Puteoli in *War* 2., 104 and *Ant.* 17., 328.

30. The Western Text of Acts adds at verse 16 that in Rome Paul was handed over to the *stratopedarch*, who seems to have been the official responsible for Paul's custody in the city. The title is otherwise not known. Many feel the Western Text reflects the actual situation. Various suggestions have been offered in the attempt to define the *stratopedarch* more precisely, such as the commander of the foreign forces (*princeps peregrinorum*), the supreme commander of the praetorian guard (*praefectus praetorii*), or the latter's immediate subordinate, the commander over the praetorian headquarters (*princeps castrorum*). For the various options, see B. Rapske, *The Book of Acts and Paul in Roman Custody*, vol. 3 of *The Book of Acts in its First Century Setting* (Grand Rapids: Eerdmans, 1994), 174–177.

31. H. J. Leon, *The Jews of Ancient Rome*, updated ed. (Peabody, Mass.: Hendrickson, 1995), 135–166.

32. J. C. Walters, *Ethnic Issues in Paul's Letter to the Romans: Changing Self-Definitions in Earliest Roman Christianity* (Valley Forge, Penn.: Trinity Press International, 1993), 56–66.

33. R. Penna, "Les Juifs à Rome au temps de l'apôtre Paul," *New Testament Studies* 28 (1982): 321–347.

34. V. Fusco shows how in Luke's Gospel, as well as Acts, there is a strong emphasis on the *inclusion* of the Jews at the Parousia: "Luke-Acts and the Future of Israel," *Novum Testamentum* 38 (1996): 1–17. See also H. van Sandt, "Acts 28:28: No Salvation for the People of Israel? An Answer in the Perspective of the LXX," *Ephemerides Theologicae Lovanienses* 70 (1994): 341–358.

35. Verse 39 is poorly attested in the early manuscripts and was probably not a part of the original text of Acts. It is a western reading designed to smooth the transition in the text by relating the exit of the Jews.

36. A rare word is used in verse 30 to describe Paul's living at his own expense or wage (*misthōma*). It may be legal language for rented property. See D. L. Mealand, "The Close of Acts and its Hellenistic Greek Vocabulary," *New Testament Studies* 36 (1990): 583–597. Rental property was not cheap in Rome. See Rapske, *The Book of Acts and Paul in Roman Custody*, 228–239.

37. If Paul had a hearing at all in Rome, it still may not have been before the emperor. Nero does not seem to have sat in judgment in the early years of his rule (cp. Tacitus, *Annals* 23.4), although he is said to have judged a case in A.D. 62 (*Annals* 14.50). Nero seems to have delegated cases of appeal for the judgment of others.

38. A. T. Robertson, *Epochs in the Life of Paul* (New York: Scribners, 1909), 270.

39. Acts was almost certainly written after the Gospel of Luke. Luke probably used Mark as a source for his Gospel, and reliable early tradition dates Mark after Peter's death (A.D. 65 or later).
40. K. Lake, "What Was the End of St. Paul's Trial?" *Interpreter* 5 (1908–1909): 147–156; W. M. Ramsay, "The Imprisonment and Supposed Trial of St. Paul in Rome: Acts xxviii," *Expositor*, series 8, no. 5 (1913): 264–284.
41. See Sherwin-White, *Roman Society and Roman Law*, 112–117.
42. For example, see J. Munck, *Paul and the Salvation of Mankind* (Richmond: John Knox, 1959), 320–322.

SUGGESTED FURTHER READING

Bruce, F. F. *Paul: Apostle of the Heart Set Free.* Grand Rapids: Eerdmans, 1977, pp. 354–392.

Leon, Harry J. *The Jews of Ancient Rome.* Updated edition. Peabody, Mass.: Hendrickson, 1995, pp. 135–166.

Polhill, John B. *Acts.* New American Commentary. Nashville: Broadman, 1992, pp. 488–548.

Rapske, Brian. *The Book of Acts and Paul in Roman Custody.* Vol. 3, *The Book of Acts in Its First Century Setting.* Grand Rapids: Eerdmans, 1994, pp. 151–241.

Sherwin-White, A. N. *Roman Society and Roman Law in the New Testament.* Oxford: Clarendon, 1963, pp. 57–70.

Smith, James. *The Voyage and Shipwreck of St. Paul.* Fourth, revised edition of 1880. Grand Rapids: Baker [reprint], 1978.

Tajra, H. W. *The Trial of St. Paul.* Tübingen: Mohr/Siebeck, 1989, pp. 135–201.

Tannehill, Robert C. *The Narrative Unity of Luke-Acts, A Literary Interpretation.* Vol. 2, *The Acts of the Apostles.* Minneapolis: Fortress, 1990, pp. 305–357.

Walters, James C. *Ethnic Issues in Paul's Letter to the Romans: Changing Self-Definitions in Earliest Roman Christianity.* Valley Forge, Penn.: Trinity Press International, 1993, pp. 5–66.

Witherington, Ben, III. *The Acts of the Apostles: A Socio-Rhetorical Commentary.* Grand Rapids: Eerdmans, 1988, 717–816.

19

1 TIMOTHY AND TITUS:
CONDUCT IN THE HOUSEHOLD OF GOD

*P*aul was a church planter with a pastor's heart. From the time of his first mission, he made it his practice to revisit the congregations he had established and to make certain they had stable leadership (cp. Acts 14:21–23; 15:41). In his catalog of apostolic trials in 2 Corinthians, he listed in the climactic position the stress he experienced over his concern for his churches (11:28). Often in his letters he expressed the desire to visit the congregation he was writing, a desire that seems to have been frequently frustrated. Sometimes he sent trusted personal representatives to the churches, coworkers like Timothy, Epaphroditus, and Tychicus. His letters were another means of maintaining contact with the churches, and they were often preoccupied with pastoral concerns.

None of Paul's letters are more reflective of his pastoral orientation than the group known appropriately as the "Pastoral Epistles," consisting of 1 and 2 Timothy and Titus. As early as the late second century, the Muratorian Canon remarked how these three Pauline epistles were devoted to matters of church organization ("ecclesiastical discipline"). The term *Pastoral Epistles* is of more recent vintage, seemingly having first been applied to these epistles in the early eighteenth century. The term is not altogether accurate. Timothy and Titus were not pastors. They were Paul's temporary, personal representatives to the churches of Ephesus and Crete. Paul gave them extensive directions about the management of the churches, however. He dealt with such matters as the character and qualifications of church leaders, the proper conduct in worship, the maintenance of purity in doctrine, and the projection of a healthy image in the larger community so as to enhance the church's evangelistic outreach. Paul challenged Timothy and Titus personally to nurture the qualities they would need if they were to be effective leaders of the congregations. In these ways the epistles are indeed "pastoral" and have provided guidelines for the ministry of the church on down to the present time.

The three Pastoral Epistles form a natural group among the Pauline letters. They were addressed to individuals rather than churches, although they were concerned with issues that involved the entire congregation. Paul may have intended Timothy and Titus to share them with the larger congregation. His final greeting in each of the letters wished grace to "you" in the plural (1 Tim. 6:21; 2 Tim. 4:22). This is most evident in Titus, which he concluded by addressing "you all" (3:15). Philemon was also written to an individual, but it was a true private letter, dealing with a personal matter. The Pastorals are church letters, addressed to Timothy and Titus in their role as congregational leaders. The language and contents of the three Pastorals are also distinctive. Though they have much in common with Paul's other epistles, they resemble one another more closely than any of them resembles any other Pauline epistle. Still, they are separate letters, written under separate circumstances. Their similarities lend to their being treated as a group, and this is the usual procedure in New Testament introductions and in commentaries. It will be followed in this chapter in setting forth the main issues surrounding these epistles.[1] We will, however, defer the treatment of the *content* of 2 Timothy to the next chapter. First Timothy and Titus probably were written during the same period of Paul's life, a period of freedom between two imprisonments in Rome. Second Timothy came later, during Paul's second imprisonment. It was his last epistle, not long before his martyrdom in the imperial capital.

The Pastorals form a closely related group, and they *are* different. Many scholars consider them so different from Paul's other epistles that they deny Paul's having written them. They would attribute them to a later personality writing in Paul's name. Even a number of conservative scholars have viewed the Pastorals as post-Pauline.[2] The question of authorship is the dominant issue in scholarship on the Pastorals. One's stance on authorship will affect one's approach on almost every issue surrounding the epistles. Because of this, we have chosen to organize the introduction to the three epistles around the main issues in the authorship debate. On each point we will first give the arguments of those who consider the epistles not to have been written by Paul. Then the alternative view will be presented, based on the assumption of Pauline authorship.

THE QUESTION OF AUTHORSHIP

No early Christian writer ever questioned Paul's having written the Pastorals. The first to have suggested that he may not have written them seems to have been F. Schleiermacher in 1807. Others quickly picked up on his idea. Among them was F. C. Baur, who saw the Pastorals as dating from the second century and as written to combat Gnosticism. H. J. Holtzmann (1880) refined the post-Pauline position, offering five major arguments against Paul's having written the letters. First, the vocabulary and style were said to be atypical of Paul. Second, with Baur he saw the Pastorals as written in opposition to second-century Gnosticism. Third, Holtzmann argued that the theology was un-Pauline. Fourth, he considered the church organization of the Pastorals to be later than Paul. Fifth, he argued that the personal details of the letter would not fit what is known of the historical Paul.[3] These five arguments are still today the mainstay for those who maintain that the Pastorals are pseudonymous. In the discussion below, we have added two other categories in light of the current discussion. The first is the claim that important second-century sources did not include the Pastorals among the Pauline epistles. The second is really a division of Holtzmann's church-organization argument into two: one dealing with the organization of the church, and the other with the church's sense of ethic. The latter was suggested by Dibelius, who argued that the author of the Pastorals reflected a "bourgeois" ethic.

THE EVIDENCE OF EARLY SOURCES

Those who see the Pastorals as non-Pauline sometimes argue that the earliest evidence for the Pauline epistles does not include them. In particular, Marcion (ca. A.D. 140) did not list them in his collection of Pauline epistles, although he did include the other ten. Likewise, our earliest extant manuscript containing the Pauline epistles does not include the Pastorals. This is a papyrus manuscript, identified by text critics with the symbol P⁴⁶. It dates from A.D. 200 or perhaps earlier. It also lacks Philemon, and its last seven leaves are missing.

The evidence from Marcion is questionable. It is doubtful Marcion would have included the Pastorals in his canon because of the outright rejection of "opposing ideas" (*antitheses*) and "what is falsely called knowledge" (*gnōsis*) in 1 Timothy 6:20. Marcion's prime work was known as *The Antitheses*, and he was a purveyor of a *gnosis*. Tertullian, our source of information on Marcion's canon, considered his rejection of the Pastorals as something of an anomaly (*Adv. Marc.* 5:21). The evidence of P⁴⁶ is at best an argument from silence. Some have suggested that the missing leaves may actually have contained the Pastorals. The scribe who produced the collection seems to have been writing in a progressively smaller hand in order to "get it all in." Allowing for this, the seven missing pages could possibly have had space for the Pastorals.[4]

More significant is the evidence for *inclusion* of the Pastorals among Paul's letters. It is possible the Pastorals were echoed by Clement of Rome in his letter to Corinth (ca. A.D. 95) and in the letters of Ignatius (A.D. 105–110). It is *likely* that Polycarp drew from the Pastorals in his letter to the Philippians (ca. A.D. 135). In fact, all the earliest commentators on the Pauline epistles included the Pastorals among their number. This included Irenaeus, Tertullian, Clement of Alexandria, and the Muratorian Canon, all dating from the late second to early third century. On the other hand, the Gnostics consistently excluded the Pastorals, which is no surprise, given the stance of the letters against pseudo-knowledge (*gnōsis*).

VOCABULARY AND STYLE

From the very beginning of the authorship debate, the vocabulary and style of the Pastorals have been a major consideration in arguments against accepting them as Pauline. Any second-year Greek student moving from Romans or Philippians into 1 Timothy is immediately aware of being in a different world. The vocabulary *is* different. Words appear which are found only in the Pastorals among all the books of the New Testament—175 of them all told. An additional 131 words occur in the Pastorals that are not found in Paul's other epistles, making for a total of 306 words unique to the Pastorals among the letters of Paul. Not only is it a different vocabulary, but different words are used for the same ideas when compared with the other epistles. The style differs too—more uniform, less animated, more typical of Hellenistic Greek, less of the jolting breaks in thought (*anacolutha*) characteristic of Paul's other epistles. Some have compared the vocabulary of the Pastorals with the Christian writings of the early second century and found much in common between them. On this basis they have argued that the Pastorals date from the second century. It is just as possible that the second-century writings knew the Pastorals and echoed their language.[5]

Paul made heavy use of traditional material in the Pastorals. He drew from Christian sources, as seems to be evidenced in stereotypical phrases like "knowing this" (1 Tim. 1:9–10; 2 Tim. 3:1–5) and "this is a trustworthy saying" (1 Tim. 1:15; 3:1;

4:9–10; 2 Tim. 2:11–13; Titus 3:3–8a). He drew from contemporary Hellenistic sources, such as lists of qualities that make for good leaders. Such traditional materials are responsible for much of the unique vocabulary in the Pastorals. There are undoubtedly some passages in which the style *is* more typical of Paul's other letters, particularly in the personal sections, such as 2 Timothy 4:9–21. Wishing to strike a middle ground between pseudonymity and Pauline authorship, a number of scholars have argued that a later disciple of Paul found a number of genuine fragments of Pauline letters and constructed the three Pastorals around these.[6] A major problem with this view is the difficulty in explaining why such personal notes would have been preserved apart from the rest of the letters and by what conceivable motive a later disciple of Paul would have spun letters around them.

We have noted previously how arguments against Pauline authorship based solely on matters of vocabulary and style cannot carry conviction because of Paul's use of coauthors and amanuenses. Many have suggested that the different style of the Pastorals may be due to Paul's use of an amanuensis whom he gave a degree of freedom. In particular, Luke has been mentioned. Those making this suggestion note many similarities in style, language, and theology between the Pastorals and Luke-Acts. Some have seen Luke as Paul's amanuensis.[7] Others have suggested that Luke was the redactor or even the author of the Pastorals.[8] It has even been argued that Luke produced the Pastorals as a third volume, designed to conclude the story of Paul begun in Acts.[9] Perhaps the Lukan affinities in the Pastorals have a simpler explanation. Luke was Paul's longtime companion. It is likely that the two would have had some mutual influence on the language and expression of each other.[10]

THE NATURE OF THE FALSE TEACHING

F. C. Baur and his followers argued that the Pastoral Epistles were written in the second century to combat rising Gnosticism. Few specific characteristics of the false teaching are mentioned in the Pastorals, and it is difficult to pin it down. One should also bear in mind that Paul was dealing with two separate congregations. Timothy was at Ephesus, Titus on the island of Crete. The false teaching was probably not exactly the same in the two locales. The false teachers at Ephesus seem to have advocated dietary regulations and to have forbidden marriage (1 Tim. 4:3). This could possibly have come from an early form of Gnostic-like dualistic speculations but could just as easily be traced to ascetic groups in Judaism like the Essenes. The teachers may have espoused a realized eschatology, because they claimed that the resurrection had already taken place (2 Tim. 2:16–18). They emphasized knowledge (*gnōsis*, 1 Tim. 6:20–21), and they had their own myths and genealogical speculations (1 Tim. 1:4; 4:7; 2 Tim. 4:4). This could refer to Gnostic-style speculations on the aeons emanating from the Spirit world but could just as well be linked to Jewish speculations on the genealogies of Genesis. In fact, the Jewish characteristics of the false teachers are striking. In addition to the ascetic dimensions of their system, they claimed to be teachers of the law (1 Tim. 1:7). Titus may have been contending with a different form of teaching on Crete, but it too seems to have had a primarily Jewish orientation. It involved circumcision (Titus 1:10), "Jewish myths" (Titus 1:14), and "quarrels about the law" (Titus 3:9).

Attempts have been made to designate the false teachings more specifically. Some have suggested that the teachers were followers of Marcion. This is based on the reference to "antitheses" (NIV, "opposing ideas") in 1 Timothy 6:20, but no particular teachings of Marcion are reflected in the Pastorals. Others have suggested that the Pastorals were written to combat an early form of Montanism, a second-century Asian heresy. The Pastorals make little mention of the Spirit. Their reticence in this regard is seen as an attempt to offset Montanist excesses in the Spirit.[11] But nothing in the Pastorals points to any Montanist distinctive. The important thing to note is that there was no tendency afoot in the congregations of the Pastorals that goes beyond what is already found in Paul's other epistles. The denial of the resurrection reminds one of the problems at Corinth, as does the marital asceticism. The dietary regulations are reminiscent of Colosse. One certainly doesn't need to look to later Gnosticism to account for the problems in the congregations of the Pastorals.

For those who deny Pauline authorship, it has become popular to describe the heresy of the Pastorals as a "stock" creation of the author rather than as a reality.[12] It is noted that in general the Pastorals simply denounce the false teachers with stereotypical traits such as greed (1 Tim. 6:5; Titus 1:11), deceit (2 Tim. 3:13), hypocrisy (2 Tim. 3:5; Titus 1:16), and contentiousness (1 Tim. 1:4, 6; 4:2; 6:4; 2 Tim. 2:14, 16, 23; Titus 1:10; 3:9). This observation is accurate to a certain extent. Paul seemed more concerned with condemning the heresy than with refuting it. He appeared more disturbed by its social disruption than by its erroneous views.[13] But, the heresy was not "stock"; it was real. It involved leaders who arose within the church, like Hymenaeus and Alexander (1 Tim. 1:20; cp. 2 Tim. 4:14). The false teachers preyed upon the church. Particularly vulnerable were the women of the congregation.[14] The young widows who did not remarry but flitted about from house to house were probably victims of their teaching (1 Tim. 5:11–15; cp. 2 Tim. 3:6–7). Some of the women, although unqualified to teach, may have attempted to do so, urged on by these self-proclaimed teachers (1 Tim. 2:12). Some of the wealthier members may have experienced their greed firsthand (1 Tim. 6:3–10). In the Pastorals Paul advocated a very conservative social ethic. This approach was altogether necessary if order was to be restored out of the chaos created by the false teachers.[15]

THE THEOLOGY OF THE PASTORALS

Those who see the Pastorals as written by a later Paulinist often argue that the theology of the three epistles is not compatible with that of Paul. They admit that the epistles echo Paul's theology but more as a hardened body of doctrine, lacking the freshness of the "genuine" Pauline epistles. In other words, they view the Pastorals as a later development, the work of an imitator rather than Paul.

In some instances they argue that the thought of the epistles is actually in conflict with that of Paul. The eschatology is said to be un-Pauline. Gone is Paul's expectation of the imminent return of Christ. In its place appears a more "realized eschatology," emphasizing the Christian's existence in the world. In response, it should be noted that the future dimension of salvation is found in the Pastorals, and the present life of the church is depicted in terms of living in the last times and in light of the impending judgment (1 Tim. 4:1–4; 2 Tim. 3:2–4; 4:1). As in Paul's other letters, salvation is seen as beginning in the present and consummated in the future.[16]

Often the different flavor of the Pastorals is more a matter of vocabulary than of theological difference. For instance, some have maintained that the preexistence of Christ is never mentioned in the Pastorals. It is present, however, in different terminology.[17] The word *epiphany* (appearance) is used in the Pastorals to refer to both the incarnation (2 Tim. 1:10) and to the Second Coming of Christ (1 Tim. 6:14;

2 Tim. 4:1, 8; Titus 2:13). Some have said that the Spirit is rarely mentioned in the Pastorals and that this is atypical of Paul. However, the Spirit *is* mentioned in the Pastorals, in significant places, once in each of the epistles (1 Tim. 4:1; 2 Tim. 1:14; Titus 3:5). The Spirit is *implicit* in other places, such as in the references to the "gift" with which Timothy was endowed as a minister (1 Tim. 4:14; 2 Tim. 1:6).[18] Arguments based on missing themes are precarious. One would not expect Paul to mention all his theology in every epistle. For example, the Spirit is mentioned only once in Colossians, once in 2 Thessalonians, and not at all in Philemon.

Faith and works is perhaps the key issue for those who see the thought of the Pastorals as un-Pauline. No one would question that the Pastorals present salvation as being based on God's grace. This key Pauline theme is found in each of the epistles (1 Tim. 1:12–16; 2 Tim. 1:9–10; Titus 3:3–8). But there is a strong emphasis on works. The phrase *good works* occurs fourteen times in the Pastorals (e.g., 1 Tim. 2:10; 6:18; 2 Tim. 2:21; 3:17; Titus 2:7; 3:1). The idea that good works result from salvation is not alien to Paul's other letters (cp. 2 Cor. 9:8; Col. 1:10; Eph. 2:10). Faith is not explicitly contrasted with works in the Pastorals, but the idea is present in Titus 3:5, where salvation is attributed to God's mercy rather than to righteous deeds. The term *faith* occurs thirty-three times in the Pastorals. Often it occurs as one Christian virtue among others, especially joined with love (e.g., 1 Tim. 1:14; 2 Tim. 1:13; 2:22; 3:10; Titus 2:2). Sometimes it is used with the article to describe "*the* faith," the body of Christian belief (1 Tim. 4:1, 6; 5:8; 6:12; 2 Tim. 4:7; Titus 1:13). This latter sense is very close to the term *deposit* (*parathēkē*), a term which occurs three times in the Pastorals and is unique to them among the New Testament writings (1 Tim. 6:20; 2 Tim. 1:12, 14). It is argued that this concept of faith reflects the church subsequent to Paul's time, when doctrine was no longer alive and forming but had hardened into a body of tradition.

In response, it should be noted that Paul often spoke of faith as a virtue (e.g., 1 Cor. 13:13; 2 Cor. 8:7; Gal. 5:22; 1 Thess. 1:3) and sometimes of "*the* faith" as a body of belief (e.g., Phil. 1:27; Col. 2:7).[19] Paul elsewhere often appealed to tradition but used different language (*paradidōmi* rather than *parathēkē*; cp. 1 Cor. 11:23; 15:3). The difference in the Pastorals is the strong emphasis on tradition. Two things probably account for this. One is the instability of the church. The rise of false teachers *from within* the congregation made it necessary to define with some precision the parameters of belief. The second factor is the nature of the Pastorals. Paul was urging his coworkers to stand firm against the false teachers. Timothy and Titus knew already the main contours of "the faith." Paul did not need to elaborate, only to urge them to stand firm in the "healthy teaching" they already knew well.

CHURCH ORGANIZATION IN THE PASTORALS

It has often been argued that the Pastorals reflect a post-Pauline church organization. On this basis, many would place them as late as the early second century. They maintain that the Pastorals reflect the type of church order that one finds in the letters of Ignatius, that is, a monarchical bishop responsible for appointing elders over the regional churches. It is true that the word *bishop* (overseer) always occurs in the singular in the Pastorals, but there is no evidence that he functioned like the bishops of the second-century church. It is probably best to translate the title (*episcopos*) as "overseer," as in the NIV (1 Tim. 3:1; Titus 1:7). The role of the overseer is unclear. The term may be synonymous with that of elder (they *are* synonymous in

Acts 20:17, 28). A bishop/overseer was possibly an elder with a special role, such as that of teacher.[20]

The offices mentioned in the Pastorals are bishops/overseers, elders, deacons, and perhaps deaconesses. First Timothy 3:11 refers to a group of "women," who may either have been wives of the deacons or an order of women deacons. It is also possible that the widows on the list referred to in 1 Timothy 5:9 were an order of older widows who had a special ministry, perhaps to the women of the congregation. There is no reason any of these offices should not have been in existence during Paul's lifetime. According to Acts, Paul appointed elders over his mission churches (14:23). Timothy ministered in the churches of Ephesus, and Acts 20:17 indicates that the leaders of the Ephesian congregation whom Paul summoned to Miletus were designated as "elders." Paul probably established his churches along the pattern of the elder system in the Jewish synagogue. In Philippians 1:1 Paul singled out the leaders of the Philippian church as bishops/overseers (*episcopoi* = elders) and deacons. The order of widows, if there was one, may well have developed along the pattern of godly, ministering women like Dorcas (Acts 9:39), and the deacons along the line of practical ministry like the seven of Acts 6:1ff. There is no reason to see the church offices of the Pastorals as post-Pauline.

Those who see the Pastorals as late point to the qualifications for office which are listed in 1 Timothy 3:1–13 and Titus 1:6–9. The Pastorals are viewed as a kind of church handbook which documents the regulations of a time later than Paul. The leadership of the churches of Paul's own lifetime are viewed as being determined charismatically, by their spiritual gifts, rather than appointed to an office by a set of rigid qualifications. But the qualities listed in the Pastorals are *not* a list of qualifications to be met but rather a description of the type of exemplary character that should belong to those who lead the church. The supposed charismatic leadership of Paul's earlier congregations is probably also not an altogether accurate picture. People did use their gifts to serve the Lord, as they still should today. But from the start Paul's churches seem to have had leaders to administer the work of the church (cp. 1 Thess. 5:12). Quite likely, the patrons and patronesses of the house churches had leadership roles from the very beginning.

THE ETHIC OF THE PASTORALS

Martin Dibelius popularized the idea that the Pastorals reflect a "bourgeois" ethic.[21] By this he meant a way of life that attempts to make peace with its social context, a "middle class" adaptation to the world. He saw this in such things as the appeal to pray for the authorities (1 Tim. 2:1–2), the traditional role ascribed to women (1 Tim. 2:9–15), and the qualities descriptive of church leadership. In particular, he showed how the latter were strikingly similar to Hellenistic lists of qualities desired in various leaders, such as military officers. The household orders of the Pastorals were viewed as betraying the same tendency of supporting the existing social order. Unlike the lists in the Prison Epistles, the Pastorals do not exemplify reciprocity. Only the subordinate group is addressed—slaves, but not masters; women, but not men. All in all, this is viewed as a conservative social perspective.[22] Some would even see it as an attempt of those in power to secure their status.[23]

In the picture furnished by Acts, the early Christians always took a socially conservative stance, attempting to create as little offense to society as possible. Of course, those who see the Pastorals as "bourgeois" see Acts in the same light and date it late as well. Even in the undisputed Pauline epistles, however, Paul often took a socially conservative stance. He did not want Christians to hang out their disputes in pagan law courts for everyone to see (1 Cor. 6:1–6). He urged Christians to respect the governing authorities and to pay their taxes (Rom. 13:1–5). His missionary strategy was to adapt as much as possible to his cultural context in order to "save some" (1 Cor. 9:22). In the Pastorals he was concerned that the Christians live quiet and peaceful lives in the community with the ultimate purpose that some of those outside would be saved (1 Tim. 2:3–4). Of course, there was also the dimension of the false teachers within Timothy's Ephesian congregations. They were disrupting both church and family. Paul urged Timothy to apply a traditional, conservative ethic in order to restore stability.

The idea is quite open to challenge that the Pastorals reflect the "middle-class" mentality of a period in the early church much later than Paul. Paul reflected socially conservative viewpoints in his other epistles. The rise of the false teachers within the Ephesian church probably forced him to recommend even stricter guidelines in the Pastorals. There is no reason this development could not have taken place in the eight years or so between his farewell address to the Ephesian elders and the writing of 1 Timothy.[24] Often in the life of the church it is necessary to consolidate, to draw clear doctrinal boundaries, to establish strong social guidelines, all to protect the integrity of the fellowship. The risk, of course, is that the church might become too fixed, too rigid, too incapable of adapting to changing times.[25] Somehow the church has to steer a middle course between the freedom of Galatians and the control of the Pastorals. Paul did. Both are a part of our heritage from him.

THE SETTING OF THE PASTORALS IN PAUL'S LIFE

The personal details mentioned in the Pastorals do not fit well into the ministry of Paul as depicted in Acts or in his other epistles. According to 1 Timothy 1:3, Paul was writing from Macedonia, having left Timothy in Ephesus to contend with the false teachers there. Nothing like this is mentioned in the Acts account of Paul's Ephesian ministry (Acts 19). Likewise, neither Acts nor Paul's other epistles mention any of the Ephesian Christians who are listed in Paul's letters to Timothy: Hymenaeus and Alexander (1 Tim. 1:20), Onesiphorus (2 Tim. 1:16; 4:19), Phygelus and Hermogenes (2 Tim. 1:15), and Carpus of Troas (2 Tim. 4:13). Paul was free when he wrote 1 Timothy but in prison in Rome at the time of 2 Timothy (2 Tim. 1:16–17). Timothy was evidently still ministering in Ephesus, but Paul wanted him to leave and come to him quickly (2 Tim. 4:9).

The concluding verses of 2 Timothy (4:9–21) contain a wealth of personal detail, which is difficult to fit into the framework of Acts: Crescens has gone to Galatia, Titus is in Dalmatia, Demas has abandoned Paul and gone to Thessalonica, Erastus has decided to remain in Corinth, Tychicus has gone to Ephesus, Timothy is to fetch Paul's cloak and parchments from Carpus at Troas, Paul has left Trophimus sick at Miletus, and Luke alone remains to keep Paul company in prison. To make things even more difficult, the letter to Titus informs us of a Pauline ministry to the island of Crete which we would never have known about apart from the letter itself. Paul had evidently started work on the island and left Titus to strengthen the ministry there (Titus 1:5). This could not be the occasion of Paul's ship putting in at Fair Havens (Acts 27:8). That is the only time Acts ever connects Paul with Crete, and the prisoner Paul did not seem at that time to have left the ship, much less started a mission on the island. At the conclusion of Titus, Paul mentioned a visit to Crete by the lawyer Zenas and Apollos (3:13). Apollos is never elsewhere connected with Crete in Acts or the Pauline epistles. Paul asked Titus to join him at Nicopolis on the Adriatic coast of Greece and promised to send Artemis or Tychicus to him (Titus 3:12). There is no evidence elsewhere of Paul being at Nicopolis.

Those who view the Pastorals as pseudepigraphical often see these details as part of the writer's fiction of Pauline authorship. However, the details are quite vivid. If they are fiction, it is a very high-handed pseudepigraphy indeed. Thus, many have claimed they are genuine Pauline fragments worked into the text by the post-Pauline writer of the epistles. This fragment hypothesis, however, does not solve the historical problem of fitting these details into Paul's ministry as known from Acts and his other epistles. The easiest solution is to see them as referring to events *subsequent to* the ministry of Paul that is depicted in Acts and also subsequent to the other ten Pauline epistles.

Some who advocate Pauline authorship of the Pastorals would still work them within the framework of Acts. The most unique position places them during the course of Paul's second mission and argues that they are the earliest extant Pauline epistles, dating from A.D. 42–44.[26] This is most unlikely, as one can only arrive at such a position by treating the text of Acts with some violence and not allowing at all for the developed state of the churches of the Pastorals. A few scholars argue that Paul was never released from the Roman imprisonment of Acts 28, seeing him as condemned to death at that time and as writing all three Pastorals during that period of incarceration.[27] A more widely held viewpoint would place 1 Timothy and Titus during Paul's third (Ephesian) mission and 2 Timothy at the time of Paul's imprisonment in Caesarea or Rome (Acts 28).[28] These scholars account for the personal details of the Pastorals by noting how Luke provided a selective treatment of Paul's missionary work. For instance, Timothy could well have been placed over the Ephesian churches for a period during Paul's three-year ministry there (Acts 19), and Paul could have sailed to Crete for a mission during the same time frame. Although this reconstruction remains possible, the simplest solution is the time-honored view that Paul was released from his first Roman imprisonment. On this assumption, the Pastorals were written subsequent to Paul's ten other epistles and the narrative of Acts.[29]

Paul's release from his first Roman imprisonment must have occurred around A.D. 62/63. He seems to have been rearrested and martyred prior to the death of Nero in A.D. 68. This would allow for a period of four or five years of freedom and missionary activity. During this period he may have worked for a period in Spain, as he wanted to do (Rom. 15:24, 28). Sources like 1 Clement, the Muratorian Canon, and *The Acts of Peter* all point to Paul's work in Spain. He also must have returned to the churches of the east. The Pastorals would indicate as much. Perhaps he began on the island of Crete, leaving Titus to continue the work there. He traveled on to Asia with Timothy. Finding the churches at Ephesus infected with false teaching, he left Timothy there to deal with the situation. He set out for Macedonia by way of Troas, where he left a coat and some parchments. Traveling to Macedonia, he wrote 1 Timothy and Titus. He planned to travel the Egnatian Way all the way to the coast and then south to Nicopolis, where he intended to spend the winter. He wrote Titus to join him there. Somewhere between Macedonia and Nicopolis he seems to have been arrested, probably as a result of Nero's attack on the Christians at that time.

The date would have been some time around A.D. 66 or 67. From prison in Rome Paul wrote a second epistle to Timothy in Ephesus. He urged his "son in Christ" to come visit him soon. He knew that this time he would not likely survive the imprisonment. He had finished his race. He was ready to join his Lord. Second Timothy is our last extant epistle from the apostle.

THE CASE FOR PAUL: A FINAL ASSESSMENT

Much of the reasoning against the Pauline authorship of the Pastorals is a rather subjective developmental argument which holds that the letters reflect the organizational and doctrinal perspective of a church well after the lifetime of Paul. As we have attempted to show, within the apostle's own lifetime Paul's churches could easily have developed the structure and the problems that are addressed in the Pastorals. On the other hand, the theory of their pseudonymity has its own problems. Why, for instance, were *three* letters written? First Timothy and Titus are strikingly similar. Remove the material from Titus that parallels 1 Timothy and little would be left. It is easy to see why Paul would have written the same things to two different coworkers. But why would a later writer attempting to combat heresy have wasted his time on two works that said virtually the same thing? The question of pseudonymity is, of course, a problem in itself. It is often maintained that this was a common practice in the early centuries and not ethically suspect.[30]

However, most examples of Hellenistic pseudonymity were written *centuries* later than the figure in whose name they were written, not just decades, as would be the case with the Pastorals. Early Christians were very careful on the question of authorial authenticity. They excluded many "apocryphal" writings from the canon because they were known to be pseudonymous. Known pseudepigraphers like the author of the spurious *Acts of Paul and Thecla* were severely disciplined. Those who were close to the time of the Pastorals accepted all three into the canon in the name of the apostle. Each of the epistles identifies Paul as author in its salutation. No voices were raised in the early centuries questioning the accuracy of this designation, none until modern times.

OVERVIEW OF 1 TIMOTHY

THE RECIPIENTS

The letter is addressed to Timothy, who on the evidence of Paul's epistles was the apostle's most constant coworker. Timothy came from Lystra, where Paul established work on his first missionary journey (Acts 14:8–20). Evidently at that time Timothy was led to Christ along with his mother Eunice and his grandmother Lois (2 Tim. 1:5). Timothy accompanied Paul on his second missionary journey. Although Timothy's father was a Gentile, Eunice was Jewish, making Timothy a Jew by Jewish law. So Paul had him circumcised (Acts 16:1–3). Timothy was thus particularly well qualified to assist in Paul's congregations, which were often of mixed Jewish and Gentile composition.

Timothy served as Paul's personal representative to his churches on several occasions—to Thessalonica (1 Thess. 3:1–10), to Corinth (1 Cor. 4:16–17), and to Philippi (Phil. 2:19–24). In the latter, Paul spoke of Timothy's selfless ministry and the close "father-son" relationship between himself and his young coworker. Of the ten Pauline epistles apart from the Pastorals, Paul included Timothy as coauthor in the address of six, indicating at the very least a close relationship with the addressees (1 and 2 Thess., 2 Cor., Col., Philem., and Phil.). Timothy was probably in his late teens when he first joined Paul (around A.D. 49). By the time of 1 Timothy (around A.D. 65), he was probably in his mid-thirties. Paul referred to his "youth" in 1 Timothy 4:12, using a Greek word (*neotēs*) that was used of individuals up to the age of forty. Timothy was not the bishop of Ephesus; he was not even pastor. He was the apostle's personal representative among the Ephesian house-churches, and he carried Paul's full apostolic authority. The epistle was primarily addressed to Timothy, but Paul surely intended him to share it with the entire church.

THE PURPOSE OF 1 TIMOTHY

From the time of the Muratorian Canon, the Pastorals have been recognized as being concerned with church order. They have been viewed as a sort of handbook, laying down the discipline and regulations for the church and the qualifications for its various ministries. The primary purpose of 1 Timothy, however, was to combat the false teaching that had risen within the church.[31] The teaching was disrupting the fellowship, wreaking havoc on individuals and families. Paul's socially conservative agenda was surely designed to combat this threat, as was his emphasis on sound teaching and on solid exemplary leadership. He wanted the leaders to be good managers of their own households so that they might effectively manage the household of God (1 Tim. 3:15). As always, he had an evangelistic purpose in mind. Christians were called upon to live an exemplary life so that all those in their community might be led to a saving knowledge of God's truth. God wills nothing less than the salvation of all (1 Tim. 2:1–4).

A STUDY OUTLINE OF 1 TIMOTHY

Epistolary Introduction (1:1–2)
I. Initial Charge to Timothy (1:3–20)
    A. Confronting the False Teachers (vv. 3–11)
    B. Remembering Paul's Example (vv. 12–17)
    C. Contending for the Faith (vv. 18–20)
II. Conduct Within the Household of God (2:1–3:16)
    A. Prayer for All People (2:1–7)
    B. The Deportment of Men and Women in Worship (2:8–15)
    C. Qualities Befitting Congregational Leaders (3:1–13)
        1. Qualities of "overseers" (vv. 1–7)
        2. Qualities of deacons (vv. 8–10, 12–13)
        3. Qualities of "the women" (v. 11)
    D. The Confessional Foundation of God's Household (3:14–16)
III. Instructions for Various Groups (4:1–6:2)
    A. For Timothy (4:1–5:2)
        1. Exposing the false teachers (4:1–8)
        2. Setting a positive personal example (4:9–16)
        3. Relating properly to all in the church (5:1–2)
    B. For Widows (5:3–16)
        1. The support of the widows (vv. 3–8)
        2. The enrollment of the widows (vv. 9–16)

HIGHLIGHTS OF 1 TIMOTHY

CONFRONTING THE FALSE TEACHERS (1:1–20)

All of chapter 1 is related to the problem of the false teachers. Paul began with his usual salutation. As in Philippians 2:22, he designated Timothy as his "son" in the faith (v. 2). He applied the title *Savior* to God, a title also applied to Christ in the Pastorals. It is a unique usage among the Pauline epistles and is characteristic of the Hellenistic language found in the Pastorals. *Savior* was a term used in the Greek cults to designate the pagan gods as deliverers. Paul reminded the Greek Christians of Ephesus that God alone through Jesus Christ was their deliverer.

In verses 3–7 Paul moved directly to the false teachers. He detailed very little about their specific belief system. He spoke of their myths and genealogies and endless speculation and how they prided themselves on being interpreters of the law. Though some would see this as referring to Gnostic myths about emanations from the spirit world, "genealogies" sounds more like Hellenistic Jewish speculations on the tribal genealogies of Genesis, and the emphasis on law likewise smacks of a Jewish background. Paul seemed less concerned about the exact teachings of their system than about their promotion of controversy and schism in the fellowship.

The mention of the law led Paul to a digression on the nature of law in verses 8–11. As in Romans 7:12, he affirmed the basic goodness of the law—when used in the *right* way. The false teachers were using the law in the *wrong* way, for speculation and to promote division. Paul enunciated a commonplace of Hellenistic thought when he stated that the law was not for good people but for bad people.[32] In his other epistles Paul reflected the same principle by speaking of the *Spirit* as one's inward moral guide. Through the Spirit one does what is right without any external coercion. Paul then proceeded with a vice list in verses 9–11, a characteristic form in his moral teaching. This one is of particular interest because it seems to be arranged according to the Ten Commandments, all the way from ungodliness to false witness.[33]

In verse 10 Paul spoke of "sound" doctrine, using a word which literally means "healthy." Throughout the Pastorals Paul used medical language. He depicted the false teaching as "unhealthy," a disease that ate away at the fellowship like gangrene (2 Tim. 2:17).[34] Paul moved on to speak of his own conversion in verses 12–17 as a kind of foil to the false teachers. *They* began from within the congregation and turned into blasphemers and destroyers of the fellowship. *Paul* began as a persecutor and destroyer of the church, a blasphemer of Christ. But God in his mercy had saved him and made him his faithful servant. Paul gave the first of the "faithful sayings" in verse 15. Four others occur in the Pastorals (1 Tim. 3:1; 4:9; 2 Tim. 2:11; Titus 3:8). They seem to be confessional statements, all introduced by the same stereotyped formula: "the saying is trustworthy/faithful." In this instance, the trustworthy saying was that Jesus came to save sinners. Paul was a prime example of that. He often spoke of how God had turned him around, the chief enemy of Christ, the persecutor of the church (cp. Gal. 1:13–16; 1 Cor. 15:9–10; Eph. 3:7–8).

In verses 18–20 Paul returned to his appeal for Timothy to contend with the false teachers. He reminded Timothy of the prophecies formerly made about him, recalling an earlier experience, perhaps Timothy's ordination (cp. 1 Tim. 6:12; 2 Tim. 1:6). The false teachers had made shipwreck of their faith. Paul urged Timothy to hold firm to his own faith and to keep a clear conscience (cp. 1 Tim. 1:5; 3:9). Conscience is a Hellenistic concept. In the Pastorals the "good" conscience is one clearly informed in the gospel, firm in sound doctrine. Hymenaeus and Alexander (v. 20) had "seared" consciences (cp. 4:2). Evidently Paul had already disciplined them, removing them from the fellowship. That seems to be the meaning of "handing them over to Satan" (cp. 1 Cor. 5:3–5). If they are the same two men who are mentioned in 2 Timothy 2:17 and 2 Timothy 4:14, they do not seem to have repented but to have persisted in their error.

PRAYER FOR ALL (2:1–7)

Chapters 2 and 3 focus on the life of the church under three aspects: (1) the central role of prayer, (2) the proper deportment of men and women in worship, and (3) the qualities requisite for good leadership. The theme of the whole section is summarized at the end: "how people ought to conduct themselves in God's household" (3:15).

Central to the worship of the church is its prayer (2:1–7). Christians are to pray for *all people*. Paul emphasized the inclusiveness of our prayer life. We are to pray for "all" (vv. 1, 4, 6). This includes rulers and civil authorities (v. 2). Paul elsewhere urged Christians to respect and pray for the governing authorities (Rom. 13:1–5; Titus 3:1). Paul's reference to living a quiet and peaceful life (v. 2) could be taken to mean that Christians will find peace with the world if they are law-abiding citizens who pray for the authorities and do not ruffle the feathers of those in power. His real meaning, however, is found in verse 4: God intends for *all* to be saved, including rulers and authorities, Jews and Gentiles. When Christians live exemplary, peaceful lifestyles, it sets a healthy context for witness to the surrounding culture. Paul reminded Timothy of the inclusiveness of his own apostolic ministry—to Gentiles as well as to Jews. We do not know all the contours of the false teaching in the Ephesian church. It may have had a strongly exclusivistic element.

In the form of a brief confessional statement, verses 5–6 give the evidence for God's concern for the salvation of all. God is the one God of all people; thus, he desires the salvation of all his creatures. He proved that desire by sending Christ as the intermediary between himself and sinful humanity. Christ gave himself as a ransom for all people (cp. Mark 10:45). Paul did not state that all will be saved but rather that God's *will* is for all to be saved. The accomplishment of God's will is up to the faithfulness of his people in their prayerful witness to all. The ultimate goal of all our worship is thus evangelism. First Timothy 2:1–7 is one of the great missionary statements of the entire Bible.

THE DEPORTMENT OF MEN AND WOMEN IN WORSHIP (2:8–15)

In the remainder of chapter 2, the context seems still to be that of worship. Paul turned first to the proper attitude of *men* in worship (v. 8). They are to pray with clean hands and hearts. They are to avoid anger and dissension. Paul may well have had in mind the disruptive, contentious behavior of the false teachers.

Paul then turned to the women of the congregation. Evidently some of them had become the particular targets of the false teachers. The Pastorals give ample attestation of this. Some of the young widows of the congregation were being overwhelmed by sensual desires (1 Tim. 5:11). They were idle and flitted about from house to house with destructive gossip (1 Tim. 5:13). Some had already fallen into Satan's snare (1 Tim. 5:15). Second Timothy 3:6–7 gives an even bleaker view of the vulnerable women of the congregation. The false teachers had wormed their way into homes and gained "control over weak-willed women, who are loaded down with sins and are swayed by all kinds of evil desires." The false teachers were probably persuading the young women not to marry (1 Tim. 4:3). The whole situation was a blight on the congregation, a bad example before the larger community, and a threat to the stability of the Christian families. Paul urged a very conservative social pattern to restore some sort of order and to provide some constructive purpose for these women. He urged them to marry and manage families (1 Tim. 5:14), which was the traditional and primary role for women in the society of that day.[35]

In 1 Timothy 2:9–15 Paul seems to have been reacting to some such disruptive pattern among some women of the congregation. He urged them to dress modestly, adorning themselves with charitable deeds rather than finery. Often in Hellenistic society overdressing was seen as a form of seduction. Paul urged that the women dress decently as an expression of their commitment to God (vv. 9–10). He further stated that he would not allow the women to teach the men of the congregation or to exercise any position of authority over them.[36] Quite possibly the false teachers were using the women to propagate their own erroneous views as the women flitted about from house to house. In their social context the women would have had little formal education and were scarcely qualified to teach. Paul wanted the women to be educated, so he urged them to sit quietly in the assembly and to learn.

In verses 13–15 he gave a basis for his instruction by appealing to the tradition about Eve related in Genesis 3:13–16. Like Eve, the Ephesian women had been deceived. Like Eve, they had fallen into the serpent Satan's snare (1 Tim. 5:15). They were coming perilously close to perdition, but there was a way to redeem their situation—through childbearing, that is, through assuming a traditional family role as managers of their households (cp. 1 Tim. 5:14). This was indeed *the* characteristic female role in the first century in both Jewish and Greco-Roman society. The false teachers of Ephesus seem to have promoted an agenda that threatened the Ephesian church with massive social upheaval, not least to the family structure. Paul's recourse was to call the Christian community back to very traditional values and structures lest it lose its moorings and fall into disorder.

QUALITIES BEFITTING CONGREGATIONAL LEADERS (3:1–13)

In chapter 3 Paul enumerated the requirements for three groups of leaders within the church—the bishop ("overseer"), deacons, and the "women." The qualities he listed are to a large extent stereotypical and frequently paralleled in the Hellenistic literature. Biographers like Suetonius described their heroes as having these same characteristics. Many of these qualities are listed as ideal traits for various sorts of leaders and professionals, such as military commanders and physicians.[37] They were viewed as "standard" qualities for good leaders.

The first leadership group addressed is that of the "overseer," or "bishop" (*episcopos*). The nomenclature and function of leaders in the Pastorals is not altogether clear. First Timothy 5:17–25 deals with a group of "elders" (*presbuteroi*). The office of elder may or may not be the same as that of the overseer in chapter 3. Chapter 3 also lists the desirable qualities for "deacons" (*diakonoi*). It is possible that "elder" was the general term for the church leadership, and the "overseers" and "deacons" were subgroups within the body of elders. The "overseers" may have been "teaching elders," with the deacons subordinate to them and responsible for the practical ministries of the church. Since the "overseer" is always addressed in the singular in the Pastorals, there may have been only one to a congregation. He may have fulfilled the same role as the pastor-teacher of Ephesians 4:11 and been roughly equivalent to the pastor of present-day churches.

Many of the qualities expected of the overseers were those generally expected of respectable leaders in Hellenistic society: above reproach in the community, level-headed, respected, self-controlled, not given to heavy drinking. Other qualities may have been more specific to his duties as a church leader. He was to be hospitable, because he may well have been responsible for entertaining visiting Christian workers. He was to be noncontentious, a quality which the false teachers decidedly lacked. Greed seems to have been a particular problem with the false teachers (1 Tim. 6:3–10). Paul therefore urged overseers and deacons alike not to be greedy or lovers of money (vv. 3, 8). He likewise emphasized that both should be a "one-woman" man (vv. 2, 12). The meaning of the phrase is anything but clear. It has been interpreted in at least five different ways.

First, it may mean that these leaders were to be married, to have a wife, not to be single. Second, it may mean that they were to have only one wife at a time, not to be polygamous. Third, it could mean that they were not to be divorced. Greek, however, had a word for divorce, and it is difficult to see why Paul would have used this strange circumlocution in its place. A fourth possibility is that Paul was referring to those who had only a single wife for the length of their lifetime, including widowers who never remarried. Being married to only one husband for their whole life made a woman worthy of special honor in the Hellenistic world (cp. 1 Tim. 5:9; lit., a "one-man woman"). Paul may have applied this special virtue to the male leadership as well. The fifth possibility is that Paul meant a man who was faithful to his wife, a man of one woman.[38] Prostitution and mistresses were a way of life for the first-century Greeks. Paul may well have held up the ideal of marital fidelity for the leaders of Ephesus, a characteristic that would have stood out as an exception and an example to the surrounding culture.

The overseer was also to be a Christian of some maturity, not a neophyte, not someone new to the faith and still learning the rudiments. Overseers were to manage their own families well. The leaders were a model and example for the church. How could they manage God's household if their own family life set a poor example? Finally, the overseer/pastor was to win the respect of the community so as to enhance the witness of the church to those outside. In a real sense, all of the qualities were essential to that goal.

Basically the same qualities were expected of deacons: they were not to be greedy, not given to wine, sincere, managing their households well, men of one woman (vv. 8, 12). Paul added that one should not be allowed to enter the office hastily but should first be tested and proven (v. 10). His statement that their faithful service procured for them a good standing (v. 13) may indicate that the diaconate was a stage in attaining a higher level of service, such as that of overseer.

The reference to "the women" in verse 11 is tantalizing. It is sandwiched in the middle of Paul's treatment of the deacons. It could refer to the wives of the deacons. It is just as possible that it referred to an order of deaconesses. The qualities listed for them are not so much domestic as leadership traits, the same kind as those laid down for the men.

THE CONFESSIONAL FOUNDATION OF GOD'S HOUSEHOLD (3:14–16)

Writing from Macedonia, Paul expressed his desire to return to Ephesus. He probably did not realize this desire but was instead arrested and taken to Rome. In verse 15 he set forth his main purpose in writing: to make clear to Timothy (and to the Ephesians) the proper conduct and order for the church. The purpose went further, however. Paul described the church as "the pillar and foundation of the truth." As guardian of the truth, the church is the main witness to the gospel and thus a key component in the salvation which God intends for all people (1 Tim. 2:4). Paul thus ended the section on an evangelistic note. He gave a confessional summary of God's salvation in Jesus Christ (v. 16).

The Christological confession of verse 16 is hymnic in structure. It is constructed of six parallel clauses which in Greek have both rhythm and assonance. It speaks of the work of Christ from his incarnation to his exaltation. The exact structure and interpretation of the hymn has been the object of much discussion.[39] One of the simplest approaches sees the hymn as composed of three couplets, each contrasting a divine with an earthly dimension. The first couplet refers to Christ's *incarnation*: he appeared in both flesh and in Spirit. The second couplet refers to the witness of Christ as *risen Lord*: he witnessed both to the earthly "nations" and to the heavenly "angelic" beings. The third couplet focuses on the twofold *reception of Jesus*: both on earth ("the world") and in heaven ("taken up"). In its context the hymn reminded Timothy of the whole purpose for God's household—to witness to the salvation which is found alone in the incarnate, risen, and exalted Lord.

INSTRUCTION TO TIMOTHY (4:1–16)

In chapter 4 Paul picked up on his charge to Timothy that he had begun in chapter 1. He advised Timothy about how to lead the church. His advice can be summarized in three general areas.

First, he advised Timothy to point out for the congregation the errors of the false teachers (vv. 1–7a). He reminded Timothy how the Spirit had warned that such false teachers would arise in the last times (v. 1). They were obviously present at Ephesus. With these words Paul reflected his conviction that we are already living in the last days. He described the false teachers in lurid terms. They had fallen prey to Satan, who had so branded their consciences that they were no longer capable of moral discernment. He pointed to two specific errors which they promulgated—abstinence from certain foods and abstinence from marriage. Paul had encountered ascetic tendencies previously in congregations like Colosse. In his epistle to that church he had argued that ascetic practices provide no effective base for controlling one's moral life. Here he argued directly against the dualistic basis of asceticism, which views the physical world negatively. Paul reminded Timothy that

God created everything, and all is thus intrinsically good. Thus, we can gladly say grace over all foods as we acknowledge them as God's gracious gift (v. 4).

In the second place, Paul urged Timothy to train himself in godliness (*eusebeia*, vv. 7b–10). "Godliness" is a favorite word in the Pastorals. It is a sort of shorthand to represent all that pertains to the life lived under Christ's lordship. The third of the "faithful" sayings occurs in verse 9. This time it most likely refers back to the previous verse: though physical exercise is of some profit, vigorous training in godliness is far more valuable, equipping one for life eternal.

Paul's third line of advice to Timothy was to set himself up as a model for the whole congregation (vv. 11–16). This would have not been altogether natural in the social context of first-century Ephesus. People generally looked up to the elders of the community, not young adults like Timothy. But Timothy represented Paul and embodied true Christian godliness. Paul probably targeted the Ephesian Christians with the words about not despising Timothy's youth. Timothy had a special gift of ministry endowed by the Holy Spirit and acknowledged when the elders laid their hands on him, probably in much the same manner as the Spirit and the church together had set Paul himself aside for ministry (Acts 13:2–3). The qualities which Paul urged Timothy to model are the essence of godliness: exemplary speech and lifestyle, love, faith, and personal purity (v. 12). Timothy was not only to model godliness; he was to preach it. Verse 13 probably refers to the ministry of the Word, consisting of opening up the Scripture, preaching it, and teaching it. Paul's advice to Timothy is suitable for the Christian servant in any generation. The minister is to persevere in all these areas: in refutation of error, in personal discipline for godliness, in the modeling of the Christian life, and in the proclamation of the Word. The minister who faithfully fulfills these charges will "save both [himself] and [his] hearers" (v. 16).

INSTRUCTIONS REGARDING WIDOWS (5:1–16)

All of 5:1–6:2 deals with how Timothy was to behave toward various groups within the church. The introductory pair of verses sets forth the general principle: Timothy was to relate to all members of the congregation as he would to members of his own family circle—dealing gently with elders as he would his own mother and father, treating young men as peers, relating to the younger women in all purity as he would his own sisters (5:1–2). The remainder of the section deals with groups who seem to have presented special problems in the church.

The first group was the widows. The Old Testament enjoined Israel to provide for orphans and widows (e.g., Deut. 10:18). From the start, the Christian community picked up on this ideal (Acts 6:1; 9:36–41). By the time of the Pastorals, the ministry seems to have grown to the point that it was creating a financial burden on the church. The ministry may have attracted many widows to the faith. The support of the church afforded these widows a degree of freedom and independence from family members and others.[40] The independence was badly managed by some, who were becoming idle and particularly vulnerable to the false teachers. Paul addressed these problems with a three-pronged solution.

First, families were instructed to provide for their own (vv. 3–5, 7–8). Children and grandchildren were to provide for their widowed parents. This is the requirement of the fifth commandment and an expression of minimal Christian piety. Adult Christian children who do not provide for their elders are worse than the pagans, who do in fact provide for their own. Verse 16 seems to be dealing with the same issue, focusing on the particular responsibility of the female family members to provide for the widows in their extended households. It is possible that this verse refers to a special circumstance where women of means (like Lydia and Phoebe) had taken destitute widows into their own homes.[41] Paul's basic principle was clear: the church was to be relieved of the financial burden of such support wherever possible.

Paul's second solution was to tighten up the qualifications for widows to receive church support (vv. 9–10). He spoke of a formal list for enrolling widows and laid down three qualifications: they were to be over sixty years of age, were to have been the spouses of only one husband (a "one-man woman") and were to have been noted for their good deeds. As examples of good deeds, Paul listed the raising of children, the practice of hospitality, "washing the feet of the saints" (probably both literally and in the general sense of menial service), and helping the needy. A true widow was to be a model of piety, giving herself to continual prayer and devotion (v. 5). Some see the list as indicative of an official ministry of widows who worked among the women of the church.[42] There is little evidence in the Pastorals or elsewhere for such an order, and it is more likely that the "list" simply contained the names of those who received church support.

Paul's third line of solution was to urge the younger widows to marry (vv. 11–15). Evidently some of them were creating a major problem for the church. They were "living for pleasure" (v. 6), their passions working against their devotion to Christ. They desired to remarry, and this was a breach of their pledge (vv. 11–12). Probably enrollment on the widow's list carried with it a pledge that one was not only a widow but would continue to remain so. Paul was a realist. He had advised the single Corinthians that they were better off to marry than to burn with passion (1 Cor. 7:9). But the Ephesian problem went deeper than uncontrolled passion. Some of the young widows were becoming idle and busybodies, flitting from house to house with destructive talk. They had probably succumbed to the deceit of the false teachers and were being used by them (cp. 2 Tim. 3:6–7). Paul urged them to remarry, raise families, manage their households, in short, to recover a constructive role in their society. As it was, they were a basis for slander of the Christian community by those outside (v. 14). Throughout the Pastorals Paul was concerned that Christians project an image that would win the respect of the larger community. He always had an evangelistic goal in mind.

INSTRUCTIONS REGARDING ELDERS (5:17–25)

All of 5:17–25 seems to relate to the question of elders.[43] Some of the false teachers may have come from the ranks of the elders of the church. Hymenaeus and Alexander may have been among their number (1 Tim. 1:20). Having dealt with the out-of-control youthful widows who had probably come under their influence, Paul now turned to these wayward leaders. He began on a positive note. Elders who manage the church well, who are effective in preaching and teaching, are worthy of "double honor." The honor included some sort of material support (v. 18), and the support may have itself been a source of abuse on the part of the problem elders.

In verses 19–20 Paul moved to his real concern with the elders—the need to discipline some of them. Paul followed biblical guidelines. They were not to be condemned hastily, but only on the evidence of two or three witnesses (cp. Deut. 19:15; 2 Cor. 13:1). When found guilty, they were to be rebuked publicly. They were highly visible figures in the church, and this demanded visible discipline. It went without saying that all discipline should be done without partiality of any kind.

Paul does not seem to have been speaking hypothetically but in light of the actual situation at Ephesus. Some elders had already been disciplined (cp. 1:20), and with their removal it was now necessary to replace them. Paul warned Timothy not to be hasty in that process either. In the laying on of hands, Christian leaders identify personally with those they are setting aside for service. They express their confidence in them. The highest standards should be maintained, and a known transgressor never appointed to office (v. 22). Unfortunately, mistakes can occur. The sins of some leaders will become evident only later (v. 24). If church leaders cannot guarantee the purity of all the leadership, they can at least take heed to their own. Paul told Timothy to keep himself pure. He also reminded him that there is a pseudopurity that does not come from the heart but only deals with externals, such as the asceticism of the false teachers. Paul may have had their dietary regulations in mind when he instructed Timothy to take a little wine for his ailments (v. 23). Wine was frequently used for medicinal purpose in the ancient world.

INSTRUCTIONS FOR SLAVES (6:1–2)

The third problem group in the church were the slaves. Paul urged Christian slaves to be respectful of their masters, thus projecting a positive image in the community (v. 1). A particular problem had developed with the slaves of Christian masters. The slaves were using their status of equality in Christ as a basis for insubordination. Paul insisted that their shared faith should make them all the more eager to please their Christian masters.[44]

FINAL ADMONITIONS (6:3–21)

Paul concluded 1 Timothy with two words about wealth: the pitfalls of greed and enslavement to money (vv. 3–10), and the blessings of good stewardship of one's material goods (vv. 17–19). Each of these treatments is followed by a charge to Timothy: verses 11–16 and verses 20–21.

The wrong attitude toward money (vv. 3–10). Paul turned to the false teachers for the last time. He again used medical language. In contrast to the healthy teaching of Christ was the disease of the false teachers. They had a sick craving for controversy that led to a vicious cycle of social disintegration—from envy to strife to accusation to suspicion to total loss of the truth. The root problem was selfishness. Like the Ephesian silversmiths (Acts 19:23–41), they viewed religion as a means to personal gain. In verses 6–10 Paul spelled out why the craving for material goods is self-destructive. The desire for gain sets up a trap, a vicious cycle of always reaching for more, of never being content. True godliness is to be content with God's provision of the necessities of life. We do not need more than that; we cannot take it with us when we leave this life (cp. Job 1:21). Paul quoted a familiar Greek proverb when he spoke of money as a root of all kinds of evil. By it he did not imply that greed is the *sole* source of the world's ills but rather that it *is* a prime source of almost endless human grief.

In verses 11–16 Paul turned again to Timothy himself, once more urging him to fight courageously for the faith. He warned him to guard his own integrity as a man of God, fleeing the contentiousness and greed of the false teachers and pursuing the things which lead to godliness, like faith and love and steadfastness (v. 11). He reminded Timothy of his first confession of Christ before many witnesses (v. 12). He reminded him how Christ in the time of Pilate had borne the ultimate confession, a confession even to the cross (v. 13). He reminded him of the certainty that God would in his own good time bring Christ back in ultimate fulfillment of his promises (v. 14). He concluded on a triumphant doxology to the majesty of God in whom all Timothy's assurances rested (v. 15). Timothy faced difficult adversaries: the pagan cult of Ephesian Artemis, the false teachers within the church. He could take courage and fight the good fight, for the King of kings and Lord of lords had called him and stood by his side.

In verses 17–19 Paul returned to the subject of wealth, showing how wealth is not inherently evil. It can be a path of destruction for people like the false teachers who invest all their hope in it. It can, however, be a blessing for those of means who place their hope in God and who are generous with his gifts, helping the needy, being rich toward God, and thus storing up treasure for the life to come.

Verses 20–22 conclude the epistle with a final charge to Timothy to "guard the deposit," that is, to be a faithful steward of the Christian truths with which he had been entrusted. Once again Paul warned Timothy of the "pseudoknowledge" of the false teachers. He concluded with a benediction in the second person plural, indicating he was addressing the whole church. Though addressed to Timothy, ultimately the epistle was for all the Christians of Ephesus.

SETTING OF THE EPISTLE TO TITUS

Titus was one of the coworkers whom Paul often mentioned in his epistles, although not as frequently as Timothy. He was an uncircumcised Gentile. Paul took him to the Jerusalem Conference where the church leaders debated the issue of requirements for Gentile admission to the church (Gal. 2:1ff.; Acts 15:1ff.). Titus seems to have personally embodied the final agreement of the conference that Gentiles would not have to be circumcised. Titus was Paul's emissary in the extensive conflict with the Corinthian church during his third mission (2 Cor. 2:13; 7:6, 13–14). He also administered Paul's collection in Corinth along with two other brothers (2 Cor. 8:6, 16, 23; 12:18).[45] He was thus well-seasoned in dealing with difficult situations.

According to Titus 1:5, Titus was serving the churches on the island of Crete at the time of the epistle. We do not know exactly when this work was established. Possibly the ministry on Crete was founded during Paul's third mission. More likely, the work was established after Paul's release from the first Roman imprisonment. Titus 1:5 seems to indicate that Paul left Titus on Crete to further the work there. The work seems to have been fairly recently established at the time of the letter. The newness of the churches is indicated by Paul's instruction to Titus to set up leaders over the churches.

Where Paul was located when he wrote Titus is uncertain. He may have written it at the same time as 1 Timothy. There are many similarities between the two letters. If so, Paul was in Macedonia, having recently left Timothy in Ephesus (1 Tim. 1:3). According to Titus 3:12, Paul planned to spend the winter in Nicopolis on the Greek Adriatic coast and wanted Titus to join him there. When Paul later wrote 2 Timothy from his second Roman imprisonment, Titus was located in Dalmatia (2 Tim. 4:10). Dalmatia (also called Illyricum) was also on the Adriatic, north of Nicopolis. In Romans Paul spoke of having ministered in this area (Rom. 15:19). Conceivably, during this time Paul did return to this area of his work, with Titus joining him there and continuing to minister in the area. In any event, Paul seems to have been arrested and taken to Rome not long after writing Titus.

A STUDY OUTLINE OF TITUS

Salutation 1:1–4
I.   Instructions to Titus (1:5–16)
    A.   To Appoint Elders (vv. 5–9)
    B.   To Confront the False Teachers (vv. 10–16)
II. Instructions for Various Groups (2:1–15)
    A.   Older Men (vv. 1–2)
    B.   Older Women (vv. 3–5)
    C.   Young Men (vv. 6–8)
    D.   Slaves (vv. 9–10)
    E.   The Entire Congregation (vv. 11–15)
III. Reminders for the Church (3:1–11)
    A.   Their Example Toward Outsiders (vv. 1–2)
    B.   Their Experience in Christ (vv. 3–8)
    C.   The Dangers of Divisive Controversies (vv. 9–11)
IV. Personal Messages (3:12–15)

HIGHLIGHTS OF TITUS

THE SALUTATION (1:1–4)

The salutation of Titus is unique among Pauline greetings in its providing a summary of the apostle's message. It emphasizes the faith and knowledge rooted in the gospel, the assurance of eternal life based on God's eternal plan, and Paul's own role in proclaiming this salvation (vv. 2–3). Paul addressed Titus as his true child in the "common faith." By "common" he probably meant the faith shared by all peoples, as exemplified by himself, a Jew, and Titus, a Gentile.

PAUL'S INSTRUCTION TO APPOINT ELDERS (1:5–9)

The churches of Crete were new and lacked leadership. Paul began his letter by instructing Titus to select leaders. As in 1 Timothy, he listed the qualifications of good leaders. These are similar to the qualifications given for the overseer/bishop and deacons in 1 Timothy 3. In Titus 1:5 Paul spoke of elders (*presbuteroi*) and in Titus 1:7 of the "overseer" (*episcopos*). Seemingly the terms were interchangeable, referring to the same group (cp. Acts 20:17, 28). They probably refer to the same group in 1 Timothy also.

There are significant differences between the qualifications listed for overseers and deacons in 1 Timothy and those in Titus. In common are such qualities as being above reproach in the community, the husband of one wife, not given to excessive drinking, sober, hospitable. As in 1 Timothy, he is to manage his household well. His children (obviously older) are to be believers, not rowdy, and not insubordinate (v. 6). Several pairs of negative traits are listed as disqualifying. He is not to be arrogant or quick-tempered, not a drunkard or belligerent person. Positively he is to love what is good and to be holy, righteous, and self-controlled. Above all, he is to be an apt teacher of the gospel who is capable of refuting false doctrine (v. 9). In 1 Timothy Paul gave Timothy the role of confronting the false teachers; in Titus he told Titus to instruct the church leaders so that they could contend with the false doctrine. The difference may be that in Ephesus some of the church leaders had themselves been tainted with the false doctrine. The churches of Crete were new, and Paul wanted to prepare the leadership in sound doctrine from the start.

CONFRONTING THE FALSE TEACHING (1:10–16)

The false teaching on Crete was not necessarily the same as at Ephesus. It does not seem to have been very developed. What little Paul said about it is similar to the Ephesian heresy. The Jewish dimension seems to have been strong in the Cretan aberration. Paul described them as belonging to the "circumcision group" and as teaching Jewish myths and laws ("commandments," v. 14). Like the heretics of Ephesus, they taught for a "dishonest" profit (v. 11). They probably had some ascetic rules. Paul's insistence that all things are "pure" for those whose minds are pure (v. 15) sounds very much like his argument about the goodness of God's creation in 1 Timothy 4:4. In both places the Jewish and ascetic characteristics were present, much as in the false teaching of Colosse. It does not seem to have been Judaizing but a later aberration with Jewish characteristics.

In verse 12 Paul quoted Epimenides, a Cretan wonder worker of the sixth century B.C., who stated that Cretans were always liars, beasts, and lazy gluttons. Paul probably did not intend this for all those of Crete—just the false teachers. Titus was to remind the Cretan Christians of their unsavory reputation and the fact that there were *some* in their midst who fit the bill. They were ruining "whole households" (v. 11), probably some entire congregations among the house-churches of Crete. Paul's most devastating comment was his last. These would-be teachers of God in fact did not know God at all. Their actions showed this (v. 16). Paul did not give us enough to know what these disqualifying actions were, perhaps such things as their avarice and divisiveness.

THE EXEMPLARY BEHAVIOR OF VARIOUS GROUPS IN THE CHURCH (2:1–10)

In chapter 2 Paul singled out specific component groups of the church. With the exception of the final group, they are arranged by age and sex, as in 1 Timothy 5:1–2: older men (v. 2), older women (vv. 3–4), younger women (vv. 4–5), younger men (vv. 6–8), slaves (vv. 9–10). This section has often been likened to the "household orders" of Colossians and Ephesians. It is in fact a summary of Paul's instructions to the members of "God's household" in 1 Timothy 2:8–6:2.[46]

Paul described this community order as "healthy" (sound) teaching, employing the familiar medical language found in 1 Timothy (v. 1). He urged the older men of the church to be "temperate, worthy of respect, self-controlled" (v. 2). These are the same qualities expected of overseers and deacons in 1 Timothy 3. The same qualities are expected of the older women as well (v. 3; cp. 1 Tim. 3:11). The relationship is logical, since in first-century society leadership would mainly be drawn from the older population. According to 1 Timothy 2:12, women were not to teach men. Titus provides the positive counterpart: they *were* to train the younger women (v. 4). The qualities desired in these younger women were primarily domestic, the same roles recommended for the young widows in 1 Timothy 5:14. They were to be subject to their husbands (cp. 1 Tim. 2:11).

The younger men were urged to be "self-controlled" (*sōphrōn*), a quality required of *all* the groups in this section: older men (v. 2), older women (v. 4),[47] and younger women (v. 5). In verses 7–8 Paul moved from instructions for the young men to instructions for Titus himself, urging him to present himself as a model for the young men. Perhaps the linkage is indicative that Titus like Timothy was still a relatively young man. The advice to Titus largely parallels the charge to Timothy in 1 Timothy 4:11–12. Titus 2:8 presents the goal of the exemplary behavior expected from Titus—to put the opposition to shame. Their shame would be due to their having no basis for criticism of the Christians. They would also be shamed in the contrast of their own behavior with the exemplary deportment of the Christians. Who the "opponents" were is uncertain. They may have been the false teachers within the Christian community. More likely they were the outside critics of the church. A major concern running throughout 2:1–10 is that Christians should project a positive image in the larger community, that they appear above reproach (vv. 5, 8, 10).

The instruction for slaves parallels 1 Timothy 6:1–2. As there, Paul was concerned with insubordination on the part of some. Distinct to the treatment in Titus is the reference to the perennial problem of slaves stealing from their masters (vv. 9–10). Verse 10 provides the basis for Paul's concern that all Christians project a wholesome image in the community: to make the gospel attractive. Christians were to gain the trust and respect of the outside community with the goal of winning them to Christ.

THE BASIS OF THE CHRISTIAN'S EXEMPLARY BEHAVIOR (2:11–15)

Verses 11–15 provide the confessional basis for the behavior of Christians. In words reminiscent of 1 Timothy 2:4 Paul spoke of God's concern for the salvation of *all*. That obviously includes all *outside* the Christian community. The positive Christian behavior that Paul has urged throughout 2:1–10 is necessary if Christians are to gain the respect of outsiders and lead them to Christ. But even apart from its mission, consistent Christian behavior is the logical response to the grace of God which all believers have experienced. In his grace, Christ gave himself as a sacrifice to free (redeem) us from our sins (v. 14; cp. 1 Tim. 2:6; Mark 10:45). The life under grace is thus one that has repented of ungodliness and worldliness, saying no to them once and for all (v. 12). On the positive side, the person educated in God's grace will live a life which is self-controlled, morally upright, and godly. These three qualities were considered cardinal virtues by the Greek philosophers. They are minimal expectations of one saved by and trained in the grace of God.

The Christian has been saved by God's grace in the past through the redemptive work of Christ. The Christian lives by God's grace in the present. There is, of course, the future dimension to the Christian life as well. Christ appeared a first time for our redemption; he will make a second appearance (*epiphaneia*) in the future for the ultimate fulfillment of our salvation, when his full glory will be revealed. Much discussion surrounds verse 13 and whether to separate "God our Savior" from "Jesus Christ." The most natural rendering of the Greek would be that of the NIV, "our great God and Savior, Jesus Christ."[48] As in Romans 9:5, Paul seems to have professed the identity of Christ with God. God's ultimate purpose in sending Christ was to set aside ("purify") a people fit for his own possession. Christians are thus to live the pure lives of God's own people, both because they *are* God's people and live under his gracious guidance, and because they are a witness and example to the rest of the world whom God wishes to save.

Verse 15 concludes Paul's directions about the Christian community's exemplary behavior. It forms an *inclusio* (a framing device) with verse 1. These opening and concluding verses directed Titus to teach the instructions contained in verses 2–14. Paul concluded by urging Titus to be firm in his teaching, not allowing anyone to look down upon him. Perhaps, as with Timothy (1 Tim. 4:12), Titus was still young and subject to the disdain of a society that usually reserved authority for its elder members. Timothy and Titus bore a special authority, however; they were representatives of the apostle Paul himself.

CHRISTIANS AND OUTSIDERS (3:1–8)

In 3:1–8 Paul continued his emphasis on witness to outsiders. Much as in 1 Timothy 2:1–7, he spoke of being respectful of the governing authorities and the importance of living a quiet and peaceful existence in the larger community. In both places the evangelistic concern is unmistakable. In verses 3–7 Paul contrasted the former life of the Christians with their new life in Christ, giving the type of summary of the gospel that one often finds in his letters (cp. Eph. 2:1–10). The connection with verses 1–2 is close. Christians should win the trust of their fellow citizens in order to witness to them. They too once stood in the lostness of a life without Christ.

In verse 3 Paul described their former sinful life, marked by ignorance, hedonistic desires, social strife, and malice. Salvation came with the coming (epiphany) of Christ (v. 4). Salvation came through his act of mercy and not through their own meritorious deeds (v. 5). It was expressed through their being cleansed by the power of the Holy Spirit (vv. 5–6). The references to the "washing of rebirth" and the "renewal by the Holy Spirit" both refer to the Spirit's work of cleansing and providing spiritual rebirth in the lives of believers. The *symbolism* of baptism may be present in the reference to "washing," but the power and the reality of regeneration is the work of the Spirit, not of the water. Verse 7 could not be more Pauline: we have been set right with God (justified) by God's grace through Christ so that we might be joint heirs with him of life eternal (cp. Rom. 8:17).

Verses 4–7 likely preserve a confessional statement. In verse 8 Paul referred to it as a "trustworthy" (faithful) word.[49] He urged Titus to insist on these "excellent and profitable" things so that the Christians of Crete would set their minds on doing good. By "these things" he probably meant all the exhortations from 2:1–3:2. As always his concern was that Christians lead an exemplary lifestyle which would be a beacon in the community, lighting the way to Christ.

AVOIDING MINDLESS CONTROVERSIES (3:9–11)

Paul concluded the body of his letter by returning to the subject of the false teachers. The Jewish elements of the teaching are again evident (cp. 1:10–16). The heretics argued over genealogies (probably those of Genesis) and quibbled about the law (probably the Jewish law). What concerned Paul most was not the actual content of their teaching but their divisiveness. He urged Titus to shun such people who tore up the fellowship (cp. Rom. 16:17–20). In accordance with the instructions of Jesus in Matthew 18:15–17, they were to be disciplined only after at least two warnings. In reality, their excommunication was their own doing. Their thinking had become perverted, and they stood self-condemned.

PAUL'S PERSONAL MESSAGES TO TITUS (3:12–15)

Paul concluded the letter with some personal instructions to Titus and with his customary final "grace greeting." First, he urged Titus to hasten to him at Nicopolis, where he planned to spend the winter himself. Titus was to come as soon as Paul sent someone to replace him in the ministry on Crete. It was to be either Artemas or Tychicus. At this point Paul was not sure which. Tychicus was one of Paul's most trusted coworkers. He had been a member of the delegation that accompanied Paul to Jerusalem with the collection (Acts 20:4). He was Paul's personal emissary who carried the letters from the imprisoned Paul to the churches of Asia Minor, the circular Ephesian epistle and those to Colosse and Philemon (Eph. 6:21; Col. 4:7). We know nothing else about Artemas apart from the reference in Titus. Judging from 2 Timothy 4:12, Paul sent Tychicus a couple of years later to Ephesus to replace Timothy. Tychicus thus does not seem to have been occupied with Crete at that time. It is thus quite possible that Artemas was sent as the replacement for Titus.

In verse 13 Paul urged Titus to provide for the needs of Zenas the lawyer and Apollos. Quite likely the pair of travelers had brought the letter from Paul to Titus. They were journeying on farther, and Paul urged Titus to see that the Christian community send them forth with the necessary provisions for their trip. We know nothing more about Zenas, but Apollos is a well-known New Testament figure. He worked with Aquila and Priscilla at Ephesus (Acts 18:24–26). From there he went to Corinth and continued the ministry which Paul had begun there (Acts 18:27–19:1; 1 Cor. 1:12; 3:4–6, 22; 4:6; 16:12). He evidently continued serving as a Christian missionary. From the time of the church fathers he has sometimes been proposed as the author of Hebrews, but that is speculative. He and Zenas were probably on mission, but where they were headed after Crete is anybody's guess.

PAUL'S CIRCUMSTANCES AFTER WRITING TITUS

Paul concluded the letter to Titus with his typical exchange of greetings (v. 15). A final grace-benediction was given to "all of you," which would indicate that Paul intended for Titus to share the letter with the Christians of Crete. What then happened to Paul is uncertain. The striking resemblances between 1 Timothy and Titus indicate that Paul wrote the two letters at the same time. According to 1 Timothy 1:3, Paul was in Macedonia. He hoped to come to Timothy at Ephesus soon (1 Tim. 3:14). On the other hand, he planned to spend the winter on the western coast of Greece at Nicopolis (Titus 3:12). Second Timothy was probably written a year or two later from prison in Rome. According to 2 Timothy 4:13, Paul had left a coat, some books, and some parchments at Troas. He wanted Timothy to bring them to him.

What happened to Paul between the writing of 1 Timothy and Titus and his second Roman imprisonment? Did he succeed in returning to Ephesus? When did he leave the things in Troas—on the return trip to Ephesus, or earlier, when he traveled to Macedonia, before writing 1 Timothy and Titus? Did he ever get to Nicopolis? Where was he arrested—in Macedonia, Troas, Nicopolis, or even in Rome itself? We have seen the pieces of the puzzle. How to put them together is guesswork. What does seem a likelihood is that somewhere, sometime after the writing of Titus, Paul was arrested and once again imprisoned in Rome. This time the circumstances were different. Nero had been persecuting the Roman Christians. Paul no longer enjoyed a liberal household custody as in his former imprisonment. Now he suffered a much harsher confinement and faced a far bleaker general prospect.

NOTES

1. L. T. Johnson rightly emphasizes the importance of considering each in its separate setting rather than viewing the three exclusively as a group: *Letters to Paul's Delegates,* The New Testament in Context (Valley Forge, Penn.: Trinity Press International, 1996), 32–33.

2. For example, F. F. Bruce, "The Enigma of Paul: Why Did the Early Church's Great Liberator Get a Reputation as an Authoritarian?" *Bible Review* 4 (1988): 32–33.

3. For the history of the authorship debate, see E. E. Ellis, "Pastoral Letters," in *Dictionary of Paul and His Letters,* ed. G. F. Hawthorne and R. P. Martin (Downers Grove, Ill.: InterVarsity, 1993), 659–660.

4. J. D. Quinn suggests that there were two separate Pauline collections—one for church letters, the other for letters to individuals. He sees P⁴⁶ as a "church collection," which would not have included Philemon or the Pastorals: "P⁴⁶—the Pauline Canon?" *Catholic Biblical Quarterly* 36 (1974): 379–385.

5. The fullest argument against Pauline authorship based on language and style is that of P. N. Harrison, *The Problem of the Pastoral Epistles* (London: Oxford University Press, 1921). Guthrie has shown that the language of the Pastorals is for the most part not distinctive of the second century but well evidenced in Greek literature prior to A.D. 50: D. Guthrie, *The Pastoral Epistles and the Mind of Paul* (London: Tyndale, 1955), 6–12. For a recent stylistic analysis, see K. J. Neumann, *The Authenticity of the Pauline Epistles in the Light of Stylostatistical Analysis,* SBL Dissertation Series #120 (Atlanta: Scholars, 1990). B. M. Metzger's observation is still valid that the Pastorals do not provide sufficient vocabulary to draw statistically valid conclusions: "A Reconsideration of Certain Arguments Against the Pauline Authorship of the Pastoral Epistles," *Expository Times* 70 (1958–1959): 91–94.

6. Harrison espoused this position, as did E. F. Scott, *The Pastoral Epistles,* Moffatt New Testament Commentary (New York: Harper, 1936), xxxvi–xxxviii.

7. C. F. D. Moule, "The Problem of the Pastoral Epistles: A Reappraisal," *Bulletin of the John Rylands Library* 47 (1964–1965): 430–452.

8. S. G. Wilson, *Luke and the Pastoral Epistles* (London: S.P.C.K., 1979).

9. J. D. Quinn, "The Last Volume of Luke: The Relation of Luke-Acts to the Pastoral Epistles," *Perspectives on Luke-Acts,* ed. C. H. Talbert (Edinburgh: T. and T. Clark, 1978), 62–75.

10. G. W. Knight III, *The Pastoral Epistles,* The New International Greek Testament Commentary (Grand Rapids: Eerdmans, 1992), 50–51.

11. J. M. Ford, "A Note on Proto-Montanism in the Pastoral Epistles," *New Testament Studies* 17 (1971): 338–346. M. Goulder sees a form of Jewish mysticism reflected in the Pastorals: "The Pastor's Wolves: Jewish Christian Visionaries Behind the Pastoral Epistles," *Novum Testamentum* 38 (1996): 242–256.

12. R. J. Karris, "The Background and Significance of the Polemic of the Pastoral Epistles," *Journal of Biblical Literature* 92 (1973): 549–563.

13. J. M. Bassler, *1 Timothy, 2 Timothy, Titus,* Abingdon New Testament Commentaries (Nashville: Abingdon, 1996), 24–31.

14. D. C. Verner, *The Household of God, the Social World of the Pastoral Epistles,* SBL Dissertation Series #71 (Chico, Calif.: Scholars, 1981), 175–180.

15. For a discussion of the setting of the heresy within the ministry of Paul, see P. H. Towner, "Gnosis and Realized Eschatology in Ephesus (of the Pastoral Epistles) and the Corinthian Enthusiasm," *Journal for the Study of the New Testament* 31 (1987): 95–124.

16. P. H. Towner, "The Present Age in the Eschatology of the Pastoral Epistles," *New Testament Studies* 32 (1986): 427–448. See also R. M. Kidd, *Wealth and Beneficence in the Pastoral Epistles*, SBL Dissertation Series #132 (Atlanta: Scholars, 1990), 185–194.

17. I. H. Marshall, "The Christology of the Pastoral Epistles," *Studien zum neuen Testament und seiner Umwelt* 13 (1988): 157–177.

18. M. A. Haykin, "The Fading Vision? The Spirit and Freedom in the Pastoral Epistles," *Evangelical Quarterly* 57 (1985): 291–305.

19. I. H. Marshall, "Faith and Works in the Pastoral Epistles," *Studien zum neuen Testament und seiner Umwelt* 9 (1984): 203–218.

20. J. P. Meier, "*Presbyteros* in the Pastoral Epistles," *Catholic Biblical Quarterly* 35 (1973): 323–345.

21. M. Dibelius and H. Conzelmann, *The Pastoral Epistles*, trans. P. Buttolph and A. Yarbro, Hermeneia (Philadelphia: Fortress, 1972).

22. A. J. Malherbe, "Paulus Senex," *Restoration Quarterly* 36 (1994): 197–207.

23. The exploitative element is emphasized by L. A. Brown, "Asceticism and Ideology: The Language of Power in the Pastoral Epistles," *Semeia* 57 (1992): 77–94; W. Munro, *Authority in Paul and Peter*, SNTS Monograph Series #45 (London: Cambridge University Press, 1983); M. McDonald, *The Pauline Churches: A Socio-historical Study of Institutionalization in the Pauline and Deutero-Pauline Writings*, SNTS Monograph Series #60 (New York: Cambridge University Press, 1988), 159–238.

24. E. E. Ellis, "The Pastorals and Paul," *Expository Times* 104 (1992–1993): 45–47.

25. R. E. Brown, *The Churches the Apostles Left Behind* (New York: Paulist, 1984), 31–46. See Also D. Horrell, "Converging Ideologies: Berger and Luckmann and the Pastoral Epistles," *Journal for the Study of the New Testament* 50 (1993): 85–103.

26. H. Ponsot, "Les Pastorales, Seraient-elles les premières lettres de Paul?" *Lumière et Vie* 231 (1997) 83–93, 232 (1997) 79–90, 233 (1997) 83–89.

27. J. V. Bartlet, "The Historic Setting of the Pastoral Epistles," *The Expositor*, series 8.5 (1913): 325–347.

28. Johnson, *Letters to Paul's Delegates*, 10–11; B. Reicke, "Chronologie der Pastoralebriefe," *Theologische Literaturzeitung* 101 (1976): 81–94; G. S. Duncan, *St. Paul's Ephesian Ministry* (London: 1929).

29. For a discussion of the evidence for Paul's release from the first Roman imprisonment, see chapter 18. See also M. Prior, *Paul the Letter-Writer and the Second Letter to Timothy*, JSNT Supplement Series #23 (Sheffield: Academic Press, 1989), 81–83; O. F. Meinardus, "Paul's Missionary Journey to Spain: Tradition and Folklore," *Biblical Archaeologist* 41 (1978): 61–68.

30. The carefully placed personal material in the Pastorals would make the pseudonymity deliberate and blatant; the imitator would have *intended to deceive*: L. R. Donelson, *Pseudepigraphy and Ethical Argument in the Pastoral Epistles* (Tübingen: Mohr/Siebeck, 1986).

31. G. D. Fee, "Reflections on Church Order in the Pastoral Epistles, with Further Reflection on the Hermeneutics of *Ad Hoc* Documents," *Journal of the Evangelical Theological Society* 28 (1985): 141–151.

32. S. Westerholm, "The Law and the 'Just Man' (1 Tim. 1:3–11)," *Studia Theologica* 36 (1982): 79–95.

33. N. J. McEleney, "The Vice Lists of the Pastoral Epistles," *Catholic Biblical Quarterly* 36 (1974): 204–210.

34. A. J. Malherbe, *Paul and the Popular Philosophers* (Minneapolis: Fortress, 1989), 121–136.

35. Alan Padgett, "Wealthy Women at Ephesus: 1 Timothy 2:8–15 in Social Context," *Interpretation* 41 (1987): 19–31. See also G. D. Fee, "Issues in Evangelical Hermeneutics, Part III: The Great Watershed—Intentionality and Particularity/Eternity: 1 Timothy 2:8–15 as a Test Case," *Crux* 26 (1980): 31–37.

36. To "exercise authority" seems to be the correct understanding of *authenteō* rather than "to domineer": G. W. Knight, "ΑΥΘΕΝΤΕΩ in Reference to Women in 1 Timothy 2:12," *New Testament Studies* 30 (1984): 143–157.

37. Dibelius and Conzelmann, *The Pastoral Epistles*, 50–51.

38. E. Glasscock, "The 'Husband of One Wife' Requirement in 1 Timothy 3:2," *Bibliotheca Sacra* 140 (1983): 244–258.

39. R. H. Gundry, "The Form, Meaning and Background of the Hymn Quoted in 1 Timothy 3:16," in *Apostolic History and the Gospel*, ed. W. W. Gasque and R. P. Martin (Grand Rapids: Eerdmans, 1970), 203–222.

40. J. M. Bassler, "The Widow's Tale: A Fresh Look at 1 Tim. 5:3–16," *Journal of Biblical Literature* 103 (1984): 23–41.

41. Kidd, *Wealth and Beneficence*, 102–106.

42. Verner, *Household of God*, 161–166.

43. J. P. Meier argues that verses 17–25 form a chiasm: "*Presbyteros* in the Pastoral Epistles," 325–337.

44. Kidd, *Wealth and Beneficence*, 140–156. Kidd argues that *the masters* should be seen as the "benefactors" of verse 2.

45. For the unlikely possibility that Titus was Luke's *brother*, see A. Souter, "A Suggested Relationship Between Titus and Luke," *Expository Times* 18 (1906–1907): 285.

46. This is strong evidence that Paul wrote 1 Timothy and Titus at the same time. Titus is almost a condensation of 1 Timothy.

47. Verbal form of *sōphrōn*, meaning "restraining, training in self-control" and translated as "train" in NIV.

48. M. J. Harris, "Titus 2:13 and the Deity of Christ," in *Pauline Studies*, ed. D. Hagner and M. J. Harris (Grand Rapids: Eerdmans, 1980), 262–277.

49. G. W. Knight III, *The Faithful Sayings in the Pastoral Letters* (Grand Rapids: Baker, 1979), 80–111.

SELECTED COMMENTARIES ON THE PASTORAL EPISTLES

BASED ON THE GREEK TEXT

Dibelius, Martin and Hans Conzelmann. *The Pastoral Epistles*. Trans. P. Buttolph and A. Yarbro. Hermeneia. Philadelphia: Fortress, 1972.

Knight, George W. III. *The Pastoral Epistles*. The New International Greek Testament Commentary. Grand Rapids: Eerdmans, 1992.

Lock, Walter. *A Critical and Exegetical Commentary on the Pastoral Epistles*. The International Critical Commentary. Edinburgh: T. & T. Clark, 1924.

BASED ON THE ENGLISH TEXT

Barrett, Charles K. *The Pastoral Epistles*. The New Clarendon Bible. Oxford: Oxford University Press, 1963.

Bassler, Jouette M. *1 Timothy, 2 Timothy, Titus*. Abingdon New Testament Commentaries. Nashville: Abingdon, 1996.

Davies, M. *The Pastoral Epistles: I and II Timothy and Titus*. Epworth Commentaries. London: Epworth, 1996.

Easton, Burton S. *The Pastoral Epistles*. New York: Scribner's, 1948.

Fee, Gordon D. *1 and 2 Timothy, Titus*. Good News Commentaries. San Francisco: Harper and Row, 1984.

Fee, Gordon D. *1 & 2 Timothy and Titus*. New International Biblical Commentary. Peabody, Mass.: Hendrickson, 1988.

Guthrie, Donald. *The Pastoral Epistles: An Introduction and Commentary*. Second edition. The Tyndale New Testament Commentaries. Grand Rapids: Eerdmans, 1990.

Hanson, A. T. *The Pastoral Epistles*. New Century Bible Commentary. Grand Rapids: Eerdmans, 1982.

Houlden, James L. *The Pastoral Epistles: I and II Timothy, Titus*. The Pelican New Testament Commentaries. New York: Penguin Books, 1976.

Hultgren, Arland J. *I–II Timothy, Titus*. Augsburg Commentary on the New Testament. Minneapolis: Augsburg, 1984.

Johnson, Luke Timothy. *Letters to Paul's Delegates*. The New Testament in Context. Valley Forge, Penn.: Trinity Press International, 1996.

Kelley, John N. D. *A Commentary on the Pastoral Epistles*. Black's New Testament Commentaries. London: Black, 1963.

Lea, Thomas E. and Hayne P. Griffin Jr. *1, 2 Timothy, Titus*. The New American Commentary. Nashville: Broadman, 1992.

Oden, T. C. *First and Second Timothy and Titus*. Interpretation. Louisville: Knox, 1989.

Quinn, Jerome D. *The Letter to Titus: A New Translation with Notes and Commentary and an Introduction to Titus, I and II Timothy, the Pastoral Epistles*. Anchor Bible. New York: Doubleday, 1990.

Scott, E. F. *The Pastoral Epistles*. The Moffatt New Testament Commentary. New York: Harper and Brothers, 1936.

Towner, Philip H. *1–2 Timothy and Titus*. IVP New Testament Commentary Series. Downers Grove, Ill.: InterVarsity, 1994.

20

"To Die Is Gain"

*T*he New Testament is silent about Paul's final years. The Acts account ends with his two-year house arrest in Rome. Some scholars believe Paul's career ended at that point, that his trial went badly and that he was martyred at that time. In the previous chapter we have taken the position that Paul was released from this first Roman imprisonment and that he returned to work in the churches of the east. Some ancient sources like 1 Clement 5 and the Muratorian Canon indicate that Paul also worked for a while in Spain during this period, although we have no early narratives dealing with a Spanish mission. In his *Ecclesiastical History* 2.22, Eusebius related the tradition of Paul's release, saying that when he visited the city a second time he suffered martyrdom under Nero.[1] The best evidence for Paul's release is the existence of the three Pastoral Epistles. The personal details in the Pastorals are most easily accounted for as having occurred subsequent to the Roman imprisonment of Acts 28. On this assumption, 1 Timothy and Titus would have been written during a further period of ministry in Asia and Macedonia after Paul's release. The personal details in 2 Timothy point to a still later period, that of a second Roman imprisonment, when Paul's prospects were far more ominous and another release was unlikely.

THE SECOND IMPRISONMENT

If Paul was arrested a second time and eventually martyred, what would account for the change of mood between his two times in prison? The first imprisonment was brought about by the accusations of the Palestinian Jews against Paul. The narrative of Acts 28:17–31 may imply that Paul's case never came to trial. In any event, it seems to have gone well with Paul, and he was released. The accusers at the second trial were probably not the Jews but the Romans. The different mood was due to the emperor himself and his effort to make the Christians a scapegoat for the great fire of Rome.

The fire broke out in the summer of A.D. 64. It seems to have originated in some shops in the Circus Maximus that were stocked with inflammable goods. A long dry spell and a strong breeze combined to envelop much of the city in flames. The fire raged unabated for six nights and seven days. Tacitus gives a full account of the conflagration and its aftermath (*Annals* 15.38–44).[2] Of the fourteen divisions of the city,

426

three were reduced to ashes, and seven others suffered major devastation. Rumors quickly circulated that soldiers had been seen running here and there with firebrands and that the emperor himself had ordered the burning of the city to make way for his grandiose urban renewal program. It was even said that he positioned himself on the palace roof and gave a performance of *The Destruction of Troy* as the city burned beneath him. To scotch such rumors, Nero sought a scapegoat and latched onto the Christians. Christians were rounded up and forced to inform on their fellows. Great numbers were arrested, summarily sentenced, and executed in the most cruel manner. Some were enshrouded in the skins of wild animals and thrown to dogs that tore them to pieces. Others were impaled on stakes and set afire at night to serve as torches in Nero's gardens. Tacitus did not himself have a very high opinion of the Christians. He considered them a pestilent lot, "loathed for their vices." Still, he noted that the Roman populace were rightly revulsed by the excesses of Nero's ferocity vented on the Christians (*Annals* 15.44).

Nero's persecution seems to have begun soon after the fire, as early as A.D. 65. The most likely explanation for Paul's arrest is his association with the Christians during the period of persecution. We are not certain where Paul was arrested. In his letter to Titus, Paul expressed his desire to spend the winter in Nicopolis on the Adriatic coast (Titus 3:12). It is possible that he was arrested there and taken to Rome.[3] It is also possible that Paul hurried to Rome when he heard that the Christians there were being persecuted. The earliest account of Paul's martyrdom is the last portion of The Acts of Paul, an apocryphal writing of the late second century.[4] The Acts of Paul is primarily a fanciful and tendentious rewriting of the story of Paul, which is based on the canonical Acts and Paul's letters. There may well be some reliable traditions embedded in it that are not covered in the New Testament, but they would be difficult to establish. According to The Acts of Paul, Paul entered Rome a free man at the time of his martyrdom and was greeted by Luke and Titus at the gates of the city. The detail about his greeters is suspect, but his free status may be accurate.[5] In any event, Paul would not have remained free for long. He would have been quickly arrested as a leader of the persecuted sect.

One can only make educated guesses when attempting to reconstruct Paul's last days. Patristic tradition places Paul's martyrdom in A.D. 68. We do not know how long his second imprisonment lasted. Paul's ministry in Spain and the east must have lasted three or four years. This would place his arrest some time around A.D. 66. This time he did not enjoy the freedom of house arrest but was confined to a more customary prison. The traditional site is the Mamertine Prison at the Roman forum. According to tradition, Peter and Paul were imprisoned there together. Guides point out a place at the top of the stairs which lead to the lower dungeon where Peter is supposed to have struck his head, leaving a pronounced indentation in the solid rock. In the dungeon beneath is a pool of water where the two apostles are said to have baptized their guards, Processus and Martinianus, who themselves also later became martyrs.

All of this is quite fanciful, of course. Peter and Paul do not seem to have been imprisoned or martyred at the same time, despite a persistent tradition to that effect. Paul probably was not taken to the Mamertine Prison. It was used primarily for significant political prisoners of the state, not leaders of a persecuted religious sect. Paul may possibly have been held in a cell at the Praetorian barracks.[6] We simply do not know.

INTRODUCTION TO 2 TIMOTHY

According to Eusebius, Paul wrote 2 Timothy during his second Roman imprisonment. He noted how Paul indicated in the epistle that his martyrdom was at hand (*Eccl. Hist.* 2.22). Eusebius was undoubtedly referring to the familiar "fought the good fight passage" (2 Tim. 4:6–8). Paul reflected a spirit of resignation, of loneliness and abandonment in the epistle. At the same time he was ready to end the race. He felt good about his ministry and was ready to entrust the work to others like Timothy.

Second Timothy has much in common with the first epistle. In both, Paul devoted considerable space to the threat of the false teachers. In both, women seem to have been vulnerable to the erroneous teaching (2 Tim. 3:6–7). From 2 Timothy we learn that the teachers taught the resurrection had already taken place (2 Tim. 2:18). Evidently, the two whom Paul had previously disciplined in Ephesus were still active (cp. 1 Tim. 1:20): Hymenaeus was one of those teaching that the resurrection had already occurred (2 Tim. 2:17), and Alexander had caused Paul considerable harm (2 Tim. 4:14). In 2 Timothy other Asians are mentioned as having deserted Paul, such as Phygelus and Hermogenes (1:15) or as having participated in the false teaching, such as Philetus (2:17). There were friends as well among the Asians. Outstanding among them was Onesiphorus (2 Tim. 1:16; 4:19).[7] It is possible that Timothy was no longer in Ephesus when Paul wrote the second epistle; 2 Timothy 4:12 may indicate as much. On the other hand, Paul may have been sending Tychicus to Ephesus as Timothy's replacement. The personalia of the letter point to Ephesus, and the problems in the church appear to be the same as those addressed in the first epistle. The most likely conclusion is that Timothy was still in Ephesus or the general region of Asia Minor.

For all they have in common, 2 Timothy differs from the first epistle in significant ways. For example, Paul gave no instructions about church order. He wanted Timothy to leave the church and come to his side; regulating the church was now in Tychicus's hand. Paul was much more concerned to exhort Timothy to be faithful to his ministry. The first epistle contained several similar charges (4:1–16; 6:11–21), but they are more pervasive in the second epistle. Paul may have realized that Timothy did not want to miss his sharing these final words of advice with him. Because Paul repeatedly urged Timothy to be strong, persistent, and courageous, some have seen him as being somewhat weak and insecure. This need not have been the case at all. Paul's strong encouragement was probably due more to Paul's own personal situation than to Timothy's character. Facing death, Paul knew he would be turning the helm over altogether to coworkers like Timothy. The apostle was used to overseeing his entire ministry. He had always depended on faithful coworkers to serve as his right arm in the churches, among whom Timothy was foremost (cp. Phil. 2:20–22). It wasn't that Timothy was weak. It was rather that the two had always shared the bond of father and son in the faith. As Timothy's spiritual father, Paul used this one final opportunity to remind his "son" of the things that really counted in his ministry. Ministers of every generation since have owed a debt of gratitude to Paul's advice to Timothy. Through his instructions to Timothy, Paul has in a real sense become their own father in the ministry.

Of the three Pastorals, 2 Timothy is by far the most personal in tone. The personalia of the letter are more extensive, particularly the concluding section (4:9–20). Even among those who deny the Pauline authorship of the Pastorals, many would see these personal details as genuine fragments of the apostle's correspondence. Some have even maintained that 2 Timothy is an authentic letter while seeing the other two Pastorals as pseudepigraphical.[8] As we have argued in the previous chapter, the most likely solution is to see all three as products of Paul's final years of ministry. It is interesting, however, that even some of the more skeptical have granted that 2 Timothy betrays the familiar style and passion of the apostle.

Second Timothy has often been described as Paul's "last will and testament," as his "farewell discourse." It is indeed probably his last extant letter. It really does not fit the genre of a farewell discourse, however. Paul did not formally pass on his ministry to Timothy. Instead, he challenged Timothy to exercise his gifts for ministry to the fullest extent, and he presented himself as a model. Second Timothy is more like the protreptic literature of the Greek philosophers in which a father passes advice on to his son. L. T. Johnson labels it a "paraenetic" letter (a letter of exhortation).[9] This suggestion seems to fit best the overall content of the letter. Paul's expressed purpose in the letter was to summon Timothy to his side (2 Tim. 4:9). On the other hand, judging from the actual content of the letter, Paul was equally concerned to challenge Timothy to the faithful discharge of his ministerial calling and to present Timothy with models for ministry.

A STUDY OUTLINE OF 2 TIMOTHY

Salutation (1:1–2)
I. Following Good Examples (1:3–2:13)
   A. The Example of Godly Forebears (1:3–5)
   B. The Example of Paul (1:6–14)
   C. The Good and Bad Examples of the Asians (1:15–18)
   D. Examples from the Secular World (2:1–7)
   E. The Example of Christ (2:8–13)
II. Rightly Dividing the Word of Truth (2:14–3:9)
   A. Confronting Unhealthy Teaching (2:14–21)
   B. Instructing with Kindness and Gentleness (2:22–26)
   C. Avoiding the Ways of the False Teachers (3:1–9)
III. Thoroughly Equipped for Ministry (3:10–4:8)
   A. Instructed in the Word (3:10–17)
   B. Faithful in Ministry (4:1–5)
   C. Steadfast to the End (4:6–8)
IV. Personal Matters (4:9–22)
   A. Instructions to Timothy (vv. 9–15)
   B. The First Defense (vv. 16–18)
   C. Exchange of Greetings (vv. 19–22)

HIGHLIGHTS OF 2 TIMOTHY

THE SALUTATION (1:1–2)

The salutation of 2 Timothy (1:1–2) is very similar to that of 1 Timothy. Paul addressed Timothy as his "son" and used the threefold benediction of "grace, mercy, and peace." In other respects the salutation of 2 Timothy resembles Paul's other epistles. Paul noted that his apostleship was "by the will of God," as in the two Corinthian epistles, Colossians, and Ephesians. He used his familiar "in Christ" language to express the certainty of life eternal through union with Christ.

FOLLOWING GOOD EXAMPLES (1:3–2:13)

The opening section of the epistle presents a series of models for Timothy to follow in his ministry. The first model is that of his forebears (1:3–5). The form is Paul's customary opening thanksgiving and prayer. The emphasis is on Timothy's predecessors in the faith, whom he is called upon to emulate. First there is Paul himself (v. 3). His "clear conscience" was because he had been faithful to God in the discharge of his ministry. The mention of "forebears" in verse 3 probably anticipates verse 5 with its reference to Timothy's grandmother Lois and mother Eunice. According to Acts 16:1, Eunice was a Christian. Second Timothy 1:5 indicates that Lois was as well. They were from Lystra and were probably converted along with Timothy during the course of Paul's first missionary journey. Before their conversion Lois and Eunice seem to have been pious Jews who trained Timothy in the Scripture from the time of his infancy (2 Tim. 3:15). They had been models of faith in God throughout Timothy's childhood. Paul knew Timothy well. He needed no proof of Timothy's faith. But we all need to return periodically to our roots in order to renew and fortify our faith, and Paul was calling Timothy back to those roots.

When Paul spoke of Timothy's "tears" in verse 4, he probably had in mind their parting when Paul left Timothy behind in Ephesus and moved on to Macedonia (1 Tim. 1:3). In any event, verse 4 presents at the very outset of the letter Paul's major expressed purpose for writing: he wanted to see Timothy. Things were not going well in Paul's imprisonment. He knew that the "time of [his] departure" was near (4:6). He wanted to see Timothy one last time before his death (4:9).

The example of Paul (1:6–14). Throughout the letter Paul presented himself as a model for Timothy. Paul had been Timothy's mentor from the very start. He reminded Timothy of his own personal role in kindling the gift of God through his laying hands on him. This is usually seen as a reference to Timothy's ordination, the same occasion as when the elders laid their hands on Timothy (1 Tim. 4:14). But in the Book of Acts the laying on of hands is also connected with conversion and the receipt of the Spirit at that time (cp. Acts 9:17; 19:6). Paul may have been reminding Timothy of the time when he first believed and received the gift of the Spirit. In that light, verse 7 may not be referring to Timothy's human spirit but to God's Holy Spirit. Paul would have been calling Timothy to yield himself to God and to the power of his Spirit.[10] Verses 6–7 thus form an *inclusio* with verse 14, where the Spirit is explicitly mentioned.

In verse 8 Paul continued the emphasis on the power of God's Spirit. His point was that God's power would grant Timothy the courage to bear witness to Christ, even if that should involve suffering. Through the remainder of chapter 1, the theme of "not being ashamed" runs like a thread (vv. 8, 12, 16). The context is that of the Christian persecution and of Paul's imprisonment. Paul urged Timothy not to be ashamed either of Christ or of his own imprisonment (v. 8). He then proceeded to set forth in greater detail the objects for which Timothy should feel no shame: the gospel of Christ (vv. 9–10), and Paul's own ministry (vv. 11–12).

Paul was not ashamed of bearing witness to the gospel of God's atoning work in Christ: "It is the power of God for the salvation of everyone who believes" (Rom. 1:16). In 2 Timothy 1:9–10 Paul expounded on God's saving work in Christ with a terse summary of the gospel. God planned it from all eternity. He revealed it in the coming (epiphany) of Christ to earth. He accomplished it through the work of Christ, destroying death and bringing life and immortality in him. This salvation was not of our own doing but solely due to God's own grace, though through it God calls us to a holy life. In the Neronic persecution Christians were tempted to deny the name of Christ in order to save their lives. Paul reminded Timothy that eternal life lies alone in a positive response to what God has done in Christ.

Paul was not ashamed of Christ. He lay in prison in Rome precisely because of his witness to the gospel. He now called on Timothy to follow his example of bold witness, even if it should lead to suffering (vv. 11–12). Paul described himself as a herald, an apostle, and a teacher. The herald proclaims the gospel. The apostle goes forth to share the gospel with those who have not heard it. The teacher applies the lessons of the gospel to life. Paul had fulfilled all of these roles and lay in chains for having done so. Paul was faithful to his calling because he trusted in the faithfulness of the God who had called him. Verse 12 is ambiguous. It literally speaks of "my trust" and could refer either to the gospel which God had entrusted to Paul or to Paul's life that he had entrusted to God. In the context, the latter is the more likely. Paul could be bold, unashamed, even willing to suffer in his testimony to Christ, because the God who had called him was trustworthy. Paul was secure in the promises of a gracious God who would keep him safely in trust until the life to come.

Verses 13 and 14 apply the lesson to Timothy, calling upon him to follow Paul's example. Once again Paul talked of the sacred trust. This time he meant the true gospel which he had shared with Timothy. He called on Timothy to guard it against falsehood and to teach it faithfully and in love. God's Spirit would empower him to discharge his ministry faithfully (v. 14; cp. v. 6).

The good and the bad examples of the Asians (1:15–18). Evidently not everyone had been unashamed of Paul or of his gospel. Perhaps, having heard of his imprisonment some had deserted Paul. It must have involved a great number of persons, since Paul spoke of "everyone" abandoning him (v. 15). He specifically mentioned two, who must have once been loyal to Paul. We know nothing more of Phygelus and Hermogenes. They may have joined the false teachers. They may simply have denied all acquaintance with the imprisoned apostle, perhaps out of concern for their own safety. In any event, they were negative examples for Timothy, those who proved to be "ashamed" of the gospel.

In contrast was the positive example of Onesiphorus (vv. 16–18). Onesiphorus was an Ephesian who had evidently come to Rome to see Paul.[11] Paul must have been in an unusual place of imprisonment, because Onesiphorus had considerable difficulty finding him. When he finally did so, he ministered to Paul, probably "refreshing" him with physical as well as spiritual provision. He was "not ashamed" of Paul's chains (v. 16). One must bear in mind that Paul was now a political prisoner, probably charged with crimes against the state. To visit Paul under such circumstances would have likely been at considerable personal risk. Paul expressed his gratitude toward Onesiphorus by wishing that he would experience God's mercy on the last day (v. 18) and by wishing God's mercy on his household (v. 16). Both wishes may indicate that Onesiphorus was dead when Paul wrote 2 Timothy.

Examples from the secular world (2:1–7). In 2:1 Paul returned to his charge to Timothy, encouraging him to allow God to strengthen him "in the grace that is in Christ Jesus." It is Paul's "mystical" language: all Christian ministry is performed within the sphere of God's grace. Ministers work in the power of grace; they breathe the air of grace. Verse 2 has often been viewed as depicting "apostolic succession," with the presence of witnesses indicating ordination and the passing of the teaching from one group to another in a succession within the ranks of ministers. The phrase "in the presence of many witnesses" would better be translated "through many witnesses."[12] The witnesses are not witnesses to ordination but witnesses to Paul's preaching. Paul's concern was not with a legitimate succession of ministers but with a faithful transmission of the Word. Verse 3 serves as a heading for verses 4–7. If Timothy is to be a faithful minister of Christ, he must serve as a soldier of Christ, and soldiers can expect their share of hardship and suffering.

Paul returned to the theme of examples in verses 4–7. Here the examples are three models taken from secular life—the soldier, the athlete, and the farmer. Paul used the same three examples in 1 Corinthians 9. There the examples of the soldier and the farmer illustrated how the workman is worthy of his hire (1 Cor. 9:7). The example of the athlete emphasized the need for rigorous discipline and training (1 Cor. 9:24–27). In 2 Timothy the main emphases are on hardship and effort and on future reward. The soldier gives his undivided attention and loyalty to his commanding officer and does not allow himself to be distracted by outside concerns. The soldier of Christ likewise concentrates on his commander, Christ. The athlete competes by the rules. In the Olympic games, the rules prescribed a rigorous training period of ten months before one could participate in the games (Pausanias, *Description of Greece* 5.24.9). The successful athlete received a victor's crown. The farmer likewise could expect to receive from the fruits of his labor. The idea of reward was present in each of Paul's metaphors: the faithful servant of Christ can expect the eschatological reward. But the ideas of concentrated service, discipline, and hardship are the strongest emphases in the three metaphors. The servant of Christ can expect a share in hardship.

The example of Christ (2:8–13). The supreme example for every believer is Christ himself. Christ suffered and died; the faithful servant of Christ must be willing to share in suffering. Paul often saw his ministry in terms of sharing Christ's sufferings (cp. Rom. 8:17; Col. 1:24). He was doing so now in the confines of a Roman prison, treated like a common criminal (v. 9). Yet, though he was in chains, the gospel itself remained unchained, just as it had in an earlier imprisonment (Phil. 1:12–18), just as it had in his first Roman imprisonment (Acts 28:30–31). Paul had no doubts about his own salvation; God would hold him in trust until the final day (2 Tim. 1:12). Paul wanted all God's chosen to experience the same assurance of salvation, and so he boldly shared the gospel, willing to endure whatever hardship might result, whether chains or even death. He urged Timothy to have the same resolve, the same willingness to suffer.

The reminder of Christ's suffering and of his own suffering led Paul to include a fifth and final "faithful saying."[13] Like the others, this one is confessional and poetic. Paul may have taken it from the worship of the church. More likely, he composed it himself; it is thoroughly within his own language and thought. It consists of four balanced couplets, each beginning with a conditional ("if") clause. The first looks to the initial Christian conversion experience of dying with Christ and rising to new life (cp. Rom. 6:8). The second focuses on perseverance: if we endure in our commitment to Christ, we will reign with him in his heavenly kingdom. The third couplet is the tragic counterpart to the other two. If we deny him, he will deny us at the final judgment. The statement ultimately goes back to Jesus himself (Matt. 10:33). The fourth is the most difficult to interpret: "If we are faithless, he will remain faithful, for he cannot disown himself." It can be taken negatively to mean that God is true to his nature as a just God. If we are faithless (in the sense of "unbelieving"), he will be just and condemn us. More often the couplet is taken in a more positive sense, as a softening of the statement about denial. The denial couplet dealt with unbelievers. The last couplet is seen to refer to believers and to mean that God remains true to his own and will not go back on his promises even when his people fail him.

RIGHTLY DIVIDING THE WORD OF TRUTH (2:14–3:9)

All of this middle portion of 2 Timothy is directed against the false teaching. Although the problems in Ephesus were foremost in his mind, Paul probably intended on instructing Timothy about the confrontation of error in broad terms. Throughout this section he contrasted the ways of faithful ministers of the gospel with those of the errorists.

Confronting unhealthy teaching (2:14–21). Paul urged Timothy to instruct his people both positively and negatively. Positively, he was to remind them of the truth of the gospel and the need for perseverance, as he had just set it forth in the "faithful saying" of verses 11–13. Negatively, he was to warn them about the dangers of the false teachers. Their teachings were worthless and divisive, having no redeeming value, destroying those who listened to them (v. 14). Paul's main charge against the false teachers was that they were argumentative, warring over words, dividing and perverting people with their talk. They were a sickness, like a creeping gangrene that ate at the flesh of the church (v. 17). He singled out two of the leaders of the heresy, Hymenaeus and Philetus. Hymenaeus was one of the pair that Paul had earlier put out of the church (1 Tim. 1:20). The fact that he was still having an impact on the church indicates the difficulty of the situation Timothy was facing in the Ephesian congregation. Paul pointed out a specific tenet of their false teaching: they maintained that the resurrection had already occurred (v. 18). This probably meant that they claimed believers were already perfected in the Spirit and thus already shared the life to come. Such was a common belief in later Gnostic systems. It was often accompanied by a libertine lifestyle. This may have been the case at Ephesus and a possible source of Paul's concern over the guilt-ridden consciences of some within the congregation (3:6).

Paul urged Timothy to avoid the useless, godless argumentation of the false teachers. They had missed the path, straying from the truth (v. 18). In contrast, Timothy was to make every effort to win God's approval by not being ashamed of the gospel (1:8, 12, 16) and by "correctly handling" (KJV, "rightly dividing") the word of truth (2:15). The word for "correctly handling" literally means "cutting straight" and was used of such things as fitting stone masonry, plowing straight furrows, and cutting a path. Paul may have intended a contrasting image. The false teachers had missed the path altogether; Timothy was to cut a straight path for his people in his faithful presentation of the truth of the gospel.

In verses 19–21 Paul continued his contrast of the true and the false. The true are God's own people, the church, God's solid foundation. The two quotations of verse 19 come from the account of Korah's rebellion during Israel's wilderness period. God distinguished his own true people from the rebellious followers of Korah (Num. 16:5) and urged them to separate themselves from the wicked ways of the rebels (Num.

16:26). The image of the vessels in verses 20–21 is reminiscent of Romans 9:21, though Paul's application is somewhat different. In 2 Timothy the emphasis is on becoming a clean vessel. The gold and silver vessels, the "noble" ones are the "best china," that which is used for special occasions. The "ignoble" vessels (lit. "dishonorable") are probably those used to remove refuse and excrement from the house. Paul had the false teachers in mind. He called on Timothy to keep himself pure from the filth of their ways in order that he might be a holy instrument for the master's work.

Instructing with kindness and gentleness (2:22–26). Timothy was not only to be a contrast to the false teachers in the purity of his life; he was also to differ from them in his manner of presenting the truth. They were quarrelsome and contentious, argumentative and divisive. Paul urged Timothy to take a more constructive approach. In this context, Paul's reference to Timothy's "youthful passions" probably did not refer to his sexual drive but rather to the kind of headstrong, belligerent nature that young men often display. Timothy was not to follow the ill-informed, argumentative ways of the false teachers (v. 23). Instead, he was to be gentle, a patient teacher, holding back even when personally wronged (v. 24). Paul called on Timothy to discipline others in all humility (v. 25). Who the opponents of verse 25 were is not altogether clear. Paul certainly had in mind those who had been taken in by the false teachers. He may even have had the false teachers themselves in mind; even *they* were not beyond the possibility of God's forgiveness. God could capture them from the devil's clutches if they genuinely repented (v. 26). Paul's lesson to Timothy was an important one. Even the truth when presented in a mean and contentious spirit can be divisive. But the truth spoken in love might overcome even the most stubborn opponent.[14]

Avoiding the example of the false teachers (3:1–9). In words reminiscent of 1 Timothy 4:1, Paul reminded Timothy that the last days would be "terrible times," marked by all sorts of sin and rebellion. Of course, Paul believed that in Christ the last times had already begun. The sinful lives of the false teachers already manifested this fact. He used a long vice list to describe the sins of the day (vv. 2–5). Of many such lists in Paul's letters, this one most resembles that of Romans 1:29–31. It contains eighteen vices, some of which are arranged in pairs. The list may have been designed for commitment to memory in the largely illiterate, oral culture of the day. It contains considerable assonance (repetition of similar sounds), which would aid in memorization. Several words are compounds of the noun for love (*phil-*), the suffix "oi" occurs on a number of words, and an initial alpha is especially frequent. (In Greek, the latter is a form of the negative, equivalent to the prefix "un-" in English). All in all, the list presents a grim picture of self-centered living. It describes those whose lives are wrapped up solely in self rather than showing any concern for others or for God. The traits were those which characterized the false teachers. These teachers may have had a certain external appearance of godliness, but at heart they shared neither the depth nor the power of genuine piety (v. 5).

The description in verses 2–5 would fit much false religion in most times and places. Verses 6–9 are more specific to the problem at Ephesus. The false teachers were preying upon the women in the church. They were "worming their way" into homes, making captives of women (lit. "little women"), who were guilt-ridden with past sins and inflamed with present desires. They were always seeking to learn but never obtaining true knowledge. The picture is the same as that of 1 Timothy. It is an accurate picture of women in first-century hellenistic society who had little role outside the home. Particularly vulnerable were the well-to-do widows, who had time and means but no real social role to fulfill. In 1 Timothy Paul dealt with the problem, urging the younger widows to marry and have families and the older ones to assume roles of ministry to the younger women of the congregation. Without such healthy roles to fulfill, the women were an easy target for the greedy false teachers.[15] Paul likened the latter to Jannes and Jambres, the magicians of Pharaoh whom Moses confronted (Exod. 7:11–12). They are given no name in the Book of Exodus, but later Jewish tradition attributed them these two names. They were charlatans too, and Moses in the end confounded them (cp. Exod. 9:11). Paul predicted that the false teachers of Ephesus would also fail in the end (v. 9).

THOROUGHLY EQUIPPED FOR MINISTRY (3:10–4:8)

Continuing steadfast in Scripture (3:10–17). Having addressed the negative example of the false teachers, Paul now turned to positive influences for Timothy to follow in his ministry: the example of Paul himself (vv. 10–13) and the guidance of the Holy Scripture (vv. 14–17).

As in 1:8–14, Paul reminded Timothy of his own example as a minister. No one knew Paul better than Timothy. He knew Paul's teachings, his manner of life, his faith in Christ, the resolute purpose with which he pursued his witness, his patience and endurance even through the worst of trials. From the time of Timothy's conversion, during the course of Paul's first mission, Paul's young coworker had been familiar with the apostle's suffering—at Antioch (Acts 13:50) and at Iconium (Acts 14:2–6). Timothy may well have personally witnessed the stoning of Paul which took place at Timothy's native town of Lystra (Acts 14:19–20). Timothy knew how Paul had been delivered from those trials. Paul now reminded him that he too could expect persecution but that he could also expect God's protection. He went on to tell Timothy of a major reality that faces all God's servants. Sometimes the false and the wicked seem to flourish while true servants suffer (vv. 12–13). In the end, however, the false will fail (v. 9) while God will rescue those who are truly his (v. 11).

In verses 14–17 Paul pointed to the most important guide of all for Timothy as he sought to be a servant of Christ—the Scripture. Timothy knew the Word of God. He had learned the Scriptures at his mother's knee (v. 15). Paul had in mind the Old Testament, which Timothy had learned from his pious Jewish mother and grandmother; the New Testament did not yet exist as a canon of Scripture.[16] Everything he said about Scripture, however, is certainly applicable to the totality of God's Word, both old and new covenants. The sacred Scripture is inspired, "God-breathed," spoken through humans by the word of God (cp. 2 Pet. 1:19–21).[17] Paul, however, was not primarily interested in convincing Timothy of the Scripture's inspiration; Timothy already believed in that. Paul was most concerned to challenge Timothy with the Scripture's *usefulness.*[18] It was his indispensable tool as a minister—for teaching, for confronting error, for straightening out those who strayed, for instruction in the standards of God. If Timothy was to do the good work of a minister, he had to be thoroughly equipped in the Word.

Faithfully preaching the Word (4:1–5). Paul urged Timothy throughout the letter to be bold, unashamed, and faithful in preaching the gospel. Now, at the close of the letter, he once again emphasized that this was the central task of ministry—to preach, to correct, to reprove, to encourage, to teach. All these are aspects of the ministry of the Word. Timothy was to preach with urgency, "in season and out of season" (v. 2). The expression "in season" may derive from the Greek philosophers, who insisted on finding just the right time for sharing their teaching in order to make the greatest impact.[19] Paul insisted that the luxury of waiting for the opportune moment no longer existed. The time had grown short (v. 1). The false teachers were on the increase, leading astray more and more whose ears were itching to hear the latest novelty (vv. 3–4). Paul himself was positioned at death's door, uncertain when he would hear the executioner's footsteps (vv. 6–8). He challenged his young colleague to be true to his calling, to be always self-controlled, ever alert, a faithful witness to the gospel, even if it should mean suffering hardship and persecution as Paul was now experiencing himself.

Keeping the faith (4:6–8). Paul's charge to Timothy was the more urgent because he himself was facing death, as is clear in these verses. Much as in Philippians, Paul spoke of pouring his life out as a "drink offering" (Phil. 2:17). Also as in Philippians, he spoke of the prospect of death as the time of his "departure" (Phil. 1:23).[20] There is a major difference between the two letters, however. In Philippians Paul had a prospect of release and further ministry (Phil. 1:19–26). During his second Roman imprisonment, Paul entertained no such hope. A martyr's death seemed inevitable. Nowhere is that more apparent than in these verses.

Paul's work as an apostle was now over. As he often did, Paul used athletic imagery.[21] He spoke of having struggled in the grand struggle. This is variously translated as "fighting the good fight" or as "running the good race," depending on whether one sees it as a reference to a boxing match or a foot race. The latter seems the more likely, as the racing image carries over in the reference to "completing the course" in the next clause. Paul had run in the greatest race of them all as he bore his testimony to Christ, and he had finished his course, the ministry which God had entrusted to him. He had indeed "kept the faith." By this he probably meant that he had "kept the trust," had been faithful to the ministry which God had entrusted to him. Verse 8 completes the racing metaphor. Paul awaited the victor's garland, the crown of righteousness which God would give him on judgment day. It was not a righteousness which Paul had earned, but a righteousness given by God in his grace and mercy, a righteousness manifested in Paul's faithful ministry. Paul had no doubts about receiving a victor's crown. It already existed, awaiting him in heaven, and not only him but all those who love Christ and await the final victory in him.

PERSONAL MATTERS (4:9–22)

Instructions to Timothy (4:9–15). As Paul contemplated his "departure," he urged Timothy to come to his side as soon as possible. Paul was lonely. The only one of his coworkers still with him was Luke (v. 11). Paul paired Demas with Luke in Colossians 4:14, but Demas was not now present with the apostle and the "beloved physician." He had evidently abandoned Paul and gone off to Thessalonica. Paul accused Demas of having fallen in love with the present age. This is eschatological language; the "present age" is the counterpart to the "age to come." Worldliness had evidently led Demas to abandon his ministry, if not his faith as well. In contrast, Titus was off on mission, ministering in Dalmatia on the Adriatic coast north of Macedonia. Another coworker, Crescens, had gone to serve in Galatia. Except for Luke, Paul was alone. He urged Timothy to pick up Mark along the way and bring him with him. Paul's disagreement with Mark had healed long ago, and he now was Paul's trusted fellow worker (cp. Col. 4:10). Paul owed Mark's restoration in no small part to Barnabas's encouragement of the young Christian minister (cp. Acts 15:39–40). Once Paul had considered Mark to be a "quitter." Now he viewed him as helpful for his ministry.

The most likely route for Timothy to travel between Ephesus and Rome was by way of Troas to Macedonia and then along the Egnatian Way to Dyrrhachium and Brundisium. Paul told Timothy to stop by the house of Carpus in Troas, where he had earlier left a coat and some parchment books (v. 13). Winter was approaching, and Paul needed the coat for warmth in his prison cell. We can only guess about the contents of the parchments. They may have been blank and needed for Paul's writing.[22] More likely they were Old Testament scrolls. Paul told Timothy that he was sending Tychicus to Ephesus, probably to replace Timothy. Tychicus was a trusted representative of the apostle. He had earlier carried the Ephesian and Colossian epistles (Col. 4:7–9; Eph. 6:21–22). He probably was the bearer of 2 Timothy.

Paul warned Timothy that as he made his way to Rome he should look out for Alexander the copper worker. He said that Alexander had done him a great deal of harm personally (v. 14). We are not certain who Alexander was. He was possibly the Alexander whom Paul had disciplined at Ephesus along with Hymenaeus (1 Tim. 1:20). Paul used a Greek word to describe Alexander's wrong that was often used for one who informed on someone. This has led some to see Alexander as the person who reported Paul to the Roman authorities. A possible scenario would have Alexander going from Ephesus to Troas after Paul had excommunicated him. At Troas Alexander would have reported Paul to the authorities, who thereupon arrested the apostle. When he was taken captive to Rome, Paul left some of his belongings behind at Troas with Carpus.[23] Whether this reconstruction of events is correct or not, it remains likely that the embittered Ephesian heretic had in some manner rendered damaging testimony against the apostle. If not at Troas, it may have been at Paul's "first defense."

The first defense (4:16–18). Paul now informed Timothy about his "first defense" in Rome. He probably was not referring to his first Roman imprisonment. Paul had been with Timothy for some length of time after his release from that imprisonment. He had surely informed Timothy already of those events. By "first defense," Paul was probably talking about a preliminary hearing in connection with his present, second imprisonment. It was standard Roman juridical procedure to have a preliminary hearing to determine the parameters of a case before setting the main trial. Paul was likely referring to such an occasion in verses 16–18. He felt abandoned on that occasion. The rest of the Christians deserted him, almost certainly because the charges against Paul were *maiestas* (treason) and those supporting him risked having the same charges brought against them. Just being identified as a Christian could be fatal during the madness of Nero.

Of course, Paul was *not* alone. The Lord Jesus stood by his side, giving him the strength to bear his Christian testimony before the Gentile court (v. 17). According to the Acts narrative, it was always that way for Paul. Rather than defend himself at his trials, he generally always used them as a time for witness. Paul came safely through his first defense. He described himself as being "delivered from the lion's mouth." The expression was proverbial for being delivered from extreme danger (cp. Ps. 22:21). In 1 Peter 5:8 it refers to deliverance from Satan's snare. In Revelation 13:2, Rome is the lion. Eusebius saw Paul as referring here to Nero himself (*Eccl.*

Hist. 2.22.4). The Acts of Paul took the reference quite literally and saw Paul as being thrown to the lions in a Roman arena.[24] However, Paul was simply using a metaphor to express the Lord's having delivered him on the occasion of his first hearing. Paul felt secure in his Lord. Christ would continue to deliver him in the "ultimate" sense: he would preserve him safely for his heavenly kingdom. Verses 6–8 make clear that Paul did not expect to survive indefinitely. He knew that death was close at hand. He praised God that death meant a crown of life, a heavenly kingdom, to be with Christ. And in the end, for the faithful apostle, that prospect was "far better." For him, to die was to be with Christ, and that was gain (Phil. 1:21–23).

Exchange of greetings (4:19–22). Paul concluded the epistle with his customary greetings. He sent greetings to Priscilla and Aquila, who evidently had returned to Ephesus. He mentioned the whereabouts of two other coworkers whom he failed to mention in verses 10–12. He had left Trophimus the Ephesian sick at Miletus (cp. Acts 20:4; 21:29). Erastus remained on the home front at Corinth (cp. Rom. 16:23). Paul sent greetings from "all" the brothers and sisters and singled out four. Three of them had Latin names—Pudens, Linus, and Claudia. They were almost surely members of the Christian community in Rome. According to Irenaeus, Linus later served as the bishop of Rome (*Adv. Haer.* 3.3.3). The Roman Christians may not have dared to appear at Paul's first hearing, but they still stuck by the apostle and were with him at a time when his missionary companions were away on duties elsewhere. Paul missed his companions and longed to see them in the short time that remained for him. He urged Timothy to come before winter (v. 21). Perhaps he was thinking of the warmth of his coat. Certainly Timothy *had* to leave before winter, when the sea would be closed to traffic and the mountain passes clogged with snow. A certain symbolism may also be present in Paul's reference to the winter, as the winter of his martyrdom would soon bring his ministry to a close.

Whether Timothy reached Paul before his death we do not know. Legend says that he did, but we only have legend. The biblical evidence ends with the closing words of 2 Timothy. For Paul's martyrdom, we are left solely with tradition, tradition overlaid with much fancy.

THE MARTYRDOM OF PAUL

THE TIME

The tradition is well-established and probably reliable that Paul died a martyr's death in Rome under Nero. Exactly when is uncertain. Nero died at his own hand on June 9, A.D. 68. Patristic tradition places Paul's death in close proximity to Nero's, seeing the tyrant's death as divine retribution for the deaths of Peter and Paul. Some modern scholars would date Paul's martyrdom closer to Nero's persecution of the Christians or even prior to the persecution.[25] If the Pastoral Epistles are taken as authentically Pauline, a date in late 67 or early 68 seems more likely.

The tradition arose quite early that Peter and Paul were martyred on the same day. It is reflected by Eusebius, who quoted the testimony of a Roman Christian named Caius to the effect that Peter and Paul's remains were to be found in Rome at the Vatican Hill and on the Ostian Way. According to Caius, the two were martyred at the same time (*Eccl. Hist.* 2.25). In the same place Eusebius cited Dionysius, bishop of Corinth, for the tradition that the two apostles were cofounders of both the Corinthian and Roman churches and that they were martyred in Rome at the same time. Jerome was also familiar with this tradition of the two apostles suffering martyrdom on the same day. He dated it in the fourteenth year of Nero's reign, A.D. 68 (*de Viris Illustribus* 5). Augustine was familiar with the tradition that the two apostles died on the same date, but he placed their deaths a year apart, Peter's preceding that of Paul (*Sermon for the Feast of St. Peter and St. Paul* 295.7).

It is not likely that Peter and Paul were martyred at the same time. The earliest sources, the second-century Acts of Peter and Acts of Paul do not indicate that such was the case. Probably the tradition of their simultaneous martyrdom arose when the two martyrs came to be venerated together on the same feast day by the Roman church.

The reasons for Paul's martyrdom are not clear. He may have been executed in connection with Nero's persecution of the Roman Christians. The excesses of that period were over by A.D. 67, but Paul in Nero's mind may have stood out as a ringleader of the Christians and a continuing threat. It may have been Paul's preaching which finally brought him at cross-purposes with the emperor, either as one who refused to participate in the imperial cult or as one who worshiped another king. The latter could be viewed by the Romans as *maiestas* (treason), an offense which demanded the immediate execution of the offender. It is unlikely that Paul actually appeared before Nero in person. Nero rarely heard cases himself but delegated the responsibility to others. Paul may have been tried by the urban prefect. Paul's would have been a case *extra ordinem*, that is, without ordinary legal precedents. In such instances the prefect would have had full jurisdictional powers—judge, jury, and executioner.[26]

The final section of The Acts of Paul deals with the apostle's death and is often designated separately as The Martyrdom of Paul. It spins an elaborate and fanciful tale of Paul's last days. According to this account, the apostle maintained a powerful witness in a barn outside Rome. Patroclus, Nero's own cupbearer, went to hear Paul. Perched in a window of the barn, he fell to his death but was miraculously raised through Paul's intercession. (The influence of the Eutychus incident of Acts 20:7–12 is unmistakable.) When the resuscitated cupbearer informed the emperor of the miracle and of his new faith in Christ the eternal king, Nero was not overjoyed. Paul had won over others of his retinue as well. The emperor accused the apostle of proclaiming a rival king and condemned him to death. Paul told the emperor that he would appear to him after his execution. In the meantime Paul witnessed to those entrusted with carrying out his sentence, the prefect Longus and Cestus the centurion. They would have released him, but Paul would not shrink from this ultimate witness unto death. When the executioner's sword fell, severing Paul's head from his body, milk rather than blood spattered all over the soldier's garment.[27] True to his promise, Paul appeared to Nero and warned him of bad times that were coming for him. Cestus and Longus repaired to a place where Paul had instructed them to go. There they were met by Titus and Luke, who baptized them.

Other traditions elaborate on the role of Nero. In a story related by John Chrysostom, Nero's anger is said to have been kindled against Paul when the apostle converted his favorite concubine and persuaded her to take a vow of celibacy (*Contra Oppugnatores Vitae Monasticae*, 1.3). The tradition that Paul died by the sword has a greater claim to reliability. Paul was a Roman citizen and would probably not have been subjected to the kind of death that other Christians experienced at Nero's hand, such as crucifixion and burning. During the Roman Republic, beheading was usually performed by the lictor's axe, but during the empire a sharp sword was the usual method (cp. Acts 12:2; Rev. 20:4). The legends elaborate on every detail of Paul's martyrdom. For instance, a fourth- or fifth-century account of Paul's death, known as *Pseudo-Linus* (or *Passio Sancti Pauli Apostoli*), tells how all along the road to the place of execution Paul preached to the crowds who lined the way.

THE PLACE OF MARTYRDOM

There are rival sites for Paul's martyrdom. A place connected with Byzantine tradition is at Aquae Salviae, some two miles south of Rome on the Ostian Way and then another three quarters of a mile on the Ardentine Way. Now known as "Three Fountains" (*Tre Fontane*), a fifth-century chapel stands there by the name of the Church of St. Paul at Tre Fontane. According to the local tradition connected with the chapel, Paul is said to have been beheaded at that very spot, under a pine tree. The site became known as Three Fountains because of three springs which are said to have appeared there at the time of Paul's death. His head is supposed to have bounced three times on the ground after the executioner's blow severed it. It is said that a spring appeared on each spot where the head bounced.

The rival site is the traditional site for the Roman church. It is located at the third mile marker on the Ostian Way. The emperor Constantine built a basilica there around A.D. 324. It was replaced by a larger one in A.D. 395. Destroyed by fire in 1823, it was rebuilt and rededicated in 1854 and is known as St. Paul's Outside the Walls. A third-century tradition claims that a certain Lucina gathered up Paul's remains and buried them on the very spot of his execution, which supposedly is the site of St. Paul's Outside the Walls.[28] This tradition also appears in *Pseudo-Linus*. Originally a pagan cemetery was located there, which lends some credence to the tradition that Paul was buried on the spot. A pagan cemetery would not likely be a spot favored by Christians unless strong tradition designated it as the actual site. Of course, the place of execution and place of burial need not be the same. In fact, the tradition connected with Tre Fontane has Lucina carrying Paul's remains from Three Fountains to the burial place at St. Paul's Outside the Walls.[29]

Other traditions exist about the whereabouts of Paul's remains. The traveler to Rome has all sorts of choices. Two fourth-century sources place the remains of both Peter and Paul at the site of the church of St. Sebastian on the Appian Way. Good evidence exists that in one period this was a favorite visiting place of pilgrims. It is possible that at one time the apostles were buried there and then later removed to St. Peter's and to St. Paul's Outside the Walls. It is also possible that during a time of persecution the remains of the apostles were removed from St. Peter's and St. Paul's and taken to the more protected site of San Sebastian.[30] To add to the confusion, there is the strong Roman Catholic tradition that the *heads* of both Peter and Paul have resided in the church of the Lateran since the ninth century. No one knows for sure where the remains of Peter and Paul really lie. The Christians of the second and third centuries probably didn't know any better than we do.[31]

THE LEGACY OF PAUL

Paul was what literary critics call a "round character"; he was many different things to many different people. This was true in his own lifetime and has continued to be so throughout the centuries. The church of Rome from its earliest days considered Paul and Peter together as its cofounders and as *martyrs* who sacrificed themselves for it. In subsequent centuries, the Roman tradition elevated Peter alone to the role of founder and first pontiff, eclipsing Paul. Still, Paul continued to be venerated in the role of martyr and saint.

Paul, of course, saw himself primarily as an *apostle* of Jesus Christ. In his own use of the word, an apostle was a sort of pioneer missionary who had received a direct calling from the risen Christ to establish work on a new field. An apostle was a groundbreaker. An apostle did not work in the field of another apostle. Above all, Paul saw himself as the *apostle to the Gentiles*. Paul's apostleship and his gospel were intimately related. The gospel of God's grace which he preached at Galatia was challenged along with his apostolic status by the legalists who had infiltrated the community. In Corinth, likewise, Paul had to defend his apostleship against the false apostles who challenged him with their impressive words and deeds. Paul withstood them with his message of servanthood. As a true apostle, Paul viewed himself as being most powerful when he was most vulnerable, in his human weakness rather than his strength. His own weakness made it apparent that whatever was accomplished was through God's grace rather than through his own effort. This paradox of power in weakness was at the very center of Paul's self-understanding as an apostle. The role of apostle gave him both power and authority, but always and only as a "slave" of Christ. Paul's power was in his weakness; his apostolic role was at one with his identity as Christ's slave.

Paul also described himself as a *pastor*, as one who had a daily concern for all his churches (2 Cor. 11:28). Paul's pastoral concerns shine through in all his epistles, from the earliest to the latest. To the Thessalonians, who worried over the deaths of fellow Christians, Paul provided pastoral care, assuring them of the certainty of the resurrection. With a pastor's insight, he realized the threat of disunity in the Philippian congregation and urged them to be more selfless and concerned for one another in the example of Christ. In the Pastoral Epistles Paul recommended to Timothy and Titus a pattern which Acts shows he regularly followed—establishing good leadership over all the churches. In the Pastorals, Paul was likewise concerned with special problems that had arisen in the churches—the image and impact of the church on the outside community and the problems of individual groups within the church, such as the widows. These were all, of course, pastoral concerns. Even Paul's socially conservative stance in Philemon probably derived ultimately from his concern for the image and witness of the church in the larger community.

Many would describe Paul as being primarily a *theologian*. They would point to such things as his profound discussion of revelation and reason in 1 Corinthians, his contrast of divine with human wisdom. They might note the exalted Christology of Colossians or the treatment of freedom in the Galatian epistle. Above all, they would point to Paul's analysis of human sin and divine righteousness in Romans. Through the centuries, Paul has been the seminal theologian for the Christian church with his powerful life-changing influence on such giants as Augustine and Luther. But Paul would probably not have described himself as a theologian. He would have been more comfortable with terms like *missionary* and *evangelist*.

Paul's theology was greatly influenced by two factors: his mission and his call. Paul's *missionary* experience as apostle to the Gentiles must have sharpened his understanding of God's grace and its relation to the law. The Jewish system of Torah presented a real barrier to the Gentile mission. As a Jew, Paul was convinced that God was one. As a Christian, he was convicted that Christ was at the center of God's work of salvation. The oneness of God demanded an equal pattern of salvation for all people, but the law was in many aspects quite narrowly Jewish. The centrality of Christ ruled out any other source of salvation, including the Torah. Paul probably already was exposed to such convictions among the Christians of Antioch. His missionary experience served to crystallize his thinking.

No description fits Paul better than that of missionary. Acts consistently portrays him in this role. The patterns of missionary activity established by Paul are in many aspects still followed today. Paul's missionary concerns are found in all his letters, from Thessalonians to the Pastorals. First Timothy 2:4 epitomizes that concern: God "wants all men to be saved." Of all Paul's letters, Ephesians is perhaps the crowning statement of his missionary concern, with its emphasis on the unity of the body of Christ, the one new humanity in Christ Jesus. At the very heart of all Paul's ministry lay the idea of the one people of God in Christ, where all the walls have fallen.

For many, Paul is primarily seen as the *convert*. The subject of conversion immediately brings Paul to mind as a sort of quintessential model of the Christian convert. This is an error, of course. The Lord comes to his own in many different ways. There is no single pattern, and Paul's experience was uniquely his. His was a radical conversion, a transformation from maligner of Christ to proclaimer, from persecutor to persecuted. Paul's entire pilgrimage began on the Damascus road. That is where he first saw the Lord, where his call as an apostle began. That is where the seeds of his theology were sown. That is where his pastor's heart came into being, his devotion to the body of Christ which once he persecuted but now he cherished. His encounter with Christ must have been a lifelong reference point for Paul, undergirding all his suffering as Christ's herald, fortifying his witness even to the point of the executioner's sword in Rome.

NOTES

1. See L. P. Pherigo, "Paul's Life After the Close of Acts," *Journal of Biblical Literature* 70 (1951): 277–284.

2. Suetonius also gives an account of the fire in his *Life of Nero*, 38. He elsewhere discusses Nero's making scapegoats of the Christians (*Nero*, 16).

3. A. T. Robertson, *Epochs in the Life of Paul* (New York: Scribner's, 1909), 303.

4. Tertullian (*de baptismo*, 17) relates that *The Acts of Paul* was compiled by an elder from Iconium who was removed from office for producing a work that was not considered to be true to Paul, particularly in its emphasis on celibacy and its portrayal of women in the roles of teaching and baptizing. The first part of *The Acts of Paul*, known as *The Acts of Paul and Thecla*, contains the famous physical description of Paul discussed in chapter 2.

5. J. Murphy-O'Connor, *Paul, A Critical Life* (Oxford: Clarendon, 1996), 368–371.

6. H. W. Tajra, *The Martyrdom of St. Paul: Historical and Judicial Context, Traditions, and Legends*, WUNT, 2. Reihe, 67 (Tübingen: Mohr/Siebeck, 1994).

7. The Acts of Paul shares several persons in common with 2 Timothy—Alexander, Demas, Hermogenes, and Onesiphorus, which may well reflect that it has a relationship of dependency on the Pastorals. For a discussion, see R. A. Wild, "The Image of Paul and the Pastoral Letters," *Bible Today* 23 (1985): 239–245.

8. This position is advocated by Murphy-O'Connor, *Paul, A Critical Life*, 356–366. See also J. Murphy-O'Connor, "2 Timothy Contrasted with 1 Timothy and Titus," *Revue Biblique* 98 (1991): 403–418.

9. L. T. Johnson, *Letters to Paul's Delegates*, The New Testament in Context (Valley Forge, Penn.: Trinity Press International, 1996), 39–41.

10. G. D. Fee, *God's Empowering Presence: The Holy Spirit in the Letters of Paul* (Peabody, Mass.: Hendrickson, 1994), 785–789.

11. Paul sends greetings to the "household" of Onesiphorus in 2 Timothy 4:19. He is mentioned nowhere else in the New Testament. His character is much more fully developed (probably fictitiously) in The Acts of Paul, where he resides at Iconium and frequently entertains Paul. Hermogenes also appears in The Acts of Paul, where he is consistently portrayed as Paul's opponent (along with Demas).

12. G. D. Fee, *1 and 2 Timothy, Titus*, A Good News Commentary (San Francisco: Harper and Row, 1984), 190–191.

13. "Here is a trustworthy saying" (NIV). The other four are 1 Timothy 1:15; 3:1; 4:9; Titus 3:8. For 2 Timothy 2:11, see G. W. Knight III, *The Faithful Sayings in the Pastoral Letters* (Grand Rapids: Baker, 1979), 112–137.

14. J. M. Bassler sees God's faithfulness as applying to all his elect, even to the false teachers should they repent: "'He Remains Faithful' (2 Tim. 2:13a)," *Theology and Ethics in Paul and His Interpreters*, ed. E. H. Lovering Jr., and J. H. Sumney (Nashville: Abingdon, 1996), 173–183.

15. D. R. MacDonald argues that *The Acts of Paul and Thecla* reflects an egalitarian movement in Asian Christian circles, where women took on traditional male roles such as preaching and baptizing and maintained their liberation through celibacy. He sees the Pastorals as written to combat this movement: D. R. MacDonald, *The Legend and the Apostle: The Battle for Paul in Story and Canon* (Philadelphia: Westminster, 1983). E. M. Howe notes that the women of *The Acts of Paul and Thecla* were scarcely "liberated," as they had to abandon their femininity and their sexual identity, disguising themselves as men: E. M. Howe, "Interpretations of Paul in *The Acts of Paul and Thecla*," in *Pauline Studies*, ed. D. A. Hagner and M. J. Harris (Grand Rapids: Eerdmans, 1980), 33–49.

16. For the view that these verses were aimed at the Marcionite rejection of the Old Testament, see C. M. Nielsen, "Scripture in the Pastoral Epistles," *Perspectives in Religious Studies* 7 (1980): 4–23.

17. Verse 16 can be rendered either "all Scripture is inspired and useful for" *or* "all inspired Scripture is also useful for." The former is grammatically and contextually the most likely translation. On the Jewish concept of scriptural inspiration, see A. T. Hanson, *Studies in the Pastoral Epistles* (London: SPCK, 1968), 42–55.

18. E. W. Goodrick, "Let's Put 2 Timothy 3:16 Back in the Bible," *Journal of the Evangelical Theological Society* 25 (1982): 479–487.

19. A. J. Malherbe, "'In Season and Out of Season': 2 Timothy 4:2," *Journal of Biblical Literature* 103 (1984): 235–243.

20. M. Prior argues that Paul's reference to his "departure" refers to his upcoming departure for a Spanish mission, not to his death: *Paul the Letter-Writer and the Second Letter to Timothy*, JSNT Supplement Series, 23 (Sheffield: JSOT Press, 1989), 91–112.

21. V. C. Pfitzner, *Paul and the Agon Motif: Traditional Athletic Imagery in the Pauline Literature*, Supplements to Novum Testamentum, xvi (Leiden: Brill, 1967).

22. Among those who see Paul as author of Hebrews, some have maintained that he used the parchments to write that epistle. This is based on the late scribal note at the end of Hebrews which states that Paul wrote Hebrews from Italy with Timothy as amanuensis. (These notes were added late to the text of the Vulgate and are not historically reliable.) As an example of one who holds this view, see N. Hugedé, *Saint Paul et Rome* (Paris: Desclée de Brouwer, 1986), 215–223.

23. G. D. Fee, *1 and 2 Timothy, Titus*, 244–245.

24. According to the legend, the incident occurred in Ephesus. (Paul's reference in 1 Corinthians 15:32 to "fighting with wild beasts at Ephesus" undoubtedly also played a part in the formation of the legend.) According to the legend, Paul was delivered from the lion. The lion did not harm him. Paul recognized that it was a lion which he had con-

verted on an earlier occasion. (The lion had also taken a vow of chastity.) The legend of Androcles and the Lion also almost certainly influenced this later Christian legend.

25. Paul's martyrdom is placed at A.D. 63 or 64 by H. W. Tajra, *The Martyrdom of St. Paul,* 31. Tajra sees Paul's preaching in Rome as the cause for his martyrdom and as a precipitating factor in Nero's latching on to the Christians for his scapegoat.

26. See Tajra, *Martyrdom,* 7–17.

27. The milk is a standard feature in subsequent stories of Paul's martyrdom. Other legends soon arose, such as that of Plautilla's scarf, found in *Pseudo-Linus.* In this story, a certain Plautilla loaned Paul her scarf to cover his eyes during the execution. After his beheading, the scarf could be found nowhere. Later, however, the risen Paul appeared to Plautilla and returned the blood-stained scarf. A later version is found in the sixth-century *Acts of Peter and Paul.* In this form, the woman's name was Perpetua, and she was blind in one eye. The handkerchief which she had given Paul to cover his eyes was returned by the soldiers after the execution. When she tied it around her own eyes, she was healed of her blindness.

28. Lucina is a stock figure of early Christian legend. Her name is derived from the Latin word for *light (lux).* She is named as the one who buried various martyrs over a period of several centuries.

29. F. F. Bruce, *Paul: Apostle of the Heart Set Free* (Grand Rapids: Eerdmans, 1977), 451–454.

30. For a full discussion of the various traditional burial sites and the excavations at them, see E. Kirschbaum, *The Tombs of St. Peter and St. Paul,* trans. John Murray (London: Secker and Warburg, 1959).

31. H. Chadwick, "St. Peter and St. Paul in Rome: The Problem of the Memoria Apostolorum ad Catacumbas," *Journal of Theological Studies,* n.s. 8 (1957): 31–52.

SUGGESTED FURTHER READING

ON 2 TIMOTHY:
See the commentaries on the Pastoral Epistles listed at the end of chapter 19.

ON PAUL'S SECOND ROMAN IMPRISONMENT AND MARTYRDOM:

Bruce, F. F. *Paul: Apostle of the Heart Set Free.* Grand Rapids: Eerdmans, 1977, pp. 441–474.

Chadwick, Henry. "St. Peter and St. Paul in Rome: The Problem of the Memoria Apostolorum ad Catacumbas," *Journal of Theological Studies,* n.s. 8 (1957): 31–52.

Kirschbaum, E. *The Tombs of St. Peter and St. Paul.* Trans. John Murray. London: Secker and Warburg, 1959.

Murphy-O'Connor, Jerome. *Paul, A Critical Life.* Oxford: Clarendon, 1996, pp. 341–371.

Tajra, Harry W. *The Martyrdom of St. Paul: Historical and Judicial Context, Traditions and Legends.* WUNT, 2. Reihe, 67. Tübingen: Mohr/Siebeck, 1994.

Index of Modern Authors

INDEX OF ANCIENT AUTHORS AND SOURCES

INDEX OF TOPICS

INDEX OF NAMES AND PLACES

Scripture Index

Acts 21:26   26
Acts 21:27–32   77
Acts 21:27–36   317–318
Acts 21:28   319, 379
Acts 21:29   438
Acts 21:36   321
Acts 21:37–40   318–319
Acts 21:39   5, 319
Acts 22   48, 50, 51
Acts 22–24   20
Acts 22–26   380
Acts 22:1–21   88, 319–320
Acts 22:3   5, 8, 25, 30, 45, 51, 381
Acts 22:3–5   24, 45, 48
Acts 22:3–16   45
Acts 22:4   37, 45
Acts 22:4–5   51
Acts 22:5   46
Acts 22:6   47
Acts 22:6–11   47
Acts 22:7   47, 103
Acts 22:8   47
Acts 22:9–12   48
Acts 22:12–16   48, 50
Acts 22:14   50, 52
Acts 22:15, 21   52
Acts 22:17–21   68, 111
Acts 22:21   49
Acts 22:22   5
Acts 22:22–24:27   306, 320–326
Acts 22:22–29   321
Acts 22:25   5, 318
Acts 22:25–29   15
Acts 22:28   5, 16
Acts 22:30–23:11   321–322
Acts 23–26   322
Acts 23:1–10   319
Acts 23:6   30, 381, 391
Acts 23:6–10   33, 113
Acts 23:8   29, 33
Acts 23:11   68, 386, 393
Acts 23:12–22   322–323
Acts 23:16   30
Acts 23:23–35   323–324
Acts 23:26   123, 318
Acts 23:26–24:26   18
Acts 23:27   15
Acts 23:30   119, 325
Acts 23:35   165
Acts 24–26   77
Acts 24:1–23   324–326
Acts 24:5–6   379
Acts 24:6b–7   328

Acts 24:8   328
Acts 24:10–21   88, 319
Acts 24:15   391
Acts 24:17   310
Acts 24:21   381
Acts 24:23   326, 378, 389
Acts 24:24   324
Acts 24:24–27   326
Acts 24:25   383
Acts 24:27   77, 78, 378
Acts 24:27–26:32   18
Acts 25:1–12   378
Acts 25:3   379
Acts 25:4–5   379
Acts 25:5–12   78
Acts 25:6–12   165, 379
Acts 25:10–12   15
Acts 25:11b   45
Acts 25:13–22   379–380
Acts 25:13–26:32   378
Acts 25:16   325
Acts 25:18   381
Acts 25:19   382
Acts 25:23–27   380–381
Acts 26   48, 50, 51, 320
Acts 26:1–32   381–383
Acts 26:2–29   88
Acts 26:4   45
Acts 26:4–5   24
Acts 26:4–5, 9–12   45
Acts 26:4–18   45, 319
Acts 26:5   45, 51
Acts 26:6–7   391
Acts 26:9–11   51
Acts 26:10   37, 45
Acts 26:10–11   37
Acts 26:11a   45
Acts 26:12–16a   47
Acts 26:14   47, 103
Acts 26:16   49, 52
Acts 26:16–18   51, 52
Acts 26:17   49
Acts 26:18   49
Acts 26:23   91
Acts 26:28   72
Acts 26:32   381
Acts 27   20, 21, 67, 385
Acts 27–28   77
Acts 27:1   20
Acts 27:1–8   383–384
Acts 27:1–28:16   378, 383–389
Acts 27:2   188, 226
Acts 27:8   404

Romans

Galatians

Ephesians

Colossians

Col. 1:1   54
Col. 1:1–4:18   338–339
Col. 1:1–14   339–340
Col. 1:4, 9   330
Col. 1:7   330
Col. 1:10   402
Col. 1:14   103
Col. 1:15–16   351
Col. 1:15–20   121, 337, 340–342, 343
Col. 1:16   336, 362
Col. 1:17–18a   351
Col. 1:18   363
Col. 1:18b–20   351
Col. 1:19   336
Col. 1:20   362, 366, 367
Col. 1:21–2:19   342–343
Col. 1:24   363, 432
Col. 1:24–29   334
Col. 1:26–27   54, 362, 368
Col. 2:1   330
Col. 2:1, 13, 16   330
Col. 2:4   335, 337
Col. 2:7   402
Col. 2:8   335, 336, 337
Col. 2:9   336
Col. 2:10   363
Col. 2:10, 15   336
Col. 2:11–12, 20   344
Col. 2:16   343
Col. 2:16–20   339
Col. 2:16–23   335–336, 338
Col. 2:18   337, 338
Col. 2:19   357
Col. 2:20–4:6   339, 343–346
Col. 3:1   358
Col. 3:1–4:6   125
Col. 3:5–17   351, 369
Col. 3:8–10   357
Col. 3:11   333, 348, 349
Col. 3:16–17   370
Col. 3:18–19   371
Col. 3:18–4:1   14, 351
Col. 3:22–25   349
Col. 3:25   371
Col. 4:3   126
Col. 4:5   370
Col. 4:7   421
Col. 4:7–8   329, 354, 357
Col. 4:7–9   128, 437
Col. 4:9   329, 346
Col. 4:10   71, 85, 87, 110, 135, 383, 437

Col. 4:10–14   329
Col. 4:10–15   126
Col. 4:12   330
Col. 4:13   330
Col. 4:14   436
Col. 4:16   100, 121, 129, 348, 355
Col. 4:17   329, 348
Col. 4:18   125, 126, 127

1 Thessalonians

1 Thess. 1–3   180, 183–184
1 Thess. 1:1   116, 123
1 Thess. 1:1–2:12   186
1 Thess. 1:1–5:28   189
1 Thess. 1:1–10   189–190
1 Thess. 1:3   122, 194, 402
1 Thess. 1:4   194, 195
1 Thess. 1:4–2:16   183
1 Thess. 1:5   87, 183
1 Thess. 1:6   184, 185
1 Thess. 1:7   184
1 Thess. 1:8   184
1 Thess. 1:9   95
1 Thess. 1:9–10   183, 185, 212
1 Thess. 2:1–2   183
1 Thess. 2:1–12   190
1 Thess. 2:1–16   190
1 Thess. 2:2   163, 184
1 Thess. 2:3–12   183
1 Thess. 2:7   184, 185
1 Thess. 2:7, 11   185
1 Thess. 2:9   182, 184, 216
1 Thess. 2:11   185
1 Thess. 2:11–12   184
1 Thess. 2:13   186, 198
1 Thess. 2:13–4:1   186
1 Thess. 2:13–16   185, 186, 196, 199
1 Thess. 2:14   102, 184, 185
1 Thess. 2:14–16   184, 186, 190
1 Thess. 2:15   186
1 Thess. 2:15–16   185
1 Thess. 2:17   185
1 Thess. 2:17–3:10   183, 184, 198
1 Thess. 2:17–3:11   125
1 Thess. 2:17–3:13   190–191
1 Thess. 2:17–20   184
1 Thess. 2:19   183
1 Thess. 3:1   207
1 Thess. 3:1–2   184
1 Thess. 3:1–5   184
1 Thess. 3:1–10   187, 207, 406
1 Thess. 3:2   128, 137
1 Thess. 3:3–4   185, 190

2 Thessalonians

1 Timothy